ATLA Monograph Series
edited by Don Haymes

16. Irene Lawrence. *Linguistics and Theology: The Significance of Noam Chomsky for Theological Construction.* 1980.
17. Richard E. Williams. *Called and Chosen: The Story of Mother Rebecca Jackson and the Philadelphia Shakers.* 1981.
18. Arthur C. Repp Sr. *Luther's Catechism Comes to America: Theological Effects on the Issues of the Small Catechism Prepared in or for America prior to 1850.* 1982.
19. Lewis V. Baldwin. *"Invisible" Strands in African Methodism.* 1983.
20. David W. Gill. *The Word of God in the Ethics of Jacques Ellul.* 1984.
21. Robert Booth Fowler. *Religion and Politics in America.* 1985.
22. Page Putnam Miller. *A Claim to New Roles.* 1985.
23. C. Howard Smith. *Scandinavian Hymnody from the Reformation to the Present.* 1987.
24. Bernard T. Adeney. *Just War, Political Realism, and Faith.* 1988.
25. Paul Wesley Chilcote. *John Wesley and the Women Preachers of Early Methodism.* 1991.
26. Samuel J. Rogal. *A General Introduction of Hymnody and Congregational Song.* 1991.
27. Howard A. Barnes. *Horace Bushnell and the Virtuous Republic.* 1991.
28. Sondra A. O'Neale. *Jupiter Hammon and the Biblical Beginnings of African-American Literature.* 1993.
29. Kathleen P. Deignan. *Christ Spirit: The Eschatology of Shaker Christianity.* 1992.
30. D. Elwood Dunn. *A History of the Episcopal Church in Liberia.* 1992.
31. Terrance L. Tiessen. *Irenaeus on the Salvation of the Unevangelized.* 1993.
32. James E. McGoldrick. *Baptist Successionism: A Crucial Question in Baptist History.* 1994.
33. Murray A. Rubinstein. *The Origins of the Anglo-American Missionary Enterprise in China, 1807–1840.* 1996.
34. Thomas M. Tanner. *What Ministers Know: A Qualitative Study of Pastors as Information Professionals.* 1994.

35. Jack A. Johnson-Hill. *I-Sight: The World of Rastafari: An Interpretive Sociological Account of Rastafarian Ethics.* 1995.
36. Richard James Severson. *Time, Death, and Eternity: Reflections on Augustine's "Confessions" in Light of Heidegger's "Being and Time."* 1995.
37. Robert F. Scholz. *Press toward the Mark: History of the United Lutheran Synod of New York and New England, 1830–1930.* 1995.
38. Sam Hamstra Jr. and Arie J. Griffioen. *Reformed Confessionalism in Nineteenth-Century America: Essays on the Thought of John Williamson Nevin.* 1996.
39. Robert A. Hecht. *An Unordinary Man: A Life of Father John LaFarge, S.J.* 1996.
40. Moses Moore. *Orishatukeh Faduma: Liberal Theology and Evangelical Pan-Africanism, 1857–1946.* 1996.
41. William Lawrence. *Sundays in New York: Pulpit Theology at the Crest of the Protestant Mainstream.* 1996.
42. Bruce M. Stephens. *The Prism of Time and Eternity: Images of Christ in American Protestant Thought from Jonathan Edwards to Horace Bushnell.* 1996.
43. Eleanor Bustin Mattes. *Myth for Moderns: Erwin Ramsdell Goodenough and Religious Studies in America, 1938–1955.* 1997.
44. Nathan D. Showalter. *The End of a Crusade: The Student Volunteer Movement for Foreign Missions and the Great War.* 1997.
45. Durrenda Onolehmemhen and Kebede Gessesse. *The Black Jews of Ethiopia: The Last Exodus.* 1998.
46. Thomas H. Olbricht and Hans Rollmann. *The Quest for Unity, Peace, and Purity in Thomas Campbell's Declaration and Address,* Text and Studies. 2000.
47. Douglas W. Geyer. *Fear, Anomaly, and Uncertainty in the Gospel of Mark.* 2002.
48. Ronald B. Flowers, *To Defend the Constitution: Religion, Conscientious Objection, Naturalization, and the Supreme Court.* 2002.

To Defend the Constitution

Religion, Conscientious Objection, Naturalization, and the Supreme Court

Ronald B. Flowers

ATLA Monograph Series, No. 48

The Scarecrow Press, Inc.
Lanham, Maryland, and Oxford
2003

SCARECROW PRESS, INC.

Published in the United States of America
by Scarecrow Press, Inc.
A Member of the Rowman & Littlefield Publishing Group
4720 Boston Way, Lanham, Maryland 20706
www.scarecrowpress.com

PO Box 317
Oxford
OX2 9RU, UK

British Library Cataloguing in Publication Information Available

Library of Congress Cataloging-in-Publication Data

Flowers, Ronald B.
To defend the constitution : religion, conscientious objection,
naturalization, and the Supreme Court / Ronald B. Flowers.
     p. cm. -- (ATLA monograph series ; no. 48)
Includes bibliographical references and index.
  ISBN 0-8108-4544-X (hardcover : alk. paper)
  1.   Naturalization--United States. 2. Religion and law--United
States. I. Title. II. Series.
  KF4710 . F58 2003
  342. 73 ' 083--dc21
                                           2002010780

To

Leah Flowers

who makes life good

When an alien resides with you in your land, you shall not oppress the alien. The alien who resides with you shall be to you as the citizen among you; you shall love the alien as yourself, for you were aliens in the land of Egypt: I am the Lord your God.

Leviticus 19:33-34
New Revised Standard Version

It is safe to assert that nowhere in the world today is the right of citizenship of greater worth to an individual than it is in this country. It would be difficult to exaggerate its value and importance. By many it is regarded as the highest hope of civilized men.

Justice Frank Murphy
Schneiderman v. United States
320 U.S. 118 at 122 (1943)

Contents

Table of Appendixes

Preface and Acknowledgments

"That woman got a *raw deal!*" That was my reaction when I first read *Rosika Schwimmer v. United States*, in which the United States Supreme Court denied Mme. Schwimmer citizenship in 1929 because she was a conscientious objector to war. Because of both her gender and her age (she was around 50), she could not have served in the military if she had wanted to. But the Court denied her citizenship. For a few years thereafter, every time I read that case with my students in my Church and State Relationships in America course, the thought recurred. Schwimmer had not been treated fairly. I found another woman, Marie Averil Bland, who had also been denied for the same reason. At that point I decided to investigate further. Soon after that decision, I read Peter Irons's *The Courage of Their Convictions: Sixteen Americans Who Fought Their Way to the Supreme Court*, an extremely interesting book. Irons tells the stories of common people whose cases reached the Supreme Court and made a difference. I was inspired by that book to emulate Irons and tell the stories of people who were denied citizenship (or not) because they had conscientious objections to war or at least combatant service. After many years (prolonged by nine distracting years as a department chair), this book is the result.

I believe *To Defend the Constitution: Religion, Conscientious Objection, Naturalization, and the Supreme Court* may make a contribution to the histories of pacifism, immigration and naturalization, law, religion in America, and feminism. But for me, the most interesting dimension of the book, that which sustained me in the writing, is what journalists would call "the human interest stories." Of the four principal characters, two were women, two were men; two were famous, two were completely obscure; they represented four very different approaches to religion: atheist (Rosika Schwimmer), American (as opposed to Southern) Baptist (Douglas Clyde Macintosh), Episcopalian (Marie Averil Bland), and Seventh-day Adventist (James Louis Girouard). Accordingly, they personified four different kinds of conscientious objection to war: philosophical absolute pacifism (Schwimmer), Christian-based absolute pacifism (Bland), Christian-based selective conscientious objection

(Macintosh, who wanted to be able to choose in which wars he would fight), and Christian-based noncombatantancy (Girouard, who would serve in the military, but only in a noncombatant role). It is easy to forget, when one reads about legal proceedings and Supreme Court cases, that they involve real people. These are not just abstract issues that may have wide (in this case, national) significance. Lives are affected, hardships endured, bitterness or happiness engendered by court decisions. Real people were involved in these matters. I hope this book humanizes these issues and events.

No author singlehandedly brings a book into existence, but rather each is the beneficiary of the work of many others. Recognizing that, I gratefully acknowledge the work of all those whose works appear in the bibliography. I especially thank the staffs of the New York Public Library Manuscripts Division, the Seeley G. Mudd Manuscripts Library at Princeton University, the National Archives, the Library of Congress Law Library, the Swarthmore College (Pennsylvania) Peace Collection, the Yale Divinity School Library, the Seventh-day Adventist Historical Society, and the Supreme Court Historical Society for their generous help in facilitating my research in their institutions. Each of the institutions, where appropriate, gave permission to quote the material I obtained there. I thank them for that. I gratefully acknowledge assistance to visit those libraries provided by a faculty research grant from the Texas Christian University Research Foundation and a Travel to Collections grant from the National Endowment for the Humanities. Persons who provided information and encouragement were Edith Wynner, longtime friend and assistant to Rosika Schwimmer and the curator of the Schwimmer-Lloyd collection at the New York Public Library; Paul Douglas Macintosh Keane, who initiated various efforts to memorialize Douglas Clyde Macintosh at Yale Divinity School and the United States Congress; Professor Emeritus Julian N. Hartt, former graduate student of Professor Macintosh; and Holly Medler Howes and Harvey Medler, grandchildren of James Louis Girouard.

My Texas Christian University Religion Department colleague Nadia Lahutsky collaborated with me on an early article about Schwimmer in the *Journal of Church and State*. Although when I decided to do the book she declined to join the project, she has given continual support, for which I thank her. James E. Wood, editor of that journal and John F. Woolverton, editor of *Anglican and Episcopal History*, gave me permission to incorporate material from my earlier articles on Schwimmer and Bland into the appropriate chapters.

In addition, several people read the manuscript, in whole or in part. Those who read a chapter or more were Morrie Wong, William H. Harbaugh, Julian N. Hartt, Paul Douglas Macintosh Keane, Donald W. Jackson, and Holly Medler Howes. Maggie B. Thomas, professor of journalism at Texas Christian University, and my student assistant for 1999-2002, Jennifer Heim, read the entire manuscript, much to my benefit. Jennifer, unflappable, always of good spirit, and wise beyond her years, did much more—library research, data input, even formatting camera-ready pages. Finally, Don Haymes, assistant librarian at Christian Theological Seminary and editor extraordinare for the American Theological Library Association/Scarecrow Press, made my writing much smoother and more concise. I thank all these, especially the last three named, for making this a much better book.

To my family, for their unflagging support, and especially to my wife, Leah, who understood my preoccupation with the book and who heard me talk about Rosika, Marie, Douglas, and James enough that they probably felt like intrusive house guests, I express my love and gratitude.

One

Immigration and Naturalization

Standing for the first time before a "Continental Congress" of the Daughters of the American Revolution on 21 April 1938, Franklin Delano Roosevelt turned to the 3,001 sumptuously dressed and decorated delegates and—according to a later witness—solemnly intoned, "Fellow Immigrants."[1] Contemporary reports do not quote that opening line, and perhaps President Roosevelt did not say exactly that. What Roosevelt did say was shocking enough to an official gathering of aristocracy-minded women who celebrated their "American" ancestry and assumed "an almost proprietary interest in the kind of immigrants who enter this Republic and what happens to them once they get here."[2]

Apologizing for appearing before this august body in a business suit rather than formal attire, Roosevelt asked the delegates to "take me as I am, with no prepared remarks." He had "thought of preaching on a text," Roosevelt continued, "but I won't. I will only give you the text, and I won't preach on it." He could "afford to give you the text," Roosevelt interjected parenthetically, because "through no fault of my own" he was "descended from a number of people who came over in the Mayflower." Indeed his ancestors on both sides of the family were "in this land in 1776" with "only one Tory among them." As heir to such a pedigree, Roosevelt could offer his text: "Remember always that all of us, and you and I especially, are descended from immigrants and revolutionists."[3]

"Bravely and politely," *Time Magazine* commented, "the Continental Congress remembered to applaud." The President's "text" was a headline in the next morning's *New York Times*. In the context of contemporary politics and the recent history of immigration in the United States, the assembled delegates of the DAR may have found this "text" not only unwelcome but also deeply disturbing. It is, I believe, a fitting text for an overview of immigration in American history and an introduction to the twentieth-century immigrants and applicants for citizenship whose stories I seek to understand in this book.

1

As President Roosevelt knew, and his audience was reluctant to acknowledge, immigration defines American history. From the earliest Spanish, English, French, and Dutch settlements to the present—with significant restrictions after the 1920s—people have streamed to the shores of America from virtually every point on the compass. All human beings living in the United States, except so-called "Native Americans," are descended from immigrants who arrived at some time since 1492. William H. A. Williams argues that immigration is integral to American culture:

> If . . . we consider . . . the *effects* of the physical, social, and cultural series of acts involved in abandoning home and homeland, crossing the ocean, and settling in a new place amid strangers, then we might conclude that the *impact of immigration is the quintessential American experience, establishing a pattern that is replicated in almost every aspect of American life.* . . . [I]n our leave taking and our arriving; in our loss and our discovery; in our rejection of the past and our embrace of the future; in our surrender of the familiar and our confrontation with the new—in our bewildered efforts to see in the mirror of our endless diversity the unifying effects of sharing this strange national experience—in all of this we can discern the patterns of immigration deep within our culture, deep within ourselves.[4]

Those who first came to the new world had mixed motives. Some came for religious reasons, to bring the gospel of Christ to the "heathen." Others came for adventure or for commerce, with the hope they could improve their lot in life. Many likely came for a combination of reasons. Indeed, corporations chartered by the English Crown governed the earliest colonies, Virginia, Massachusetts Bay, Plymouth, Connecticut, and Rhode Island. Yet even these colonies had distinctly religious characteristics.[5] Usually an established religion maintained theological uniformity. Most early immigrants sought to maintain "a pure religion," neither diluted nor perverted by heresy. As the Rev. Nathaniel Ward of Massachusetts Bay, writing as "The Simple Cobbler of Aggawam" in 1647, pithily expressed it,

> I dare take upon me, to be the Herauld of New-England so farre, as to proclaime to the world, in the name of our Colony, that all Familists, Antinomians, Anabaptists, and other Enthusiasts, shall have free Liberty to keep away from us, and such as will come to be gone as fast as they can, the sooner the better.[6]

The Simple Cobbler shows us more than the desire to maintain religious purity. All kinds of people were arriving in North America. The earliest settlers were all English, although soon enough they were of different views about religion. Ethnic pluralism soon also appeared. For example, the Dutch founded New Amsterdam in 1626 and some Spanish and Portuguese Jews settled in New Amsterdam, by way of Holland and Brazil, in 1654.[7]

Immigration continued well beyond the first wave of settlers. Indeed, it extended until the American Revolution. In the early days, the bulk of immigrants were English, Anglicans, Congregationalists, Quakers, and Roman Catholics. During the reign of Charles II (1660-85), the government decided that so many people leaving the country would weaken England, and thus curtailed emigration. As the numbers of English immigrants declined, the numbers of other nationalities increased. French Huguenots came in the late seventeenth century. In the eighteenth century large numbers of Scotch-Irish, primarily Presbyterians, and Germans— Moravians, German Reformed, and mainly Lutherans—arrived. Jews from a variety of countries trickled in.[8]

Why did these later immigrants come? The principal motive, throughout the colonial period, was the search for a better life. Those already in America capitalized on this desire to find adventure and work. Indeed, they recruited people to come. Colonial governments and private entrepreneurs developed programs encouraging people to come to improve property values, rents, and profits. Recruiters were sent to Europe to entice people to come; sometimes colonial governments paid bonuses for every immigrant recruited. Sponsors often provided transportation and subsidies for the purchase of land and tools. Yet commerce was not the only appeal. Religious opportunities were important to immigrants, especially to those people who were dissenters in their home countries. As more people of different faiths came, the various colonies became even more tolerant.[9] For example, the directors of the Dutch West India Company, a business venture interested in profits, reprimanded Peter Stuyvesant, governor of New Amsterdam, for arresting and fining a man who allowed Quakers to use his home. They told Stuyvesant that he ought to be more tolerant of minority religions so that more people would come:

> Wherefore, it is our opinion, that some connivance would be useful; that the consciences of men, at least, ought ever to remain free and unshackled. . . . This maxim of moderation has always been the guide of the

magistrates of this city [Amsterdam], and the consequence has been
that, from every land, people have flocked to this asylum. Tread then in
their steps, and, we doubt not, you will be blessed.[10]

Likewise, the Lords of Trade in London wrote to the Council of Virginia:

A free exercise of religion . . . is essential to enriching and improving a
trading nation; it should be ever held sacred in His Majesty's colonies.
We must, therefore, recommend it to your care that nothing be done
which can in the least affect that great point.[11]

Yet not all who came to work in the new world were willing immigrants. In the eighteenth century the British Crown sent about 50,000
convicted felons to America and the West Indies. The colonies became a
dumping ground for people who had been convicted of crimes, major or
minor. This was an exception to the English discouragement of emigration.
Africans also were brought to be slaves. By the middle of the seventeenth
century, black people resided in all of the colonies. By the end of the
century, slavery was well established in the southern colonies. Throughout
the eighteenth century about 200,000 Africans were brought to that area.[12]
Fewer immigrants came during the time leading up to the Revolutionary
War and the war itself (1775-83). No matter how difficult one's lot in life
or how attractive a new country may be, people usually do not willingly
put themselves in harm's way. The turmoil in Europe surrounding the
French Revolution and the Napoleonic Wars also prevented masses of
people from leaving their native countries. Consequently, the annual
number of immigrants to North America declined from the early 1770s
until 1815; yet an estimated 250,000 came to America even during these
years. Although some were persons of outstanding intellectual and
political gifts, many were indentured servants and/or refugees from
France.[13]

The convention that drafted the Constitution of the United States
heard considerable debate about immigration. Some of the founders spoke
positively, believing that immigrants could make constructive contributions to the new nation. Others were concerned that immigrants from
monarchical societies would import a preference for despotism and thus
would threaten the welfare of a democratic country. Probably because the
founders disagreed about the impact of immigration, the Constitution is
essentially silent on the subject. Immigration is mentioned only in Art. 1,
Sec. 9, which deals with those special immigrants, slaves.[14] Article 1, Sec.

8 empowered Congress "to establish a uniform Rule of Naturalization," and the Constitution refers to requirements of citizenship in two other places. Naturalization and citizenship will be examined later in this chapter.

Lack of any restriction on immigration in the Constitution and conditions in both Northern Europe and the United States determined that after 1815 the quantity of immigration would increase dramatically. Many historians speak of a flood tide of immigration beginning around 1830. The number of immigrants who came between 1815 and 1860 far surpassed the number who had come during the colonial period. As Maldwyn Allen Jones wrote in a landmark study of American immigration, "They came in a series of gigantic waves, each more powerful than the last and separated from one another only by short periods of time." After the final defeat of Napoleon Bonaparte, the first wave gradually rose through the 1830s and 1840s to reach its crescendo in 1854. Although the United States only began to record numbers of immigrants in the 1820s, 151,000 new arrivals came ashore in that decade. In the 1830s immigration increased almost fourfold to 599,000, and that figure was nearly tripled in the 1840s, which saw 1,713,000 arrivals. The flood tide of the 1850s would equal and surpass the previous two decades at 2,314,000. The shock of this wave as it landed on the American shore cannot be overestimated. Jones counts five million immigrants between 1815 and 1860, more people than the first federal census found in the United States in 1790. As Jones notes, "The three million who arrived in the single decade 1845-54 landed in a country of only about twenty million inhabitants and thus represented, in proportion to the total population, the largest influx the United States has ever known."[15]

Who were these people? They were, predominantly, Northern Europeans from the British Isles, Germany, Scandinavia, Switzerland, and Holland. Canadian immigrants, about 250,000, also arrived between 1815 and 1860. Those from the British Isles came primarily from Ireland. Principally because of the potato famine (1845-49), huge numbers of Irish migrated to America. In 1816, 6,000 Irish resided in the United States; by 1850 there were 961,719.[16] Generally they were unskilled or underskilled people who, like their earlier counterparts, were looking for a better life. Most of them had little money, having spent their resources on the voyage to America. Several agencies organized efforts to help these impoverished people find their way in their new environment.

Of these immigrants, the majority settled in the North and Midwest. The largest numbers found their way to New York, Pennsylvania, Ohio, Illinois, Wisconsin, and Massachusetts. Among slave states, Missouri, Maryland, Louisiana, and Texas attracted the most immigrants. The majority lived in cities. By 1860 immigrants made up nearly half of the population of New York, Chicago, Cincinnati, Milwaukee, Detroit, and San Francisco (where newcomers were primarily Asian). Three-fifths of St. Louis's inhabitants were immigrants.[17]

Why did they come in such numbers? The answer is complex and grossly oversimplified here. There was a push-pull dynamic: the push of principally demographic and economic factors such as war, famine, persecution, and social upheaval in Europe and the pull of perceived advantages in America. Population pressures stimulated immigration. Between 1750 and 1850 the population of Europe doubled, as a result of better medical care, sanitation, the lack of any major plagues, and increased food supply. By 1815 Ireland had the greatest population density of any country in Europe. Population pressure by itself probably did not cause many people to decide to immigrate, but it interacted powerfully with other simultaneous developments, primarily the industrial revolution. Development of manufacturing, the factory system, stimulated profound changes in European society, causing unemployment of great numbers of artisans and craftsmen. Those people who still made their living from the soil—and they were legion—suffered the same kind of devastation from the development of scientific farming. Cultivation of large units of land supplanted the family farm, displacing countless thousands. Some people came because of political unrest in their countries, but this was not a major cause of migration. Others left their homelands in order to obtain religious freedom or to be with coreligionists, among them Mennonites who migrated into Pennsylvania, Ohio, and Indiana, and British converts of Mormon missionaries coming to the mountain states to join the Mormon colonies there. Others came because of catastrophic events such as the Irish potato famine. But unemployment and population pressures were the predominant forces that pushed people out of familiar surroundings.[18]

Industrialization in America pulled immigrants out of Europe, for what was causing unemployment in Europe was generating need for laborers in America. Many who were losing or in danger of losing status in Europe perceived America as "a land of opportunity." Enormous amounts of information and misinformation about America—disseminated in newspapers, immigrant guidebooks, literature published by companies recruiting workers, promotional brochures by land agents, and advertisements by shipping companies—circulated in Europe. It is not surprising that many decided to come to see it for themselves. Yet perhaps the greatest inducement came in letters from previous immigrants extolling the wonders of their new homeland. In spite of the hardships many endured to get to America, after they arrived multitudes wrote letters home describing their adopted land in quite positive terms. What did these hawkers and new residents most praise about America? Opportunity and freedom. Even though many immigrants found it difficult to obtain employment in trades they had followed at home and though often working conditions were difficult, they wrote of economic and social opportunity. America was a place where one, by diligence in education and/or the workplace, could better one's status in life—if not for oneself, then surely for one's children.[19] Yet they not only celebrated opportunity through free enterprise, they also extolled political freedom. The American Constitution was a continuing source of security and satisfaction. Immigrants frequently contrasted the liberty of their new home with the despotism of the places they had left. This theme attracted those in the old country who received their letters, providing another incentive to family and friends to make the passage also.[20]

An explosion in transatlantic commerce beginning about 1815, particularly in the timber trade, became a catalyst enabling this massive immigration. Europe hungered for American raw materials, especially timber, cotton, and tobacco. Ships regularly sailed to Europe filled with such commodities. On their return they carried manufactured goods, which generally took up less space. Ship captains filled their surplus space with immigrants, and soon learned that immigrants were a lucrative cargo, so they made more room for them. On these sailing ships, small by today's standards and slow, a voyage could take one to three months. Cargo ships, not designed for the comfort of passengers, crowded them below deck in steerage compartments. It was not an easy passage. During congressional debate about the Passenger Act of 1819, it was reported that during 1817, of the 5,000 people who sailed from Antwerp toward America, 1,000 died.[21]

During the colonial period, when there was no national government, each of the colonies regulated immigration within its borders. Regulation principally involved which, if any, immigrants should be denied entrance to the colony. Colonies with major ports—points of entry for immigrants—were most concerned. Colonial governments tried to screen out diseased, impoverished, and criminal individuals who were unlikely to become good citizens or would drain the resources of the colony. Because, at the time of nation-building, the Constitution did not address immigration, regulation of immigration continued to reside in the states. The Passenger Act of 1819 made passage on ships safer and somewhat more comfortable, prohibited importation of indentured labor, and required the State Department to record immigration statistics beginning in 1820. Although this act represents the first federal attempt to regulate immigration, immigration remained principally under the laws of the various states until after the Civil War. The U.S. Supreme Court, in *City of New York v. Miln*,[22] affirmed this arrangement in 1837. Miln, the captain of a ship that carried immigrants, sued New York on the grounds that the city's restrictions on the admission of immigrants were obstructions of interstate and foreign commerce. The Court found against that contention, arguing that a state had legitimate police power to regulate who entered its boundaries. The decision affirmed that state regulation of immigration was permissible; states could set standards for admission of immigrants and reject those who did not meet the standards.[23]

How did immigration affect immigrants? Generally, immigration was traumatic. Immigrants left the familiar to go to the unfamiliar. They were torn from their familiar lives, often by hardship, sometimes by suffering, occasionally by disaster. That was distressing enough. But they came to a new environment that increased the psychological tension. They were forced to cope with living in a country that was experiencing growing pains of its own, a country on the move. America was a new nation, trying to understand what independence meant, how to be a democracy, how to interpret and implement religious freedom, how to tame the frontier. Immigrants encountered enormous social changes, some brought about by immigration itself. Industrialization generated need for immigrant labor and questions about working conditions and acceptable salaries. Growth of cities raised questions of adequate housing, sanitation, education, health and other social services. Toward the middle of the nineteenth century, slavery and sectional hostilities became a national obsession. Many descendants of seventeenth- and eighteenth-century immigrants did not care at all for those who came later, and they did not welcome newcomers to America, particularly if they were Roman Catholic. "Nativist" attitudes often issued in not-so-subtle hostility and sometimes in physical harassment or violence. It was into this boiling cauldron that immigrants were thrust.

The immigrant experience of trauma is understandable. People, usually from a rural setting, found themselves, more often than not, in an urban environment and faced with questions of how to make a living. Survival could become exceedingly difficult if one did not have skills appropriate for the new environment. Often working conditions in a factory or home sweatshop were oppressive and dangerous. Even if one's language was English, and it frequently was not, one had to learn, understand, and adapt to American customs as a stranger in a strange land. Adapting to American society raised questions of acculturation, particularly for one's children. Housing was often crowded, dirty, unsanitary, and backbreakingly expensive. Yet, in spite of all these things, immigrants wrote letters home encouraging family members and friends to come. They found, still, a land of opportunity.

Immigrants coped with their problems practically. They tried to blunt the newness of their situation by preserving as much of their traditional culture and their traditional self-identity as they could. They lived in enclaves with others of the same nationality, usually by choice, although the hostility of the society, real or perceived, sometimes compelled this choice. Community with others of common heritage and language extended especially to religion. In friends, customs, foods, drama, dress, language, self-created social organizations, and worship, immigrants sought to preserve as much of the old country as possible. Yet they had come to a new world, and they tried to make the best of it. They worked hard. They used educational opportunities made available by states or social welfare agencies. They began to try to understand the political systems of the nation and the place where they lived. In many ways, they were caught between two cultures—belonging completely to neither.[24]

Immigration declined dramatically during the time the nation tore itself apart over the issue of slavery. After the war, immigration resumed. Until about 1880 the majority still came from northern Europe, but after 1880 more new arrivals originated in eastern and southern Europe, and they came in greater numbers than ever before.

These "new immigrants"—as they were called then and as they are still designated by most historians—came from Italy, Greece, Poland, Russia, and Austria-Hungary. They also came from China and Japan. (Indeed Asian immigration had begun before the Civil War. Asians, primarily Chinese, began to come to California during the gold rush in 1849, then later to work on the railroads. By 1869, 63,000 Chinese had come to the United States; by 1879, another 126,000 had arrived.) Other migrants came from Canada and Mexico. Yet the predominant immigration was of southern and eastern Europeans. The numbers were huge. In the decade 1880-89, 5,248,568 came; 1890-99, 3,694,294; 1900-09, 8,202,388; 1910-19, 6,347,380, for a total in that forty-year period of 23,492,630. Some of these returned home. Figures on departures from America are not nearly so precise. But the vast majority remained.[25]

Faster, cheaper transportation accelerated this massive migration. Steamships replaced sailing ships. These ocean liners were larger, faster, and safer. Passage was more comfortable and took about ten days rather than one to three months. As late as 1856, 96.4 percent of immigrants arriving in New York came on sailing ships. By 1873, a higher percentage arrived by steamship. Because these ships were so much larger than sailing ships, they contributed, in an economy of scale, to the larger number of people arriving in America.[26]

Why did the "new immigrants" come? They came for the same reasons as earlier arrivals. By the late nineteenth century, the population of southern Europe was expanding rapidly, and industrialization was taking its toll. Employment was difficult; the family farm was shrinking. Comfortable living was increasingly problematic. Political oppression also motivated emigration. Russian Jews provide the classic, heartrending example.

A bomb killed Czar Alexander II in 1881, touching off a series of pogroms in the spring and summer of that year and causing the government, under Alexander III, to promulgate the "May Laws" of 1882. Enforcement of those laws made the lives of Russian Jews more miserable than they ever had been before. Jews lost what few rights they had and were forced to give up their property. Conditions became so intolerable that multitudes fled the country, often with little more than the clothes they were wearing, arriving in America in staggering numbers—1,314,000 in the twenty-five years before World War I.[27]

Like their predecessors, the new immigrants settled in cities in New England, New York, Pennsylvania, New Jersey, and the eastern Midwest. Few of them went to the southern states or to the farms of the plains states. The favored destination of Asian immigrants was San Francisco. By 1916, 72 percent of the inhabitants of that city spoke a language other than English as their primary language. Like earlier immigrants, the new immigrants found themselves challenged by their new environment. Most of the cities where they settled were already crowded, often overcrowded, by earlier arrivals. New immigrants, coming in hordes, compounded the congestion and thereby found themselves in ever more difficult housing and working conditions. Like their predecessors, they did their best to preserve the ethos of the old country, particularly language and religion. But they also had high motivation to change, especially to give up their language for English. English was essential for commerce. Immigrant children, embracing acculturation and seeking to cast off the foreignness of their parents, strongly pressured them to learn the language of their adopted country. Difficulties abounded.[28] As Alan Kraut has observed, the new immigrants "most frequently intended their stay to be temporary, and for some it was, but for millions more, the umbilical cord that tied them to their birthplaces was irreparably severed. Most of those in motion were from society's poor, and many oppressed as well." Men led the swelling parade, but married and single women soon joined them in increasing numbers.[29]

As the tide of immigrants continued to sweep upon America's shores, government at both the state and federal levels began to realize that state regulation of immigration alone was not sufficient. The federal government needed to be more directly involved. Indeed this process began shortly before the Civil War. In 1855, Congress mandated that the Customs Service should compile quarterly and annual statistics on immigration, transferring this responsibility to the more experienced Bureau of Statistics in the Treasury Department in 1867.[30] In 1876 the Supreme Court enabled a major revision in immigration policy. In *Henderson v. Mayor of New York*,[31] the Court ruled that all state regulations of immigration were unconstitutional because they usurped Congress' power to regulate foreign commerce, overturning its earlier ruling in *City of New York v. Miln*. As a result of *Henderson*, states began to dismantle their port authorities and mechanisms for screening immigrants.[32] In the 1880s, Congress passed a series of laws that brought immigration under federal control. It also set categories and standards for denial of admission.

Many established Americans looked on this massive immigration disapprovingly. Resistance to immigration was so widespread and vigorous (and sometimes so violent) that historians have given it a name: "nativism." One of the more celebrated students of nativism, John Higham, identified three causes of this anti-immigrant attitude: anti-Catholicism, antiradicalism, and racism.[33] Alan Kraut correctly believes that a fourth cause, anti-Semitism, ought to be added.[34]

Nativism began early in the colonial period. The first permanent settlers were English, and even by the end of the seventeenth century, about 90 percent of all settlers were of British birth or descent. Although they received hospitality and assistance from Indians in the early days of settlement, relationships between English and Indians soon turned sour. Forgetting that *they* were the immigrants, the white people began to dominate the Indians and to expect them to conform to English/European ways. Racism here, as elsewhere, prevailed.[35]

The earliest settlers were Protestants. Although they represented different kinds of Protestantism, they all brought memories of the Protestant Reformation and the problematic (to say the least) relationship between the papacy and the English monarchs of the sixteenth century. They remained staunchly anti-Catholic throughout the colonial period. Because Catholics were scarce during that time, it was not until the early nineteenth century, when Catholics began arriving in massive numbers, that anti-Catholicism became a movement—sometimes silly, more often malicious–that would dominate anti-immigrant attitudes and activities for the rest of the nineteenth century and beyond.[36]

Antipopery, as it was sometimes called, emerged from concerns both theological and social. Protestants, who found their source of faith and theology in the Bible, were convinced that Catholics placed their faith in the church and its leadership more than in Jesus Christ and in the Bible, the revealed Word of God. For Protestants, then, Catholic reliance on the church and its tradition for true theology made it a religion essentially false. (Even now, in the early twenty-first century, some undergraduates commonly ask their religion professors, "Are Catholics Christians?") Most, if not all, American Protestants believed that Catholicism threatened the theological health of the nation. Catholicism would lead people to a false understanding of Christianity and put the salvation of many in the population in jeopardy. For many, fear of Catholicism and its teachings and tendencies was a genuine concern.

Yet these theological concerns also became excuses that masked social fears and prejudices. Many argued that Catholicism and its adherents were antidemocratic. Americans embraced representative government, government for the people and by the people, while Catholics offered allegiance to the Pope. Countries that were predominantly Catholic were monarchical and opposed to democracy. Nativists argued that Catholicism was inimical to the American way of life; that a dramatic increase in Catholics would subvert American constitutional government. Conspiracy theorists even asserted that the Roman Catholic Church was encouraging massive immigration into the country to accomplish that goal.

"Trusteeism" controversies in local Catholic parishes provided nativists with a useful example of what they saw as the problem. As Catholics had to open more churches to accommodate the flood of immigrants, many congregations wanted the authority to appoint their priests and to have the title to their church property reside with the trustees of the local parish. Catholic bishops asserted their traditional prerogatives and decreed that church buildings would be owned and priests appointed by the bishops of the various dioceses. Nativists found in this assertion of episcopal authority an ideal illustration of the imperious, rather than democratic, nature of Catholicism.[37]

Education also appeared to illustrate of what opponents of immigration perceived as the subversive nature of Catholicism. Nineteenth-century Americans believed that public schools needed to teach morality by infusing nonsectarian religious values into the curriculum. The essentially Protestant ethos of the country dictated that those religious values pervading the public school curriculum would come largely from the Bible. Catholics exposed to this curriculum objected to the "Protestant" tenor of the public schools.[38] They did not want to expose their children to teaching that ran counter to their faith. So the Catholic church began to build parochial schools. When American bishops met in conferences in 1829, 1833, and 1852, each time they declared parish schools a high priority across the country. Yet not all Catholic children could attend parochial schools, either because the schools were unavailable or they lacked financial resources. Believing that local governments should support the education of all children, Catholic bishops tried to obtain public money their schools or, alternatively, to make curricula of public schools less Protestant, even less religious.[39] Americans regarded the developing public school system as a mechanism for assimilating immigrants into the American way of life, for teaching the morality that would develop children into law-abiding adults. Nativists saw Catholic initiatives to modify curricula of public schools—or, worse yet, to avoid public schools by starting parochial schools—as clear signs of a Catholic conspiracy to subvert American principles. Catholics, they said, did not want to be assimilated into America and showed profound contempt for this most important of American institutions, the public schools.[40] Catholic resistance to public education, they argued, demonstrated how a great influx of Catholics would endanger the country.

Often anti-Catholicism focused on alleged immorality in the church. Celibacy of priests and nuns inflamed rumors of sexual impropriety between the two. Purported confessions of young nuns who had been ravished by priests or had, at least, consensually engaged in sexual intercourse with them became a popular literary genre, at once pious and lurid. Babies born to these illicit unions were said to have been murdered (after being baptized) and concealed by the offending priests or sometimes by Mother Superiors. The alleged autobiography of one Maria Monk, the *Awful Disclosures of the Hotel Dieu Nunnery of Montreal*, published in 1836, became a classic of the genre. Discredited thoroughly as a fabrication among the learned, this book nonetheless set the tone for American anti-Catholicism for decades.

Belief that immigrants were taking jobs from Americans also motivated nativist responses. Because the majority of immigrants were poor and came to America to better their lives, they would work for low wages. Economic arguments moved nativism more powerfully and more broadly than anti-Catholicism, but sometimes these forces combined and even led to violence. On 11 August 1834 workers in a local brick factory burned the Ursuline Convent in Charlestown, Massachusetts, because they believed that Irish immigrants threatened their jobs.[41]

Anti-Catholic opposition to immigration before the Civil War focused primarily on Irish and German Catholic immigrants. Protestant and Jewish immigrants were perceived as threatening the labor market, but the racial and anti-Semitic dimensions of nativism did not come to the fore until after the war. Northern and western European immigrants, even Irish Catholics, were, after all, "like us." The "new immigrants" were another matter. Now came Italian, Mexican, and Polish Catholics; Jews from Russia and Austria-Hungary; Greeks, whose Eastern Orthodox religion looked enough like Catholicism to concern nativists; and Asians, whose religions were conundrums to Americans, and who were not "white." In the face of the legions of strange-looking and behaving people pouring into America, nativism increased beyond its mid-nineteenth century intensity. Added to earlier fears—of pernicious religion, economic competition, and immoral influences—was a powerful anxiety about dilution, some said "mongrelization," of the Anglo-Saxon race. Not only were there now multitudes of former slaves, no longer confined "in their place" by slavery, but also strange and disagreeable looking people from Asia and the less desirable parts of Europe seemed to be overrunning American society. In a nation of immigrants, descendants of previous generations of immigrants were uneasy about these new immigrants. As one student of this phenomenon has written, "natives and newcomers" had always "viewed each other through a prism of racial, religious, and cultural rivalries," yet "most Americans and most early immigrants were willing to coexist, however warily." It was "the new immigrants, even more alien than the Irish," who "stirred latent fears that a time was coming when a majority of the population would no longer be of Anglo-Saxon Protestant stock."[42] Through the years, nativism found expression in various organizations, among them the Protestant Reformation Society (1836), the American Protestant Society (1844), the Native American Party (1845), and the Order of the Star-Spangled Banner (1849), which evolved into the best-known of nativist organizations, the Know-Nothing Party (1854),[43] and the American Protective Association (1887). In the twentieth century two other well-known organizations, while formed for other purposes, nonetheless generally opposed open immigration: the Daughters of the American Revolution[44] and the American Legion.[45]

As noted earlier, for most of the time after America became a nation, the various states regulated immigration. The Supreme Court's decision in *Henderson v. Mayor of New York* in 1876 opened the way for the federal government to assume that responsibility. Fears on the West Coast about Chinese immigration motivated the federal government to begin to assert itself in this area. Many argued that large numbers of Chinese laborers imperiled American jobs, but there was no small amount of racism in the call for restrictions. Nativists widely assumed Chinese to be primitive, backward, inherently servile and unassimilable, labeling them "the Yellow Peril." In 1882 Congress passed the Chinese Exclusion Act,[46] prohibiting immigration of Chinese laborers for ten years. It was a law clearly based on race, the first law to exclude a specific racial or ethnic group from entrance into the country. It was also the beginning of the federal government's authority over immigration. Congress passed some other immigration laws in the same year, including one that identified categories of immigrants who could be excluded—for example, mentally handicapped persons and those unable to support themselves.[47]

In 1884 Congress, with the urging of the Knights of Labor, passed the Foran Act,[48] prohibiting any company or other employer from assisting importation of any laborer under prior contract. Skilled laborers whose work Americans were unable or unavailable to do were exempt from the exclusion. In 1888 Congress prohibited immigration of all Chinese, not just laborers, for twenty years.[49] As if that were not enough, the Chinese Exclusion Act was extended for another ten years in 1892 and indefinitely in 1904. In 1907, President Theodore Roosevelt reached a "Gentlemen's

Agreement" with Japan that limited entry of Japanese laborers in exchange for eliminating discrimination against Japanese students in California schools.

In this context of concern about and restriction of immigration the Statue of Liberty was dedicated on 28 October 1886 amid a flurry of speeches by dignitaries, including President Grover Cleveland. Already in 1883 the poet Emma Lazarus, descended from Sephardic Jews who had immigrated to New York in the seventeenth century, had composed the lines that in 1903 were inscribed on a plaque placed on the statue's pedestal.

> Give me your tired, your poor,
> Your huddled masses yearning to breathe free,
> The wretched refuse of your teeming shore.
> Send these, the homeless, tempest-tost to me,
> I lift my lamp beside the golden door.[50]

As this monument to America's open door was dedicated, the door was already beginning to close and the inviting lamp to dim. Congress would complete that process in the 1920s.

In 1891 the first comprehensive (as opposed to targeted) national law controlling immigration, the Immigration Act of 1891,[51] established the Bureau of Immigration in the Treasury Department. States now were relieved completely of responsibility of screening immigrants. In 1892 Ellis Island opened as the main entry point for immigrants from Europe. There procedures to screen and exclude immigrants with health problems or moral deficiencies—for example, convicts—were honed to an efficiency previously unknown.[52]

By 1903 Congress had transferred the Bureau of Immigration to the new Department of Commerce and Labor (after 1913, the Department of Labor), where it remained until 1940 when it was moved to the Department of Justice. Renamed the Bureau of Immigration and Naturalization in 1906, the agency became the Immigration and Naturalization Service in 1933.[53]

In 1907 Congress created a commission, chaired by Senator William P. Dillingham, a Vermont Republican, to study immigration problems. In its forty-one-volume report, released in 1910, the commission outlined assumptions that would influence immigration policy for decades. America was about to be inundated by immigrants, the "new immigrants" were racially inferior to those who had come prior to 1860, and comprehensive restriction of immigration was imperative.[54]

To curtail immigration, the Dillingham Commission proposed a literacy test; no persons sixteen or older could be admitted unless they could read a portion of the Constitution in English or some other language.[55] Congress passed that proposal twice, but two different presidents vetoed it. Finally, in the Immigration Act of 1917,[56] Congress enacted the literacy test over President Wilson's veto. The Act also barred immigrants from Asian countries other than China and Japan, who were already excluded by previous laws. The literacy test proved ineffective in reducing the flow of immigrants,[57] so in the 1920s Congress turned to a different strategy, quotas based on national origin.

In 1921 the Quota Act[58] restricted the number of immigrants of each nationality to be admitted to three percent of the foreign born of that nationality counted in the census of 1910. Immigrants from the Western Hemisphere were not subject to quotas, but Japanese were included now in the category of Asians barred totally. Actors, singers, artists, lecturers, nurses, ministers, and professors—those who might contribute to "uplifting"American society—were offered exemptions from European quotas.[59] Yet the effect, indeed the intent, of the law was to restrict numbers of immigrants coming into the country. Congress enacted the law for one year, but renewed it twice.

With the legislation of 1917 and 1921 racial and religious prejudice became more visible, and anti-Semitism dramatically increased. The Ku Klux Klan, characterized by anti-Catholicism as well as hatred of blacks and Jews, spread across the Midwest and the South. From 1920 until 1927 Henry Ford's newspaper, *The Dearborn Independent*, published anti-Semitic articles claiming that Jews threatened America. To bolster that theme, the *Independent* published a document written about twenty years earlier, the *Protocols of the Elders of Zion*. Purported to be a document written by an international group of Jewish leaders, the *Protocols* detailed their plans to take control of the economic and political centers of the world. Already the *Protocols* had been proven to be a fraud, but the *Independent* published thousands of copies that helped to inflame anti-Semitism across the country.[60]

World War I had made Americans much more wary of foreigners. Although the war was not fought on American soil, many Americans died in it because of the machinations of other nations. Americans did not feel as insulated and safe as they previously had. Meanwhile the war had encouraged that sort of "America first" patriotism that promoted a more skeptical attitude toward those who came to America from elsewhere. Because of the Russian Revolution and the resulting "red scare" about Communism, Americans would not forget that many immigrants in those years came from eastern Europe, including large numbers of Russians.[61]

Beyond all these things, the quota system of 1921 had not restricted immigration enough to satisfy the Immigration Restriction League and similar pressure groups, prompting Congress to enact new legislation. The Immigration Act of 1924,[62] based on a national-origins quota system, now limited immigration permanently. This law mandated a quota of 2 percent of foreign born persons of each nationality based on the census of 1890. Because fewer immigrants from southern and eastern Europe were coming in 1890 than in 1910 (the census benchmark for the 1921 law), the quota diminished the numbers coming from those regions in favor of "Anglo-Saxon" immigrants. The total number that could come in any one year was 164,667. "With the enactment of this law, an epoch in American history came to an end. After three centuries of free immigration America all but completely shut her doors on newcomers."[63] The law would not become fully operational until 1929, but it turned back "the new immigration" and, as Kraut observes, "finally slammed 'the golden door' celebrated by Emma Lazarus."[64]

In 1927, Congress reduced the number of immigrants who could enter in any one year to 150,000. The method of calculation was no longer a straight two percent. Each country received the percentage of 150,000 that was equal to the percentage of persons from that country, foreign born or by descent, living in the United States according to the 1920 census. This set the pattern for decades to come.[65]

In the aftermath of world war and the beginning of the so-called Cold War came the Immigration and Nationality Act of 1952,[66] usually called the McCarran-Walter Act from the names of its sponsors in the Senate and House of Representatives.[67] This act brought all immigration laws into one comprehensive statute, abandoning the previous piecemeal approach. Hearings and floor debate on this bill in the two houses of Congress took two years. Passions ran high as one political faction sought to preserve traditional immigration policy and another tried to reconstruct it in order to create goodwill in countries around the world. Debate centered on four points. First was an economic dimension, protecting American workers from foreign competition. Although jobs had been a major issue earlier in the century, the primary motivation of the 1952 bill seems not to have been the protection of the standard of living of American laborers.

The ethnic or racial identity of immigrants and their assimilation into American society became a second major contention, since it clearly had been a major consideration in enacting the 1921 and 1924 laws. In the debate on McCarran-Walter, restrictionists seemed reluctant to express any sort of racial rationale for their preferences for retaining national quotas. Antirestrictionists were outspoken in their desire to rid immigration policy of racism, either explicit or implicit. Yet all sides agreed to retain some sort of quota system based on national origins. Ethnic considerations weighed significantly in the passage of the act.

The importance of immigration policy to the foreign relations of the United States arose as a third major component in the debate. Antirestrictionists argued that the national origin quotas of traditional immigration policy damaged the image of America with countries around the world. In a postwar environment of fear about advancing Communism, some argued that maintaining restrictions against Asians would enable Communists to discredit America in Asia. Restrictionists granted that argument, to a slight degree, but "national security" was more important to them. They wanted immigration policy to bar those who would "endanger" the nation. That was a weightier value than the image of immigration policy in foreign relations.

That leads to the fourth factor in the debate over the bill, nationalism. The specter of the Soviet Union, Communism, and the Cold War loomed over the debate. Restrictionists expressed concern about the internal security of America; to preserve it they wanted to keep out persons whose loyalty to America was suspect. They believed that loyalty to the nation depends on birth in the United States and is virtually impossible to instill in the foreign born. No proposal for education in Americanism for immigrants could shake that conviction. Strict control of immigration seemed essential to national security.

The last remarks in Senate debate on the omnibus immigration bill summed up the two perspectives. Senator Hubert Humphrey, who led the charge for new policies, declared, "The issue is whether we shall have the respect of people around the world." Senator Patrick McCarran responded, "If we destroy the internal security of this country by opening the floodgates of unlimited immigration, without screening and without curtailment, we will have destroyed the national security of the United States."[68]

Under the McCarran-Walter Act the United States continued to admit immigrants according to their national origin. Northern and western European nations accounted for 85 percent of the annual total, as the prejudice against southern and eastern Europeans (many of whom were now under Communist influence and were Jews) continued. The Act barely relaxed the restrictions on Chinese, Japanese, and other Asians. Japan was given a quota of 185 and China a total of 105 immigrants a year.[69]

President Harry S. Truman vetoed the bill, although it had passed by large majorities in both houses of Congress, objecting to its retention of the national-origin quotas. "The greatest vice of the present quota system," Truman wrote in his veto message, "is that it discriminates, deliberately and intentionally, against many of the peoples of the world." He asked Congress to send him a different kind of immigration bill that would be "a fitting instrument for our foreign policy and a true reflection of the ideals we stand for, at home and abroad."[70]

Congress overrode Truman's veto and the McCarran-Walter bill became law on 27 June 1952.[71] In the Immigration and Nationality Act Amendments of 1965,[72] however, Congress abolished national-origin quotas, eliminating national origin, race, or ancestry as a basis for immigration.[73]

In this book the dimension of immigration that raises fundamental issues of justice and humanity is naturalization. Coming to the United States and becoming inhabitants did not automatically bestow rights and privileges of citizenship. Citizenship does not naturally follow from residence. As Reed Ueda, a scholar of citizenship, has written, in America society "admission to the political community as a citizen involves a voluntary pledge of allegiance and an agreement to follow the laws of the country's sovereign government." For that pledge the United States "confers legal, constitutional status and political privileges on its citizens." Applicants can obtain citizenship "by *jus soli* (birth within the borders of the United States or its possessions), by *jus sanguinis* (the inheritance of the nationality of the parents), or through the process of naturalization." Citizens by birth or blood are assumed to offer an allegiance identical to that sworn in solemn oath when a person becomes a naturalized citizen.[74]

As laws govern immigration, laws also govern acquisition of citizenship. Naturalization legislation has developed slowly and ambiguously. To these laws we now turn, for they are at the heart of the human drama in this book.

In laws of American citizenship the principal ambiguity stems from relations between the states and the federal government. This ambiguity emerges from the experience of the various colonies before independence from England. Citizenship in the colonies derived from sixteenth-century English concepts of subjectship. The Crown would provide its subjects with protection and the subjects would respond with loyalty and obedience. In the American colonies, English settlers were still expected to be subjects of the Crown. Soon, however, the Crown, Parliament, and the governments of the respective colonies competed for the authority to declare a person a citizen of the colony, an issue of particular pertinence to persons arriving in the colonies from places other than England or its possessions. In the late seventeenth century, British courts and Parliament ruled that colonial governments could not bestow citizenship on alien residents. These people had to petition either Crown or Parliament for citizenship. Virginia and New York early ignored that requirement and awarded citizenship on their own authority. Finally, in 1740, Parliament authorized American colonies to grant citizenship. Applicants were required to reside in any of the colonies for at least seven years without having been absent for more than two consecutive months. Two witnesses had to attest that an applicant, during the previous three months, had taken the Lord's Supper in a Reformed Protestant congregation.[75] An applicant had to swear loyalty to the Crown and profess Christian belief in open court. Quakers and Jews were exempt from the sacramental requirement, but Catholics were not. One who received citizenship in the American colonies would be recognized as a British subject anywhere in the empire.

Colonial governments were not yet satisfied. They continued to press for more autonomy in granting citizenship. Because they wanted to attract more people, the colonies continued to pass citizenship laws that did not require the seven-year residency. Consequently, many immigrants applied for colonial citizenship. Finally, as part of a more comprehensive effort to assert more authority in the colonies, Parliament in 1773 prohibited any sort of independent naturalization process in the colonies; all colonial citizenship would have to be granted by Crown and Parliament. In response to this, the Second Continental Congress, in its Declaration of Independence on 4 July 1776, complained that the King of England "has endeavored to prevent the Population of these States; for that Purpose obstructing the Laws for Naturalization of Foreigners."[76]

After the colonies declared independence, something like thirteen autonomous republics existed in America, each of them developing its own procedures to regulate citizenship and naturalization. No uniformity existed among the states; some were considerably more lenient than others. Prior to the adoption of the Constitution, "citizen" denoted citizenship in the states.[77]

Delegates to the Constitutional Convention, addressing citizenship first in regard to qualifying federal officers, concluded that representatives must be citizens for at least seven years (Art. 1, Sec. 2, part 2) and senators for nine years (Art. 1, Sec. 3, part 3) at the time of election. Article 2 specifies that the president (and vice president) must be "a natural born Citizen." By specifying that the president must be a citizen by birth, they clearly distinguished that representatives and senators may be naturalized. Yet the Constitution affirmed the same rights for citizens, native-born and naturalized, rather than giving the former more rights than the latter, as some delegates had advocated.

The Constitution also specifies the process to institute naturalization laws and the privileges of citizenship. According to Article 1, Sec. 8, "The Congress shall have Power . . . To establish a uniform Rule of Naturalization . . . throughout the United States." Article 4, Sec. 2, known as the Comity Clause, adds, "The Citizens of each State shall be entitled to all Privileges and Immunities of Citizens in the several States," thereby making citizenship awarded in any state applicable in all states.

Yet ambiguities remained. The founders assumed that the states would continue to legislate naturalization and that national citizenship would derive from acquisition of state citizenship. The "uniform rule of naturalization" provision apparently was intended to assure that states would not abuse the naturalization power. The Constitution does not specify what the "privileges and immunities of citizens" are, thereby leaving those definitions to the states. It did not clearly define the relationship between federal and state citizenship.[78] Ambiguity between federal and state regulation of citizenship would persist until 1870.

Consistent with the power granted by the Constitution, the First Congress passed the Naturalization Act of 1790,[79] providing that any "free white person" who had lived for two years "within the limits and under the jurisdiction of the United States" could be naturalized. The two-year residence requirement was designed to give immigrants a period of time to learn the American governmental system and culture before they became citizens. The act also granted the power to confirm naturalization to "any common law court of record in any one of the States." The act did not settle questions about the authority of the national and the various state governments over naturalization, and many states continued to administer their own naturalization laws.[80]

At that point, partisan politics began to play a role in the formulation of naturalization rules. Federalists were troubled that many "radicals," influenced by the French Revolution, were entering the country. The Jeffersonians, on the other hand, were anxious about the arrival of royalists from France. So, for different reasons, in the Naturalization Act of 1795, the two parties agreed on a five-year residence requirement, again in the belief that such a time was necessary for the applicant to understand and accept the American system of government. The act required applicants to renounce their former political allegiance and also any titles of nobility they might hold.[81]

Meanwhile the Northwest Ordinance of 1787 had opened up new territory for settlement, but it contained no provision for citizenship of the inhabitants of the area. To correct that problem, the Naturalization Act of 1795 was amended to enable territorial courts to naturalize people. Since there was no state structure in the Northwest Territory, persons so naturalized were citizens of the United States, but not citizens of a state—in contrast to the general principle that the various states would grant citizenship.[82]

Federalists were not satisfied, however, with the five-year waiting period of the Act of 1795, believing that too many foreigners sympathetic to the Jeffersonians were still entering the country. The Naturalization Act of 1798[83] extended the required time of residence making one eligible for naturalization to fourteen years. Federalists hoped this long waiting period would discourage Federalist opponents from coming to apply for citizenship. Many states were, however, still naturalizing people after only two or five years. This situation did not last. As President, Thomas Jefferson advocated repeal of the fourteen-year waiting period, accomplished in passing the Naturalization Act of 1802.[84]

The Act of 1802 essentially removed the Naturalization Act of 1798 from the books and restored the provisions of the Act of 1795. Since with only slight modifications the provisions of this law governed United States naturalization procedures for more than a century, it may be useful to enumerate the conditions of naturalization. The Act of 1802 required (1.) five years' residence in the United States; (2.) declaration of intention filed three years before naturalization in either a state or a federal court; (3.) renunciation of any foreign allegiance and titles of nobility; (4.) swearing an oath to support the Constitution of the United States; and (5.) satisfying a common law court of record—state or federal—that these conditions had been fulfilled and that the applicant had maintained good character throughout the five-year period.[85]

Some groups were not pleased with the five-year waiting period for naturalization; they thought it entirely too short. The American Republican Party, founded in New York in 1843, advocated a waiting period of twenty-one years. The Know-Nothing Party, approximately a decade later, advanced the same idea. Both groups hoped that such a long waiting period would discourage immigrants from coming to America. If they did come, a long wait before naturalization would assure that they could learn thoroughly the American way. Since native-born Americans were required to live twenty-one years before they could vote, no shorter period should be required of immigrants, given that they often came from despotic lands and were, in any case, ignorant of the American system.[86] These views, often proposed, never were adopted into law.

Slavery brought to a head the continuing ambiguity about the role of the states and the federal government, particularly in the controversy about admission of Missouri to the Union in 1820. Missouri's constitution prohibited free blacks and mulattoes from entering the state. Northerners claimed that the prohibition was contrary to the Comity Clause of the Constitution, which obligated each state to honor citizenship conferred by any other state. Southerners argued that Missouri's constitution did not violate the Comity Clause because blacks and mulattoes were not citizens. But as nonslave states were admitted from the western areas of the country, southerners challenged the traditional assumption that federal citizenship derived from state citizenship. If they could not prove that state citizenship was local only in application, they would have to grant citizenship to free blacks under the mandate of the Comity Clause. That, in turn, could raise questions about the citizenship of slaves. The Supreme Court completely muffed an opportunity to clarify these issues in the case of *Dred Scott v. Sandford*.[87] Dred Scott was a slave who had lived in a free state and a free territory before coming to Missouri. He filed suit to obtain his freedom in Missouri, arguing that since he had lived in a free state, Missouri also ought to recognize his freedom. The Court found against Scott in a variety of ways. He could not legitimately bring suit in a federal court; he actually never had been free, even though he had lived in a free state; and that no black person could ever be naturalized, given that all the naturalization acts had reserved naturalization for "free white persons." *Dred Scott* reaffirmed the concept of dual citizenship, preserving the idea of state and federal citizenship, with the latter flowing from the former. It consequently provided opportunity for continuing conflict between states and the federal government in conferring and defining citizenship.[88]

Inflamed passions about race and slavery, to which *Dred Scott* significantly contributed, led to the bloodletting of the Civil War. In spite of tremendous loss of life, destruction of property, and long-lasting sectional animosities, the Civil War contributed signifcantly to statecraft and citizenship through the Thirteenth, Fourteenth, and Fifteenth Amendments to the Constitution. The Fourteenth Amendment is central to the development of citizenship.

> All persons born or naturalized in the United States and subject to the jurisdiction thereof, are citizens of the United States and of the State wherein they reside. No State shall make or enforce any law which shall abridge the privileges or immunities of citizens of the United States.

Several states at first refused to ratify the amendment. But Congress, in the Reconstruction Act of 1867,[89] formally declared that no state could be readmitted to the Union unless it had ratified the Fourteenth Amendment and until the amendment had become part of the Constitution. Legislatures of the southern states then capitulated, and the amendment was ratified on 9 July 1868. The amendment clarified that national citizenship was prior to state citizenship, and it affirmed the primacy of birthright citizenship, *jus soli*, rather than *jus sanguinis*, citizenship based on the national status and allegiance of one's parents.[90]

From its ratification in 1868, the Fourteenth Amendment became, as John P. Roche has observed, a "watershed in citizenship." Now a United States citizen's allegiance belongs primarily to the national government, and only secondarily to the authority of the state where the citizen resides. Before 1868 the states determined national citizenship, although, as Roche notes, "in practice the national government exercised (or perhaps usurped) direct jurisdiction, particularly in the territories." Until the Civil War confusion prevailed, for national leaders were reluctant to challenge contradictory regulations or to define citizenship specifically, fearing that attempts to impose clarity and coherence would exacerbate tensions between North and South. "The realists of the day," Roche writes, "intent on compromises, avoided clarification, and United States citizenship remained undefined until 1868." The Fourteenth Amendment reversed the earlier process, making state citizenship depend on national citizenship.

"In citizenship, as in many other fields," Roche concludes, "the United States did not attain sovereignty until after Appomattox."[91]

In 1905 President Theodore Roosevelt appointed a commission to prepare a revision of the Naturalization Act of 1802 and to devise a bureau to supervise naturalization. Although the federal government began supervising immigration in 1891 in the Bureau of Immigration, there was no comparable structure for naturalization. The Naturalization Act of 1906,[92] the last major development in citizenship and naturalization law pertinent to this study, placed the Bureau of Immigration and Naturalization in the Department of Commerce and Labor.[93]

The 1906 Act laid out three steps in the naturalization process. An applicant had to file a declaration of intention (first papers), and then a petition for naturalization (second papers). Between the first papers and the second would come a time interval of no less than two years nor more than seven. A hearing in open court, no less than ninety days after the filing of the petition, would award or deny the certificate of naturalization (final papers). In both the petition and the hearing, an applicant had to convince the court that she or he was a person of good moral character, not an anarchist or a polygamist, that he or she had lived continuously in the country for at least five years and at least one year in the state where the hearing occurred, and that she or he could speak English.[94]

Before a certificate of naturalization could be granted, an applicant had to renounce any title of nobility, if he or she had one, and to swear an oath in open court. The requirement to shed nobility and the wording of the oath are in the law.

> Third—He shall, before he is admitted to citizenship, declare on oath in open court that he will support the Constitution of the United States, and that he absolutely and entirely renounces and abjures all allegiance and fidelity to any foreign prince, potentate, state, or sovereignty, and particularly by name to the prince, potentate, state, or sovereignty of which he was before a citizen or a subject; *that he will support and defend the Constitution and laws of the United States against all enemies, foreign and domestic*, and bear true faith and allegiance to the same.[95]

To facilitate getting applicants for naturalization to the final hearings in open court and to ensure that they met standards and requirements for citizenship, the Bureau of Naturalization employed naturalization examiners. As they worked with applicants these people would judge whether persons fit the requirements for naturalization. Judges relied heavily on the recommendations of naturalization examiners in the final hearing process. The naturalization service developed a form that had to be completed as a part of the petition for naturalization (second papers). This form requested information such as one's previous country, method of passage to the United States, current address, and marital status. In addition, it asked some more substantive questions in reference to requirements for citizenship. Applicants were asked, for example, whether they understood the system of government in the United States, whether they had read the required oath of citizenship and were willing to take it, and whether they were polygamists or anarchists. In 1922 or 1923, question 22—"If necessary, are you willing to take up arms in defense of this country?"—was added to the form. Therein lies the seed of the human conflict recounted in this book. Yet before that tale can be told, it is necessary to understand pacifism in its historical development.

Notes

1. Frank Kingdon, *As FDR Said: A Treasury of His Speeches, Conversations, and Writings.* (New York: Duell, Sloan and Pearce, 1950), 30.

2. See Martha Strayer, *The D.A.R.: An Informal History* (Westport, Conn.: Greenwood Press, 1958), 57.

3. See Winifred Mallon, "President Reminds D.A.R. Forefathers Shed Fascist Yoke; 'You and I Are Descended From Immigrants and Revolutionists,' He Says," *New York Times*, 22 April 1938, 1, 9; "Daughters of Rebels And Also of Immigrants, Roosevelt Reminds D.A.R.," *Newsweek* 11 (2 May 1938):10; "Continental Congress," *Time Magazine* 31 (2 May 1938): 13. See also "Extemporaneous Remarks Before the Daughters of the American Revolution. Washington, D.C. April 21, 1938," in *The Public Papers and Addresses of Franklin D. Roosevelt 7: The Continuing Struggle for Liberalism,* Samuel I. Rosenman, ed. (New York: Macmillan, 1941), 259. On the same day President Roosevelt spoke to some newspaper editors and explained his remarks to the D.A.R. "I am going to tell you what I said to the D.A.R. today. (*Laughter*) I am going to preach the same sermon to you that I preached to them. It is a perfectly good text. I said that I probably had a more American ancestry than nine out of ten of the D.A.R. I had various ancestors who came over in the *Mayflower* and similar ships—one that carried the cargo of furniture—and furthermore that I did not have a single ancestor who came to this country after the Revolutionary War; they were all here before the Revolution. And, out of the whole thirty-two or sixty-four of them, whichever it was, there was only one Tory. (*Laughter*) Well, they began to wonder if they ought to applaud that or not. And, I said, now I will come down to the text. It is just as good for your people as it was for the D.A.R. I am putting you

in the same category. (*Laughter*) I said, Here is the text: Keep in the front of your heads all of the time, dear ladies, first, that you are the descendants of immigrants. And they did not know whether to applaud that or not. Secondly, that you are the descendants of revolutionists. They did not know whether to applaud that or not." "A Special Press Conference with the Members of the American Society of Newspaper Editors. Washington, D.C. April 21, 1938." *Papers of Franklin D. Roosevelt*, 7: 260-61.

4. William H. A. Williams, "Immigration as a Pattern in American Culture," in *The Immigration Reader: America in a Multidisciplinary Perspective*, David Jacobson, ed. (Malden, Mass.: Blackwell Publishers, 1998), 19, 27. Emphasis in original.

5. Maldwyn Allen Jones, *American Immigration*, 2d ed. (Chicago: University of Chicago Press, 1992), 7; *American Christianity: An Historical Interpretation with Representative Documents* 1: *1607-1820*, H. Shelton Smith, Robert T. Handy, and Lefferts A. Loetscher, eds. (New York: Charles Scribner's Sons, 1960), 7-8.

6. Nathaniel Ward, "The Simple Cobbler of Aggawam," in *American Christianity 1607-1820*, 127.

7. Nathan Glazer, *American Judaism* (Chicago: University of Chicago Press, 1957), 12-13.

8. Jones, *American Immigration*, 15, 23, 26.

9. William S. Bernard, "A History of U.S. Immigration Policy," in *Immigration: Dimensions of Ethnicity*, Stephan Thernstrom, ed. (Cambridge, Mass.: Belknap Press, 1982), 76-78.

10. William Warren Sweet, *Religion in Colonial America* (New York: Charles Scribner's Sons, 1953), 151-52. The letter is dated 17 April 1663.

11. Winthrop S. Hudson, *Religion in America* (New York: Charles Scribner's Sons, 1965), 11.

12. Jones, *American Immigration*, 18, 27.

13. Bernard, "A History of U.S. Immigration Policy," 81; Jones, *American Immigration*, 54, 57, 59.

14. Bernard, "A History of U.S. Immigration Policy," 80-81; Roger Daniels, "What Is an American? Ethnicity, Race, the Constitution and the Immigrant in Early American History," in *The Immigration Reader*, 40. Article 1, Sec. 9 reads: "The Migration or Importation of such Persons as any of the States now existing shall think proper to admit, shall not be prohibited by the Congress prior to the Year one thousand eight hundred and eight, but a Tax or duty may be imposed on such Importation, not exceeding ten dollars for each Person."

15. Jones, *American Immigration*, 79.

16. Jones, *American Immigration*, 153, 91-93, 97; Martin E. Marty, *Righteous Empire: The Protestant Experience in America* (New York: Dial Press, 1970), 127-28.

17. Jones, *American Immigration*, 100.

18. Jones, *American Immigration*, 80-83, 108-09; Richard A. Easterlin, "Economic and Social Characteristics of Immigrants," in *Immigration*, 26-28; Edwin Scott Gaustad and Philip L. Barlow, *New Historical Atlas of Religion in America* (New York: Oxford University Press, 2001), 123-28.

19. Marcus Lee Hansen, *The Immigrant in American History* (New York: Harper Torchbooks, 1964), 81. Professor Hansen explains immigrant motives: "What poor people wanted was freedom from laws and customs that curbed individual economic enterprise. . . . In other words, they wanted the freedom to buy, sell and bargain, to work or loaf, to become rich or poor. Little wonder that free enterprise was the thought that predominated when immigrants reported the blessings of the New World. . . . To enjoy the opportunities of free enterprise and to preserve the fruits thereof—this was the aspiration of the rank and file of immigrants."

20. Hansen, *Immigrant in American History*, 77-79.

21. Jones, *American Immigration*, 87-88; Edward P. Hutchinson, *Legislative History of American Immigration Policy, 1798-1965* (Philadelphia: University of Pennsylvania Press, 1981), 21. For an account of the nature of the passage, see Hansen, *Immigrant in American History*, 30-52.

22. 11 Peters 102 (1837). Until 1874, when for the first time Congress fully funded reporting of Supreme Court cases, beginning the series *United States Reports*, volumes of case reports carried the names of court reporters–in this case, Richard Peters.

23. Bernard, "A History of U.S. Immigration Policy," 80-83; Jones, *American Immigration*, 57; Hutchinson, *Legislative History of American Immigration Policy*, 21-22.

24. Williams, "Immigration as a Pattern in American Culture," 22; Jones, *American Immigration*, 109-117. A moving, poignant scholarly presentation of immigration from the immigrants' point of view is Oscar Handlin's *The Uprooted: The Epic Story of the Great Migrations That Made the American People* (New York: Grosset and Dunlap, 1951). Some scholars think Handlin's account romanticized, yet it remains a classic in immigration literature.

25. Bernard, "A History of U.S. Immigration Policy," 87; Alan M. Kraut, *The Huddled Masses: The Immigrant in American Society, 1880-1921* (Arlington Heights, Ill.: Harlan Davidson, 1982), 16-25.

26. Jones, *American Immigration*, 158.

27. Kraut, *Huddled Masses*, 28-40; Howard Morley Sachar, *The Course of Modern Jewish History*, rev. ed. (New York: Dell Publishing, 1977), 243-46, 305-14.

28. Kraut, *Huddled Masses*, 76-77, 115-22.

29. Kraut, *Huddled Masses*, 27.

30. Bernard, "A History of U.S. Immigration Policy," 85.

31. 92 U.S. 259 (1876).

32. Reed Ueda, "Immigration," in *The Oxford Companion to the Supreme Court of the United States*, Kermit L. Hall, ed. (New York: Oxford University Press, 1992), 420-21.

33. John Higham, *Strangers in the Land: Patterns of American Nativism 1860-1925* (New York: Atheneum, 1963), 5-9.

34. Kraut, *Huddled Masses*, 151.

35. Daniels, "What Is an American?" 31-32.

36. Ray Allen Billington, *The Protestant Crusade, 1800-1860: A Study of the Origins of American Nativism* (Chicago: Quadrangle Books, 1964), 1-4, 32-33.

37. Jones, *American Immigration*, 126-29; Billington, *Protestant Crusade*, 38-47. See also Charles R. Morris, *American Catholic: The Saints and Sinners Who Built America's Most Powerful Church* (New York: Vintage Books, 1998), 74-75.

38. Robert Michaelsen offers a classic treatment of this characteristic of public education and the controversy surrounding it in *Piety in the Public School: Trends and Issues in the Relationship Between Religion and the Public School in the United States* (New York: Macmillan, 1970), particularly 45-108.

39. Archbishop John Hughes of New York played a major role in all these efforts; see Andrew M. Greeley, *The Catholic Experience* (Garden City, N.Y.: Doubleday Anchor Books, 1969), 102-26. Greeley argues that the belligerent, combative Hughes played right into nativist propaganda. In 1850 Hughes declared, speaking of the Catholic Church and its objectives, "There is no secret about this. The object we hope to accomplish in kindness is to convert all pagan nations and all Protestant nations. . . . Everybody should know that we have for our mission to convert the world, including the inhabitants of the United States, the people of the cities, the people of the country, the officers of the Navy and the Marines, commanders of the Army, the legislatures, the Senate, the Cabinet, the President, and all" (Greeley, *The Catholic Experience*, 107-8).

40. In 1922 Oregon, by public referendum, required all children without special education needs to attend public school, intending to Americanize immigrant children. Challenged by a parochial school and a secular military academy, the law was struck down by the Supreme Court in *Pierce v. Society of Sisters* 268 U.S. 510 (1925), which declared the law unconstitutional because the Fourteenth Amendment protected the right of private entities to make a living unforbidden by the state and the right of parents to direct the education of their children. See Michaelsen, *Piety in Public Schools*, 149-56.

41. Billington, *Protestant Crusade*, 98-117, 53-84.

42. Kraut, *Huddled Masses*, 151.

43. Its constitution clearly reveals the objectives of this organization: "The object of this organization shall be to protect every American citizen in the legal and proper exercise of all his civil and religious rights and privileges; to resist the insidious policy of the Church of Rome, and all other foreign influence against our republican institutions in all lawful ways; to place in all offices of honor, trust, or profit, in the gift of the people, or by appointment, none but native-born Protestant

citizens, and to protect, preserve, and uphold the Union of these states and the Constitution of the same" (Billington, *Protestant Crusade*, 386). All the groups mentioned so far in this paragraph opposed open immigration and Catholicism.
44. The DAR thoroughly supported immigration restriction legislation of 1924. The President-General, Mrs. Anthony Wayne Cook, spoke to the DAR's 1924 annual convention in foreboding terms of the masses of immigrants in Europe poised to flood into America if Congress lifted immigration restrictions. "A two per cent quota of admission, based upon the naturalization of alien immigrants during 1890," Mrs. Cook concluded, "would prove a mighty bulwark to stem the flood of foreign immigrants." Yet the DAR prided itself on helping immigrants to learn about America, to learn English, to acquire domestic skills, and to qualify for naturalization. The organization operated an aid program at Ellis Island for many years and published an educational book to accomplish the goals just mentioned. Included in the 1921 edition of the book was a "Message to the Immigrant": "America expects that those who come here shall accept its institutions, obey its laws and be peaceful, honest, industrious naturalized citizens. America expects them to respect and defend the flag that protects them; to love, honor, and pay loyalty to the country that gives them this peace, happiness and prosperity; to make themselves worthy to receive the great gift of American citizenship; to become true Americans in heart and soul." Consequently, a historian of the DAR speaks of one of its "prime inconsistencies—opposition to increased immigration and great pride in its record of aid to immigrants in the past" (Strayer, *The D.A.R.*, 58, 62-63, 58).
45. Raymond Moley, Jr. *The American Legion Story* (New York: Duell, Sloan, and Pearce, 1966), 175. Roscoe Baker (*The American Legion and American Foreign Policy* [New York: Bookman Associates, 1954], 65) offers a good summary of attitudes of the American Legion, founded in 1919, toward immigration and immigrants. "At various times in the period 1919 to 1948, the Legion called for banning of immigration for periods of five, ten and two years. None of these was adopted by Congress. When complete banning of immigration was not adopted, the Legion accepted the quota system based on national origins. From time to time the Legion tried to get tighter restrictions enacted into laws regulating immigration and naturalization. The Legion's policies have been partly accepted in these matters. The Immigration Act of 1924, based on national origins, has become the policy of the United States in handling the immigration problem. The Legion has favored immigration restrictions to bar aliens who were considered 'slackers' in that they would not bear arms in the defense of the United States, to prevent aliens from adding to unemployment problems in the United States, to prevent subversive activity, to prevent aliens from being a threat to the national security, and to prevent aliens from competing with veterans for jobs and for housing."
46. 22 *Statutes at Large* 59. This citation form refers to *The Statutes at Large of the United States of America* (Washington: United States Government Printing Office, 1845-1936) and its annual volumes.

47. Jones, *American Immigration*, 212-14; Kraut, *Huddled Masses*, 156; Bernard, "A History of U.S. Immigration Policy," 97-89. See Lawrence H. Fuchs, "Immigration Policy," in *The Encyclopedia of the United States Congress*, Donald C. Bacon, Roger H. Davidson, and Morton Keller, eds. (New York: Simon and Schuster, 1995), 2: 1093 for a useful overview with a chart of major legislation.

48. 23 *Statutes at Large* 58.

49. 25 *Statutes at Large* 476. These regulations excepted government officials, teachers, students, and tourists; see Fuchs, "Immigration Policy," 1093-94; Marion T. Bennett, *American Immigration Policies: A History* (Washington: Public Affairs Press, 1963), 15-21, 25, 37-39.

50. Lazarus wrote the poem to be auctioned at a gala in 1883 in an effort to finance the pedestal on which the Statue would stand in New York harbor. Her poem was not read at the dedication, and the inscribed plaque was not even placed on the pedestal until 1903. (Lazarus died in 1887.) See Bette Roth Young, *Emma Lazarus in Her World: Life and Letters* (Philadelphia: Jewish Publication Society, 1995), 3. Despite this time lapse, most historians see the connection between the poem and the Statue as coterminous; see Kraut, *Huddled Masses*, 1-2, and Edwin Scott Gaustad, *A Religious History of America*, rev. ed. (New York: Harper and Row, 1990), 181. Young (p. 11) writes that Lazarus gave the Statue an identity. By 1883, when she wrote the poem, Emma Lazarus had become keenly aware of the plight of Jewish immigrants to America. "Calling her [the Statue] 'Mother of Exiles,' [in an earlier part of the poem] she brought America's most illustrious immigrant [the Statue had been given to America by France] down to earth to welcome exiles from around the world. Her Statue could not wait for the concept of liberty to triumph in distant lands; she offered liberty now, to the globe's great unwashed. Lazarus' poem reinforced the concept of America as a haven for the homeless. It came, appropriately, at a time when this country was overwhelmed by an unending torrent of immigrants" (Young, *Emma Lazarus in Her World*, 4).

51. 26 *Statutes at Large* 1084.

52. Bernard, "A History of U.S. Immigration Policy," 90-91; Fuchs, "Immigration Policy," 1098.

53. *INS Fact Book* (Washington, D.C.: Department of Justice, Immigration and Naturalization Service, January 1997), Foreword.

54. Bernard, "A History of U.S. Immigration Policy, 93-94; Fuchs, "Immigration Policy," 1094.

55. Proposals for a literacy test predated the Dillingham Report, as congressional debate in 1906 demonstrates, even as it exhibits racist attitudes among some members of Congress and use of the test to exclude "undesirables." According to Representative Oscar W. Underwood, Democrat of Alabama, on 25 June 1906, "The educational test will not only separate the ignorant, vicious, and the lazy from the intelligent and industrious classes that are coming to this country, but to a large extent it will eliminate the lower classes of immigrants from the countries that are not of Teutonic and Celtic origin, and to some degree will solve the problem of the assimilation of the dissimilar races" (Hutchinson, *Legislative*

History of American Immigration Policy, 141).

56. 39 *Statutes at Large* 874.

57. The literacy test proved ineffective because there were too many exceptions to it. People under sixteen did not have to take it. Family members of admitted aliens, if they were over fifty-five, could be admitted even if they were illiterate. The test required reading forty words, not forty sentences, in any language, so one could be admitted without any knowledge of English. Political refugees and those escaping religious persecution were also exempt from the test. Bennett, *American Immigration Policies*, 27, 302-303.

58. 42 *Statutes at Large* 5.

59. Bernard, "A History of U.S. Immigration Policy," 94-95; Fuchs, "Immigration Policy," 1095; Jones, *American Immigration*, 236.

60. Jones, *American Immigration*, 235; See Arthur Hertzberg, *The Jews in America: Four Centuries of an Uneasy Encounter: A History* (New York: Simon and Schuster, 1989), 249-54.

61. Kraut, *Huddled Masses*, 171-76.

62. 42 *Statutes at Large* 153.

63. Jones, *American Immigration*, 238.

64. Kraut, *Huddled Masses*, 177.

65. Bernard, "A History of U.S. Immigration Policy," 97-98.

66. 66 *Statutes at Large* 163.

67. This and several ensuing paragraphs rely on the research of Robert A. Divine, *American Immigration Policy, 1924-1952* (New Haven: Yale University Press, 1957), 187-91. Divine offers a helpful and readable overview (164-91) of the McCarran-Walter Act.

68. *Congressional Record* (27 June 1952), 8267, quoted in Divine, *American Immigration Policy, 1924-1952*, 191.

69. Bernard, "A History of U.S. Immigration Policy," 102-103.

70. *Congressional Record* (25 June 1952), 8082-3, quoted in Divine, *American Immigration Policy, 1924-1952*, 184.

71. 66 *Statutes at Large* 163.

72. 79 *Statutes at Large* 911.

73. Fuchs, "Immigration Policy," 1099.

74. Reed Ueda, "Naturalization and Citizenship," in *Immigration*, 107.

75. James H. Kettner, *The Development of American Citizenship, 1608-1870* (Chapel Hill: University of North Carolina Press, 1978), 74-75. Church of England (Anglicans), Presbyterians, Congregationalists, Baptists, German Reformed, Dutch Reformed, French Reformed, and probably Lutherans would have been included in this category; see Gaustad and Barlow, *New Historical Atlas of Religion in America*, 46-48.

76. Ueda, "Naturalization and Citizenship," 109-112.

77. John P. Roche, *The Early Development of United States Citizenship* (Ithaca, N.Y.: Cornell University Press, 1949), 2-3.

78. Ueda, "Naturalization and Citizenship," 114-15; Daniels, "What Is an American?," 40-41; Kettner, *Development of American Citizenship*, 224-25, 230-32; Roche, *Early Development of U.S. Citizenship*, 5-7.

79. 1 *Statutes at Large* 103.

80. Roche, *Early Development of U.S. Citizenship*, 10; Kettner, *Development of American Citizenship*, 238-39; For congressional debate leading to the passage of the Naturalization Act of 1790, see Frank G. Franklin, *The Legislative History of Naturalization in the United States* (Chicago: University of Chicago Press, 1906; repr., New York: Arno Press, 1969), 33-48.

81. Daniels, "What Is an American?," 42-54; Kettner, *Development of American Citizenship*, 239-43; Franklin, *Legislative History of Naturalization in the U.S.*, 49-71.

82. Roche, *Early Development of U.S. Citizenship*, 11.

83. 1 *Statutes at Large* 566; Jones, *American Immigration*, 72-75.

84. 2 *Statutes at Large* 153.

85. Roche, *Early Development of U.S. Citizenship*, 14.

86. Billington, *Protestant Crusade*, 200-203; Jones, *American Immigration*, 134.

87. 19 Howard 393 (1857).

88. Ueda, "Naturalization and Citizenship," 121-22; Walter Erlich, "Scott v. Sandford," in *The Oxford Companion to the Supreme Court of the United States*, Kermit L. Hall, ed. (New York: Oxford University Press, 1992), 759-61.

89. 14 *Statutes at Large* 428.

90. Roche, *Early Development of U.S. Citizenship*, 24; Ueda, "Naturalization and Citizenship," 122-23; Kettner, *Development of American Citizenship*, 342.

91. Roche, *Early Development of U.S. Citizenship*, 26.

92. 34 *Statutes at Large* 596. Another Nationality Act, in 1940, would be crucial to the Supreme Court's determination of *Girouard* v. *United States*.

93. Luella Gettys, *The Law of Citizenship in the United States* (Chicago: University of Chicago Press, 1934), 31-33. In 1909 the Department of Commerce and Labor differentiated the Division of Naturalization in a discrete unit. In 1913 the Bureau of Naturalization was placed under the supervision of the newly independent Department of Labor. In 1933, by executive order, President Roosevelt consolidated the Bureau of Immigration and the Bureau of Naturalization into the Immigration and Naturalization Service (Gettys, 34).

94. Ueda, "Naturalization and Citizenship," 127-28; Gettys, *Law of Citizenship*, 37-42. These requirements are laid out the Naturalization Act of 1906 itself: "Fourth—It shall be made to appear to the satisfaction of the court admitting any alien to citizenship that immediately preceding the date of his application he has resided continuously within the United States five years at least, and within the State or Territory where such court is at the time held one year at least, and that during that time he has behaved as a man [*sic*] of good moral character, attached to the principles of the Constitution of the United States, and well disposed to the good order and happiness of the same. In addition to the oath of the applicant, the

testimony of at least two witnesses, citizens of the United States, as to the facts of residence, moral character, and attachment to the principles of the Constitution shall be required, and the name, place of residence, and occupation of each witness shall be set forth in the record" (34 *Statutes at Large* 596, chapter 3592, sec. 4).

95. Naturalization Act of 1906, 34 *Statutes at Large* 596, chapter 3592, sec. 3 (italics added). The italicized clause is that part of the oath that is absolutely crucial to the stories told in this book. This clause did not appear in naturalization laws until this 1906 Act. From 1790 until 1906, applicants were not required to pledge to defend the Constitution against all enemies.

Two

Peace and War

"There are few finer or more exalted sentiments than that which finds expression in opposition to war," Justice George Sutherland wrote in the Supreme Court case *United States v. Macintosh*. "Peace is a sweet and holy thing, and war is a hateful and abominable thing to be avoided by any sacrifice or concession that a free people can make."[1] Justice Sutherland here defined one of the perennial dilemmas of humankind. Although the term "pacifist" was not invented until 1901,[2] modern historians have labeled as "pacifists" some people who through the centuries have attempted as best they could to make peace in human relationships and eliminate war.

Pacifist impulses may be traced to antiquity, perhaps as early as Akhenaton, king of Egypt in the fourteenth century before the Christian era (B.C.E.). Lao-Tse, in China in the seventh century B.C.E., Gautama Buddha and Mahavira, the founder of Jainism, in India in the sixth century B.C.E., and Herodotus, Euripides and Aristophanes in Greece in the fifth century B.C.E. are among those who thought peace more desirable than war. Buddhism and Jainism continue to teach *ahimsa*, the concept of noninjury.[3]

In the Western world from antiquity onward Christianity has provided the primary rationale and principal locus for pacifism. The first three centuries of Christian history became a laboratory for Christians to formulate and live out principles of nonviolence and antimilitarism. Rooted deeply in Jewish soil, the earliest Christians inherited Jewish attitudes toward war and peace. On these issues Jewish tradition, like every other tradition, bore a burden of ambiguity.

An essential element of Israel's religious consciousness is found in the command "You shall not kill." Scholars debate whether the original Hebrew is more properly translated "kill" or "murder," the latter seeming to have a more restricted meaning than the former. Yet even if the command is translated "You shall not kill," the people Israel did not understand it to prohibit taking of all life. It did not forbid killing of animals or capital punishment, nor did it prohibit war, in which Israel was often engaged.[4]

Yet as an extension of the command not to kill we find a continuing quest for peace in Israel's consciousness. *Shalom* is a central concept of Hebrew Scripture with many dimensions. The root meaning of the word seems to be "wholeness," "completeness," "healthfulness." Individual peace is health and the good life. Peace is restoration to health after illness, as is safe return from battle. Likewise, communal peace is the prosperity and security of the family, community, or the nation. Certainly peace follows an end of warfare; yet, more profoundly, it is absence of war. For both individual and community, peace comes from righteousness, as the consequence of a virtuous life. To be at peace is to be upright, faithful, trustworthy, and just. God determines and gives peace, *shalom*. Peace is the presence of God. A person's or a nation's righteousness makes peace. The wholeness—*peace*—of a person's or a nation's life depends on obedience to God.[5]

Peace did not pervade the history of Israel. War played a significant role in that history. In Exodus 15:3, as praise and thanksgiving for deliverance from the bondage of Egypt, Israel sang, "Yahweh is a man of war." Deliverance from Egypt and God's promise of a homeland become the foundation for "holy war" in Israel's history. Holy war is, by definition, warfare inspired, directed, blessed, and even carried out by God. A military commander leading troops or a ruler who ordered war did not act alone, but were thought to have divine authorization for their actions. Neither did a soldier fight alone: "Yahweh your God is the one who goes with you, to fight for you against your enemies, to give you victory" (Deut. 20:4).

Israel developed the holy war idea and used it most frequently during the period of the Judges, when, after the Exodus, they were retaking possession of Canaan, the land God had promised them. During the period of monarchy, the kings imposed more regulation on the military activities of the nation. Holy war continued. Although the prophets often opposed wars, frequently they did so because they believed the people had lost their devotion to God and consequently were in danger of losing. Holy war was not incompatible with prophetic faith. Holy war resurfaced during the Maccabean rebellion against Hellenistic rulers in the period just prior to the rise of Christianity. How the people of God shall conduct war is clearly defined and graphically presented in Deuteronomy 20.[6] Holy war in

Hebrew Scripture is sometimes described as a "crusade" concept of war, fighting intended to spread the faith—a philosophy that we shall examine more thoroughly.[7] Some scholars disagree with that designation. According to Everett E. Gendler, "To attempt to spread one's faith by force of arms was utterly foreign to Israel, and until the time of the Maccabees the concept of a war of religion had not appeared." Gendler cites the work of Roland de Vaux: "This is the principal fact: it was Yahweh who fought for Israel, not Israel which fought for its God. The holy war, in Israel, was not a war of religion. . . . Israel is not fighting (directly) for its religious freedom, but for its existence as a people."[8]

Israel without doubt endorsed war and the belief that God fought on behalf of the people of God—but that was not the entire tradition. There was that statement in the Decalogue, "You shall not kill," and there was more. From at least the eighth century B.C.E., Judaism looked forward to a Messiah, an "anointed one" of God who would create a new world. In that new world Israel would find peace, an absolute cessation of war. The prophet Isaiah wrote of that future time when natural enemies would coexist.

> The wolf shall dwell with the lamb,
>   and the leopard shall lie down with the kid,
> and the calf and the lion and the fatling together,
>   and a little child shall lead them. . . .
> The sucking child shall play over the hole of the asp,
>   and the weaned child shall put his hand on the adder's den.

Government in those times would be transformed, by peace and for peace. A "great light" would illumine the way for a people hitherto "in darkness." The boots and blood-soaked garments of warriors would be "burned as fuel for the fire."

> For to us a child is born, to us a son is given;
>   and the government will be upon his shoulder,
> and his name will be called "Wonderful Counselor, Mighty God,
>   Everlasting Father, Prince of Peace."
> Of the increase of his government and of peace
>   there will be no end.

In the most famous, perhaps the most pertinent passage, God "shall judge between the nations" and end their ancient rivalries,

and they shall beat their swords into plowshares,
    and their spears into pruning hooks;
nation shall not lift up sword against nation,
    neither shall they learn war any more.[9]

One can read these texts to teach that the people of God should abstain
from war-making, and so contemporary pacifists regularly interpret them.[10]

Christians in the early church knew this prophetic tradition. Indeed
they believed that the Messiah had come in the person of Jesus Christ and
that those who believed in him should adhere to his ethic of peace. Jesus'
teachings centered on the Kingdom of God, not as a political entity but as
the reign of righteousness to come. God would not establish or maintain
the kingdom by force of arms. Jesus' sayings are remarkably devoid of
statements about war, given that it does not seem to have been a central
concern for him. Yet Jesus repeatedly speaks of peace and love. This is
particularly true of sayings found in the so-called Sermon on the Mount
(Matt. 5:1-7:29). "The meek," Jesus says, "shall inherit the earth," and
"the peacemakers . . . shall be called sons of God." While the ancients had
heard "an eye for an eye and a tooth for a tooth," Jesus says, "Do not resist
one who is evil. But if any one strikes you on the right cheek, turn to him
the other also." Heretofore Jesus' own people—and indeed all humankind—had been instructed to "love your neighbor and hate your enemy,"
but Jesus says, "Love your enemies and pray for those who persecute you,
so that you may be sons of your Father who is in heaven." These teachings
bring us to Jesus' so-called, summary Golden Rule: "So whatever you wish
that people would do to you, do so to them; for this is the law and the
prophets."[11]

According to Peter Brock, a noted historian of pacifism, Jesus'
importance to the pacifist tradition "does not depend on any one text" but
rather "emerges from a consideration of his total outlook on God and
humankind." Jesus never teaches directly about war, but given his
"message of nonviolence" and especially "his love commandments," Brock
concludes that "it requires considerable ingenuity to show how the waging
of war can be squared with his injunctions as these are presented to us in
the Sermon on the Mount or the Beatitudes."[12]

Although Jesus founds the Christian ethic of peace, he is not alone in
teaching it. His messenger Paul, writing to Christians at Rome itself, urges
them to "Bless those who persecute you; bless and do not curse them."
Again echoing the words of Jesus, Paul admonishes his readers to "repay

no one evil for evil, but take thought for what is noble in the sight of all. If possible, so far as it depends on you, live at peace with all." Christians are never to seek vengeance, "but leave it to the wrath of God," as Moses in Deuteronomy had taught: "Vengeance is mine, I will repay, says the Lord." Paul repeats the advice of ancient wisdom: "If your enemy is hungry, feed him; if he is thirsty, give him drink; for by so doing you will heap burning coals upon his head." "Do not be overcome by evil," Paul concludes, extending the teaching of Jesus, "but overcome evil with good."[13]

Christians in the early church did not serve in the Roman military. There were some practical reasons for this. Until about 170 in the Christian era (C.E.), given the stability and the efficiency of the *Pax Romana*, there was little demand for recruits in the Roman army. Citizenship was a requirement for military service, but most Christians were not Roman citizens. Indeed Rome regarded Christians as disloyal and subversive, both politically and theologically, and periodically prosecuted them.[14]

Theological reasons also explain why Christians did not serve in the military. Christians obeyed teachings of Jesus and other New Testament worthies. In obedience to Jesus' teachings, early Christians were pacifists. Christians would not serve in the military because, as peacemakers, they sought to be meek and to "turn the other cheek." Soldiers often engaged in blackmail, intimidation, extortion, fornication, and other "vulgar" or immoral acts. Christian moral teaching forbade that kind of behavior. In Rome the emperor had been deified and was worshiped as one of the gods. The army required soldiers to worship the emperor and required military officers to offer sacrifices to the gods, including the emperor, while soldiers witnessed and assisted in the ceremonies. Soldiers venerated military insignia as divine objects. Christians, as monotheistic worshipers of one true God, would not subject themselves to such demands. For all these reasons Christians avoided service in the military.[15]

After about 170 C.E. Rome began to conscript Christians. Sometimes pagan soldiers converted to Christianity. Christians in the military either found their way around some offensive practices or compromised their values. Some studies suggest that Christian soldiers made a "sign of the cross" before witnessing or participating in a ceremony of worship of the emperor, thereby assuaging their consciences. Some Christian soldiers, however, were executed or otherwise severely punished for not following orders that they considered contrary to their faith. Military service placed

Christians in a morally difficult position. Through the first century and most of the second, Christians—in obedience to the teachings of Jesus, were absolute pacifists. In the latter part of the second century and throughout the third, some Christians served in the military, but most Christians maintained the pacifist tradition.[16]

The fourth century brought dramatic change. Early on the Emperor Constantine recognized Christianity as a legitimate religion. Imperial persecution stopped. Christians no longer had to fear mistreatment by those in authority. Constantine began a process that eventually made Christianity the official religion of the Roman Empire. Once it had been a political liability to be a Christian; now it was a political asset. In contrast to the pre-Constantinian world, Emperor Theodosius II ruled in the early fifth century that only Christians could serve in the military.

With this changed relation to the human order came a new view of war. Now that Christians governed, they had to contemplate maintaining order in society and defending the empire against invaders. Protecting the empire was not a hypothetical abstraction. In the late fourth and early fifth centuries "barbarians" who spoke neither Greek nor Latin began to raid deep into the empire. In 410 Rome fell to the Goths; sending shock waves throughout the empire. Ambrose, Bishop of Milan, and Augustine, Bishop of Hippo in North Africa, began to think of "just war."[17]

Augustine articulated the "just war theory," or, better, the "justifiable war theory," in *The City of God*, a history and analysis of the relation of the church to the world. According to Augustine, there are two cities, each based on love. The city of God is built on love of God, while the earthly city rests on love of self. In the real world, these two cities are intertwined and inseparable. Thus Christians, while devoted to God, must be concerned with affairs of this world. In Augustine's own time, Christians had to defend both the earthly city and the city of God against the hordes of barbarians threatening to overrun the Roman Empire. This practical necessity stimulated Augustine to propose just war theory in order to defend civilization and Christendom in a manner consistent with Christian ethics. Augustine hoped to bring warfare within the purview of moral law. War was not to be just wanton destruction, but was to be conducted by rules that would make it humane—as humane as war ever could be. The characteristics that make war "just" deserve careful examination. For now it is enough to say that Christian attitudes toward war had moved from absolute pacifism to justifiable—that is, ethical—warfare a remarkable transition. Just war theory has persisted to become the dominant concept in Roman Catholicism and most Protestant groups to the present time.[18] Yet just war was not the last permutation on themes of war and peace in the history of the church. In the eleventh century, the crusade arose in response to several crises in the history of the church. From its beginning in the seventh century Islam expanded rapidly, largely through conquest. Muhammad, the founder of Islam, died in 632 C.E. Under his successors, Jerusalem came under Muslim control in 638 and by 640 all the region Christians call "the Holy Land" was under Islamic rule. Much later, in 1054, the Eastern branch of the church separated from Rome over a variety of theological issues, including the authority of the papacy, to form the Eastern Orthodox Church. The Roman Catholic Church was catholic (the word means "universal") no more. Western Christians feared that the entire Byzantine Empire might fall to Islam, thus exposing territory influenced by the Roman Church to the Muslims. Therefore, Pope Urban II challenged those assembled at the Council of Clermont in November 1095 to launch a campaign—a crusade—to liberate the Holy Land from the Muslims, to protect the Byzantine Empire, and to reunite western and eastern Christianity. Such a campaign would, of course, have to proceed by the edge of the sword. Those who heard this challenge responded with enthusiasm, crying, "God wills it." They launched almost 200 years (the last crusade ran its course in 1270) of crusading spirit and activity. In the latter part of the period crusaders in the south of France attacked Christians accused of heretical beliefs. Although the crusades never accomplished the specific goals that called them into being, they produced incredible brutality and loss of life among both crusaders and their enemies.[19]

With the cry "God wills it," the just war became the crusade. As in the holy war of Old Testament times, war received divine authorization. Yet the parallel is not precise. Israel was not spreading its faith by force of arms, but the same cannot be said for the crusade. The church inaugurated crusades save "the holy land" from "infidels." Crusaders enlisted to save the faith and to advance the faith in the name and under the guidance of God. While just war theory attempts to make war ethical, a crusade tends to disregard moral imperatives in its sacred mission. Fighters for God (or nation) tend to "go all out" to eliminate the evil of those perceived to be apostates from the true religion (or political system). God's approval excuses excesses of zeal, even if they result in atrocities.

From this historical survey we may begin to analyze the three ways Christians have understood peace and war—the crusade, the just war, and pacifism.[20] The crusade understands war as conflict between good and evil; there is no "gray area." Crusaders tend to demonize and stereotype the enemy; they hate the enemy more for who he is than for what he does. Our side is righteous, the other side represents abject evil. The crusade's cause is righteous because "God is on our side" or "God wills it." The crusade is God's war; crusaders are God's warriors. Therefore, crusades seek absolute and unlimited goals. Because crusaders wage war against the enemies of God, the goal is the annihilation of the enemy, or, at the very least, unconditional surrender. In crusade the means of war are unrestrained. If the goal is the eradication of the enemy, then it makes no sense to hold back the resources of war-making available. The crusade is the waging of total war, by implication ignoring any difference between combatants and noncombatants. In crusade the latter are just as much subject to destruction as the former. The same is true of property; civilian homes are just as likely to be in the line of fire, beneath the bombs, as military installations.[21]

Just war advocates conceive of war quite differently. Although others beside Christians use just war theory, Christians developed it and I shall discuss it from that perspective. Just war theory begins with a conviction that Christians are called to be peacemakers. Yet it also recognizes that sin in the world causes people to make war. The state thus has an obligation to wage war to protect citizens from aggressors and to restore what has been unjustly taken. Rulers may use force to try to restore peace and to preserve or recover a just order in society. Just war thinkers, beginning with Augustine, have insisted that warring people remember that God is God of all, the enemy as well as the friend. This prevents one side from deifying its cause and demonizing the enemy.

Just warriors must initiate war with ethical principles in mind. First, the war must have a justifiable cause. Such causes would be to protect people from attack, to restore rights that illegitimately have been taken away, or to defend or restore a just social order. This usually, but not always, means that the just warrior will defend rather than attack. Second, the highest authority possible must declare war. Nations should never wage war for private purposes, but to serve a public good. Only those who speak for the population and who are accountable to the people should make the decision to wage war. When a nation declares war, it should state its war aims or goals. The nations waging war should know what the purpose of the war is. Third, the war should be a last resort. Nations should wage war only after all other means of conflict resolution between the parties have failed. War should happen only after intense diplomacy and negotiation. Fourth, nations should initiate war only after a cost-benefit analysis. It must be clear that the evil war inflicts will not be greater than the evil it is trying to correct. Fifth, there should be a reasonable chance of success. War should not be waged if there is no reasonable chance that legitimate objectives of the conflict can be achieved. The ultimate goal of any just war should be a durable and moral peace. Without probable opportunity to achieve such peace, war cannot be justified.

These motivations for war have implications for how a war is fought. The just war will be waged with discrimination, that is, to distinguish between combatants and noncombatants, between military and nonmilitary targets. Innocent bystanders, civilians, even though they may politically support the enemy regime, should not be objects of military action. Combat should not destroy property that has no military function or usefulness. Often there are unintended consequences, but just warriors intend to wage war against the enemy regime and its soldiers and collaborators, not against the innocent. Just war will be waged under the principle of proportionality, which limits the amount of force, or destructive power, unleashed. Just warriors should use no more force than is necessary to achieve stated objectives. Adhering to this principle will prevent the inclination to wage total war, to resort to the kind of "overkill" characteristic of the crusade.

Even as just war theory begins with a theological assumption that all humans, friend and enemy alike, are children of God, so it concludes with a theological principle—that all who wage war, friend and enemy alike, are sinners, that sin always pervades war-making. This principle should prevent waging war with self-righteousness characteristic of crusaders.[22]

Pacifist thinking is not as elaborate as just war theory. The difference between a just war advocate and a pacifist is the absolutism of the pacifist. Just war proponents think there may be circumstances in which it is appropriate to wage war, but pacifists believe there are no circumstances in which it is legitimate to engage in war. A pacifist believes that war—in any and all circumstances, times, and places—is wrong. Yet not all pacifists are the same. Scholars frequently distinguish between "pragmatic pacifism" and "witnessing pacifism."[23]

Pragmatic pacifism simply argues that in situations of potential violence, pacifism works. Nonviolence is morally preferable to war because it produces better results. Pragmatic pacifism operates on the assumption that aggressors will respond to nonviolence in a nonviolent manner. It calls attention to the high cost of violence, cost calculated not only in terms of money, but also in loss of life and the hatred engendered by war, which ignites desire for revenge in the losers and victims.

If pragmatic pacifism makes its arguments on philosophical and psychological grounds, and nonreligious persons could easily hold it, witnessing pacifism is founded on the theological understanding of violence and nonviolence in the teachings of Jesus and early Christianity. War is not wrong just because nonviolence produces better results; war is wrong because it is contrary to the will of God—always. As a primary witness to the love of God in Jesus Christ a believer will oppose and refuse to participate in war. God will bring peace in God's own way on God's own time, and humans should not presume to interfere. A Christian's obligation is to obey God. The Christian must be meek, be a peacemaker, be willing to "turn the other cheek," and be willing to bear the scorn and ridicule of others, even when that takes the form of accusations of cowardice and betrayal of nation. In any and all cases, the Christian must reject war and practice nonviolence.[24]

The pacifist period of Christian history ended with the accession of Constantine and establishment of Christianity as the state religion of the empire. Yet pacifism did not disappear. Although just war principles prevailed throughout the medieval period—while failing to discipline the crusade mentality—from time to time the pacifist impulse appeared in what we may best describe as fringe groups in Catholic Christendom. The Protestant Reformation of the sixteenth century provided a context for formation of pacifist churches that have persisted into the present.

The Reformation fragmented the unity of Western Christendom. The Anabaptists, who began in Switzerland in 1525, believed that previous attempts to reform the medieval church had not gone far enough. They intended to take reformation to its logical conclusion, which is why some historians call the Anabaptists the "Radical Reformation," or the "Left wing of the Reformation." To accomplish complete reform, Anabaptists attempted to restore the pattern of the New Testament church, patterning their Christian lives after the lives of the first Christians. They took the New Testament literally. They interpreted Romans 13:1-7[25] to mean the separation of church and state. They recognized the legitimacy of the state, but, as Paul says, its purpose is to control evildoers. Anabaptists believed that because Christians are not evildoers, they should not participate in the affairs of the state. They believed that the church is to be a community of saints, those who live by a rigid Christian ethic, and consequently separate from the world.[26] That meant, among other things, that Christians should not participate in the military. Their attitude was not simply noncooperation with the military, however, but rather was nonviolence. They believed the statements of Jesus in the Sermon on the Mount were to be the pattern of their lives. A Christian should never resort to violence in any circumstance, even in self-defense. Historians of the Anabaptist movement always refer to their attitude as "nonresistance."[27]

"True, believing Christians are as sheep in the midst of wolves, wrote Conrad Grebel, one of the founders of the Anabaptist movement.

> They . . . must reach the fatherland of eternal rest, not by overcoming bodily enemies with the sword, but by overcoming spiritual foes. They use neither the worldly sword nor engage in war, since among them taking human life has ceased entirely, for we are no longer under the old covenant.[28]

Within two years of their beginning, Anabaptists drafted a statement of faith that contains a simple but powerful assertion.

> Jesus Christ has made us free from the servitude of the flesh and fit us for the service of God through the spirit which he has given us. Therefore we shall surely lay down the unchristian, yea, satanic weapons of force, such as sword, armor and the like, together with all their use, whether for the protection of friends or against personal enemies; and this in the strength of the words of Christ, "I say unto you that ye resist not evil."[29]

One of the principal architects, although not a founder, of the Anabaptists was a Dutch former Catholic priest, Menno Simons—so influential that the movement since his time has been called "Mennonite." According to Menno,

> Christ is our fortress; patience our weapon of defense; the Word of God our sword; and our victory a courageous, firm, unfeigned faith in Jesus Christ. And iron and metal spears and swords we leave to those who, alas, regard human blood and swine's blood about alike. He that is wise let him judge what I mean.[30]

As among the early Christians, after whom Anabaptists patterned their lives, concepts of nonresistance were not just abstract principles. Anabaptists practiced their principles, for they were widely and severely persecuted. Because of their theological principles—believers' baptism is one example—Protestants and Catholics alike regarded Anabaptists as heretics. Because of their separation from the evil world, so that they refused to participate in government and the military, they were regarded as political subversives. In the first ten years of the movement's existence, more than 5,000 Swiss Anabaptists were put to death. They were also executed in other parts of Europe.[31] Many of them were drowned, as a parody of their belief in baptism as immersion, but many others were beheaded or burned at the stake, usually after a period of excruciating torture. They did not resist and endured persecution with courage they derived from their faith in God.[32]

In England in 1652, a young man named George Fox founded another movement, the Society of Friends, commonly called Quakers. They also developed a pacifist doctrine, although more gradually than the Anabaptists. The context of the founding of the movement was complex, with crosscurrents of ideas about religion and about the use of violence.

In 1534 King Henry VIII had separated the Church in England from Rome. Soon a popular movement arose to purify the Church of England, claiming that it still had too many elements of Roman Catholicism. These purifiers were called "Puritans." In some ways, Quakers were a more radically purifying manifestation of Puritanism.

In the seventeenth century the Church of England and Puritan forces competed to define the established church in England, just as the monarchy and parliament contested the form of government England should have. George Fox, as a young man, became well acquainted with war, as controversies, ecclesiastical and political, became military campaigns. King Charles I was executed in 1649. Later, again through military means, the monarchy was restored. So George Fox's experience of war influenced his thinking about war, but that was not all. Fox also knew of the pacifist tradition. As early as the fourteenth century, John Wyclif introduced pacifist ideas, and his followers, known as Lollards, kept this tradition alive. By 1530, the Anabaptist movement began to be known in England and some people followed that line of pacifism. They influenced the English Baptist movement, which organized its first church in 1609. Although Fox was an unschooled man and did not read widely or deeply in theological literature, he nonetheless was aware of religiously based pacifism.[33]

Fox perceived that English religion, including the Puritan reform, was more a matter of form than feeling. Religion, as he saw it, was essentially sterile ritual dominated by clergy. People "went through the motions" of religion rather than making it the rule of life. This sterility of religion, accompanied by the political machinations typical of an official state church, caused Fox to seek a life-transforming religious experience. In his journal Fox offers posterity first-hand knowledge of his activities and thinking. When he was twenty-three, he was thinking about what a minister is and how disappointed he was in the clergy of the major churches of his time.

> And when all my hopes in them, and in all men was gone, so that I had nothing outwardly to help me, nor could tell what to do; Then, O! then I heard a voice, which said, "There is one, even Christ Jesus, that can speak to thy condition": and when I heard it, my heart did leap for joy.[34]

Fox saw immediately that one could have a religious experience without the mediation of clergy or church. One could know God through Christ experientially, personally. This experience led to the defining characteristic of Quakers, belief in the "Inner Light." Quakers described the Inner Light as "that of God within," "resembl[ing] the doctrine of the Holy Spirit." Consistently with Fox's original statement, Quakers perceive the Inner Light as Christ within the individual, a person's direct acquaintance with Christ.[35] But because Christ is the personification of God, one can properly return to the expression that the Inner Light is "God within." All humans have this Light, although most are not aware of it. For Quakers, the Inner Light is a source of direct revelation from God, the opportunity for an intimate relationship with God. It also means that human life is sacred. The Inner Light reveals an ethical imperative, to treat someone in whom God dwells with utmost respect. According to a manual used by American Friends, "The idea of the Inward Light enters all concerns of Friends. The recognition that others share the Inward Light leads to a sympathetic awareness of their need and a sense of responsibility toward them."[36] To kill someone would be to take a life that the indwelling presence of God has sanctified. One might even say that, from the Quaker perspective, killing is not only homicide but also deicide.

This Quaker pacifist perspective did not emerge full-blown at the founding of the Friends, as it had among Anabaptists. Many Quakers in the seventeenth-century English army were converted to the Society of Friends during their time of service. Apparently they saw no incompatibility between their faith and their military service. When military leaders became uneasy at high concentrations of Quakers in the ranks and began to discharge them, the Quakers were indignant that they had been removed from the service.

Fox was ambivalent about pacifism in the 1650s. In 1651, while he was imprisoned for his faith (one of four times), officers of the Commonwealth army against the King offered to arrange his release from prison if he would take a command position in the army. Some soldiers even asked him to command them. Fox refused, saying that he would not engage in war. "But I told them I lived in the virtue of that life and power that took away the occasion of all wars," Fox wrote in his journal, "and I knew from whence all wars did rise from the lust according to James his doctrine [*sic*]. . . . I told them I was come into the covenant of peace which was before wars and strifes was."[37] Yet Fox also encouraged the English government to pursue military action against Catholics on the continent. Here Fox's attitude seems similar to that of Anabaptists. God instituted government to maintain order and suppress evil persons in the society. For that they needed to use force. But God's people, the church separated from society, not having the responsibility to regulate society, should not use weapons. So Fox was not of a single mind about pacifism in the early days of the movement. By 1659, however, he seems to have come to clarity of mind. In that year he wrote an open letter to all Quakers, declaring that "Ye are called to peace, therefore follow it, and that peace is in Christ, not in Adam in the Fall." Therefore, he wrote,

> All that pretend to fight for Christ they are deceived, for his kingdom is not of this world, therefore his servants do not fight. Therefore fighters are not of Christ's kingdom, but are without Christ's kingdom; for his kingdom stands in peace and righteousness, but fighters are in the lust, and all that would destroy men's lives are not of Christ's mind, who came to save men's lives. . . . All such as pretend Christ Jesus, and confess him, and yet run into the use of carnal weapons, wrestling with flesh and blood, throw away the spiritual weapons. . . . All Friends everywhere, this I charge you, which is the word of the Lord God unto you all, Live in peace, in Christ, the way of peace, and therein seek the peace of all men, and no man's hurt.[38]

Quaker peace testimony became solidified just after 1660, when the monarchy was restored.[39]

As the political situation clarified, Quakers apparently wanted to reassure the king that they would not be political subversives. Another group, the Fifth Monarchy Men, had attempted to overthrow the government. Hundreds of Quakers were imprisoned. So Fox and other Quaker leaders signed an official declaration, presented to the king in 1661. That statement announced to the crown and to all Friends the Quaker position on warfare and arms bearing.

> So we, in obedience unto his Truth, do not love our lives unto the death, that we may do his will, and wrong no man in our generation, but seek the good and peace of all men. And he that hath commanded us that we shall not swear at all (Matt. v. 34), hath also commanded us that we shall not kill (Matt. v. 21), so that we can neither kill men, nor swear for nor against them. And this is both our principle and practice, and hath been from the beginning, so that if we suffer, as suspected to take up arms or make war against any, it is without any ground from us; for it neither is, nor ever was in our hearts, since we owned the truth of God; neither shall we ever do it, because it contrary to the spirit of Christ, his doctrine, and the practice of his apostles, even contrary to him for whom we suffer all things, and endure all things.[40]

The pacifist declaration of 1661 decisively influenced the Society of Friends. "Henceforward pacifism became a hallmark of Quakerism," Peter Brock writes, "and for the next two centuries and more the nonpacifist Friend was the exception, whose minority stand might get him in trouble with his Society, especially if he chose actually to bear arms." Quaker pacifism found authority in the commands of God in the Bible and in personal experience. According to Elton Trueblood, "They acted in obedience to God's command as recommended by the Inner Light and confirmed in the text of the New Testament."[41]

In seventeenth-century Germany, Protestants and Catholics fought several severe religious wars, including the Thirty Years' War (1618-1648). Perhaps as many as three-fourths of the population died. These wars left behind continued hostility, a shattered economy, and an eroded morality. In the culture of the time the Lutheran church had become rigid in doctrine and polity, and formal in liturgy. "True religion" was perceived to be "correct doctrine." Preaching was often reduced to dry, ponderous theological exposition. Clergy dominated the church while laypeople generally "went through the motions" of being religious.

Pietism, inspired by Philipp Jakob Spener, sought to reform cold, formal religion. Spener wrote *Pia desideria* (*Pious Desires*) in 1675, hoping to replace the sterile religion of his time with a heart-felt religion of warmth and emotion. He called Christians, clergy and laity alike, to make religion more than a merely intellectual exercise. The essence of religion is reformation of life. Religion must challenge people to live praiseworthy, moral lives. In facing postwar moral decadence with this powerful message, Pietism became a powerful movement.[42]

Deeply influenced by Pietism, in 1708 five men and three women met at a stream near Schwarzenau, in central Germany, to baptize one another and start a new church. Like others before them, they sought to recover the New Testament pattern of religion, which meant their church should differ radically from the society around it. So began the Church of the Brethren.[43]

The devastation of the Thirty Years' War and its demoralizing consequences lived in the historical memory of Brethren. They determined to live by the standard of New Testament Christianity, putting Jesus' teaching of love, peacemaking, and nonresistance into practice. They followed the theology and witness of the Anabaptists as role models of the Christian life. Brethren today continue as a pacifist, nonresistant church.[44]

Anabaptist/Mennonites, Quakers, and Brethren have become the principal "peace churches" in American history. In the story of pacifism in the United States, they are predominant. They were joined in the middle nineteenth century by the Seventh-day Adventist Church, which I shall survey in a later chapter, and in the twentieth century by the movement that since 1931 has been known as Jehovah's Witnesses. Witnesses, like other peace churches, believe in obedience to government, following Paul's admonition in Romans 13:1-7 that Christians are to obey civil rulers. But Witnesses also believe that governments, all governments, are essentially controlled by Satan and therefore disobey God's will. When government commands something contrary to God's will, Witnesses believe Christians *must* obey God's law rather than government's. Because one of God's laws is "You shall not kill," Witnesses have tended to become conscientious objectors.[45]

Although modern pacifism has antecedents in early Christianity and the development of peace churches, pacifism became a movement only in the nineteenth century. Development of reform movements characterized early-nineteenth-century America. Often, although not exclusively, Protestant revivalism stimulated these reform efforts. Revivalism generated religious energy that worked itself out in a host of "societies" dedicated to uplifting American society—societies aimed at temperance, Sabbath observance, profanity, vice, women's rights, slavery, conditions in penitentiaries, and education. Among these reforming groups were some dedicated to world peace.[46] Reacting to the War of 1812, the New York Peace Society and the Massachusetts Peace Society both began in 1815, one founded by a Presbyterian minister, the other by a Unitarian minister. In 1816 Quaker activists organized The Society for the Promotion of a Permanent and Universal Peace and in 1828 the American Peace Society. The latter was a national organization, combining several state and local groups that had sprung up by that time, all committed to the proposition that war was unchristian and should be abolished.[47]

Although evangelical Christianity, along with a memory of the historic peace churches, inspired these societies and others, many of them were not exclusively religious. Not all who joined peace societies were ministers, nor were they all even Christians. Another source of the impulse to peace originated in the Enlightenment. Christian pacifists condemned war as sin, but others influenced by rationalism argued that war was irrational and inhumane, destroying human kinship and unity. From early on both religious and secular arguments for the abolition of war persisted side by side, sometimes in the same society, sometimes in different organizations.[48] In general the leadership and most of the membership of peace societies were educated, middle- to upper-class individuals, the literary and professional elite.[49]

Not all was pacific, however, even in peace societies. People disagreed on how absolutely one ought to oppose war. Many of those influenced by the theology of the historic peace churches could not condone violence in any circumstance. They advocated a position traditional among peace churches, nonresistance. Others distinguished between aggressive war, which was unacceptable, and defensive war. In case of war to defend one's homeland, or even to defend a third party, they believed war was acceptable, a version of traditional just war theory. Those who disapproved of all war thought those who defended defensive war were not true pacifists. Those who condoned defensive war thought the nonresistant folk were fanatics—noble, perhaps, but out of touch with reality. This dispute has persisted in some form or other throughout the history of peace movements.[50]

The debate moved beyond the abstract to the practical toward the middle of the nineteenth century, as national passions became inflamed over slavery. In the North, Quakers, among others, had opposed slavery for as long as they had opposed war. As it became apparent that war would be the mechanism to abolish slavery, Quakers and other pacifists pondered a cruel dilemma. Was it justifiable to go to war to eliminate slavery and preserve the Union? Or did their principled aversion to war take precedence over their opposition to slavery? Many northern Quakers did take up arms. Other pacifists, not members of peace churches, joined them. William Lloyd Garrison was an absolute pacifist, but he was also an ardent abolitionist. When it became clear that war was inevitable, Garrison supported it. He believed that the war would be God's instrument to purge the nation of the evil of slavery. A crusading spirit pervaded the nation, both North and South. One wanted to abolish slavery and preserve the Union, the other wanted to preserve slavery and assert states rights. For both, the war was a crusade. In either context, it was not easy to be a pacifist. Many members of the American Peace Society supported the war to preserve the Union and took up arms.[51]

The religion-inspired peace movement—especially the American nonresistance movement, the explicitly theological dimension of pacifism—never quite recovered from the Civil War. Other elements of the peace movement did recover, principally by becoming more secular. Although peace movements had arisen in other Western nations, especially England, in the first half of the century and there had been some communication between these and the American groups, internationalism became a much more significant component of American pacifism in the last third of the century. International commerce had flourished, so financiers and business leaders on both sides of the Atlantic instinctively realized that business would grow more surely in a peaceful world. With greater participation from the business community, the peace movement tended to focus on international law and world government. These interests succeeded, primarily through treaties, in settling international disputes before they broke into war. To bring peace through world order, the movement focused on five goals: (1) arbitration of international disputes, (2) arbitration clauses in treaties, (3) development of international tribunals, (4) codification of international law, and (5) disarmament. The American Peace Society adopted arbitration as its primary focus after the Civil War. In 1899, an international conference at The Hague discussed rules of war and peaceful settlement of disputes, producing a Permanent

Court of Arbitration. However, religiously based pacifism, understood as humanitarianism, was not dead. Beginning in 1866, the Universal Peace Union, inspired by Quaker principles, promoted peace as a principle of a morally pure society.[52]

By 1900 there were about 425 peace organizations in the world, 63 of them in the United States and exhibiting considerable energy.[53] That dynamism continued into the new century. Between 1900 and 1914, about 45 new peace groups formed in America. The variety of approaches to pacifism increased. Some groups focused on arbitration, others on the formulation of international law, others on a world court or some sort of assembly of nations. Many espoused more than one of those positions, in various combinations. Others, particularly those with religious faith, believed that peace depended more on reforming human nature and eliminating the impulse to violence than on tinkering with international politics.[54]

Leaders of these peace societies tended to be obscure people, although most of them were middle class, educated, and professional. Most of them had not held political positions, nor were they prominent business leaders. In 1895 two Quaker brothers, Albert and Alfred Smiley, who owned a resort hotel in the Catskills, on the shores of Lake Mohonk, offered use of their hotel for a conference about formulating a system of world law that would guarantee peace. Meetings that influenced the peace movement convened at Lake Mohonk regularly for many years, but the Smiley brothers remained in relative obscurity. In 1910, however, two well-known benefactors brought financial assistance and considerable notoriety to the peace movement. Publisher Edwin Ginn established the World Peace Foundation with the promise to give $50,000 annually and $1 million at the time of his death. Andrew Carnegie founded the Carnegie Endowment for International Peace with a gift of $10 million. He distributed another $50,000 to sixteen peace societies in the same year.[55]

When war broke out in Europe in 1914, the growing concern for world peace was cast into considerable doubt. Many pacifists—among them some strong and visionary women—believed that it was imperative to keep America out of the war and to try to end the war in Europe as quickly as possible. For women at the beginning of the twentieth century, the peace movement offered an exceptional opportunity. The traditional role of women in times of war is passive and often tragic, issuing from an enforced inequality of the sexes that has characterized much of human culture. As Jo Vellacott, a historian of women pacifists, has written, "where women are relegated to the private sphere, and where they are not organized to reclaim equality or push back the frontiers, women do not emerge as forceful opponents of war, demanding to be heard." In the usual pattern of "widely differentiated traditional roles of men and women," Vellacott writes, women will, inevitably and dutifully,

> fulfill, instead, their assigned role in war as in peace, sacrificing their sons and lovers without complaint (mourning, yes, but complaining, no), keeping the home fires burning, loving soldiers, being sexually available, bearing and nurturing cannon-fodder for future wars, enduring hardships, taking on extra tasks for the duration and relinquishing them without a murmur when the men come home.

"This," Vellacott rightly observes, "is the role of 'our' women," those on "our" side of the conflict. We should not be surprised that "the 'enemy's' women also have a role: they are to be part of the bait, part of the prize; and humiliation through use and abuse of conquered women is part of the punishment to be inflicted on defeated warriors." Such suffering of women—noncombatants by definition through most of human history—is not, in the current Newspeak, merely "collateral damage," but a goal of war waged by men. "Women are not expected to like all this," Vellacott concludes, "but the role allowed them in war has not included any mandate to resist it."[56]

As American entry into "world war" loomed, a cadre of women chose not to respond passively to the threat of war, but to confront the challenge and try to change the outcome for the better. Many of these women had been active in the women's suffrage movement. Women should be empowered with the vote, suffragists argued, because, as people perceived (by men) to be morally superior, they could help to protect society from corruption and decay. When war broke out, it seemed natural to think that the nurturing, moral spirit of women might alleviate the warring spirit of the nations. Suffrage had given many women visibility, helped them to develop organizational skills, and offered them opportunity to speak persuasively in public.

Rosika Schwimmer—one of the principal characters discussed in this book—embodied a combination of suffrage background and international public presence that transformed the peace movement on the eve of world war. Born in Hungary in 1877, she early became interested in women's suffrage. By 1913 she was an internationally known figure in the suffrage movement and, in that year, led in organizing the meeting of the International Women's Suffrage Alliance. In 1914 she went to London to work as the press secretary of the alliance. When war began, she realized war would devastate Europe, with terrible consequences for women. Schwimmer now dedicated herself to pacifist causes, with particular emphasis on mediating between belligerent nations. If they could settle their differences through mediation, the war could be stopped. Schwimmer came to the United States intending to persuade President Woodrow Wilson to initiate an attempt by leading neutral nations to mediate the differences between the belligerents. In the company of Carrie Chapman Catt, president of the alliance, and bearing a petition that had been signed by women from all over Europe, Schwimmer met President Wilson on 18 September 1914, urging him to bring together neutral and belligerent nations for mediation.[57]

Rosika Schwimmer did not stop there. With a peace leader from England, Emmeline Pethick-Lawrence, she began a lecture tour of the United States. The two women made a compelling case for mediation to end the war before it spread further, pleading for women to take up the cause. Schwimmer, fluent in eight languages, spoke powerfully and persuasively. Speaking as many as six times a day, she and Pethick-Lawrence had addressed audiences in sixty cities in twenty-two states by December 1914. Carrie Chapman Catt, sensing that their campaign had aroused great interest in a women's peace movement, resolved to call a conference to build on that beginning. Catt asked one of the more notable women in America, Jane Addams, to serve as chair of the conference. Addams, an ardent pacifist, readily agreed.[58]

On 10 January 1915 about 3,000 women met at Washington, D.C., to hear speeches and to debate what women could do for the cause of peace. They formed a Woman's Peace Party, presenting a platform that specifically proposed strategies to promote peace. (See Appendix A). "The women of the country were lulled into inattention to the great military question of the war," Carrie Chapman Catt proclaimed in a speech at the end of the conference,

> by reading the many books put forth by great pacifists, who had studied the question deeply and who announced that there would never be another war. But when the great war came and the women waited for the pacifists to move, and they heard nothing from them, they decided all too late to get together themselves and try to do something at this eleventh hour.[59]

Try they did. The Woman's Peace Party had called for an international conference of neutral nations to find peaceful solutions to the conflict. By April 1915 some Dutch women had convened a conference of women at The Hague in the interest of peace. The Woman's Peace Party sent a large delegation and Jane Addams presided at the meeting. The International Conference of Women adopted the continuous mediation program that had been the primary feature of the American women's platform, putting a plan into action. The Conference appointed two delegations to go to heads of state of neutral nations and the belligerents to present a plan of continuous mediation. They asked the neutral nations to form a committee to mediate differences between the combatants. The nations would consider and modify proposals repeatedly until they arrived at a plan acceptable to all for ending the war. The women were to attempt to convince the neutrals to initiate the process and the belligerents to employ it. Jane Addams and two other women visited the belligerent nations. Rosika Schwimmer and three other women visited the heads of state of several neutral nations. From May until August 1915 the two groups of women made thirty-five visits to leaders in various countries, including the United States. In every case, they were received politely, but their plan for continuous mediation found little support. As Anne Wiltsher has observed, "the leaders of the neutral countries were too frightened, or unimaginative, or selfish, to act collectively. The idea of acting for humanitarian purposes and not for state power was beyond the mentality of national politicians."[60]

Although delegates from the International Committee of Women for Permanent Peace (the name the ongoing organization created at The Hague conference) could not bring interested parties to the negotiating table, another mechanism to promote continuous mediation presented itself. In late 1915 Rosika Schwimmer (who never passed up an opportunity to try to stop the war) persuaded Henry Ford to charter a ship to carry American pacifists to Europe to establish their own committee for continuous mediation—just the sort of bold proposal that the entrepreneur liked. The *Oscar II* sailed from New York on 4 December 1915—an object of considerable ridicule from the national media—transporting about sixty delegates who were to become the core and the staff of the committee on continuous mediation. Despite controversy about Schwimmer's "domineering" nature and the shock of Ford's departure to the United States shortly after the boat landed, eventually a mediation committee made its headquarters in Stockholm and labored heroically for months to persuade the belligerents to settle their differences. When, inevitably, the committee's efforts came to naught, it was not because the delegates did not try. They espoused the method first proposed by the Woman's Peace Party and championed by Rosika Schwimmer, perhaps its most flamboyant member.[61]

Secular groups could not claim an exclusive franchise in articulating the pacifist message as America was drawn into World War I. In 1911 the Federal Council of Churches of Christ in America organized a Peace and Arbitration Commission. With a gift of $3,000,000 from Carnegie in 1914, the Commission became the Church Peace Union. By 1915 Quakers and others had formed the Fellowship of Reconciliation, which provided a pacifist home for many clergy and laypeople from liberal Protestant denominations. The "social gospel" movement attempted to apply Christian moral teaching to social problems of the time. Most social gospelers who were pacifists joined the Fellowship, which rejected war completely. It was not designed to be politically active, but sought, instead, to appeal to the consciences of Americans. Early in 1917, however, the Fellowship attempted to prevent American intervention in the European war.[62]

These efforts and those of other pacifist groups proved futile. When America entered the war on 6 April 1917 the pacifist movement was transformed. Except for the Fellowship and the peace churches, virtually all pacifists endorsed the war. The transition from pacifism to militarism was rapid and dramatic. "Up to this time I had believed in pacifism," Clarence Darrow wrote. "When Germany invaded Belgium I recovered from my pacifism in the twinkling of an eye."[63] According to Caroline Moorehead, "Thousands who had willingly given hours of their time to crusading for peace now threw themselves, with frantic endeavor, into recruiting for war."[64] Campaigns for peace, conducted in peacetime, swiftly turned in wartime to assaults on all who might continue to seek peace. Intolerance disguised as "patriotism" was the order of the day. War hysteria gripped even the clergy. Except among the "peace churches" ministers expressed virtually unanimous support for the war. One historian of the phenomenon aptly titled his book *Preachers Present Arms.*[65] Preachers and politicians demonized the enemy and sanctified the Allied cause in which America had now joined, denouncing Germany as the tool of Satan. The evangelist Billy Sunday, delivering a prayer in the U.S. House of Representatives, enlisted God against the Germans: "Thou knowest, O Lord, that no nation so infamous, vile, greedy, sensuous, bloodthirsty ever disgraced the pages of history." Americans with German names suffered ridicule and sometimes physical abuse. Some states enacted laws forbidding the German language to be spoken or taught in schools. Some hostility to things German now seems ridiculous, as when "sauerkraut" was called "liberty cabbage," "German measles" were named "liberty measles," and dachshunds became "liberty pups."[66]

America represented the cause of righteousness. President Wilson had nobly proclaimed the war to end all wars, the war to make the world safe for democracy. Wilson and many Americans found religious meaning in the war, seeing a kind of salvation in defeating the evil represented by the enemy. Preachers argued that God would not allow civilization to be destroyed. America, fighting for the cause of righteousness, justice, and liberty, embarked on a holy war, a crusade to preserve and promote the Kingdom of God on earth. God and country became synonymous.[67]

Meanwhile the government sought to prevent opposition to the war. The Espionage Act of June 1917 made it illegal to obstruct recruiting for the armed service of the United States, which the Wilson administration interpreted to prohibit any criticism of the war. By 1918 the Sedition Act prohibited any language that scorned or brought into disrepute the form of government of the United States. These laws primarily targeted pacifists. People were sent to prison for proposing to make peace with Germany. Clarence Darrow, in other times a defender of the defenseless, now claimed that pacifists were anti-American.

> The pacifist speaks with the German accent. Even if his words are not against America, the import of all he says is to aid Germany against America and its allies in the war. Pacifism is a religious and philosophical theory which has no relation to life and no practical place in the world today.[68]

Many ministers vociferously attacked pacifists. According to a rector of a Chicago church, a pacifist was the "most despicable and craven creature that crawls the earth" and "pacifist" was "the most disgraceful word in the English language." Another minister addressed a patriotic meeting at Carnegie Hall in rhetoric truly incendiary.

> Whoever now talks of peace is no real friend of peace nor true friend of freedom, no loyal son of America. Our danger today is not from the Germans in the trenches, but from the so-called pacifists, the American bolsheviki, who are seeking by peace talk to break down the morale of our fighting men. We want no talk of negotiation, or indemnity, no

restatement of war aims; we have only one war aim, the complete and decisive overthrow of the Prussian military machine, its crushing defeat on the field of battle. Till then any talk of peace is dangerous or thinly disguised treason.[69]

Had not the President of the United States, in his Flag Day speech on 14 June 1917, declared the peace movement was "the new intrigue," and that pacifists were "tools" of "the masters of Germany"? "This is a People's War," Woodrow Wilson had proclaimed,

> a war for freedom and justice and self-government amongst all the nations of the world, a war to make the world safe for the people who live upon it and make it their own. . . . Woe be to the man or group of men that seeks to stand in our way in this high day of resolution when every principle we hold dearest is to be vindicated and made secure for the salvation of the nations.[70]

Woe, indeed. As Melvin Endy has observed of the orchestrated national campaign to promote the war and to silence those who labored for peace,

> All of the elements of the crusade were present: the God of salvation-history was calling to battle; the cause was the final triumph of Christian civilization; and participants were what Wilson called "disinterested champions of right" against the minions of the devil.[71]

One might think—given the intense nationalism, enthusiasm for war, and the criticism of pacifism during the war—that postwar America might not be a hospitable place for pacifism. Just the opposite was true. Various forms of pacifism became more vital than they had been before the war. Several conditions motivated this renewed interest in pacifism: love teachings of Jesus, disillusion over the vindictive Treaty of Versailles, and—perhaps most of all—horror at the terrible destruction of war. As Caroline Moorehead has observed, "The principle, for liberals and radicals, believers and atheists, was clear: war was wrong and there should be no more of it."[72] Consequently pacifists redoubled their efforts to prevent recurrence of war.[73]

Religious and secular pacifists agreed on many themes in the postwar period, although some distinctions remain. Historic peace churches remained consistent in opposing war and advocating nonresistance. Now many religious groups that had no pacifist history became adversaries of war and preparation for war. Episcopalians, Lutherans, Methodists, Presbyterians, Baptists, Christian Churches (Disciples of Christ), Congregationalists, Unitarians, and the Evangelical and Reform Churches all took pacifist positions, usually through resolutions at their conventions.[74] Roman Catholics, who had not previously been inclined toward pacifism—given the church's historic association with just war theory and crusades—in 1927 organized the Catholic Association for International Peace.

Many Protestant ministers now advocated pacifism from their pulpits. Harry Emerson Fosdick, one of the most prominent ministers in New York City, sailed to Europe just after the armistice. The devastation of the war, particularly the human suffering, profoundly affected him. Although he still saw some grim necessity in the war to defeat rampant evil, he soon became a pacifist. According to Fosdick's biographer, "before many years he could say with Whitman, 'God damn every war'—and mean it."[75]

Although no one knew it then, in the 1920s the social gospel was already beginning to decline. It was based on a kind of optimism about human nature and history that the combination of world war, perceived immorality, and the depression eventually discredited. Yet many still believed that humans could cooperate with God to create the Kingdom of God on earth. Certainly a peaceful world was part of that picture. The social gospel influenced most religious pacifists of the time.

The armaments industry, feeding the habit of governments to stockpile munitions in preparation for war, was, for peace-minded Christians, a primary contributor to continuing warfare. Most religious pacifists sought disarmament. After the war many religious pacifists took membership in the American Union Against Militarism, organized in 1915-1916, and others worked closely with that organization to promote universal disarmament. After an international disarmament conference in Washington, D.C., in November 1921, the Federal Council of Churches encouraged ministers, priests, and rabbis to preach about the need for disarmament. Many did. The Fellowship of Reconciliation was active on that front and many others, as the most evident manifestation of religious pacifism in the 1920s and 1930s.[76]

Postwar secular pacifists focused on internationalism—not that religious pacifists ignored that issue[77]—continuing the campaign of prewar pacifists to prevent war by producing mechanisms to mediate international disputes. They had high hopes for the League of Nations. American internationalists were mystified and angry when the U.S. Senate kept this country out of the League. Internationalists believed that the American system of democracy was a model for the world and they attempted to work through diplomacy to make a world safe from war. They were not monolithic in their views; some favored collective security and international organizations, some focused on international law and a world court, others stressed international education, others believed that trade agreements would promote international cooperation. All believed that the United States should in some way assume more responsibility for world order, optimistically thinking that peace could be maintained through some kind of international cooperation.[78]

Some pacifists turned to socialism. Not all socialists were pacifists, for some argued for the necessity of a class war, but many believed that a classless society would be a peaceful society. Many socialists worked against militarism and "preparedness"—stockpiling weapons and maintaining standing armies—because they identified armament manufacturers as the worst sort of capitalists. They believed that in war the workers suffered, but not the capitalists, who in fact profited from war.[79]

Many women remained pacifist activists after the war. Immediately after the armistice, they began work to guarantee that such a conflict would never happen again. A conference at Zurich in 1919 brought together women from defeated, victorious, and neutral countries. They opposed the repressive and vindictive terms of the Treaty of Versailles, presciently believing that it would cause another war. Recognizing the need for structure and organization in lobbying and negotiating for peace, they formed the Women's International League of Peace and Freedom. Jane Addams was again elected president. Many of these women—like many other, particularly secular, pacifists—recognized that sometimes force was necessary to protect social order and justice. They believed that, as women, they had a particular instinct for cooperation and compassion that would make peace. They insisted on making their views known in international fora. Through the 1920s the Women's International League of Peace and Freedom provided such a forum for women worldwide, who were, as Vellacott notes,

> speaking out from a feminist perspective, urgently informed by a belief that, on the one hand, there was no place for women's equality or freedom in a militaristic society and that, on the other, women's insight and experience provided the greatest hope for a world which the spirit of domination had to be replaced by new values.

These women "challenged the premises, methodology, and effectiveness of male statesmanship, and went far towards demonstrating by their example the alternative potential in which they believed."[80]

Postwar pacifists were a diverse movement divided into many more organizations than I have mentioned. Yet they all had something in common, a moral protest against war. Christian pacifists, especially in historic peace churches, appealed to the teachings of Jesus and the pacifist example of the early church, to the moral precept of "love your neighbor." Secular pacifists hearkened back to the Enlightenment's moral principle of reasonableness. They believed that rational people are teachable, that they could be persuaded that war is counterproductive and that international cooperation is beneficial. For those influenced by Darwin, peace rather than war became the means for the survival of the fittest.[81]

The American Legion personified another approach to peace very different from pacifism: military preparedness. The Legion was outspoken in its belief in and hope for peace, as in its founding document (1919): "That the purpose of this corporation shall be: to promote peace and good will among the peoples of the United States and all the nations of the earth."[82] The Legion has maintained that guiding principle throughout its history. Its way to peace, however, is not disarmament or antimilitarism, but adequate military strength: preparedness. In its national conventions the Legion has offered several statements on the subject through the years, as in this one from 1933:

> We believe that America will never seek a war and that a war will never seek a prepared America. We believe in an America, peace-loving and intent on peace but strong enough to insure and enforce the peace. We know that the pitiably small army in existence at the start of every war has never kept us out of war.[83]

The Legion opposed pacifist movements, however, and not only those that advocated disarmament. The Legion believed that pacifists in general were naive and too willing to try a quick fix for peace. A 1938 statement summed up the Legion's attitude toward pacifism: "To the ardent pacifist, peace is all that counts—but to the legionnaire, peace with honor is more desirable."[84] America's other great patriotic organization, the Daughters of the American Revolution, shared the Legion's views.[85]

In 1928 Aristide Briand, the French foreign minister, suggested to the American Secretary of State, Frank B. Kellogg, that their two nations join in a treaty to renounce war as an instrument of national policy. Eventually most of the world's major powers signed the Kellogg-Briand Peace Treaty. (See Appendix B.) Many people thought the treaty outlawed war. Internationalists of various nations welcomed it, as did pacifists of every variety. Even the American Legion and the DAR approved it, especially since a memorandum to the treaty exempted wars of self-defense from the ban. The Federal Council of Churches presented to the White House petitions with 185,333 signatures of people from about thirty denominations, urging the Senate to ratify the treaty. The day following ratification, the Federal Council urged church leaders everywhere in the nation to celebrate: "Let church bells be rung, songs sung, prayers of thanksgiving be offered and petitions for help from God that our nation may ever follow the spirit and meaning of the Pact." Charles Clayton Morrison, editor of *The Christian Century* and an ardent pacifist, exulted, "Today international war was banished from civilization."[86]

Pacifist activity continued in the 1930s. On 2 May 1935, in Riverside Church, New York City (Harry Emerson Fosdick's church), 254 ministers, priests and rabbis clad in clerical garb joined in a pledge.

> In loyalty to God I believe that the way of true religion cannot be reconciled with the way of war. In loyalty to my country I support its adoption of the Kellogg-Briand Pact which renounces war. In the spirit of true patriotism and with deep personal conviction, I therefore renounce war and never will I support another.

By 1941, 1,900 ministers and thousands of laypeople had signed this or similar pledges.[87]

In December 1935 a coalition of pacifist groups, many of them strongly religious, formed the Emergency Peace Campaign, a nationwide peace education and propaganda effort. The campaign sought to foster international cooperation and avoid war. To those ends, it sent speakers to about 1,000 events, conducted workshops, taught short courses to high school and college students, launched a "neutrality campaign" and a "no-foreign-war crusade." The word "emergency" in its title is instructive. War was again threatening and, of course, broke out in Europe in 1939. America was attacked in 1941. Crusades or ministerial pledges could not prevent war. The Emergency Peace Campaign stalled and ceased to exist by late 1937. When war became a reality, most pacifists reluctantly supported it. Pacifist groups were not verbally attacked and physically abused in World War II as they had been in World War I. Most pacifists were isolated and ignored rather than attacked. They put their energy into refugee work and helping conscientious objectors.[88]

Although the term "conscientious objection" can have several connotations,[89] James F. Childress articulates the common understanding, the one pertinent here, as "refusal to participate in military service on moral or religious grounds." A conscientious objector "claims that the refused act, if undertaken, would violate his or her conscience and would result in a loss of integrity and wholeness in the self, along with heavy guilt and shame."[90]

Modern conscientious objection was born in America when members of sixteenth- and seventeenth-century peace churches migrated to America and asserted their pacifism against various colonial governments. British colonies (except Quaker Pennsylvania) organized militias and called the adherents of peace churches to serve. They responded that they could not bear arms as a matter of conscience, pointing out that they were not just trying to be contrary. As one request for exemption put it, they were not objecting from "obstinate humor or contempt for your authority [but] purely in obedience as we apprehend to the doctrine of our Beloved savior & the discharge of a good conscience." Consequently various colonies exempted the pacifists, but several governments required objectors either to pay a fee or to hire a substitute. Mennonites were generally willing to do that, but Quakers were not.[91]

When the colonies fought for their independence from England military service became a profoundly practical matter. The Army of the Continental Congress needed able-bodied men. Yet even in this extremity, members of peace churches were exempted, albeit with the requirement to pay the fee or provide a substitute. On 18 July 1775 the Continental Congress appealed to the consciences of Christian pacifists.

> As there are some people who from Religious Principles cannot bear Arms in any case, this Congress intend no Violence to their Consciences, but earnestly recommend it to them to *Contribute Liberally*, in this time of universal calamity, to the relief of their distressed Brethren in the several Colonies, and to do all other services to their oppressed country, which they can consistently with their Religious Principles.[92]

This resolution raises a possibility of alternative service to the government rather than bearing arms, which later became a major issue. Some Quakers and perhaps more Mennonites and Brethren in fact fought for the colonies, only to be excommunicated by their churches.[93]

The Civil War presented a new problem for nonresisters, national conscription. Although in the earliest months of the war, on both sides raising the army was the responsibility of the states, that situation soon changed. The Confederacy resorted to universal conscription first. In April 1862, legislation gave the raising of military forces to the central government. On 11 October 1862, a new law exempted from induction members of certain church groups.

> All persons who have been and are now members of the society of Friends, and the association of Dunkards, Nazarenes, Mennonists in regular membership in their respective denominations: *Provided*, Members of the society of Friends, Nazarenes, Mennonists and Dunkards shall furnish substitutes or pay a tax of five hundred dollars each into the public treasury.[94]

The Union did not craft a conscription law until March 1863. That law was replaced with a new draft act, passed on 24 February 1864. Section 17 of that provided exemptions similar to the Confederate law.

> *And be it further enacted*, That members of religious denominations, who shall by oath or affirmation declare that they are conscientiously opposed to the bearing of arms, and who are prohibited from doing so by the rules and articles of faith and practice of said religious denominations, shall, when drafted into the military service, be considered noncombatants, and shall be assigned by the Secretary of War to duty in the hospitals, or to the care of freedmen, or shall pay the sum of three hundred dollars, to such person as the Secretary of War shall designate to receive it, to be applied to the benefit of the sick and wounded soldiers: *Provided*, That no person shall be entitled to the benefit of the provisions of this section unless his declaration of conscientious scruples against bearing arms shall be supported by satisfactory evidence that his deportment has been uniformly consistent with such declaration.[95]

Peace churches, especially the Quakers, had traditionally opposed slavery, posing a dilemma for young men in the North. Slavery was an overriding issue in the conflict. Should one fight for such a noble cause, or should one be faithful to one's pacifist heritage? Many remained true to their pacifism, especially given opportunity to assist the country through alternative service, but large numbers of Quakers and other pacifists did enter combat. Many of them were not disciplined by their churches, since they were bearing arms in opposition to slavery. Antislavery pacifists in the South did not face the same dilemma since their government was fighting to preserve slavery. So a much larger proportion of peace church adherents in the South refused to fight than those in the North. Of course, this did not endear them to their government or to fellow southerners.[96]

When America entered the World War in April 1917, it was clear that conscription would be necessary, even though some pacifist groups petitioned Congress not to pass such a law. On 18 May 1917 the Draft Act again exempted some Christian pacifists.

> [N]othing in this Act contained shall be construed to require or compel any person to serve in any of the forces herein provided for who is found to be a member of any well-recognized religious sect or organization at present organized and existing and whose existing creed or principles forbid its members to participate in war in any form and whose religious convictions are against war or participation therein in accordance with the creed or principles of said religious organizations, but no persons so exempted shall be exempted from service in any capacity that the President shall declare to be non-combatant.[97]

Previous requirements to hire a substitute or pay a fee were eliminated from this act and never again appeared in American conscription law. Again the exemption was reserved for members of peace churches.[98]

President Wilson took ten months to designate what qualified as noncombatant service, as provided in the last clause of the law. By Executive Order on 20 March 1918, he designated the Medical Corps, the Quartermaster Corps, and the Engineering Corps. Significantly, Wilson opened the possibility of noncombatant service to pacifists who did not have religious objections to war. On 1 June 1918, the Secretary of War appointed a board of three men to examine all those who had applied for conscientious objector status to see whether or not they were religious and sincere. Of more than 4,000,000 men drafted, 3,989 claimed objector status. The board examined only 2,294 of them. About 1,300 accepted noncombatant service, 504 were court-martialed (those judged insincere or defiant and those who propagandized other soldiers), and the remainder (about 490) were sent to farms to work or confined in military camps doing menial labor.[99]

When Congress revised the draft law in 1940, it treated the issue of conscientious objectors very differently. Whereas before it had restricted objector status to those who were members of peace churches, it now broadened the category of those who could qualify.

> Nothing contained in this Act shall be construed to require any person to be subject to combatant training and service in the land or naval forces of the United States who, by reason of religious training and belief, is conscientiously opposed to participation in war in any form.[100]

This change was urged on Congress by religious groups, both historic peace churches and others. Religious people of any faith could qualify, but nonreligious people could not. The law also provided that objectors in the military would be assigned to noncombatant roles, or, if they objected to that, be assigned to civilian work of national importance. Between 50,000 and 72,000 people were classified as conscientious objectors in World War II.[101]

The 1940 statute did not define "religious training and belief." Soon some men went to court, applying for conscientious objector status, although they were not members of any church and their conscientious opposition to war seemed to be based more on philosophy than religion. In *Kauten v. United States*[102] the Second Circuit Court of Appeals ruled that one could be an objector even if his conscientious scruples were not based on a belief in God; if his objection to war was of compelling importance to him, it was the equivalent to "religious training and belief." Later, in *Berman v. United States*[103] the Ninth Circuit Court of Appeals disagreed with the *Kauten* test and asserted that an applicant for objector status must have a deity concept in order for his objection to be based on "religious training and belief."[104] Faced with this conflict between courts, Congress rewrote the law. The Selective Service Act of 1948 says, in pertinent part,

> Nothing contained in this title shall be construed to require any person to be subject to combatant training and service in the armed forces of the United States who, by reason of religious training and belief, is conscientiously opposed to participating in war in any form. Religious training and belief in this connection means an individual's belief in a relation to a Supreme Being involving duties superior to those arising

from any human relation, but does not include essentially political, sociological, or philosophical views or a merely personal moral code.[105]

Later, beyond the time frame of this book, Congress again changed the standards for qualifying for conscientious objector status in the Selective Service Act of 1967. Some Supreme Court cases, to be addressed later, compelled this change. Although a person must still show a religious basis for objection to war, the Act of 1967 removed any reference to a Supreme Being.

> Nothing contained in this title shall be construed to require any person to be subject to combatant training and service in the armed forces of the United States who, by reason of religious training and belief, is conscientiously opposed to war in any form. As used in this subsection, the term 'religious training and belief' does not include essentially political, sociological or philosophical views, or a merely personal moral code.[106]

Although the law, in some form, has exempted conscientious objectors in all of America's major wars, objectors have not always been respected or well-treated. In fact, the opposite has generally been true. War often evokes the crusade mentality, white-hot patriotism, and contempt for all who do not support the war effort. Conscientious objectors have frequently been regarded as cowards and shirkers of duty, if not traitors—attitudes often manifested in actions of derision, or even actual violence, against conscientious objectors.

In the Revolutionary War, Quakers, Mennonites, and other objectors were often thought to be sympathizers with Britain. That they would not fight for independence was obvious evidence to patriots that they were loyalists. Sometimes their property was confiscated, they were fined more than the law allowed, or their churches were turned into barracks for soldiers or field hospitals. Often they were criticized severely and accused of cowardice. In the Civil War, under the theory that "one who is not my friend must be the friend of my enemy," conscientious objectors were widely suspected of sympathizing with the other side. Many ascribed religious meaning to the Civil War: God supported slavery or, alternatively, God intended that the pernicious institution of slavery should be destroyed. Thus those who refused to fight abstained from a divine cause. Again property was confiscated, people attempted to shame objectors into army service, and objectors faced verbal (and occasionally physical) harassment.[107]

When America entered World War I, objectors endured more than ridicule. Because initially all conscientious objectors were inducted into the military, they were commingled with other draftees and, frequently, treated in shameful ways. Although officers were instructed to assure that objectors in their camps were treated civilly, it frequently did not happen. Because objectors usually called attention to themselves by refusing to wear military uniforms or to follow orders, they were generally harassed. Some objectors were willing to do alternative, noncombatant service, and they were not harassed as much. But some, especially religious pacifists, were convinced that any sort of cooperation with the military was a violation of their objection to war. They steadfastly refused to cooperate. In efforts to break the objectors' resolve, they were sometimes subjected to solitary confinement, frequently manacled in uncomfortable positions for the better part of a day, occasionally "given showers" and rubbed with stiff-bristled brushes until they bled, sometimes fed barely enough to sustain life. On at least one occasion an objector died from the pneumonia he contracted during his solitary confinement in a pitch-black hole partially filled with water. His body was shipped home to his parents wearing the military uniform he would not wear while alive. As a result of such treatment, many objectors abandoned their principles and agreed to fight.[108]

The three-member Board of Inquiry appointed to separate the sincere from the insincere conscientious objectors interviewed objectors one by one. Those judged to be sincere, who continued to refuse to bear arms, were sent to work on farms. Objectors who were judged insincere, or who refused the farm furlough, or who engaged in political propaganda were court-martialed and often sentenced to between twenty and twenty-five years in prison. One hundred forty-two were sentenced to life and seventeen received the death penalty. Because of the armistice, however, no person was imprisoned ·more than three years and none were executed.[109] The task of the Board of Inquiry was extraordinarily difficult and apparently it proceeded fairly; it did not conduct the court-martial proceedings. One of its members, Harlan Fiske Stone, respected the authority of conscience and disapproved of the abusive treatment of the objectors. "However rigorous the state may be in repressing the commission of acts which are regarded as injurious to the state," Stone wrote,

it may well stay its hand before it compels the commission of acts which
violate the conscience.

It is the easy but undiscriminating and shallow way to dispose of
the case of the conscientious objector by denouncing him as a coward
and slacker.[110]

Not all held Stone's views. Bitterness against pacifists and harassment of
conscientious objectors brought two organizations into being to assist
objectors. The American Union Against Militarism in 1917 spawned a
branch organization, the Civil Liberties Bureau. As war frenzy intensified,
as Congress passed the Espionage and Sedition Acts, democracy at home
seemed to be in danger. The Union leadership, seeking to assure that
soldiers coming home from the war would find a democratic society,
formed the Civil Liberties Bureau to advocate and defend civil rights in a
nation at war. Almost immediately the organization took up the cause of
conscientious objectors, advising objectors of their legal rights and
assisting and defending them in the army camps. When the Union finally
passed out of existence, defeated by the overwhelming militarism of the
time, the Civil Liberties Bureau remained alive as an independent
organization, in 1920 becoming the American Civil Liberties Union. Under
the leadership of Roger Baldwin, it broadened its scope to protect a vast
array of civil rights, not just those of conscientious objectors. Had it not
been for the horrific treatment of conscientious objectors, the ACLU might
never have come into being.[111]

Also in 1917 Quakers organized the American Friends Service
Committee. Although the AFSC was also concerned about preserving the
civil rights of conscientious objectors, it was founded to relieve suffering
of victims of war in Europe. As such, it provided a place where conscientious objectors could do humanitarian service. In fact, the government's
Board of Inquiry, designed to examine the claims of conscientious
objectors, allowed some sincere objectors to do their alternative service
with the AFSC in European war relief.[112] The AFSC today continues its
humanitarian service, with particular emphasis on the Quaker "peace
testimony," just as the ACLU has continued to be a staunch defender of
civil liberties.

Conscientious objectors in World War II were treated differently than
in World War I. Peace churches lobbied for legislation that broadened the
category of conscientious objector beyond those who were members of
historic peace churches to any person whose objection was based on

"religious training and belief." Peace churches also influenced the government to adopt more regulated and humane ways to process, employ, and treat conscientious objectors. Objectors were assigned to Civilian Public Service camps. There they worked with other objectors, not with soldiers who resented them, in the national public interest, avoiding the hostility and brutality of the earlier war. By the time the camps were abolished in 1947, about 11,000 objectors had worked in them. Most labored in conservation projects, while others worked on farms, in mental hospitals, or in training schools. About 500 served as "guinea pigs" for medical and scientific projects. Significantly, the government allowed peace churches to play a significant role in the program. The government provided sites, transportation, technical supervision and equipment for the camps. But the peace churches provided for day-to-day administration and the cost of the camps. They were the camp managers.[113]

The Supreme Court has several times been asked to decide cases of conscientious objection and to interpret the conscription acts of Congress. The Draft Act of 1917 exempted from combatant service all those who were members of peace churches. Soon people who were not members of peace churches challenged the Act on the grounds that it gave preferential treatment to some religions. The challengers argued that the law exempting peace church believers but not all religious believers violated the Establishment Clause of the First Amendment, which mandates that government should be neutral in matters of religion, not preferring one over another. Opponents believed that the law violated the Free Exercise Clause because it restricted nonpeace church conscientious objectors from practicing their religion. The Supreme Court was not impressed with that contention. Chief Justice Edward D. White, for a unanimous Court, wrote:

> And we pass without anything but statement the proposition that an establishment of a religion or an interference with the free exercise thereof repugnant to the First Amendment resulted from the exemption clauses of the act . . . because we think its unsoundness is too apparent to require us to do more.[114]

The Selective Service Acts of 1940 and 1948 changed the exempting language. The former provided that exemption was based on "religious training and belief," thus accomplishing what the religious plaintiffs requested and the Supreme Court denied in the *Selective Draft Law Cases*. Any religious person could potentially qualify as a conscientious objector.

But in 1948 Congress narrowed the definition of "religious training and belief," saying that it must derive from "a relation to a Supreme Being involving duties superior to those arising from any human relation." The meaning of that qualification would be tested during the Vietnam War, certainly the most unpopular war in American history.

The issue presented to the Court was whether a person who did not believe in a personal God could qualify for conscientious objector status under the "Supreme Being" language. Three applicants conscientiously objected to the war, but none of them could claim traditional theology. That is, none of them acknowledged belief in God, although they variously used language such as "belief in and devotion to goodness and virtue for their own sakes, and a religious faith in a purely ethical creed," a belief "in 'Godness' which was 'the Ultimate Cause for the fact of the Being of the Universe,'" and a belief "in our democratic American culture, with its values derived from the western religious and philosophical tradition" which the applicant equated with "a belief in the Supreme Being or God." The cases the three applicants initiated were consolidated under the title *United States v. Seeger.*[115]

The Court, in an opinion written by Justice Tom Clark, ruled that in despite untraditional views of religion and morality, the appellants could qualify as conscientious objectors. When it wrote the draft law of 1948, Congress chose to use the phrase "Supreme Being," rather than "God." That left open the way for the government to accommodate people with theories of divinity and ethics broader than a belief in a personal God. One could comply with the statute with a belief in a being or impersonal power on which all else was dependent in a person's life. That is the equivalent to religious training and belief in relation to a Supreme Being. The Court laid down a test as to how a government official could determine if the nontraditional believer would qualify. "A sincere and meaningful belief which occupies in the life of its possessor a place parallel to that filled by the God of those admittedly qualifying for the exemption comes within the statutory definition."[116] This interpretation of the language of the statute clearly broadened the grounds to grant conscientious objector status.

In 1970, the Court was presented with a conscientious objector whose religious belief was even less precise and theistic than Seeger's. On his application to be a conscientious objector, Elliott Welsh marked out the word "religious," signifying that his objection to war was not based on religion. He confirmed that in a letter to his draft board, in which he asked that the question about whether or not he believed in a Supreme Being be left open. The Court approved his application for objector status anyway. Justice Hugo Black wrote that few applicants are aware of how broadly the concept of "religious training and belief, . . . in a relation to a Supreme Being" had been interpreted in *Seeger*. Welsh was more religious than he realized, in relation to the elastic interpretation of the law in *Seeger*. The Court was now willing to say that he came within the statutory language. After this, virtually anyone could qualify as a conscientious objector.[117]

At one point, however, the Court interpreted the language of the statute quite literally. In every version of conscription legislation from 1917 until the present, the law has said that in order to qualify, an objector must be "conscientiously opposed to war in any form." One could not be a selective conscientious objector, picking and choosing the wars in which one was willing to fight. The Supreme Court upheld that principle in *Gillette v. United States*.[118] Guy Gillette opposed participation in the Vietnam war, which he considered to be unjust, but he could agree to fight in, say, defensive wars or United Nations-sponsored peacekeeping wars. Louis Negre, a plaintiff in a companion case, was a Roman Catholic who adhered strongly to theories of just war and unjust war. His selective conscientious objection rested on a theological tradition of his church. Writing for the Court, Justice Thurgood Marshall ruled that there was only one reading of the statutory language possible. In order to qualify as an objector, one had to object to war in any form. Selective conscientious objection was not permissible. To the question as to whether this discriminated against some religious groups, such as Catholics, which would violate the Establishment Clause, the Court answered negatively. The language requiring objection to war in any form was not aimed at any religious group, it "simply does not discriminate on the basis of religious affiliation or religious belief. . . . The section says that anyone who is conscientiously opposed to all war shall be relieved from military service."[119]

As Caroline Moorehead observes, pacifism "is basically the most lonely of beliefs, held for the most part in private, and sustained in isolation, often in the face of powerful opposition." Among modern mass movements, Moorehead ranks pacifism "with the battle for women's suffrage as the one most tenaciously, most lastingly and most universally held." Pacifism "has pushed people to the most remarkable feats of endurance." For those who do not share its vocation, Moorehead concludes, "There is a stubbornness, an obduracy, about pacifism that can be infuriating; it can also be heroic, admirable."[120]

Notes

1. 283 U.S. 605 at 621 (1931).

2. Emile Arnaud, a French lawyer and president of the *Ligue Internationale de la Paix et de la Liberté*, devised the term *pacifisme* in 1901 to describe a peaceful process to resolve conflict and avoid warfare, without implying lack of patriotism or defeatism. See Charles Chatfield, "Thinking About Peace in History," in *The Pacifist Impulse in Historical Perspective*, Harvey L. Dyck, ed. (Toronto: University of Toronto Press, 1996), 37 n2.

3. *Instead of Violence: Writings by the Great Advocates of Peace and Nonviolence Through History*, Arthur and Lila Weinberg, eds. (Boston: Beacon Press, 1965), 443-47, 466-74; Peter Brock, *Varieties of Pacifism: A Survey from Antiquity to the Outset of the Twentieth Century* (Syracuse, N.Y.: Syracuse University Press, 1998), 1-2; Duane L. Cady, *From Warism to Pacifism: A Moral Continuum* (Philadelphia: Temple University Press, 1989), 127-28.

4. J. Edgar Park, "The Book of Exodus: Exposition," in *The Interpreter's Bible* (Nashville: Abingdon Press, 1952), 1:986.

5. E. M. Good, "Peace in the Old Testament," in *The Interpreter's Dictionary of the Bible: An Illustrated Encyclopedia,* George A. Buttrick, and others, eds. (Nashville: Abingdon Press, 1962), 3:704-706.

6. See L. E. Toombs, "Ideas of War," in *Interpreter's Dictionary of the Bible*, 4:796-801.

7. Roland H. Bainton, *Christian Attitudes Toward War and Peace: A Historical Survey and Critical Re-evaluation* (Nashville: Abingdon Press, 1960), 44-52. Virtually all scholars in the field regard this book as a classic.

8. Everett E. Gendler, "War and the Jewish Tradition," in *A Conflict of Loyalties: The Case for Selective Conscientious Objection*, James Finn, ed. (New York: Pegasus, 1968), 84; Roland de Vaux, *Ancient Israel: Its Life and Institutions*, trans. John McHugh (New York: McGraw-Hill, 1961), 262.

9. Isaiah 11:6, 9; 9:2, 5-7a; 2:4; Brock, *Varieties of Pacifism*, 2

10. See Guy Franklin Hershberger, *War, Peace, and Nonresistance* (Scottsdale, Pa: Herald Press, 1944, 1953, 1969, renewed, 1981), 15-41.

11. Matthew 5:5, 9, 38-39, 43-45a; 7:12.

12. Brock, *Varieties of Pacifism*, 3.

13. Romans 12:14, 17-21; Deuteronomy 32:35; Proverbs 25:21-22.

14. See the fascinating correspondence of Pliny "the Younger" (Gaius Plinius Luci Caecilius Secundus), provincial governor of Bithynia, and the emperor Trajan concerning legal issues that prosecution of Christians presented, in *Pliny: Letters and Panegyricus* 10.96-97, trans. Betty Radice, Loeb Classical Library (Cambridge, Mass.: Harvard University Press, 1969), 285-93. See also Stephen Benko, *Pagan Rome and the Early Christians* (Bloomington: Indiana University Press, 1984), 4-14, 127-28.

15. Knut Willem Ruyter, "Pacifism and Military Service in the Early Church," *Cross Currents* 32 (Spring 1982): 54-60; see also Bainton, *Christian Attitudes Toward War and Peace*, 66-84; Hershberger, *War, Peace, and Nonresistance*, 64-70.

16. Ruyter, "Pacifism and Military Service in the Early Church," 56-62; Bainton, *Christian Attitudes Toward War and Peace*, 66-81.

17. Justo L. Gonzalez, *The Story of Christianity* 1: *The Early Church to the Dawn of the Reformation* (San Francisco: Harper & Row, 1984), 113-25, 189-93, 207-219; Bainton, *Christian Attitudes Toward War and Peace*, 85-95; Brock, *Varieties of Pacifism*, 5-8.

18. Bainton, *Christian Attitudes Toward War and Peace*, 91-100; Chatfield, "Thinking About Peace in History," in *The Pacifist Impulse in Historical Perspective*, 39-41.

19. Gonzalez, *The Story of Christianity* 1:248-50, 262-65, 292-300; Bainton, *Christian Attitudes Toward War and Peace*, 109-16.

20. Apparently Bainton, in *Christian Attitudes Toward War and Peace*, is the first to formulate this threefold description, but it is used by other scholars. See Dennis Byler, *Making War and Making Peace: Why Some Christians Fight and Some Don't* (Scottsdale, Pa.: Herald Press, 1989) and "Introduction" in *The Wars of America: Christian Views*, Ronald A. Wells, ed. (Macon, Ga.: Mercer University Press, 1991), 9-11.

21. Joseph L. Allen, *War: A Primer for Christians* (Nashville: Abingdon Press, 1991), 7-15; Edward LeRoy Long, Jr., *War and Conscience in America* (Philadelphia: Westminster Press, 1968), 33-41.

22. Allen, *War: A Primer for Christians*, 31-52; Long, *War and Conscience in America*, 22-33.

23. See John Howard Yoder, *Nevertheless: Varieties of Religious Pacifism*, rev. ed. (Scottsdale, Pa.: Herald Press, 1992), who discusses many permutations of pacifism.

24. Allen, *War: A Primer for Christians*, 16-30.

25. "Let every person be subject to the governing authorities. For there is no authority except from God, and those that exist have been instituted by God. Therefore he who resists the authorities resists what God has appointed, and those who resist will incur judgment. For rulers are not a terror to good conduct, but to bad. Would you have no fear of him who is in authority? Then do what is good, and you will receive his approval, for he is God's servant for your good. But if you do wrong, be afraid, for he does not bear the sword in vain; he is the servant of God to execute his wrath on the wrongdoer. Therefore one must be subject, not only to avoid God's wrath but also for the sake of conscience. For the same reason you also pay taxes, for the authorities are ministers of God, attending to this very thing. Pay all of them their dues, taxes to whom taxes are due, revenue to whom revenue is due, respect to whom respect is due, honor to whom honor is due."

26. Because the church was meant to be a community of saints, only those people who could confess their faith and promise to live by the stringent Christian ethic should be members of the church. Obviously infants could not do that, so Anabaptists rejected infant baptism, which other Christians practiced, calling for "believer's baptism." Any person who had been baptized as an infant had to be baptized again when he/she became a true believer. "Anabaptist" means "rebaptizer" and was a term of derision on the lips of opponents.

27. Hershberger, *War, Peace and Nonresistance*, 81-86; Brock, *Varieties of Pacifism*, 13-23; Franklin H. Littell, *The Origins of Sectarian Protestantism: A Study of the Anabaptist View of the Church* (New York: Macmillan, 1964), 79-108, especially 101-108.

28. Hershberger, *War, Peace and Nonresistance*, 82.

29. "The Schleitheim Confession of Faith," in John Horsch, *The Principle of Nonresistance as Held by the Mennonite Church: A Historical Survey* (Scottsdale, Pa.: Mennonite Publishing House, 1951), 8-9. For a rather different translation see *The Schleitheim Confession*, John Howard Yoder, ed. (Scottsdale, Pa.: Herald Press, 1977). In his introduction to this translation, Yoder writes that the Confession testifies "that peace as a way of life is the only option for those attempting to live faithfully as the people of God" (3).

30. Menno Simons, "Foundation of Christian Doctrine," in *The Complete Writings of Menno Simons, c. 1496-1561*, Leonard Verduin, trans., J. C. Wenger, ed. (Scottsdale, Pa.: Herald Press, 1984), 198.

31. Hershberger, *War, Peace, and Nonresistance*, 85.

32. See, for example, "The Trial and Martyrdom of Michael Sattler," in *Spiritual and Anabaptist Writers*, *The Library of Christian Classics* 24, George H. Williams, ed. (Philadelphia: Westminster Press, 1957), 136-44.

33. D. Elton Trueblood, *The People Called Quakers* (New York: Harper and Row, 1966), 1-39; Peter Brock, *The Quaker Peace Testimony, 1660 to 1914* (York, Eng.: Sessions Book Trust, 1990), 1-8.

34. George Fox, *The Journal*, Nigel Smith, ed. (London: Penguin Books, 1998), 13.

35. Trueblood, *The People Called Quakers*, 30-33, 63-84; Richmond P. Miller, "What is a Quaker?" in *Religions of America: Ferment and Faith in an Age of Crisis*, Leo Rosten, ed. (New York: Simon and Schuster, 1975), 223.

36. *Faith and Practice: A Book of Christian Discipline* (Philadelphia: Philadelphia Yearly Meeting of the Religious Society of Friends, 1978), 8.

37. Fox, *Journal*, 54. See James 4:1-2.

38. *The Journal of George Fox*, John L. Nickalls, ed. (Cambridge: Cambridge University Press, 1952), 357.

39. Brock, *The Quaker Peace Testimony*, 9-23; Brock, *Varieties of Pacifism*, 27-32.

40. *The Journal of George Fox* (Nickalls ed.), 401. See the complete text of the declaration, 398-404.

41. Brock, *The Quaker Peace Testimony*, 25-26, 29; Trueblood, *The People Called Quakers*, 187-207.

42. Dale W. Brown, *Brethren and Pacifism* (Elgin: Ill.: Brethren Press, 1970), 21-23; Justo L. Gonzalez, *The Story of Christianity.* 2: *The Reformation to the Present Day* (San Francisco: Harper and Row, 1984), 203-208.

43. They have been known by a number of names, "Fraternity of German Baptists," "German Baptist Brethren," "Dunkers," or "Dunkards." The latter two, which Brethren do not like, are derived from the German *tunken*, to immerse. From the beginning the movement centered on baptism, in the New Testament form of immersion, to form the true church separate from society. See Donald F. Durnbaugh, "Early History," in *Church of the Brethren: Yesterday and Today*, Donald F. Durnbaugh, ed. (Elgin, Ill.: Brethren Press, 1986), 1-2.

44. Durnbaugh, "Early History," 3-9; David B. Eller, "Social Outreach," in Durnbaugh, *Church of the Brethren: Yesterday and Today*, 119-20; Brown, *Brethren and Pacifism*, 17-25. One other voice favored pacifism in the sixteenth century: the Roman Catholic humanist Desiderius Erasmus, who in several writings ridiculed the folly of war and extolled the virtue and value of peace. Erasmus is one of the first writers in the West to question the divine right of kings to wage war; see Cady, *From Warism to Pacifism*, 132-34; David P. Barash, *Introduction to Peace Studies* (Belmont, Calif.: Wadsworth Publishing, 1991), 59.

45. *Jehovah's Witnesses: Proclaimers of God's Kingdom* (Brooklyn: Watchtower Bible and Tract Society, 1993), 189-96; *The Truth That Leads to Eternal Life* (Brooklyn: Watchtower Bible and Tract Society, 1968), 157-65; "Government," in *Reasoning from the Scriptures* (Brooklyn: Watchtower Bible and Tract Society, 1985), 152-56. For an overview of some of the Witnesses' legal battles because of their refusal to serve in the military, see Shawn Francis Peters, *Judging Jehovah's Witnesses: Religious Persecution and the Dawn of the Rights Revolution* (Lawrence: University of Kansas Press, 2000), 260-84. Marley Cole *(Jehovah's Witnesses: The New World Society* [London: George Allen and Unwin, 1956], 134-37) notes that Witnesses are conscientious objectors but not pacifists. They use warlike terms to describe their campaign against the sins of the world and false religion, which includes all others. They also speak of the coming battle between Jehovah and the powers of Satan, Armageddon, in which they believe very strongly. They anticipate fighting on the side of God at Armageddon. This point is dramatically illustrated by the Supreme Court case *Sicurella v. United States* 348 U.S. 385 (1955). A Jehovah's Witness was denied conscientious objector status because he said he would participate in a "theocratic war" and would fight at Armageddon with spiritual, rather than carnal, weapons. The Court ruled that Sicurella should be granted C.O. status because Congress did not have in mind spiritual wars when it required all conscientious objectors to object to "war in any form."

46. Winthrop S. Hudson, *Religion in America* (New York: Charles Scribner's Sons, 1965), 197-98.

47. Barash, *Introduction to Peace Studies*, 61; Charles Chatfield, *The American Peace Movement: Ideals and Activism* (New York: Twayne Publishers, 1992), 3-6; Barbara S. Kraft, "Peacemaking in the Progressive Era: A Prestigious and Proper Calling," *Maryland Historian* 1 (Fall 1970): 121.

48. Kraft, "Peacemaking in the Progressive Era," 121; Peter Brock, *Twentieth-Century Pacifism* (New York: Van Nostrand Reinhold, 1970), 9; Cady, *From Warism to Pacifism*, 134-36 cites Immanuel Kant as an example of rationalist influence on pacifism. Kant's "Idea for a Universal History from a Cosmopolitan Point of View" (1784) and "Perpetual Peace" (1785) argue for the necessity of international law. Some sort of international civility is imperative to achieve the goal of a universal civic society. It is only reasonable that humans should live together in peace and that they can devise a method of international cooperation to accomplish that aim.

49. Chatfield, *American Peace Movement*, 11.

50. Brock, *Varieties of Pacifism*, 62-63.

51. Chatfield, *American Peace Movement*, 7, 11; Brock, *Varieties of Pacifism*, 69-72; Vernon H. Holloway, "A Review of American Pacifism," *Religion in Life* 19 (Summer 1950): 368; Melvin B. Endy, Jr., "War and Peace," in *Encyclopedia of the American Religious Experience: Studies of Traditions and Movements*, Charles H. Lippy and Peter W. Williams, eds. (New York: Charles Scribner's Sons, 1988) 3: 1416-18.

52. Brock, *Varieties of Pacifism*, 76-78; Brock, *Twentieth-Century Pacifism*, 8; Endy, "War and Peace," 1419-20; Chatfield, *American Peace Movement*, 12-15; David S. Patterson, "Citizen Peace Initiatives and American Political Culture, 1865-1920," in *Peace Movements and Political Cultures,* Charles Chatfield and Peter van den Dungen, eds. (Knoxville: University of Tennessee Press, 1988), 187-89.

53. Kraft, "Peacemaking in the Progressive Era," 122.

54. Patterson, " Citizen Peace Initiatives and American Political Culture," 192-94; Harold Josephson, "Introduction," in *Biographical Dictionary of Modern Peace Leaders*, Harold Josephson, and others, eds. (Westport, Conn.: Greenwood Press, 1985), xiv; Michael A. Lutzker, "Themes and Contradictions in the American Peace Movement, 1895-1917," in *The Pacifist Impulse in Historical Perspective*, Harvey L. Dyck, ed. (Toronto: University of Toronto Press, 1996), 321.

55. Josephson, "Introduction," xiv; Kraft, "Peacemaking in the Progressive Era," 123, 127-32; Patterson, "Citizen Peace Initiatives and American Political Culture," 192-94; Chatfield, *American Peace Movement*, 21.

56. Jo Vellacott, "Women, Peace and Internationalism, 1914-1920: 'Finding New Words and Creating New Methods,'" in *Peace Movements and Political Cultures*, 115.

57. Barbara J. Steinson, *American Women's Activism in World War I* (New York: Garland Publishing, 1982), 4-6, 16-18; Anne Wiltsher, *Most Dangerous Women: Feminist Peace Campaigners of the Great War* (London: Pandora Press,

1983), 11-13, 30-33, 43-45; Edith Wynner, "Rosika Schwimmer," in *Biographical Dictionary of Modern Peace Leaders*, 862-65; Marie Louise Degen, *The History of the Woman's Peace Party* (Baltimore: Johns Hopkins Press, 1939; New York: Garland Press, 1972), 28-30. According to Degen, the *New York Times* (19 September 1914) reported that Schwimmer and Catt presented to Wilson an appeal of 1 million women from thirteen countries urging the president "to invite the neutral countries of Europe to send envoys to meet the delegates he will appoint to carry the message of our nation, and these envoys shall unite in a demand upon the nations now at war that they declare a cessation of hostilities until this message shall have been delivered, being confident that this armistice would be the first step toward permanent peace." See "Women and War," *Outlook* 109 (24 March 1915): 676, which also contains an announcement of the international women's conference at The Hague, 28-30 April 1915.

58. Rebecca S. Stockwell, "Bertha von Suttner and Rosika Schwimmer: Pacifists from the Dual Monarchy," *Seven Studies in Medieval English History and Other Historical Essays*, Richard H. Bowers, ed. (Jackson: University of Mississippi Press, 1983), 147-50; Degen, *History of the Women's Peace Party*, 30-37; Steinson, *American Women's Activism in World War I*, 23-30; Wiltsher, *Most Dangerous Women*, 45-48, 53; Nancy Ann Slote, "Jane Addams," in *Biographical Dictionary of Modern Peace Leaders*, Josephson, ed., 5-8.

59. Degen, *History of the Woman's Peace Party*, 38-53; Wiltsher, *Most Dangerous Women*, 53-54.

60. Wiltsher, *Most Dangerous Women*, 89-105, 125; see also Chatfield, *American Peace Movement*, 33-34; Degen, *History of the Woman's Peace Party*, 64-126; Harriet Hyman Alonso, *Peace as a Women's Issue: A History of the U.S. Movement for World Peace and Women's Rights* (Syracuse, N.Y.: Syracuse University Press, 1993), 66-69.

61. Degen, *History of the Woman's Peace Party*, 127-50; Stockwell, "Bertha von Suttner and Rosika Schwimmer," 150-56; Mark Sullivan, *Our Times, 1900-1925* 5: *Over Here, 1914-1918* (New York: Charles Scribner's Sons, 1939), 162-83; Burnet Hershey, *The Odyssey of Henry Ford and the Great Peace Ship* (New York: Taplinger Publishing, 1967); Barbara S. Kraft, *The Peace Ship: Henry Ford's Pacifist Adventure in the First World War* (New York: Macmillan Publishing, 1978). For Schwimmer's life see Beth Wenger, "Rosika Schwimmer (1877-1948)," in *Jewish Women in America: An Historical Encyclopedia*, Paula E. Hyman and Deborah Dash Moore, eds. (New York: Routledge, 1997) 2: 1220-22. See also Janet Stevenson, "Lola Maverick Lloyd: 'I Must Do Something for Peace!'" *Chicago History* 9 (Spring 1980): 47-57.

62. Chatfield, *American Peace Movement*, 38-39; Charles Chatfield, "Pacifists and Their Publics: The Politics of a Peace Movement," *Midwest Journal of Political Science* 13 (May 1969): 300, 306; Brock, *Twentieth-Century Pacifism*, 29; Holloway, "A Review of American Religious Pacifism," 374; Kraft, "Peacemaking in the Progressive Era," 134. On the social gospel, see C. Howard Hopkins, *The Rise of the Social Gospel in American Protestantism, 1865-1915*

(New Haven: Yale University Press, 1940).

63. Clarence Darrow, *The Story of My Life* (New York: Grosset and Dunlap, 1932), 210.

64. Caroline Moorehead, *Troublesome People: The Warriors of Pacifism* (Bethesda, Md.: Adler and Adler, 1987), 66-67; Brock, *Twentieth-Century Pacifism*, 29-30.

65. Ray H. Abrams, *Preachers Present Arms* (New York: Round Table Press, 1933, Scottsdale, Pa.: Herald Press, 1969).

66. Sullivan, *Our Times* 5: *Over Here*, 467-76.

67. Endy, "War and Peace," 1421; Abrams, *Preachers Present Arms*, 56-57.

68. Clarence Darrow, *The War* (New York: National Security League, 1917), 13-14.

69. Abrams, *Preachers Present Arms*; 131-33; Brock, *Twentieth Century Pacifism*, 31; Samuel Walker, *In Defense of American Liberties: A History of the ACLU* (New York: Oxford University Press, 1990), 14.

70. Blanche Wiesen Cook, "Democracy in Wartime, Antimilitarism in England and the United States, 1914-1918," in *Peace Movements in America*, Charles Chatfield, ed. (New York: Schocken Books, 1973), 44.

71. Endy, "War and Peace," 1421.

72. Moorehead, *Troublesome People*, 89. See Robert Moats Miller, *American Protestantism and Social Issues: 1919-1939* (Chapel Hill: University of North Carolina Press, 1958), 336.

73. Josephson, "Introduction," xi-xii; Harold Josephson, "The Search for Lasting Peace: Internationalism and American Foreign Policy, 1920-1950," in *Peace Movements and Political Cultures*, 204; Barash, *Introduction to Peace Studies*, 62-63. Barash, 76, 75, makes a useful generalization: "Peace movements have typically grown when the threat to peace was great, and/or when the memory of recent carnage was particularly acute and painful. Ironically, they have done best—in terms of enthusiasm, membership and financial contributions—when the situation seemed darkest. . . . Nonetheless, peace movements often have a difficult time. During war, they are typically denounced and often banned or even attacked as unpatriotic, cowardly, or traitorous for giving 'aid and comfort to the enemy.' And during time of peace, they often are hard-pressed to make a dent in public complacency."

74. Holloway, "A Review of American Religious Pacifism," 372-73. As an example, see *Hamilton v. Regents of the University of California*, 293 U.S. 245 (1934). The case contested a request for exemption from military training in a university ROTC, based on the resolutions of the Methodist General Conferences of 1931 and 1932, which renounced war as a national policy and requested conscientious objector status for Methodist youth.

75. Robert Moats Miller, *Harry Emerson Fosdick: Preacher, Pastor, Prophet* (New York: Oxford University Press, 1985), 88, 92.

76. Brock, *Twentieth-Century Pacifism*, 108, 142-44; Endy, "War and Peace," 1422-23; Holloway, "A Review of American Religious Pacifism," 372; Miller, *American Protestantism and Social Issues*, 327-29; Charles Chatfield, *For Peace and Justice: Pacifism in America, 1914-1941* (Knoxville: University of Tennessee Press, 1971), 21-24.

77. The Federal Council of Churches, the Church Peace Union, and the World Alliance for International Friendship Through the Churches urged clergy to petition the Senate to ratify American participation in the League of Nations; 14,450 clergy signed a petition to that effect, to no avail. The same kinds of massive efforts were made in favor of the World Court, with somewhat more success. Miller, *American Protestantism and Social Issues*, 319-20, 324-25.

78. Josephson, "The Search for Lasting Peace," 205; Chatfield, *The American Peace Movement*, 169.

79. Josephson, "Introduction," x; Chatfield, "Pacifists and Their Publics," 307; Brock, *Twentieth-Century Pacifism*, 11-12, 30-31.

80. Vellacott, "Women, Peace, and Internationalism," 120; see also Moorehead, *Troublesome People*, 81-83.

81. Brock, *Twentieth-Century Pacifism*, 114, 117.

82. Roscoe Baker, *The American Legion and American Foreign Policy* (New York: Bookman Associates, 1954), 29.

83. Baker, *American Legion*, 116.

84. Baker, *American Legion*, 223, see also 113, 221-22; Raymond Moley, Jr., *The American Legion Story* (New York: Duell, Sloan, and Pearce, 1966), 86-87, 151-60, 165, 178-79, 188, 226-27.

85. Martha Strayer, *The D.A.R.: An Informal History* (Westport, Conn.: Greenwood Press, 1958), 116, 121-26.

86. Miller, *American Protestantism and Social Issues*, 326-27; Barash, *Introduction to Peace Studies*, 360-61; Chatfield, *American Peace Movement*, 60-61; Moley, *American Legion Story*, 179; Strayer, *D.A.R.*, 116; Josephson, "Internationalism and American Foreign Policy," 211.

87. Miller, *American Protestantism and Social Issues*, 340.

88. Chatfield, *The American Peace Movement*, 64-72, 75-76; Josephson, "Introduction," xii.

89. See Ronald B. Flowers, "Government Accommodation of Religious-Based Conscientious Objection," *Seton Hall Law Review* 24 no. 2 (1993): 695-735.

90. James F. Childress, "Conscientious Objection" in *The Westminster Dictionary of Christian Ethics*, James F. Childress and John Macquarrie, eds. (Philadelphia: Westminster Press, 1986), 118.

91. John Whiteclay Chambers II, "Conscientious Objectors and the American State from Colonial Times to the Present," in *The New Conscientious Objection: From Sacred to Secular Resistance*, Charles C. Moskos and John Whiteclay Chambers II, eds. (New York: Oxford University Press, 1993), 23-26; Brock, *Varieties of Pacifism*, 23, 34; Brock, *Twentieth-Century Pacifism*, 4-6. A helpful survey of the history of conscientious objection is found in volume one, chapter

three of *Conscientious Objection*, 2 vols. (Washington, D.C.: Selective Service System, special monograph # 11, 1950). Volume one is narrative, volume two is documentary.

92. *Conscientious Objection*, 1:33-34. Emphasis in original.

93. Chambers, "Conscientious Objectors and the American State," 27-28; Brock, *Varieties of Pacifism*, 23-25, 38, 42-44; C. Henry Smith, *The Story of the Mennonites*, 4th ed. (Newton, Kans.: Mennonite Publication Office, 1957), 787.

94. Confederate States of America, *Statutes at Large*, 8 February 1861-18 February 1864, ch. 45, p. 78. "Dunkards" is a name used for Church of the Brethren.

95. 13 *Statutes at Large* 6.

96. *Conscientious Objection*, 1: 45, 41-42; Chambers, "Conscientious Objectors and the American State," 29-31; Brock, *Varieties of Pacifism*, 69-74.

97. 40 *Statutes at Large* 76 at 78 § 4.

98. *Conscientious Objection*, 1:49; Steinson, *American Women's Activism*, 254; Chambers, "Conscientious Objectors and the American State," 32-35.

99. Endy, "War and Peace," 1421-22; Smith, *Story of the Mennonites*, 792-99; *Conscientious Objection*, 1:49-66; Harlan Fiske Stone, "The Conscientious Objector," *Columbia University Quarterly* 21 (October 1919): 255, 257, 270-71. Stone, at the time Dean of Columbia Law School and one of three members of the examination board, describes the process in considerable detail. Stone later became a Justice and then Chief Justice of the Supreme Court and was the only Justice involved in all four cases that are the subject of this book.

100. 54 *Statutes at Large* 885 at 889 § 5(g).

101. *Conscientious Objection*, 1:67-90; Smith, *Story of the Mennonites*, 811-13; Chambers, "Conscientious Objectors and the American State," 35-38; Endy, "War and Peace," 1423-25.

102. 133 F.2d 703 (1943).

103. 156 F.2d 377 (1946), cert. denied 329 U.S. 795 (1946).

104. See Francis M. Nevins, Jr. "The Conscientious Objector and the Constitution," *Intramural Law Review, New York University School of Law* 22 (May 1967): 253-55.

105. 62 *Statutes at Large* 604 at 612-613 § 6(j); Chambers, "Conscientious Objectors and the American State," 39. The modification of "religious training and belief" is taken from Chief Justice Hughes's dissent in *United States v. Macintosh*, one of the subjects of this book, 283 U.S. 605 at 633-34. Congress, however, used the phrase "Supreme Being" rather than Hughes's "God."

106. 81 *Statutes at Large* 100 at 104 § (7).

107. Chambers, "Conscientious Objectors and the American State," 25-31; Hudson, *Religion in America*, 124-25; Mark A. Noll, *A History of Christianity in the United States and Canada* (Grand Rapids: William B. Eerdmans Publishing, 1992), 130-32, 314-17.

108. Chambers, "Conscientious Objectors and the American State," 32-34; Moorehead, *Troublesome People*, 68-71; Brock, *Twentieth-Century Pacifism*, 41-56. Ernest L. Meyer *Hey! Yellowbacks!* (New York: John Day, 1930) offers a frequently cited, autobiographical account of shameful treatment inflicted on conscientious objectors.

109. Moorehead, *Troublesome People*, 70; Brock, *Twentieth-Century Pacifism*, 56-59.

110. Stone, "The Conscientious Objector," 268-69.

111. Mark Lieberman, *The Pacifists: Soldiers Without Guns*. (New York: Praeger Publishers, 1972), 71; Christine A. Lunardini, *The American Peace Movement in the Twentieth Century* (Denver: ABC-Clio, 1994) 6-7, 17-18; Chambers, "Conscientious Objectors and the American State," 33-35; Cook, "Democracy in Wartime," 48-49.

112. Lunardini, *American Peace Movement*, 7-8; Chatfield, *American Peace Movement*, 45-46.

113. Chatfield, *American Peace Movement*, 78-79; Albert N. Keim and Grant M. Stoltzfus, *The Politics of Conscience: The Historic Peace Churches and America at War, 1917-1955* (Scottsdale, Pa.: Herald Press, 1988), 103-126; *Conscientious Objection*, 1:157-249, 291-311.

114. *Arver, et al. v. United States* (also commonly called *Selective Draft Law Cases*) 245 U.S. 366 (1918). The law in this case was also challenged on other grounds, irrelevant to this study.

115. 380 U.S. 163 (1965). Peter Irons, *The Courage of Their Convictions: Sixteen Americans Who Fought Their Way to the Supreme Court* (New York: Penguin Books, 1990), 152-78 presents a fascinating account of the case of Daniel Seeger.

116. *United States v. Seeger* 380 U.S. 163 at 176. I call this a "double sincerity test." For a government official to determine whether an unconventional believer qualifies, he or she must compare the sincerity of that person to the sincerity of a conventional believer, real or hypothetical, who clearly qualifies as a conscientious objector. If their respective sincerities are comparable, then the unconventional believer qualifies. See Ronald B. Flowers, *That Godless Court?: Supreme Court Decisions on Church-State Relationships* (Louisville: Westminster John Knox Press, 1994) 58-59.

117. *Welsh v. United States* 398 U.S. 333 (1970). The statute did exclude those whose objection rested on "essentially political, sociological or philosophical views, or a merely personal moral code." 81 *Statutes at Large* 100 at 104 § (7). That would seem to exclude Welsh, but the Court said that it did not. This language excludes only "those whose beliefs are not deeply held and those whose objection to war does not rest at all upon moral, ethical, or religious principle but instead rests solely upon considerations of policy, pragmatism, or expedience." 398 U.S. 333 at 342-43.

118. 401 U.S. 437 (1971).

119. 401 U.S. 437 at 450.

120. Moorehead, *Troublesome People*, xiii.

Three

Rosika Schwimmer:
". . . You Led the Way"[1]

She was female and fifty-one years old, yet the Supreme Court of the United States denied American citizenship to Rosika Schwimmer because she would not agree to bear arms in defense of the country. *United States v. Schwimmer*[2] is one of the celebrated cases of 1929—noteworthy because some considered Schwimmer "the most powerful woman in the world"[3] because of her international campaigns for feminism and pacifism. Her case was the first in Supreme Court history to raise the question of whether an alien conscientious objector to war could qualify for citizenship.[4] It set a temporary precedent in American jurisprudence and stimulated considerable congressional and public debate.

Born in Hungary in 1877, Rosika Schwimmer was the daughter of Max B. Schwimmer, a dealer in agricultural products and fine horses, and Bertha (Katscher) Schwimmer. In this upper-middle-class family of Jewish background, Rosika's father was an agnostic, her mother was a freethinker, and an uncle was a rabbi. Her parents sent her to a Catholic school for girls in Romania, although she received only eight years of formal schooling, probably because of health problems; she had been born two months prematurely and was a sickly child.

When Rosika Schwimmer was eighteen, family financial reverses forced her to seek employment. She worked as a bookkeeper or office manager for a variety of companies and soon, dissatisfied with working conditions for women, began to organize women to improve their political, economic, and social status. She organized the National Association of Women Office Workers in 1897 and cofounded the Hungarian Feminist Association in 1904. For a number of years she edited the feminist magazine *A Nö* (*Woman*). She organized the Seventh Conference of the Woman Suffrage Alliance in 1913 and served in London in 1914 as the press secretary for the Alliance. From the beginning of World War I, she gave her total time and considerable talents to pacifism,[5] and some of her activities in that cause are described in Chapter Two.

Although Madame Schwimmer (as she was called by friends and enemies alike) had visited the United States several times in the years leading up to and including World War I, she came to live in America in 1921—arriving in a rather frightening way.

In 1918 Schwimmer became Hungarian ambassador to Switzerland, the first woman to hold an ambassadorial-level diplomatic post. She was appointed to this position by Count Michael Károlyi, the prime minister of Hungary and a pacifist. Under the Károlyi regime, Hungary remained a democratic republic, but, after a few months, Károlyi was deposed and replaced by the communist regime of Béla Kuhn. A short time after that Hungary came under the control of a fascist "white terror" government. The Kuhn government removed Schwimmer from her post in Switzerland, and now she feared for her life, because she was identified with the former democratic government. In February 1920 she was smuggled out of Hungary to Vienna with the aid of English and American Quakers, Swedish war relief workers, a member of the British Parliament, and others. She lived in Vienna as a political refugee until, with an emergency passport from Austria, she was granted permission to enter the United States in 1921.[6] She settled in Chicago on 8 September 1921.[7]

Schwimmer filed her first papers with naturalization authorities, declaring her intent to petition the government for citizenship, on 16 November 1921.[8] As an applicant for citizenship, Schwimmer was required to "declare on oath in open court" that she would "support and defend the Constitution and laws of the United States against all enemies, foreign and domestic, and bear true faith and allegiance to the same."[9] This oath would follow on five years of residence demonstrating "to the satisfaction of the court" that the applicant had "behaved as a man [sic] of good moral character, attached to the principles of the Constitution of the United States, and well disposed to the good order and happiness of the same."[10] To determine whether an alien conformed to the requirements of the law, the Department of Naturalization employed a questionnaire, to be completed prior to filing her petition for naturalization ("second papers"). Question 20 was crucial.

20. Have you read the following oath of allegiance?
"I hereby declare, on oath, that I absolutely and entirely renounce and abjure all allegiance and fidelity to any foreign prince, potentate, state or

sovereignty, and particularly to [the country of origin], of which I have heretofore been a subject; that I will support and defend the Constitution and laws of the United States of America against all enemies, foreign and domestic, and that I will bear true faith and allegiance to the same."

Are you willing to take this oath in becoming a citizen?"[11]

Schwimmer answered both questions "Yes." Question 22 asked, "If necessary, are you willing to take up arms in defense of this country?" Number 23 inquired, "Did you file a questionnaire with a draft board during the war?" She answered neither question, thinking they applied only to men.[12]

Her papers returned from Washington with the directive to answer question 22—the first salvo in her battle to become a citizen. Schwimmer believed that the American Legion Auxiliary had fomented the problems that were developing in her naturalization process. When Schwimmer's friend and patron Jane Addams happened to mention, in a meeting of the Washington Congress of the Women's International League for Peace and Freedom in May 1924, that Schwimmer had filed "first papers" in applying for citizenship, she set off an "alarm signal" among what Schwimmer called "the militarist and so called patriotic organizations." At a meeting of the Auxiliary of the American Legion in Indianapolis in June 1924, two years before Schwimmer could advance to the next stage in the application process, "they passed a resolution of protest against my admittance and presented the resolution in Washington to the Labor Department, to which naturalization matters belong." Schwimmer's friends, she lamented, "refused to take this step seriously" and "unopposed the other side organised [sic] and carried a vigorous campaign to the bitter end." When in 1926 Schwimmer "applied for final papers and filled out a four page questionnaire" her enemies were prepared. "When the papers were returned from Washington," she wrote, "the District Director of Naturalization was another man."[13]

The District Director of Naturalization in Chicago was Fred Schlotfeldt, born in Germany, himself a naturalized citizen.[14] When Schwimmer's papers returned from Washington with the requirement to answer question 22, he suggested that she answer it in the affirmative. But Schwimmer insisted on honesty and standing on principle. She answered question 22: "I would not take up arms personally."[15] In spite of Schlotfeldt's advice, "I insisted on going through the whole process of examination, unable to believe the U.S.A. would be the first civilized country to compel women to take up arms."[16]

Schwimmer's determination led to a formal hearing on 22 September 1926, when she discussed with Schlotfeldt what he considered to be the inconsistencies between her answers to questions 20 and 22. Her words would follow her up the legal ladder. On the subject of her willingness to take the oath, rejecting loyalty to any other country and promising to support and defend the Constitution, Schwimmer said that she "could and can say 'Yes' because I do not want to remain a subject of Hungary" where indeed her life was threatened by a hostile regime. She had "found the Constitution and the institutions of the United States of America nearest to my ideals of a democratic republic governed by the people for the people on the basis of independence and tolerance." In her search for "an adoptive country" the United States had seemed to her "a haven of refuge from a country where social prejudices and feudal institutions have grown intolerable to self-respecting men and women." She was "therefore whole-heartedly prepared to 'bear true faith and allegiance.' And just as unreservedly am I ready 'to support and defend the Constitution and the law against all enemies foreign and domestic.'"[17]

Yet Schwimmer's defense of the Constitution would not, she told Schlotfeldt, extend to bearing arms. She could not "see that a woman's refusal to take up arms is a contradiction to the oath of allegiance." She would have "other ways and means" to fulfill that duty. She could imagine that she might attend "meetings" or read "publications" in which she might find "attacks against the American form of government" or "praise of undemocratic forms, in which I do not believe." Confronted with such statements, Schwimmer would, "according to my conception of 'support and defense' . . . consider it my duty to uphold most emphatically the American constitution [*sic*] and the American form of government in which I believe, and to oppose such forms of government which are not based on Democracy and Self-government." She could claim "practical experiences" as well as "theoretical convictions" that "qualify me to take this stand." For Schwimmer, "It would be denying the force of spiritual influences, of mental energies, if we defined the word 'defense' solely as a physical act." Elsewhere she pointed out that a lawyer defends a client with words, not physical activity. She would refuse, in theory or in fact, to bear arms.

If, however, it is a fact that the Government of the United States can compel its women citizens to take up arms in defense of the country—something that no other civilized government has ever attempted, I would not be able to comply with this requirement of American citizenship. In this case I would recognize the right of the government to deal with me as it is dealing with its male citizens who for conscientious reasons refuse to take up arms.[18]

At this interview Schlotfeldt urged Schwimmer to withdraw her petition for naturalization because he could not recommend its approval, given what he still saw as inconsistencies in her responses to questions 20 and 22.[19] This she refused to do.

Shortly thereafter Schlotfeldt informed Schwimmer that he had received a copy of a letter to Col. L. A. Stone in which she had written, "I am an uncompromising pacifist for whom even Jane Addams is not enough of a pacifist. I am an absolute atheist. I have no sense of nationalism, only a cosmic consciousness of belonging to the human family." Schlotfeldt wanted to know whether this statement accurately reflected her views.[20] This query became the turning point in Schwimmer's naturalization process; her reply reverberated in all her legal proceedings through her Supreme Court case.

Yes, Mme. Schwimmer replied, these were her views. "Col. Stone," to whom the letter was addressed, was Dr. Lee Alexander Stone, a physician and commander of the Military Intelligence Association of Chicago. In the latter role, he spied on "subversive" or "dangerous" people and then warned the public about them. Stone and his organization spread the story that Schwimmer had been a German agent during the war and that she was dangerous to American security because of her pacifism.

Stone's organization did not spread this propaganda alone. Because Schwimmer had been so active in trying to end World War I, she was plagued with charges that she was a German operative. The *New York Herald* published two articles in 1917 alleging that Schwimmer advanced the interests of the German government in trying to end the war. Many pacifists were accused of being German agents, but articles about Schwimmer were more specific, charging that she had brokered some meetings between a Russian agent and the German Ambassador to the United States as Germany was trying to get Russia to surrender. The same articles accused Schwimmer of tricking Henry Ford into his ridiculous effort to try to end the war, also an act consistent with German interests.[21] *The Woman Patriot*, antifeminist and antisocialist, also published a series of articles accusing Schwimmer of being a German agent. The massive

Report of the Joint Legislative Committee of the New York Legislature investigating seditious activities—the so-called Lusk Report—mentioned Schwimmer several times as a "known German agent" during the war, lending legitimacy to the postwar campaign. Henry Ford's newspaper, *The Dearborn Independent*, launched a series of anti-Semitic articles in the early 1920s. The idea circulated widely that Rosika Schwimmer had aroused his anti-Jewish venom by duping him into the Peace Ship fiasco and taking some of his money in the process. This accusation appeared in both Jewish and Gentile publications. Schwimmer strongly denied it.[22] In coming to America in 1921, Schwimmer planned to live by writing and lecturing. Because of all the negative publicity, speaking invitations declined appreciably, leaving her in a precarious financial condition. Indeed, as Beth Wenger has noted, "the Peace Ship debacle signaled the beginning of a smear campaign" against Schwimmer that eventually ended her career as a public intellectual and political activist and continued beyond the grave to treat her as a danger to the United States.[23]

Schwimmer reacted with indignation to the campaign of Col. Stone's Chicago Military Intelligence Association and initiated steps to get Stone and his group to stop. At her request, Stone and some of his colleagues spoke with Schwimmer personally about her views and became convinced that she was not dangerous but dedicated to America and its survival. Stone publicly recanted his earlier criticism and even asked her to speak to his organization. He lent her some of his books and she wrote him a long letter endorsing many of his ideas. The lines about which Schlotfeldt inquired came from that correspondence.[24]

Schwimmer sent Stone a telegram, asking how Schlotfeldt had come to have a copy of her private letter to him. Stone responded by telegram that he was attempting to help Schwimmer's cause with Schlotfeldt. To that end he had shared with Schlotfeldt all of their correspondence. Stone thought that Schlotfeldt favored Schwimmer's naturalization.[25]

Schwimmer now told Schlotfeldt that the views expressed in her letter to Stone were her views. She was, indeed, "an uncompromising pacifist." She acknowledged that she was an atheist. One characteristic that made America so attractive to her was the separation of church and state, "which makes one's religious belief a strictly private matter." She assumed that the same was true for applicants for naturalization. The fact that she had "no sense of nationalism" was illustrated by the fact that she was willing to give up the nationality of her birth. Her "consciousness of belonging to the human family" simply meant that she would not be willing to do to others what she would not want done to her.[26]

"I am able to take the oath of allegiance without any reservations," Schwimmer asserted. "I am willing to do everything that an American citizen has to do except fighting." Were American women "compelled" to fight, Schwimmer "would not do that. I am an uncompromising pacifist." How far would she carry her "uncompromising" pacifism? Did she "disapprove of the government fighting"?

> I answer, it means I disapprove of the government asking me to fight personally with my fists or carrying a gun. I do not care how many other women fight, because I consider it a question of conscience. I am not willing to bear arms.

"In every other single way," Schwimmer argued, "I am ready to follow the law and do everything that the law compels American citizens to do. That is why I can take the oath of allegiance, because as far as I can find out, there is nothing that I could be compelled to do that I cannot do." Surely, she had thought, women would not be compelled to fight. "If it is a question of fighting, as much as I desire American citizenship, I would not seek the citizenship." Responding to accusations that she was "spreading propaganda among the women throughout the country, about my being an uncompromising pacifist and not being willing to fight," Schwimmer affirmed that "I am always ready to tell anyone who wants to hear it that I am an uncompromising pacifist and will not fight. In my writings and in my lectures I take up the question of war and pacifism if I am asked for that."

Schwimmer was qualified for naturalization, Schlotfeldt concluded, except that her views on bearing arms suggested that she was not attached to the principles of the Constitution and well disposed to its good order, and that she might not be able to take the oath of allegiance without a mental reservation.[27] Schlotfeldt forwarded his conclusion to the Federal District Court before which Schwimmer's application would be heard.

Somewhere along the way Schwimmer engaged a lawyer, Olive Rabe, of the Chicago firm of Zimring and Rabe. The two became close friends as well as counselor and client. Rabe was Schwimmer's lawyer throughout her struggle for citizenship. Others also represented her at points in the process. In a way I have not been able to determine, William B. Gemmill of the Chicago firm of Urion, Drucker, Reichmann and Boutwell became involved in Schwimmer's case. Gemmill had served in the military, but apparently dedicated himself to the task of gaining citizenship for his pacifist client. Rabe charged no fee except expenses and Gemmill may also have worked *pro bono*, given that Schwimmer had no money. In September 1926 she moved to New York City,[28] although her case remained under the jurisdiction of the Chicago naturalization office. Her sister, Franciska (known as Franzi), and her mother, Bertha, lived with her. They had no money to spend on legal work because Rosika received no invitations to lecture and Franciska, a musician, had very few students. What money they had beyond living expenses went for the treatment of Bertha, who in the early days of the citizenship battle was gravely ill with stomach cancer. At one point Schwimmer wrote Schlotfeldt that "my dear mother is since May, bleeding her life away with cancer of the stomach." Her mother's illness exacted its toll on Schwimmer, financially and psychologically.[29]

In the early stages of Schwimmer's campaign for citizenship, Olive Rabe questioned whether Schwimmer should have been compelled to answer question 22. Article 1, Section 8 of the Constitution says that Congress shall establish a uniform rule of naturalization, but Schwimmer, Rabe, and others learned that in some areas of the United States, the page of the naturalization questionnaire containing question 22 was not used. That some applicants had to answer the question and others did not seemed unfair and unconstitutional. A "uniform rule of naturalization" was crucial to Schwimmer's effort to become a citizen. Olive Rabe wrote to the Commissioner of Naturalization, asking questions about whether different jurisdictions used different versions of the form or whether women were exempt from answering the questions about defense of the country. The reply was emphatic.

> You are advised . . . that the forms in use in each of the naturalization districts are the same in all respects excepting the mailing address of the naturalization officer to whom they are to be delivered or mailed by the applicants for naturalization.
>
> As a response to your question as to whether it is the intention that women applying for naturalization should answer question 22 on Form 2214, it may be stated that no statement is printed on the form excepting female applicants for naturalization from answering this question, and the form in addition contains in its upper right-hand corner a notice to the alien that all blanks are to be filled out.

Later a lawyer told Schwimmer that the issue of the form would not determine her case; the real issue would be her attachment to the principles of the Constitution. That prediction turned out to be true.[30]

After the formal hearing on 22 September 1926 Schlotfeldt delayed the required appearance before a judge of a federal district court. Such a court appearance was inevitable; the question was about when it would happen. Before Schwimmer's day in court, there was some negotiation about who would represent her. Roger Baldwin and his associate Forrest Bailey, of the American Civil Liberties Union, wanted Schwimmer to engage Clarence Darrow for the court appearance; a lawyer of his fame would help her cause. Schwimmer appeared interested, but Olive Rabe dissuaded her. Rabe was willing to contact Darrow, but believed that the conservative judges available in the District Court would not be favorably disposed to him. Schwimmer agreed with that and wrote "You remember perhaps that I never thought of Mr. Darrow as useful in my affairs, but obviously he has here admirers who think him effective in everything he does. But your explanation makes it clear that his assistance would be undesirable."[31] The ironic possibility of Darrow, the harsh critic of pacifism, as part of her legal team never came up again.

As weeks of delay turned into months,[32] Rabe and Schwimmer's other attorney, William Gemmill, lobbied Naturalization Director Schlotfeldt on her behalf. At one point Schlotfeldt felt that there were two or three things in her application that might cause her to be denied citizenship, although he did not specify them. Later he told Gemmill that there was only one problem: her answer to question 22. Schlotfeldt said she was an excellent person, except for her unwillingness to fight in defense of the country. Her statements about being an atheist or having no sense of nationalism would not make any difference to her naturalization petition. The government regarded her as a perfect candidate for citizenship except that her refusal to bear arms meant that she could not support and defend the Constitution.

Somehow, in July 1927, newspapers began to report that Mme. Schwimmer had been denied citizenship. She issued a news release refuting such reports, saying that her court appearance was set for the week of 8 July. The court hearing did not happen at that time, but the press reports irritated Schlotfeldt because he thought they reflected badly on him. All through this period Rabe worked on a brief in preparation for the court appearance. "From a purely legal point of view," Rabe wrote, "we can make Schlotfield [sic] look ridiculous."[33]

In mid-September, Rabe persuaded Schlotfeldt to accompany her to the chambers of Judge George A. Carpenter of the United States District Court for the Northern District of Illinois to set a date for Schwimmer's day in court. That interview was unsatisfactory. When Schlotfeldt told the judge the nature of the case, "The Judge, in a very decided manner, said I could tell you [Schwimmer] that unless you were willing to give the very last drop of your blood in defense of this country, you would not get citizenship through his court." The judge asked Rabe what arguments could be made on her client's behalf. She responded that the Constitution authorized only Congress to raise an army and provide a navy. Congress had, in several Acts, provided for the military and a militia, but in every case had specified that only males could serve. Judge Carpenter replied that Congress, however, in times of emergency, could require women to serve and they consequently must be willing to do so. Rabe also said that only Congress had the authority to make uniform laws of naturalization. Congress had not authorized the preliminary form with question 22, so the Bureau of Naturalization had no right to insert additional requirements for naturalization, as it had with this question. "Judge Carpenter maintained insistently that it was not possible to take the oath of allegiance unless the applicant was willing to bear arms in defense of the country. He said there was no doubt what his decision would be." When they left the judge's chambers, "Mr. Schlotfeldt looked very jubilant and said, 'I told you so,' or something to that effect."[34]

A few days before this encounter, Rabe had written to Schwimmer that the Supreme Court, in *Tutun v. United States* had ruled that a judgment in a naturalization case could be appealed. She said that surely Judge Carpenter would not decide Schwimmer's case negatively, but if he did, they would appeal.[35] After her conversation with Judge Carpenter, Rabe probably did not feel as sanguine about his impending decision and was glad of the potential opportunity to appeal.

Schwimmer finally appeared in Judge Carpenter's court on 13 October 1927, more than a year after her initial formal hearing before the naturalization examiner. In this proceeding she was interrogated by the government's lawyer and the judge. Schwimmer did not qualify or recant any of the views she had formerly articulated. At one point, she was asked whether she expected others to follow her example.

Q. You say you are an uncompromising pacifist?
A. Yes.

Q. How far does that go? Does it refer only to yourself?

A. Yes.

Q. That you are not going to use your fists on somebody?

A. Yes.

Q. Or do you disapprove of the Government fighting?

A. It means that I disapprove of the Government asking me to fight.

Q. You mean fight personally?

A. Yes, physically.

Q. Carrying a gun?

A. Yes.

Q. Is that as far as it goes?

A. That is as far as it goes.

. . . .

Q. The time will never come, I venture to say, when the women of the United States will have to bear arms.

A. Well, I am not willing to bear arms. In every other single way, civic way, I am ready to follow the law and do everything that the law compels American citizens to do. I am willing to do that. That is why I say I can take the oath of allegiance because as far as I, with the able help of my lawyers, could find out there is nothing that I could be compelled to do that I could not do.[36]

Finally Judge Carpenter interrupted.

THE COURT: Let me ask you this one question:

A. Yes, sir.

Q. If you were called to the service, and the kind of work that women usually can perform better than the men can—say as a nurse or as someone to give cheer to the soldiers—and you were at some place in a war, which I hope never will come, and you saw someone coming in the headquarters or the barracks, wherever it was, with a pistol in his hand to shoot the back of an officer of our country, and you had a pistol handy by, would you kill him?

A. No, I would not.

THE COURT: The application is denied.[37]

Later in the proceeding, the judge remarked, "Otherwise, except on this one point, I think the Government will admit that the applicant is entirely qualified." He told Mme. Schwimmer that there was nothing personal in his denial of her application and she assured him that she understood. Schwimmer's lawyers *and* Judge Carpenter said that the question should be reviewed on appeal.[38] (See the text of this proceeding in Appendix D.[39])

Most newspapers found the judge's decision wrong, if not incredible. The *New York World* reported that papers across the country opined that if another judge had heard Schwimmer's case, she would have gained citizenship. Officers from the Naturalization Bureau and from other U.S. District Courts said that it was exceedingly rare to ask an applicant for citizenship such a hypothetical question as Judge Carpenter had asked Schwimmer. "The general reaction here and in Washington was that it bordered on absurdity to ask a fifty-year-old woman anything about her willingness to bear arms for her country." An editorial in the *World* questioned Judge Carpenter's own penchant for patriotic sacrifice.

> In 'Who's Who' we find no mention of military service on his part. If he had borne arms himself he might know that the situation with which he confronts Mme. Schwimmer could not occur except in comic opera. In short, we believe that his exhibition was poor law, poor patriotism and poor sense. And we are glad that Mme. Schwimmer has decided to carry her case to the higher courts.[40]

The decision at this hearing, however, was not the final order of the court. Rabe had prepared a brief to support her argument that Schwimmer should be granted citizenship, repeating the argument she had made previously to Judge Carpenter in his chambers. The judge had not read it before the hearing, and Gemmill asked Judge Carpenter to read it before issuing his final order. The judge readily agreed. "I will be glad to see it. It is a matter of education for me." The judge also instructed Schlotfeldt to work with Schwimmer's lawyers to produce an "agreed statement of facts" to accompany the case on appeal.

Schlotfeldt did not follow the judge's instructions, but issued an order denying Schwimmer citizenship without telling her lawyers about it. Apparently he intended to close their avenue of appeal or, alternatively, if they did appeal, to include more information adverse to Schwimmer in the record that went to the appeals court. Some time early in November, when Schwimmer's lawyers were trying to get Schlotfeldt to work with them to produce the agreed statement of facts, he told them he had "inadvertently" filed a final order denying her citizenship. Furious, they determined to meet with Judge Carpenter to tell him of Schlotfeldt's inappropriate activity. By the time they met, on 14 November, Judge Carpenter had become irritated by the press coverage of the 13 October hearing. He accused Schwimmer's lawyers of making their case in the press. He vacated Schlotfeldt's earlier order and reinstated it on that date with the same language. So, on 14 November 1927, Judge Carpenter issued his final order, denying Rosika Schwimmer citizenship.

[I]t appearing that the said petitioner is not attached to the principles of the Constitution of the United States and well disposed to the good order and happiness of the same, and further that she is unable to take the oath of allegiance prescribed by the Naturalization Law without a mental reservation, it is therefore ordered that the said petition be and is hereby denied.[41]

Thereafter Schwimmer's lawyers and Schlotfeldt worked out an agreed statement of facts (see Appendix E).

The following week Schwimmer appealed her case to the United States Circuit Court of Appeals for the Seventh Circuit. In spite of Schlotfeldt's shenanigans, her lawyers believed that the record of the case strongly favored her. Rabe was working on a brief to the court; the government's brief was due soon. She believed that the Court of Appeals would surely overturn Judge Carpenter's order.[42]

Olive Rabe argued the appeal for Schwimmer; Fred Schlotfeldt represented the government. On 29 June 1928, the court unanimously found in Schwimmer's favor. Reviewing some of her previous testimony the court concluded that, aside from her refusal to bear arms, she showed a good understanding of the Constitution, appeared to be attached to its principles, and to be well disposed to the welfare of the United States. The decision next reviewed pertinent portions of the law, observed that the opportunity to become a citizen is a privilege and not a right, and asserted that all statutory requirements must be complied with to gain the status. In the light of that, in Schwimmer's case,

The question for judgment was, Did she make it appear that she had behaved, that is, conducted herself, as a person of good moral character, attached and disposed as the statute requires, during the time fixed by it? . . . [M]ere views are not, by the statute, made a ground for denying a petition.[43]

Noting that Schwimmer was both female and fifty years old, the court concluded:

Women are considered incapable of bearing arms. Male persons of the age of the appellant have not been compelled to do so. Appellant, if admitted, cannot by any present law of the United States be compelled to bear arms. Judging by all the conscription acts of which we have knowledge, she never will be required to do so; yet she is denied admission to citizenship because she says she will not fight with her fists or carry a gun.

In other words, there is put to her an hypothetical question—what would she do under circumstances that never have occurred and probably never will occur—and upon her answers to this supposed case her petition is denied. A petitioner's rights are not to be determined by putting conundrums to her.

The views of appellant relied upon to support the denial of her application have no substantial relation to the inquiry authorized by the statute. They were immaterial to that inquiry and do not furnish sufficient basis for the decree.[44]

In a letter of glowing praise—"you have brought my citizenship matter to a victorious end"—Schwimmer thanked Rabe profusely for her legal work and reminded her of the larger implications of their triumph. "It must give you satisfaction to know that your work has not only helped me but will also benefit all the others who might have citizenship difficulties on similar grounds as I had."[45] Schwimmer also put on paper what apparently are musings to herself about the progress of her case to this time and her attitude toward American citizenship (see Appendix F).

On the same day Schwimmer won a libel judgment against Fred R. Marvin, making the decision of the Court of Appeals even sweeter. As leader of "The Key Men of America," a columnist for the *New York Commercial*, and an adviser to the DAR, Marvin attacked pacifists and liberals, whom he generally labeled as communists. In columns in May and June 1924, he had joined others in accusing Mme. Schwimmer of being a German spy during World War I and a communist. Marvin derived much of his material for his columns from the Lusk Committee Report published by the New York Legislature. Schwimmer filed a libel suit against Marvin and the *Commercial*. Her attorney was Arthur Garfield Hays, whom she had obtained through the American Civil Liberties Union. After lengthy legal proceedings, Schwimmer won a judgment of $17,000. Marvin's attorney had argued that because much of the information in the columns had come from the state legislature's Lusk Committee, it was privileged and not subject to legal attack. He also admitted that his client had called Schwimmer a "bolshevik" and a "German spy," but argued he was free to do so because "it is well known that she is a pacifist and you can say anything about a pacifist." On the former point, the trial judge said: "Libel does not become privileged matter because published by a legislative committee" and that "such a report, to be privileged, must be fair and honest," which the Lusk report was not. The ACLU was delighted with Schwimmer's vindication, believing that it might bring smear campaigns against "liberal" activists to an end. There were reports that Marvin and his organization would quit their publications because of lack of funds.[46]

In the proceedings of the Marvin case Schwimmer learned something unexpected—the perfidy of Col. Lee Alexander Stone of the Chicago Military Intelligence Society. "Imagine my surprise when Marvin's lawyer pulled out the two letters I had addressed to Dr. Stone and used them against me!" Schwimmer wrote to Olive Rabe. "Dr. Stone has turned out to be more of a scoundrel than I had believed him during his worst campaign against me." She would "keep the expression of my contempt against him" to herself until her naturalization proceedings were complete and she could "speak to him as an American to an American." Yet she now saw quite clearly that Stone had "handed the same two letters first to Schlotfeldt with a malicious intent."[47]

The decision of the Court of Appeals entitled Rosika Schwimmer to citizenship, and indeed it might have followed. Yet many continued to oppose her naturalization. Schwimmer had already accused the Women's Auxiliary of the American Legion of being a prime mover in stimulating government opposition to her citizenship. I have not been able to find much interest in her at all on the part of the American Legion prior to the Supreme Court decision. As government officials debated whether or not to ask the Supreme Court to review Schwimmer's case, many individuals and groups urged them to do so. Among the most vocal of these were the National Patriotic Association and the Junior Committee of the National Patriotic Association. Harry A. Jung of Chicago, representing the American Coalition of Patriotic Societies: An Organization to Coordinate Patriotic Efforts to Keep America American, sent to the Solicitor General a nineteen-page, single-spaced document "giving the life's history of an individual whom I consider one of the most dangerous propagandists in the country today and one who is indefatigably working to render us a defenseless nation."[48] Generally, Schwimmer's opponents claimed that she was a Bolshevik, she had been a German agent during World War I, she was a Communist sympathizer (after all, she was supported by the ACLU), she was an atheist (although this was least mentioned by opponents), and she was a pacifist. If followed by others, they argued, she would weaken the nation.

The most sustained attack against Schwimmer, and the one most nettlesome to her, appeared in *The Woman Patriot*, a magazine "Dedicated to the Defense of the Family and the State AGAINST Feminism and Socialism." In a series of five consecutive issues after the Court of Appeals decision, *The Woman Patriot* concentrated almost exclusively on Schwimmer and the danger she posed to the naturalization process. These articles rehearsed, in considerable detail, Schwimmer's role in the international meeting at which the Women's International League for Peace and Freedom was formed. (The magazine insisted on calling this meeting by its German title, *Internationaler Frauenkongress*, apparently to bolster its contention that Schwimmer was a German agent during those years.) In its wide-ranging attack on Schwimmer *The Woman Patriot* argued that when Schwimmer told the District Court "I do not care how many other women fight, because I consider it a question of conscience," she lied. Schwimmer was instrumental in the adoption by the Women's International League of what the magazine called the "slacker oath," alleged to be a resolution by the League for a universal strike by women against any effort to wage war. In the event of war or threat of war, women everywhere were encouraged to be nonparticipants and nonsupporters. Far from thinking of war as a matter of individual conscience, *The Woman Patriot* charged, Schwimmer had earlier gone on record that all people opposed to war should adamantly resist it. Schwimmer had testified before the District Court that she appreciated the American government so much that she saw it as a model for a peaceful federation of nations. Each nation could keep its identity just as the American states have, but the nations would enter into cooperative arrangements to preserve peace. *The Woman Patriot* charged that before the Women's International League Schwimmer had argued for a new international order, in which the nations would give up sovereignty, or, alternatively, they would live under a communist form of government. According to her critics, Schwimmer did not appreciate American democracy, but just said these things to please immigration officials and the judge of the District Court.[49]

Schwimmer contended that these magazines were filled with "infamous, also libelous, material," asking Rabe if it were possible to do something about it. I have found no evidence that they ever took any legal or public opinion action to answer these attacks.[50]

It is not clear that any of these anti-Schwimmer groups actually influenced the government's decision to petition the Supreme Court for a writ of certiorari[51] in the hope that the Court of Appeals decision would be overturned. The Attorney General, the Solicitor General, and the Department of Labor were primarily involved in making that decision. On 18 July 1928 Robe Carl White, Acting Secretary of Labor, articulated the Department's views about the Appeals Court decision favoring Schwimmer. White believed the court had erred and that a Supreme Court review of the case would be of great importance. The lower court had distinguished between Schwimmer's *conduct* in relation to good moral character and her *views* about bearing arms. The Secretary argued that to be a false distinction, referring to Section 7 of the Naturalization Act of 1906, which specified

> That no person who *disbelieves* in or who is opposed to organized government, or who is a member of or affiliated with any organization entertaining and teaching such *disbelief* in or opposition to organized government, . . . shall be naturalized. . . .[52]

Section 27 of the law, obviously aimed at Mormons, required one to state in the declaration of naturalization that "I am not a polygamist nor a *believer* in the practice of polygamy." The same affirmation was part of the questionnaire in the application for naturalization.[53] These citations showed that beliefs and attitudes were part of the statutory basis for qualification for naturalization.[54] A second answer to the Court of Appeals was that courts regularly used hypothetical questions in interviewing applicants for naturalization. Third, the attitude of the applicant had a material relationship to the inquiry required by the statute—that is, whether she were "attached to the principles of the Constitution of the United States, and well disposed to the good order and happiness of the same." Schwimmer insisted on inserting a proviso into her agreement to support and defend the Constitution; that she would not do so by bearing arms. The citizen is obligated to support the government in return for the protection the government owes the citizen. An alien should not be granted citizenship unless he or she shows a willingness to give that support in the way that those in authority consider necessary. Finally, by considering Schwimmer's sex a factor in the granting of citizenship, the court had established a rule that granted her a preferred status over a male applicant, contrary to the constitutional requirement that the rules of naturalization be uniform.[55] Because the case raised questions about the eligibility of applicants for citizenship, it potentially involved every petition for naturalization and consequently was of greatest importance.[56]

William D. Mitchell, the Solicitor General, believed that the Court of Appeals had made a valid point about Schwimmer's age and sex, but there was an issue broader than that—namely, Schwimmer was a public speaker and writer and could influence others to refuse military service. "She is very clever," Mitchell wrote. He thought she should have been questioned concerning "whether her attitude on pacifism is such that in time of war she could not refrain from action influencing the conduct of others." Failure to press that line of inquiry had, in Mitchell's view, weakened the government's case. "She speaks only of propaganda among women, who are not usually supposed to bear arms, and she cleverly dodges the issue concerning those who are required to bear arms." "Under present conditions," Mitchell concluded, "I think it likely the Supreme Court would not care particularly about considering such a case as this, with such a slim record to go on."[57]

Debate continued when Assistant Attorney General Oscar R. Luhring wrote to Mitchell offering reasons why the Supreme Court should be asked to review the case. Clearly the law should apply equally to men and women. Although military service was not required of women, that did not negate the requirement of a state of mind [attachment to the Constitution] in the applicant. Luhring cited the 1875 Supreme Court decision in *Minor v. Happersett*.

> There cannot be a nation without a people. The very idea of a political community, such as a nation is, implies an association of persons for the promotion of their general welfare. Each one of the persons associated becomes a member of the nation formed by the association. He owes it allegiance and is entitled to its protection. Allegiance and protection are, in this connection, reciprocal obligations. The one is a compensation for the other; allegiance for protection and protection for allegiance.[58]

Given the nature and necessity of "allegiance" and the importance of the case for administration of naturalization, Luhring—a former prosecutor and congressman from Indiana who had served in the Department of Labor—found it imperative to ask the Supreme Court for review.[59]

Soon Harry S. Ridgely, a career Justice Department lawyer, sent a memorandum to Mitchell arguing against application for certiorari. "On the cold record facts," Ridgely wrote, "there is no indication of any past, or of any suggested future activity on her part, which would indicate a spirit of disloyalty." Ridgely agreed with Mitchell's earlier assessment that the record from the courts below made it doubtful the Supreme Court would agree to hear the case. If the case were heard, Ridgely added, the government would be forced to argue that the oath would require Schwimmer to do what women have never been called upon to do and probably never will be asked to do—bear arms.[60]

Leaving on an extended vacation, Solicitor General Mitchell gave charge of Schwimmer's case to Gardner P. Lloyd, who was, in his absence, Acting Solicitor General. Responding to pressure from the Department of Labor to petition for certiorari, Lloyd "studied the files very carefully in an effort to find some basis for such a petition" but confessed himself "unable to find that there is any real question of law involved." Lloyd found "nothing in the record to show that the woman is not attached to the principles of the Constitution." While the Department of Labor might have "information concerning Rosika Schwimmer which is not contained in the record," Lloyd noted, "and while this may show that the woman should not have succeeded in the courts below it furnishes no ground for an application for certiorari."[61]

A decision soon followed. On 31 August 1928 Luhring wrote on behalf of the Attorney General to the Secretary of Labor, declaring the record in the Schwimmer case was insufficient to elicit a writ of certiorari from the Supreme Court and no writ would be requested.[62]

The Department of Labor did not give up. Robe Carl White, Assistant Secretary of Labor, wrote to Attorney General John G. Sargent urging the Justice Department to reconsider its decision. "This case is regarded both by the department and the naturalization officials as involving the most vital question which has arisen in a naturalization case during the period of governmental supervision." If Schwimmer were successful in qualifying the oath of naturalization to fit her own views, others could do the same and consequently "transfer to the applicants for citizenship the determination of the conditions of support and defense of the United States. This but paves the way for the immediate breakdown of the naturalization law." The case had already received much publicity. If no attempt were made to get the Supreme Court to hear the case, great harm would likely come to administration of naturalization law. "The matter is one of grave public concern," White emphasized; indeed "the department can hardly conceive of one which could be more important—and it is again respectfully urged that the Supreme Court be given the opportunity to pass upon the issue."[63]

That plea marked the turning point for Rosika Schwimmer. Acknowledging the letter, Acting Solicitor General Lloyd responded that, since receiving it, he had "read with great care everything we have here relating to the case." Reviewing the record "in view of your very emphatic request for a reconsideration and reversal of our decision," Lloyd had "felt that there was upon me a responsibility to form my own opinion irrespective of the views heretofore expressed by others." Lloyd confided that "I approached the case from a standpoint favorable to your contention," since,

> like most everybody else who reads the papers and tries to keep informed about what is going on in the world, I have from time to time read a good deal about the activities of Rosika Schwimmer and had formed a pretty definite opinion that she was a most pestiferous woman of the kind likened in the Scriptures to the continual dropping on a rainy day[64] and one whose congenial and appropriate habitat would be almost anywhere in the world except the United States.

"I found, however," Lloyd confessed, "that the evidence in the case was wholly insufficient to enable a court, proceeding in a judicial manner, to find such to be the fact." Indeed the record would have convinced him, had he not heard of her previously, that Schwimmer

> was rather a fine type of woman, conscientious, idealistic, honest, with something of the martyr's spirit, perhaps a bit of fanatic, disposed to accept more literally than most of us the commands not to kill and to love one's neighbor as one's self, but not hostile to the fundamental principles of our civilization or a menace to our political or social institutions, and, with-al [sic], a woman of unusual intelligence, education and ability.

"The trouble with this case," Lloyd asserted, "is the record." If indeed Schwimmer had long been "engaged in activities sinister in character, it would seem as if with all the publicity she has had that could have been shown to the court by evidence." No such evidence existed in the record. "Personally, after a most serious consideration," Lloyd wrote, "I would not be disposed to overrule the decision heretofore made." Lloyd was, however, a political appointee, and he now realized that he could no longer sustain politically his personal judgment against such a plea from the highest levels of the Department of Labor. "In deference to these views so solemnly expressed," Lloyd concluded, bowing to the inevitable, "I have decided to prepare and have ready for filing a petition to be submitted to the Solicitor General on his return, for his decision."[65]

On returning to his office, Solicitor General Mitchell wrote to the Department of Labor affirming the decision to file a petition for certiorari with the Supreme Court. He was not optimistic. "The state of the record" made Schwimmer's case "a desperate one" for the government, "and I greatly regret that we are forced to present to the Supreme Court, as a test case of an important question, a record which is so deficient." In completely ignoring "Rosika Schwimmer's past activities and record" the prior proceeding "wholly fails to give any adequate picture of these things, which are matters of common knowledge, but of which, of course, the Supreme Court cannot take judicial notice." Schwimmer had, Mitchell noted, "endeavored, with some success, to give the impression that her opposition to bearing arms is personal and partly because of her sex and that she has no objection to others following their conscience in such matters." Mitchell did not doubt that "it could have been shown that she is violently opposed to armed defense by others who are fit for military service and that she has preached and taught that doctrine," but the government had not shown that. "With these handicaps about the case," Mitchell continued, "I am not at all sanguine that we will gain anything by filing the petition." He would prefer "some other case" to test "the question whether those who are opposed to armed defense of the Constitution and laws of the United States against invasion and insurrection are eligible to citizenship." Yet the Department of Labor had, effectively, handed him a mandate. So "because of the unanimity in your Department and the emphatic statements in your letter of September 10th I have concluded to yield my own judgment in the matter and proceed as you have requested."[66]

Once committed to proceed against Schwimmer, despite its reluctance and perhaps because of its lack of confidence in its case, the Department of Justice produced a powerful petition for certiorari, arguing that Schwimmer was a dangerous person. The Constitution provides for the defense of the country through the military. A person opposed to bearing arms is thus neither attached to the Constitution nor believes completely in organized government. Although Americans are a peace-loving people, common defense against foreign aggressors or domestic insurrection is still necessary. Any applicant for naturalization who is not willing to participate in the common defense is a dangerous person. Schwimmer's age and sex were irrelevant; whether an "applicant for citizenship may or may not be able to bear arms is not the sole consideration."

> The mental attitude of the individual towards the Government and its defense, with its necessary influence on others, is a vital matter. The applicant's intellectual attitude towards the institutions of the country are of importance. The applicant in this case says she has "no sense of nationalism, only a cosmic consciousness of belonging to the human family": also that "she is an uncompromising pacifist for whom even Jane Addams is not enough of a pacifist."

These assertions, the government argued, demonstrated that Schwimmer was "an extremist." She would never "be called upon personally to bear arms in defense of the country,"

> but she does not believe in other people bearing arms in defense of the country, and she is a writer, author, and propagandist by profession. She does not believe in organized government as we understand it, because organized government can not exist without military defense. She is not attached to the principles of our Constitution and Government when she rejects the fundamental principle that they must be defended by military force if necessary. She would see the Constitution and the Government of the United States destroyed by an enemy rather than have one citizen lift a finger in their defense. If every citizen believed as she does, and acted as she will, we would have no Constitution and no Government.

Repeatedly the government pressed its central point. Because Schwimmer was a conspicuous public person, a persuasive lecturer and writer, she might persuade others to believe and act in the same manner, rejecting their patriotic, military duty. Her pacifism "has been and will be actively reflected in her speeches and writings, and . . . she can be depended upon to agitate against the discharge by others of this duty of citizenship." Consequently, the Supreme Court should accept this case, in order to affirm the District Court's denial of citizenship.[67]

On the last day possible under the rules of the Supreme Court, 29 September 1928, the government filed its petition for certiorari. Given his doubts about the strength of the case, Solicitor General Mitchell must have been pleased and amazed when the Court granted certiorari on 19 November 1928. Schwimmer was dismayed. "Even if one expects bad news one is always stunned when they actually arrive," she wrote to Olive Rabe. "So it was with the news of the Government's appeal. . . . I wonder how long the process will last. When may I expect to know the final decision? I think I shall not live to see the end of the matter."[68]

When it became clear that the case would go to the Supreme Court, Schwimmer had to raise some money. Although Rabe never charged for her services to Schwimmer, there were still expenses associated with the case. Schwimmer received almost no income from lecturing because, as she believed, the patriotic societies had so defamed her name that no group dared ask her to address them, and she had no personal resources to contribute to the work on her case. The ACLU had previously expressed strong interest in her case, and now Schwimmer applied to the ACLU to underwrite her legal expenses. The appropriate committee deferred action on that request, but conveyed its sentiment that Schwimmer's case of was of signal importance "and deserves our moral support." Moral support was not enough, Schwimmer replied; financial support was necessary. "I should be terribly sorry if there were not interest enough to back the appeal financially." In Chicago Jane Addams began to solicit money from friends and others interested in Schwimmer's case. Apparently, through small contributions, she was able to raise enough to cover the presentation of the case to the Court of Appeals. Because of those efforts and because the ACLU had agreed to finance the presentation of the case to the Supreme Court, Addams was relieved of any further fund-raising responsibility, with thanks from Schwimmer and her attorney.[69]

The ACLU had not budgeted money to finance the case, and estimated that the expense would be about $500. With Jane Addams out of the picture, the ACLU enlisted Robert M. Lovett, a professor of English at the University of Chicago, to head a committee to raise money for the case. In an illuminating exchange of letters, Lovett and Forrest Bailey of the ACLU focused on the difficulty of the task and the difficulty of representing Schwimmer. "We have a committee in Chicago on Rosita [sic] Schwimmer," Lovett wrote to Bailey early in January 1929, "but I am obliged to say that this community is completely tired of the lady. You have no idea to what extent she has imposed herself upon the good will of this community." Lovett was committed to "make another appeal," although he was "not at all sure of the result." Lovett related a startling conversation with his wife. "I said to Mrs. Lovett a day or so ago, 'I wish they would deport her.' She replied, 'I wish they would drown her.'"

By return mail, Bailey of the ACLU responded, "For my part, I hope she chokes."

These were Schwimmer's allies, not her enemies. Whatever they thought of her, they saw the principles for which she was struggling as greater than Rosika Schwimmer. "Considering that it involves issues that are not at all personal," Bailey told Lovett, "we feel that the appeal deserves every bit of support we can give it." From the ACLU's perspective, "It seems quite logical that the money should be raised in Chicago, as Chicago must accept responsibility for the presence of Judge Carpenter who made all the trouble." The ACLU foresaw "a number of other cases in the offing which will depend upon the decision in the Schwimmer case," making a "favorable" decision, of which the ACLU was confident, even more significant. Bailey could "hope that when the Chicago committee tackles the problem in this spirit it will not find much difficulty to raise the money."[70] Although fund raising for Schwimmer continued to be difficult, eventually the ACLU found enough money to cover all expenses for the case.[71]

As preparations for a Supreme Court hearing began, once more the ACLU questioned whether Olive Rabe should continue as Schwimmer's counsel. Roger Baldwin and Forrest Bailey invited Schwimmer to meet with them to decide on an attorney who would share time with Rabe arguing the case before the Supreme Court. Given that the ACLU was now covering costs, Schwimmer apparently acquiesced and informed Rabe of the arrangement. Baldwin secured the services of a prestigious New York lawyer, Joseph F. Cotton, a former Undersecretary of State who had argued many cases before the Court.[72] Rabe expressed surprise that the ACLU wanted a change in counsel, especially since the organization had never yet supported the case financially as it had promised to do. "After I have contributed many hundreds of dollars in services because I was interested in the principle involved and because of my friendship for Madame Schwimmer," Rabe wrote to Bailey, "it would seem that I ought to be entitled to some recognition in the matter, especially since my argument in the Circuit Court of Appeals resulted in a favorable decision." To Schwimmer she was grieved but conciliatory. "Of course, I should have been much disappointed if you had consented to their first suggestion of taking the case out of my hands. I feel that it is not the standing of the counsel but the essential merit of your case that will win in the Supreme Court, and I am confident that we will win."

Rabe was clearly pained by the ACLU's initiative, but she agreed to cooperate with Cotton or whomever was chosen to help her. Bailey wrote to Rabe, trying to soothe her feelings, and also sent a telegram to

Schwimmer regretting that Rabe seemed to think that the ACLU was trying to get rid of her. Such was not the case, Bailey contended; the organization had complete confidence in her ability. Yet the proposal for co-counsel remained on the table. To make matters worse, when Baldwin engaged Cotton, he had not made it clear to him what the ACLU had in mind. When Rabe visited Cotton to discuss how they would divide the time of the argument, he had not agreed to that arrangement and refused to participate. Cotton told Rabe that he thought her case was a sure winner and it would be a detriment to her and the case to have anyone else with her on the brief or in argument before the Court. Forrest Bailey now wrote to Arthur Garfield Hays asking his advice in the matter of counsel—a letter not so much requesting suggestions as admitting how badly the ACLU had bungled its intrusion. Bailey confessed that he had favored Mrs. Rabe's handling of the case alone all along, and also acknowledged how stingy the ACLU had been in supporting her efforts. "We have done so little in the actual sponsorship of the case from the very beginning that it would come with bad grace from us to begin dictating policies at this stage." Hays agreed. "I think it is quite right that Mrs. Rabe handle this case in the Supreme Court," he told Bailey. "You know I have always been of the opinion that the persons best qualified to handle these cases are those who take them up at the beginning." That settled the matter. Olive Rabe would take the case to the Supreme Court.[73]

Although the Solicitor General had told Rabe that he intended to file an entirely new brief, the government's brief to the Supreme Court was, with the addition of a few sentences, identical to its petition for certiorari. In adding to its previous arguments, the government pointed out that the Constitution enables the nation to defend itself through raising military forces. Preservation of the government depends on the existence of these forces and willingness of citizens to fight. It follows that those who are not willing to fight do not believe in ordered government—that is, they subvert the welfare of the nation. Section 7 of the Naturalization Act provided that no person who disbelieves in organized government or belongs to an organization that teaches disbelief in organized government shall be naturalized. On this logic, given her pacifism, Schwimmer did not believe in organized government and should not be naturalized. The Court of Appeals had erred, in holding that her age and sex exempted her from bearing arms, because her pacifism and her inclination and ability to persuade others to join her in that belief was the real problem. The government's brief concluded with the Supreme Court's recent declaration in *United States v. Manzi* (1928): "Citizenship is a high privilege, and when doubts exist concerning a grant of it, generally at least, they should be resolved in favor of the United States and against the claimant."[74]

Olive Rabe's brief began aggressively, asserting that only Congress can establish the qualifications for naturalization, not the courts nor even the Bureau of Naturalization. The Constitution, in Article 1, section 8, authorizes Congress to create a uniform rule of naturalization. The Naturalization Act of 1906 did not require an applicant for citizenship be willing to bear arms. Question 22 in the preliminary questionnaire for naturalization, which asks if one is willing to bear arms in defense of the country, had become part of the naturalization process without the authorization of Congress. If the courts could prohibit applicants from citizenship for holding beliefs not expressly prohibited by Congress, then the courts would be usurping the function and power of Congress. That was precisely what the government was asking the Supreme Court to do. For various courts to reach decisions in such a manner would be contrary to a uniform law of naturalization.[75]

The government had argued from section 7 of the Naturalization Act that since any person who disbelieves in organized government is not entitled to naturalization, therefore any person who did not believe in bearing arms did not believe in organized government and should be disqualified. Rabe responded that the section would not bear that construction. Because Congress had not included language in the law specifying characteristics indispensable to "organized government," Rabe argued, "we are forced to conclude that Congress meant by persons 'opposed to organized government' those opposed to government *as such*—in other words anarchists." For the government to assert that pacifism is equivalent to disbelief in organized government goes much beyond what Congress seems to have meant. Schwimmer had explicitly testified before the District Court that she believed in organized government and especially in democratic government.

> No argument whatsoever has ever been able to sway me from my deep-rooted opposition to any undemocratic form of government, like the dictatorship of the proletariate [*sic*], or dictatorship of Fascism, or the rule of white terror, or military dictatorship. All my past work proves that I have always served democratic ideals and fought—though not with arms—against undemocratic institutions.[76]

The government had sought to disqualify Schwimmer because of her beliefs. That, Rabe asserted, was wrong. According to paragraph 4, section 4 of the Naturalization Act, an applicant for citizenship must show that "he has behaved as a man [*sic*] of good moral character, attached to the principles of the Constitution of the United States and well disposed to the good order and happiness of the same." Rabe argued that the phrase "attached to the principles" "must depend upon the verb 'has behaved' since there is no other verb in the sentence."

The government had made much of Schwimmer's declaration, "I am an uncompromising pacifist. I am an absolute atheist. I have no sense of nationalism, only a cosmic consciousness of belonging to the human family." Rabe responded that "nationalism" would have a different meaning for a person of European origin, such as Schwimmer, than for a native-born American. For an American, nationalism includes goodwill toward other nations as well as loyalty to one's own. That was not true for Europeans. Realizing that nationalism, to a European, meant attachment to one's own nation only, it is not surprising that Schwimmer should renounce nationalism when her experience of nations had been that of hostility and warfare. "It is worthy of comment here," Rabe noted, "that nationalism is not given in any dictionary as a synonym for patriotism."

The government had argued that since Schwimmer was not willing to bear arms, she was not able to take the oath of naturalization without mental reservation. Rabe could find no case law at the appellate level supporting such a conclusion. Rather, the law states that one must "support and defend *the Constitution and laws* of the United States," not the country. Given the referent of the words "support and defend," one could offer defense in more ways than only by bearing arms. Rabe pointed out that the Constitution required the President of the United States to take an oath or affirmation to "preserve, protect and defend the Constitution of the United States." If "defend" meant what the government argued in its brief, by physical defense, "there would seem to be no sound reason why it should not be construed in the same manner in the President's oath so as to bar from the Presidency a member of any religious sect whose principles forbid its members to bear arms."[77] Rabe did not have to mention that her argument was not hypothetical, since the current President was Herbert Hoover, a Quaker.

Rabe's final argument rested on something "which does not seem to have sufficiently impressed the petitioner—the respondent is not a man, but a woman." In 1929 the armed services did not want women in their ranks and neither did the Congress. The law specifically excluded women from the Army, the Navy, the National Militia, and the National Guard. Each of the states covered by the naturalization district in which Schwimmer filed her application also forbade women to serve in their militias. "Women are not required to render military service in any civilized country in the world," Rabe wrote. "In this country women are not even permitted to render military service and there is not the slightest agitation to change the law in this respect. Yet the petitioner seeks to have respondent denied citizenship for not being willing to do what the law does not permit her to do!"[78]

Rabe declined to address only one issue that the government had raised—Schwimmer's reputation and ability as a writer and public speaker, which would undoubtedly lead to spreading influence of her pacifist message among others. On this point that the government had stressed Rabe's brief was completely silent.

The Supreme Court heard the case on 12 April 1929. Schwimmer thought that for a principal to be in the courtroom when her case was argued might be poor etiquette. "Of course, I am dying to be present when you plead the case," she wrote to Rabe, "but should you consider it better if I kept away, please let me know frankly. I must, however, say that I will be terribly disappointed if I were not to be in court on that particular day." Rabe replied that it was certainly all right for her to attend arguments and encouraged her to do so. "I am so convinced that the Supreme Court will grant you citizenship," Rabe wrote, "that I feel that the Washington trip will be a turning point for you and will open doors now closed, and to have this happen in cherry blossom time will be a good omen."[79]

Schwimmer was struck by the "funereal" solemnity of the Court, with its rituals: "The dim quiet hall, the ceremonious bowing of the clerks, the constant stream of visitors, moving soundless, the judges old and bowed, and in robes." Feeling that she was to be "the corpse of the occasion," Schwimmer kept wondering, "When will they bring in the remains?" Bringing to bear her considerable powers of observation, Schwimmer watched and listened closely as Alfred A. Wheat, a veteran of appeals involving immigrants, presented the government's case. In Schwimmer's view, "He hardly made a legal argument but put all his strength on the fact that 'she is an exceptionally brilliant mind, unusually intelligent and extraordinary intellect [sic] and therefore the more dangerous.' This is an actual quotation of what he said three times over." In his summing up, Schwimmer recalled, Wheat "rubbed it in": "If she were a simple housewife and held these views, it would not matter, but since she is 'and so on as above,' she would have an immense influence." Wheat had "stopped to find the word 'immense' to make it more impressive."

Olive Rabe had not indulged Wheat's "purely personal argument," but had in her argument to the Court presented "a concise strictly legal argument, bringing out chiefly the point that refusal on the ground claimed by the lower court would be an infringement on Congressional prerogatives." Schwimmer thought that Rabe "was very good and we all thought the judges were impressed." As Schwimmer watched, "During the preceding technical cases some of the judges plainly slept. None of the eight present did sleep during our brief trial."

Brief it was. Olive Rabe expressed disappointment to Schwimmer "that hardly any questions were asked." Alone among the justices, James McReynolds posed several queries to Rabe and Wheat that to Schwimmer "all sounded rather hostile." Court historians know McReynolds as not only irascible but also disdainful of female lawyers. He asked Rabe "something about anarchists being barred, to which she could read out of my former written statements, that I was not an anarchist, that I was not opposed to organized government, as the Government asserts, but to the contrary, believed in highly organized government." In "hardly more than half an hour" the hearing was over. Chief Justice William Howard Taft "and several others bowed politely and smilingly to Mrs. Rabe." Schwimmer's informal poll "of those who pretend to read faces" found "*that six of the judges will be in favor, one, Reynolds* [*sic*], opposed and one, Butler, doubtful." Schwimmer left the Court guardedly optimistic: "*Vederemo!*"[80]

In its decision, handed down on 27 May 1929, the Court almost exactly reversed Schwimmer's reading of faces, denying her quest for citizenship by a vote of 6-3. Justice Pierce Butler, whom Schwimmer had thought "doubtful," wrote the majority's definite opinion. Justice Butler was born in Minnesota in 1866. His parents were immigrants from Ireland. Although educated at Carleton, a Congregationalist college, he was a lifelong, staunch Roman Catholic. Admitted to the bar in 1888, at age twenty-two, Butler soon excelled as a corporate lawyer, especially as an advocate for railroads in rate valuation cases. He was a senior partner in one of Minnesota's richest corporate law firms, Butler, Mitchell, and Doherty, when he was appointed to the Supreme Court in 1923.

As a lawyer with a taste for detail, Butler was known as a ruthless cross-examiner. One biographer found Butler lacking "political finesse, a compromising spirit, an ability to straddle issues, and any demagogic appeal . . . brilliancy or any touch of genius." He was "direct, honest, trustworthy, realistic, dogmatic, and intense . . . oppressed with no inferiority complex, personal or racial or religious." Another saw Butler as burdened with "no feelings for the rights of the radical dissenter." Yet William O. Douglas, a justice often perceived as liberal, remembered Butler as a friendly and very able judge.[81]

As a Regent of the University of Minnesota between 1907 and 1924, Butler was instrumental in dismissing four "liberal" faculty members. President Warren G. Harding's nomination of Butler to the Supreme Court aroused considerable opposition. Many ardently supported Butler as a remarkable lawyer, among them Chief Justice Taft, who had witnessed his work firsthand. Butler's opponents feared his bullying nature, his conservatism, and his corporate advocacy as a source of bias on the bench. Yet Harding, a Republican, appointed Butler, a Democrat, and he served on the Court from 1923 until he died in 1939. As a conservative and Social Darwinist, Butler attributed a person's lack of success to personal fault, not economic disadvantage. As one of the "Four Horsemen" of a conservative Supreme Court, he regularly opposed New Deal legislation.

Butler came to Schwimmer's case with definite ideas about the duties of citizens. In a 1915 lecture, "Educating for Citizenship," he asserted that an American citizen owes the country unqualified allegiance. The citizen must be faithful to the nation; the nation must protect the citizen. Patriotic citizens are obliged to defend the federal and state constitutions because they are safeguards of individual freedoms. A citizen's support of country requires a strong morality. Although Butler did not mention Schwimmer's atheism in his opinion in her case, in his 1915 lecture he had considered a learned person whose conscience is not grounded in religion as a threat to society. Justice Butler returned to these themes in 1926, three years before he wrote the opinion in *Schwimmer*, as a speaker at the International Eucharistic Congress in Chicago. In a passage echoing the naturalization oath, Butler declared, "The Church would have every citizen contribute all that is his to support and defend the Government, that justice and domestic peace and tranquility may continue, and that the blessings of liberty may be retained by us and handed down unimpaired to posterity."[82]

Justice Butler made fairly short work of denying citizenship to Schwimmer, reviewing the pertinent law and Schwimmer's previous testimony, including those famous words from her private correspondence, "I am an uncompromising pacifist. . . . I have no sense of nationalism, only a cosmic consciousness of belonging to the human family." Pointing to the reciprocal obligations of citizens and nations, allegiance for protection, Butler observed that aliens can enter such a relationship only by obedience to the requirements for naturalization set forth by Congress, including attachment to the Constitution and willingness to support and defend it, which may require bearing arms. Contrary to Schwimmer's contention that it is possible to defend the Constitution in a variety of ways, including with words and ideas, Butler affirmed that defense is possible only through bearing arms. "That it is the duty of citizens by force of arms to defend our government against all enemies whenever necessity arises is a fundamental principle of the Constitution." On that premise, the Court decreed that a pacifist or one who might promote pacifism should not be allowed to become a citizen.

> Whatever tends to lessen the willingness of citizens to discharge their duty to bear arms in the country's defense detracts from the strength and safety of the government. . . . The influence of conscientious objectors against the use of military force in defense of the principles of our government is apt to be more detrimental than their mere refusal to bear arms. The fact that, by reason of sex, age or other cause, they may be unfit to serve does not lessen their purpose or power to influence others. . . . [Schwimmer] may be opposed to the use of military force as contemplated by our Constitution and laws. And her testimony clearly suggests that she is disposed to exert her power to influence others to such opposition.
>
> A pacifist in the general sense of the word is one who seeks to maintain peace and to abolish war. Such purposes are in harmony with the Constitution and policy of our Government. But the word is also used and understood to mean one who refuses or is unwilling for any purpose to bear arms because of conscientious considerations and who is disposed to encourage others in such refusal. And one who is without any sense of nationalism is not well bound or held by the ties of affection to any nation or government. Such persons are liable to be incapable of the attachment for and devotion to the principles of our Constitution that are required of aliens seeking naturalization.

In the abstract, a pacifist is one who refuses to bear arms and, at least by implication, will encourage others to refuse. One with no sense of nationalism is not likely to be attached to the principles of a country. Schwimmer's testimony persuaded the Court majority that she personified the abstraction and she was quite likely to convert others to her views. The District Court was correct in denying her citizenship.[83]

Justice Oliver Wendell Holmes, Jr., dissented—but not because he sympathized with Schwimmer's pacifism. As a young man, Holmes served with the Twentieth Massachusetts Volunteer Infantry in the Civil War. He was wounded three times; twice he was near death. He cherished his days as a soldier. He knew the hatefulness of war, but accepted its necessity in some circumstances. "I believe in 'my country right or wrong,'" Holmes wrote in 1914, adding that this war "shows us that . . . nations that mean to be in the saddle have got to be ready to kill to keep their seat." In 1917 he wrote to Felix Frankfurter that when his pacifist secretary "talks of more rational methods [of resolving international disputes] I get the blood in my eye and say that war is the ultimate rationality." In that same year he witnessed a reunion of Confederate Veterans that united veterans of both North and South to support America in World War I. Of all the signs, the one that pleased Holmes the most said "Damn a man who ain't for his country right or wrong." As late as April 1929, before *Schwimmer* was decided, he wrote: "All 'isms [including pacifism] seem to me silly—but this hyper-aetherial respect for human life seems perhaps the silliest of all."[84]

Holmes was no pacifist,[85] but he preached and practiced freedom of speech. Following passage of the Espionage and Sedition Acts in 1917 and 1918, the Supreme Court began hearing cases of persons accused of violating those acts by criticizing the government and encouraging men to resist conscription. Was that speech protected by the First Amendment? In *Schenk v. United States*[86] Holmes, writing for a unanimous Court, convicted a conscription protester. Yet in the process he declared that government could suppress speech only if it presented a "clear and present danger" to the government's interests. In *Abrams v. United States*[87] Holmes, joined by Louis D. Brandeis, dissented from the conviction of another accused of harming the government by his speech. He now believed that the First Amendment protected all speech unless it presented such an immediate threat to the process of law that it endangered the country. The Court wrestled with the scope of freedom of speech for the next decade. In 1927, concurring in *Whitney v. California*,[88] Justice Brandeis wrote an impassioned defense of a broad interpretation of freedom of speech. When confronted with *Schwimmer*, Holmes and Brandeis saw it as a free-speech case, and Brandeis encouraged Holmes to dissent from the majority opinion.[89]

During the time he was considering *Schwimmer*, Justice Holmes experienced tragedy. In February 1929 eighty-eight-year-old Fanny Holmes, recovering from "the grippe," fell and broke her hip. For a while she appeared to improve, but then began to decline. In mid-April (*Schwimmer* was argued 12 April) Holmes began missing sessions of the Court, and may have been the Justice absent at Schwimmer's hearing. On 30 April, Holmes's wife of fifty-seven years died. For a while, as he grieved Fanny's death, he wanted no companionship, nor did he work much. Toward the end of May, he began to brighten, and took up his work at the Court again. On 27 May, he delivered his dissent in *Schwimmer*.[90]

Noting that Schwimmer was a woman of character and intelligence, exhibiting character desirable in a citizen, Holmes endorsed the argument that Schwimmer's age and sex rendered moot the question of her bearing arms. To seek to improve the Constitution, Holmes noted, does not demonstrate a lack of attachment to it. That Schwimmer might attempt to improve the Constitution by advocating the abolition of war did not make her dangerous to the country in the same manner as the man convicted in *Schenk*. She was perhaps naively optimistic about abolishing war, yet "the notion that the applicant's optimistic anticipations would make her a worse citizen is sufficiently answered by her examination which seems to me a better argument for her admission than any that I can offer."

> Some of her answers might excite popular prejudice, but if there is any principle of the Constitution that more imperatively calls for attachment than any other it is the principle of free thought—not free thought for those who agree with us but freedom for the thought that we hate. I think that we should adhere to that principle with regard to admission into, as well as to life within this country.

Although Holmes did not mention the First Amendment's Free Speech Clause, he was clearly advocating an advanced understanding of freedom of speech that he and Brandeis—Brandeis more than Holmes—had worked out over the years since *Schenk*. Holmes comes in *Schwimmer* to the summit of his faith in free speech.[91] He could defend the cause of Schwimmer the avowed atheist by chiding his patriotic and nominally Christian colleagues in the majority, pointing out that "many citizens agree with the applicant's belief and . . . I had not supposed hitherto that we regretted our inability to expel them because they believe more than some of us do in the teachings of the Sermon on the Mount."[92]

Notified of the decision by telegram from the Clerk of the Supreme Court, Olive Rabe immediately telegraphed her client and friend: "Shocked beyond words by wire from Clerk that Supreme Court reversed appellate Court much love and sympathy in this disappointment." A few days later Schwimmer telegraphed Rabe, commenting on some of the press coverage of the decision and on other reaction she had heard. She mentioned that she had received three marriage proposals, apparently from men who thought that marriage would get her citizenship. Rep. Anthony Griffin of New York, a Democrat, had introduced a bill in Congress the day after the decision to make her citizenship possible (see Chapter Six). "First shock of disappointment passed," Schwimmer could say of herself. "Physically very tired but in good spirits." Rabe replied, "I know how you felt when you got the news, because of the terrible shock I got myself. I am still dazed by the decision."[93]

"I just want to express a word of indignation at this most reactionary decision of the Supreme Court," Roger Baldwin of the ACLU wrote to Rabe. "It is incredible after the splendid presentation you gave the case and the weakness of the government's contentions, that these old gentlemen should have fallen for the prejudices of unthinking men in the streets." Among Baldwin's allies, "not even the most pessimistic" had "predicted any such result, despite the Supreme Court's bad record since the war on all such issues." Writing to Schwimmer, Baldwin extended his assessment of the postwar climate, but offered admiration and encouragement. "I suppose you have got to charge this reversal of all that America stood for in the old days to the times we live in," Baldwin wrote. Yet he found Schwimmer "a pioneer of new ideals, and all pioneers have paid a price." Schwimmer's price was "high," Baldwin concluded, "but you are a fighter and I know you will not complain of risk or defeat, for the future belongs to us."

In a long letter to Forrest Bailey of the ACLU, Rabe, still expressing shock, pondered whether "we might petition for a rehearing," but thought it unlikely because "the dissenting judges were unable to sway the majority, it would be unlikely that anything that could be said on the subject would have any effect on them." Rabe deeply regretted the outcome, but thanked Bailey and the ACLU for their support. Bailey for his part conveyed to Rabe "how deeply we all feel the upset in the Supreme Court." He assured the attorney he had once tried to replace "that there is nobody who raises the slightest question as to your having done everything that could be done in the best possible way."[94]

Throughout this correspondence, the parties discussed whether or not to petition the Supreme Court for a rehearing. Most thought such a petition probably would not succeed, but might be worth a try. That discussion ended when Mme. Schwimmer vetoed the idea. She had concluded that because the United States did not want her to be a citizen; she was not going to continue the struggle.[95]

When reporters asked for her reaction to the Court's decision, Schwimmer replied that she was a woman without a country. The United States did not regard her as fit to be a citizen, yet she had no passport to go anywhere else. Indeed, other countries took their lead from America; since she was denied citizenship here, surely she would not be welcome elsewhere. For her pacifist cause, worse consequences loomed: when other countries saw that America now expected its women to bear arms, they might do likewise. "I can see no other result than the super-militarism of the world."[96] Rather typical of her response in the press is the interview she gave to the *New York American* (for an excerpt see Appendix H).

Various publications criticized the Court's decision. The *Outlook and Independent* found irony abounding: "Cynics chortle over this decision from the highest court of a Nation which has just elected a Quaker President, which has just renounced war and pledged itself to the peaceful settlement of all disputes. . . . Certainly there are other proofs of loyalty than willingness to go to the front." The *Cleveland Plain Dealer* lamented that freedom of opinion and expression, "fundamental to the American conception of government," were now diminished by the Court. "Millions" who might "hate the thought of the 'uncompromising pacifist' . . . will regret to see the great Supreme Court make that thought a bar to American citizenship. That branch of government, even if no other, should be a defender of tolerance." Fiorello H. La Guardia, self-described as "America's most liberal Congressman," wrote in the *New York Evening Graphic* that while munitions manufacturers had derided Schwimmer, "her name will be known to future generations and inscribed in history's roll of honor when the names of the war profiteers will be carded and indexed along with the criminals of the twentieth century." La Guardia joined the *Plain Dealer* in calling attention to the absurdity of a nation denying citizenship to a pacifist when it had just agreed to the Kellogg-Briand Treaty. La Guardia lauded Schwimmer for courageous service to peace for the nation and the world. In the *New York World* Walter Lippmann reflected on similar themes. The ACLU issued a sixteen-page booklet containing the testimony of Mme. Schwimmer at the District Court level, an excerpt from the Court of Appeals' decision, and the Supreme Court opinions. In its commentary the ACLU expressed outrage at the final disposition of the case and lobbied for legislation, already introduced in Congress, to allow naturalization to conscientious objectors. The booklet sold for ten cents a copy.[97]

Virtually alone among religious journals, *The Christian Century* supported Schwimmer, praising Justice Holmes for writing "another of those great dissenting opinions which, in some future day, will be gathered as milestone documents in the struggle to keep this country true to the ideals of liberal democracy." The Court had said that Schwimmer's avowed refusal to bear arms might influence others, including "possible combatants," to follow her. The *Century* agreed:

> So it might. And so it may whether she is a citizen or not. She is here. She can talk—eloquently in several languages. And this appallingly stupid decision has put behind her a sounding-board which will make her voice heard as it never could have been without it.

How, the *Century* wondered, could the nation resolve the incongruity between this Supreme Court decision and the Kellogg-Briand Treaty renouncing war as a means of solving international disputes?

> Is it superfluous to remind the learned justices that treaties duly ratified are part of the organic law of the country? And that the recently ratified treaty outlawing war is as much a part of that body of law of the United States as any other law?

"Those who bear true faith and allegiance to this nation now and who support and defend its institutions most loyally," the *Century* proclaimed, "are not those who express the greatest willingness to fight, but those who are most loyal to the new law of peace—our law." Finally, the journal urged Americans to petition Congress to undo *Schwimmer* through legislation.[98]

Dr. Henry Sloane Coffin, the president of Union Theological Seminary in New York, called the decision an abridgement of the American tradition of free speech and "a disgrace to our country." About 300 ministers applauded his remarks. Some ministers mentioned the decisions in their Sunday sermons. The Rev. John Haynes Holmes, a Unitarian, found the principle of nonresistance at the heart of the Sermon on the Mount. He compared Schwimmer, the avowed atheist, to the early

Christians who refused to bear arms in the Roman legions. According to Dr. Walter Russell Bowie of Grace Episcopal Church in New York, the *Schwimmer* case alerted Christians that good will should supersede warmaking, or "this world as we know it is headed for certain destruction." The Rev. C. E. Wagner, a Methodist, called the decision "a vicious blow at free thought and hopes for peace," adding that its inconsistency with efforts toward peace "makes us a laughing stock before nations." Rabbi Jacob Katz of Montefiore Synagogue in the Bronx said, "The majority is correct for the time being, but the minority is right and will yet triumph."[99]

On the day of the decision, the Women's Peace Society in New York passed a resolution deploring it, saying its members "do hereby express their deep sorrow that, by this action, our Country the United States of America, is to be deprived of the benefits which would accrue to it by conferring citizenship upon this noble woman." The resolution was sent to the President, the Senate, the Supreme Court, the press, to Schwimmer and to Rabe. Jane Addams and some of her friends circulated a petition in Chicago urging Congress to act in support of Schwimmer.[100]

Some newspapers supported the decision of the Court. The New York *Evening Post* declared that the Court acted properly "if there is any meaning in nationalism and the duties of citizenship." The Washington *Evening Star* supposed that except for "peace-at-any-price groups, the republic will applaud the Supreme Court's ruling." Loran W. Warner, a columnist for the Winamac, Indiana, *Democrat*, cleverly derided Schwimmer and her case a little later, as Schwimmer was listening to the cases of Douglas Clyde Macintosh and Marie Averil Bland before the Supreme Court (see Chapters Four and Five). "Madame Schwimmer is downright disgusted" with the Supreme Court's disposition of her case, Warner reported, and placed in her mouth a quotation I have elsewhere been unable to verify.

> "When I first started my battle to obtain Americanship," says she, "I was eager to become a citizen of this country, but now I no longer believe American citizenship worth having. I have become thoroughly disgusted by the injustice I have received in the courts here, and the way I have been generally treated by others."

"For such beautiful remarks," Warner suggested, "the lady should be sweetly requested to close the door from the outside." The United States need no advice from outsiders: "When the lady from a foreign neighborhood questions the soundness of our institutions it is time to remind her that 'if you must pincha da fruit, pincha da coconut.'" For all his folksy, nativist sarcasm, Warner was deadly serious.

> The obligation to bear arms for America has long been regarded as a sacred privilege and the adopted son or daughter should be tickled to death to be accorded that opportunity. If the foreign applicant can not find himself in accord with that spirit, then his bump of loyalty is not sufficiently developed to grow a true American scalp lock. He should be given a one-way ticket.[101]

Schwimmer's journalistic nemesis, *The Woman Patriot*, printed the Court's decision and Holmes's dissent, followed by a series of newspaper editorials praising the decision.[102] In a subsequent issue, the magazine attacked on a different front. In early 1929 Schwimmer, confident that the Supreme Court would rule in her favor, had planned a trip to Europe to attend pacifist conferences. When the Court postponed the argument of her case, she worried that she would not have a passport in time to make the trip. She asked Rabe to try to arrange for her to take the oath immediately after the Court's decision so she could obtain a passport and make the trip. When the Court denied citizenship, Schwimmer somehow got an emergency passport and made the trip anyway. While she was out of the country, Mary G. Kilbreth, president of the Woman Patriot Publishing Company, wrote a letter to President Herbert Hoover, urging him not to allow her back into the country, printing her letter in *The Woman Patriot* as an open letter.[103] Obviously Kilbreth's petition was not granted, for Schwimmer lived the rest of her life in the United States; yet her request illustrates the animosity to Schwimmer in some circles.

Law journal commentary on *Schwimmer* published soon after the case was decided, principally of the "case note" variety, simply described the facts of the case and its disposition by the Supreme Court. Typically the notes did not contest the validity of the decision.[104] Some articles, however, evaluated the verdict. Robert C. Pugh argued that the Court was right in denying citizenship—since Schwimmer might encourage others to shirk their duty to bear arms, the Court appropriately assessed what she might do after she was naturalized. Against Justice Holmes's judgment that what Schwimmer wanted to do was to improve the Constitution, Pugh claimed that she would abet resistance to military service whether or not changes were made in the Constitution. "Unfortunate as it may be, under present world conditions," Pugh wrote, "governments cannot be based on the precepts of the Sermon on the Mount. Unhappily, we do not dwell in

Utopia and for all practical purposes must deal with human nature as we find it and not as we would like it to be." Ernest Freund took the opposite tack, pointing out that all the naturalization statute required was that an applicant during the previous five years had behaved as a person of good moral character and attached to the principles of the Constitution. "Congress, then, it appears was content to abide by the relatively practicable test of actual conduct, and there is no statutory authority to go beyond that." In reference to the statute, what Schwimmer might do in the future is irrelevant.[105] Herman A. Gray agreed with the Court's decision, but disagreed with the government policy that elicited it. "Despite the pious phrases of the Kellogg Pact," armed forces remain necessary to the nation. Yet a citizen has a right to protest. "[E]ach citizen must be left free to refuse support in any course of action which does violence to his sense of right," Gray wrote. "Authority being based upon consent, it becomes invalid when the consent is unwillingly given. Loyalty can be voluntary only and must born of satisfaction. The power to coerce is a dangerous one and inevitably leads to perversion."[106] Still another analyst argued that Schwimmer's sex should have determined the case. Women are inherently opposed to war, so "the expression of a natural feeling against war by a fifty year old woman, otherwise qualified for citizenship, is not a sufficient ground for holding that such a woman will not make a good citizen." Elmer Brown made a similar argument, invoking Justice Holmes's dissent to ask whether "free thought" is a "constitutional principle" that "should apply not only to life within the country, but also to admittance into the country?"[107] Henry B. Hazard, Chief Counsel of the Bureau of Naturalization, contributed the most substantive article involving the case, a comprehensive piece reviewing disputes about conscientious objection and naturalization in American jurisprudence up until *Schwimmer*, including some that interpreted the critical phrases in the oath of naturalization, "to support and defend the Constitution and laws of the United States" and to "bear true faith and allegiance to the same." Hazard devoted little attention to *Schwimmer* itself, although clearly he believed that the Court decided correctly. He concluded that "the 'conscientious objector' has not been regarded favorably by either the law-making or law-interpreting agency of government" and saw "a duty on the part of all citizens—male and female alike—to defend the government by force of arms in case of necessity" to be "a fundamental principle of the Federal Constitution." While "the attitude of an applicant is usually made manifest by acts," Hazard wrote, "opinions, views and beliefs may also disqualify for naturalization, as witness the case of Madam Schwimmer."[108]

Despite her shock and dismay at denial of her citizenship, Schwimmer greatly appreciated Justice Holmes's dissent. She wanted to write him a letter of thanks, but Olive Rabe advised that it was not appropriate to do so. Toward the end of January 1930, when Schwimmer read that the aging Holmes was ill, human feeling overcame proper protocol. She wrote the first of several letters that expressed sincere admiration and released some of her pent-up emotion.

> At the risk of violating legal etiquette I will no longer refrain from expressing my deep-felt gratitude for your dissenting opinion in my Citizenship [*sic*] case.
>
> My impulse to do so at the moment of its publication was checked by my legal advisors. "You don't thank Judges," I was told. "It is not done." I let legal etiquette suppress common sense and carried my unexpressed gratitude as a moral debt.

Whatever her personal feelings, Schwimmer had, with the help of Holmes, been able to comprehend the decision in historical perspective.

> But whatever rules I am breaking, I must at last thank you with profound gratitude for your magnificent expression of true Americanism. I am grateful for it because it did justice to my motives for seeking American citizenship. And also, it saved me from feeling a perfect fool. A person born into the wrong family and choosing another wrong one when chance permits a selection of a new family—that seemed to be my foolish position.
>
> Your, and your dissenting colleague's statements, reassured me that my conception of the ideal standards of the new family I was seeking, was justified. The family I chose is not wrong, there is only temporarily something wrong with it.
>
> The magnificence of your dissenting opinion has helped me to take the blow of the refusal without loss of faith in the inherent idealism of your nation.

Schwimmer signed herself "With greatest admiration for your life's work, and Sincere respect. . . ."

Justice Holmes responded with a handwritten note.

> You are too intelligent to need explanation of the saying that you must never thank a judge—which I often heard quoted from a judge who was

on the bench when I was young. If his decision was of a kind to deserve thanks, he would not be doing his duty. A case is simply a problem to be solved, although the considerations are more complex than those of mathematics. Even when as in your case it was only to interpret a statute, Madam, you appreciate that the opinion of the majority simply meant that they did the sum differently—that duty and reason seemed to them to require a different conclusion from that which the minority reached. After which protestation, I must add that of course I am gratified by your more than kind expression, and that I thank you.[109]

Schwimmer sent two books to Holmes—her own *Tisza Tales*, a collection of children's stories set in Hungary, and *Great Musicians as Children*, written by her sister, Franciska. Holmes sent a letter of thanks.

Will you and your sister please accept my thanks for the two charming books that you have been good enough to send me. I say charming and I mean charming. I become a child again on reading them and sentimental tears drop from my eyes as I follow the boy chasing the rainbow or the youth of the other boys who followed the rainbow music. The law also is a rainbow, but to older eyes, and you have made me forget it. I am truly much obliged to you both. . . .

Schwimmer replied that she and her sister were "deeply touched" by the knowledge that he enjoyed their books. At the end of that letter she returned to the subject of thanking judges for their opinions. She acknowledged that while no thanks is due those who do their duty, " your exquisite minority opinion was not a verdict giving me favorable judgment. It was a precious document of American idealism for which I will always be grateful to you."[110]

When Justice Holmes retired in January 1932 Schwimmer wrote to say that "Your retirement from the judicial service of the United States is darkening the legal horizon." Annually she sent short birthday greetings, typically answered by Holmes's secretary (a different one each year, the precursors to today's clerks for the various Justices).[111]

In 1933 Schwimmer visited Holmes in person. Apparently they had a genial conversation, principally about Justice Holmes's age, how he read murder mysteries more than substantive books, and how the Court should not have denied her citizenship. Holmes wondered if Schwimmer might introduce him to Albert Einstein.[112] Early in 1935 Schwimmer, herself in the hospital at the time, heard that Holmes was ill. She wrote him a letter of wishes for a full and speedy recovery and how she would like to visit him again when they both regained their health. Holmes died 5 March 1935. Schwimmer wrote a "Letter of condolence to the American Nation!" in tribute to Holmes that she released through the Associated Press and the United Press. She claimed that it appeared in newspapers throughout the country. Later she led a group of pacifists to Arlington Cemetery to decorate Holmes's grave.[113]

Schwimmer sent a copy of the open letter to Holmes's good friend Felix Frankfurter, then a professor at Harvard Law School. Frankfurter agreed with Schwimmer's assessment of Holmes, thanked her for sending it to him, and promised to send a copy to Justice Brandeis. Frankfurter recalled that "The Judge once spoke to me of the pleasure you gave him and especially the delight he found in a volume either by yourself or your sister, which you had sent him." In 1941, the hundredth anniversary of Holmes's birth, Schwimmer sent to Frankfurter, now a Supreme Court Justice, transcripts of all her correspondence with Holmes because Frankfurter was Holmes's "official biographer." She also sent copies to the Library of Congress and the Harvard Law School library.[114] Clearly Schwimmer cherished her relationship with Holmes because he, of all the people who could have made a difference, had argued most vigorously for her naturalization.

Rosika Schwimmer had been denied citizenship, but she lived the rest of her life in America, a resident alien. She never again earned her living as a writer or lecturer, yet she apparently never thought of herself as anything else.[115] Her sense of vocation and her rather fragile health prevented her from seeking any other gainful employment. She was supported for nearly twenty years by contributions from admirers.[116]

Schwimmer's concern for world peace never diminished.[117] In 1924, with her lifelong friend, fellow feminist, and warrior for pacifism, Lola Maverick Lloyd, she wrote *Chaos, War, or a New World Order: What We Must Do to Establish the All-inclusive, Non-military, Democratic Federation of Nations*, in which they proposed a world parliament made up of elected delegates from all the countries of the world. They reissued the booklet in 1937, 1938, and 1942.[118] Lloyd died in 1944, but Schwimmer published yet another edition of her plan in 1945.[119] In 1939 she wrote a monograph arguing that the attempt to create a world government should not begin only with those nations currently most democratic, as some had suggested, but should include all nations from the outset, in order to put them all on an equal basis. A passage from that publication sums up her thinking in these years. Schwimmer recognized that spreading "totalitarianism is driving mankind towards a cataclysm" but argued that doom "cannot be averted by the frenzied war preparations now bankrupting the world economically and morally." She hoped that "the first active public step towards the creation of an all-inclusive World Union and the knowledge of this step would relieve the world immediately of its agonized fear of world dictatorship and stop the militarization of the human family from the cradle to the grave.[120]

In mid-1928, before the Court of Appeals had reversed the District Court, Franciska Schwimmer wrote to Lola Maverick Lloyd to relate a startling development. She had been contacted by a Miss Dumont, who wanted to begin an international movement to nominate Rosika Schwimmer for the Nobel Peace Prize. Franciska understandably wanted to keep this initiative secret from her sister, but she wanted Lloyd to know of it. This Miss Dumont wanted to begin the effort by contacting Charles Lindbergh or, if he were not interested, Mrs. Lindbergh. She also wanted to enlist the support of Henry Ford.[121]

I find no evidence that Schwimmer ever knew of this effort to nominate her for the Nobel Peace Prize. In 1932 she wrote an article accusing the trustees of the Nobel Peace Prize of subverting the intention of the founder. They had routinely given the prize to older people, often rich and frequently famous, as a reward for past work done in the interest of peace. Schwimmer contended that Alfred Nobel had intended for the prize to be given to younger people who had begun to work for peace so they could intensify their efforts. He wanted the prize to relieve relatively young people of the responsibility of their own financial maintenance so they could give undivided attention to promoting peace. She called for the Peace Prize Committee to return to the intention of the founder.[122] Although she was 55 when she wrote the article, Schwimmer may have had herself in mind. She was bothered that she had to live on "charity," and she certainly had an interest in peace. Surely she had considered what she could do if she had the Nobel money to enable her to give full attention to peacemaking!

In May 1937, 181 people from America and western Europe, including Carrie Chapman Catt, Albert Einstein, Fiorello La Guardia, Margaret Sanger, and Rep. Caroline O'Day of New York, signed an appeal asking people to contribute money to an award for Schwimmer, a peace prize that would rival the Nobel prize in monetary value and prestige. This letter from the "International Committee for World Peace Prize Award to Rosika Schwimmer" outlined several bases for the appeal, recognizing

Schwimmer's status among those who had long worked for peace, that she was compiling a history of peace activities during World War I (which admirers, in 1927, petitioned her to do, in honor of her fiftieth birthday), that she had been libeled as a German sympathizer, that she had been a victim of diabetes since 1916, and that she had been denied citizenship by the Supreme Court. The Committee hoped to acknowledge Schwimmer's work in the interest of peace, putting the lie to calumnies heaped upon her through the years, as a fitting recognition of her sixtieth birthday. The appeal was successful, although surely it did not yield as much revenue as the committee had hoped. In December 1937, at a banquet in New York, Schwimmer was presented the "World Peace Prize" and a cash gift of $8,500. The Committee also published *Rosika Schwimmer, World Patriot: A Biographical Sketch*. In accepting the prize Schwimmer proposed a World Federation of Nations, but lamented that the prize money would cover only her "most pressing" debts.[123]

In her sixtieth year Schwimmer received the World Peace Prize. For nearly another decade afterward she campaigned for peace as she could, but nothing else of importance addressed her public life or the question of her citizenship.

Notes

1. Carrie Chapman Catt to Rosika Schwimmer, 15 October 1946, Schwimmer-Lloyd Collection, box G-24. Catt's comment responds to the Supreme Court's decision in *Girouard v. United States* (see Chapter Seven), which finally allowed applicants for citizenship who were conscientious objectors to receive citizenship, if they were qualified in all other ways. "Therefore, the obstacle to your citizenship no longer exists, Catt wrote. "You may die if you wish without a country, but if that is not satisfactory you may have a country now by asking for it, and I think it may be written about you that you led the way. I think no other woman before you was ever asked if she would be willing to bear arms in case of war, because no nation expects its women to bear arms, although they might do so."

2. 279 U.S. 644 (1929).

3. Paul S. Rundquist, "Rosika Schwimmer," *Ms.* 3 (January 1975): 58-59.

4. Henry J. Abraham, *Freedom and the Courts: Civil Rights and Liberties in the United States*, 4th ed. (New York: Oxford University Press, 1982), 246; "Union to Aid Peace Sect," *New York Times*, 1 June 1929, 16.

5. Interview of Edith Wynner by Ronald B. Flowers, New York City, 15 January 1992. Edith Wynner was friend, confidant, protégée, and secretary to Rosika Schwimmer for many years. In addition to her personal relationship with Schwimmer, she is the supervisor of the Schwimmer-Lloyd collection of papers in the New York City Public Library. Wynner is probably the leading authority on the life and thought of Rosika Schwimmer. See also Edith Wynner, "Rosika Schwimmer," in *Dictionary of American Biography, Supplement Four 1946-1950*, John A. Garraty and Edward T. James, eds. (New York: Charles Scribner's Sons, 1974), 724-28; Martin David Dubin, "Rosika Schwimmer," *Notable American Women: A Biographical Dictionary*, Edward T. James, Janet Wilson James, and Paul S. Boyer, eds. (Cambridge: Harvard University Press, 1971) 3: 246-49; John F. McClymer, "Schwimmer, Rosika," *European Immigrant Women in the United States: A Biographical Dictionary*, Judy Barrett Litoff and Judith McDonnell, eds. (New York: Garland Publishing, 1994), 272-3.

6. Beth S. Wenger, "Radical Politics in a Reactionary Age: *The Unmaking of Rosika Schwimmer, 1914-1930*" *Journal of Women's History* 2 (Fall 1990): 77; *Rosika Schwimmer: World Patriot, A Biographical Sketch* (International Committee for World Peace Prize Award to Rosika Schwimmer, 1937), 6 (in a revised and enlarged edition of this booklet published in 1947, the same information appears on page 8); Peter Pastor, "The Diplomatic Fiasco of the Modern World's First Woman Ambassador, Roza Bedy-Schwimmer," *East European Quarterly* 8 (September 1974): 273-82. Her mission was a "fiasco" primarily because the Swiss were not willing to receive a woman ambassador.

7. Schwimmer found the United States "so much to my taste that I decided to establish a home there," but she did not at first "contemplate change of citizenship"; formal citizenship had "meant nothing" to her. "The formality of citizenship to me, I always felt at home in any part of the world." The end of the war and the change of regime in Hungary forced her "to look for a country." She "wanted a Democracy where women were not merely females, but citizens, and a nation most likely to lead in building a world federation which would end the militaristic epoch of mankind and inaugurate the co-operative epoch. I chose the U.S.A. as adoptive [*sic*] country, it came nearest to my ideals. In its success to unite 48 states within the superstructure of a co-operative federation seems to me the most admirable example of state-craft in history. The U.S.A. seemed to me to be called to lead the world toward the final step in the evolution of human co-operation which had advanced from the single savage to a formation like the U.S.A." (Rosika Schwimmer, "Citizenship Case," 27 August 1929). At the top of the typescript is written, in Schwimmer's hand, "Report of address at W.I.L.P.F. [Women's International League for Peace and Freedom] Congress in Prague, explaining why R.S. sought American citizenship." ACLU Archives, vol. 417. A Freedom of Information Act request filed with the Federal Bureau of Investigation revealed that in 1928, as the government was considering referring her naturalization case to the Supreme Court, the FBI was investigating the number of times, and when, Schwimmer had entered the country. The report does not

suggest why this information was pertinent. Someone may have wanted to see whether she had entered illegally. See Agent R. P. Burruss to J. Edgar Hoover, with accompanying document New York file #58-41, 8 October 1928. Freedom of Information Act request to Federal Bureau of Information #302395, 1993. The FBI also actively investigated Schwimmer just after she had landed in the country permanently in 1921. The State Department informed J. Edgar Hoover that she could be located "for 'observation purposes'" at the home of Lola Lloyd (Schwimmer's friend and pacifist ally) in Winnetka, Ill. Hoover dispatched an agent to Winnetka "to make a complete and thorough investigation of the present activities of this subject." Although the subsequent report was censored heavily by the Freedom of Information personnel, enough remains to see that the agent remarked that Schwimmer went often to Chicago, the Hull House (founded and operated by Schwimmer's ally, suffragist and pacifist Jane Addams) and the offices of the Federated Press. The agent noted that Schwimmer went repeatedly to Winnetka. "Subject will be kept under surveillance and any developments will be reported." See unsigned letter from Department of State to Hoover, 23 September 1921; Hoover to C. Walker, 3 October 1921; FBI Report entitled "ROSIKA SCHWIMMER: Hungarian Suffragist & Pacifist: RADICAL MATTER," 6 October 1921. Freedom of Information Act request to Federal Bureau of Investigation #302395, 1993.

8. Apparently Schwimmer thought about moving to New York and wrote to attorney Arthur Garfield Hays about transferring her naturalization case there. Hays advised against it. Transfer of residence would delay the case for a year. Although it would be a tough fight in Chicago, the federal judges there "are of the highest type." See Arthur Garfield Hays to Schwimmer, 15 September 1922. Schwimmer-Lloyd Collection, Box G-2. Schwimmer moved to New York City in 1925-26, but she kept her naturalization case in Chicago. As it happened she drew a judge whom she did not find "of the highest type."

9. 8 U.S.C. § 381, the Naturalization Act of 1906, in effect at the time of Schwimmer's attempt.

10. 8 U.S.C. § 382.

11. Transcript of Record, *The United States Court of Appeals for the Seventh Circuit, Rosika Schwimmer* v. *United States*, filed 31 December 1927, 8.

12. Nearly two years after she filed her petition for naturalization, Schwimmer wrote to her friend, the women's suffrage leader Carrie Chapman Catt, asking her opinion about the proper interpretation of questions 22 and 23. Catt replied indignantly that the question about bearing arms was for men only. That was reinforced by question 23, inquiring whether the applicant registered with a draft board during World War I. That question, she said, was for men only and so was the question about the willingness to bear arms. "Of course, you cannot give a pledge to take up arms in defense of this or any other country, Catt wrote in a later letter. "That is not, and never has been, a woman's work. . . . if they refuse your citizenship . . . I am perfectly sure this will not be the real reason. The real reason will be that they are not sure of your loyalty. They are not sure but that you are not

a Bolshevik in disguise who might place a bomb under some persons [*sic*] chair, for there are a lot of people in this country who are just this scared. They know they cannot prove this, so they will not say it to you or publish it as a reason for refusing you." Carrie Chapman Catt to Rosika Schwimmer, 9 October 1926, 6 December 1926. Hoover Collection.

13. Rosika Schwimmer, "Citizenship Case," 27 August 1929. At the top of this document Schwimmer wrote in longhand "Report of address at W.I.L.P.F. Congress in Prague, explaining why R.S. sought American citizenship." In her "An Adventure in Citizenship," 3 (see Appendix C) Schwimmer wrote, "In May 1924 a patriotic bird whispered the frightful news into their shocked ears that I had applied in November 1921 for first papers. . . . In the last analysis these valiant ladies can claim full credit for having saved the U.S.A. from destruction by my admission to citizenship. A heroic deed worthy to go down in history along with the saving of the Capitol by the patriotic Roman geese." I have not confirmed any of Schwimmer's accusation against the American Legion Auxiliary. The "Summary of Proceedings" of the Auxiliary"s national convention, held in Saint Paul in September 1924, does not mention Schwimmer. The only reference to naturalization in those minutes is a resolution to work with immigrants to help them become Americanized and to welcome qualified immigrant women into the membership of the Auxiliary. A hagiographic history of the American Legion Auxiliary for 1924-1934 does not refer to Schwimmer but does indicate that by 1924 the Auxiliary was past its growing pains and had reached a maturity that enabled it to be active on many fronts, including urging Congress to enact the 1924 law restricting immigration. Although the Auxiliary opposed pacifism and advocated military preparedness to guarantee peace, which it fervently desired, it did not on the record specifically oppose Schwimmer's naturalization. See Frank Ernest Hill, *The American Legion Auxiliary: A History: 1924-1934* (Indianapolis: American Legion Auxiliary, 1935), 1-20, 29-38.

14. Schlotfeldt began work in the U.S. Immigration office in Chicago in 1910 and directed it from 1919 until his retirement in 1943, helping 580,000 persons become naturalized. He died at his home in New Braunfels, Texas, 8 June 1961. "Fred J. Schlotfeldt," *Chicago Daily Tribune*, Friday, 16 June 1961, part 1, page 18.

15. Transcript of Record, *Seventh Circuit Court of Appeals, Schwimmer v. United States*, 8.

16. Schwimmer, "Adventure in Citizenship," 5. This is a draft of a manuscript she wrote describing her efforts to obtain citizenship, dated in her handwriting "30 July 1930." I can find no evidence that it was ever published. The text of this document appears as Appendix C . Hoover Collection.

17. Transcript of Record, *Seventh Circuit Court of Appeals, Schwimmer v. United States*, 11.

18. Schwimmer, "Adventure in Citizenship," 6; Transcript of Record, *Seventh Circuit Court of Appeals, Schwimmer v. United States*, 11-14.

19. Schwimmer, "Adventure in Citizenship," 6.

20. Transcript of Record, *Seventh Circuit Court of Appeals, Schwimmer v. United States*, 14.

21. Herman Bernstein, "Great Conspiracy of Traitors Doomed Gallant Russian Armies; Plot Extended to the United States," *New York Herald* 7 October 1917, 1, 19 and 8 October 1917, 1, 11. See also Mary B. Forbes, and others, "Is Woman Suffrage Pro-German?" *The Chronicle*, Brookline, Mass., 28 September 1918.

22. Schwimmer to *The Woman Patriot*, 14 December 1925, Hoover collection; New York State Senate, Report of the Joint Legislative Committee Investigating Seditious Activities, *Revolutionary Radicalism: Its History, Purpose, and Tactics* (Albany: J. B. Lyon, 1920) 1: 971, 985, 988, 992; "Reds and the Law," *New York Times*, 19 March 1920, 12; Beth Wenger, "Radical Politics in a Reactionary Age: *The Unmaking of Rosika Schwimmer, 1914-1930*," *Journal of Women's History* 2 (Fall 1990): 76-84; "Woman Asks Ford to Vindicate Her," *New York Times*, 4 September 1927, sec. 2, 1; "Denies Peace Ship Led to Ford Attack," *New York Times*, 5 September 1927, 17; "Mme. Schwimmer Gets Ford's Reply," *New York Times*, 18 September 1927, 9; "Pacifist Disavows Influencing Ford," *New York Times*, 28 June 1928, 18.

23. Wenger, "Radical Politics in a Reactionary Age," 76. A letter in the FBI files for 1940 indicates that in 1915-1916 "[Schwimmer] was investigated to a minor degree by reason of her participation in the Ford Peace Party," Special Agent P. R. Foxworth to J. Edgar Hoover, 2 March 1940. The FBI censored much of the letter before releasing it. Six pages of documents point to an investigation of Schwimmer in late December 1915 and early January 1916, which may have been the "minor degree" investigation mentioned in 1940. These documents were censored so heavily that it is difficult to say what was learned at the time. Although Schwimmer had been dead 45 years when the documents were released to me, the government remained reluctant to reveal the substance of any of its investigations of her. Freedom of Information Act request to Federal Bureau of Information #302395, 1993.

24. Schwimmer, "Adventure in Citizenship," 8-9; Transcript of Record, 16; Schwimmer to ACLU, 12 December 1925, Hoover collection; Schwimmer to Stone, 19 September 1925, 13 October 1925, Schwimmer-Lloyd collection, box G-5.

25. Telegram, Schwimmer to Stone, 20 January 1927; telegram, Stone to Schwimmer, 21 January 1927, Schwimmer-Lloyd collection, box G-2. On the top of Stone's telegram to her, Schwimmer wrote in longhand: "This was the head of the Chicago Military Intelligence Association. He advised lieing [*sic*] myself into citizenship. It was through remarks in my private letters to him, which he showed to Schlotfeldt, that the question of atheism, cosmic against nationalistic conscience was brought into the limelight." Schwimmer seems to suspect that Stone had betrayed her, yet at this time she maintained that she had won Stone over to her side and that he was sincerely trying to reverse calumnies he had circulated about her and to rehabilitate her image. I believe that he falsely professed to be

Schwimmer's ally and intended to sabotage her naturalization initiative by giving Schlotfeldt damaging evidence. Whether or not that was his intention, he succeeded.

26. Schwimmer to Schlotfeldt, 21 January 1927, printed in the Transcript of Record, *Seventh Circuit Court of Appeals, Schwimmer v. United States*, 15-16. In that letter, Schwimmer wrote about her letter to Stone.

"There is however one point I consider necessary to explain. That is *why* I made the quoted statement in my letter to Colonel Stone. The passage lifted out of connection with my previous conversation with Colonel Stone . . . and from the rest of the three-page letter, standing bare by itself sounds like a militant flouting of my ethical principles, like an arrogant challenge to those of different views. The last thing I would ever do! . . .

"My letter of September 19, 1925—containing the passage which now enters into the question of my eligibility for American citizenship—was an enthousiastic [*sic*] approval of Colonel Stone's views on other questions in which I am interested.

"I sincerely admired Dr. Stone's broad views on women's rights and his sane and sympathetic understanding of the problems of Youth. But on the verge of getting his public amends for the public wrong he had done to me I was afraid my enthousiastic [*sic*] approval may be mistaken as a so-to-say bribe to influence his prospective action on my behalf.

"To prevent Dr. Stone from considering my complimentary comment on his books as flattery with which to make myself pleasant I balanced my remarks on his books with a reference to those of my personal traits, which I knew Dr. Stone abhorred in general. Under ordinary circumstances I am not used to write or to speak without challenge of such personal matters." Transcript of Record, 16-17.

27. Transcript of Record, *Seventh Circuit Court of Appeals, Schwimmer v. United States*, 17-18.

28. "Shall Mrs. Schwimmer be Naturalized?" *Hyde Park Herald* (Chicago), 15 July 1927.

29. Edith Wynner, Schwimmer's longtime confidant and secretary, does not know how Schwimmer met Rabe, other than that she was a famous person living in Chicago and Rabe was a promising young lawyer looking for business. Wynner, Flowers interview, 15 January 1992; Ernest R. Reichmann to Forest Bailey (ACLU), 16 October 1927, ACLU archives, vol. 375; Schwimmer to Schlotfeldt, 9 August, 1927, ACLU archives, vol. 325, reel 51.

30. Schwimmer to Rabe, 20 December 1926, Schwimmer-Lloyd collection, box G-5; Rabe to Schwimmer, 19 September 1927, ACLU archives, vol. 325, film reel 51; Raymond Crist, Commissioner of Naturalization, to Zimring and Rabe, 24 September 1927, Schwimmer-Lloyd collection, Rabe papers, box G-5; Schwimmer to Rabe, 28 September 1927, Schwimmer-Lloyd collection, box G-5; Joseph Cassidy for Hays, St. John & Buckley, New York, 4 October 1927, Hoover collection.

31. Schwimmer to Rabe, 20 December 1926, Schwimmer-Lloyd collection, box G-5; Rabe to Schwimmer, 6 January 1927; Schwimmer to Rabe, 9 January 1927, box G-2. Darrow renounced his pacifism during World War I (see Chapter Two).

32. On 3 December 1926, W. K. Wilson, Chief, War Plans and Training Branch of the War Department, wrote to J. Edgar Hoover, Director of the Bureau of Investigation (later the FBI), about Schwimmer. Hoover already had an active file on her. Wilson offered general information about her application for citizenship, remarking that "She told a party here the other day that just as soon as she secured her naturalization papers, she proposed to be a candidate for the State Legislature." I have seen no other reference to this proposal; it does not appear in Schwimmer's personal correspondence about her naturalization case. Letter obtained through Freedom of Information Act request # 1738F-89 from the Department of the Army, 24 October 1989.

33. Rabe to Schwimmer, 7 February 1927, 21 March 1927, 27 April 1927, 12 July 1927; United Press news release, 3 July 1927, 21 July 1927, all in Schwimmer-Lloyd collection, box G-2; Gemmill to Rabe, 28 March 1927, box G-5.

34. Rabe to Schwimmer, 19 September 1927, ACLU archives, vol. 325, reel 51, also Schwimmer-Lloyd collection, box G-5.

35. Rabe to Schwimmer, 10 September 1927, Schwimmer-Lloyd collection, box G-5; *Tutun v. United States* 270 U.S. 568 (1926).

36. Unpublished transcript of hearing before the District Court of the United States for the Northern District of Illinois, Eastern Division, 23 October 1927, 3-4, Hoover collection.

37. Transcript of Record, *Seventh Circuit Court of Appeals, Schwimmer v. United States*, 5.

38. Transcript of Record, *Seventh Circuit Court of Appeals, Schwimmer v. United States*, 5, 9, 8. See "Mme. Schwimmer Is Barred from Citizenship: Asserts She Would Not Kill Nation's Enemy," *New York Times*, 14 October 1927, 1.

39. The text of the hearing is not included in the Transcript of Record of the case. It may be found in *The Case of Rosika Schwimmer: Alien Pacifists Not Wanted!* (New York: American Civil Liberties Union, 1929), 9-14.

40. "Schwimmer Bar Is Surprise Here," "Judicial Nonsense," *New York World*, 15 October 1927.

41. Transcript of Record, *Seventh Circuit Court of Appeals, Schwimmer v. United States*, 19; Rabe to Schwimmer, 7 November 1927, 15 November 1927, Schwimmer-Lloyd collection, box G-2 and box G-5; Gemmill to Schwimmer, 9 December 1927, ACLU archives, vol. 325, reel 51. Rabe could not believe what Schlotfeldt said and reported that she found him so disagreeable it gave her indigestion. Of Judge Carpenter's action, Rabe wrote, "I never saw such high-handedness on the part of a Judge before."

42. Gemmill to Schwimmer, 9 December 1927, ACLU archives, vol. 325, reel 51; Rabe to Schwimmer, 24 February 1928, Schwimmer-Lloyd collection, Rabe papers, box G-5. Neither Schwimmer's nor the government's brief are preserved in the Transcript of Record.

43. *Schwimmer v. United States* 27 F.2d 742 at 743-44. The time period cited is the five years prior to the application for citizenship.

44. 27 F.2d 742 at 744.

45. Schwimmer to Rabe, 4 July 1928, Schwimmer-Lloyd collection, box G-5.

46. "Mme. Schwimmer on Stand in Suit," *New York Times*, 27 June 1928; "Peace Ship Leader Wins Suit for Libel," *New York Times*, 30 June 1928, 19; "Fred Marvin Loses $17,000 in Libel Suit of Mme. Schwimmer," *National Council for Prevention of War News Bulletin*, 1 July 1928, ACLU Archives, vol. 362. Schwimmer did not realize any money from the suit for more than a year because Marvin appealed the ruling twice, to no avail. Harvey O'Connor, "Pauperism Price of Patrioteering?" *Federated Press Eastern Bureau*, Sheet 3, No. 3606, 19 June 1929; "Marvin, Key Men Fink, Must Pay Out 17 'Grand,'" *Industrial Solidarity*, 3 July 1929; Ray Tucker, "Marvin, Red-Baiter, Loses Backing for His Daily Alarum," *Washington D.C. News*, 1 July 1929; "Great Loss: Key Men of America Give Up Their Daily Data Sheet—Marvin in a Bad Way," *New Leader*, 13 July 1929; "Skating Close to Libel," *New York Telegram*, 2 December 1929, ACLU Archives, vol. 362. Schwimmer squabbled with Hays and the ACLU about legal fees. Hays persuaded her to pay one-half of any settlement to his firm. Later she asked whether she could spread payments over three years. Hays would not agree to that, but asked the ACLU to mollify Schwimmer. Hays to Schwimmer, 18 October 1928; Schwimmer to Hays, 21 October 1928; Hays to Roger Baldwin, 9 August 1929; Baldwin to Schwimmer, 26 August 1929, ACLU Archives, vol. 375.

47. Schwimmer to Rabe, 4 July 1927, Schwimmer-Lloyd collection, box G-5.

48. Harry A. Jung to Solicitor General William Mitchell, 4 October 1928, *United States v. Schwimmer*, Appellate case file, Records of the Supreme Court of the United States, Record Group 267, National Archives, Washington, D.C. (hereinafter cited as "Archives collection").

49. See *The Woman Patriot*, 1 October, 15 October, 1 November, 15 November, 1 December 1928, in Archives collection. In the first of these issues the magazine printed the government's entire petition for a writ of certiorari to the Supreme Court in the *Schwimmer* case.

50. Helen Tufts Bailie to Schwimmer, 28 May 1928, Schwimmer-Lloyd collection, box G-3; Schwimmer to Rabe, 17 November 1928, Schwimmer-Lloyd collection, box G-5; Bailey to Schwimmer, 27 March 1929, ACLU Archives, vol. 373, reel 67.

51. In a writ of certiorari a superior court commands a lower court (in this case, the Supreme Court to the Court of Appeals, Seventh Circuit) to send up the record of a case so the higher court may review it for irregularities. See Steven H. Gifis, *Law Dictionary* (Woodbury, N.Y.: Barron's Educational Services, 1975), 31.

52. Letter of Robe Carl White, Acting Secretary of Labor, to John G. Sargent, Attorney General, 18 July 1928, 2, Archives collection; emphasis in original. The statute cited is 8 U.S.C. § 364.

53. White to Sargent, 18 July 1928. Emphasis in original. 8 U.S.C. § 409.

54. The language cited shows that the statute was specific about references of these attitudes—disbelief in organized government or belief in polygamy. Schwimmer did not hold either of those views. To make its case the government had to stretch the content of the statute.

55. Question 22 was not present on the questionnaire in all districts, which weakens the uniformity argument.

56. White to Sargent, 18 July 1928, 3-5.

57. Memorandum of William Mitchell, Solicitor General, to O. R. Luhring, Assistant Attorney General, 30 July 1928, 1-3, Archives collection.

58. *Minor v. Happersett* 88 U.S. 162 at 165-66 (1875).

59. Memorandum of O. R. Luhring, Assistant Attorney General, to William Mitchell, Solicitor General, 10 August 1928, 3, 5-6, Archives collection.

60. Memorandum to the Solicitor General from [Harry S.] Ridgely, 25 August 1928, 1-2, Archives collection.

61. Memorandum by Acting Solicitor General Lloyd, 27 August 1928, 1-2, Archives collection, apparently circulated to all involved, with no specific addressee.

62. O. R. Luhring, for the Attorney General, to the Secretary of Labor, 31 August 1928, Archives collection. Luhring sent a similar letter to J. Edgar Hoover, Director of the Federal Bureau of Investigation, 4 September 1928, Archives collection.

63. White to Sargent, 10 September 1928, 1-2, Archives collection.

64. Lloyd alludes to Proverbs 27:15 KJV: "A continual dropping in a very rainy day, and a contentious woman, are alike."

65. Lloyd to White, 13 September 1928, Archives collection.

66. Mitchell to White, 28 September 1928, 1-3, Archives collection.

67. William D. Mitchell, Solicitor General, *Petition for a Writ of Certiorari to the United States Circuit Court of Appeals for the Seventh Circuit and Brief in Support Thereof*, In the Supreme Court of the United States, September 1928, 11, 15, 16-17, 5.

68. "Files Plea to Bar Rosika Schwimmer," *New York Times*, 30 September 1928; Schwimmer to Rabe, 23 September 1928, Schwimmer-Lloyd collection, box G-5.

69. Forrest Bailey (ACLU) to Schwimmer, 24 October 1927; Schwimmer to Bailey, 26 October 1927, ACLU Archives, vol. 325, reel 51; Bailey to Fellowship of Reconciliation, 9 March 1929, ACLU Archives, vol. 373, reel 67; Jane Addams to Rabe, 28 October 1927; Addams to Rabe, 30 November 1928; Rabe to Addams, 5 February 1929, Olive Rabe papers, Schwimmer-Lloyd collection, box G-5.

70. Rabe to Bailey, 21 January 1929; Bailey to Rabe, 29 January 1929; Bailey to Robert M. Lovett, 29 January 1929; Lovett to Bailey, 31 January 1929; Bailey to Lovett, 5 February 1929, ACLU Archives, vol. 373, reel 67.

71. Rabe to Bailey, 2 April 1929; Bailey to Lovett, 5 April 1929; Bailey to Rabe, 9 April 1929; Lovett to Bailey, 11 April 1929; Bailey to Rabe, 19 April 1929; Rabe to Bailey, 29 May 1929; Bailey to Rabe, 3 June 1929; Rabe to Bailey, 6 June 1929, ACLU Archives, vol. 373, reel 67.

72. Mary G. Kilbreth of *The Woman Patriot* magazine, an archenemy of Schwimmer, identified "Cotton" as Undersecretary of State Joseph F. Cotton. Since Kilbreth thought Cotton was a liberal, she used this brief effort to get Cotton on Schwimmer's legal team as one more example of Schwimmer's disrespect for democracy and lack of patriotism. See Mary G. Kilbreth, "Statement of Miss Mary Kilbreth, President of the Woman Patriot Publishing Co.," Hearings Before the Committee on Immigration and Naturalization, House of Representatives, Seventy-First Congress, Second Session, on H.R. 3547, 8-9 May 1930, 198.

73. Bailey to Schwimmer, 2 October 1928; Rabe to Bailey, 6 October 1928; Rabe to Schwimmer, 6 October 1928; Bailey to Rabe, 8 October 1928; telegram Bailey to Schwimmer, 8 October 1928; Bailey to Hays, 22 December 1928; Hays to Bailey, 26 December 1928; Bailey to Rabe, 27 December 1928, ACLU Archives, vol. 362.

74. Rabe to Bailey, 21 January 1929; Transcript of Record, U. S. Supreme Court, *Brief for the United States, United States v. Schwimmer*, 6, 10-11, 17. *United States v. Manzi* 276 U.S. 463 at 457 (1928).

75. Transcript of Record, U. S. Supreme Court, *Brief for Respondent, United States v. Schwimmer*, 7-8. Forrest Bailey of the ACLU had written to Rabe, on 8 March 1929, "I have just been reading the government's brief and have a strong feeling that you will have no difficulty demolishing it." Rabe sent Bailey a copy of her brief, saying "I hope you feel as I do that it fully answers the points raised by the Government." ACLU Archives, vol. 373, reel 67.

76. Transcript of Record, U. S. Supreme Court, *Brief for Respondent, United States v. Schwimmer*, 9-12.

77. Transcript of Record, *Brief for Respondent, U. S. v. Schwimmer*, 12-17.

78. Transcript of Record, *Brief for Respondent, U. S. v. Schwimmer*, 18-20. Rabe cites statutes for the various services: for the Army 10 U.S.C. § 621; Navy, 10 U.S.C. § 1; National Militia, 32 U.S.C. § 1; National Guard, 32 U.S.C. § 4; Naval Militia, 34 U.S.C. § 841. For the state Militias, she cites state constitutions: Indiana, Art. 12, § 221; Illinois, Art. XII; Michigan, Art. XV, § 1; Wisconsin Statues 1925, §§ 21.01, 21.05, 22.01.

79. Schwimmer to Rabe, 21 February 1929; Rabe to Schwimmer, 12 March 1929, Schwimmer-Lloyd collection, box G-6. Schwimmer wrote when they thought the case was going to be argued in early March. The Court postponed it to April, enabling Rabe to rhapsodize about cherry blossoms.

80. Schwimmer to Lola Maverick Lloyd, 1-2 May 1929, Lloyd papers 0-108, Schwimmer-Lloyd collection. The Italian "Vederemo" means "we shall see." On Justice McReynolds's personality and his hostility to women lawyers, see David T. Pride, "James C. McReynolds," in *The Supreme Court Justices: Illustrated Biographies, 1789-1993*, Clare Cushman, ed. (Washington, D.C.: Congressional Quarterly, 1993), 326-30. Mme. Schwimmer saw only eight justices hearing oral arguments. I have found no record of who, if anyone, was absent. No justice excused himself from the decision and opinions.

81. "High Court Bars Mrs. Schwimmer," *New York Times*, 28 May 1929, 1; Richard J. Purcell, "Mr. Justice Pierce Butler," *The Catholic Educational Review* 42 (April 1944): 197, 198, 201; David Burner, "Pierce Butler," in *The Justices of the United States Supreme Court: Their Lives and Major Opinions*, Leon Friedman and Fred L. Israel, eds. (New York: Chelsea House, 1997) 3: 1090; William O. Douglas, *The Court Years, 1939-1975: The Autobiography of William O. Douglas* (New York: Vintage Books, 1980), 15-16.

82. Purcell, "Mr. Justice Pierce Butler," 202, 204; Burner, "Pierce Butler," 1082-90; William Reilly, "Pierce Butler," in *The Supreme Court Justices*, Chushman, ed. 351-55; John T. Noonan, Jr. "The Catholic Justices of the Supreme Court," *Catholic Historical Review* 67 (July 1981): 369-85. Noonan (374-76) finds a fascinating coincidence between Butler and John W. Davis and Martin T. Manton, who were instrumental in the *Macintosh* and *Bland* cases (see Chapters Four and Five). President Harding believed it would be politically advantageous to name a Democrat to the Court. The appointee had to be conservative, a southerner, from New York, and an able lawyer. He offered the appointment to Virginian John W. Davis, a noted lawyer practicing in New York, but Davis did not want to leave his corporate law practice. By this time the New York lobby had added Catholicism to its list of requirements, offering Appeals Court Judge Martin T. Manton as its candidate. Manton did not have a good reputation elsewhere—he was later convicted of bribery—so Harding, on advice of Chief Justice Taft, turned to Pierce Butler. Noonan says that Butler would not have been appointed if he had not been Catholic, but a Catholic would not have been appointed at all if the New York lobby had not promoted Manton. Justice Douglas later wrote, "What influenced Harding toward Butler rather than Manton is not known, but the choice protected the Supreme Court against what would have left an awful scar" (*The Court Years*, 16).

83. *United States v. Schwimmer* 279 U.S. 644 at 646-53 (1929). For the full text of the opinion see Appendix G.

84. Sheldon M. Novick, *Honorable Justice: The Life of Oliver Wendell Holmes* (New York: Dell, 1989), 315, 322, 471 n50; Liva Baker, *The Justice from Beacon Hill: The Life and Times of Oliver Wendell Holmes* (New York: HarperCollins, 1991), 497; G. Edward White, *Justice Oliver Wendell Homes: Law and the Inner Self* (New York: Oxford University Press, 1993), 583 n292.

85. Holmes expressed his contempt for pacifist sentiment in a letter to John Wigmore. "Doesn't this squashy sentimentality of a big minority of our people about human life make you puke? . . . of pacifist—of people who believe there is an onward and upward—who talk of uplift—who think that something in particular has happened and that the universe is no longer predatory. Oh bring in the basin." See Novick, *Honorable Justice*, 469 n11.

86. 249 U.S. 47 (1919).

87. 250 U.S. 616 (1919).

88. 274 U.S. 357 (1927).

89. White, *Justice Oliver Wendell Holmes*, 412-49; Melvin I. Urofsky, "Justice Louis Brandeis," in *The Jewish Justices of the Supreme Court Revisited: Brandeis to Fortas*, Jennifer M. Lowe, ed. (Washington, D.C.: Supreme Court Historical Society, 1994), 9-34; Novick, *Honorable Justice*, 353. "The wife of Judge Brandeis is very friendly to me," Schwimmer had written two years earlier. "I called on her last year when we stopped in Washington with Mother, and I told her about my naturalization difficulties. She was shocked and thought it was the most absurd thing that can be imagined. If Judge Brandeis has anything to do with it I am sure to get a sane, which means favorable judgment" (Schwimmer to Rabe, 12 September 1927, Schwimmer-Lloyd collection, box G-2). I have found no evidence that Schwimmer's friendship with Mrs. Brandeis influenced his attitude toward her case.

Emmet Lavery's 1945 play about the life of Justice Holmes portrays a dialogue in Act Three between Holmes and Brandeis about Schwimmer's case. Brandeis seems to be trying to persuade Holmes to come to Schwimmer's side. For his part, Holmes regards Brandeis as "a poor benighted optimist" as "all crusaders are . . . or they wouldn't be crusaders." Yet Holmes, thinking that "they're going to lick us on this Rosika Schwimmer decision," is "spoiling for a good fight," and Brandeis is urging him to become "a crusader . . . just once." Holmes sees the Schwimmer case as "a big fight" that might become his crusade. "This isn't just a matter of denying citizenship to a sincere woman pacifist. It's a matter of denying to ourselves just what that citizenship means . . . freedom of opinion doesn't mean merely freedom for the ideas we happen to like . . . it means just as much freedom for the ideas we happen to despise. For either this country of ours is a country where each man's right to his own point of view is respected and protected by every other man or—or—I'm sorry, Brandeis. My heart's with you but I can't seem to make my mind behave." Holmes is consumed with concern for his ailing wife, and in a later dialogue with her husband it is Fanny Holmes who breaks down her husband's remaining doubts about the pacifist Schwimmer who "thinks like a woman." Fanny apposes to her husband's "soldier's faith" "the faith that takes the Sermon on the Mount as gospel truth." Her remark that "we have never held it against the Quakers that they seemed to take the Sermon on the Mount a little more seriously than some of us do or can" at last provides to Holmes the "twist" he has been seeking. See Emmet Lavery, *The Magnificent Yankee: A Play in Three Acts* (New York: Samuel French, 1945,

1946), 91-93, 99-101. During the play's New York run, the principals in the cast—Louis Calhern, Dorothy Gish, and Edgar Barrier—had tea with Schwimmer in her home; see Edith Wynner, "Schwimmer-Lloyd Papers Open for Research," *World Peace News* (February 1974): 6, Schwimmer-Lloyd collection; I. Scott Messinger, "Legitimating Liberalism: The New Deal Image-makers and Oliver Wendell Holmes, Jr.," *Journal of Supreme Court History* (1995): 57-72.

90. Baker, *The Justice from Beacon Hill*, 619-21. In her account of the oral argument of her case Schwimmer mentions only eight justices present. Perhaps Holmes did not hear oral arguments because of his wife's illness. If that were the case, it did not cause him to recuse himself from the decision.

91. White, *Justice Oliver Wendell Holmes*, 446-48.

92. 279 U.S. 644 at 653-55. Justice Brandeis joined Holmes's dissent. Justice Edward T. Sanford dissented in one sentence endorsing the opinion of the Court of Appeals.

93. Telegram, Charles Elmore Cropley, Clerk of the Supreme Court, to Rabe, 27 May 1929; telegram, Rabe to Schwimmer, 27 May 1929; telegram, Schwimmer to Rabe, 30 May, 1929; letter, Rabe to Schwimmer, 3 June 1929, Schwimmer-Lloyd collection, Olive Rabe files, box G-6.

94. Letters, Baldwin to Rabe, 26 May 1929; Baldwin to Schwimmer, 28 May 1929; Rabe to Bailey, 29 May 1929; Bailey to Rabe, 1 June 1929; ACLU Archives, vol. 373, reel 67.

95. Schwimmer to Rabe, 6 June 1929, Schwimmer-Lloyd collection, Olive Rabe files, box G-6.

96. "Mrs. Schwimmer Without a Country," *New York Times*, 29 May 1929, 11; "Madame Schwimmer—'Without a Country,'" *Literary Digest*, 8 June 1929, 9; Ernest K. Lindley, "Mme. Schwimmer Universal Alien," *New York World*, 2 June 1929.

97. "Arms and the Woman," *Outlook and Independent* 162 (12 June 1929): 250; "Unwisely Barred" *Cleveland Plain Dealer*, 31 May 1929; F. H. La Guardia, "I'm Telling You Confidentially!" *New York Evening Graphic* 25 June 1929; Walter Lippmann, "The Schwimmer Case," *New York World*, 31 May 1929, 14, reprinted in *The New York Review*, 19 March 1981, 53; *The Case of Rosika Schwimmer: Alien Pacifists Not Wanted* (New York: American Civil Liberties Union, 1929). See also Dorothy Dunbar Bromley, "The Pacifist Bogey: An Apology to Prospective Citizens," *Harper's Monthly Magazine* 61 (October 1939): 553-65. La Guardia was mistaken about Schwimmer's name living on in the honor roll of history, for she is today virtually unknown. That is one reason for the writing of this book.

98. "Citizenship for Arms-Bearers Only," *Christian Century* 46 (5 June 1929): 734; "The Case of Madame Schwimmer," *Christian Century* 46 (12 June 1929): 769-71; "Quakers Are Now Excluded From Citizenship," and "The Naturalization Law Should Be Amended," *Christian Century* 46 (19 June 1929): 795. See also William C. Allen, "What About the Christian Conscience?" *United Presbyterian*, 26 December 1929, ACLU Archives, vol. 362.

99. "Calls on Churches to Fight Humanism," *New York Times*, 29 May 1929, 30; "Schwimmer Ruling Held Un-Christian," *New York Times*, 3 June 1929, 28. The ACLU also announced that it had sent letters to 150 religious denominations and church peace groups requesting aid in supporting legislation to overcome *Schwimmer*. See "Asks Law to Aid Pacifists," *New York Times*, 23 June 1929, 13.

100. Women's Peace Society Resolution, 27 May 1929; Rabe to Forrest Bailey, 9 July 1929. The Addams petition charged that the Court's decision in *Schwimmer* would "exclude from citizenship many highly desirable applicants," whereas "the signing and ratification of the Kellogg Treaty the renunciation of war as an instrument of national policy has been made a part of that body of Law which all loyal citizens are bound to support and defend" and "the Constitution of the United States vests in Congress the power to prescribe qualifications for citizenship." The petition therefore urged Congress "to amend the Naturalization Law so as to make it clear that persons otherwise eligible, shall not be barred from citizenship because of conscientious objections to bearing arms." ACLU Archives, vol. 373, reel 67.

101. "Madame Schwimmer—Without a Country,"*Literary Digest* (8 June 1929): 9; Loran W. Warner, "Smart Weed and Tickle Grass With a Varying Mixture of Nettles, Burrs and Posies, Plucked from the Fields of Current Thought," Winamac, Indiana *Democrat*, 30 April 1931. I have no direct statement from Schwimmer that conveys the idea that Warner attributes to her at the beginning of his remarks.

102. "United States of America v. Rosika Schwimmer," *The Woman Patriot* 13 (1 June 1929): 83-87.

103. Schwimmer to Rabe, 23 May 1929; Rabe to Schwimmer, 3 June 1929 (Rabe wrote: "I can't tell you how much disappointed I am that you should be deprived of your trip to Europe. It just seems preposterous."); Rabe to Schwimmer, 7 June 1929 (Rabe wrote: "Congratulations. So glad you can have the three months trip."). Rabe papers, Schwimmer-Lloyd collection, box G-6. Mary G. Kilbreth, "Government Considering Plea for Frau Schwimmer's Exclusion," *The Woman Patriot* 13 (1 August 1929): 113-15.

104. "Right of Alien 'Pacifist' to Obtain Citizenship," *Law Notes* 33 (September 1929): 111; "Constitutional Law —Naturalization—Aliens—Taking Oath of Allegiance with Mental Reservations," *Southern California Law Review* 3 (February 1930): 224-25; "Aliens—Naturalization," *Michigan Law Review* 28 (February 1930): 445; "Aliens—Naturalization—Doctrine of the Schwimmer Case," *Michigan Law Review* 29 (December 1930): 241-42; "Naturalization of Aliens—Duty to Bear Arms in Defense of United States, *Illinois Law Review* 25 (February 1931): 723-25; Henry B. Hazard, "Supreme Court Holds Madam Schwimmer, Pacifist, Ineligible to Naturalization," *American Journal of International Law* 23 (July 1929): 626-32. Hazard's case note is atypically long, but remains essentially a digest of the case.

105. Robert C. Pugh, "Pacifism and Citizenship—The Case of Rosika Schwimmer," *University of Cincinnati Law Review* 3 (November 1929): 462-71; Ernest Freund, "United States v. Schwimmer," *New York University Law Quarterly Review* 7 (September 1929): 157-59.

106. Herman A. Gray, "Willingness to Bear Arms as a Prerequisite to Naturalization," *New York University Law Quarterly Review* 7 (March 1930): 723-27. The government's answer to the argument was that applicants for citizenship are treated differently from citizens.

107. W. E. M., "Naturalization—Effect of Woman Applicant's Expression of Unwillingness to Personally Bear Arms," *Virginia Law Review* 16 (December 1929): 169-74; Elmer Brown, "Aliens—Right of Naturalization—Unwillingness to Bear Arms," *Boston University Law Review* 9 (November 1929): 263-65.

108. Henry B. Hazard, "'Attachment to the Principles of the Constitution' as Judicially Construed in Certain Naturalization Cases in the United States," *American Journal of International Law* 23 (October 1929): 783-808. Hazard addresses *In re Roper* 274 F. 490 (1921) and *In re D*—— 290 F. 863 (1923), neither of which was cited in *Schwimmer*, nor have I explicated them here.

109. Schwimmer to Holmes, 28 January 1930; Holmes to Schwimmer, 30 January 1930, Schwimmer-Lloyd collection, box G-14.

110. Holmes to Schwimmer, 5 February 1930, Schwimmer-Lloyd collection, box G-14. Holmes had received Rosika Schwimmer, *Tisza Tales* (Garden City, N.Y.: Doubleday, Doran, 1928), and Franciska Schwimmer, *Great Musicians as Children* (Garden City, N.Y.: Doubleday, Doran, 1929). The copy of Holmes's letter in the Schwimmer-Lloyd collection is a carbon that she had sent to Olive Rabe. At the top Schwimmer wrote that she wanted no publicity whatsoever about this letter. At the bottom she added, "Don't you think this is the most touching appreciation imaginable?" The first mention of rainbows in Holmes's letter refers to one of the *Tisza Tales*, "Chasing the Rainbow." The reference to "rainbow music" refers to stories in Franciska's book. Schwimmer to Holmes, 10 February 1930, Schwimmer-Lloyd collection, box G-14.

111. Schwimmer to Holmes, 16 January 1932; Schwimmer to Holmes, 7 March 1931; Robert W. Wales to Schwimmer, 10 March 1931; Schwimmer to Holmes, 7 March 1932; Horace Chapman Rose to Schwimmer, 16 March 1932; Schwimmer to Holmes, 8 April 1934 (In this letter Schwimmer was in the hospital and a month late with the birthday greeting, for which she apologized.); Mark DeWolfe Howe to Schwimmer, 11 April 1934. Schwimmer-Lloyd collection, box G-14.

112. "Mme. Schwimmer Calls on Holmes," *New York Times*, 22 January 1933; see also Rosika Schwimmer, "Friend Tells of Holmes [*sic*] Great Charm," *Hartford Daily Courant*, 10 March 1935, a recapitulation of her visit with Holmes, written at the time of his death and somewhat embellished compared to the earlier article. "I told him," Schwimmer wrote, "that some papers had predicted his minority opinion in my case would become a classic in American letters, along with Washington's Farewell Address and Lincoln's Gettysburg Address. 'Now,

I call that an exaggeration,' he said laughing, 'but I admit I consider it one of the best bits I have ever written.' A personal friend of Justice Holmes's later told me the old man really liked that 'bit' so much that he sometimes would read it to guests." In the same article Schwimmer reflected that "No property measurable in money could make me feel richer than the few letters I have from Justice Holmes. And the memory of the visit in his home, his brilliant, scintillating conversation, his warm laughter, his gentle interest in a tolerated alien will always belong to my most cherished spiritual possessions."

113. Schwimmer to Holmes 28 February 1935. In her "open letter," dated 6 March 1935, Schwimmer wrote, "The death of Justice Oliver Wendell Holmes means immeasurably more than the passing of a grand old man. It means the closing of an intellectual and spiritual frontier, following by some decades the closing of the physical frontiers of the United States.

"Justice Oliver Wendell Holmes glamorously personified all that was genuinely ideal in the nation which attracted dissenters from all other countries to find here a haven of liberty, tolerance, and freedom of conscience.

"They brought spiritual and intellectual gifts, and enthusiasms for which their old countries saw no use, and which enriched the young new world. As the frontiers became narrower there was also less and less hospitality for intellectual and spiritual dissenters from other shores. It was the towering grand American, Oliver Wendell Holmes, who to the last raised his majestic voice in welcome to them, and who warned his country against abandoning its old ideals of tolerance and respect for individual conscience that were always one of America's proudest distinctions among the nations.

"As one who had served as the subject of one of Justice Holmes' most striking minority opinions, and who had also the unforgettable privilege of personal contact with the great American, after his retirement from the bench, I feel the need to express my condolence to the American nation which suffered an irreparable loss in the death of its greatest man, Justice Oliver Wendell Holmes." Schwimmer-Lloyd collection, box G-14. "Decorate Justice Holmes's Grave," *New York Times* 2 May 1935, 23.

114. Frankfurter to Schwimmer, 14 March 1935; Schwimmer to Frankfurter, 26 March 1941; Schwimmer to Archibald MacLeish, Librarian of Congress, 28 March 1941; Schwimmer to Librarian, Harvard Law School, 28 March 1941; MacLeish to Schwimmer, 31 March 1941; Helen Sherman, Harvard Law School Library, to Schwimmer, 31 March 1941, Schwimmer-Lloyd collection, box G-14. In 1991, on the 150th anniversary of Holmes's birth, Anthony Lewis wrote a tribute to Holmes's advocacy of free speech, quoting from two of Holmes's dissents, *Abrams v. United States* 250 U.S. 616 (1919), and from *Schwimmer*, his famous sentence, "If there is any principle of the Constitution that more imperatively calls for attachment than any other, it is the principle of free thought—not free thought for those who agree with us but freedom for the thought that we hate." Anthony Lewis, "The Poet Judge," *New York Times* 8 March 1991, 29-A.

115. Edith Wynner, Schwimmer's longtime friend and assistant, wrote to me, "It is untrue that she never thought of herself as anything else than a writer or lecturer. She placed a position wanted ad in the papers. The job offers that came to her were weird: one offer wanted her to model silk stockings. (It is true that she had very handsome legs; one Hungarian friend visiting her in New York City said: 'Thank God you still have slender ankles.') Another job offer wanted her to sit in an expensive car (expensively dressed) to camouflage liquor deliveries by a bootlegger. She found both offers unacceptable." Edith Wynner to Ronald B. Flowers, 12 May 1993. Wynner did not mention any jobs that Schwimmer accepted, and acknowledged in the same letter that Schwimmer's friends supported her, with the principal contributions coming from Lola Maverick Lloyd and Schwimmer's sister Franciska.

116. John Bainbridge and Russell Maloney, "Where Are They Now? The Innocent Voyage," *New Yorker* 16 (9 March 1940): 29; Wenger, "Radical Politics in a Reactionary Age," 90.

117. Schwimmer is quoted as having said that since she had become an "undesired alien," she was determined not to make any more peace propaganda; "Pacifists Demand Citizenship Rights," *New York Times*, 18 January 1931, 2. She did continue to campaign for peace, although she did not make a living at it.

118. Edith Wynner and Georgia Lloyd describe the plan in *Searchlight on Peace Plans: Choose Your Road to World Government* (New York: E. P. Dutton, 1949), 107-12.

119. Rosika Schwimmer and Edith Wynner, *Memorandum on Immediate Action for World Government* (New York, n.p., 1945); see Edith Wynner, *World Federal Government: Why?, What?, How?* (Afton, N.Y.: Fedonot Press, 1954), 74-76.

120. Rosika Schwimmer, *Union Now for Peace or War?: The Danger of the Plan of Clarence Streit* (New York: The Author, 1939), 11.

121. Franciska Schwimmer to Lola Maverick Lloyd, 9 March 1928, Schwimmer-Lloyd collection, box G-3.

122. Rosika Schwimmer, "The Nobel Peace Prize," *The World Tomorrow* 15 (January 1932): 20-22.

123. Open letter from International Committee for World Peace Prize Award to Rosika Schwimmer, May 1937; unsigned letter and petition to Rosika Schwimmer asking her to write a history of pacifism in World War I on "this Fiftieth Anniversary of your birthday" (which was 1927); *Rosika Schwimmer: World Patriot: A Biographical Sketch* (International Committee for World Peace Prize for Rosika Schwimmer, 1937 [published again in an updated version, 1947]; "People," *Time* 30 (13 December 1937): 48. Schwimmer elaborated her plan for a World Federation of Nations in an open letter "To my Friends: the Initiators, Sponsors and Contributors of the World Peace Prize 1937," 10 February 1938. Swarthmore Peace collection.

Four

Douglas Clyde Macintosh:
Alien Theologian

United States v. Macintosh,[1] decided by the Supreme Court of the United States on 25 May 1931, was one of the most famous cases of its era. *The Christian Century*, comparing *Macintosh* to the infamous *Dred Scott*[2] decision, exclaimed that it "outrages the national conscience," and called it "incredible . . . monstrous . . . the inevitable death of spiritual religion."[3] Who then was Douglas Clyde Macintosh? Why did he have a case before the Supreme Court? Why did so many become so exercised about it?

Born in Canada in 1877, Douglas Clyde Macintosh was descended on both sides of his family from people steeped in religion. His mother, Elizabeth Everett, was a seventh-generation descendant of John Cotton (1584-1652), an eminent Puritan divine of colonial Boston. At some point some of Cotton's descendants returned to England. Macintosh's maternal grandfather, Cotton Mather Everett, a Wesleyan Methodist, migrated to Canada. His large family was religiously diverse; some were evangelical Protestants, others were rather rationalistic, and one was a skeptic known in his community as an "infidel." Macintosh's mother was thoroughly religious and theologically conservative. His paternal great-grandfather, Donald Roy McLaurin, emigrated from Scotland to Canada in the late eighteenth or early nineteenth century and somewhere along the way converted from Congregationalism to Baptist beliefs. Macintosh's grandfather, John Macintosh, and his father, Peter, served as deacons in their local Baptist church. All three men were soundly orthodox Baptists, although grandfather John had his doubts about predestination.

Macintosh earned his undergraduate degree from McMaster University in Toronto. In 1904 he began graduate work at the University of Chicago. Ordained to the ministry of the American Baptist Church in 1907, Macintosh returned to Canada to teach in a small college. In 1909, the same year he completed his Ph.D. at the University of Chicago, he was invited to join the faculty of Yale Divinity School.[4] As he traveled to America to accept that appointment in the summer of 1909, Macintosh suffered his first difficulty with the immigration laws of the United States. He had boarded a train in Canada. "As we neared the border," he later recalled,

> the American immigration official came around, asking the usual questions:
> "Are you a citizen of the United States?" I was not.
> "Are you going to reside in the United States?" I was.
> "Are you going to work?" "Yes."
> "Have you got a job?" This, too, had to be answered in the affirmative.
> "Where were you when the contract was made?" I had to say, "I was in Canada."
> "Well! You can't go any farther. You must get off the train." I smiled incredulously.
> "Yes, I mean it! You must get off at the next station. You are violating the Alien Labor Law."
> "That's very strange," I replied. "The President of the United States was a member of the corporation that hired me." (President Taft was at the time a member of the Yale Corporation.)
> The officer eyed me narrowly. "What are you going to do?" he asked. I answered apologetically to the effect that I was going to be a professor in Yale University.
> "Oh well!" said the agent, "if you're going to be a professor, that's all right. I thought you said you were going to *work*!"[5]

When the Supreme Court heard his case, Macintosh was Chaplain of the Yale Graduate School and Dwight Professor of Theology in the Divinity School, one of the luminaries of the Yale faculty, American citizen or not.

In 1925 Macintosh filed with the U.S. District Court in New Haven, Connecticut, a declaration of intent to become a United States citizen. On 18 March 1929 he filed his application for naturalization. As part of that process, an applicant had to complete a form that provided pertinent information for the application. On that form was question 20, "Have you read the following oath of allegiance?" which was then quoted. The form then asked, "Are you willing to take this oath in becoming a citizen?" Macintosh answered both halves of this question "Yes." Question 22 asked: "If necessary, are you willing to take up arms in defense of this country?" Macintosh answered the question: "Yes, but I should want to be free to judge of the necessity."[6] In the United States of 1929, that was not an acceptable answer.

The Naturalization Act of 1906, normative at the time of Macintosh's application, required an applicant for citizenship to swear an oath promising to "support and defend the Constitution and laws of the United States against all enemies, foreign and domestic, and bear true faith and allegiance to the same," thereby demonstrating that one was "attached to the principles of the Constitution of the United States and well disposed to the good order of the same."[7] Consequently, the oath of naturalization read:

> I hereby declare, on oath, that I absolutely and entirely renounce and abjure all allegiance and fidelity to any foreign prince, potentate, state or sovereignty, and particularly to_____, of whom I have heretofore been a subject; that I will support and defend the Constitution and laws of the United States of America against all enemies, foreign and domestic; and that I will bear true faith and allegiance to the same.[8]

The oath appeared as question 20 on the preliminary form. The applicant was asked if he was willing to take the oath to become a citizen. Macintosh answered "Yes." His response to the oath satisfied the requirement, but his desire to qualify his answer about bearing arms troubled those who would pass judgment on his qualifications.

Douglas Clyde Macintosh's application for naturalization was considered in a preliminary hearing before John F. Davis, a Naturalization Examiner, on 10 July 1929. Because he had responded to question 22 with a conditional answer, he submitted a statement to the examiner to clarify his answer. "I am willing to do what I judge to be in the best interest of my country," Macintosh wrote,

> but only insofar as I can believe that this is not going to be against the best interests of humanity in the long run. I do not undertake to support "my country, right or wrong" in any dispute which may arise, and I am not willing to promise beforehand, and without knowing the cause for which my country may go to war, either that I will or that I will not "take up arms in defense of this country," however "necessary" the war may seem to the Government of the day. It is only in a sense consistent with these statements that I am willing to promise to 'support and defend' the Government of the United States 'against all enemies, foreign and domestic.' But, just because I am not certain that the language of questions 20 and 22 will bear the construction I should have to put upon it in order to be able to answer them in the affirmative, I have to say that I do not know that I can say 'Yes' in answer to these two questions.[9]

Even this preliminary hearing attracted public attention. American Legion Hughson Post 71, West Haven, Connecticut, passed a resolution 10 June 1929, calling attention to the Legion's effort to "perpetuate one hundred per cent Americanism" and deploring the attempt by Professor Macintosh to try to become a citizen "with any reservation whatsoever." It also questioned the judgment of Yale University in having such a man as Macintosh as the Dwight Professor of Theology, a teacher educating young people.[10] Macintosh also received a letter from some Quakers in Philadelphia expressing interest in his case and promising to become advocates on his behalf if he were denied citizenship.[11]

In a formal naturalization hearing before District Court Judge Warren B. Burrows on 24 June 1929 Macintosh elaborated his views on bearing arms. According to the court record, Macintosh declared that

> his first allegiance was to the will of God, defined as what was morally right and for the ultimate well-being of humanity, and that after that he would put allegiance to one's country as coming before all merely individual and private interest. He stated further that he was ready to give to the United States, in return for citizenship, all the allegiance he ever had given or ever could give to any country, but that he could not put allegiance to the government of any country before allegiance to the will of God.[12]

Macintosh added that he did not anticipate engaging in propaganda against any war in which the United States might fight, but that he could not even promise that in advance, without knowing the circumstances.[13] He may have sought to avoid one of the controversies that cost Rosika Schwimmer her citizenship, but the caveat was not categorical enough to accomplish that goal.

Another way that Macintosh tried to distinguish himself from Schwimmer and to clarify his own position on war was to say that he was not a pacifist. Macintosh had served in World War I. In June 1916 he was appointed a chaplain in the Canadian army and served at the front in the area of Vimy and in the battle of the Somme. When the Dean of Yale Divinity School would not extend his leave of absence, Macintosh returned in November 1916 to teach. In the next year, he made about forty speeches rallying support for the Allied war effort. In the spring of 1918 he became an American YMCA agent, working in France, including service at the front near St. Mihiel until the war was over.[14]

After establishing this war record, of which he seemed to be proud, Macintosh first addressed questions of war and peace as a scholar in an article written in 1918. There Macintosh confronted the question of God's action in history—specifically, how God could allow war to happen. Macintosh explicitly asserted that sometimes war could be God's will. As moral righteousness is consistent with God's will, so a war fought for causes of justice and right is consistent with God's will. "Right has to be worked for, and sometimes it has to be fought for." If war is a necessary alternative to national betrayal of trust, or ignoble servitude, or any other evil that is greater than the evil inflicted by war, and if war is entered into with a brave and self-sacrificing spirit, then war-making is "in accord with the will of God. Indeed, if we may regard the divine spirit as immanent where we find the divine qualities present in human life, we may go further and say that such righteous participation in the war is the work of God within the soul of man, fighting against the forces of evil."[15]

Macintosh's experience in the war and reflection on it had led to some conclusions. While serving as a chaplain, he had firmly believed in the cause of the Allies and in the effort to fight a war that was supposed to end all wars. He exhorted soldiers to serve their country and the future welfare of humanity in general by fighting in that noble cause. But the end of the war and how badly the peace turned out taught him "a profound distrust of war as a way of settling anything. And in view of the menace to civilization of unnecessary war, it now seems to me highly immoral for an individual to promise beforehand to support what he may have to regard at the time as an unnecessary and immoral war."[16]

Macintosh's understanding of "immoral war" is crucial to his willingness to bear arms in some wars and not others—his answer to question 22. It was the basis for his application for citizenship as a nonpacifist, religious, selective conscientious objector to war. A war may be morally unjustified for several reasons. Its motivation may be unjust. It may have just cause, yet be launched prematurely, before all legitimate means of conflict resolution have been tried. It may be a war from which justice can never result. Injustices inflicted on the opposing side may be out of proportion to the injustices originally experienced. It may be better to suffer some injustices than to inflict the devastation associated with modern warfare. Given the destructive quality of contemporary warfare, a huge burden of proof rests on any leader who advocates or nation that launches a war, even a "defensive" war. A war of self-defense would be, in the abstract, a morally justified war. Yet, coupled with the terrible destruction of modern warfare, nations distressingly tend to justify any war they begin as defensive.[17]

In light of this understanding, Macintosh believed that neither citizens nor applicants for citizenship should promise categorically to fight in all future wars. Indeed the government should not demand such a promise. The government should have a conscience, too, and decide conscientiously what to demand of citizens in the event of national crisis. Then every citizen must decide conscientiously—in light of all information available, including what the government has demanded—what to do. Every citizen should decide whether to accede to the government's demand or take the course of civil disobedience. Then the government should have to decide conscientiously how to do deal with the civil disobedience of a citizen or a naturalization applicant.[18] Obviously, since Macintosh vigorously pursued citizenship, he did not believe that the government could legitimately deny citizenship.

On the basis of the statements accompanying the preliminary form and in open court, the recommendation of the Naturalization Examiner, and, perhaps, the precedent of *Schwimmer*, Judge Burrows denied Macintosh's application for citizenship: "Attachment to the principles of the Constitution not shown."[19]

The next day American Legion Hughson Post 71 in Macintosh's hometown broadcast its resolution to

> applaud and approve the decision of Judge Warren B. Burrows denying citizenship to Professor Douglas Clyde Macintosh or anyone who seeks citizenship in part and not completely and entirely in accord with the principles set forth in the Constitution of the United States of America, and the oath of Allegiance.[20]

This statement was widely reported in local and regional newspapers. Yet a lawyer who was a member of the American Legion wrote, "May I extend my good wishes for you. I admire your courage."[21]

Commentary in the secular press mostly deplored the court's denial of citizenship. "No sensible government would do what has now been done," the *New York World* asserted. No government should "deliberately, by a trick question, provoke a purely theoretical debate over whether the will of the majority or the will of God is to prevail in a hypothetical case." However "interesting" they may be, "such debates" should be avoided. Governments "ought not to ask elderly women and superannuated professors of divinity whether they are prepared to surrender their convictions in advance in the event of a war against X."[22] Columnist Heywood Broun wrote that "if the wisdom of Judge Burrows is sustained it will be necessary to change our coinage so that the familiar slogan shall read, 'In God we trust so long as He does not get in the way of any act of Congress.'"[23] According to the *Washington Daily News*, "the absurd and dangerous decision of Federal Judge Burrows" forced citizens to choose between "allegiance to conscience" and "the principles of the United States Constitution."

> For a country founded on the principles of religious freedom, such a dictum is untrue. For a country with a Quaker President [Herbert Hoover], it is inconceivable. For a country in which millions of splendid citizens hold the views thus outlawed, it is a mockery. For a country which initiated and signed an international treaty for the renunciation of war, it is hypocrisy.[24]

Hickman Powell interviewed Professor Macintosh for the *New York World*, finding "little about this Yale theologian to identify him with the usual articulate ecclesiastical foes of war." Macintosh was, rather, "a small, gray, mild-looking man in tweed knickers . . . a man who has tried to keep his mind free . . . a Baptist, but far from fundamentalism . . . a man of good will." Macintosh "doesn't speak at peace conventions" and "there is nothing violent about him, not even his opinions or his cry for peace." Significantly, "though religion is his profession," Macintosh "has never signed a creed. He has always been wary of pledges for the future." Macintosh's position on war was a matter of principle, not taken because he was repulsed by the horrors of war, as some commentators had said. He believed any future war would be "such an irreparable calamity for the world" that he could not promise in advance to support it, although he would be willing to fight for the welfare of the world. He believed in America there ought to be room for a person to follow his conscience. That was the reason he intended to appeal his case. "For such a man," Powell wrote, "'the supreme sacrifice' is not to be killed, but to kill."[25]

The Christian Century noted about 200 applicants for citizenship were in the courtroom on the day that Judge Burrows questioned and rejected Macintosh. "Who could blame them," the *Century* asked, "if they drew the inference that willingness to fight was the most highly prized qualification for citizenship, and that the government is so uncertain of the justice of its cause in the 'next war' that it must make all new citizens commit themselves in advance to blind obedience?" Macintosh's case, which dramatized the possible conflicts between government policy and the consciences of its citizens, was destined to be even more significant than *Schwimmer*. Christianity would not have survived in the ancient world if Christians had not "believed that they must obey God rather than man." Now, if Judge Burrows were to be upheld, "there might as well be written over the doors of our naturalization courts: 'No Christians need apply.'" In a subsequent editorial the *Century* called the theory of government articulated by Judge Burrows "completely pagan" because it subordinated the conscience of any person, citizen or applicant for citizenship, Christian or not, to "the absolute and unlimited power" of the state. Burrows had made a mockery of the naturalization oath, or any other civil oath, usually affirmed with the phrase, "So help me God." The challenge to Christians, according to the *Century*, was clear. Any church that would not "rise in protest against the monstrous paganism and tyranny" that "refuses civil rights to those who will not agree to stifle the voice of conscience" and subordinate "the voice of God" to "the voice of Caesar" would be "a church whose candlestick has been removed and whose light has gone out."[26]

One critic upbraided Macintosh's lawyer, Charles E. Clark, Dean of Yale Law School, for taking the case, since Macintosh was surely undermining "the morale of the young students who are in your university." Clark replied that he did not share "Dr. Macintosh's position on war as stated by him before the Federal Court,"

> but I do honor his attempt to think out his view on public affairs, and to stand by them after he has thought them through to his satisfaction. I think this is a higher form of citizenship than a mere blind acceptance of the views of any merely temporary political leaders.[27]

Although Dean Clark represented Macintosh before the District Court, discussion of continuing counsel was already under way. Following the informal hearing, before Judge Burrows denied citizenship, Forrest Bailey of the American Civil Liberties Union wrote to Macintosh offering its services if they were needed. The ACLU had been active in the case of Rosika Schwimmer. That she had been denied citizenship on 12 May 1929 intensified the ACLU's interest in Macintosh's case. Macintosh expressed thanks for the offer of help and promised to be back in touch if the need should arise. It did arise on 24 June, when Judge Burrows rejected his application for citizenship. The next day, Roger Baldwin, the director of the ACLU, wrote to Macintosh that it was not surprising that he had been denied, given the precedent of *Schwimmer*. "But you have laid an excellent basis for an appeal on grounds both moral and legal. Your position strikes squarely for the right of a citizen to have a conscience at all." He asserted the desire of his organization to help as Macintosh's attorneys thought appropriate, including raising money to pay court costs. Macintosh responded with gratitude and said that he would decide soon whether or not he wanted the ACLU's help.[28]

At this point the New York law firm of Davis, Polk, Wardwell, Gardiner and Reed entered the picture.[29] The Davis of this firm was John W. Davis, one of the most esteemed lawyers in America. Macintosh could have hardly had more respected counsel.[30] By 1929 Davis had been a member of the U.S. House of Representatives for two terms, Solicitor General of the United States, U.S. Ambassador to Great Britain, and the Democratic candidate for President in 1924 (a compromise selection after the 103d ballot at the Democratic convention) against Calvin Coolidge. During his years as Solicitor General and in private practice, he argued 141 cases before the Supreme Court, sixty-seven of those in five years, more than any other lawyer up to his time. He was known as an advocate of consummate skill.[31] "Of all the persons who appeared before the Court in my time," Justice Oliver Wendell Holmes recalled, "there was never anybody more elegant, more clear, more concise or more logical than John W. Davis."[32] Justice Felix Frankfurter would tell Davis in 1953, "The biggest debt we all owe you is the debt that you have paid to our great profession. . . . As law teacher and as judge I have often referred to you as one of the finest exemplars of what Elihu Root called 'the public profession of the law.'"[33] Justice William O. Douglas called Davis "debonair and eloquent," among three advocates "who knew no equal."[34] In 1953, at the end of his career, *Time Magazine* remarked that

> In the 29 years since his defeat [for the presidency], Davis has all but faded from popular memory; in his own profession, he is a living legend. Most Davis Polk business never reaches a courtroom at all. But the courtroom is still the showcase of the legal profession, and John W. Davis the acknowledged star of the show.[35]

Davis was eager to argue the case. He had strongly supported the presidential candidacy of Al Smith on religious freedom grounds. American Protestants and other groups had attacked Smith, charging that a Roman Catholic President would not be able to govern freely in a democratic society because he must submit to the authority of the Papacy. Davis, incensed by that prejudice, argued that the American tradition of religious freedom should determine that one would never be denied the presidency because of religious beliefs. Now the Macintosh case would enable him to argue similarly that one's conscientiously held religious beliefs about war should not preclude citizenship. Davis could express his abiding belief in the primacy of personal rights over government power. He believed that a person of Macintosh's intellectual and moral caliber was eminently qualified for citizenship. According to his biographer, Davis "felt more keenly about this case than almost any he ever argued."[36]

The brief that Davis and his colleagues prepared for the Court of Appeals attempted to distinguish Macintosh from the views of Rosika Schwimmer, who had been denied citizenship only a month before Judge Burrows's ruling. Whereas Schwimmer was an absolute philosophical pacifist, Macintosh accepted a rationale for armies and navies and simply wanted to reserve the right to refuse to participate in wars he believed to be unjust, based on his conscience as a Christian. That he was not a pacifist clearly meant that he could not be denied citizenship on the same grounds as Mme. Schwimmer. Furthermore, Congress had not required the promise to bear arms in defense of the country as a requirement for admission to citizenship. Although question 22 on the preliminary naturalization form asked about an applicant's willingness to bear arms in national defense, that question was not the result of an act of Congress and was intended only to inform the Naturalization Service, not restrict it.[37]

Question 22 now drew considerable legal attention. Roger Baldwin of the ACLU, probably motivated by *Schwimmer*, wrote to the Bureau of Naturalization asking when and why the question was added to the application for naturalization. He also asked whether the Bureau had any record of the number of people who had been denied naturalization because of the question. The Bureau of Naturalization responded that the question had been added "about six years ago" (about 1923). Many courts began asking such a question after World War I as a way of ascertaining whether applicants for citizenship were attached to the principles of the Constitution, properly disposed to the good order and happiness of the same, and were able to take the oath to support and defend the Constitution against all enemies, foreign and domestic, as required by law. Since the question was being asked in courts, it was added to the preliminary form. Some people had been denied citizenship on refusal to bear arms before question 22 was added to the form. Roger Baldwin thanked the Bureau for the information, but asked for specific case names of those who had been denied prior to the inclusion of question 22. That letter was never answered.[38]

Macintosh's case was heard by Judges Martin T. Manton, Learned Hand, and Thomas W. Swan of the Court of Appeals for the Second Circuit on 19 May 1930. Rosika Schwimmer attended the oral argument, reporting later to her attorney that "John W. Davis spoke very oratorically but terribly weak in logic and argument. The Government's representative opposing him was from his point of view exceedingly good."[39] On 30 June a decision in Macintosh's favor came down, Judge Manton writing for a unanimous court.[40] The same Martin T. Manton had been rejected for the Supreme Court in favor of Pierce Butler, who wrote for the majority in *Schwimmer* (see Chapter Three).

Manton asserted that it was appropriate for the Naturalization Examiner to inquire into the religious and philosophical beliefs of an applicant for naturalization. Since the naturalization law requires an applicant be of good moral character, attached to the principles of the Constitution, and willing to support and defend the Constitution, it is only natural that the government, through the Examiner, may explore the beliefs of the applicant. Yet "Question 22 is merely informative" to the court and not dispositive of the case at hand. Citizens have a duty to fight in defense of the country, but it is "well-recognized" that if one has a religiously based conscientious objection to fighting, that person "does not lack nationalism or affection for his government." Judge Manton demonstrated that the principle was "well-recognized" by citing, in two footnotes, statutes from six states and constitutional provisions from twenty-two states that exempted persons with religious scruples against bearing arms from that responsibility. He also declared that "Congress has recognized that persons having conscientious scruples against bearing arms shall be exempt," citing and describing as principal examples the Militia Act of 2 June 1916[41] and the Selective Draft Act of 18 May 1917.[42] "This federal legislation," Manton wrote, "is indicative of the actual operation of the principles of the Constitution."[43]

Manton next equated the beliefs of selective conscientious objectors, who refuse to fight in wars considered to be unjust, and persons who object to fighting in all wars. The two kinds of objectors are the same because of their common desire to preserve peace and eliminate war. Manton rather incongruously illustrated that equation by asserting that a distinction between just and unjust war could be found in international law and in the recent Kellogg-Briand Peace Treaty, ratified 15 January 1929. Manton declared rights of conscience to be inalienable and out of the reach of government; for that assertion he cited the famous Supreme Court justice and constitutional scholar Joseph Story: "The rights of conscience are, indeed, beyond the just reach of any human power. They are given by God and cannot be encroached upon by human authority, without a criminal disobedience of the precepts of natural, as well as revealed religion."[44]

According to the Court of Appeals, a person who refuses to enter military service because of conscientious scruples, so long as there is no effort to obstruct the war effort or to persuade others to do so, does not act against either society or the Constitution. Whether the objector is a member of a sect that teaches conscientious objection does not matter. While membership in a peace church is convincing evidence of religious scruples against participation in warfare, nonmembership in such a group does not suggest that one is incapable of possessing such scruples. The government should not treat applicants for citizenship differently than native-born citizens. "No more is demanded of an alien who becomes a citizen than a natural-born citizen, and, when an alien becomes a citizen, he is accorded all the rights and privileges afforded to a natural-born citizen except eligibility to the presidency."[45]

Finally, Manton distinguished Macintosh from Schwimmer. She was a strict pacifist; Macintosh was willing to fight in wars he considered just. She was an atheist, Macintosh based his conscientious objection on his understanding of the will of God. "From his answers," Manton wrote, Macintosh "indicates an upright sense of obligation to his God, and has carefully explained his willingness to be a citizen of the United States, assuming the responsibilities and obligations of its form of government." Meanwhile Macintosh had exhibited "a high regard for his general duty to humanity. He wishes to keep pure his religious scruples." The Court of Appeals therefore concluded that his "application for citizenship should have been granted. The order is reversed, with directions to the District Court to admit appellant to citizenship."[46]

Apparently responding to a note of thanks for his argument that led to this victory, John W. Davis wrote to Macintosh, "I am as much gratified by the decision as you can be, and I consider it a privilege to have been afforded an opportunity to argue the case."[47] William Lyon Phelps, a professor of English literature at Yale and a committed, public Christian, wrote to "confess I was surprised at the decision of the U.S. Court of Appeals, but how I rejoice in it! HURRAH!" Phelps thought that Macintosh had accomplished a "great thing":

you have brought the Christian religion into contact with its most dangerous and powerful enemy, the religion of nationalism. And you have won a great victory. I did not think you would get the decision. But even if you had not, you would have accomplished what you set out to do. You have done more for the Christian religion than can be expressed in words.

"I am proud to know you," Phelps concluded, "and that you belong to Yale."[48]

Several major newspapers carried the story of Macintosh's victory at the Court of Appeals,[49] but few commented on the case. In *The Open Road*, the "official organ of the Society of the Universal Brotherhood of Man," Bruce T. Calvert lamented the decision, thinking it gave preference to religious objectors. In *Schwimmer* an atheist pacifist had been denied citizenship, but the Court of Appeals had now awarded citizenship to one whose decision to participate in war would be based on his awareness of the will of God. "A God-spooked, fundamentalist religioner is entitled to conscientious scruples," Calvert wrote. "A free thinker, atheist or agnostic, is not." Calvert faulted the Court of Appeals for "putting God into the Constitution . . . and setting up a religious test for citizenship, a thing the founders intended forever to prohibit." If the decision "does not wreck our Constitution I don't see what could."[50]

Taking note of similar press commentary and assuming that the government would appeal his case to the Supreme Court, Macintosh wrote to Charles Poletti, a member of his legal team, crafting an argument that would not rely on an appeal to God and offering it for their consideration, if they should need it. Macintosh said that his objection to a promise in advance to fight in any and all wars was a moral argument that could be made without reference to God. He interpreted duty as God's will, but it was also possible to cast duty in secular terms. One is morally obligated to do whatever one can for human welfare, but "it is not this explicitly religious consideration which first makes the moral law binding; as moral it is binding already, whether one believes in a moral Lawgiver or not." On these grounds, one could take exactly the same position on bearing arms for the country, even if he did not believe in the existence of God. In this light, "it becomes clear that a favorable decision in my case does not involve imposing subscription to any particular religious creed, even belief in God, as a condition of admission to citizenship."

Poletti responded that he, Davis, and Wardwell had read Macintosh's argument with interest. They had not yet decided the tack they would take in making the argument to the Supreme Court. Poletti agreed with Macintosh that the government would probably argue that the Court of Appeals' decision established a religious test for naturalization. "I believe we can crush such an argument."[51] As it happened, the government did not use that argument.

The United States filed a petition for the Supreme Court to grant a writ of certiorari on 7 October 1930. The Court agreed on 24 November 1930 to hear the case. The government's argument in its brief laying out its case against Macintosh, submitted over the name of the Solicitor General, Thomas D. Thacher, was fairly simple. Macintosh did not deserve to be naturalized because he had reserved to himself the right to determine when he would fight in a war and therefore did not conform to the requirements of the Naturalization Act of 1906.

The Court of Appeals had held that once a person is admitted to citizenship, that person has equal rights with the native-born citizen. That means that "his conscientious or religious scruples against bearing arms *prior* to naturalization should be as tenderly regarded as if he were a citizen." The government's brief to the Supreme Court argued that the Court of Appeals was wrong. The only grounds on which a person may be granted citizenship are those explicitly contained in the Naturalization Act, which do not make any exceptions for those who have conscientious scruples against participating in warfare. The Court of Appeals had wrongly asserted that Macintosh was a religiously based conscientious objector! Macintosh from the beginning had argued that he was not a pacifist, distinguishing himself from the thoroughgoing pacifists denied citizenship in *Schwimmer*. He was not a pacifist because he was willing to participate in wars he considered to be just, as his own service in World War I showed. Now the government turned that argument back on him. Because he wanted to judge for himself about the justification of a war, he was not opposed to all war on the basis of conscientious or religious scruples. Apparently the Department of Justice believed that an individual's judgment about whether a war is just could not be based on religious beliefs. "The position of respondent is *merely* that of a highly educated man with that deep sense of right and wrong which every applicant for citizenship is presumed to possess, seeking to transfer from Congress to himself, the right to determine whether the defense of this country requires him to bear arms." If he seeks to transfer that determination to himself rather than Congress, he does not conform to the Naturalization Law. Applicants for citizenship cannot be naturalized unless they have strictly complied with statutory requirements.

In passing, the brief noted that not only did Macintosh reserve to himself the judgment as to whether or not he would fight in a particular war, but he also reserved to himself any decision about whether or not he would engage in propaganda against any war he considered unjust.[52] This, without mentioning the case, also tied him to a behavior rejected by the Supreme Court in *Schwimmer*.

According to the government's brief, Macintosh's inability to take the oath of naturalization without mental reservation mitigates the nature of the oath itself. An oath has no sanction, no authority, if it is taken with mental reservations. When, on question 20 of the preliminary form, Macintosh was asked "Are you willing to take this oath in becoming a citizen?" he answered "Yes." Yet he could not answer affirmatively "unless his interpretation of the oath was adopted." To allow him to interpret the oath for himself freed him "to use his own judgment, or follow his own conscience as to what were the best interests of the United States." Macintosh had testified that "his judgment and conscience in this respect would be governed by his views as to the best interests of humanity." The oath was now meaningless.

> It is difficult to conceive of a more vague and intangible basis for allegiance than this. . . . It is not the degree or quality of qualification or reservation in taking the statutory oath which governs. Such an oath can not be taken with any qualifications or reservations if the statute is to be satisfied.[53]

In *United States v. Schwimmer* the Supreme Court had decreed that to qualify for citizenship one must be willing to bear arms. That decision, the government now argued, made it simply impossible for one who wants to become a citizen to avoid military service because of conscientious or religious views. The Court of Appeals had granted Macintosh citizenship because Congress had provided exemptions for native-born citizens who were conscientious objectors, declaring that no more should be required of an applicant for citizenship than for a natural-born citizen. The Department of Justice now called that argument irrelevant. "The test is not what rights are permitted to citizens after citizenship," the government asserted, "but what requirements are imposed by the naturalization statutes." The United States deal with "conscientious objectors whom we have among our citizens . . . in the best way possible, but the naturalization statutes afford no ground for inferring that Congress intended to show the slightest tolerance for the individual view of alien applications which might interfere with full and complete performance of the duties of citizenship."[54]

Aside from what motivated them to object to war, religiously informed conscience or conscience alone, the government saw *Schwimmer* and Macintosh's case as exactly parallel and the differences between them as "superficial." Whether one admired or condemned their motives for refusing to bear arms, "the fact remains that in each case the applicant was willing to assume only a qualified allegiance." If then "unwillingness to bear arms in all wars disqualifies an alien for citizenship," as the government contended that the Court had held in *Schwimmer*, Macintosh's "somewhat more discriminating unwillingness to bear arms . . . is an equal disqualification." The government found "inconceivable" the prospect "that any naturalizing court may transfer from Congress to the citizen applicant the power to determine the necessity of war or the obligatory duty of the citizen to bear defensive arms."[55]

For all these reasons, it seemed clear that Macintosh could not wholeheartedly swear "to support and defend the Constitution and laws of the United States against all enemies, foreign and domestic" and satisfy the Court that he was "attached to the principles of the Constitution" as required by law. Consequently, the Solicitor General urged the Supreme Court to reverse the Court of Appeals and affirm the decision of the District Court.

The brief for Macintosh, prepared by John W. Davis's firm and considerably more elaborate than the government's, concentrated on four points. First, it asserted that Congress had not demanded that applicants for citizenship promise in advance to bear arms in any and all future wars. Congress had, at various times, excluded Chinese, those who are opposed to organized government, and polygamists, among others. But Congress had never explicitly excluded those with conscientious objections to war, although it could have done so. Although the government had claimed that Macintosh had attempted to vitiate the oath of naturalization by taking it with mental reservations, Macintosh's legal team pointed out that at no time had he sought to alter the oath; he was willing to take it as it was written. One does not take an oath with mental reservation unless one's beliefs and attitudes are inconsistent with the oath. Since the Constitution and statutes did not demand that an applicant for citizenship bear arms contrary to religious objections, his lawyers argued that Macintosh's mental reservations were not inconsistent with the oath.

Taking a different tack, Macintosh's lawyers pointed out that when the Constitution and the statutes mention an oath, they also provide opportunity for a person to make affirmation rather than swear—principally out of deference to Quakers, who historically have conscientiously objected to war. The oath of allegiance required of all persons being naturalized is essentially the same as that administered to all public officials, except the President. Article 2, sec. 1 of the Constitution details the words the President is to say on taking office, but allows choice of "oath or affirmation." Article 6 of the Constitution requires that all office holders "shall be bound by Oath or Affirmation." Such language implies that those having religious objections to war are not to be excluded from any public office, even the presidency. Furthermore, Article 6 specifically excludes any "religious Test . . . as a Qualification to any office or public Trust under the United States." Macintosh's counsel concluded that since Congress did not preclude persons "with conscientious religious scruples against bearing arms" from swearing or affirming an oath of office or an oath of allegiance, "it is idle to contend that the respondent in entertaining such scruples 'refused to take the oath without qualification or mental reservation' and that consequently he should be denied citizenship."[56]

Although the government had attempted to show that Macintosh objected to unjust wars only on his own judgment rather than on defined religious scruples, his lawyers argued that Macintosh had explicitly asserted in his statement before the District Court that "his first allegiance was to the will of God, defined as what was morally right and for the ultimate well-being of humanity." Macintosh's decision not to bear arms "is dictated solely and directly by what he considers to be the will of God speaking through his conscience." On that foundation "any attempt by the Government to assert that the respondent does not act from religious scruples is unjustified by the facts."[57]

As its second major point, the brief supporting Macintosh's case asserts that the Constitution and the laws of the United States do not require a person to bear arms over religious objections. The argument begins with a survey of laws of several of the original states before ratification of the Constitution, showing that they rather uniformly made some provision for those who had religious objections to military service. It then turns to the debate in the First Congress. James Madison, acutely conscious of concerns in the various states to accommodate matters of conscience, introduced into the House on 8 June 1789 a list of amendments to the Constitution, including language that would excuse from military service those who had religious scruples against such service. Deeming brevity of language necessary, Congress "merged and incorporated" the provision for excusing objectors from bearing arms "into Article I of the Bill of Rights." A survey of laws pertaining to formation of militias and conscription of soldiers for them "further proves that the Constitution and laws of the United States have *always* recognized that persons having religious scruples against bearing arms need not do so." Many states incorporated the same principle in their constitutions after formation of the United States. Although the Supreme Court had established the government's constitutional "right to compel military service from its citizens . . . the Constitution and laws of the United States recognize that along side this general principle exists an exception—a privilege that persons with conscientious religious scruples need not bear arms."[58]

Continuing on this point, the brief notes that the Court's previous interpretations of the Free Exercise Clause of the First Amendment in *Reynolds v. United States*[59] and *Davis v. Beason*[60] support Macintosh's request for exemption from bearing arms. Those cases articulate a principle that free exercise of religion may be limited by government, but only when religious behavior contravenes the peace and good order of society. Conscientious objection to war, particularly selective conscientious objection such as Macintosh's, is not religious behavior inimical to the welfare of society, especially since most people are willing to fight in any and all wars. Legal precedent demonstrated "that the constitutional protection of religious freedom does embrace conscientious scruples against bearing arms in a war." Macintosh's lawyers could not see

> the slightest indication that this Court would countenance any attempt by Congress to compel a citizen to flout the will of God and commit what in his sincere belief is none other than murder. The distinction between prohibiting an overt act against peace and good order and ordering affirmative action is not a shallow one.[61]

Since not all wars are just, it is logical to think that some citizens should have religiously based conscientious objections to unjust wars. The distinction between just and unjust wars is recognized in international law and in the recently ratified Kellogg-Briand Peace Treaty. His lawyers found the kind of distinction Macintosh makes embedded in the law of the land. Sensitivity to the consciences of citizens is embodied in the Ninth Amendment to the Constitution, which assumes rights that are not granted to government are "retained by the people."[62] For all these reasons, the Constitution and laws of the United States protect conscientious objections to bearing arms.

In its third point Macintosh's brief argues that the government may not require an applicant for citizenship to forego a privilege held by native-born citizens. The government must treat citizens and applicants for citizenship alike. A naturalized citizen enjoys all the privileges of the native-born except eligibility for the presidency.[63] Naturalization is not a favor the government confers. Once Congress has established conditions for citizenship, "the alien has a right which no court can deny him."[64] To require an applicant for citizenship to promise to bear arms in wars against which he might have religious scruples puts that person in an unequal relationship to the native-born. As a price of citizenship an applicant must relinquish a privilege enjoyed by the natural-born citizen. "That is the manifest result of the fixed principle of our Constitution, zealously guarded by our laws, that a citizen cannot be forced and need not bear arms in a war if he has conscientious scruples against doing so."[65] We shall have occasion to recall that language.

Finally, the brief asserts that the decision of the Court of Appeals granting Macintosh citizenship is consistent with *United States v. Schwimmer*. Professor Macintosh and Mme. Schwimmer were very different people. Invidiously the brief casts Schwimmer in the worst possible light. Recalling her statements that she had "no sense of nationalism," "no nationalistic feeling," and "only a cosmic consciousness of belonging to the human family,"[66] the brief concludes that she would not "recognize or give to the United States the modicum of allegiance" that citizens should. On the other hand, Macintosh had testified to the District Court "that he was ready to give to the United States, in return for citizenship, all the allegiance he . . . ever could give to any country, but that he could not put allegiance to the government of any country before allegiance to the will of God."[67] (These words are almost identical to Schwimmer's. At her hearing before the District Court she said: "I am willing to do everything that an American citizen has to do except fighting. . . . I am not willing to bear arms. In every other single way I am ready to follow the law and do everything the law compels American citizens to do."[68] The difference between these two applicants was in Macintosh's reliance on religion and his willingness to fight in just wars, not in the extent of the allegiance they offered to America.) The brief says that no thinking Christian could promise more to the country than Macintosh had. It also pointed out that, unlike Schwimmer, Macintosh was willing to fight in wars he thought were justified, as his war record showed; unlike Schwimmer, he was not a pacifist.

The government had noticed that Macintosh did not unequivocally promise that he would not engage in antiwar propaganda. His lawyers responded that he claimed no more than any citizen guaranteed freedom of speech by the Constitution. He does not want to promise to forfeit his rightful freedom of speech. "More and more it becomes evident that the government contends in this case for the naturalization only of persons who will become uniform, unthinking, slavish robots. The government would demand that right and wrong, God and conscience be bent to nationalism. It is a doctrine fit only for despots." The Supreme Court can hold to its precedent in *Schwimmer*, that citizens must bear arms in times of necessity in defense of the country. Macintosh agrees with it. But in *Schwimmer* the Court did not hold that one must promise in advance to violate one's conscience.[69]

An *amicus curiae* brief filed by the American Friends Service Committee, reflecting the views of the Society of Friends, framed the issue of this case in terms of the historic teaching of Jesus, that his followers are to give to Caesar what is Caesar's and to God what is God's. This presents a threefold problem: "(1) What is the duty to God? (2) What is the duty to the Civil Authority? (3) How can these duties be harmonized? Treason is a great wickedness, but not less awful is breach of faith with Jehovah."[70]

The Friends' brief assumes that the government, in this case, asserts that the state is absolute, that no exception is allowed to the sovereignty of the state, and offers a history lesson in what happens when states are declared to be all-powerful. "The voice we are quoting is the voice of the learned Assistant District Attorney who argued the Macintosh case in the Circuit Court of Appeals, but the hand is the Iron Hand of Prussian history." The brief then recounts several instances in history when people of conscience and courage stood up against absolute government.

The oath of naturalization itself requires a would-be citizen to promise "to support and defend the Constitution and laws of the United States." War does not need to be in progress for the Constitution and laws to need defense. Such defense can be accomplished in ways other than bearing arms. That such defense is understood only in military terms is simply a reaction to World War I. The oath did not have that meaning from the 1790 Naturalization Act through the Act of 1906. Only recently did it acquire such a militaristic interpretation.

After briefly explaining that one can be religious and object to war without being a member of a "peace church" such as the Society of Friends, the brief concludes, "There is no duty in Christian ethics so profound as obedience to conscience. . . . This Court should not declare the oath or affirmation to mean 'I promise to render unto Caesar the things which are God's.'"[71]

John W. Davis argued Macintosh's case before the Supreme Court on 27 April 1931, pointing out how ridiculous it was to expect that all persons applying for naturalization should promise to bear arms. He suggested that priests, nurses, women with young children, and handicapped in wheelchairs ought to be exempt. He told the Justices that "what we want now is not more men who agree with the majority but [more] who are willing to go against the majority on occasion." He stressed the government's inconsistency as a leader in formulating the Kellogg-Briand Treaty renouncing war as a means of settling international disputes while demanding commitment to war from Macintosh and other applicants for citizenship.[72]

Solicitor General Thomas D. Thacher, arguing the government's case, also pointed to inconsistency. When Davis, as Solicitor General, had argued the *Selective Draft Law* cases,[73] he had asserted that it is a citizen's duty to defend the country by bearing arms. Now he was claiming that rights of conscience, including a choice to not bear arms, are inalienable rights. Later Davis said that he did not retract what he had argued earlier. Thacher acknowledged that the government's only problem with Macintosh was his reliance on his own judgment in deciding whether to bear arms; in every other way "we most frankly concede that he is an estimable Christian gentleman."[74]

Davis was disappointed in his performance. "The truth is," he wrote to a colleague, "I feel this case so deeply that it is hard for me to do it justice." Davis thought himself "sufficiently irreligious . . . to have a profound respect for the religion of others, and the result reached in this case seemed to me so absurd from any standpoint of practicality—having so little relation, indeed, to the personality and fitness of the applicant—that I get hot all over whenever I think about it."[75]

The Court announced its decision on 25 May 1931, five to four against Macintosh. Justice George Sutherland wrote for the Court, Chief Justice Charles Evans Hughes in dissent. Appointed to the Court by President Warren G. Harding in 1922, Justice Sutherland had served one term in the U.S. House of Representatives and two terms in the Senate from Utah. Sutherland came on the Court with a "conservative" reputation and joined with other conservative Justices. He tended to argue for individual rights against government interference,[76] but in this case he placed congressional power above individual conscience.[77]

"Naturalization is a privilege," Sutherland asserted, "to be given, qualified, or withheld as Congress may determine, and which the alien may claim as of right only upon compliance with the terms which Congress imposes."[78] He proceeded to justify government inquiry into applicants' beliefs on certain issues, including whether they are willing to bear arms in national defense, in order to determine whether they are fit to become good citizens. Part of being a good citizen is to be willing to support the government in war as well as peace, and a prospective citizen must be ready to help defend the country, "not to the extent or in the manner he may choose, but to such extent and in such manner as he lawfully may be required to do." Macintosh had been examined and found to be of good character and conduct. The case revolved on his willingness to participate in national defense. After reviewing Macintosh's statements in his application and in the hearing before the District Court, Sutherland concluded that he was unwilling to take the naturalization oath except on his own terms. Consequently, the case would be decided by *Schwimmer*, in which the Court had ruled that it is the duty of citizens to defend the country by force of arms when it becomes necessary. Also, when objectors to war influence other people to do the same, that may be more harmful to the nation than their own refusal to participate in war. Because Macintosh qualified his willingness to fight or to refrain from propaganda, *Schwimmer* required that he be denied.[79]

Sutherland acknowledged that war is a terrible thing and peace is to be desired by all civilized people. Yet, so far in human history, the impulse to war has seemed to be stronger than the inclination to peace. Consequently, the Founders wrote war powers into the Constitution; one of its purposes is to "provide for the common defense." And when the nation calls to implement the war powers of the Constitution, there can be no exceptions to service except for those provided in the Constitution itself or in international law. Whatever exemptions from waging war there may be must be derived from acts of Congress, not from the scruples of any individual.[80] The Congress had repeatedly made exemptions for native-born conscientious objectors. That record had been so long it seemed that some thought the situation was permanent. That was particularly so in this case. Then Sutherland quoted a rather long passage from "the carefully prepared brief of respondent," focusing on a crucial sentence: "it is the manifest result of the fixed principle of our Constitution, zealously guarded by our laws, that a citizen cannot be forced and need not bear arms in a war if he has conscientious scruples against doing so." Sutherland professed himself astounded by "an astonishing statement." He found "no such principle of the Constitution, fixed or otherwise." In the view of the Court's majority, "The conscientious objector is relieved from the obligation to bear arms in obedience to no constitutional provision, express or implied; but because, and only because, it has accorded with the policy of Congress thus to relieve him."[81]

Contemporary news accounts of the reading of this opinion report that Sutherland raised his voice to emphasize some points.[82] This was surely one of those places. Following hard on that was another, in which Justice Sutherland delivered an astonishing statement of his own, probably raising his voice. Sutherland declared that the flaw in Macintosh's attitude toward defending the country was that he wanted to reserve to himself the judgment as to when he should fight. Macintosh wanted to base his choice on the will of God. God's will, Sutherland countered, must encompass something more than Macintosh's private judgment.

> When he speaks of putting his allegiance to the will of God above his allegiance to the government, it is evident, in the light of his entire statement, that he means to make *his own interpretation* of the will of God the decisive test which shall conclude the government and stay its hand. We are a Christian people (*Holy Trinity Church v. United States* 143 U.S. 457, 470-471), according to one another the equal right of religious freedom, and acknowledging with reverence the duty of obedience to the will of God. But, also, we are a Nation with the duty to survive; a Nation whose Constitution contemplates war as well as peace; whose government must go forward upon the assumption, and safely can proceed upon no other, that unqualified allegiance to the Nation and submission and obedience to the laws of the land, as well those made for war as those made for peace, are not inconsistent with the will of God.[83]

To affirm Macintosh in his heresy against the civil religion of "unqualified allegiance," Sutherland wrote, would take the Court down a slippery slope. Macintosh refused to take the oath except in an altered form, a form consistent with his understanding of just war. If his attitude were to prevail, if the Court should allow him citizenship, where should the line be drawn? The courts would be bargaining continually with applicants for naturalization. "It is not within the province of the courts to make bargains with those who seek naturalization. They must accept the grant and take the oath in accordance with the terms fixed by the law, or forego the privilege of citizenship." Professor Macintosh refused to accept the terms of the oath as prescribed by law. He must forego citizenship.[84]

Chief Justice Charles Evans Hughes served on the Supreme Court as an Associate Justice from 1910 to 1916, having been appointed by President William Howard Taft. He resigned from the Court to run for President, but was defeated by Woodrow Wilson. He served as Secretary of State under Presidents Harding and Coolidge. He was appointed Chief Justice by Herbert Hoover, serving from 1930 until 1941. In his confirmation some progressive senators depicted Hughes as conservative and a lawyer subservient to corporate interests. His dissent in *Macintosh*, some news articles pointed out, as his first dissent allied him with the more liberal wing of the Court.[85]

Like Macintosh, Hughes was a Baptist, reared in a pious home, who entered college to study for the ministry. As frequently happens to students, Hughes changed his mind and, by the time of graduation, he wrote to his parents that he no longer desired the ministry as a profession, but wanted to pursue a career in law. Baptists in those days strongly emphasized religious liberty, and apparently Hughes remained faithful to that emphasis on "soul freedom" throughout his life. In his presidential address to the American Bar Association in 1925 Hughes called attention to the ominous growth of a spirit of intolerance. That dreadful tendency could "be exorcised only by . . . the American spirit of civil and religious liberty." To be faithful "to the ideal of religious liberty the power of government is not to be used to propagate religious doctrines or to interfere with the liberty of the citizen in order to maintain religious doctrines." Power exercised on behalf of religion could be brutal, for "If kings and princes, or the legislative majorities which have succeeded them, may enter the domain of conscience it is certain that they will make this entry with the most fiery zeal, the most profound conviction, the most ruthless determination of which the human heart is capable." Hughes concluded that "The highest interests of the soul demand freedom, not fetters, and the immunity of the domain of conscience from the control of government is the assurance of the richest fruitage of the spiritual life."[86]

Hughes began his dissent (closely following Macintosh's brief) by acknowledging that citizenship is a privilege that the government may grant or withhold, that Congress sets the conditions by which citizenship may be granted, and even that Congress has the authority to require an applicant for citizenship to promise to bear arms in the event of war. But Hughes questioned whether Congress had, in fact, required such a promise. For him, the answer was clearly "No." To provide clarity and certainty, Congress should express its intent on the matter in explicit language, as it had on other matters, such as excluding polygamists. It had not done so. Macintosh was unjustly denied citizenship because he had expressed no forbidden belief or behavior, while Congress had not explicitly required a promise to bear arms.

Hughes noted that the oath of naturalization is essentially the same as the oath required of officeholders and similar to that required of the President. The officeholder promised "that I will support and defend the Constitution of the United States against all enemies, foreign and domestic; that I will bear true faith and allegiance to the same." Since Article 6 of the Constitution stipulates that "no religious Test shall ever be required as a Qualification to any Office or public Trust under the United States" and since many have struggled heroically to establish and maintain religious freedom, it is impossible that Congress should frame the oath to require a religious test. Congress had not required those with religiously based objections to war to promise to fight as a condition of being naturalized. There are other ways of defending the country than actually wielding arms. Native-born office holders are not required by their oath to violate their religious beliefs or practices, or their consciences. The naturalization oath should be understood in the same way, given that the language of the two oaths is virtually identical. Applicants for citizenship should be treated the same as native office holders, not differently.[87]

Hughes did not allow Sutherland's identification of the will of the government with the will of God to go unanswered. He acknowledged that government has the power to enforce obedience to laws in spite of private scruples. "When one's belief collides with the power of the State, the latter is supreme within its sphere and submission or punishment follows," Hughes wrote. "But, in the forum of conscience, duty to a moral power higher than the State has always been maintained." One's relation to God involves "duties superior to those arising from any human relation." Citing the opinion of Justice Stephen J. Field, in *Davis v. Beason*—"The term 'religion' has reference to one's views of his relations to his Creator, and to the obligations they impose of reverence for his being and character and of obedience to his will."[88]—Hughes asserted that "One cannot speak of religious liberty, with proper appreciation of its essential and historic significance, without assuming the existence of a belief in a supreme allegiance to the will of God." Beyond "dogmas with their particular conceptions of deity, freedom of conscience itself implies respect for an innate conviction of paramount duty." Hughes found

> abundant room for enforcing the requisite authority of law as it is enacted and requires obedience, and for maintaining the conception of the supremacy of law as essential to orderly government, without demanding that either citizens or applicants for citizenship shall assume by oath an obligation to regard allegiance to God as subordinate to allegiance to civil power.[89]

Congress had historically sought to preserve religious liberty, and Hughes could see no evidence that its intention had been reversed in the naturalization oath.

The government had made much of Macintosh's refusal to promise to fight in those wars he considered unjust, claiming that he would take the oath with mental reservations. Hughes found no grounds for exclusion in this, for Macintosh's attitude was not novel. Many people of great political importance have held similar views. If Congress had recognized refusal to fight in all wars as legitimate, as it had in conscription laws and, at least by implication, in the oath of office, there was no reason why it could not be equally solicitous of those who object only to some wars. "Attachment to the principles of the Constitution" is not inherently opposed to freedom of conscience.

Finally, in two sentences, Hughes disposed of *United States v. Schwimmer*. That case rested on special facts, but it does not require reversal of the decision in favor of Macintosh by the Court of Appeals, which decision should be affirmed.[90] (For the text of the opinion, see Appendix K.)

Justices Oliver Wendell Holmes, Louis Brandeis, and Harlan Fiske Stone joined Chief Justice Hughes in dissent. The prestige of these Justices did not prevail. Professor Macintosh was denied citizenship.

On the day after the decision was announced, John W. Davis wrote one line to Macintosh: "I blush for my country." Other members of Davis's law firm also wrote. Allen Wardwell said that they felt strongly about the case and were frustrated by the decision, but he was glad they had the opportunity to make the fight. Charles Poletti was surprised by the breadth of Justice Sutherland's opinion, effectively making all citizens subservient to the state, regardless of their religious convictions. "At any rate, I feel that you should be partly elated by the realization that your case has permitted us to learn from the august Supreme Court how inconsequential a citizen's personal feelings are." Dean Clark of Yale Law School told Macintosh that his case now had been before thirteen judges, seven of whom had decided in his favor. Clark thought lawyers everywhere would say that those who found in favor of Macintosh had considerably more ability than those who had decided against him. He noted that the case elicited one of the ablest opinions of the Chief Justice, one that far overshadowed "the very drab" effort of the majority. Yet Clark lamented that Justice Owen Roberts had voted with the majority. He had previously tended to vote with more liberal members of the Court. Clark assumed that Justice Roberts voted against Macintosh because of "some emotional complex he had. I still hope he is out of place in the company which he is now keeping."[91]

Newspapers throughout the United States carried the story of Macintosh's defeat. In an interview a United Press reporter found Professor Macintosh "disappointed but philosophical." When told "that his stand had won the support of the famous liberal trio of the supreme court [*sic*]—Holmes, Brandeis, and Stone and caused Chief Justice Hughes to align himself with the minority and write his first dissenting opinion," Macintosh's "face brightened with evident satisfaction." He told the reporter, "I'm not budging from my stand one bit. . . . I will make no further attempt to obtain citizenship if my point of view is unacceptable."[92] Apparently Macintosh gave only this interview concerning the case. One newspaper mentioned that he steadfastly refused to talk about it. Julian N. Hartt, who became Macintosh's graduate student in 1937 and remained in close contact until he died, reminisced in 1978 that Macintosh was reluctant to talk about his case. Hartt recalled Macintosh as "a person of daunting reserve."[93] Surely he was disappointed in his defeat. His frustration surfaced in 1939, in a preface to his *Social Religion*, an application of religion to social problems: "[T]his overgrown volume is the abnormal expression of my repressed (or suppressed) desire to vote!"[94]

In the weeks immediately following the decision, journalists gave the case considerable attention. Marie Averil Bland's case had been proceeding through the courts and had been argued and decided in tandem with Macintosh's. As a psychiatric nurse Bland had gone to France to treat "shell-shocked soldiers" among the American forces for some nine months after the war. From this experience and her strong Christian faith (she was Episcopalian), she came to the conviction that war was contrary to the ethics of Christ. Unlike Macintosh, she was a pacifist, objecting to fighting in any war, although she would be quite willing to be a nurse in wartime.

A native of Canada, she applied for citizenship and was denied. The District Court cited *Schwimmer* as precedent. The Court of Appeals for the Second Circuit, the same judges who heard Macintosh's case, awarded her and Macintosh citizenship on the same day. Her case was argued before the Supreme Court the same day as Macintosh's and was decided the same day. She was also denied citizenship. Both the opinion and the dissent in her case were quite brief, for all acknowledged that the decision in her case was controlled by the reasoning in *Macintosh*. I shall examine her case in Chapter Five.[95]

Press coverage of the two cases focused on Macintosh. He was, after all, a much more public person than Bland, and all the interesting rhetoric emerged in the majority and dissenting opinions in his case. Some accounts ignored Bland's case entirely. Yet when, on the day after the decision, the *Washington Daily News* reported that "U.S. Won't Deport Professor, Nurse, Denied Citizenship," both may have taken some comfort in that. But the same article also reported that the Labor Department, which oversaw naturalization, would henceforth be more aggressive in barring pacifists from citizenship.[96]

Just as secular press coverage began to wane, Bland's and Macintosh's attorneys decided to petition the Supreme Court to rehear the cases, hoping to persuade Justice Roberts to change his votes and overturn the five to four decisions. The request for rehearing stimulated another round of newspaper articles, as did the Court's decision, on 12 October 1931, to deny a rehearing.[97]

Journalists not only reported facts of the Court decisions, filing of petitions, and denials of them, but also offered editorial commentary. Syndicated columnist Heywood Broun wrote of the Justices, "nine human beings concerned in handing down a verdict," that they "behaved in accordance with their glandular alignment and their personal prejudices." Yet Broun found "no nine men in any kind of robes . . . sufficiently powerful to alter the fact that the chief duty of the individual is not and never has been to the Constitution alone. There is no sort of law or amendment which can wipe out the human conscience."[98]

The Baltimore Sun responded in typically Menckensque rhetoric: "As an expression of a national ideal, the decision of the majority of the Supreme Court of these United States is disheartening. They have made the nation safe for morons." The *Tacoma Ledger* was pleased that President Hoover's "Quaker family got into this country before the Supreme Court delivered that arms-bearing decision." In Salem, Oregon, the *Statesman* declared, "The court draws the line on finespun and senseless theory while opening the floodgates to the riff-raff of the world."[99] Jerome Davis, a Yale Divinity School colleague of Macintosh and a theologian and sociologist by training, wrote an article showing that many naturalized immigrants were problems for the society, offering statistics and historical examples of how many new citizens were in trouble with the law, were dependent on the state, or were unemployed; scientific support for the "riff-raff" argument. Davis strongly criticized the immigration and naturalization process, in order to reveal the bitter irony that Macintosh—good, intelligent, productive—had been denied citizenship while many ne'er-do-wells received it.[100] The *New York Times* expressed doubt that the decision denying Macintosh citizenship would pass the "rule of reason," given Macintosh's character.[101] *The People's Business* depicted Jesus in the Supreme Court room, listening to the *Schwimmer* and *Macintosh* decisions being read.

> A smile, half of pity, half of humor plays upon His face. The smile vanishes. He murmurs, "Inexcusable." He steps up and across the small room and around behind the Bench. As the Court turns its questioning eyes upon Him, with His ageless finger He touches the forehead, first of Justice Butler and then of Justice Sutherland, saying to them, one after the other, in the calm, commanding voice of one delivering the opinion of the Judge Eternal, "THOU FOOL."[102]

In Reading, Pennsylvania, the *Labor Advocate* favored "a new declaration of 'inalienable right' which will confirm the right of judges to be perfect asses." After examination of the majority and dissenting opinions "we favor conferring the degree of Doctor of Asinity upon members of the majority."[103] The *Milwaukee Leader* found the decision "a strong assertion of the theory of the legitimate authority of the state to overrule any and all scruples of individual conscience."[104]

Not all the editorial comment in the secular press supported Macintosh. Many agreed with the decision, arguing that those applying for citizenship want something from the country and ought to be willing to give something in return. "After all," the *Ann Arbor News* declared, Bland and Macintosh "have no inherent right to become Americans." The nation, not individuals must set "the conditions for citizenship." Any who find the conditions a "hardship . . . too severe . . . are privileged to change their minds." When crises come, the nation "has a right to expect every citizen to perform his duty." Natives "cannot be required to fight" when "naturalized citizens" are "given immunity." The *News* echoed a common refrain: "If America is worth living in, it is worth fighting for."[105]

Also in Michigan, the *Pontiac Press* agreed: "No one wants war and no one wants oppression, but when the structure of the democracy is threatened, under which thrive our liberties, base, indeed, is the man or woman who will not lend a shoulder to its support. No other sort is entitled to American citizenship."[106] The *Philadelphia Record*, in a column sensitive to the complexities of the cases, finally supported the decision. One could assume that Macintosh and Bland were people of high quality, but personal excellence is not the issue. Naturalized citizens share equal obligations with native-born citizens. "True liberalism champions individual rights—but does not exalt them to the point of countenancing philosophic anarchism."[107]

Predictably Rosika Schwimmer's old enemy, *The Woman Patriot* ("Dedicated to the defense of the Family and the State AGAINST Feminism and Socialism"), vigorously approved the Macintosh decision, publishing the full texts of *Macintosh* and *Bland* and commenting on them. Far beyond the particular conscientious objections to war of the plaintiffs, these cases concerned the power of government, especially its war power. The power to compel is inherent in government, especially in war. Macintosh, Schwimmer, and Bland would limit that power with their conscientious objections. The *Patriot* did not focus on citizenship questions so much as on the potential of these objections to war to "stay the hand" of government. Objectors "seek to *'stay the hand'* of the Government in defending its existence, and to abolish the war power of Congress to compel military service!" Macintosh and his allies are really tools of the "slacker organizations," principally the ACLU, to challenge the war powers of Congress. "The Baldwin [Roger Baldwin, director of the ACLU]-Schwimmer scheme ever since 1917 has been to give *organized slackers* a 'constitutional right' to refuse either to fight or to 'knit a sock, nurse a soldier or buy a bond' in defense of the United States in the 'next war.'" These cases have enormous scope, since objectors attempt to destroy the war power of government, and no government can survive, remain sovereign, without its power to compel, especially in time of war. The Court rightly decided the Macintosh case, holding off "slacker organizations" for another day.[108]

Prominent ministers mentioned the case in sermons and some devoted entire sermons to it. Dr. Harry Emerson Fosdick, pastor of the Riverside Church in New York, said that he, like Macintosh, would not support a morally wrong war. He affirmed Chief Justice Hughes's dissent as representative of true religion and true Americanism. He noted that the dissent represented the thinking of the stronger Justices of the Court. Just a few days after the decision was announced, Fosdick also articulated a theme repeatedly asserted by the religious community. The decision "announces in a particularly obnoxious form the doctrine of the nation's right to conscript conscience. . . . The nation in war time will conscript our children, conscript our property, conscript our business. . . . Has the nation, however, so taken the place of God Almighty that it can conscript our consciences?" The Reverend George A. Crapullo, pastor of the Irvin Square Presbyterian Church in Brooklyn, supposed that "If Jesus were here today and applied for American citizenship, he would be politely informed that he was not eligible." Pro-Macintosh sermons were preached by the Rev. Lester Ward Auman at First Methodist Church of Jamaica, Queens; and by Dr. Malcolm James MacLeod at Collegiate Church of Saint Nicholas, the Rev. George Maychin Stockdale of Saint James Methodist Episcopal Church, and Rabbi Jacob Katz of Montefiore Congregation, all in Manhattan.[109] Macintosh's friend and Yale colleague Jerome Davis addressed the 109th graduating class of Yale Divinity School to plead the issues in the case, although he did not mention Macintosh by name. Davis told the graduates and assembled guests that every Christian must place faith in God and religiously informed conscience ahead of loyalty to country. Neither legislation nor court decisions could endure if they were contrary to morality and human welfare. "The motto, 'My country, right or wrong,' must be refined to read, 'My country, in so far as she stands for Christ and humanity,'" Davis proclaimed. "Just because humanity has not achieved a warless world, we must not lose faith. . . . It is possible to create a warless world if we christianize our nationalism, but never if patriotism dechristianizes our religion."[110]

Several denominations passed resolutions in their conventions expressing discontent with the Macintosh decision. Macintosh himself received letters from four denominational conventions, three Baptist and one Presbyterian.[111] The Texas Baptist Convention offered a strong statement in the Baptist tradition of support for religious liberty, freedom of conscience, and the belief that loyalty to the will of God supersedes loyalty to the state. Its statement was typical of denominational resolutions. (See Appendix L.[112])

The religious press exploded in anger against the Supreme Court: "No more serious this announcement," the Northern Baptist *Baptist* asserted. "In the event of another war, it is likely, under the law as the Supreme Court has defined it, that the jails will be filled to overflowing. There may come a time when it will be a disgrace for a Baptist, with his spiritual heritage, to be out of jail." According to the Methodist *Christian Advocate*, "The highest interests of the nation are safe only in the hands of those who refuse a blind allegiance to any requirement or practice which violates the sense of their own most sacred obligations to God." The Church of the Brethren *Gospel Messenger* thought that the United States had "begun the suicidal business of refusing to accept the sort of people who have made civilization possible." In the opinion of the Seventh-day Adventist *Liberty*, "The decision of the Court puts the government in the position of attempting to coerce the conscientious convictions of citizens rather than to punish them for outright violations of the law."[113]

Most outspoken was the nondenominational *Christian Century*. Its editor, Charles Clayton Morrison, a minister of the Christian Church (Disciples of Christ), applied Christianity to social problems and devoted much of his magazine to that interest. Perhaps Morrison was so engaged in and incensed by the Macintosh case because he held a similar pacifist position. The *Century* criticized the government's position from the time Macintosh was first denied citizenship by the District Court, saying of Judge Burrows's decision, "Never has a completely pagan theory of government been stated with more rigorous consistency or more unambiguous clarity."[114] Justice Sutherland's equation of the will of the government with the will of God raised the *Century*'s indignation to white-hot levels. "For once," in this case "the religion of Christ comes squarely and uncompromisingly face to face with the religion of nationalism."[115]

According to the Supreme Court, all those who believe in God and seek to live by the will of God will now have to look to the government, which will tell citizens what the will of God is. The Court's doctrine is equivalent to Prussianism—a deification of the state and a denial of monotheism. It portends the death of spiritual religion. The Court's decision in *Macintosh* "is the most complete and clear-cut enunciation of the doctrine of the supremacy of the state over the individual conscience—or in other words, of the Cult of the Omnipotent State—ever formulated." Lest one think that the case involves only applicants for citizenship, the doctrine of the state asserted by the Court applies equally to native-born citizens. All people who live in the country are subject to the "Omnipotent State." That is why the decision is so morally monstrous and intolerable. "It stretches over all citizens the pagan panoply of a nationalistic God before whom all must bow in reverence." The doctrine propounded by the Court "is tyranny in its worst form." Every citizen who believes in God is affected. Indeed, every citizen who believes in freedom and rights of conscience is affected. For the *Century*, the way of radical resistance seemed clear, inevitable, and necessary.

> The Christian Century, on its part, takes its place beside Dr. Macintosh. We refuse to accept the constitution as interpreted by this decision of the supreme court. Our conscience is not for sale. We give no government the power to conscript our religion. We refuse to bow down and worship the state. We refuse to bear arms or to aid in any way a war which we believe contrary to the will of God.
>
> This may be treason—it is not for us to say. But if it be treason, let the defenders of tyranny make the most of it![116]

Not content merely to rail against the Supreme Court and the doctrine of the state that it had posited, the *Century* formulated a "Declaration of an American Citizen" (the Seventh-day Adventist *Liberty* called it "a new declaration of independence"[117]) and encouraged all Americans to sign it and send it to Congress and the President. The "Declaration" appeared in the *Century* and thirty-two other religious or denominational papers, which encouraged readers to cut it out, sign it, and return it to the *Century* or to the journal in which they read it. Editors of the various papers would compile the responses and send them to Washington. The *Century* had launched a grassroots movement to express to Congress and the President the people's dissatisfaction with the state of affairs created by *Macintosh*.

The "Declaration" contained ten "Whereas" clauses, including one quoting Justice Sutherland's equation of the will of the nation with the will of God and another citing Chief Justice Hughes's refutation of that concept. Other "Whereas" clauses comment on the dire implications of the Court's doctrine or praise America's tradition of liberty of conscience. The heart of the document (for the full text, see Appendix M), expressed the action that the signer promised to carry out.

> Therefore, I, a native-born citizen of the United States, solemnly refuse to acknowledge the obligation which the supreme court [*sic*] declares to be binding upon native-born citizens. I have not promised, expressly or tacitly, to accept an act of Congress as the final interpretation of the will of God, and I will not do so. In my allegiance to my country I withhold nothing, not even my life. But I cannot give my conscience. That belongs to God. I repudiate the obligation which the Supreme Court's decision

would impose upon me, and declare that the imposition of such an
obligation is the essence of tyranny. I refuse to be bound by it.[118]

Independently of the *Century* campaign, some prominent clergy and
other religious leaders inspired by Reinhold Niebuhr, Professor of
Theology at Union Theological Seminary in New York, composed a
statement to be sent to the President and Congress expressing dissatisfaction with the *Macintosh* decision. Forty-eight persons initially signed the
petition, but they hoped to add 2,000 signatures before sending it to
Washington. For Niebuhr the petition was "not a matter of indignation, but
of common sense." Some of its signers could not, because of conscience,
participate in any war. Others, like Macintosh, would judge the legitimacy
of the war before they would decide whether to participate. All agreed with
Chief Justice Hughes that it was imperative to recognize a duty to a power
higher than the state.[119] (See Appendix N for the full text of the petition and
a list of initial signers.)

"Without claiming the gift of prophecy, we predict that this will mark
the beginning of an era of intolerance," Heber H. Votaw, the editor of
Liberty, remarked, summing up the foreboding of many religious leaders.
"It is dreadful to contemplate what might occur when the war dogs are
loosed, if in times of peace an unbiased tribunal like the Supreme Court of
this nation can so far misunderstand the spirit of America."[120]

This wide press coverage brought Macintosh many letters from people
he did not know. Henry E. Jackson, who was writing a book about Thomas
Jefferson's fight for religious liberty in Virginia, wrote, "You are a worthy
ally of Jefferson and would be a source of great satisfaction to him were he
living today." A sixteen-year-old student in a military academy wrote that
he had been interested in Professor Macintosh's case from the beginning,
but now even more. At his school they were singing "The Star Spangled
Banner" in chapel when he noticed this line in the third stanza: "Then
conquer we must, when our cause it is just." For the student it now seemed
"that this statement sung by all good Americans should have some influence
to bear on your case. Since the United States Government refuses to grant
you your citizenship papers, because of your refusal to fight in an unjust
war, it would be pertinent to ask why this statement could not be used as a
defense." He then wished Macintosh the best of luck in his efforts for
citizenship.[121]

In addition to wide coverage in the secular and religious press, there
were also commentaries about the case in law journals. Most of these

involved reporting, "case notes," rather than analysis. Some of them supported the majority opinion,[122] some the dissent.[123] Some argued that Macintosh's petition for naturalization was unsound because he was not willing to submit to all laws, but just some laws. The oath demands a pledge to obey the laws as a system, not just those with which the applicant agrees. "In short," John H. Wigmore wrote in an *Illinois Law Review* symposium, "the Macintosh principle is nothing less than the *right of individual secession*." If the Court had agreed to that principle, it would have opened a door to ever greater exceptions to the law on the part of succeeding waves of applicants. The dissent failed to hold Macintosh to the standard of the religious exemptions laws. The law required religious objectors to war to be members of "peace churches," which have a historic aversion to war. Macintosh was not a member of such a group, but he simply wanted to assert his personal religious objections to war. "Why did Congress limit its tolerance to members of 'well-recognized religious sects or organizations?' For the very practical reason that by this limitation alone could the masses of weak-kneed intellectual slackers be prevented from sheltering under, and abusing, this privilege."[124]

Against the decision other analysts argued that an oath is not taken with mental reservation unless there is some likelihood that the event at issue will occur. In this case, there was no possibility that the government would call a man in his fifties to serve in the military, even in the event of war. "An oath to support and defend the Constitution and laws," Frederick Green asserted in the same issue of the *Illinois Law Review*, "should not be construed as a promise to do what cannot be compelled under the Constitution and laws as they now are." To equate the will of the government with the will of God is to create a fiction of government infallibility. The Constitution itself recognizes the limitations of government. The founders established courts and formulated a system of checks and balances, showing that they recognized the possibilities of abuses of power in the government they had designed. Certainly the idea that the government does not have absolute sway over citizens is affirmed by the Ninth Amendment. "The enumeration in the Constitution of certain rights shall not be construed to deny or disparage others retained by the people."[125]

After *Schwimmer*, members of Congress began attempting to modify the Naturalization Act of 1906 to accommodate applicants for citizenship who had conscientious objections to war. They attempted to motivate Congress to do what the Supreme Court failed to do. After *Bland* and *Macintosh*, those efforts intensified. Macintosh continued to teach and write, as one of the luminaries of the Yale Divinity School faculty, but in America irremediably an alien.

Notes

1. 283 U.S. 605.

2. *Dred Scott v. Sandford* 19 Howard 393 (1857).

3. "An Astounding Decision," *Christian Century* 48 (10 June 1931): 766-67.

4. Douglas Clyde Macintosh describes his family tree and offers an autobiographical account of his intellectual history in "Toward a New Untraditional Orthodoxy," in *Contemporary American Theology: Theological Autobiographies*, Vergilius Ferm, ed. (New York, Roundtable Press, 1932) 1:277-319.

5. Douglas Clyde Macintosh, *Social Religion* (New York: Charles Scribner's Sons, 1939), x. In 1885 Congress had forbidden contract labor immigrants to enter the United States, but excepted professionals, such as teachers and lecturers.

6. Transcript of Record, *United States v. Macintosh*, 5.

7. 34 *Statutes at Large* 596, c. 3592; 8 U.S.C. §§ 372, 381, 382. For the text of the pertinent part of the Naturalization Act of 1906 see Appendix I.

8. Transcript of Record, *United States v. Macintosh*, 5.

9. Transcript of Record, *United States v. Macintosh*, 11-12.

10. Open Letter of American Legion Hughson Post #71, West Haven, Connecticut, to the American Legion, Department of Connecticut, 12 June 1929. Douglas Clyde Macintosh kept a large scrapbook of items relating to his naturalization case, now in the Library of Yale Divinity School, record group 30. Items contained in it, such as this resolution, will be identified as "DCM Scrapbook."

11. William B. Harvey of the Religious Society of Friends of Philadelphia and Vicinity wrote to Macintosh on "Sixth Month 18, 1929."

"As Friends, we are particularly interested in thy case, and I have been requested to write thee to ask whether we can render assistance of any kind.

"There is much criticism of the U.S. Supreme Court in its majority decision in the Rosika Schwimmer case. As I see it, there is a great difference between you.

"By the ruling we might infer that William Penn would be refused U.S. Citizenship, if living. If a prominent Christian leader is not given favorable consideration by the Federal Judge on the 24th, we shall have even greater reason to openly express our views on the whole situation." DCM Scrapbook

12. Transcript of Record, *United States v. Macintosh*, 12. As a theologian and faithful Christian, Macintosh defined the will of God "as what is right and for the highest well-being of all humanity." As much as he loved America, he could not put his loyalty to country higher than his allegiance to the will of God, as he understood it; see Macintosh, *Social Religion*, 286. In his scrapbook Macintosh

preserved another manuscript prepared to help Judge Burrows understand his position. It is not identical with anything that appears in the Transcript of Record, but it may facilitate understanding of his mind (see Appendix J).

13. Transcript of Record, *United States v. Macintosh*, 13.

14. Transcript of Record, *United States v. Macintosh*, 8-11. Macintosh's war service had delayed his efforts to become an American citizen. He had come to America in 1909 and within the first year of residence had declared his intention to apply for citizenship. He had to wait five years to file his application. Before the end of that period Canada had become embroiled in the war. Believing he ought not to give up his citizenship while his country was at war, he became a chaplain. By the time he returned to America, the time limit for his declaration of intention to become a citizen had expired. He had to submit his "first papers" again, in February 1919. Other complications arose because naturalization authorities had lost his record of entry into this country. Applying again for naturalization, he chose November 1916, when he returned from service with the Canadian army, as the date of his entry into the United States. Macintosh was one of 25,926 persons who served American soldiers at home and abroad during World War I. The YMCA received its commission 28 August 1917 "to provide for the amusement and recreation of the troops by means of its usual program of social, physical, educational and religious activities." Workers provided food, recreation, nursing services, reading material, athletic equipment, musical and dramatic entertainment and education, often very close to battle zones, as Macintosh's service illustrates. Consistent with its religious origin and nature, YMCA workers distributed Bibles, assisted chaplains, and in the absence of chaplains, led soldiers in religious services. General Pershing and his commanders wrote of the YMCA, "There is no one factor contributing more to the morale of the Army in France than the Y.M.C.A. The value of the organization cannot be overestimated. Give me 900 men who have a Y.M.C.A. rather than 1000 men who have none, and I will have better fighters every time." *Summary of World War Work of the American YMCA* (Young Men's Christian Associations, National War Work Council, 1920), v-vi, 26-41, 179-85.

15. Douglas Clyde Macintosh, "God and History," in *Religion and the War: By Members of the Faculty of the School of Religion, Yale University*, E. Hershey Sneath, ed. (New Haven, Conn.: Yale University Press, 1918), 24, 29.

16. Macintosh, "Toward a New Untraditional Orthodoxy," 307-8.

17. Macintosh, *Social Religion*, 139, 145-47.

18. Macintosh, *Social Religion*, 288. Macintosh wrote about his case in this book, describing the position he had tried to explain to the Naturalization Examiner and Judge Burrows on 285-87.

19. Transcript of Record, *United States v. Macintosh*, 15. The final decree denying citizenship was issued 8 January 1930; Transcript of Record, 16.

20. Open Letter of American Legion, Hughson Post #71, New Haven, Conn. To the American Legion, Department of Connecticut, 25 June 1919. DCM scrapbook.

21. A. Henry Wiseman of Waterbury, Connecticut to Macintosh, 31 July 1929. DCM Scrapbook. In his scrapbook, Macintosh saved letters from all over the United States congratulating him for his stand. Many were from ministers; some were former students, many apparently were strangers to him. Some were from well-known people, among them Harry Emerson Fosdick, minister of Riverside Church in New York, and Henry P. Van Dusen, President of Union Theological Seminary, New York.

22. "Fool Question," *New York World*, 27 June 1929, reprinted in *National Council for Prevention of War News Bulletin*, 1 July 1929. From the Swarthmore College Peace Collection (hereinafter cited as Swarthmore Collection). See "Believe Professor Got War Horror at Front," *New York Times*, 12 June 1929, 12; "Professor Macintosh's Conscience," *San Francisco News*, 25 June 1929, which called Judge Burrows's decision "silly"; "Denies Citizenship to Yale Professor," *New York Times*, 25 June 1929, 1, American Civil Liberties Union Archives, Seeley G. Mudd Library, Princeton University, vol. 358, reel 61 (hereinafter cited as ACLU Archives).

23. Heywood Broun, "It Seems to Me," *Washington Daily News*, 27 June 1929, 13; see also "Will the Supreme Court Dethrone God?" *National Council for Prevention of War News Bulletin*, 15 January 1930, 5; Edwin D. Mead, "Is Fighting the Test of Loyalty?" *New Republic* 59 (17 July 1929): 236, Swarthmore Collection; "Whose a Good Citizen?" *Passaic* [New Jersey] *Herald*, 19 June 1929. DCM Scrapbook .

24. "Can a Baptist Minister Be a Good American Citizen?" *Washington Daily News*, 11 January 1930, quoted in "Shall Militarism Determine Citizenship Qualification?" *Liberty* 25 (Second Quarter 1930): 48. Seventh-day Adventist Historical Society, hereinafter known as SDA Archives. *Liberty* was and is a magazine of religious liberty published by the Seventh-day Adventist Church.

25. Hickman Powell, "Macintosh Charges Laws Bar True Christian," *New York World*, 30 June 1929. ACLU Archives, vol. 358, reel 61. In the copy of this article in Macintosh's scrapbook, he attached a note in his handwriting, saying that he granted the interview to Powell to give the public a more accurate version of his position than was available in most of the articles about his case.

26. "No Christians Need Apply!" *Christian Century* 46 (10 July 1929): 888-89; "So Help Me God!" *Christian Century* 47 (22 January 1930): 102-4.

27. Major General I. Thord-Gray to Charles E. Clark, 26 June 1929; Clark to Thord-Gray, 27 June 1929. DCM Scrapbook.

28. Forrest Bailey to Macintosh, 12 June 1929; Macintosh to Bailey, 13 June 1929; Roger Baldwin to Macintosh, 25 June 1929; Macintosh to Baldwin, 26 June 1929. ACLU Archives, vol. 372, reel 67.

29. William H. Harbaugh reports that Macintosh's Yale Divinity School colleague Jerome Davis, within hours of Judge Burrows's ruling, contacted his friend Allen Wardwell, a partner in John W. Davis's prestigious Wall Street law firm, asking the firm to take the case; see William H. Harbaugh, *Lawyer's Lawyer: The Life of John W. Davis* (New York: Oxford University Press, 1973; University

Press of Virginia, 1990), 286. Wardwell wrote to Macintosh on 19 July 1929, "I have given further consideration to the question of your appeal from the decision of the District Court with regard to your naturalization application and we will be very glad to undertake this appeal on your behalf if you wish it." DCM Scrapbook.

30. Ironically, in the process of finding counsel for Macintosh, someone had approached the firm of Hughes, Rounds, Schurman & Dwight. Charles E. Clark wrote to Macintosh saying that he had taken the liberty of writing to John Caskey, of that firm, "thanking him for his interest in the matter and telling him that in view of Mr. Davis's willingness to take the case, we had decided not to trouble Judge Hughes." The "Judge Hughes" of that firm was Charles Evans Hughes; apparently someone had asked Hughes to take Macintosh's case. The request would probably have been in vain, given that Charles Evans Hughes, Jr. was Solicitor General at the time and the senior Hughes refused to take any cases against the government. Charles Evans Hughes was confirmed as Chief Justice of the Supreme Court on 13 February 1930 and wrote a strong dissent in Macintosh's case. See Charles E. Clark to Macintosh, 26 July 1929 (DCM Scrapbook); *The Autobiographical Notes of Charles Evans Hughes*, David J. Danelski and Joseph S. Tulchin, eds. (Cambridge, Mass.: Harvard University Press, 1973), 285; Burnett Anderson, "Charles Evans Hughes," in *The Supreme Court Justices: Illustrated Biographies*, 1789-1993, Clare Cushman, ed. (Washington, D.C.: Congressional Quarterly, 1993), 310.

31. William H. Harbaugh, "John W. Davis," *American National Biography*, John A. Garraty and Mark C. Carnes, eds. (New York: Oxford University Press, 1999) 6:209-10; "John W. Davis," *The National Cyclopædia of American Biography Being the History of the United States* (New York: James T. White, 1962) 45:26-27; Harbaugh, *Lawyer's Lawyer*; Irving Stone, *They Also Ran: The Story of the Men Who Were Defeated for the Presidency* (Garden City, N.Y.: Doubleday, Doran, 1943), 321-39.

32. Harbaugh, "John W. Davis," 209.

33. Felix Frankfurter to John W. Davis, 13 June 1953, quoted in Harbaugh, *Lawyer's Lawyer*, 317.

34. William O. Douglas, *The Court Years, 1939-1975: The Autobiography of William O. Douglas* (New York: Vintage Books, 1980), 183-84.

35. "May It Please the Court . . . ," *Time* 62 (21 December 1953): 18-19, quoted in Harbaugh, *Lawyer's Lawyer*, 514.

36. Harbaugh, *Lawyer's Lawyer*, 271-80, 286-87. Davis and Macintosh shared a melancholy parallel in their personal lives—their first wives died in childbirth. Davis married Julia McDonald on 20 June 1899. She died 17 August 1900; her baby survived. Macintosh married Emily Powell on 13 February 1921. She and her child died 2 November 1922. One week after Emily's death, it was Professor Macintosh's turn to lead worship in the Divinity School Chapel. He did not excuse himself, but read as his text Habakkuk 3:17-18: "Although the fig tree shall not blossom, neither shall fruit be in the vines; the labor of the olive shall fail, and the fields shall yield no meat; the flock shall be cut off from the fold, and there shall

be no herd in the stalls: Yet I will rejoice in the Lord, I will joy in the God of my salvation." Harbaugh, *Lawyer's Lawyer*, 33-34; Roland H. Bainton contribution, "Douglas Clyde Macintosh: A Centennial Tribute at Yale University Divinity School, 11-17 September 1978, Paul Douglas Macintosh Keane, ed., 11, unpublished, Douglas Clyde Macintosh papers, record group 50, Yale Divinity School Library. See also Roland H. Bainton, *Yale and the Ministry: A History of Education for the Christian Ministry at Yale from the Founding in 1701* (New York: Harper and Brothers, 1957), 233.

37. Harbaugh, *Lawyer's Lawyer*, 287-89.

38. Roger Baldwin to Bureau of Naturalization, Department of Labor, 24 June 1929 (coincidentally the very day Judge Burrows denied Macintosh citizenship); Acting Commissioner of Naturalization (signature undecipherable) to Baldwin, 8 August 1929; Baldwin to Acting Commissioner of Naturalization, 26 September 1929. ACLU Archives, vol. 359, reel 62. Naming Secretary of Labor James J. Davis as the person responsible for the inclusion of question 22 on the application form, the National Council for Prevention of War called it "this ungodly policy" ("Will the Supreme Court Dethrone God?" *National Council for Prevention of War News Bulletin*, January 1930, 5). One commentator cited the case of a Quaker, Francis Wills Wood, who was denied citizenship in Camden, New Jersey, in 1916, long before question 22 was added to the form; see Dorothy Dunbar Bromley, "The Pacifist Bogey: An Apology to Prospective Citizens," *Harper's Monthly Magazine* 161 (October 1930): 554.

39. Rosika Schwimmer to Olive Rabe, 22 May 1930, Schwimmer-Lloyd collection, Box G-5.

40. *Macintosh v. United States* 42 F.2d 845 (1930). See "Decision Reserved in M'Intosh Case," *New York Times*, 21 May 1930, 56, for a summary of the oral arguments. In 1939 Judge Manton was tried, convicted, and imprisoned for taking money for favorable decisions. For some twenty years prior, many leaders of the bar, including Judges Hand and Swan, had been concerned about the abilities and ethics of Judge Manton. In the legal proceedings against him, John W. Davis served as an unenthusiastic character witness; see. Harbaugh, *Lawyer's Lawyer*, 313-17.

41. 32 U.S.C.A. §§ 4, 3.

42. 50 U.S.C.A. § 226n.

43. *Macintosh v. United States* 42 F.2d 845 at 847-48.

44. 42 F.2d 845 at 848; Joseph Story, *Commentaries on the Constitution of the United States* (Boston: Hilliard, Gray, 1833), § 1876.

45. 42 F.2d 845 at 849, citing *Osborn v. Bank of U.S.* 9 Wheat. (22 U.S.) 738 (1824); *Boyd v. Thayer* 143 U.S. 135 (1892); *Luria v. United States* 231 U.S. 9 (1913); *Tutun v. United States* 270 U.S. 568 (1926).

46. 42 F.2d 845 at 849. See "Dr. Macintosh Wins Right to Citizenship," *New York Times*, 1 July 1930. Rosika Schwimmer wrote a letter to the *New York Herald-Tribune* concerning the cases of Macintosh and Marie Averil Bland, decided the same day. I have not determined that it was published.

"It gives me great pleasure to learn that Professor Macintosh and Miss Bland were granted citizenship in spite of their objection to bearing arms," Schwimmer wrote. "Permit me, however, to express my bewilderment about the comparison made between their attitude and mine in points that determined my rejection.

"According to newspaper reports the two successful applicants' cases differed from mine in so far that I admitted a lack of sense of nationality.

"It may be due to the proverbial lack of feminine logic that I am unable to see a difference in their attitude and mine on this point. To my mind, Professor Macintosh and Miss Bland exhibited the same lack of sense of nationality when they renounced the nationality of their birth. Persons with a sense of nationality stick to their country, right or wrong. The newspapers further report that, according to the decision, my 'cosmic sense of belonging to the human family' is an attitude of mind which properly disqualifies me for American citizenship. I wonder whether a professor of Christian theology and an applicant basing her refusal to bear arms on the teachings of Christ can fail to have a sense of belonging to the human family, since one of the fundamental tenets of Christianity is the belief that all human beings are God's children?" See Schwimmer to *New York Herald-Tribune*, 1 July 1930. ACLU Archives, vol. 373, reel 67.

47. Davis to Macintosh, 7 July 1930. DCM Scrapbook.

48. William Lyon Phelps to Macintosh, 2 July 1930. DCM Scrapbook. The theme of this letter would be argued again and again in the religious press, and indeed Phelps developed this theme in print; see William Lyons Phelps, "Christianity and Nationalism," *Christian Century* 47 (8 August 1930): 961-63.

49. "Two Pacifists Win Citizenship Rights," *New York World*, 1 July 1930; "Citizenship Right is Won by Macintosh, *New York Herald-Tribune*, 1 July 1930; "War Nurse, Cleric Denied Citizenship, Win on Appeal," *Washington Post*, 1 July 1930; "Dr. Macintosh Wins Right to Citizenship," *New York Times*, 1 July 1930.

50. Bruce Calvert,"Citizenship and Religion," *Open Road* 20 (August 1930): 1.

51. Macintosh to W. Charles Poletti, 7 September 1930; Poletti to Macintosh, 11 September 1930. DCM Scrapbook.

52. Transcript of Record, *United States v. Macintosh*, "Brief for the United States," 9-14; emphasis added.

53. Transcript of Record, *United States v. Macintosh*, "Brief for the United States," 15-16.

54. Transcript of Record, *United States v. Macintosh*, "Brief for the United States," 18-19.

55. Transcript of Record, *United States v. Macintosh*, "Brief for the United States," 19-20, 25.

56. Transcript of Record, *United States v. Macintosh*, "Brief for Respondent," 8-14.

57. Transcript of Record, *United States v. Macintosh*, "Brief for Respondent," 15-16.

58. Transcript of Record, *United States v. Macintosh*, "Brief for Respondent," 20-27; emphasis added. The brief cited the *Selective Draft Law Cases*, 245 U.S. 366 (1918), at that point.

59. 98 U.S. 145 (1879).

60. 133 U.S. 333 (1890).

61. Transcript of Record, *United States v. Macintosh*, "Brief for Respondent," 27-35.

62. Transcript of Record, *United States v. Macintosh*, "Brief for Respondent," 35-37.

63. As authority the brief cites *Osborn v. Bank of the United States* 22 U.S. 738 at 827 (1824) and *Luria v. United States* 231 U.S. 9 at 22 (1913), "Brief for Respondent," 40. See the U.S. Constitution, Article 2, Sec. 1, par. 5.

64. Citing *Tutun v. United States* as authority: "A court, in passing upon a petition for naturalization, 'exercises judicial judgment' and 'does not confer or withhold a favor.'" 270 U.S. 568 at 578 (1926); "Brief for Respondent," 40.

65. Transcript of Record, *United States v. Macintosh*, "Brief for Respondent," 40-42.

66. *United States v. Schwimmer* 279 U.S. 644 at 648 (1929).

67. Transcript of Record, *United States v. Macintosh*, "Brief for Respondent," 44-45.

68. *United States v. Schwimmer* 279 U.S. 644 at 648

69. Transcript of Record, *United States v. Macintosh*, "Brief for Respondent," 46-51.

70. Transcript of Record, *United States v. Macintosh*, "Amicus Brief for American Friends Service Committee," 5.

71. Transcript of Record, *United States v. Macintosh*, "Amicus Brief for American Friends Service Committee," 8-26. The brief includes a four-and-one-half page appendix, "Oaths of Allegiance in English and American History."

72. Harbaugh, *Lawyer's Lawyer*, 291-92; "High Court Hears Citizenship Suits," *New York Times*, 28 April 1931, 55.

73. 245 U.S. 366 (1918).

74. Harbaugh, *Lawyer's Lawyer*, 292; "High Court Hears Citizenship Suits," *New York Times*, 28 April 1931, 55. The subheadline reads "Old Brief by John W. Davis, Counsel for Macintosh, Turned Against Him."

75. Davis to William A. Bell, 28 May 1931, quoted in Harbaugh, *Lawyer's Lawyer*, 292.

76. See Ellen Frankel Paul, "George Sutherland," in *The Oxford Companion to the Supreme Court of the United States*, Kermit L. Hall, ed. (New York: Oxford University Press, 1992), 848-49; Jay S. Bybee, "George Sutherland," in *The Supreme Court Justices*, Cushman, ed., 346-50.

77. Ironically, Justice Sutherland was appointed in 1922 to replace Justice John H. Clark, who resigned from the Court to pursue peace work. Clark spent several years in writing and speaking, trying to persuade the American people and Congress to support the League of Nations and peace causes in general. Had Clark

remained on the Court, he might have supported Macintosh's selective conscientious objection and application for citizenship. See Clare Cushman, "John H. Clark," in *The Supreme Court Justices*, Cushman, ed., 336-40.

78. *United States v. Macintosh* 283 U.S. 605 at 615.

79. 283 U.S. 605 at 616-21.

80. 283 U.S. 605 at 621-23.

81. 283 U.S. 605 at 623.

82. See "Citizenship Denied to Arms Objectors," *New York Times*, 26 May 1931, 1, "In delivering their opinions today before a crowded courtroom, both Justice Sutherland and Chief Justice Hughes were more than ordinarily emphatic. Justice Sutherland especially stressed the duties of the citizen." ("Court Denies Citizenship to Macintosh," *New York Herald Tribune*, 26 May 1931), "Justice Sutherland delivered the majority opinion emphatically, raising his voice until it resounded throughout the room, laying stress especially on those portions of the opinion in which he outlined the duties of citizens." ("High Court Bars MacIntosh, Yale Professor, as Citizen," *New York Evening Post*, 26 May 1931).

83. 283 U.S. 605 at 624-25; emphasis in original.

84. 283 U.S. 605 at 625-26.

85. Anderson, "Charles Evans Hughes," *Supreme Court Justices*, Cushman, ed., 306-10; Raymond Clapper, "Hughes Goes Over to Dissenters' Side of the Supreme Court," *Washington Daily News*, 26 May 1931. Swarthmore Collection; "Allegiance Oath Is Held Necessary," *Buffalo Evening News*, 26 May 1931; "MacIntosh Gives Up Fight for Citizenship," *Hartford Times*, 26 May 1931. ACLU Archives, vol. 781.

86. *Autobiographical Notes of Charles Evans Hughes*, Danelski and Tulchin, eds., 6-11, 24-27; Charles Evans Hughes, "Liberty and Law," *American Bar Association Journal* 11 (September 1925): 564, 567.

87. 283 U.S. 605 at 627-33.

88. 133 U.S. 333, 342 (1890).

89. 283 U.S. 605 at 633-35.

90. 283 U.S. 605 at 635.

91. Davis to Macintosh, 26 May 1931; Wardwell to Macintosh, 26 May 1931; Poletti to Macintosh, 27 May 1931; Clark to Macintosh, 28 May 1931. DCM Scrapbook. On Roberts's vote, see "Roberts Swings Supreme Court Over to Militarism," Washington, D.C. *Open Forum*, 6 June 1931, and generally, Jay S. Bybee, "Owen J. Roberts," in *Supreme Court Justices*, Cushman, ed., 366-70.

92. Boyd Lewis, "MacIntosh Gives Up Fight for Citizenship," *Hartford Times*, 26 May 1931; "Prof. Macintosh Not to Change Stand on Oath," *Boston Traveler*, 26 May 1931.

93. See Julian N. Hartt's contribution to "Douglas Clyde Macintosh: A Centennial Tribute at Yale University Divinity School," 11-17 September 1978, Paul Douglas Macintosh Keane, ed., 11, unpublished, Douglas Clyde Macintosh papers, record group 50, Yale Divinity School Library. See also Hartt to Ronald B. Flowers, 7 February 2000.

94. Macintosh, *Social Religion*, ix.

95. 283 U.S. 636 (1931); see Ronald B. Flowers, "In Praise of Conscience: Marie Averil Bland," *Anglican and Episcopal History* 62 (March 1993): 37-57. The *amicus* brief of the American Friends Service Committee, summarized earlier, applied to *Bland* as well as *Macintosh*.

96. "U.S. Won't Deport Professor, Nurse, Denied Citizenship," *Washington Daily News*, 26 May 1931.

97. "I do not think any of us have any real hope of a change in the Court's decision, but in view of the five to four decision we feel that we would like to file the petition so that we can comport ourselves with the thought that everything possible has been done" (Allen Wardwell to Macintosh, 12 June 1931). Charles Poletti to Macintosh, 17 June 1931. DCM Scrapbook.

98. Heywood Broun, "It Seems to Me," New York Telegram Corporation, 25 May 1931.

99. Heber H. Votaw, "Some Press Comments on the MacIntosh Citizenship Cases," *Liberty* 26 (Fourth Quarter, 1931): 105-6, 119-20. SDA Archives.

100. Jerome Davis, "The Assimilation of Immigrants and Our Citizenship Process," *Social Forces* 12 (May 1934): 579-85. DCM Scrapbook. Davis earlier published a similar, but shorter, critique of the naturalization system, charging that many who are let in are undesirable; see Jerome Davis, "If Not Dr. Macintosh, Who?" *Christian Century* 50 (8 March 1933): 322-24.

101. "The Macintosh Case," *New York Times*, 26 May 1931, 26. ACLU Archives, vol. 471.

102. "Supreme Judicial Folly," *The People's Business* 6 (June 1931): 1. This periodical was published by The People's Legislative Service, Washington, D.C. ACLU Archives, vol. 455.

103. "Five Noble Judges," *Reading* [Pa.] *Labor Advocate*, 5 June 1931. ACLU Archives, vol. 471.

104. "Wisconsin Views," *Milwaukee Leader*, 2 June 1931. See also editorials critical of the Court's decision in "Citizenship and War," *Philadelphia Inquirer*, 27 May 1931; "An Incomprehensible Decision," *Alpena* [Mich.] *News*, 29 May 1931; "Bearing Arms," *Michigan City* [Ind.] *News*, 29 May 1931; "A Strange Decision, But a Fine Dissent," *Milwaukee Leader*, 11 June 1931. All in ACLU Archives, vol. 471. "Justice Sutherland's words in denying citizenship to Professor Macintosh had a historical connection worth noting," one reader wrote to the *New York Times*. "He said flatly and without equivocating, that this country is no place for persons who put the law of God above the law of man.

"The New York Times Magazine of May 24 had an article about Joan of Arc. Her judges asked her if she presumed to interpret the law of God for herself and to hold it higher than the laws of man. She admitted to the charge, so they burned her up.

"The progress made by humanity during the intervening centuries lies in this—that we haven't burned Professor Macintosh and that the Supreme Court's decision had four dissenters" (R. W. Riis, "We Have Made Progress Since Joan of

Arc's Day." *New York Times* 31 May 1931, sec. III, 2).

105. "Supreme Court Upholds Duties of Citizenship," *Ann Arbor News*, 28 May 1931. ACLU Archives, vol. 471.

106. "Duty of Citizenship," *Pontiac* [Mich.] *Press*, 29 May 1931. ACLU Archives, vol. 471.

107. "The Decision Barring Aliens Asking Special Privilege as Citizens," *Philadelphia Record*, 28 May 1931. See also "No Citizenship with Reservations," *Shepherd* [Mich.] *Republic*, 19 June 1931. ACLU Archives, vol. 471.

108. "An Essential Decision," *Woman Patriot* 15 (June 1931): 7-11. Emphasis in original. The magazine made its points in strong language, see also p. 8:

"If Professor Macintosh has received a special new personal commandment from on high: *'Thou shalt choose thy own wars; in them only shalt thou serve,'* it is the strangest—and most dangerous—doctrine in relation to the right of a state to defend its existence since Moses came down from the Mount. It bears a stronger resemblance to the Kaiser's *'Me und Gott'* than to any other 'religious' view we have ever heard of. And if every citizen—and every alien, to boot—can nullify every Federal law against which he brings the *'Me und Gott'* objection, and *he can if the Macintosh reservation is valid*, then as the Pennsylvania Supreme Court held in the Clark case, *"anarchy will stalk in unmolested"* and orderly government will perish from the earth." Emphasis in original.

109. "Preachers Assail Citizenship Ruling," *New York Times*, 1 June 1931, 19; "Supreme Court Decision on Macintosh Criticized," *New York Herald Tribune*, 8 June 1931. ACLU Archives, vol. 471. This was not the first time ministers had defended Macintosh. Clergy supporting him after he was denied citizenship by the District Court included the Rev. Walter Russell Bowie of Grace Episcopal Church, Dr. Joseph Sarachak, rabbi of the Jewish Centre of University Heights, Bronx, Dr. Peter Ainslie of Baltimore's Christian Temple, and Rabbi Stephen S. Wise of the Free Synagogue of Carnegie Hall. "Declares Patriot May Renounce War," *New York Times*, 1 July 1929, 32; "Myriads Would Not Bear Arms, He Says," *Baltimore Sun*, 1 July 1929; "Dr. Wise Sees God Dethroned by Courts," *New York Times*, 3 February 1930. Swarthmore Collection.

110. "Yale Speaker Hits Court Arms Ruling," *New York Times*, 1 June 1931, 9. Earlier Davis had spoken to 130 students from fourteen New England colleges at a conference devoted to study of issues in Macintosh's case. Students heard speakers for and against Macintosh's position. "130 Attend Conference at Northfield." *Hartford Daily Courant*, 17 February 1930. Both clippings in the Swarthmore Collection.

111. The Presbyterian General Assembly (30 June 1930), the Seventh Day Baptist General Convention (23 August 1931), the Connecticut Baptist Convention (6 November 1931) and the Texas Baptist Convention (13 November 1931). DCM Scrapbook. South Carolina Baptists rejected the right of governments to pass judgment on any individual's conscience "whose religious convictions forbid him to sanction war"; see "Carolina Baptists Uphold Rights of Conscience," *Christian Century* 49 (23 March 1932): 388. The Federal Council of Churches also passed

a resolution supporting Macintosh; "Citizenship Bar on Peace Plea Called Unwise," *Christian Science Monitor*, 7 December 1929. So did the Quakers; see "Conscience and Citizenship: A Statement by the Religious Society of Friends (Quakers)," *Friends Intelligencer*, Second Month 22, 1930, 146; "Denial of American Citizenship in Case of Macintosh Reviewed," *Christian Science Monitor*, 15 July 1931. All in Swarthmore Collection.

112. In June 1931, the Northern Baptist Convention met and failed to express itself about the Macintosh case. Precisely the same resolution passed by the Texas Baptist Convention in November was read to the convention and referred to committee. Nothing else happened. *The Christian Century* criticized the Northern Baptists, calling attention to their long tradition of "soul liberty" and devotion to religious freedom; see "Have Baptists Lost Their Courage?" *Christian Century* 48 (1 July 1931): 862-63. Many Baptists had spoken out at the time of the District Court opinion. See "Baptists Deplore Exclusion of Yale Professor," *Washington Daily News*, 13 January 1929, Swarthmore Collection. The Seventh Day Baptist General Conference passed a resolution critical of the Supreme Court decision; "Declarations Regarding the MacIntosh Case," 23 August 1931, Record Group 267, National Archives, *United States* v. *Macintosh* folder.

113. "The Religious Press on the MacIntosh Case," *Liberty* 27 (First Quarter, 1932): 6-7, 22-23.

114. "So Help Me God!" *Christian Century* 47 (22 January 1930): 102-4. See also "Theirs Not to Reason Why" *Christian Century* 46 (3 July 1929): 859-60; "Only Killers Need Apply!" *Christian Century* 46 (4 December 1929): 1493-94.

115. William Lyon Phelps, "Christianity and Nationalism," *Christian Century* 47 (6 August 1930): 961-63, written before the Supreme Court decision. Justice Sutherland's *dicta* focused the problem even more sharply. Most of the *Century*'s vituperation against the Court and the religion of nationalism was in editorials, although it published signed articles on the general topic; see Ralph E. Kinsley, "Conscience and the Constitution," *Christian Century* 49 (24 June 1931): 835-38; Vernon Nash, "If All Wars or None, Then None!" *Christian Century* 48 (11 November 1931); 1415-16; Charles P. Howland, "Consciences in Regimentals," *Christian Century* 49 (20 January 1932): 84-86.

116. "An Astounding Decision," *Christian Century* 48 (10 June 1931): 766-67; "Christianity at a Crisis," *Christian Century* 48 (24 June 1931): 832-33; "Dr. Macintosh Asks a Rehearing," *Christian Century* 48 (22 July 1931): 942-43; "Re-open the Macintosh Case," *Christian Century* 48 (30 September 1931): 1199-1201. In its passion about this issue, the *Century* occasionally resorted to hyperbole. "The dissenting opinion of Chief Justice Hughes . . . may in time come to be regarded as a charter of liberty for the individual conscience comparable in importance to the Mayflower pact, the Virginia bill of rights, or the first ten amendments to the federal constitution"; "The Office Notebook," *Christian Century* 49 (20 January 1932): 76.

117. "Conscience vs. Congress," *Liberty* 27 (Second Quarter, 1932): 49.

118. "Declaration of an American Citizen,"*Christian Century* 49 (20 January 1932): 75. See also "A Call to Patriots," *Christian Century* 49 (20 January 1932): 80-81; "Conscience and the Law," *Christian Century* 49 (17 February 1932): 214-15; "Macintosh Oath Ruling Flouted in Church Press," *New York Herald Tribune*, 21 February 1932; "Declaration of an American Citizen," *The Baptist*, 16 January 1932, 76; "A Revolt of Conscience," *The Baptist*, 30 January 1932, 140.

119. "Churchmen Ask Action to Annul Macintosh Bar," *New York Times*, 24 September 1931.

120. Heber H. Votaw, "Rehearing for Dr. MacIntosh Denied," *Liberty* 27 (First Quarter, 1932): 11.

121. Henry E. Jackson to Macintosh, 9 July 1931; M. Polasky, student at Miami Military Institute, Germantown, Ohio, to Macintosh, 17 October 1931. DCM Scrapbook. The line to which Polasky refers is in the fourth stanza of the "Star-Spangled Banner." Congress had made the song the national anthem on 3 March 1931 (46 Stat. 1508, ch. 436; 36 U.S.C. § 301[a]), not quite three months before Macintosh was denied citizenship.

122. Eugene Wambaugh, "The Oath Required for Naturalization—The Macintosh Case," *Tulane Law Review* 6 (1931-32): 132-35; S.S., "The Macintosh Case," *University of Pennsylvania Law Review* 80 (December 1931): 275-81.

123. John B. Hennessy, "Aliens—Naturalization—Duty to Bear Arms," *Dakota Law Review* 3 (December 1931): 429-30; Morris Melnick, "Aliens—Right of Naturalization—Oath of Allegiance with Qualification," *Boston University Law Review* 11 (November 1931): 532-37; John S. Tennant, "Aliens—Naturalization—The Promise to Bear Arms," *Michigan Law Review* 30 (November 1931): 133-37.

124. John H. Wigmore, "United States vs. Macintosh—A Symposium," *Illinois Law Review* 26 (December 1931): 375-82.

125. Frederick Green, "United States vs. Macintosh—A Symposium," *Illinois Law Review* 26 (December 1931): 386-96.

Five

Marie Averil Bland:
In Praise of Conscience

Marie Averil Bland walked into a courtroom in New York City, 14 April 1930, to become a citizen of the United States. She was one of about 500 aliens who were, collectively, about to take the oath of naturalization.

> I hereby declare, on oath, that I absolutely and entirely renounce and abjure all allegiance and fidelity to any foreign prince, potentate, state, or sovereignty, and particularly to [the country and sovereign] of whom I have heretofore been a subject (or citizen): that I will support and defend the Constitution and laws of the United States of America against all enemies, foreign and domestic; that I will bear true faith and allegiance to the same; and that I take this obligation freely without any mental reservation or purpose of evasion; So help me God.

When the clerk of the court administering the oath came to the phrase "that I will support and defend the Constitution and Laws of the United States against all enemies," Marie Bland lowered her hand and did not repeat the words. In that throng, no one noticed her action, certainly neither the judge nor the clerk of the court. When the proceedings were over, Bland approached the court clerk and told him what she had done. When he had ascertained that she had conscientious objections to that part of the oath, he said that she must have an individual hearing before a naturalization examiner and before the Judge of that same United States District Court to determine her eligibility for citizenship.[1] So began an episode of some legal significance and great personal importance. Why had Bland refused to complete the oath of naturalization and then called attention to herself?

Marie Bland was not the first woman to object to the wording of the naturalization oath. In 1929, the United States Supreme Court had decided the case of Rosika Schwimmer.[2] Marie Bland filed her petition for citizenship (21 May 1929) six days before the *Schwimmer* decision was handed down (27 May 1929). At the time of her filing, Bland saw no problem with the oath; what it required was consistent with her own conscience. By the time of the oath ceremony on 14 April 1930 Bland had become aware of the Court's ruling in *Schwimmer*, and she felt that she could not take the oath as it was now interpreted—that the only way to "defend the Constitution" was to serve in the military. What had brought her to that conclusion?

Marie Averil Bland was born 1 April 1883 in Ingersoll, Ontario, Canada. Her parents, Marie Augusta Bland and Edward Michael Bland, had come to Canada from England. Edward Bland was an Anglican clergyman on missionary assignment to Canada from 1875 to 1906. One of several small towns in southwestern Ontario, in an area between Michigan and New York surrounded on three sides by Lakes Michigan, Erie, and Ontario, southwest of Toronto and due west of Niagara Falls, Ingersoll in the 1880s was a typical small town surrounded by rich farmland. Its principal industries were small businesses, many related to farming. Religiously, the largest Protestant denomination was Methodist, followed by Baptists and smaller numbers of Presbyterians and Anglicans. The Anglican church could not afford to pay a minister, hence the Rev. Bland's missionary assignment. There were also some Irish Catholics in the area. In the same year Marie was born, a Salvation Army barracks opened in Ingersoll, much to the fascination of many of its residents. Marie Averil Bland spent her early childhood in a small community, undoubtedly influenced by the values of community loyalty, appreciation for the land, and, through her family, a love for the church.[3]

Marie Bland came to the United States in February 1914—when she was nearly 31—from England, where, by this time, her father served a church. (From 1913 to 1916 he was Rector of Langton-by-Horncastle and Vicar of Woodhall Spa, both in Lincolnshire.[4]) As a nurse by profession Bland, during World War I, had not considered bearing arms, since the possibility had never occurred to her. Yet on 11 November 1918, Armistice Day, she sailed for France, employed by the United States government, as part of a reconstruction unit, sent to serve the needs of soldiers injured in the war. "Reconstruction" was the word for "therapy" in those days. "Reconstruction aides" or "re-aides" were either physical therapists or occupational therapists. Physical therapists gave the soldiers massages, electro or hydro treatments, or other therapeutic procedures, while the occupational therapists taught skills such as crocheting, weaving, reading and writing, math, typing and mechanical drawing. The first re-aides sent to France in June 1918 initially were not welcomed in Army hospitals and combat medical facilities. Their profession was new and previously not recognized in the military, The re-aides gradually gained acceptance because of the good they did for wounded soldiers. Not only was their profession not traditional in the military; but their status in the military was also ambiguous. They were civilian employees, but subject to Army regulations. They had to take the oath of induction and serve until they were released. They had to be United States citizens or citizens of countries at war with Germany, as was Bland.[5]

Bland worked for nine months as a psychiatric nurse in Brest, France. (That Bland was a psychiatric nurse meant she served, strangely enough, as an occupational therapist re-aide, for they worked with neuropsychiatric patients, or NPs, as they were called.[6]) Her patients were American soldiers who had fought in the war and suffered from battle fatigue and from other psychological disorders resulting from the stress and trauma of combat. "For nine months," she recalled, "I nursed shell shocked soldiers."[7] "Shell shock" was a term commonly used for combat soldiers who were debilitated but had not suffered physical wounds. Many Army doctors preferred the term "war neurosis," but "shell shock" captured the public's imagination. These neuropsychiatric disabilities manifested themselves in a variety of ways—from convulsions, coma, deafness, and paralysis, to emotional reactions such as depression, fear, anger, and suicidal or homicidal tendencies.

Working with traumatized soldiers affected Bland profoundly, as it did many of the re-aides. As one re-aide remembered, "We saw wholesale suffering; wholesale, but game, suffering. No motion pictures can ever show or lecturers tell; one must have been actually in the hospitals to know what this victory had cost. . . . [T]here are far worse things than death."[8] Seeing firsthand the suffering and waste produced by war, Bland began to think about its morality. Her religious faith contributed significantly to her reflections. She measured war against her conception of Christian ethics. She found it wanting. "Since the date of my return from France," she wrote, "I have come to realize that the abolition of war is in accord with the teachings of Jesus Christ and that He would have condemned fighting and bearing arms."[9] She arrived at that conclusion not only by witnessing personal tragedies in military hospitals and by her religious training as the daughter of a minister, but by participating in her parish, Grace Episcopal Church in New York, where Dr. Walter Russell Bowie was rector from 1923 until 1939.

In 1918 Bowie took leave from St. Paul's Church of Richmond, Virginia, where he was then rector, to serve as chaplain in a Red Cross field hospital based near combat zones in France. Bowie worked daily with wounded soldiers, conducted worship for those who wanted it, arranged for the burial of the dead, and wrote letters of condolence to the families of the deceased. He also witnessed at firsthand the devastation wrought by war.

Bowie returned to the United States with an interest in promoting pacifism. He was a progressive minister convinced that to preach the "simple gospel" as a fundamentalist recital of personal salvation was not faithful to the Christian's call. Bowie believed in personal salvation, but he also was convinced that the Christian message had to be applied to social problems. Among the social gospel issues he addressed in sermons was the propriety of war. After the war was over, Bowie reluctantly dedicated a plaque in Grace Church with the names of those from the congregation who had died in the conflict, commenting that to have a plaque with the names of conscientious objectors who had been incarcerated in the federal prison in Leavenworth would be equally appropriate. In 1939, the Episcopal Church, building on the foundation laid earlier by the Fellowship of Reconciliation, founded the Episcopal Peace Fellowship. Bowie was one of five priests who planned the founding of this organization and one assumes that he signed its pledge: "In loyalty to the Person, Spirit, and teachings of Jesus Christ, my conscience commits me to His way of redemptive love and compels me to refuse to participate in or give moral support to any war." In 1940 the Episcopal Church issued a new hymn book containing a subsection of eight hymns on world peace. One of those was Bowie's "Lord Christ, when first thou cam'st to men."[10] Bowie wrote that hymn in 1928, suggesting that his pacifist views were fully developed in the days when Bland was attending Grace Church and listening to his sermons.[11] She interpreted many of his sermons as opposition to war and she applied them to her life in such a way that she became a conscientious objector.[12] These experiences and influences led Bland to refuse to repeat that part of the naturalization oath requiring one to "defend the Constitution."

Bland's hearing before the Naturalization Examiner, J. A. G. Stitzer, occurred on 24 April 1930, just ten days after she had failed to complete the oath. Its purpose was to determine whether she was qualified for naturalization—in light of her reservations previously stated. Stitzer asked Bland, accompanied by her attorney, Emily Marx, whether she persisted in the view that she could not take the prescribed naturalization oath without reservations. Bland affirmed that she understood the *Schwimmer* case to require bearing arms, which she could not do.[13] She said she could take the oath in a modified form. She wanted to replace the phrase "I will support and defend the Constitution and laws of the United States" with the phrase "I will support the Constitution and laws of the United States and will, as far as my conscience as a Christian will allow, defend it against all enemies." There was precedent within the government for such a modification. The State Department allowed similar words to be inserted into the oath required to obtain a passport, out of deference to Quakers and other pacifist groups.[14]

Roger Baldwin, the director of the ACLU and a pacifist, had written in early October 1926 to the Passport Division of the State Department, inquiring about the oath required to obtain a passport. His specific question was whether the phrase "to support and defend the Constitution" obligated the one taking the oath to bear arms or to support the nation's wars. The director of the Passport Division had replied that his department did not

> construe the oath or affirmation of allegiance prescribed by the passport regulations as necessarily involving physical defense of the Constitution and consequently does not perceive any good reason why non-resistants should decline to accept it, especially as it is administered to women and children old enough to understand its nature. However, if you have conscientious scruples against taking the oath as it now stands, the Department will consider the matter of issuing a passport to you if you will file formal application for such a document supported by an oath or affirmation of allegiance to the Constitution in the following form:
>
> "Further, I do solemnly affirm that I will support the Constitution of the United States and will, *so far as my conscience will allow*, defend it against all enemies, foreign and domestic; that I will bear true faith and allegiance to the same; and that I take this obligation freely without any mental reservation or purpose of evasion. So help me God."[15]

Bland referred to this precedent on the advice of her legal counsel. Significantly, however, she wanted to add the word "Christian" to the conscience clause allowed in applications for passports and to use that word in the naturalization oath.

Naturalization Examiner Stitzer asked if her objections to bearing arms were based on her view of Christian morality. She replied: "Yes. According to the ethics of Christ, I would not conscientiously bear arms." In the affidavit she submitted with her testimony, she had written, "I believe that it is my duty as a Christian to refuse to bear arms or kill my fellow men, even in the event of war."[16] She acknowledged that she derived this view in part from the preaching she heard at Grace Episcopal Church in New York City. Stitzer noted that pacifism was not a theological tenet of the Episcopal church. Bland acknowledged that, but said she did not represent the Episcopal church. Her views were her own interpretation of the concepts preached at Grace Church. (For the text of Bland's testimony before the Naturalization Examiner, see Appendix O.) She believed, however, that other Episcopalians might agree with her, even though pacifism was not an official doctrine of the denomination.[17]

Many Episcopalians did agree with Marie Bland's views on war. The House of Deputies and House of Bishops of the Episcopal Church, meeting in New Orleans in 1925, had resolved that "*We assert our solemn judgment that aggressive warfare is a crime on the part of a nation and so to be held by followers of Christ*, Who has commanded that we make disciples, not enemies, of the peoples of this world." The statement was signed by 131 bishops. Just after Bland's hearing before Mr. Stitzer, the World Conference of the Bishops of the Anglican Communion, meeting in Lambeth, England, in July and August 1930, proclaimed, "The Conference affirms that war as a method of settling international disputes is *incompatible with the teaching and example of Our Lord Jesus Christ. . . .* For the Christian must condemn war not merely because it is wasteful and ruinous, a cause of untold misery, but far more *because it is contrary to the will of God.*" Among the signatories of this resolution were 53 American bishops.[18] Despite these statements, neither Bland nor her attorney, Emily Marx, challenged Stitzer's assumption that pacifism was not a teaching of the Episcopal Church. Stitzer concluded that Bland's pacifism was based on her interpretation of the sermons she heard at Grace Episcopal Church and her own moral reflection.

The Supreme Court majority's belief that she might try to influence others toward a pacifist position was one of the principal causes of the decision against Rosika Schwimmer. Stitzer questioned Marie Bland closely on this subject. Bland assured him that she had no intention of trying to influence others to refuse to bear arms, except insofar as her example might sway them. If she were asked specifically about her personal views, she would reply simply: "Personally, I would not bear arms." If others asked her advice on the issue, she would tell them that they would have to make up their own minds and follow their own conscience.[19]

Stitzer inquired how strongly she believed it was wrong to bear arms. She answered that she was absolutely opposed to serving in combat. "I feel that my duty to God is higher than my duty to any man-made laws in regard to carrying arms." She could not think of a circumstance that would cause her to violate her conviction, even if America were under attack and it was clear that the nation were imperiled. She would be a loyal citizen of the United States; she took citizenship very seriously. She would be willing to swear allegiance to all requirements of citizenship and to obey all laws, except the bearing of arms. When asked the hypothetical question of what she would do if she were a citizen and drafted into the military, she replied that she would go to prison. She refused to believe, contrary to the *Schwimmer* court, that bearing arms was the only way a person could be loyal to the country and defend the Constitution. "My idea of loyalty does not take that form; I think you can be loyal in ideals and ethics and you can work for the real spiritual welfare of a country even though you don't defend it by force of arms." If granted citizenship, she would be willing to serve as a nurse in time of war. "I would render service to the Government in anything but a combat capacity, and would be willing to help nurse the wounded anywhere in time of war."[20]

In the affidavit she submitted to Naturalization Examiner Stitzer at the time of the preliminary hearing, Bland had already announced her position.

> Since I believe that my obligations to my Maker impose upon me a duty to refrain from personally bearing arms, I cannot take the Oath of Allegiance without a mental reservation that as to me, [*sic*] personally, the word "defend" does not mean personally bearing arms. In the event of a war, I would willingly contribute my knowledge, experience and services as a nurse to the care of the wounded, wherever my services would be needed. But I would not personally take a gun in my hand and shoot any of my fellow men.[21]

On the basis of this testimony, Stitzer recommended on 25 April 1930 to the Federal District Court for the Southern District of New York that citizenship be denied to Bland because she was not attached to the principles of the Constitution and she was unwilling to take the oath without a mental reservation. Stitzer was joined in this objection to naturalization by the District Director of Naturalization, Merton A. Sturges. Sturges agreed with the reasons of Stitzer and added to those the precedent established in *United States v. Schwimmer*.[22]

When the Naturalization Examiner and Director sent a negative recommendation to the court, Bland's attorney, Emily Marx, prepared a brief to make her client's case. Marx was a graduate of Barnard College and Yale Law School, where she was editor of the *Yale Law Journal*. She was active in Republican politics and ran, unsuccessfully, for the State Assembly two times. During her career she served as a State Assistant Attorney General, judge in the New York City Domestic Relations Court, and enforcement attorney for the Downtown War Price and Rationing Board. But most of her career was devoted to private practice. She lectured at Barnard College and at Columbia University Institute on Arts and Sciences. For about fifteen years she wrote a column, "Our Laws," aimed at laypeople, for a weekly newspaper, *The Riverdale Press*. An excellent swimmer, she taught wimming and lifesaving at Red Cross camps during the summer months for many years and was recognized by the national Red Cross for her work in developing the organization's lifesaving program. Probably because of her involvement in Bland's case, she became interested in immigration and later worked extensively with aliens. She wrote a booklet, *Alien Into Citizen*, about how to enter, stay in, and leave America.[23]

Marx's brief to the District Court focused on three issues. First was the nature of the naturalization oath. Bland wanted to insert a phrase into the "defend" clause of the oath so that it would read "I will support and defend the Constitution and laws of the United States of America *as far as my conscience as a Christian will allow* against all enemies, foreign and domestic." Because neither the Constitution nor any statute prescribes the language of the oath, nothing "forbids the insertion of the limitation suggested by the petitioner." It is inconsistent to deny her request to insert those words. "The customary oath," Marx argued,

> relies for its effectiveness upon the petitioner's conscience as a Christian. Its last words are "So help me God." It assumes that the petitioner holds her duties to her Maker, as she sees them, above all other obligations. Yet, the customary oath would require the petitioner to disregard those duties as far as the bearing of arms is concerned. It would, in effect require her to place the obligations of citizenship above her religious obligations.

The State Department, Marx noted, allows those desiring to receive a passport to insert the phrase into the oath they swear, which set a govern-ment precedent for what Bland requests. To permit the Naturalization

Bureau to dictate the oath of naturalization to the exclusion of Bland is to go beyond congressional authorization.

Second, Bland clearly based her objection to bearing arms on her religious convictions, enabling Marx to distinguish this case from *Schwimmer*. Rosika Schwimmer was not a religious person and her objection to bearing arms was entirely philosophical. Bland's objection was based squarely on her religious conviction, so her case involved the constitutional principle of religious freedom. "The [*Schwimmer*] Court was not confronted by a conflict between the fundamental principle of religious freedom... and the 'fundamental principle' involving the duty to bear arms. The instant case presents such a conflict." Marx asserted that it was problematical that the duty to bear arms is a principle of the Constitution, but even if it were, the constitutionally guaranteed right of religious freedom superseded it. This was illustrated by various statutes—federal and state, that exempted conscientious objectors from military, or at least combatant, service—statutes she cited in her brief. The government had never required women to serve in the military. It certainly cannot be a fundamental principle of the Constitution for women to bear arms when it was not, until 1920, such a principle for women to be able to vote. "If the duty of women to bear arms is a fundamental principle of the Constitution, it must have become such a principle sometime during the past ten years. It surely did not have that status on June 16, 1906, when the Naturalization Act was passed."

Finally, Marx referred to Bland's personal qualities. She did not intend to try to persuade others to become pacifists or refuse to bear arms, again distinguishing her from Schwimmer. Further, she had been completely honest with the government, contrary to her own best interest. "To deny this petition," Marx concluded with painful irony,

> would put a premium on dishonesty. An alien who is honest with herself and with the government, would thus be automatically barred from citizenship because of her religious convictions concerning the bearing of arms; while the alien who does not bother to delve into his innermost thoughts on the subject, is welcomed as a citizen and permitted to examine his innermost thoughts more minutely when the occasion for bearing arms actually arises. Then he may claim exemption from the battlefields while his more honest fellow applicant for citizenship is imprisoned in a alien prison camp.
>
> Surely the best interests of the government are not served by such a procedure.[24]

Before submitting her brief to the court, Marx sent a copy to Rosika Schwimmer. "I am sure that you understand the reason for my assuming that the remarks made about you in the majority opinion of the Supreme Court, in *United States v. Schwimmer*, are true," Marx wrote. "I am, of course, attempting to distinguish the Bland case from yours in an effort to secure a different ruling."[25]

Marie Averil Bland appeared for her final citizenship hearing before Judge William Bondy of the United States District Court for the Southern District of New York on 28 April 1930. The proceedings were essentially the same as the hearing before the Naturalization Examiner, except that the court did not cover the ground as thoroughly.[26] Judge Bondy established that Bland was a conscientious objector whose ideas were based firmly on religious beliefs.

The Court: Can you not conceive of any circumstances under which you would [take the oath of allegiance]?
The Witness: No, I could not.
The Court: If you actually believed that the security of the homes of Americans was threatened, would you take up arms?
The Witness: No, I could not—not even then.
The Court: Are you a married woman?
The Witness: No.
Miss Marx: What is your reason for not wanting to take up arms?
The Witness: My reason is that I could not, according to my conscience as a Christian, bear arms. It is against my ethics—the ethics of Christ.
The Court: To bear arms?
The Witness: Yes.
The Court: If a person threatened you with violence, what would you do? Let him exercise violence?
The Witness: They would have to.
The Court: If a person threatened to kill you, with a gun in his hand, would you let him kill you?
The Witness: Certainly.
Miss Marx: You said that your religion forbids you bearing arms?
The Witness: Yes.
Miss Marx: For the purposes of the record, will you explain what you mean by your religion?
The Witness: Well, my religion, as far as I can explain it, is living according to the ethics of Christ, and what Christ taught—my interpretation of the Gospel.
The Court: Your interpretations are different from those of the majority of people, are they not?

The Witness: They may be. I could not say.[27]

In the hearing Emily Marx argued that *Schwimmer* could not be considered as precedent and applicable to Bland's case. The two women were different. Schwimmer was an atheist and did not base her objection to war on religious ethics. Bland was a devout Christian and grounded her pacifism on religion. Schwimmer had no nationalistic feeling, only a "cosmic consciousness." Bland had a distinct nationalistic loyalty—to the United States. Schwimmer was a lecturer and propagandist. Bland was a nurse, albeit with strong personal feelings about the evil of war, but she would not impose those feelings on others.

Marx further argued that even if the Supreme Court were right in *Schwimmer*—that the obligation to bear arms was a constitutional principle, a proposition with which she disagreed—the constitutional principle of religious freedom was more weighty. Marx contended "that this principle of religious freedom is much more important than any principle of bearing arms, and that, so far as our country is concerned, we have always insisted that if a person had religious opinions which they honestly believed, and those opinions did not conflict with our public policy, they were entitled to them." This right of religious freedom should be as applicable to the alien as to the native-born citizen.[28]

Bland's testimony and Marx's arguments did not persuade Judge Bondy. He accepted the adverse recommendation of the Naturalization Examiner and, on 7 May 1930, without a written opinion, decreed that Bland could not become a citizen, based on the precedent of *United States v. Schwimmer*.[29] The Federal Council of Churches took note and disagreed with the decision, as did a few newspapers.[30]

Emily Marx determined to appeal this judgment with all deliberate speed, but the manner in which she intended to do it precipitated a flurry of correspondence between her, Bland, and various officials of the ACLU. Douglas Clyde Macintosh had been denied citizenship by the Federal District Court of Connecticut on 8 January 1930 (see Chapter Four). His case was appealed to the Court of Appeals, Second Circuit, on 6 March 1930. Marx believed that it was important to appeal Bland's case to the same court in a timely manner so the cases could be argued together. Forrest Bailey, of the ACLU, wrote to Arthur Garfield Hays, wondering about the wisdom of Marx's strategy. Bland's case was attractive to the ACLU because its religious element was clearer than in Macintosh's. Would Hays make a judgment about whether the ACLU should grant Marx's request for funds? Marx wrote that she was willing to volunteer her services if the ACLU would pay all the costs of the appeal to the Court of Appeals and the Supreme Court, including travel, stenography, postage and other incidental expenses. She also said that she had talked with Hays and he agreed that the Bland case should be argued with Macintosh's. She and Hays also agreed that the two of them should argue Bland's case together, dividing argument time in half. Bailey sent a telegram to Marx, saying that Macintosh's attorney requested the two cases not be argued together, "believing such action would prejudice [the Macintosh case] and the whole cause. Hays [sic] advice in this matter did not have concurrence of our board. Our cooperation on Bland appeal must be conditional on your agreement to above request."[31]

Marie Bland wrote to Harry F. Ward, Chair of the ACLU Board, saying that when she had supported the ACLU earlier, she never dreamed she would become one of its cases. If her case involved only her, Bland would not pursue an appeal, but because it had broader implications, "I think it good to carry it to a higher court. Besides which I think this country should not be content with anything less than religious and ethical freedom of action in regard to war from those who wish to become citizens, and to live up to what its best citizens stand for, in this and other matters." Forrest Bailey responded to Bland on behalf of Ward[32] that the ACLU had withdrawn its support for her case because of Marx's intention to argue it in tandem with the Macintosh case. He explained that the ACLU's leaders believed that her case should be argued after a decision in the Macintosh case had been rendered. That way her case could come before a court with no similar issues before it and perhaps get a more objective hearing. Marx wrote to the ACLU saying that she persisted in wanting to argue Bland's case with Macintosh's and thus would not expect ACLU support. The standoff continued when the ACLU board reaffirmed its position in two separate votes. Marx wrote that it was regrettable that the ACLU would not financially support Bland's case. She also said that John W. Davis, Macintosh's attorney, had no objection to the two cases being argued together, contrary to the ACLU's earlier assertion. She hoped the ACLU would at least pay the printing costs for the appeal. Forrest Bailey wrote to Marx, saying the desires of the Davis firm were only incidental in the ACLU's taking the position it did. Bailey wrote to Bland, enclosing a copy of his letter to Marx and explaining that Davis's agreement with Marx was only lawyer's courtesy, not acquiescence with her plan. "As a matter of fact, in the interest of their own client and with due regard to your interests as well, the firm expressed itself as endorsing our position—namely, that it was desirable that your case should not be argued until a decision should be reached in the Macintosh case."[33]

Marx, apparently a tenacious woman,[34] argued Bland's case on the same day as Macintosh's, before the same three judges of the United States Court of Appeals, Second Circuit—Martin T. Manton, Learned Hand, and Thomas W. Swan. She argued the case alone; Arthur Garfield Hays did not assist her. Rosika Schwimmer attended the oral argument, and later wrote to Olive Rabe that "Miss Marx, to our immense surprise, was very good for Miss Bland, much better than [John W.] Davis for his client [Macintosh]. The Government's representative opposing her was very weak. She was quite matter of fact, did not try stunts, kept strictly to the legal points."[35]

The court reversed the lower court and awarded Bland citizenship. Writing for the court, Judge Manton observed that neither the Constitution nor the naturalization statute prescribed the words of the oath of naturalization. The words came from the rules of the Commissioner of Naturalization, with the implication that the words that were offensive to Bland's religious sensibilities were not mandated by the most weighty authorities. Clearly, however, Bland was willing to swear her allegiance to the country, using the customary oath, if it could be modified in one phrase only. The Constitution and the appropriate laws ask for nothing more than the expression of allegiance.

The Court of Appeals stressed that the nation protects freedom of religion through the First Amendment. True, the Constitution and laws of the land provide for the military and even drafting male citizens and aliens (who intended to become citizens) into military service. Yet in deference to religious freedom the government had consistently exempted from combat those who had religious objections to war. Such individuals were usually assigned a noncombatant role in the military. Marie Bland had testified to her willingness to serve in a noncombatant role as a nurse. The record of the case showed that she was willing

> to assume all the obligations and duties of citizenship as required by the Constitution and the laws of the country. To take the oath as phrased by the Naturalization Bureau would leave appellant free to be relieved of bearing arms in the event of war. It would not enforce arms bearing upon her or any other citizen in event of future wars, and Congress unquestionably will, as it has in the past, make provision for citizens who conscientiously, irrespective of sect, want to be relieved because of religious convictions against combatant military service. And, if this appellant was

thus informed, she, perhaps, would have been relieved of her fear of assuming an obligation which her oath did not impose upon her.

Finally, the Court of Appeals distinguished Bland's case from *Schwimmer*. In *Schwimmer*, the religious beliefs of the objector never were raised; they were important in this case. Schwimmer was a propagandist; Bland was not. The court concluded that Bland should be awarded citizenship: "The appellant may take the oath, and she will be fully protected if she will then make known her conscientious objections."[36]

Marx now wrote to ACLU director Roger Baldwin that she had won the appeal. Because of that result, "it occurred to me" that the ACLU might want to reconsider its refusal to help finance the case. Bland, after all, was a nurse and not able to underwrite the costs. Simultaneously Baldwin offered congratulations to Marx and admitted "that evidently we were wrong in our assumption that the arguing of this case at the same time with Professor Macintosh would cloud the issue. Indeed, judging by results the two cases together are stronger than one." Baldwin did not, however, "understand the reasoning of the Court of Appeals in distinguishing these cases from the Schwimmer case and for that reason I trust the government will appeal." These two letters crossed in the mail. Baldwin responded to Marx's request by asking for an accounting of expenditures so far. He said he could not promise anything, but would do his best. Marx replied with appreciation and enclosed a statement for $267.62.

Marie Bland sometime earlier had sent a contribution of $5 to the ACLU. As the letters between Baldwin and Marx were being composed, Baldwin was also writing to Bland.

> We hate to take money from you at a time when you have been put to all the expenses of carrying up your case in court. We ought to be paying you, not you us. I am asking your attorney about those expenses, because we may be able to do something both on what has already been paid out and on the possible defense of your case if the government appeals.

Baldwin also reminded Bland that she had sent $5 earlier in the year and that she had contributed $10 annually since 1925.

"If there is one thing more than another that I admire," Bland replied to Baldwin,

> it is to see anyone acknowledge they have made a mistake, and when it is the Civil Liberties that does it, adding to your already long list of

virtues, words fail to express which I think. You certainly deserve every bit of help you can get. I had not forgotten I usually contribute but thought you might have to do with $5.00 this year, and I am beginning to appreciate the high cost of liberty for myself. Many thanks for your suggestion of possible assistance but I can manage to pay what I owe Miss Marx, little by little as she kindly allows me. The defense of a further appeal would be harder to meet, though when I read of your defense of the Atlanta Communists in Jail, [sic] I should hate to take a penny from their greatly needed defense. I too agree that Mde Schwimmer should be admitted to Citizenship, if we are.

Baldwin thanked Bland for her appreciation and said the ACLU could not allow her to bear the costs in her own case. She should not worry that her expenses would detract from the defense of the Atlanta Communists.[37]

The debate about the ACLU's support of the Bland case came rapidly to a close, temporarily. According to an internal ACLU memorandum, when the case went to the Supreme Court, Marx wanted to argue it and looked to the ACLU for fees, both for the Appeals Court and the Supreme Court. "She frankly says the reason she took the case into the Court of Appeals without fee is because she knew it would do her practice good." A letter went to Marx saying that the ACLU would reimburse Bland for her out-of-pocket expenses, but could not pay Marx's fee. If the case were to go to the Supreme Court, the organization could pay court costs, but no fee for Marx. The ACLU's budget for special projects was only $1,500. Surely Marx could understand. Baldwin wrote the same information to Bland, but enclosed a check for $267.62 for her expenses. "I am very much obliged to you and the Executive Committee for their offer to pay my expenses," Bland replied. "I accept it with gratitude. I consider it very generous in view of the small amount you have at your disposal."[38]

Responding to the decisions of the Court of Appeals granting Bland and Macintosh their citizenship, Rosika Schwimmer asked her friend and legal counsel, Olive Rabe, what she thought of the "favorable decision, supported by the argument that they are so much better than I am?" Schwimmer confessed that she was "getting more than fed up to serve as a bad example to make others appear the more innocent and nice. Couldn't they give the others citizenship without making a special note of my undesirability?" Emily Marx "shouts like a peacock with her victory. I told her that you too had won an appeal."[39]

The Department of Justice could not allow the Court of Appeals's decision to go unchallenged; it eroded the government's understanding of the function and effect of the naturalization oath. The government's petition to the Supreme Court for a writ of certiorari centered on Bland's absolute conscientious objection as a Christian, her unwillingness to take the oath of naturalization unless she were able to insert the phrase "so far as my conscience as a Christian will allow," and that the Court of Appeals had erred by interposing its own judgment for that of Congress, which had prescribed the precise wording of the oath. The government also referred to the brief it was simultaneously filing in the Macintosh case as applying to this case, as well. The Supreme Court granted certiorari on 24 November 1930.[40]

In her brief arguing Bland's position, Emily Marx called attention to Bland's religious belief as the basis of her conscientious objection. Marx contrasted Bland with Schwimmer, a secular pacifist and propagandist who lacked nationalistic feeling. Bland could not be characterized that way. Because Bland was a religious pacifist, Marx thought the Justices must understand that this case was dramatically different from *Schwimmer*.[41]

Marx first noted that the wording of the oath of naturalization had been taken bodily from the oath of office required of all public officials except the President (the wording of whose oath is mandated by the Constitution). Since 1861 those taking the Oath of Office had promised to "defend the Constitution." Yet never had the oath been construed to exclude from public office persons having religious objections against bearing arms. Such a construction would violate Art. 6, cl. 3 of the Constitution: "[N]o religious Test shall ever be required as a Qualification to any Office or Public Trust under the United States." If the oath were not a barrier against office holders who were conscientious objectors, neither should it bar aliens with similar convictions.[42]

In its second argument the brief for Bland spoke to the wording of the oath itself, that neither the Constitution nor naturalization statutes demanded the language adopted by the Bureau of Naturalization. The Naturalization Act required only a promise to support and defend the Constitution and laws of the nation; it did not mandate any words about how that would be accomplished. Nothing in the Constitution or the Act forbade insertion of the phrase desired by Bland, "insofar as my conscience as a Christian will allow." The customary oath ended with the phrase, "So help me God," which meant that the oath depended for its effectiveness on the alien's conscience as a Christian. Yet the oath, as construed by the courts, required an alien to disregard her or his duties to God as far as bearing arms was concerned. The oath, as interpreted by the government in reference to those with religious objections to killing, was logically inconsistent. The Naturalization Act had implicitly recognized historical guarantees of religious freedom and its applicability to alien applicants for citizenship by listing "in detail the particular views and opinions, *religious*, philosophical and political, which will bar an alien from becoming naturalized." The Act "makes no mention of religious scruples against bearing arms; it does not prescribe a *text* for the Oath of Allegiance. It merely requires that the oath shall contain, among other promises, an agreement to support and defend the Constitution." To impose a "promise to defend by force of arms by those whose religious beliefs forbid such a promise, was clearly not within the intention of Congress or within the spirit of the Act." Bland "would have been admitted to citizenship if she had not held religious convictions concerning the bearing of arms, or if she had been less honest with herself and with the District Court." Now in Bland's behalf Marx emphasized that "*To refuse to administer to her the oath which she has suggested, would deprive her of citizenship, solely because of her religious convictions.*" Such refusal is not consistent with America's tradition of respect for religious freedom.[43]

Religious convictions against bearing arms do not demonstrate lack of attachment to the principles of the Constitution. The District Director of Naturalization and the Federal District Court both held that Bland was not attached to the principles of the Constitution on the basis of the *Schwimmer* case, in which the Supreme Court had held that one could defend the Constitution only by bearing arms. But *Schwimmer* did not involve the element central to Bland's conviction: religious belief. An extensive review of military service laws shows that the duty to bear arms had never been allowed to interfere with the principle of freedom of religious belief and conscience. People with such convictions had served the several states and the nation well. It seemed to Marx "that throughout our natural history" lawmakers had acquiesced "in the principle enunciated by the members of the First and Second Congress, *that when military obligations interfere with religious scruples, the conflict should be resolved in favor of an unhampered performance of religious duties.*" They had never "required those religiously scrupulous of bearing arms, to perform combatant military service."[44]

Bland's religious beliefs were, in fact, in accord with the public policy and ideals of the American government. As a signatory to the Kellogg-Briand Treaty of 24 July 1929, in which the treaty nations had agreed to renounce war as an instrument of national policy, the United States had made such a concept the law of the land.[45] "Surely," Marx observed, bringing to bear both the language of the treaty and Justice Homes's dissent in *Schwimmer*, "it is not against public policy of a government which has persuaded fifty-eight nations of the world to renounce war 'as an instrument of their national policy' to admit to citizenship an alien who believes 'more than some of us do in the teachings of the Sermon on the Mount.'"[46]

To deny Bland's petition for citizenship, Marx concluded, would place a premium on intellectual dishonesty and ignorance. Prevailing policy seemed to reward persons who do not take the trouble to know the interpretation of the courts, or who do not examine their attitudes toward waging war, or who even object to bearing arms but—prizing citizenship more than those convictions—take the oath without questions. Persons who are honest with the government and voice their conscientious convictions are denied citizenship.[47]

The government replied to these arguments in its own brief to the Supreme Court, but offered its primary arguments in the case of Douglas Clyde Macintosh running on a track parallel to Bland's. Macintosh and Marie Bland were both conscientious Christians; both had offered Christian service to soldiers in World War I; but while Macintosh did not object to participation in any and all wars, Bland would not promise to bear arms in any war.

Straightforwardly the government argued that while Macintosh wanted to make his own judgment about the appropriateness of a war before he would participate, Congress, in the Naturalization Act, had made no exceptions for those who were not willing to take the oath because of conscientious or religious scruples. Although the nation had made exceptions for *citizens* who were conscientious objectors, it had not made them for *aliens* applying for naturalization. In order to receive citizenship, one had to comply exactly with the naturalization laws and rules. Macintosh had refused to take the prescribed oath without qualification or mental reservation and he had failed to convince the District Court that he "was attached to the principles of the Constitution." The government said the *Schwimmer* case was controlling in this case as well. That Macintosh was religious while Mme. Schwimmer was not was without significance. Both had substituted their understanding of the oath and the necessity to go to war for that of Congress—the crucial issue in the cases. It was not possible, under the law, for a court to transfer the power to determine the necessity of war or the duty of the citizen to bear arms from Congress to the applicant for citizenship.[48] Macintosh's position "is merely that of a highly educated man with that deep sense of right and wrong which every applicant for citizenship is presumed to possess, seeking to transfer from Congress to himself, the right to determine whether the defense of this country requires him to bear arms."[49]

In arguing the *Bland* case, the government repeatedly invoked everything in its *Macintosh* brief. If anything, Bland was a worse scoundrel than Macintosh because at least he was willing to fight in some wars, whereas she refused to bear arms in any circumstance. Both cases recapitulated *Schwimmer*, even though Schwimmer was an atheist, for they all three had refused to swear to the required oath "and it makes no difference whether the refusal to take the oath, as required by Congress, is placed upon conscientious, religious, or other grounds."[50]

The government's brief, signed by Solicitor General Thomas D. Thacher, focused on Marx's argument that neither the Naturalization Act nor the Constitution authorized the language of the Naturalization Oath to which Bland objected. Although neither prescribe the exact language, the Naturalization Oath follows the substance of the Naturalization Act so closely that it is clear that the Oath is derived from the Act. Bland wanted to add the phrase "so far as my conscience as a Christian will allow," a proposition approved by the Court of Appeals. (Neither Schwimmer nor Macintosh had wanted to change the wording of the oath.) Such modification was unacceptable. "The statute recognizes no such qualification. It prescribes the substance of the oath without qualification and for the courts to qualify the substance of a statutory requirement is to amend the law. This is a task for Congress, not the courts." Although the United States had permitted citizens with religious objections to war to be exempt from participation, the same privilege could not be available to applicants for citizenship. Bland could not "be permitted to transform into a vested right those acts of mere grace by which in times of war Congress has exempted from combatant service persons whose religious convictions forbade them bearing arms." Only Congress, "not the alien applicant for citizenship," could determine "whether such exemptions shall be granted." In the government's understanding of "the qualification tests exacted by the Naturalization Act," citizenship requires "nothing less than the unqualified willingness of the alien applicant to bear arms if Congress shall deem it necessary."[51]

The American Friends Service Committee filed an *amicus curiae* brief to the Supreme Court jointly on behalf of Macintosh and Bland (see Chapter Four). Edward L. Parsons, Episcopal Bishop of California, and twelve other luminaries of the Protestant Episcopal Church in the United States, including Walter Russell Bowie, filed a brief supporting Bland.[52] In her hearing before the Naturalization Examiner, Bland had admitted that pacifism was not a tenet of the Episcopal Church, that her conscientious objection was based on her own personal faith and her interpretations of the sermons she heard at Grace Episcopal Church. Bland did say, however, that she believed that many Episcopalians agreed with her aversion to war. This *amicus* brief sought to verify that claim, describing the antiwar statements of the American Episcopal Church at its convention in 1925 and of the World Conference of Bishops of the Anglican Communion at Lambeth, England, in 1930 (see note 18 and accompanying text). In its brief, the government had asserted that Bland offered her conscience as sole judge of the meaning of the moral law of Christ, following closely its argument against Macintosh. The Episcopal leaders addressed that accusation head on. In light of the resolutions of Anglican bishops, Bland "has not set up her 'own conscience or will as the sole judge to determine what laws are not in accord with the moral law of Jesus Christ.' Her interpretation of the ethics of Christ accords with the construction placed thereon by many of the leaders of the Protestant Episcopal Church."[53]

Bland and *Macintosh* were argued before the Supreme Court on successive days—27-28 April 1931. One news account contrasted the counsel for the two plaintiffs, describing Macintosh's lawyer, John W. Davis, as "white-haired, urbane," "at home before the nation's highest court," while "Fair haired, young and pretty was Miss Bland's counsel, Miss Emily Marx, of New York, making her legal debut before the Supreme Court, but undaunted in the fervor of her appeal." When the Justices filed in and Justice James C. McReynolds saw Marx, he said, "Do we have to listen to a *fe*male?" Despite that welcome, Marx reminded the Justices of Bland's experience of the horrors of war as she nursed soldiers. She also noted that Bland had called attention to her aversion to war; to deny her citizenship would place a premium on dishonesty. Marx also called attention to the *amicus* brief written by the Episcopal Church leaders, demonstrating that many people of that faith agreed with Bland's position on war and bearing arms. Justice Butler asked her if she were arguing that the Episcopal Church taught that Christians should not bear arms in defense of the country. Justice Sutherland asked if she were arguing that if a nation invaded America, members of the Episcopal Church or any other church should refuse to take up arms in defense of the country. Marx acknowledged that pacifism was not a teaching of the Episcopal Church, but asserted that the Bishops were asking that those many Episcopalians who conscientiously objected to war, as Bland did, should be excused from military service.[54]

The cases were decided on 25 May 1931. Justice George Sutherland wrote both opinions for the majority. In his first sentence of the *Bland* decision, Sutherland announced, "This case is ruled by the decision just announced in *United States v. Macintosh*." In *Macintosh* the Court held that naturalization could be gained only on the terms set forth by Congress. The case was decided under principles set forth in *United States v. Schwimmer*.[55] Justice Sutherland drew only one distinction between *Bland* and *Macintosh*. "The only difference between the position she took, and that taken by the respondent in the *Macintosh* case, is that in addition to refusing positively to bear arms in defense of the United States under any circumstances, she required an actual amendment of the oath." As in *Macintosh*, "this is a circumstance which has no distinguishing effect" since the "substance of the oath has been definitely prescribed by Congress." The Court majority found that the "words of the statute do not admit of the qualification upon which the applicant insists." Bland's Christian conscience could not be allowed to limit the oath. "For the court to allow [the qualification] to be made is to amend the act and thereby usurp the power of legislation vested in another department of the government."[56] Marie Averil Bland was denied American citizenship.

In *Bland*, as in *Schwimmer* and in *Macintosh*, justices dissented from the majority. Chief Justice Charles Evans Hughes, joined by Justices Holmes, Brandeis, and Stone, said what he had written in dissent in *Macintosh* (see Chapter Four) applied to the *Bland* case as well. He added only that Bland understood the oath of naturalization as amounting to a promise that she would bear arms contrary to her religious convictions. The Court of Appeals had held that the oath did not imply that promise and Bland could take it without having to bear arms. Chief Justice Hughes wrote that he thought the ruling of the Court of Appeals was correct and should have been affirmed.[57] (For the full text of the Court's opinion, see Appendix R.)

Because *Bland* and *Macintosh* were handed down the same day and Macintosh was a much more public figure, most of the voluminous press commentary focused on him. In many articles, Bland was mentioned hardly at all. "We helped to put these cases before the Supreme Court," ACLU director Roger Baldwin announced, "because we believed it would stand by the old tradition of freedom for religious conscience. But this decision reveals a new dispensation—the supremacy of the State over the conscience of the individual. God officially gets second place." The Court "now decrees that the government alone shall judge what war service a citizen shall render. Thus the only war-time right left to any of us, by the implication of this decree, is the right to agree with the government." The decision would please "all professional patriots and militarists . . . in line with the widespread propaganda for militarism."[58]

The *Christian Science Monitor* reported that Bland was barred from citizenship "for refusing to promise to do something which the laws of the nation would not permit her to do." The *Philadelphia Record* exclaimed, "A strangely inflexible rule, if it is to be applied to exclude war nurses! This country has no women's Battalion of Death; its women are not expected or required to bear arms. Rejection of Miss Bland seems to be a triumph of legalism over reason."[59]

Emily Marx would not take "no" for an answer. She filed a petition with the Supreme Court for a rehearing of Bland's case. (In this she was not alone; Macintosh's counsel did the same thing.) Marx began with an ironic appeal to "manhood," pointing—as editorial commentators had already done, in *Bland* as in *Schwimmer*—to the ludicrous effect of the decision in light of traditional sex roles. Although the Court had held that exemption from military service because of religious scruples was always at the discretion of Congress, "yet when that conscientious objector happens to be a woman, she is relieved from combatant military service not by a Congressional act of grace but by virtue of the virile spirit of manhood of this nation, which has never permitted its women to engage in mortal combat." Her client "would not be permitted to bear arms even if she so desired—the men of this country will never allow the women to do their fighting for them." Indeed, Marx asserted, "By reading into the Naturalization Act a Congressional direction that women must promise to bear arms in order to become citizens, the Court is running counter to every instinct and tradition of our civilization."

Marx then invoked religious freedom, for in *Macintosh* the Court had decreed that allegiance to the nation and obedience to the laws of the land are consistent with the will of God. "If it is not possible that obedience to the laws of the land should ever be inconsistent with the will of God," Marx asked, "what further need have we of the First Amendment to the Constitution?" The decision obliterated a distinct American contribution to human liberty and religious life. "If Congress is the oracle thru [*sic*] which the will of God is announced to this Nation, what has become of the right of the individual to determine for himself 'his relations to his Creator' and 'the obligations they impose of reverence for his being and character, and of obedience to his will.'" Congress had "heretofore" respected "religious scruples against bearing arms"; now "this Court has imposed a limitation upon religious liberty in advance of Congressional action thereon. The conflict of conscience and law Congress has ever sought to avoid; should the courts bring it on?"[60]

At the conclusion of her first argument, emphasizing the disparity between the decision and traditional sex roles in American society and seeking to distinguish Bland's case, Marx had written that "Rosika Schwimmer was more than a conscientious objector. She was pledged to active propaganda against combatant service by others. Her individual refusal to promise to bear arms was merely incident to her avowed desire and purpose to persuade others to refuse to perform active military service."[61] Angered and affronted, Schwimmer wrote in the margin of her copy of the brief, "Plain lie. R.S." She sent the brief to her attorney, Olive Rabe. "You will see that she accuses me in it of things that I have never done," Schwimmer wrote.

> I wonder whether I have to stand for that? Could I not make her publicly acknowledge that I was not "pledged to active propaganda against combatant service by others." I was neither pledged nor did voluntarily do anything of that sort. My peace activities were exclusively directed to persuade the governments to mediate and stop the whole bloody business. To "persuade others to refuse to perform active military service" was not and is not in my line because that would not prevent war; would not make it impossible. What I have done all my life before, during and since the war is to try to persuade people and governments to reorganize the world so that war should become impossible.

"I am terribly mad at that little beast for misusing me this way," Schwimmer complained of Marx. "She never let me have a copy of her brief. I had to borrow one from Miss Bland and got it copied."

"Of course there was no excuse for Miss Marx' statement about you in the petition for a rehearing," Rabe responded to Schwimmer. "If she didn't know the facts she should have asked you. But if she had the transcript of your hearing here, she *had* the facts and purposely misstated them." Rabe argued against asking for a public apology, for that would mean publicity for Marx, which is what she desired, or a lawsuit, which surely could not be won (and would be counterproductive to the pacifist cause). Rabe advised requesting a written apology from Marx. Schwimmer then could decide whether to allow it to remain private or to make it public. I have found no evidence that Schwimmer ever demanded an apology from Marx. When Marie Bland learned of Schwimmer's anger about Marx's statements, she offered her "sincere sympathy in your effort to have Miss Marx retract the false statement made about you in my brief." Bland thought it "a great reflection on her probity when she stoops to such methods to make a point in her petition." Marx had injured Schwimmer, who would be "quite right, I think, not to ignore it." Bland thought the injury was more public than personal. "Your friends who know you will not believe this of you, but it is the public who are misinformed."

Bland had her own strong reservations about Marx's brief. "Miss Marx had filed a brief appealing the decision of the Supreme Court in my behalf," she wrote to Roger Baldwin, referring to a *New York Times* report.

> This she did without my knowledge, approval, or consent & I have asked her to withdraw the petition. I think it was a great mistake & I want to know if it is legal without my consent or knowledge & and if there is any way it can be [withdrawn]. I do not wish to appeal on any grounds. Will you please consider this confidential & answer me perfectly frankly if you think this ridiculous petition should stand. I enclose the petition.

Baldwin replied that there was nothing Bland could do about the filing of the petition, "foolish as it is," expressing amazement that Marx had acted without Bland's consent. Marx had asked the ACLU for $50 to finance the petition, but the organization refused the money "because it was a useless move." Baldwin assumed that Marx had hoped that Justice Owen C. Roberts, a liberal judge, would change his mind and swing his vote to the dissenters, who would then become the majority.[62] Marx filed the petition to the Supreme Court to no avail, despite the anger and dismay it caused. The Court denied the petition.[63]

Among the stories of Marie Bland, Rosika Schwimmer, and Douglas Clyde Macintosh there is one curious distinction. In her quest to become a citizen Bland got as far as her naturalization ceremony before taking action that set in motion the litigation that ultimately denied her citizenship. Schwimmer and Macintosh were identified as conscientious objectors almost as soon as they began the naturalization process. The distinction lies in the famous question 22 on the naturalization questionnaire,[64] which asked, "If necessary, are you willing to take up arms in defense of the country?"[65] Mme. Schwimmer answered "I would not take up arms personally" and Professor Macintosh answered "Yes, but I would want to be free to judge of the necessity." In each case, this answer triggered a process that eventually led to denial of naturalization. In each case, questions had been asked about whether the question was used uniformly[66] and how long it had been used;[67] yet in neither case had the question of the existence of the question been important in the outcome. Remarkably, Bland been able to get all the way to the oath-taking ceremony because the question had not been on the questionnaire she was required to complete. Article I, Sec. 8, of the Constitution requires Congress "To establish a uniform Rule of Naturalization." Congress had enacted laws that, supposedly, established that "uniform rule," but the procedures to implement those laws were not uniform.[68] The questionnaire forms were not identical in all jurisdictions and that led to different results in the naturalization process. In New York City, where Bland lived, the naturalization office apparently used older forms, composed before the question about bearing arms was included.[69] When Bland filled out the form, she was not asked to reveal her pacifist attitudes. She did not know she was on a collision course with the government until she began to see the publicity surrounding *Schwimmer*, decided six days after she filed her formal petition for naturalization. Bland's case begins and ends with a failure of "equal protection of the laws."

Marie Averil Bland's case was overshadowed by that of Douglas Clyde Macintosh. She did not make legal history.[70] She did not distinguish herself in any public way once her case was decided. Why, then, tell her story? Marie Bland exemplifies all-too-rare human virtues of honesty and integrity. American citizenship was within her grasp. Her hand was raised. She was taking the oath. Yet at those words her faith would not allow her to say, she lowered her hand and fell silent. Even then, no one seems to have noticed. She could have remained true to her aversion to militarism and still have become a citizen. No one would have been the wiser. But Marie Bland's Christian conscience would not let her lie to herself or to duly constituted authorities. She told the judge what she had done—perhaps to bear witness, perhaps because integrity would allow her to do no other. She consequently lost her opportunity to become an American citizen. But in that moment of truth she represented the finest of the human spirit. Marie Averil Bland is a woman from whom all can learn. Her story is told "in praise of conscience."

Notes

1. Testimony of Emily Marx, "Bill to Permit Oath of Allegiance by Candidates for Citizenship to Be Made with Certain Reservations," Hearings Before the Committee on Immigration and Naturalization, House of Representatives, Seventy-First Congress, Second Session, on H.R. 3547, 8-9 May 1930, 49-50; see also Marie Averil Bland, "Affidavit of Petitioner," United States Circuit Court of Appeals for the Second Circuit, Transcript of Record, *Marie Averil Bland v. United States,* 24-25, 27.

2. *United States v. Schwimmer* 279 U.S. 644 (1929).

3. The famous evangelist Aimee Semple McPherson was born in Ingersoll just seven years after Bland. Edith L. Blumhofer, (*Aimee Semple McPherson: Everybody's Sister* [Grand Rapids: William B. Eerdmans Publishing, 1993], 23-59) describes Ingersoll and the region surrounding it, recounting (39) the words of a Salvation Army battle song written on the occasion of the opening of the Ingersoll barracks.

> Our Barracks here in Ingersoll are up, up, up;
> The brickwork and the woodwork, they are all now done;
> And now the seats are in,
> Let Mr. Devil grin,
> But we shall hear the Savior say "well done."

4. For biography of Edward Michael Bland see John A. Venn, *Alumni Cantabrigienses* 2: *1752 -1900* (Cambridge: Cambridge University Press, 1940) 1:293; *Crockford's Clerical Directory 1936* (London: H. Cox, 1936), 120.

5. Lettie Gavin, *American Women in World War 1: They Also Served* (Niwot, Col.: University Press of Colorado, 1997), 101-5; Ida May Hazenhyer, "A History of the American Physiotherapy Association," *Physiotherapy Review* 26 (January-February 1946): 3-5, reprinted in *The Beginnings: Physical Therapy and the APTA* (Alexandria, Va.: American Physical Therapy Association, 1979), 60-62. See also "Recollections and Reminiscences from Former Reconstruction Aides" (in *The Beginnings: Physical Therapy and the APTA*, 10-28), which offers autobiographical statements by Reconstruction Aides that illustrate what that service was like. Its oath of induction read, "I, _____, do solemnly swear (or affirm) that I will bear true faith and allegiance to the United States of America; that I will serve them honestly and faithfully against all their enemies whomsoever; and that I will obey the orders of the President of the United States, and the orders of the officers appointed over me according to the Rules and Articles of War"; see *Manual for Noncommissioned Officers and Privates of Cavalry of the Army of the United States* (Washington: Government Printing Office, 1917), 9.

6. Gavin, *American Women in World War 1*, 242-43, 112.

7. Bland, "Affidavit of Petitioner," Transcript of Record, 25-26.

8. Gavin, *American Women in World War 1*, 110.

9. Bland, "Affidavit of Petitioner," Transcript of Record, 26.

10. Although the hymn is listed in the index of the hymnal under "Peace: International," only stanza three speaks of peace directly.

> New advent of the love of Christ,
> Shall we again refuse thee,
> Till in the night of hate and war
> We perish as we lose thee?
> From old unfaith our souls release
> To seek the kingdom of thy peace,
> By which alone we choose thee.

See *The Hymnal of the Protestant Episcopal Church in the United States of America, 1940* (New York: Church Pension Fund, 1940), 522.

11. Walter Russell Bowie, *Learning to Live* (Nashville: Abingdon Press, 1969), 109-131, 140-55, 166-77, 182. This is Bowie's autobiography. See also Nathaniel W. Pierce and Paul L. Ward, *The Voice of Conscience: A Loud and Unusual Noise?: The Episcopal Peace Fellowship 1939-1989* (Episcopal Peace Fellowship, 1989), 2-10. Richard O. Boyer ("The Gentleman in the Pulpit,"*New Yorker* 14 [22 October 1938]: 30) focuses on Bowie's liberalism and his uneasy relationship with the congregation of Grace Episcopal Church.

12. Bland, "Affidavit of Petitioner," Transcript of Record, 16-17, 21-23, 26.

13. "Preliminary Hearing Before Examiner," Transcript of Record, 15.

14. "Preliminary Hearing Before Examiner," Transcript of Record, 19-20, 25. See *United States v. Bland*, to the Supreme Court of the United States, *Brief on Behalf of Petitioner-Appellee*, 19-20.

15. M. Huddle, Chief, Passport Division, to Roger N. Baldwin, 22 October 1926, Schwimmer-Lloyd collection, box G-2, emphasis added. Baldwin subsequently obtained a passport by swearing in the manner described here.

16. Transcript of Record, 16, 26.

17. Transcript of Record, 17.

18. See *United States v. Bland*, to the Supreme Court of the United States, Brief on behalf of Edward L. Parsons, *et al.*, *Amici Curiae*, 4-5, 12; emphasis in original.

19. Transcript of Record, 16, 14.

20. Transcript of Record, 15-16, 18, 19, 21, 23.

21. Transcript of Record, 27. For the text of this hearing before the Naturalization Examiner, see Appendix O; for the affidavit attached to the text of the hearing see Appendix P.

22. Transcript of Record, 10-11, 28-29.

23. A brief biography of Emily Marx can be constructed from "To List Law Firms Which Bar Women," *New York Times*, 17 April 1927, 4; "Miss Marx to Meet Voters in Her District," *New York Times*, 21 August 1927, 5; "How Do Women Campaign?" *New York Times*, 28 August 1927, 10; "No Relative of Miss Marx," *New York Times*, 7 October 1927, 29; "Citizens Union Praises Miss Marx," *New York Times*, 6 October 1927, 6; "Will Back Miss Marx," *New York Times*, 11

October 1927, 6; "Appeals for a Dry Plank," *New York Times*, 12 October 1927, 3; "Republican Gains in the Assembly," *New York Times*, 9 November 1927, 6; "General Motors Head on Raskob's Transfer," *New York Times*, 31 July 1931, 3; "Miss Marx Wins Medal," *New York Times*, 11 September 1928, 14; "Bars Fellowship Forum," *New York Times*, 24 September 1928, 5; "Citizens Union Lauds Miss Marx," *New York Times*, 7 October 1928, 24; "Weighs Aspirants in Assembly Race," *New York Times*, 15 October 1928, 12; "Objects to Smith Pictures," *New York Times*, 28 October 1928, 24; "Asks Silence on Politics," *New York Times*, 31 October 1928, 8; "Gerard's Riding Club Faces Court Fight," *New York Times*, 3 November 1928, 3; "Lays Defeat to 'New Vote,'" *New York Times*, 8 November 1928, 6; "Riding Club Plan Dropped," *New York Times*, 17 December 1928, 46; "Koening Declares for Fusion Ticket," *New York Times*, 3 May 1929, 16; "Decision Reserved in M'Intosh Case," *New York Times*, 21 May 1930, 56; "Other Weddings: House-Marx," *New York Times*, 24 June 1931, 2; "Finds Judge Wasted Time," *New York Times*, 6 January 1934, 3; "Inflation: Control Plan," *New York Times*, 3 May 1942, E9; "Woman Ex-Judge Loses Traffic Plea," *New York Times*, 13 June 1942, 17; "Emily Marx Dead; A Lawyer Here, 63," *New York Times*, 9 June 1966, 47; Amy Schaeffer, "Meet Miss Marx!" *Barnard College Alumni Monthly* 30 (January 1941): 12-13; "Emily Marx," *Who's Who of American Women*, 3d ed. (Chicago: Marquis-Who's Who, 1964-65), 655.

24. *Brief in the Matter of the Petition of Marie Averil Bland to Be Admitted to Become a Citizen of the United States of America*, 4-5, 9-10, 12-13, 16, 24-26; Record Group 267, National Archives collection.

25. Marx to Schwimmer, 26 April 1930. Schwimmer-Lloyd collection, box G-4. Schwimmer disliked Marx; this note may have provoked that attitude.

26. One report described Bland as "subdued and gentle in manner," answering the judge's questions "with quiet dignity"; see "Anti-War Nurse Fights U.S. Ban on Citizenship," *New York Herald-Tribune*, 29 April 1930. Swarthmore Peace Collection.

27. Transcript of Record, *Bland v. United States*, 31-32. For the entire text of the court testimony see Appendix Q.

28. Transcript of Record, 32-34; "War Nurse Spurns Oath to Bear Arms," *New York Times*, 29 April 1930, 29; "Anti-War Nurse Fights U.S. Ban on Citizenship," *New York Herald-Tribune*, 29 April 1930.

29. Transcript of Record, 37-38.

30. Walter W. Van Kirk ("Conscience and Citizenship," *Federal Council Bulletin* [June 1930]: 13-14) stated that the Federal Council had already gone on record that "the United States should welcome as citizens all applicants for citizenship, otherwise qualified, who conscientiously seek to follow the highest ideals, including those who have, in their own hearts, renounced war as an instrument of dealing with others." The Council believed that naturalization laws should "be brought into harmony with the spirit and intent of the Pact by which the nations have renounced war as an instrument of national policy."; "Refusal of Nurse to Bear Arms May Cost Citizenship," *Philadelphia Inquirer*, 29 April 1930;

Ruth Millard, "Will Women Bear Arms in Next War?" *New York World*, Women's Section, 4 May 1930.

31. Bailey to Hays, 6 May 1930; Marx to Bailey, 7 May 1930; telegram, Bailey to Marx, 10 May, 1930. ACLU Archives, vol. 430, reel 78.

32. Harry F. Ward was professor of social ethics at Union Theological Seminary in New York and was not regularly present in the ACLU office.

33. Bland to Ward, 11 May 1930; Bailey [replying for Ward] to Bland, 14 May 1930; Marx to Bailey, 13 May 1930; Bailey to Marx, 13 May 1930; telegram, Bailey to Marx, 20 May 1930; Marx to Bailey, 21 May 1930; Bailey to Marx, 22 May 1930; Bailey to Bland, 23 May 1930. ACLU Archives, vol. 430, reel 78. The last four items were composed and posted after 19 May, the date Marx had requested for oral arguments at the Court of Appeals.

34. Forrest Bailey wrote to Charles Poletti, of John W. Davis' law firm, 14 May 1930, about the ACLU's attempt to get Marx to argue her case at a time different from the argument of the Macintosh case. He mentioned writing to Bland to explain the desires of the ACLU and the Davis firm. "In writing her as I have done I thought there might be some effect in presenting the situation to the party of chief interest, since there seemed to be nothing more to do with her lawyer. I am holding my breath while waiting to see if Miss Bland may not ask her lawyer to do as we have advised. *But I wonder if Miss Marx would pay any attention to anybody at all?*" Emphasis added. ACLU Archives, vol. 430, reel 78.

35. Schwimmer to Rabe, 22 May 1930, Schwimmer-Lloyd collection, box G-5.

36. *Bland v. United States* 42 F.2d 842 at 843-45. I did not find briefs from either side to the Court of Appeals, although Bland's brief was likely similar to the one written for the District Court.

37. Bland to ACLU, 27 June 1930; Marx to Baldwin, 2 July 1930; Baldwin to Marx, 2 July 1930; Baldwin to Bland, 3 July 1930; Baldwin to Marx, 3 July 1930; Marx to Baldwin, 7 July 1930; Bland to Baldwin, 7 July 1930; Baldwin to Bland, 8 July 1930. ACLU Archives, vol. 430, reel 78.

38. ACLU Memorandum, 11 July 1930; Baldwin to Marx, 14 July 1930; Baldwin to Bland, 14 July 1930; Bland to Baldwin, 16 July 1930. ACLU Archives, vol. 430, reel 78.

39. Schwimmer to Rabe, 1 July 1930. Schwimmer-Lloyd collection, Olive Rabe files, box G-6. Schwimmer had expressed similar anger to Rabe after she heard the oral arguments in the Court of Appeals. "The Government's representatives in both cases proclaimed that they stand absolutely on the decision in my case. It was very strange to listen to all the things said about me from both sides. The fact that in the Supreme Court the question at issue was a difference in our and the Government's interpretation of the word 'defend' was entirely lost, and the fact that I was a pacifist *propagandist* influencing others made most of." Schwimmer to Rabe, 22 May 1930, Schwimmer-Lloyd collection, box G-5; emphasis in original.

40. *Petition for Certiorari, United States v. Bland*, Transcript of Record, 1-11.

41. *United States v. Bland*, to the Supreme Court of the United States, "Brief on Behalf of Petitioner-Appellee," 5-8.

42. "Brief on Behalf of Petitioner-Appellee," 8-10. Marx noted that four members of Abraham Lincoln's cabinet were Quakers. John W. Davis used essentially the same argument, with the same example, in the first point of his brief for Douglas Clyde Macintosh.

43. "Brief on Behalf of Petitioner-Appellee," 18, 21; emphasis in original. See also 10-19.

44. "Brief on Behalf of Petitioner-Appellee," 22-33, quote at 26; emphasis in original.

45. Article VI, section 2, of the Constitution provides, "This Constitution, and the laws of the United States which shall be made in Pursuance thereof; *and all Treaties made, or which shall be made, under the Authority of the United States, shall be the supreme Law of the Land*"; emphasis added.

46. "Brief on Behalf of Petitioner-Appellee," 33-37. Marx quotes from Justice Holmes's dissent in *Schwimmer*–ironically, since she had tried strenuously to distinguish Bland from Schwimmer earlier in the brief. Yet Holmes's phrase more accurately described Bland, a devout Christian, than Schwimmer.

47. "Brief on Behalf of Petitioner-Appellee," 38-44. Critics frequently asserted that the country needed citizens of honesty and moral sensitivity; that it was a mistake to deny citizenship to people who thought deeply. "Some of the people denied citizenship have been of the highest type. America needs such citizens," an editorial in the Sacramento *Union* observed on 5 May 1931. "The very fact that they are willing to declare their opinions before they attempt to crash the gates is sufficient reason for admitting them to citizenship.

"To deny Miss Bland, who has long been a resident of the United States, and whose character is above criticism, the right to take part as an American in American affairs, because she realizes as does every other thinking person, the horrors of war and who in addition to a realization to the futility of fighting, has sufficient courage to come out with an opinion against it, would be to place a bar on every person who has a mind and an honest determination to use it. We need honest citizens. We need courageous ones and Miss Bland has proven herself to be of the material of which such are made. If she is refused citizenship it will be another case of the courts ignoring the spirit 'which maketh alive' and deciding with the letter of the law 'which killeth.' There is no sane reason for refusing citizenship to Miss Bland and every good reason for granting it." Swarthmore Peace Collection.

After the Supreme Court decided Bland's case, the Baltimore *Sun* reported that the nation had been "made safe for morons"; quoted in "Conscience versus Citizenship,"*Literary Digest* 109 (6 June 1931): 7.

48. *United States v. Macintosh*, to the Supreme Court of the United States, "Brief for the United States," 1-26.

49. *United States v. Macintosh*, to the Supreme Court of the United States, "Brief for the United States," 10-11, 7.

50. *United States v. Bland*, to the Supreme Court of the United States, "Brief of the United States," 13-14.

51. *United States v. Bland*, to the Supreme Court of the United States, "Brief of the United States," 15, 18.

52. Emily Marx, Bland's lawyer, also wrote this *amicus* brief.

53. *United States v. Bland*, to the Supreme Court of the United States, Brief on behalf of Edward L. Parsons, *et al.*, *Amici Curiae*, 5-16. Statements recommending conscientious objection from other Protestant denominations—among them Methodist Episcopal; Methodist Episcopal, North East Ohio Conference; Quaker Church; Northern Baptist Convention; Christian Church (Disciples of Christ); Presbyterian Church in the U.S.A.; Federal Council of the Churches of Christ in America; United Lutheran Church—are appended to this brief (18-22).

54. Max Stern, "Exemption Intended for War Objectors, Davis Tells Court," *New York News*, 29 April 1931; "Citizenship Plea Based on Religion," *New York Times*, 29 April 1931, 19; Schaeffer, "Meet Miss Marx!" 12.

55. *United States v. Macintosh* 283 U.S. 605 at 614, 620.

56. *United States v. Bland* 283 U.S. 636 at 636-37 (1931).

57. *United States v. Bland* 283 U.S. 636 at 637 (1931); "Citizenship Denied to Arms Objectors," *New York Times*, 26 May 1931.

58. "Supreme Court Bars Two as Citizens Because of Refusal to Fight," *American Civil Liberties Union Press Service*, Bulletin #458, 28 May 1931, 2. ACLU Archives, vol. 444.

59. "Can Conscience Be Mortgaged?" *Christian Science Monitor*, 28 May 1931; "The Decision Barring Aliens Asking Special Privilege as Citizens," *Philadelphia Record*, 28 May 1931.

60. Transcript of Record, *United States v. Bland*, "Petition of Respondent for Rehearing," 2-3.

61. Transcript of Record, *United States v. Bland*, "Petition of Respondent for Rehearing," 2.

62. Schwimmer copy of *United States v. Bland*, "Petition of Respondent for Rehearing." ACLU Archives, vol. 430, reel 78; Schwimmer to Rabe, 27 July 1931; Rabe to Schwimmer, 10 August 1931. Schwimmer-Lloyd collection, Olive Rabe files, box G-6. Bland to Schwimmer, 30 July 1931. ACLU Archives, vol. 430, reel 78. Bland to Baldwin, 25 June 1931 [the word in brackets is illegible in the original hand-written text]; Baldwin to Bland, 26 June 1931. ACLU Archives, Bland collection.

63. "Miss Bland Asks for a Rehearing," *New York Times*, 20 June 1931; Chief Justice Charles Evans Hughes, Order denying petition for rehearing in *United States v. Bland*, 12 October 1931. Record Group 267, National Archives, Bland folder.

64. Question number 22 on Form 2214, number 24 on Form A-2214, adopted and put into use on 1 July 1929. See testimony of Emily Marx, "Hearings on H.R. 3547," 54.

65. Because the Supreme Court had declared sex and age essentially irrelevant to the question in *Schwimmer*, Marx in her brief to the Supreme Court did not call attention to Bland's sex and the incongruity of asking a woman to promise to bear arms (although her petition for a rehearing before the Supreme Court did raise the issue). Apparently others were not willing to leave that issue aside. Bland's case attracted widespread attention among women's club leaders, social service workers, and liberals, who asked government officials about the question on the form in relation to women. Raymond F. Crist, Commissioner of Naturalization, replied, "That is a form. We ask those questions to humans, not men or women. It is a question of allegiance. I know of no plans of the War Department or the Navy Department or any other division of the Government to insist actually on women bearing arms. Of course, before that could be done, Congress would have to act. The Naturalization Bureau bases its questions on the acts passed by Congress." Responding to the same questions, Robe Carl White, Assistant Secretary of Labor in charge of the enforcement of naturalization laws, said, "We are following the decision of the Supreme Court in the Schwimmer case. The question about arms is asked men and women without regard to sex. It has been asked as far back as the records go. When applicants say that they will not obey laws, there is nothing left but to bar them." See Millard, "Will Women Bear Arms in Next War?" *New York World*, Women's Section, 4 May 1930.

66. See Chapter Three, n30.

67. See Chapter Four, n38.

68. In hearings before the House Committee on Immigration and Naturalization about H.R. 3547, Emily Marx testified that the questionnaire that Bland had to complete as part of her application for naturalization did not have the question about bearing arms. Various members of the House Committee, and the Commissioner of Naturalization, contended that there never had been a form without that question. Marx insisted that there was. She must have been correct, for otherwise how would Bland ever have come to the swearing-in ceremony without a government official's knowing of her pacifist inclination? Bland testified in the District Court that she had had such views for two or three years. See "Hearings on H.R. 3547," 51-55; Transcript of Record, 21.

69. This was the speculation of Emily Marx. See "Hearings on H.R. 3547," 54-55.

70. After Schwimmer was decided in 1929, Representative Anthony J. Griffin of New York introduced legislation in the House of Representatives to permit the naturalization oath to be taken by aliens who had philosophical and/or religious objections to war; H.R. 3547. In hearings on 8-9 May 1930 the bill engendered much opposition and considerable emotion on both sides; see "Hearings on H.R. 3547." After *Bland* and *Macintosh* were handed down, Rep. Griffin introduced his bill again, and hearings produced the same result. Because *Macintosh* had received

so much more attention from the Court itself and from the media than *Bland*, the same was true in the hearings. See "To Reconcile Naturalization Procedure with the Bill of Rights," Hearings Before the Committee on Immigration and Naturalization, House of Representatives, Seventy-second Congress, First Session, on H.R. 297 and H.R. 298, 26-27 January 1932. Marie Bland was rather "lost in the shuffle" at the time; the same has been true since.

Six

Harbingers of Change?

On 27 May 1929 the Supreme Court of the United States denied citizenship to Rosika Schwimmer. The next day Anthony J. Griffin, a Democratic Congressman from New York, read the Court's decision. Particularly impressed and persuaded by Justice Holmes's dissent, on 29 May Griffin filed a bill in the House of Representatives, H. R. 3547, for the purpose of amending the naturalization law. So began a long and often acrimonious debate about the proper form of the immigration process and the larger question of pacifism and citizenship.

Representative Griffin, born in 1866 in New York City, graduated from Cooper Union College and earned a law degree at New York University in 1892. In 1906 he founded the *Bronx Independent*, becoming its first editor. He served in the New York Senate for two terms, 1911-1915. In 1918 he was elected to Congress, from New York's Twenty-second Congressional District, to fill an unexpired term and then served full terms in the House of Representatives from 1919 until his death in 1935. Before his congressional service, Griffin served in the military. He was an officer in the New York National Guard beginning in 1888. In 1898 he organized Company F of the 69th Infantry of the New York National Guard and served as a Captain in that unit in the Spanish American War.[1] Proud of that service, Griffin referred to it often in the debate about his bill. He reminded his opponents, who accused him of being a pacifist, of his war record as proof that he was not a pacifist, although he deplored war. Griffin once declared that he did not believe in large standing armies in peacetime.[2]

Congressman Griffin was an advocate of immigration. At a time when Congress was considering legislation to suspend all immigration, Griffin argued against the bill. He believed existing law was sufficient to bar criminal, sickly, destitute, unskilled persons from America, and agreed with their exclusion. Yet Griffin believed strongly that immigration as a concept was a good thing, bringing diversity and cross-fertilization of cultures invigorating to America. "The mixture of blood in the United States," he once said, "has proven to be the salvation of our Nation."[3]

Representative Griffin denied that he introduced his bill as a way to circumvent the Supreme Court's decision and help Rosika Schwimmer achieve citizenship. "I introduced my resolution after the decision in the Schwimmer case," Griffin wrote in a letter, "because I believed it was an injustice to penalize her for honest convictions," yet he steadfastly maintained that he had a larger objective for the bill. When asked at the congressional hearings if he had introduced his bill to give citizenship to Schwimmer, he took considerable offense at the charge. "This bill was written off in five minutes after reading Justice Holmes's opinion on May 30, 1929," he replied. "I took it over instantly to the legislative bureau and had them pass upon the legality of the thing, and I introduced it the next morning in the House without consultation with a single person."[4]

Griffin's bill proposed to amend section six of the Naturalization Act of 1906 by adding the following sentence: "Except that no person mentally, morally, and otherwise qualified shall be debarred from citizenship by reason of his or her religious views or philosophical opinions with respect to the lawfulness of war as a means of settling international disputes."[5]

Apparently the bill did not attract much attention at the time it was introduced, but early in 1930 its visibility increased. Representative Griffin inserted a speech in the *Congressional Record*, a dialogue between a citizen and a soldier, in which he tried to describe the bill's objective and dispel misperceptions. Griffin emphatically did not intend the bill to relieve any citizen from defending the nation in time of war. It was, rather, designed to prevent the candidate for citizenship from having to answer a hypothetical question about what he or she might do in the event of war. Griffin insisted that every citizen, native-born or naturalized, would have to obey the law in time of war, recognizing that Congress had historically exempted conscientious objectors from combat. His bill would not offer any special privileges to a prospective citizen.[6]

A national "Griffin Bill Committee" organized on 14 March 1930. It existed for many years as a lobby group to rally support for passage of the Griffin bill in Congress. Its membership included many luminaries of pacifist and civil rights organizations, particularly on the East Coast. Lola Maverick Lloyd, longtime close friend and fellow laborer in pacifist and feminist causes with Rosika Schwimmer, chaired the Committee. The vice-chair was Emily Marx, Marie Averil Bland's attorney. Listed on the

Committee's stationery as a "National Sponsor" was Felix Frankfurter, a professor of law at Harvard.[7] That is worthy of note because he was a Justice of the Supreme Court when it decided *Girouard v. United States* (see Chapter Seven).

The House Committee on Immigration and Naturalization conducted hearings on H. R. 3547 on 8-9 May 1930. Representative Albert Johnson of the state of Washington was chair of the Committee.[8] Representative Griffin stated that his primary purpose in introducing the bill was to motivate Congress to define the word "defend" more broadly by eliminating question 24 (formerly question 22) from the naturalization questionnaire.[9] Griffin thought it inappropriate for the government to ask an applicant for naturalization, "If necessary, are you willing to take up arms in defense of the country?" He pointed out that for most of the history of the country, the question was not asked. It was only in reaction to World War I that the question was introduced to the form. Furthermore, the Department of Labor inserted the question without the authorization of Congress. For years persons were naturalized without having to declare their beliefs about bearing arms and the nation was not the poorer for it; it had caused no damage to the country. Now the question was asked and that caused problems. It was a hypothetical question. The citizenship of candidates depended on their answer to a question about what they might do in the case of a war that might not happen. In many cases people might change their minds; their belief in the future might not be what they believed now. "The heckling questions as to the nature of the service that should be given in time of war," Griffin asserted,

> have absolutely no relevancy to the question as to the qualifications of the citizen because it has to do with a contingency that is remote and many never happen. . . . The only idea at the bottom of this bill is to get rid of hypothetical questions at the time citizenship is granted, and let the question of war take care of itself when a war confronts us.

It was entirely appropriate, Griffin believed, for the government to ask applicants substantive questions about their attitude toward democracy and whether they believed in or practiced things that were inimical to public morals, like polygamy. The question about bearing arms was entirely hypothetical and inappropriate. Because of that, Griffin derisively called it a "heckling question." How could it not be thought of as a heckling question when it was asked of women such as Schwimmer, who could not serve in the military; men too old for the military, such as Macintosh; and all other applicants for naturalization, even though they might be physically or mentally disabled? When the heckler (the Naturalization Examiner) asked any and all applicants for citizenship whether they were willing to bear arms in defense of the country, Griffin declaimed, "That is a gratuitous, unwarranted, unauthorized interpolation. It is not called for by law or by the oath. The answer simply calls for an opinion. It is not an opinion as to what a person will do now, but what he thinks he will do at some future time in a contingency."[10]

Griffin explicitly stated, however, that his bill did not intend to alter the oath of naturalization. He did not object to the "defend the Constitution" clause in the oath. He believed that every naturalized citizen ought to assume the same obligations and responsibilities for national defense as native-born citizens, although he adamantly asserted that bearing arms was not the only way to defend the country. Rather than trying to screen out those who object to war at the time of naturalization, otherwise qualified applicants ought to be admitted and then, if and when war came, the government should deal with them in the same way that it deals with native-born citizens, which historically included exemptions for conscientious objectors. "The bill doesn't excuse anyone from the performance of their obligation as a citizen in time of war," Griffin concluded.

> My theory in the preparation of this bill was that if we could get an interpretation of the term "defend" large enough to embrace the . . . idea that everyone should do their duty in time of war, as they are called upon by the Government to do it; in other words, to put an interpretation upon the law which would prevent the Naturalization Bureau from asking these questions of women and old men, it would clarify it. . . . I would like to put the benevolent, broad thought into the minds of our bureaus of government that the Government ought to respect the personal opinions of individuals, their religious and philosophic and conscientious opinions, on certain matters and not go into those matters. Let those things come up when war confronts us.[11]

Proponents and opponents of the bill, most of them representing some organization or *ad hoc* group, appeared before the committee, speaking from a variety of perspectives.[12] Jeannette Rankin, who in 1917 had stood alone in Congress against the entry of the United States into World War I, saw the Griffin bill as a perfect way to help implement the Kellogg-Briand Peace Treaty. Given that Art. 6, clause 2, of the Constitution says that all treaties are the "law of the land,"[13] Rankin believed that the Kellogg Treaty was law and should be obeyed. A treaty must eventually be implemented in deeds. Passage of the Griffin bill would be a deed implementing this law. Since the Kellogg Treaty said that nations should not employ war to settle international disputes, the current question 24, asking whether applicants for citizenship are willing to bear arms, contravened the law made by the treaty. In effect the question asked, "Are you willing to violate the supreme law of the land? Unless you are willing to violate it, you can't become a citizen." Passage of the Griffin bill would remove that contradiction.[14]

Several advocates, representing traditional nonresistance groups such as Mennonites and Quakers, argued that welcoming people of conscience as citizens might uplift the moral quality of the society and the civil government. "Now it may be that the calling of some men is to go to war," the Quaker Henry M. Haviland supposed, "but I think it must be remembered that the calling of some other men may be to work for binding up, for repairing the losses of war, and that is what we felt to be our duty—not to go to war, but we won't admit that we are second to any in patriotism."[15] Another Quaker, William B. Harvey, thought that "when the nations are striving for disarmament and the pacific settlement of disputes, the conscientious objector to war will be an asset rather than a liability." Such a citizen "will not be a mere negative protester. His love of country will be as deep and genuine, and his service as helpful as that of many other citizens. He may be counted upon more than most to support his country in its efforts to abolish war."[16] Silas M. Grubb, a Mennonite pastor and publisher, reflected ruefully that "If having a conscience and consistently exercising it is an indication of undesirability as citizens, then God pity our country."[17]

Olive Rabe, Rosika Schwimmer's attorney, pointed out that from enactment of the first naturalization law of 1795 until revision of the law in 1906, the phrase about defending the Constitution and laws of the land was not in the oath required of applicants for naturalization. For most of American history, aliens had not been compelled to swear "to defend the Constitution and laws" of the nation. From 1906 until 1918 no court had interpreted "defend" to mean physical defense[18] and not until 1929, in *Schwimmer*, had the Supreme Court proposed such an interpretation. "Since the Constitution of the United States does not require Congress to exact any oath whatsoever from an applicant for citizenship," Rabe concluded, and since the word "defend" has been in the oath of allegiance only since 1906, it ought to be clear that the Griffin bill, if enacted by Congress, would be constitutional. . . . The committee can lend its weight to preserving the old-fashioned ideal of liberty of conscience by recommending the passage of the Griffin bill with full confidence that the bill is constitutional.

Rabe thought it obvious that such legislation was needed, due to the number of people denied citizenship because of conscience by various courts since *Schwimmer*.[19]

In one of those cases Martha Jane Graber, a Mennonite nurse, had said in her naturalization hearing that she would be willing to shed her blood and to serve as a nurse in war, but she would not be willing to fight or take the life of another. She was denied citizenship.[20] In another case frequently cited, Mary Boe—born in America and a citizen—married a Norwegian who had come to be the minister of the Church of the Brethren congregation in her town. Because of the citizenship laws at the time, she lost her American citizenship and became a Norwegian.[21] Just before *Schwimmer*, Mr. Boe was naturalized. Even though he was a pacifist, apparently he was not asked the question about bearing arms. Three years later, Mrs. Boe applied for naturalization.[22] Now, after *Schwimmer*, the judge quizzed her about bearing arms. She said she could not. The judge denied her citizenship. A native-born citizen was denied citizenship while her foreign-born husband, also a pacifist, became an American citizen.[23] A Quaker, Margaret Webb, came before a court in Indiana in March 1929. Because she testified that she could not and would not engage in combat in the service of the country, the Naturalization Examiner asked for a continuance of the hearing, since *Schwimmer* was pending before the Supreme Court. He wanted to postpone Mrs. Webb's case to get some guidance from the Court. When the hearing reconvened in September 1929, Mrs. Webb was denied citizenship, because of the *Schwimmer* decision.[24] For advocates of the Griffin bill, such cases made the legislation necessary.

Several opponents of the Griffin bill were members of the committee itself, including its chair. Representative Robert A. Green of Florida, among the most outspoken, believed the bill "will eventually work to encourage sovietism, socialism, and communistic tendencies, Government debauching, law destroying, un-Americanism, giving vent to cowardice and the tearing down of all things that mean American freedom and liberty."[25] Others feared that the bill would make it easier for people to become citizens who would teach the abolition of rights, disarmament, and racial intermixing.[26] Because the bill was thought to give certain naturalized citizens privileges not enjoyed by native-born citizens, it was said to be part of a continued effort of some to destroy the control of Government and to replace the control of the nation by "our own citizens" with domination by foreign influences.[27]

Much of the opposition focused more specifically on the danger to American national defense if the Griffin bill were to become law. Opponents repeatedly mentioned "reciprocity"—if people want to enjoy benefits of American citizenship, of which there are many, they must be willing to take the responsibility to defend the nation and government that provides those benefits. The Griffin bill, its opponents charged, would admit to citizenship those who were not willing to protect the benefits of citizenship that they enjoyed. If the bill passed, the government would lose its war power over citizens. As Mary G. Kilbreth, publisher of *The Woman Patriot*, declared, "You could not put a draft measure through and force men to serve the country after they had been admitted to citizenship in accordance with this bill."[28] James H. Patten represented several organizations whose members "are dedicated to the Constitution of the United States, as the greatest written charter of liberties in all history." They found in that document "a cardinal principle . . . that the first duty of every loyal and desirable citizen is to be willing to defend the United States with his or her life against all enemies designated by Congress and by the constituted governmental authorities." They were "unalterably opposed to the admission of any alien to citizenship, who is unwilling to shed blood for our country and its institutions in time of need and when necessary and when others are called upon to do so, whether that blood be his own or someone's else [*sic*]." Patten's organizations "feel intensely that the United States already has all the antination, international, and anti-American-Constitution-thinking persons we can comfortably stand, and that no more should be imported or added to our present population by the immigration or citizenship route."[29]

Some organizations passed formal resolutions urging Congress not to approve the Griffin bill. (For the text of two, fairly long, representative resolutions, see Appendixes S and T. For some shorter resolutions in opposition, see Appendix U.)

Some opponents brought up the issue of the modification of the oath to get a passport, as had been discussed in relation to Marie Averil Bland's effort to alter the language of the naturalization oath. Roger Baldwin of the

ACLU and Dorothy Detzler of the Women's International League for Peace and Freedom had each applied for a passport, knowing full well they would not take the prescribed oath requiring them to defend the country with arms if necessary. The State Department allowed them to alter the language of the oath to accommodate their pacifism. Each received a passport. Opponents insisted that such procedure should not serve as a precedent or rationale for the bill under consideration. The Supreme Court had explicitly said in *Schwimmer* that the only way one could defend the country was by bearing arms.[30]

Shortly after Representative Griffin filed H. R. 3547 in the House of Representatives, Senator Daniel F. Steck of Iowa filed S. 1506 in the Senate, a bill directly opposite to Griffin's in intent. Steck proposed to amend the Naturalization Act of 1906 by adding language to section four: "that when called upon he will bear arms in defense of the United States, its Constitution and laws; and that he will, without reservation, aid and encourage the United States against all enemies, foreign and domestic." Steck believed *Schwimmer* had been decided correctly and intended his bill to make that explicit in the naturalization law. Steck's bill never went anywhere, apparently because the Bureau of Naturalization thought it was redundant with *Schwimmer* and consequently unnecessary.[31]

But all was not peaceful among advocates of citizenship for pacifists. Almost immediately after Griffin had filed H. R. 3547, Roger Baldwin and other ACLU personnel began to question the language of the bill in the belief that it did not answer *Schwimmer* in the way Griffin thought it did. They argued that Griffin's bill addressed attitudes toward war whereas in *Schwimmer* the majority focused on unwillingness to bear arms. Convinced the bill was not a remedy for what the Supreme Court had held, ACLU attorneys suggested the last part of Griffin's bill should read: "by reason of his or her views, beliefs, personal convictions or philosophical opinions with respect to nationalism, bearing of arms, and/or the lawfulness of war as a means of settling international disputes." Griffin replied that he had considered that sort of more detailed language when he first wrote the bill, but had decided against using it. "It seemed, at the time, that there was danger in being too specific," Griffin wrote. The legislative process of hearings and debate would clarify the bill's content. In Griffin's opinion, "The words 'religious views or philosophical opinions with respect to the lawfulness of war' covers the whole subject and is all inclusive." He might change his mind, "but there is plenty of time for the consideration of that when I have a hearing on it in December."

Baldwin saw Griffin's point, that he was probably wise in allowing the discussion at the congressional hearings to clear up the specific wording: "I had not thought of that." Yet cases that had come to the ACLU for help caused him to be troubled about Griffin's language in the bill. Those cases had not focused on the beliefs of the aliens about the effectiveness or lawfulness of war, but on whether they would agree to bear arms in defense of the country. "Since, however, you have the matter in mind, we are sure that you and your conferes [*sic*] in Congress will frame a broad enough Bill to meet the practical situation." Even so, before Baldwin wrote that conciliatory letter to Griffin, he had written to ACLU attorney Arthur Garfield Hays, saying "I think he [Griffin] is wrong in his conclusions and we ought to show him why he is wrong."[32]

Baldwin raised the issue again later in the year in a letter in which he asked Griffin when the hearings on the bill would happen "and also how the amendment which we proposed strikes you personally?" Griffin replied that the amendment was fine, but he persisted in believing that it was unwise to provoke opposition to the bill. "I think it is better to allow the Committee to make the change in the Bill as reported and I will make an effort to that end." If Griffin had seen an earlier newspaper article about his bill in which the ACLU described it as "in a form not yet satisfactory," he did not remonstrate in his correspondence with Baldwin.[33]

From the hearings on H. R. 3547 in May 1930 no clarification of the language of the bill resulted. Baldwin and his colleagues persisted in their disagreement with Congressman Griffin's language. Yet infighting over language did not prevent a rally of support for the principals in the litigation and for passage of the Griffin bill. The Griffin Bill Committee hosted a dinner in New York City, attended by Rosika Schwimmer, Douglas Clyde Macintosh, Marie Averil Bland, and the chairs of the Boston and New York branches of the Griffin Bill Committee. The dinner offered support to the litigants, particularly Macintosh and Bland, whose cases were still pending before the Supreme Court at the time, but its primary purpose was to call attention to the Griffin bill and urge support for it. Albert Einstein, who could not attend, sent greetings and support. Speakers at the event included Professor Harry Elmer Barnes of Smith College, Congressman Griffin, and Mrs. Helen Tufts Bailie, who had left the DAR after a dispute and was chair of the Boston branch of the Griffin Bill Committee. According to Professor Barnes, pacifists would make better citizens than "war mongers"; the United States should welcome such high-minded persons to citizenship. Representative Griffin said that if the attitude of the opponents of his bill represented the majority of thought in the country, he would be ashamed of America. Schwimmer, Macintosh, and Bland did not make presentations at the dinner.[34]

Because the House Committee on Immigration and Naturalization did not approve H. R. 3547 and because he was under some pressure to modify the language of his proposal, Griffin considered changing the bill. "I am thinking of introducing a new bill," Griffin wrote to a friend. While the new effort would proceed "in substantial compliance with H. R. 3547," Griffin admitted that his "first bill was a generalization and I have found to my discomfort that it presumed too much on human intelligence." His new proposal "specifically provides that prospective citizens cannot be interrogated as to what they 'could, should, would or might do in the event of some future hypothetical wars.'"

Apparently those in the Baldwin camp thought that Griffin was simply not willing to change. The minutes of the ACLU meeting called to discuss the future of legislation to help pacifist aliens began, "In view of the fact that Mr. Griffin is unwilling to change the wording of his bill. . . ." Those attending the meeting agreed to try to produce different language and have that introduced in the Senate. A committee to write the proposed legislation included John W. Davis, Olive Rabe, Felix Frankfurter of Harvard Law School, ACLU attorney Arthur Garfield Hays, Professor Edwin Borchard of Yale, and Harold Evans, a lawyer from Philadelphia.[35] Davis seems to have taken the lead, for by September 1930 Charles W. Poletti, a member of Davis's law firm, had written a proposal for legislation with different language. Poletti based the document on two premises: (1) that Griffin did not do a convincing job of presenting and defending his bill during the May hearings, and (2) the language of the Griffin bill was ineffective in undoing the decisions in *Schwimmer*, *Macintosh* and *Bland*. "The dispute there arose," Poletti wrote, "not as to the views or opinions held by an alien with respect to the lawfulness of war as a means of settling international disputes but with views or opinions with respect to bearing arms in a war or otherwise participating in such war." Since Griffin's bill was "not aimed at this 'bull's-eye,'" Poletti recommended abandoning it After several pages of analysis, Poletti proposed inserting into the Naturalization Act of 1906 that "No alien otherwise qualified under this act shall be denied citizenship by reason of his refusal on conscientious grounds to promise to bear arms, but every alien admitted to citizenship shall be subject to the same obligations in all respects as a native born citizen."[36]

Representative Griffin was aware of this maneuvering behind the scenes. At some point Poletti met with Griffin, apparently to encourage Griffin to "see the light." Griffin was not impressed. "I presume Roger Baldwin imagined that, when I had once met Mr. Poletti face to face and listened to his logic and erudition," Griffin recalled, "I would immediately collapse and consent to his proposed amendment." Predictably "no such thing happened." Griffin found Poletti "a very pleasant young man" but, "as I suspected, arrogant, cocksure and self-opinionated." Griffin saw significant distinctions between his understanding and that of the ACLU.

> My position is not to emphasize that persons refusing to bear arms shall be entitled to citizenship, but that their views on the subject of war and all its consequences should not be touched upon, and that questions to ascertain their religious views or conscientious scruples should be eliminated from the questionnaire entirely. Under the Poletti bill, on the contrary, the very fact that it makes reference to persons refusing to bear arms will permit and practically invite a continuance of the very form of heckling of applicants to which I have all along objected.
>
> I am wondering why he, and others like him, cannot see that the language of his bill practically creates two classes of citizenship, namely, those who will take up arms and those who will not. The courts have for many years objected to the creation of class legislation for the benefit of certain class [*sic*] of citizens. Surely, they would not look kindly upon any proposal to create a special class of citizens distinguishable from others by their unwillingness to take up arms in time of war.
>
> The whole thing is so absurd, it really argues itself out of court. If Poletti is determined to go ahead on that line, by all means let him do it. The presentation of such a bill in Congress, I think, would help, rather than hinder, the progress of our bill.[37]

Senator Bronson Cutting of New Mexico introduced a form of the alternative language in the Senate on 25 January 1932, in a bill designated S. 3275. Cutting was born in New York in 1888, but after study at Harvard he went to New Mexico in the second decade of the twentieth century for his health. There he discovered the plight of Spanish-speaking inhabitants of the state. As he learned Spanish, Cutting soon became their advocate. He bought the Santa Fe *New Mexican*, the oldest newspaper in the territory, introducing a Spanish-language edition, *El Nuevo Mexicano*. As Richard Lowitt has observed, Cutting's newspaper championed "progressive principles by challenging corruption and calling for honesty and efficiency in public life." Cutting himself sustained a lifelong concern "about the plight of people oppressed by circumstances over which they had little control." He supported Theodore Roosevelt in his 1912 campaign for the presidency and was active in the Progressive Party for a while, but became a Republican in the 1920s. During World War I he served as military attaché in the American embassy in London, with the rank of captain, and in 1919 was awarded the British military cross. Cutting later became a principal organizer of the American Legion nationally, and in New Mexico served two years as its commander. He was appointed to the Senate to fill an unexpired term in 1927 and was elected to full terms in 1929 and 1934, serving on the Military Affairs committee. En route to vote in the Senate on veterans legislation, Cutting was killed in an airplane crash in 1935. He was an Episcopalian. Although Cutting had a strong military background and an active involvement in the American Legion, he introduced S. 3275, in language almost the same as that proposed by Poletti.

> [B]ut an alien otherwise qualified shall not be denied citizenship under any provisions of this Act solely by reason of his refusal on conscientious grounds to promise to bear arms or otherwise participate in war: *Provided*, That nothing in the foregoing provisions shall be construed to affect the obligations of aliens after their admission to citizenship.[38]

Meanwhile, on 8 December 1931, Griffin reintroduced his bill, this time in two forms. In one, H. R. 298, the language was precisely the same as his bill proposed in the previous session. In the other, H. R. 297, he added a clause—"but every alien admitted to citizenship shall be subject to the same obligations as the native-born citizen." Griffin was not enthusiastic about H. R. 297; he thought the additional language was superfluous, but he added it to benefit "those who have not intelligence enough to know that a citizen is a citizen no matter whether by birth or through naturalization and that all have equal responsibility and privileges"—for the "boneheads" who could not understand that he did not intend to give naturalized pacifists special privileges. Griffin intended to concentrate his efforts on H. R. 298, the version without the additional language.[39]

The House Committee on Immigration and Naturalization conducted a full hearing on H. R. 297, since it offered different language from H. R. 3547, considered in the previous session of Congress.[40] Representative Griffin, in introducing the bill, repeated his statements from the earlier session. A few proponents of the legislation presented new arguments. Jerome Davis, the Yale colleague of Douglas Clyde Macintosh, offered strong statements about the nature of government and conscience. In that form of government represented by the phrase *Der Stadt über alles*,[41] individual conscience is subservient to the all-powerful state, a view Davis attributed to "the Bolshevists." The United States, on the other hand, has always recognized freedom of conscience, allowing people to put their faith in God first and their loyalty to the state second. "It was never the idea of the founders of this Republic," Davis asserted, "that a man should have to obey the supreme law of the United States in contravention to his conscience and what he thought his God would want him to do." In Davis's view, opponents of the Griffin bill held a Bolshevistic understanding of freedom of conscience. Passage of this bill would affirm the American tradition of freedom of conscience. Davis obviously believed that religious freedom is inextricably related to freedom of conscience and inextricably involved in naturalization. "How absurd it would be," he concluded, "to ask the prospective citizen to read that oath and end with the words 'So help me God,' and then say, 'If God does not want me to do it, I will do it, so help me God.'"[42]

Speakers in these hearings stressed freedom of conscience and religion, since both *Macintosh* and *Bland* had been decided by this time and both applicants had based their pacifist arguments on their Christian faith. Richard A. Wood, a Quaker, likened the nation to an organism, not a static or dead entity. As a growing organism, the United States would benefit from men and women willing to criticize and even to disagree with it. Wood thought that "to exact of applicants for citizenship a promise, in advance, of unqualified obedience" would be "a bad and short-sighted policy, contrary to the permanent interest of the United States." Such a policy "deprives the Nation of precisely this stimulus to development that it has received from its rugged nonconformist patriots in the past." According to Wood, "The independent, responsible consciences of our citizens and prospective citizens are our greatest national asset, to be cherished in the interest of the Nation and at the behest of patriotism."[43]

"If a man is really convinced that the Government is wrong," John F. Finerty, another witness, admonished the congressmen, "it is his duty to resist this Government; and I need only cite you to the author of the Declaration of Independence, who said the same thing."[44] Mercer G. Johnston, arguing that religious belief often formed consciences, resented regulations for admission to citizenship that forced applicants to violate their consciences. "I resent the thought that my country would ever set up a standard for admission to citizenship which would automatically exclude from American citizenship the character in all history whose presence in our country would do most to honor and glorify it," Johnston testified, finding that "it is an almost intolerable indignity and affront to the spirit of the religious man for a standard to be set up which would automatically exclude that character from American citizenship." Johnston resented "a question like that 24 . . . because it is a good long step toward the establishment of an inquisition in the United States."[45]

Several opponents of the bill argued that it would allow naturalized citizens to enjoy privileges of citizenship without assuming one of its principal responsibilities. Such "preferential treatment" would "weaken the power of the United States to defend itself" and was clearly "backed by the communists, of course."[46] Surely, opponents argued, there were already enough conscientious objectors in the country; no need for legislation that would encourage others to come.[47]

In light of *Macintosh* and *Bland*, opponents of the legislation found religious justification for refusing to subscribe to the oath of naturalization illegitimate, arguing that God did not oppose the defense of the country. Indeed, God gave the United States to its citizens and God expects them to defend it. Those who fought in the Revolutionary War won the religious freedom Americans enjoy. According to Herman A. Miller of the Patriotic Order of Sons of America, bloodshed had been necessary "for the progress of mankind" and war had "established . . . a new Nation where the right to worship God in his own way is accorded to every citizen." In Miller's view, "This may have been the plan of God. Citizens should be willing to preserve this blessing with their life if necessary. You can serve your God with your soul, and your country with your body."[48]

Frank I. Peckham, a very religious man, offered religious objections to war, believing he was not alone in that. Yet he could not justify admitting conscientious objectors to citizenship. "I would say that 95 per cent at least of the men that served in the World War were of religious convictions that were opposed to war," Peckham told the Committee. "But it seems to me that unless and until the Almighty in his infinite wisdom sees fit to grant that supplication that we make in the Lord's Prayer ['Thy will be done on earth . . .'], that we shall have to contend with the abominations of the devil, including war." According to Peckham, "This is a religious question proponents of the bill are injecting into this. They say if they can base their opposition to war on religious grounds they can come in and be citizens of your country and my country, thus advertising the United States as a refuge for the coward."[49]

At the end of the hearings, Demarest Lloyd summed up for the opposition, calling proponents of the bill "poor sports" because they claimed to believe in democracy but supported their arguments by relying on the dissenting opinions in *Schwimmer*, *Macintosh*, and *Bland*. Prevailing law rests on what Congress has done, interpreted by Supreme Court majorities. Lloyd's coalition of patriotic societies opposed the bill on the premise that it would undercut national defense. The more sophisticated those pacifists might be, the worse the problem. As the Court majority had said in *Schwimmer*, pacifists can be propagandists for peace, persuading more and more people not to fight in defense of the country. This contributed to organized pacifism's goal of disarming the country, which would bring disaster should another war come. In that light, "the question asked by the Bureau of Naturalization is quite necessary and is in accord with the established law of the land and the spirit of the Constitution, and it should not be changed." Lloyd quoted the "very significant words" of question 24 ("If necessary, are you willing to take up arms in defense of this country?") and asked, "what does that mean? It means that if the country is in peril, if its citizens—men, women, and children—are in peril, and if force to protect them is decreed by the Government, then will you help?" The bill's advocates, Lloyd argued,

> want to have in the country a lot more of the people who, in a case like that, would sit back and say: "No; my philosophical opinions do not sanction this effort either to repel a foreign invader or suppress one of these cutthroat, communist resolutions, and I am just going to let somebody else do the job."[50]

Congressman Griffin, in his rebuttal, confessed that "I never realized until to-day how really wicked I am. I heard myself classified with Communists and Bolshevists and pacifists and all sorts of 'ists.' I assure you I am absolutely innocent of any such connection." Griffin once more emphasized that he did not intend his bill to give pacifist applicants for citizenship any special privileges, but rather to spare them harassment at the time of their naturalization. In the interest of religious or philosophical freedom, Griffin wanted to reconcile the naturalization procedure with the Bill of Rights. "In short, my sole purpose was, and is, to keep the halo around citizenship, to put it in an exalted niche, where it belongs, and to allow no snooping into a man's religious views or inner convictions. That is all there is to it."[51]

Although Griffin and members of the Griffin Bill Committee had hoped the bill would pass, the House Committee never approved it or allowed a vote in the House.[52] The same fate befell the Cutting bill in the Senate, S. 3275. A three-member subcommittee of the Senate Committee on Immigration considered that bill. On 2 May 1932 the senators on the subcommittee recommended to the full committee that the bill be rejected. "In all of our wars," they wrote, "we have been uncommonly tender to the conscientious scruples of those of our citizens whose religion taught that it was wrong to bear arms under any circumstances, but this fact affords no reason why we should take into our citizenship aliens who entertain similar principles."

> The freedom that we have and the liberties that we enjoy have been won by the bravery and sacrifice of those of our ancestors who were not restricted by conscientious scruples from defending their country. These liberties can be preserved only by a readiness on the part of our citizenry to defend the nation from every attack. Your Sub-Committee can think of no valid reason why we should be asked to furnish asylum for aliens who will not undertake their share of the common burden.[53]

Since these bills had never even made it to the floor of the House of Representatives for a vote, Representative Griffin introduced legislation of the same language and intent in the next Congress, H. R. 1528.[54] Rosika Schwimmer offered to disassociate herself from the bills in hope of aiding their passage. "I came to the conclusion," she wrote to Representative Griffin, "that if my person were removed from consideration, the liberalizing of the naturalization laws might have an easier sailing." Schwimmer had "long ago decided not to apply for American citizenship, even if the change of the laws would permit me to do so" and "intimate friends" were aware of her decision."I wonder now," Schwimmer confided,

> whether you don't think that a public statement of mine when the issue will come up for decision in Congress, would not favorably influence the vote? I would be very glad to help the passage of your Bill with a public statement as to my decision not to apply for American citizenship, if you agree with me that such a step would influence the vote of your Bill. I appreciate tremendously what you have done and what you are doing to uphold American ideas in naturalization matters, and will always be grateful for your efforts. I hope you will give me a frank

expression in the question I am asking now because you must know that my desire to be of service in the liberalizing of naturalization laws is independent from my private fate as a person without a country.

"I regret the statement you make in your letter," Griffin replied to Schwimmer, "that you have made up your mind not to reapply for citizenship in the event the naturalization law is liberalized." He "had already heard a rumor of your resolution." Griffin assured her that "your personality has nothing to do with the merits of the case." The "fools who misinterpret your ideals" would find another "exhibit to justify their bigotry and intolerance" if Schwimmer were not available. The "small minds" of her enemies would take her public statement "as a retreat or as a flash of petulance." Griffin advised Schwimmer "not . . . to put your position in their power. Simply lay low and await the coming of the dawn."[55] The dawn never came. Congressman Griffin died 13 January 1935.

The leadership of the Griffin Bill Committee recruited a new member of Congress, Representative Caroline O'Day, also from New York, to take up Griffin's torch as an advocate for pacifist aliens. Mrs. O'Day, a Democrat, elected as a representative at large from New York in 1934, served four terms in Congress. From the perspective of the Griffin Bill Committee (now renamed the Griffin-O'Day Bill Committee), she was a likely choice to take up this cause. She was a vice-president of the Women's International League for Peace and Freedom and, in Congress, sat on the House Committee on Immigration and Naturalization. On 31 January 1935 O'Day introduced H. R. 5170 with language identical to Griffin's H. R. 297.[56] She agreed, however, with Roger Baldwin "that the wording of the Bill you sent is better than the one I have already introduced." Yet "friends of Mr. Griffin" had been "most keen . . . to have the Bill go in just as he worded it." Opponents had generated "some rather violent letters on the subject" and O'Day doubted "that it will get out of committee." In that case she intended to redraft it and resubmit it in the next session.[57]

Representative O'Day did introduce legislation to the same effect in the next Congress, H. R. 8259.[58] Senator Cutting's fatal accident assured that he would never reintroduce his bill in the Senate, but Senator Gerald P. Nye of North Dakota introduced a very different and more specific bill in 1939, S. 165, providing that

any *female* alien, otherwise eligible for citizenship under the naturalization laws, shall not be denied a certificate of citizenship for the reason
that such alien is conscientiously opposed to war as a method of settling
international controversies or has expressed an unwillingness to serve in
the armed forces of the United States in time of war with a foreign
country.[59]

For a decade after the *Schwimmer* decision, bills were proposed in
Congress to enable applicants for citizenship who were conscientious
objectors to bypass the question about bearing arms in the application
questionnaire and qualify for citizenship. Aside from the hearings covered
in some detail here, I find no evidence that any other versions of the bill
received public hearings. No bills ever made it out of committee to receive
a vote of the full House of Representatives or the Senate. Legislative
efforts to undo *Schwimmer*, *Macintosh*, and *Bland* were unsuccessful.[60]

Congressional action in 1940 and 1942 does not seem, on the surface,
to have any relevance to the issue at hand, yet it figures prominently in the
dissenting opinion in *Girouard v. United States* (see Chapter Seven) and
in some cases leading up to *Girouard*. In the Nationality Act of 1940,
Congress revised the nationality laws into a comprehensive code.
Significantly, the new law did not change the language of the Oath of
Allegiance at all; like the Nationality Act of 1906, it contained the phrase
"that I will support and defend the Constitution and laws of the United
States against all enemies, foreign and domestic."[61] The law also spelled
out the contents of the Declaration of Intention[62] and the Petition for
Naturalization[63] required of applicants. Yet the law also provided that the
applicant's petition could contain other information deemed material to the
application,[64] seeming to allow use of the questionnaire that contained the
question about willingness to bear arms.

Congress enacted in March 1942 a law "to further expedite the
prosecution of the war," which contained a provision to expedite
naturalization of aliens who were currently serving or who had served in
the military. It enabled them to be naturalized without having to meet some
of the requirements of residency, filing a declaration of intent, and other
things required of regular applicants, apparently in order to reward those
aliens who served in the military. However, the law explicitly excluded
from expedited naturalization "any conscientious objector who performed
no military duty whatever or refused to wear the uniform."[65] In December
1942 Congress extended similar expedited naturalization to veterans of
World War I or the Spanish-American War, extending the favor only to

that veteran "who was not a conscientious objector who performed no military duty whatever or refused to wear the uniform."[66]

In 1940 Congress also changed the language of the selective service law (see Chapter Two), broadening the scope of conscientious objector status to include those who were not members of historic peace churches.

> Nothing contained in this Act shall be construed to require any person to be subject to combatant training and service in the land or naval forces of the United States who, by reason of religious training and belief, is conscientiously opposed to participation in war in any form.[67]

Congress seemed to maintain a distinction that many wanted to make, that applicants for citizenship had to meet a different standard than native-born citizens.

Meanwhile, as Congress considered the Griffin bill and modified naturalization laws, naturalization cases involving immigrant pacifists suggested that some judges were unhappy with the decisions in *Schwimmer*, *Macintosh*, and *Bland*. First came the case of Abraham Warkentin, a Mennonite minister. Warkentin had been born in Russia, had lived in Germany for a long time, and came to the United States in 1923. When he applied for naturalization, he answered question 24—"If necessary, are you willing to take up arms in defense of this country?"—with these words: "No. Because my church, the Mennonite Church, does not permit us to take up arms and to take the life of other people." The Naturalization Examiner recommended that Warkentin be denied citizenship. In a hearing before Judge William H. Holly of the U. S. District Court for the Northern District of Illinois, Warkentin strongly affirmed his membership in a historic peace church and demonstrated that its doctrines had shaped his beliefs. He presented as evidence a long theological statement of the church that clearly articulated its pacifist doctrine. Following that hearing, Judge Holly issued a preliminary judgment.

> While I am not in sympathy with the opinions expressed by the majority of the Supreme Court in U. S. v. Schwimmer and U. S. v. Macintosh, as a District Judge I can do no other than follow the decision of the court in these cases and I cannot distinguish between those cases and the present case. The petition for admission of petitioner to citizenship must be denied.

Holly's final judgment appeared on 28 June 1937. He did not repeat his disapproval of *Schwimmer* and *Macintosh*, but the effect was the same. Warkentin was denied citizenship.[68]

Warkentin then requested help in financing an appeal of his case, since both his lawyer and even Judge Holly thought his case should go to the Supreme Court as the vehicle to overturn *Schwimmer*, *Macintosh*, and *Bland*. The ACLU and several lawyers agreed. A flurry of letters ensued as the ACLU tried to coordinate the appeal to the Court of Appeals and, ultimately, to the Supreme Court. John W. Davis was approached to argue the case at the Appeals Court level and at the Supreme Court, under the theory that his reputation and skill would surely carry the day. Davis declined the offer. Although he was interested in the case and wanted to see *Macintosh* overturned, he decided that it might not be in Warkentin's interest to have a "defeated General" argue his case.[69]

Attorneys were optimistic that this might be the case to get a favorable ruling for alien conscientious objectors from the Supreme Court because Warkentin's beliefs could be distinguished from those of Macintosh and Bland. While both were religious, their objections to bearing arms were based on personal theology, their own understanding of the morality of war and/or the imperative of the Christian life in relation to war. Warkentin firmly based his belief on the venerable affirmation of a historic peace church. Lawyers discussing the case believed that this distinction from *Macintosh* and *Bland* (this discussion rarely mentioned *Schwimmer* because her pacifism was philosophical, rather than religious) might persuade the Supreme Court to hear the case, although Whitney North Seymour, Sr., then a former Assistant Solicitor General, candidly admitted that in terms of the Court's reasoning the distinction was tenuous.[70]

He was right. When the Court of Appeals for the Seventh Circuit decided the case, the court rejected the distinction. The court commented that the case had been an enlightening discussion on the history of the oath of allegiance, and of the theology of the Mennonite church, but that the decision reached was based on none of that, but on the precedents of *Schwimmer* and *Macintosh*. Those cases showed that citizenship is the possession of the nation to grant and that the applicant receives it as a privilege, not as a right. The way an applicant receives the grant is to comply with the requirements the state imposes. One of those is to promise to bear arms in defense of the country, if necessary. "These decisions control us here." Yet as it reached its decision, the court remarked,

Whatever might be our inclination, were the question open to us, is wholly beside the point. The settled conviction of this court upon the same issue as expressed in Schwimmer v. United States was disapproved and the decision reversed by the Supreme Court in its review. We are foreclosed from any contrary ruling.[71]

The court clearly implied that if had its own way and was not bound by precedent, it would have decided Warkentin's case differently from the way *Schwimmer* and *Macintosh* had been decided. Still it denied Abraham Warkentin citizenship, and his lawyers did not ask the Supreme Court to review the case.

Although *Warkentin* failed to present a Supreme Court challenge to an unacceptable precedent, supporters of pacifist applicants for citizenship could be interested and, at times, encouraged by a series of judicial opinions. The decision in *In re Losey* was remarkable for the candor with which the Judge expressed disapproval of the majority opinions in *Schwimmer*, *Macintosh*, and *Bland*. Mrs. Harta Inez Losey, a Seventh-day Adventist, recognized the right of the nation to declare war and of Congress to specify the requirements for naturalization. Following her religious beliefs, Mrs. Losey would support the nation in all ways except participating in combat. Judge Lewis B. Schwellenbach of the Federal District Court thought that she was a fine candidate for citizenship and would have gladly awarded it except for the precedent of *Schwimmer*, *Macintosh*, and *Bland*. Those cases, he thought, had been decided wrongly.

> My personal opinion is that these dissenting opinions clearly stated the law. I agree with Chief Justice Hughes that the inclusion of the meaning about bearing arms in the oath as administered to prospective citizens is not justified either by the law or by the form of the oath itself. The form of the oath is not materially different from the form of oath prescribed for those who may enter upon the performance of their duties as public officials in the United States. . . . I can't agree with the majority opinion in the Schwimmer case that this action results in applicants for citizenship being placed upon the same footing as the citizens themselves. These decisions require of the applicants for citizenship a higher degree of patriotism than we require of native-born citizens.

Schwellenbach recognized he was bound by precedent and consequently had to deny citizenship to Mrs. Losey. Yet he also expressed his hope that someday Mrs. Losey's case would challenge that precedent in the Supreme

Court.[72] That did not happen, but Schwellenbach's personal opinion of the precedents was extraordinary.

The case of Rebecca Shelley[73] elicited another discordant comment from judges of the Court of Appeals of the District of Columbia. Shelly had lost her citizenship by marrying a noncitizen. Later, under the Cable Act, she desired to regain her citizenship.[74] To do that she had to take the oath of allegiance. She was willing to take the oath with the proviso, because of religious and pacifistic beliefs, that she could not promise to bear arms in defense of the country. The court refused Shelley's application for citizenship on the basis of *Macintosh* and *Bland*, yet it also commented: "Justices Holmes, Brandeis and Stone joined Chief Justice Hughes in dissenting; but in view of the recent flag salute case, we cannot predict that the present Supreme Court will agree with them."[75] The "recent flag salute case" was *Minersville School District v. Gobitis*,[76] in which a sharply divided Court held that public schools could require children of Jehovah's Witnesses to recite the pledge of allegiance to the flag, contrary to their conscientious objections based on freedom of religion and freedom of speech rights. Apparently the fact that the current Court rejected the claims of children's conscientious objections to required public ceremonies in schools suggested that it would not accept the claims of aliens' conscientious objections to military service. Could it be that the judges of the Court of Appeals believed that, in other circumstances, the current Supreme Court might believe the dissenters in *Macintosh* and *Bland*? Could this cryptic remark be a source of encouragement to prospective litigants on this issue?

The Supreme Court heard *Schneiderman v. United States* in 1943,[77] which did not address the issue of conscientious objection, but offered some interesting implications for those cases. William Schneiderman became a citizen in 1927. He was a communist at the time, a fact known to the naturalization examiner and the court that heard his case. Because he met all the specific criteria necessary for citizenship—communists were not specifically prohibited—he was naturalized. In 1939 the government brought suit in a denaturalization proceeding, attempting to take his citizenship from him on the grounds that it was "illegally procured" because, at the time of naturalization and for the five years prior to then, he was not attached to the principles of the Constitution. The Supreme Court found in favor of Schneiderman and against the government, largely on the grounds that the government had not proved its case. In a denaturalization case the burden of proof against the citizen is formidable and the government had not met it. The Court, in reaching its decision, quoted several times from the dissenting opinions in *Schwimmer* and *Macintosh* with approval. Although this majority opinion by Justice Frank Murphy is long and argued meticulously, it essentially asked whether the government can revoke naturalization without a preponderance of clear, convincing evidence. As a way of saying that in cases like these the government may not go on what we would call a "fishing expedition," the majority opinion quoted in two different contexts Chief Justice Hughes's dissent in *Macintosh*: that evidence "should be construed, not in opposition to, but in accord with, the theory and practice of our Government in relation to freedom of conscience." In a concurring opinion making essentially the same point, Justice William O. Douglas cited the same passage from Hughes, again with approval. Furthermore, in the two quotations in the majority opinion, Murphy cited the entire dissenting opinion of Justice Oliver Wendell Holmes, Jr., in *Schwimmer*.[78] In saying that Schneiderman should not be penalized because he wanted to change the American form of government and even the Constitution when he was naturalized, Murphy quoted a famous passage from Justice Holmes's dissent in *Schwimmer*.

> Surely it cannot show lack of attachment to the principles of the Constitution that . . . [one] thinks it can be improved. . . . If there is any principle of the Constitution that more imperatively calls for attachment than any other it is the principle of free thought—not free thought for those who agree with us, but freedom for the thought that we hate.[79]

Finally, after quoting from the dissents in the conscientious objector cases, seemingly drawing a concept from them, Murphy wrote for the majority,

> In view of our tradition of freedom of thought, it is not to be presumed that Congress in the Act of 1906, or its predecessors of 1795 or 1802, intended to offer naturalization only to those whose political views coincide with those considered best by the founders in 1787 or by the majority of the country today. Especially is this so since the language used, posing the general test of "attachment" is not necessarily suspectable of so repressive a construction.[80]

The Court now appeared ready to consider a less wooden understanding of the concept of attachment to the Constitution than had been employed in the conscientious objector cases.

Schneiderman, obviously approving the core ideas expressed in the dissents in *Schwimmer* and *Macintosh*, and viewing more expansively what attachment to the Constitution might mean, suggested to some a possibility that the Court might decide another conscientious objection case more favorably.

In 1944 cases from the Federal District Court in the Western District of Washington injected a new element into case law on this issue. Two men, serving in the military, applied for citizenship. William Kinloch, a Seventh-day Adventist, and William McKillop, a member of the Church of the Brethren, were unwilling because of their faith to bear arms or serve in a combatant role in the military. If the oath for citizenship required such behavior, they could not take the oath. Yet they were completely willing to serve in the military, wear uniforms, submit to the discipline, so long as they could serve in noncombatant roles. At the time of their application, both men were serving in a medical unit. Soldiers serving in medical units could not bear arms. All conceded, including the commanding officer of these two applicants, that members of medical units had to be in combat zones and had to exhibit considerable heroism to carry out their duties.

Because of their refusal to take the oath with the understanding that it required them to bear arms, the Naturalization Service asked the court to deny citizenship to Kinloch and McKillop on the basis of *Schwimmer*, *Macintosh*, and *Bland.* The court acknowledged that on the basis of the precedent, their citizenship applications would have to be denied. Congress had, however, enacted additional pertinent legislation since those cases were decided—the Nationality Act of 1940 and amendments thereto in 1942. That legislation allowed naturalization of aliens serving in World War II, indeed, in an expedited fashion. The Act allowed persons in the military in noncombatant roles to be naturalized under the expedited procedures. The law explicitly excluded any conscientious objector who performed no military duty or refused to wear the uniform. The court found that Kinloch and McKillop fell squarely within the legislation and, given their noncombatant service in the military, were entitled to naturalization. "[A] conscientious objector performing military duty and wearing the uniform, if he be an alien, is, upon application, entitled to citizenship, even though he be a conscientious objector."[81] The court did not suggest that *Schwimmer*, *Macintosh*, and *Bland* were bad law, only that new rules applied to certain kinds of conscientious objector applicants for citizenship. The decision got the attention of the ACLU and its friends, who ascertained from the Justice Department that the government did not intend to appeal *In re Kinloch*. That meant they needed to search for another vehicle to take the issue before the Supreme Court again.[82]

Everett R. Sawyer was also serving in a military medical unit. The facts of his case are identical to those in *Kinloch*. In its brief opinion the Federal District Court in Delaware offered a fascinating account of what happened.

> Just as the oath of allegiance was about to be administered, the thought occurred to the Court as to whether . . . Schwimmer, . . . Macintosh, . . . and . . . Bland disqualified the applicant for citizenship. The hearing was adjourned in order that the Court might give further examination to the question which was raised by it sua sponte.
>
> After a reading of Judge Leavy's opinion in Re Kinloch, the Court is convinced by the able discussion found in that case that the applicant at bar is entitled to his citizenship.[83]

Another, similar, case resulted in a far different verdict, primarily because of the style and manner of the applicant. Verner Nielsen, a Seventh-day Adventist, had served in the military as a noncombatant medic. He took the soldier's oath, wore the uniform, performed his duties as a medic. After his honorable discharge he applied for citizenship and claimed that these facts and the precedent of *In re Kinloch* meant he was entitled to citizenship under the Selective Service Act of 1940. The Department of Justice agreed and recommended his naturalization. The judge for the U.S. District Court for the District of Columbia declined to see it that way. Nielsen's military service, even under the Selective Service Act of 1940, as amended in 1942, did not require the government to award him citizenship. Nielsen needed to remember that citizenship was a privilege, not a right, and that it would be conveyed by the Government, on its terms. The Selective Service Act of 1940, the court concluded, "neither abrogates, limits or in any other way qualifies the law as laid down in the Schwimmer, Bland, Macintosh, and Shelley cases. The application is denied."[84] Here a court was quite willing to assert the primacy of precedents in the application of alien conscientious objectors for citizenship.

The Supreme Court approached the perimeter of this issue again in 1945. Clyde Wilson Summers, an American citizen educated in the law, applied to be admitted to the bar of Illinois. He was denied only because he was a conscientious objector to war. A Christian of undisclosed denomination, Summers was convinced that the teachings of Christ—in the Sermon on the Mount (Matthew 5:1-7:28), for example—prohibit a true Christian from participating in violence, warfare, the taking of another's life. Illinois required that members of the bar swear allegiance to and be willing to enforce the laws of the Constitution of Illinois.[85] Illinois ruled that a conscientious objector cannot do that. Although Illinois recognized that Summers was denied an opportunity to earn a livelihood in his chosen profession only because of religious beliefs, guaranteed to be free by the U.S. and Illinois Constitutions, it held that he could not practice law because he could not enforce the law. The Illinois Supreme Court sustained that judgment. The U.S. Supreme Court granted Summers's petition for certiorari,[86] but affirmed the ruling of the Illinois Supreme Court, basing its decision on the precedents of *Schwimmer* and *Macintosh*. "The United States does not admit to citizenship the alien who refuses to pledge military service," Justice Stanley Reed wrote for the majority.

> Even the powerful dissents which emphasized the deep cleavage in this Court on the issue of admission to citizenship did not challenge the right of Congress to require military service from every able-bodied man. It is impossible for us to conclude that the insistence of Illinois that an officer who is charged with the administration of justice must take an oath to support the Constitution of Illinois and Illinois' interpretation of that oath to require a willingness to perform military service violates the principles of religious freedom which the Fourteenth Amendment secures against state action, when a like interpretation of a similar oath as to the Federal Constitution bars an alien from national citizenship.[87]

In a vigorous dissent, Justice Hugo L. Black met the ruling precedents of the majority head-on, and did not shrink from spelling out inevitable consequences. "It may be," Black wrote, "as many people think, that Christ's Gospel of love and submission is not suited to a world in which men still fight and kill one another." Yet Black, a Baptist and former United States senator from Alabama, could not agree "that a mere profession of belief in that Gospel is a sufficient reason to keep otherwise well qualified men out of the legal profession, or to drive law-abiding lawyers of that belief out of the profession, which would be the next logical development." Nor should "such a belief . . . be penalized through the circuitous method of prescribing an oath, and then barring an applicant on the ground that his present belief might later prompt him to do or refrain from doing something that might violate that oath." Black reminded the Court majority that "Test oaths, designed to impose civil disabilities upon men for their beliefs rather than for unlawful conduct, were an abomination to the founders of this nation." The dissents in *Schwimmer* and *Macintosh*, Black continued, "rested in part on the promise that religious tests are incompatible with our constitutional guarantee of freedom of thought and religion." By now it was clear that "I agree with the constitutional philosophy underlying the dissents of Mr. Justice Holmes and Mr. Chief Justice Hughes." From that premise, Black wrote,

> I cannot agree that a state can lawfully bar from a semi-public position a well-qualified man of good character solely because he entertains a religious belief which might prompt him at some time in the future to violate a law which has not yet been and may never be enacted. Under our Constitution men are punished for what they do or fail to do and not for what they think and believe. Freedom to think, to believe, and to worship, has too exalted a position in our country to be penalized on such an illusory basis.[88]

Justices William O. Douglas, Frank Murphy, and Wiley B. Rutledge joined Justice Black in his explicit endorsement of the dissents of Justice Holmes and Chief Justice Hughes.[89]

For those who continued to believe that the decisions in *Schwimmer*, *Macintosh*, and *Bland* had treated unjustly conscientious objectors who applied for citizenship, a decade of attempted legislation had proved unsuccessful. Yet now, courts around the country, among them the Supreme Court itself, had signaled that some judges disagreed with the precedents and were ready to correct them. Activists in search of a remedy began to believe that the Supreme Court might welcome another test case.

Notes

1. Lola Maverick Lloyd, *The Griffin Bill* (New York: Griffin Bill Committee, n.d.), 2. Lloyd was Chair of the Griffin Bill Committee. Schwimmer-Lloyd collection, Griffin bill files, box G-7; "Anthony Jerome Griffin," *Who Was Who in America*: 1: *1897-1942* (Chicago: A. N. Marquis, 1943), 487. In his opening testimony before the House Committee on Immigration and Naturalization, Griffin commented on his personal history. "My mother's great grandfather fought in the American Revolution. I think with that background I can at least lay claim that I can not, in the very nature of things, lack anything of devotion and loyalty to my country. Let that be coupled also in your minds with the thought that I am far from

being a pacifist. I served 12 years in the National Guard and in the United States Army. I was a captain during the Spanish-American War." See *Hearings Before the Committee on Immigration and Naturalization, House of Representatives, Seventy-First Congress, Second Session, on H.R. 3547,* 8-9 May 1930, 3, hereinafter designated "Hearings on H.R. 3547."

    2. Anthony J. Griffin, "Necessity for Trained Officers in Time of Peace" (10 March 1920), in *The War and its Aftermath: Speeches of Hon. Anthony J. Griffin of New York in the House of Representatives During the 65th, 66th, and 67th Congresses* (Washington: n.p., 1922), 77.

    3. Griffin, "Against Exclusion of Immigration" (10 December 1920), in *The War and Its Aftermath,* 124.

    4. Anthony Griffin to Vaughn Bachman Brokaw of Phoenix, Arizona, 22 July 1929. Schwimmer-Lloyd collection, Griffin Bill files, box G-7; Hearings on H.R. 3547, 63. Schwimmer saw a personal dimension to the bill, as she wrote to Rep. Griffin.

    "I am deeply touched to learn that you have introduced a bill in Congress to amend the naturalization laws, so that I and other pacifists, [*sic*] might be admitted as citizens.

    "I am very grateful for the step you have taken, not only because it opens the possibility of my gaining American citizenship, but because in addition to Judge Holmes and his dissenting colleagues' opinions, your action has helped me to regain faith in what I have always considered American ideas and ideals, a faith that was rudely shattered by the Supreme Court's decision.

    "The passage of your bill will also help to restore faith in multitudes of others who are bewildered by the contradiction in the fact that America stands before the world as leader for world peace, yet in the Supreme Court decision denounces pacifists as dangerous for the United States." See Schwimmer to Griffin, 31 May 1929. Schwimmer-Lloyd collection, Griffin Committee files, box G-7.

    Griffin says that the bill was filed on 30 or 31 May, while other sources say it was filed on 29 May. See Lloyd, *Griffin Bill,* 2 and Alfred Lief, "Pacifist Citizens Wanted," *The Arbitrator: A Monthly Digest of News of Social Significance* 13 (February 1931): 2. In any case, Griffin acted *very* soon after *Schwimmer* was handed down.

    5. Hearings on H. R. 3547, 1-2.

    6. "A Dialogue Between a Citizen and a Soldier on H. R. 3547," *Congressional Record—House* 72 (11 April 1930): 6966-67.

    7. Lloyd, *Griffin Bill,* 2; Press Release, "National Griffin Bill Committee Organized," 14 March 1930. Schwimmer-Lloyd collection, Griffin bill file, box G-7. "Many of us would have chosen different wording if we were consulted," Lloyd said of the Griffin bill. "We were not consulted, but, of course, when we heard of the bill we gave our support to Mr. Griffin, and we are very glad to support this bill just as it is." See Hearings on H.R. 3547, 178.

8. The Griffin Bill Committee claimed that hearings on the bill began so late because Johnson, who was hostile to the bill and did not want it considered, continually delayed them. It charged him also with obstructionism during the hearings and, later, in the production of the transcript of the hearings. See Lloyd, *Griffin Bill*, 3-4.

9. By the time of the hearings, question 22 on the naturalization questionnaire had been changed to question 24 on a revised form, although the language of the question was exactly the same.

10. Hearings on H. R. 3547, 4-5, 20, 174, 12-13, 72, 10.

11. Hearings on H. R. 3547, 150-51.

12. Two newspaper headlines reflect the diversity of perspectives: "Anti-War Sects Bill Stirs House Group to Hot Debate," *Baltimore Sun*, 9 May 1930; "Patriotic Organizations Oppose Bill Granting Citizenship to Pacifist Aliens," *Bronx Home News*, 9 March 1930. The latter paper was printed in Representative Griffin's district. Although the article anticipated that the hearings would begin on 11 March (they actually began on 8 May), it accurately reported that the Griffin bill "has suddenly loomed as the storm center of one of the bitterest controversies of recent years. From coast to coast patriotic and civic organizations have opened a campaign which will be climaxed next Tuesday by a united attack on the bill when it comes before the Congressional Committee on Immigration and Naturalization."

13. "This Constitution, and the Laws of the United States which shall be made in Pursuance thereof; and all Treaties made, or which shall be made, under the Authority of the United States, shall be the supreme Law of the Land; and the Judges in every State shall be bound thereby, any Thing in the Constitution or Laws of any State to the Contrary notwithstanding." Capitalization in original.

14. Jeannette Pickering Rankin (1880-1973), elected to Congress from Montana in 1916, helped to draft a Constitutional amendment granting women the right to vote nationally and lost her bid for the Senate in 1918 after opposing America's entry into war. Elected to Congress again in 1940, Rankin once more voted alone against joining a world war. In 1930 she spoke before the committee as a representative of the National Council for the Prevention of War. Hearings on H. R. 3547, 30-31.

15. Henry M. Haviland, representing the Religious Society of Friends; Hearings on H. R. 3547, 172.

16. William B. Harvey, a Quaker speaking for himself; Hearings on H. R. 3547, 168.

17. Rev. Silas M. Grubb, the pastor of a Mennonite church and publisher of *The Mennonite*, a denominational newspaper; Hearings on H. R. 3547, 45.

18. Rabe mentioned 1918 in her testimony without specific reference to a case. I have not found a 1918 case in which that interpretation was made.

19. Olive Rabe, speaking for herself; Hearings on H. R. 3547, 84-86.

20. Apparently the case was never reported; there is no legal citation. Her hearing was widely reported, however, as "In the Court of Common Pleas of Allen County, Ohio. In the Matter of the Petition of Martha Jane Graber to Be Admitted

a Citizen of the United States of America. Citizenship Petition No. 329. Hearing July 9th, 1929." For the transcript of the hearing, see Hearings on H. R. 3547, 36-40 and Hearings on H. R. 297, 172-75. See also "A Girl Without a Country," *Christian Century* 46 (31 July 1929): 957.

21. See the Expatriation Act of 1907, 34 *Statutes at Large* 1228, § 3 (1907). "That any American woman who marries a foreigner shall take the nationality of her husband."

22. See 42 *Statutes at Large* 1022 (1922), often called the Cable Act after its sponsor, Rep. John L. Cable of Ohio. It provided that a woman who had lost her citizenship through marriage could be naturalized, provided that she complied with all requirements of the naturalization laws, which obviously included taking the oath.

23. Apparently the case was unreported; there is no legal citation; see Hearings on H. R. 3547, 34-36; Hearings on H. R. 297, 183.

24. Although it was unreported with no legal citation, the full transcript of the hearing is printed in Hearings on H. R. 297, 175-83. Questioning of Mrs. Webb exemplified what Representative Griffin called "heckling" of applicants for naturalization.

25. Representative Robert A. Green of Florida, Hearings on H. R. 3547, 24. This speech occurred at the beginning of the hearing process, demonstrating that Green was not without bias.

26. Elizabeth G. Fries, representing the American Legion Auxiliary, District of Columbia; Hearings on H. R. 3547, 65.

27. J. Edward Cassidy, Director-General, United States Air Force Association, Hearings on H. R. 3547, 214, 216. Rep. Griffin denied that his bill would give naturalized citizens any status different from native-born citizens.

28. Mary G. Kilbreth, President of the Woman Patriot Publishing Company, Washington, D.C.; Hearings on H. R. 3547, 186. As an addendum to her brief statement, Miss Kilbreth filed a huge document (187-214) that excoriated pacifism, feminism, internationalism, communism and everything "liberal" that had happened in Europe and America in the first third of the twentieth century—the kind of material *The Woman Patriot* had been publishing for some time. Rosika Schwimmer was mentioned several times in this document. After obtaining a copy of the transcript of the hearings, Schwimmer wrote to Griffin that she was "outraged to find myself libelled in the most shameless way in the statements presented after we had left. I am positively sick with the feeling of helplessness that these so-called 'verified facts' should now go to Congressmen and other people who have no means to know that Miss Kilbreth's statement contains the most unqualified lies about me. I am physically sick with all that." See Schwimmer to Griffin, 25 May 1931, Schwimmer-Lloyd collection, Griffin bill files, box G-7.

29. James H. Patten, representing the Immigration Restriction League, the New York State Council, Junior Order United American Mechanics, and the Executive Board of Fraternal Patriotic Americans; Hearings on H. R. 3547, 182-83.

30. H. Ralph Burton, representing the National Patriotic League; Hearings on H. R. 3547, 154, 157-64, 196-98 (the latter pages derive from material submitted by Mary Kilbreth of *The Woman Patriot*.

31. S. 1506, in the Senate of the United States, 14 June 1929; Statement by Senator Steck, "Oath to Be Taken by Aliens," *Congressional Record—Senate*, 71/3 (14 June 1929): 2861-63; Robe Carl White, Assistant Secretary of Labor to Sen. Hiram W. Johnson, Chair of Senate Committee on Immigration and Naturalization, 26 June 1929. "As the oath of allegiance has been authoritatively construed by the Supreme Court in the Schwimmer case," White wrote, "the Bureau of Naturalization is of the opinion that it needs no clarification, either as to the conditions there present, or others which may arise. The bureau therefore does not look with favor upon the proposed legislation. The department, likewise, does not look upon such legislation as desirable." Record group 267, National Archives collection.

32. Baldwin to Griffin, 14 June 1929; Griffin to Baldwin, 19 June 1929; Baldwin to Hays, 21 June 1929; Baldwin to Griffin, 27 June 1929. ACLU Archives, vol. 359, reel 62.

33. Baldwin to Griffin, 12 October 1929; Griffin to Baldwin, 16 October 1929; Frederick W. Wile, "Schwimmer Case Inspires New Bill," *Washington Star*, 8 October 1929; Baldwin to Wile, 26 September 1929. In preparation for the *Star* article, Wile had written to Baldwin on 18 September asking why the ACLU thought the bill was not in satisfactory form. "We do not think it accomplishes the purpose which he has in mind," Baldwin replied, "and we have proposed to him an amendment which would read for the last three lines: 'by reason of his or her religious beliefs or personal convictions with respect to bearing arms, or the lawfulness of war as a means of settling international disputes.'" Schwimmer-Lloyd collection, Griffin bill file, box G-7.

34. "Pacifists Demand Citizenship Rights," *New York Times*, 18 January, sec. II, 2. Tickets to the Griffin Bill Committee Dinner at the Town Hall Club, 123 West 43d Street, on Saturday, 17 January 1931, are preserved in the Schwimmer-Lloyd collection, Griffin bill file, box G-7. Admission was $2.00 per person.

35. Griffin to Alfred Lief, 1 March 1931, Schwimmer-Lloyd collection, Griffin bill file, box G-7; Minutes, Conference for Joint Action, American Civil Liberties Union, 11 August 1931; Swarthmore Peace Collection.

36. Charles W. Poletti, Memorandum prepared for the American Civil Liberties Union, "Proposed amendment of the Naturalization Act to grant citizenship to aliens with conscientious scruples against bearing arms," 28 September 1931, 2, 5. Schwimmer-Lloyd collection, Griffin bill file, box G-7. The proposed language was to be inserted in the Naturalization Act in the first paragraph of subdivision 4 of section 4.

37. Griffin to Marion Tilden Burritt [a member of the Griffin Bill Committee], 6 November 1931. Schwimmer-Lloyd collection, Griffin bill file, box G-7.

38. S. 3275, In the Senate of the United States, 72nd Congress, 1st Session, 25 January 1932, ACLU Archives, vol. 532; Richard Lowitt, "Cutting, Bronson Murray," in *American National Biography* (New York: Oxford University Press, 1999) 5: 940-41. Griffin was sure that Senator Cutting was not the principal force behind his bill. "I learned that Senator Cutting intends to back the Roger Baldwin Bill supposed to have been prepared by John W. Davis. Personally, I do not think he had a thing to do with it because it has the ear marks of emanating from the brain of a clerk in Davis' office, named Poletti, influenced no doubt by Baldwin." In a later letter to the editor of *The Woman Patriot* (of all people), Griffin wrote, "There is one point on which I desire to set you right—The American Civil Liberties Union did not support my bill. They prepared a bill of their own, introduced by Senator Cutting, which, in my opinion, would perpetuate the folly of question #24 and oblige applicants for citizenship to reveal their religious or conscientious scruples—matters, in my opinion, sacred and beyond the scope of state interference. It is proper for you to know that I am opposed to it, as it is designed for the benefit of a class; although, for all that, it would not give them the exemption they evidently desire." Griffin to Alfred Lief, 18 January 1932; Griffin to J. S. Eichelberger, 15 August 1932, Schwimmer-Lloyd collection, Griffin Bill file, box G-7.

39. H. R. 297 and H. R. 298, in the House of Representatives of the United States, 72nd Congress, 1st Session, 8 December 1931; Griffin to Emily Marx, 12 January 1932; Griffin to Katherine D. Blake, Chair of Women's International League for Peace and Freedom, 4 January 1932; Schwimmer-Lloyd collection, Griffin bill file, box G-7.

40. Although *The Christian Century* had been quite vocal in its condemnation of the decisions in *Schwimmer* and *Macintosh*, it gave rather scant attention to legislative initiatives. See "Hold Hearings on the Cutting Bill," *Christian Century* 49 (6 April 1932): 436-37; "The Griffin and Cutting Bills," *Christian Century* 49 (11 May 1932): 597. The latter article pointed out that "superpatriots" were mounting furious opposition to the bills and urged all supporters to write to the members of the respective Committees on Immigration and Naturalization. In a series of editorials the *Washington Post* opposed the legislation. "Nothing could be gained by extending citizenship to such individuals," the *Post* announced in "On Bearing Arms" (23 October 1931). "On the other hand, one of the strong ties of national unity and common interest would be broken down. Citizenship would become meaningless. America has no place for those aliens who are so holy that they will not fight to defend the lives of their families and their homes, but who are nevertheless base enough to seek protection at the expense of citizens who are more courageous." In "Privileges for Aliens" (25 January 1932) the *Post* derided the aims of the Griffin Bill Committee: "Any movement to bring into the fold a group honorary citizenship, a class of privileged aliens, is too disgusting to merit serious consideration in Congress." In "To Encourage Disloyalty" (22 March 1932) the *Post* asserted that "Certain aliens of twisted mentality, who are not to be classed as criminals, have been debarred from

citizenship because they could not bring themselves to give the honest pledge to bear arms if called upon by the Government. The Supreme Court held that these aliens were not fit to become citizens. The public applauded this decision; but the 'liberals' who demand license in the name of liberty are trying to obtain special favors and exemptions for aliens who are not willing to defend the country. . . . The United States is not asking aliens to become citizens. They seek this privilege themselves. Let them give the oath to support and defend the United States against all enemies, foreign and domestic, by bearing arms, or let them be excluded as unfit to become American citizens."

41. Davis got his allusion wrong. *Der Staat über alles* would have conveyed the meaning he wanted. *Stadt* (city) is a feminine noun, *Die Stadt*.

42. Jerome Davis, speaking for himself; *Hearings on H. R. 297 and H. R. 298 Before the Committee on Immigration and Naturalization, House of Representatives, Seventy-second Congress, First Session*, 26 January 1932, 20, 23, hereinafter designated "Hearings on H. R. 297."

43. Richard A. Wood, speaking for the Society of Friends of Philadelphia and Vicinity; Hearings on H.R. 297, 57-8.

44. John F. Finerty, speaking for himself, Hearings on H. R. 297, 39.

45. Mercer G. Johnston, Director of the People's Legislative Service, Washington, D.C.; Hearings on H. R. 297, 75.

46. Major General Amos A. Fries, speaking for the National Sojourners, an organization of officers and ex-officers of the various military services; Hearings on H. R. 297, 121. See also Col. J. T. Taylor, speaking for the American Legion, H. Ralph Burton, speaking for the National Patriotic League, and Colonel Orvel Johnson, speaking for the Reserve Officers' Training Corps Association of the United States; Hearings on H. R. 297, 101-2, 98, 125-26.

47. James H. Patten, speaking for the Immigration Restriction League of New York, the New York State Council of Junior Order United American Mechanics, the Fraternal Patriotic Americans, and the Commandery General of the Patriotic Order Sons of America. "We have already in our midst, . . . quite enough conscientious objectors," Patten told the Committee, "and it is most respectfully suggested that we do not need any increase in their number or the number of war cowards and war slackers this special class legislation would certainly tend to invite and create by the immigration and naturalization routes." See Hearings on H. R. 297, 143.

48. Herman A. Miller, speaking for the Patriotic Order of Sons of America; Hearings on H. R. 297, 107. See also H. Ralph Burton, speaking for the National Patriotic League (93), and Mrs. Lowell F. Hobart, speaking for the Daughters of the American Revolution (103).

49. Frank I. Peckham, speaking for the Sentinels of the Republic; Hearings on H. R. 297, 134.

50. Demarest Lloyd, Vice Chairman of the Board, American Coalition of Patriotic Societies; Hearings on H. R. 297, 145-46.

51. "Statement by Representative Anthony J. Griffin in Rebuttal"; Hearings on H. R. 297, 146-48. See Rep. Griffin's rather elaborate statement of purpose and philosophy and his response to his opponents in "H. R. 297—An Appeal for Religious Liberty and Freedom of Thought," *Congressional Record—House* 75 (14 July 1932): 15354-57.

52. Albert Lief, national secretary of the Griffin Bill Committee, wrote, "The fact that such worthies as John W. Davis, Dean Clark of Yale Law School, and Felix Frankfurter have joined the fight for amending the law heartens us." See Lief to Olive Rabe, 26 March 1932, Schwimmer-Lloyd collection, Griffin bill file, box G-7. I have not found a statement of vote by the committee on any of these bills, but neither have I found any record of a debate or vote by the full House of Representatives.

53. The merits of the bill were argued before the subcommittee by John W. Davis, Francis J. McConnell, president of the Federal Council of Churches, Father Richard A. McGowan of the National Catholic Welfare Conference, Rabbi Edward L. Israel of the Central Conference of American Rabbis, and Francis R. Taylor of the Society of Friends. Roger Baldwin, ACLU open letter "To the organizations interested in the bills to admit alien pacifists to citizenship," 23 March 1932; ACLU report "To those interested in the Cutting and Griffin bills to admit alien pacifists to citizenship," 2 May 1932, ACLU Archives, vol. 512. Opponents of the bill also made presentations to the subcommittee, but I have not found their names or any transcript of speeches before the subcommittee. *The Woman Patriot* devoted two issues to the Griffin and Cutting bills, asserting the same kind of opposition that was presented in the hearings on H. R. 3547. Miss Kilbreth claimed the material was what she presented in the subcommittee hearings on S. 3275. See "Statement Against the Cutting and Griffin Bills," *The Woman Patriot* 16 (May 1932): 1-8; "Statement Against the Cutting and Griffin Bills (Part II)," *The Woman Patriot* 16 (June 1932): 1-8. Kilbreth comments (7) that a transcript of the hearings before the subcommittee was published, but only a limited number for the use of the Senate, which may explain why I have not found a copy.

54. *Congressional Record—House* 77 (9 March 1933): 90.

55. Schwimmer to Griffin, 11 June 1932; Griffin to Schwimmer, 13 June 1932, Schwimmer-Lloyd collection, Griffin bill file, box G-7.

56. Lola Maverick Lloyd, "Now Griffin-O'Day Bill Committee," Open letter to the Griffin Bill Committee, 20 February 1935, Swarthmore Peace Collection; "O'Day, Caroline Love Goodwin," *National Cyclopædia of American Biography* (New York: James T. White, 1942) F (1939-42): 281; Filing of H. R. 5170, *Congressional Record—House* 79 (31 January 1935): 1356.

57. O'Day to Baldwin, 11 February 1935, ACLU Archives, vol. 784.

58. *Congressional Record—House* 81 (13 August 1937): 9193. I do not know whether O'Day changed the language to the version Baldwin and the ACLU preferred, for I have not found the bill itself. Chief Justice Stone, in his dissent in *Girouard v. United States* (328 U.S. 61 at 73-74), in which this legislative history played a large part, claimed the language was "identical" with that of H. R. 297.

59. *Congressional Record—Senate* 84 (13 August 1939): 67; emphasis added.

60. Legislation failed despite a public education campaign by the ACLU. In February 1938 it published a booklet detailing the history of the issue and describing the efforts of some, particularly Abraham Warkentin and Rebecca Shelley, to win citizenship in the courts. The booklet encouraged people to contact legislators, to support one of the bills in Congress, and to send money to the ACLU. See "Citizenship for Alien Pacifists: The Issue Again Before the Courts," (New York: American Civil Liberties Union, 1938), 1-15. Swarthmore Peace Collection.

61. Nationality Act of 1940, chap. 876, 54 *Statutes at Large* 1137 at 1157 § 335 (b).

62. 54 *Statutes at Large* 1153 § 331.

63. 54 *Statutes at Large* 1154 § 332 (a).

64. 54 *Statutes at Large* 1154 § 332 (b).

65. Chap. 199, 56 *Statutes at Large* 1182 "Title X—Naturalization of Persons Serving in the Armed Forces of the United States During the Present War," §§ 701-704.

66. Chap. 690, 56 *Statutes at Large* 1041, "An Act Providing for the Naturalization of Certain Alien Veterans of the World War," § 323a.

67. 54 *Statutes at Large* 885 at 889 § 5(g).

68. Biographical statement, "Abraham Warkentin," *Agreed Statement of Facts: In the Matter of the Petition of Abraham Warkentin to Be Admitted a Citizen of the United States of America*, In the District Court of the United States for the Northern District of Illinois, Eastern Division; Judge William H. Holly, "Memorandum, *In Re Abraham Warkentin*," ACLU Archives, vol. 978.

69. Warkentin to Sherwood Eddy, 22 April 1937; A. L. Wirin [ACLU counsel] to Whitney North Seymour [former U. S. Assistant Solicitor General, now in private practice], 17 May 1937; Wirin to Charles P. Schwartz [Warkentin's lawyer], 14 September 1937; Schwartz to Wirin, 18 October 1937; Roger Baldwin to Judge Charles Poletti, 10 November 1937; Poletti to Baldwin, 18 November 1937; Schwartz to Baldwin, 22 November 1937. ACLU Archives, vol. 978.

70. Seymour to Wirin, 6 July 1937. "Plainly, the attempt ought to be to distinguish between individual conscientious scruples and those dictated by an adherence to the tenets of a church, although the distinction is really pretty tenuous." ACLU Archives, vol. 978.

71. *Warkentin v. Schlotfeldt* 93 F.2d 42 at 44 (1937); citations omitted.

72. *In re Losey* 39 F.Supp. 37 at 38 (1941).

73. Rebecca Shelley was a friend, of sorts, of Rosika Schwimmer. Schwimmer regarded Shelley as a pest. Before bringing her naturalization case to the District Court and Court of Appeals for the District of Columbia, Shelley had brought the same case to several other courts, including the Court of Appeals for the Sixth Circuit. *Shelley v. United States* 120 F.2d 734 at 735 (1941).

74. Another layer of facts is at work in this case, but it is irrelevant to the outcome and to the point here.

75. *Shelley v. United States* 120 F.2d 734 at 735 (1941).

76. 310 U.S. 586 (1940). For a useful historical treatment of *Gobitis*, see Shawn Francis Peters, *Judging Jehovah's Witnesses: Religious Persecution and the Dawn of the Rights Revolution* (Lawrence: University Press of Kansas, 2000), 19-95.

77. 320 U.S. 118 (1943).

78. *Schneiderman v. United States* 320 U.S. 118 at 132, 138, 164-65.

79. *Schneiderman v. United States* 320 U.S. 118 at 138. Murphy also cited Chief Justice Hughes's dissent in *Macintosh* at the same point.

80. *Schneiderman v. United States* 320 U.S. 118 at 139.

81. *In re Kinloch* 53 F.Supp. 521 at 523 (1944).

82. "Conscientious Objectors Admitted to Citizenship," *Press Service: American Civil Liberties Union*, 1 May 1944; "Federal Judge Admits Conscientious Objectors to Citizenship," *Interpreter Releases: Common Council for American Unity*, New York City, 13 June 1944; Albert E. Reitzel [Acting Counsel, U. S. Department of Justice] to Clifford Forester [Staff Council, ACLU], 13 April 1944, ACLU Archives, vol. 2569. "Citizenship and the Bearing of Arms: A Recent Court Decision," *Liberty* 41 (Fourth Quarter 1944): 2-3, 17; Seventh-day Adventist Historical Society.

83. *In re Sawyer* 59 F.Supp. 428 at 429 (1945); citations omitted. *Sua sponte* means "on one's own," that is, "by the court's initiative without motion from either party."

84. *In re Nielsen* 60 F.Supp. 240 at 242-43 (1945).

85. The U. S. Supreme Court described Illinois's position thusly: "The Justices [of the Illinois Supreme Court] justify their refusal to admit petitioner to practice before the courts of Illinois on the ground of petitioner's inability to take in good faith the required oath to support the Constitution of Illinois. His inability to take such an oath, the Justices submit, shows that the Committee on Character and Fitness properly refused to certify to his moral character and moral fitness to be an officer of the Court, charged with the administration of justice under Illinois law. His good citizenship, they think, judged by the standards required for practicing law in Illinois, is not satisfactorily shown. A conscientious belief in nonviolence to the extent that the believer will not use force to prevent wrong, no matter how aggravated, and so cannot swear in good faith to support the Illinois Constitution, the Justices contend, must disqualify such a believer for admission." See *In re Summers* 325 U.S. 561 at 569-70 (1945). This doctrine is perhaps better expressed by Horace B. Garman, a member of the State Board of Law Examiners for the State of Illinois, in a letter to Summers. "This reply is personal and not an expression of the Committee on Character and Fitness," Garman wrote. "Your conduct is governed by a higher law which we all hope may some day prevail. In the meantime most of us think chaos would prevail and civilization might be destroyed if the wolves are not kept at bay. Lawyers have the job of aiding in the administration and enforcement of the law—all law. What protection can the law be to the weak if lawyers do not consider its mandates to be entitled to obedience

by force if necessary? Can a man conscientiously take an oath to support the Constitution and the laws, at the same time reserving the use of force from the meaning of 'support'? I do not argue against your religious beliefs or your philosophy of non-violence. My point is merely that your position seems inconsistent with the obligation of an attorney at law." ACLU Archives, vol. 2696.

86. Clyde W. Summers to Clifford Forster of the ACLU, 23 April 1945: "Sometimes the implications of this case both for myself and for many others frightens [*sic*] me, yet I have never felt that I could with a clear conscience let the matter drop." ACLU Archives, vol. 2696.

87. *In re Summers* 325 U.S. 561 at 572-73.

88. *In re Summers* 325 U.S. 561 at 576-78.

89. Summers 326 U.S. 561 at 578. See "U.S. Supreme Court Upholds Refusal to Admit Pacifist to Bar," *Press Release: American Civil Liberties Union*, 18 June 1945. The ACLU expressed fear because of the "far-reaching implication" of Summers's case. Summers, later admitted to the New York bar, had a distinguished teaching career and also served as the ACLU's principal authority on labor questions. Samuel Walker. *In Defense of American Liberties: A History of the ACLU* (New York: Oxford University Press, 1990), 153.

Seven

James Louis Girouard:
"The Correct Rule of Law"

The defining stage of controversy concerning naturalization of conscientious objectors began quietly enough. James Louis Girouard's application for naturalization came before the United States District Court of Massachusetts in 1943. Responding to the question on the preliminary form about whether he was willing to bear arms in defense of the United States,[1] he had written, "No. (Non-combatant) Seventh Day Adventist." In spite of that and contrary to the recommendation of the Naturalization Examiner, a judge granted Girouard citizenship on 1 August 1944.[2]

James Louis Girouard was born 24 August 1902 in Moncton, New Brunswick, Canada, where he lived until he immigrated to the United States on 9 July 1923.[3] His parents, Oliver and Mary Ellen Girouard, were Roman Catholic, and James was baptized in the Catholic Church as an infant. He attended a Catholic school, although his formal education ended with the eighth grade. He began work as a painter's apprentice in the first-class coach shop of the Canadian National Railway. Girouard married Mabel Ardella Kierstead, a lifelong Seventh-day Adventist, on 9 April 1923. In anticipation of his marriage, Girouard converted to the Seventh-day Adventist Church and remained a devoted believer the rest of his life. One month after their marriage, the Girouards boarded a train for Haverhill, Massachusetts.

Girouard found a job as a painter at New England Sanitarium and Hospital, a Seventh-day Adventist institution in Stoneham, Massachusetts, moving to Stoneham in February 1924. Girouard worked as a painter for two years and then applied for a job in the sanitarium's power plant, where he worked as an electrician for forty years. He went to night school to learn the skills and obtain the proper licenses to work in the plant and eventually became assistant chief engineer.[4]

Girouard filed his intention to become a citizen on 8 August 1940, seventeen years after he entered the country. No one in his family knows why he waited so long to apply for citizenship. Several members of the family immigrated to America about the same time as Girouard. Many of them waited several years to apply for citizenship. They were legal immigrants and all were able to work. They also kept close ties with other family members still in Canada and frequently visited there. They did not feel the need to become citizens. As war clouds gathered in Europe, travel between the United States and Canada became somewhat more difficult. Several in the family applied for citizenship about that time, to make sure their positions in America were secure. It may be that Girouard thought the same way.[5] In conformity with the law, he filed his application for citizenship two years later, 26 January 1943. As part of that process he completed the preliminary form that contained the question, "If necessary, are you willing to take up arms in defense of this country?" Girouard answered, "No (Non-combatant) Seventh Day Adventist."[6]

The Seventh-day Adventist Church began in the 1840s among people who had expected the second coming of Christ to occur in 1844. When that did not happen, a believing remnant reinterpreted the prediction that had caused them to expect Christ to come, forming the Seventh-day Adventist Church. On the question of the second coming, as their name implied, they believed it would happen sooner rather than later, but they no longer would be date-setting predictors of the event. Taking the Bible as their rule, they set the seventh day of the week, God's Sabbath, as the proper day of worship. They adopted the biblical custom to worship and rest from their labors from sundown Friday until sundown Saturday. Based primarily on the teaching of its inspired prophet, Ellen G. White, the church also concentrated on health issues. The church gave advice about proper diet and lifestyle in order to maintain the body as the temple of God. It also launched formal ministries of health such as sanitaria, hospitals, and clinics, and sent medical missionaries to many parts of the world. Prophetic teaching and biblical interpretation converged to form the church's attitudes toward government and war.[7]

The church developed its formal organization just as the Civil War broke out, so it was compelled to think about the issues of government and war. The church strongly believed that Adventist Christians should give loyalty and obedience to the civil government. Paul had argued in Romans 13:1-5 that a Christian should be subject to the "powers that be," who ruled because of God's pleasure. Christians should obey civil authorities not because of fear, but for conscience's sake. Adventists must honor the state and obey its laws, including paying their taxes. Yet Christians must also obey the law of God, realizing that the law of God is higher and more compelling than the law of the state. Consequently, if the state imposes a law contrary to the law of God, a Christian is obligated to obey the law of God rather than the law of the state. About the question of war, God's teaching was clear. The Sixth Commandment reads, "You shall not kill." Jesus said, "If my kingdom were of this world, then would my servants fight." The implication is that his kingdom is not of this world, so his followers must not fight. Jesus said, "Resist not evil; but whoever strikes you on the right cheek, turn the other one to him also." Jesus said, "Love your enemies, bless those who curse you, do good to those who hate you, and pray for those who despitefully use you and persecute you." Adventists used many of the biblical texts and arguments used by other Christian pacifists (see Chapter Two). To these Adventists added that they could not engage in war because it would require them to violate the observance of the seventh-day Sabbath. These arguments could be reduced to Jesus' famous commandment, "Give to Caesar the things that are Caesar's; give to God the things that are God's."[8]

Most Adventists lived in the North, so when the Union began conscription in March 1863, the issue became urgent. Adventists took an approach more practical than ideological. The church argued that Adventists could not fight because to do so would cause them to violate their Sabbath obligations. The law, however, allowed those called to serve to send a substitute or pay a $300 commutation fee. Most Adventists did the latter. Sometimes churches even helped poor draftees to raise the money for the fee. So the church took a pacifist stand, but the practicalities of the law enabled it to avoid relying on its theological arguments. After the war ended, the General Conference, the governing body of the church, stated its position in a formal resolution.

Resolved, That we recognize civil government as ordained of God, that order, justice, and quiet may be maintained in the land; and that the people of God may lead quiet and peaceable lives in all godliness and honesty. In accordance with this fact we acknowledge the justice of rendering tribute, custom, honor, and reverence to the civil power, as enjoined in the New Testament. While we thus cheerfully render to Caesar the things which the Scriptures show to be his, we are compelled to decline all participation in acts of war and bloodshed as being inconsistent with the duties enjoined upon us by our divine Master toward our enemies and toward all mankind.[9]

World War I obviously presented a crisis for Adventists and other conscientious objectors. The church modified its position to make it much easier for Adventists to refuse to kill and, at the same time, give to Caesar what was Caesar's. In April 1917 the North American division of the church issued a statement that reproduced the Civil War resolution and added the phrase, "We have been noncombatants throughout our history." Whereas "noncombatant" previously had meant nonparticipation in the military, now it meant something entirely different. It now meant serving within the military, but in a noncombatant role. Adventists would be soldiers who did not take up arms. Calling attention to their long tradition of advocacy of good health practices and the medical facilities of the church, Adventists requested to serve as medical personnel within the ranks of the military. It was an ingenious solution, for it also circumvented the problem of doing work on the Sabbath. The church had concluded, from the teaching and example of Jesus, that helping people was always acceptable, even on the Sabbath. Adventists could give Caesar his due by serving in the military and yet be true to their pacifist history by refusing to bear arms. Medical service allowed them to be faithful to a strong tradition of their church and to justify violating Sabbath sanctity. To make sure all this would happen, in 1916 the church began to instruct its military-age men in church-run Red Cross training schools about the techniques of being a medic in the military. Military leaders were pleased to induct people already trained in the skills they would need, so they routinely assigned Adventist inductees to the roles they wanted.

In World War II Adventists followed the same procedure with more sophistication. In 1939 the church began to operate units of the Medical Cadet Training Program at its colleges, with instruction given by regular Army personnel. Now Adventists preferred to be called "conscientious cooperators." C. S. Longacre, head of the Religious Liberty Department of the General Conference, appeared before the House Military Affairs Committee in 1943 to explain the Adventist position (and terminology). "Seventh Day Adventists," Longacre announced, "are not pacifists nor militarists nor conscientious objectors, but noncombatants." A noncombatant "merely believes that he should not take human life. But he is willing to cooperate with his government in any capacity that he can, without having to violate his conscience in regard to taking a life." Adventists,

Longacre concluded, "are perfectly willing to lay down their lives in defense of their country."[10]

During World War II about 12,000 Adventists served in medical units in various branches of the armed forces. Church leaders and Adventists generally pointed out that medics were frequently in harm's way and served with valor. Adventist historians especially emphasize the story of Desmond T. Doss, an Army Private First Class, who won the Congressional Medal of Honor for his heroic medical aid to soldiers in the Okinawa battle of 1945.[11] So when James Louis Girouard refused to bear arms but indicated that he was a noncombatant Seventh-day Adventist, he acted securely in the mainstream of that tradition.

Not surprisingly, Girouard's response attracted the attention of the Immigrant Inspector in Boston, George F. Sears. On 9 March 1943 Girouard submitted to sworn testimony before Sears.

Q. It is noted on page 2 under question 26 which asks, "If necessary, are you willing to take up arms in defense of this country" your answer is "No," which has been qualified by the word "Non Combatant," [sic] have you any remark to make on this point?
A. Not except that it is a purely religious matter with me. I have no political or personal reasons other than that.
Q. Then you are unwilling to bear arms in defense of this country?
A. That is right.
Q. Have you anything further to say?
A. No, I believe there is nothing else I would add to that.

Sears then explained to Girouard that the Supreme Court had declared that an applicant for citizenship must be willing to bear arms to defend the United States. Girouard preferred to present his case to the court.[12]

Girouard had two more stops to make before his case went to a hearing before the District Court. On 3 November 1943 he appeared before his draft board to claim exemption from combatant service as a conscientious objector. This was reported to the District Director of Immigration and Naturalization.[13] On the same day he filed his petition for naturalization.[14] Therefore, James O'Sullivan, the Naturalization Examiner, recommended that the District Court deny citizenship to Girouard.

Girouard's day in court came on 1 August 1944, in a hearing before U.S. District Judge George C. Sweeney. Unfortunately, the court made no transcript of that hearing.[15] Judge Sweeney disregarded the government's recommendation and granted citizenship to Girouard, ruling

That since the selective Service and Training Act permits, as a matter of right, an applicant for the draft to express a willingness to serve in the armed forces of the United States, but as a non-combatant, then this petitioner by exercising that right is still a person who can take an unqualified oath of allegiance to the United States and is therefore eligible to citizenship.[16]

At this point the ACLU became interested in the case. Clifford Forster, an ACLU staff counsel, wrote to Harrop Freeman, the executive director of the Pacifist Research Bureau in Philadelphia, that he had "just noted" Girouard's case in the District Court. Knowing that the case was going to the Court of Appeals, Forster asked Freeman if he would write an *amicus curiae* brief for the ACLU. Somewhat later, Arthur Garfield Hays, another counsel for the ACLU, wrote to John W. Davis, the lawyer who argued Douglas Clyde Macintosh's case before the Supreme Court, asking Davis if he would be willing to write a brief if the case went to the Supreme Court, as it surely would. Davis responded that he assumed that appealing Girouard's case to the Supreme Court "would be tantamount to a petition for rehearing in the McIntosh [*sic*] case." In spite of his interest in that, Davis did not promise to write a brief on behalf of Girouard. Near the end of May, the ACLU made a public announcement of its support of the Girouard case in the Court of Appeals and its determination to assist the case in the Supreme Court in the hope of overturning *Schwimmer* and *Macintosh*. Forster also wrote to Alfred Albert, apparently then chair of the ACLU's legal committee,[17] expressing interest in this case. "Our C.O. committee has instructed us to go ahead with the case, so I would appreciate it if you would have some representative of your committee contact Girouard."[18]

During this maneuvering behind the scenes, the government filed a notice of exception to Judge Sweeney's ruling and appealed it to the First Circuit Court of Appeals.[19] Girouard's lawyers were David J. Coddaire and William J. Fitzsimmons, who had apparently represented him at the District Court level as well.[20] Girouard's case was argued at the Appeals Court 3 April 1945, before John C. Mahoney and Peter Woodbury, Circuit Judges, and Arthur D. Healey, District Judge.

Judge Mahoney wrote for the court, denying citizenship to Girouard. The opinion began with a detailed discussion of the facts of the case. It quoted the statement of Judge Sweeney of the District Court granting Girouard citizenship and then stated the court was in error. Congress had laid out the requirements for naturalization and any applicant must conform to them to gain citizenship. Among those requirements are those contained in the oath of naturalization, certainly including the promise to defend the Constitution and laws of the land. To buttress that point, the court quoted passages from *Schwimmer*, *Macintosh*, and *Bland*, especially emphasizing the points the Supreme Court had held: the Constitution requires citizens to defend the nation by force of arms when necessary[21] and the war powers of the government "to compel the armed service of any citizen in the land" are virtually limitless.[22] The Court of Appeals acknowledged that the Supreme Court had been sharply divided in these cases, but until Congress changed the law or the Court reversed itself, it said (with the slightest bit of reluctance to the discerning reader), "we are bound to accept the law as promulgated by these decisions. The facts in the instant case bring it squarely within the principles of these cases."[23]

Noting that because the Selective Service Act of 1940[24] enabled an alien to declare that he would serve in the military as a noncombatant, the District Court had permitted such a person to take the oath of naturalization, Mahoney argued that permission to serve as a noncombatant did not relieve an alien from taking the oath as the Supreme Court had interpreted it, to bear arms in defense of the country. "The naturalization laws make certain requirements of the applicant for citizenship and the consideration given to him as a draftee under the Selective Training and Service Act does not lessen those requirements."[25] The Nationality Act of 1940[26] had replicated the oath of naturalization from the 1906 law and did not modify the Supreme Court's interpretation of it. Congress amended the Act of 1940 in 1942[27] to expedite naturalization for those aliens who had served or would serve in the military during World War II. Again, no change was made in the oath of allegiance, and the law stipulated that it did not apply to those aliens who performed no military service or refused to wear the uniform. Since Girouard "has not served in the armed forces," the Court of Appeals concluded,

he is definitely denied the benefits of this amendment. . . . Congress, we think, in passing this amendment, intended to reward the conscientious objectors who had served or were serving in the armed forces by allowing them to take an oath which did not conflict with their religious scruples. It has passed no legislation expressly changing the meaning as interpreted by the Supreme Court, and we do not believe that it intended to extend this reward beyond this particular group. We do not think that it meant to give the benefit of such an inferential change in the meaning of the oath of allegiance to any alien conscientious objector who like the appellee here has not served and is not serving in the armed forces, . . . Since the petitioner is not willing to bear arms in defense of the United States, his petition must be denied.[28]

The decisions of the Courts of Appeals in *Schwimmer, Macintosh,* and *Bland* differed from this opinion in two ways. Each of these granted citizenship to the alien, but this one denied citizenship. Each of the earlier opinions was unanimous, but this one ignited a vigorous dissent by Judge Woodbury, who began by pointing out once more what had been raised so many times by previous applicants for citizenship: the question about bearing arms in the preliminary form for application had been included there by administrative initiative, not by congressional action. The question was not and had never been part of the naturalization law. Woodbury then turned to the Naturalization Act of 1940, acknowledging that it did not change the language of the oath of allegiance that Schwimmer, Macintosh, and Bland had refused, but neither did Congress, when it added several new requirements for eligibility to citizenship,[29] add a specific requirement to bear arms. Judge Woodbury inferred from that silence that Congress did not affirmatively adopt the interpretation of the Supreme Court in *Schwimmer, Macintosh,* and *Bland.* "It seems to me that the permissible inferences from that statute neutralize one another." Yet the 1942 amendment to the Nationality Act of 1940 *did* change the Supreme Court's interpretation of those cases. It applied to Girouard because it expedited the citizenship of those who had the same scruples as he. True, he could not take advantage of that law because he had not served in the military. But because it covered those with the same scruples as Girouard's and because Congress did not change the language of the oath of allegiance,

> it would seem to follow that Congress has by necessary implication expressed its intention that one who believes as the petitioner does can take that oath without reservation. It would be strangely inconsistent if Congress permitted conscientious objectors to elect service in a noncombatant capacity, gave persons so serving, if aliens, advantages in obtaining citizenship by naturalization, and then required them to take an oath actually to bear arms in defense of the United States.

"I think," Woodbury reasoned, "Congress must have intended the words of the oath to mean the same thing to one who has served in the military or naval forces as they do to one who has not."[30]

Judge Woodbury had only begun his extraordinary dissent. "I would even be willing myself to go further," he declared, "and affirm the order of the court below on a still broader ground. I would be willing to recognize frankly that the case at bar is ruled in principal [*sic*] by the *Schwimmer*, *Macintosh* and *Bland* cases, but decline to follow them."[31] Woodbury acknowledged that judges of lower courts are obligated to follow precedents set by Supreme Court decisions, that federal law would be in disarray if District Courts and particularly the Courts of Appeals decided cases only according to the legal philosophies of the various judges. Appeals court judges should, indeed must, decide cases as they think the Supreme Court would decide them. Yet on "rare occasions," Woodbury wrote,

> and I think this is one of them, situations arise when in the exercise to the best of our ability of the duty to prophesy thrust upon us by our position in the federal judicial system we must conclude that dissenting opinions of the past express the law of today. When this situation arises and we do not agree with the decisions of the Supreme Court I think it our duty to decline to follow such decisions and instead to follow reasoning with which we agree. As I see it this is the situation which confronts us here.[32]

After this startling declaration Judge Woodbury reviewed the dissenting opinions in the previous cases, especially *Schwimmer* and *Macintosh*. He found several themes. Dissenters acknowledged Congress had the power to exact a promise to bear arms in defense of the country; the question was whether it had done so. The dissent in *Macintosh* had compared the wording of the oath of allegiance with that of the oath of office, except the President's, and found them comparable. The dissents had argued that there are other ways to defend the country in addition to service in the military. They also had pointed out that laws of military service had granted exemptions since colonial times to those who had conscientious objection to military service.[33] With the Supreme Court dissents in mind and believing that appellate judges may occasionally decide differently from Supreme Court precedent, Judge Woodbury concluded that were he "to decide the question of law before us here *de novo* I would be disposed to follow the reasoning of the dissenting opinions in the *Schwimmer*, *Macintosh* and *Bland* cases and the decisions of the circuit courts of appeals reversed therein." Having found no "express statutory provision," Woodbury would "find it hard to believe that Congress intended to deny citizenship by naturalization to members of sects such as the Quakers (and I think the same may be said of Seventh Day Adventists) who, as Mr. Justice Holmes observed in his dissent in the *Schwimmer* case, 'have done their share to make the country what it is.'" As Woodbury wrestled with "the oath of allegiance in its historical setting, in connection with other statutes, and in conformity with the First Amendment," it seemed to him that

> Congress did not intend in it to exact an unconditional promise actually to bear arms in war, but instead intended to exact a promise to support and defend the Constitution, and laws of the United States in whatever way and by such means as are appropriate to an applicant's sex, age, and capabilities, and are not in violation of an applicant's religious scruples or beliefs in so far as those scruples or beliefs are either protected by the Constitution or have been consistently respected by Congress.

"However," Woodbury admitted, "the three celebrated cases above have not been overruled, and since in principle they rule the case at bar, I would probably feel compelled to follow them were it not for my view that now the Supreme Court itself would not do so." Yet in these cases "decisions of circuit courts of appeals were reversed by a divided Supreme Court" and, in *Macintosh* and *Bland*, "the ones most nearly in point, by the narrowest margin, and the decisions reversed were fully, and I think convincingly reasoned and were unanimous." That made "a substantial body of judicial opinion opposed to that of the majority" in the ruling cases. "In view of this substantial body of opinion," Woodbury wrote,

> in view of what I believe to be the intrinsic merit of that opinion, and in view of the many recent decisions of the Supreme Court giving broad definition to the scope of the guarantee of the free exercise of religion in the First Amendment,[34] I believe that the prediction can be ventured that the above cases are no longer expressive of the law. . . . Therefore I feel that we are not constrained to follow the Supreme Court cases cited last above.[35]

With this denial of citizenship and Woodbury's strong dissent recommending defiance of Supreme Court precedent, Girouard's supporters—some of whom Girouard may not have known he had—began planning an appeal. Alfred Albert wrote that he had attempted to contact Girouard about ACLU assistance and he believed a petition for certiorari to the Supreme Court ought to be filed immediately. A few days later the

General Conference Committee of the Seventh-day Adventist Church voted to use Girouard's case as a test case before the Supreme Court and to employ lawyers to argue his case. At this point neither the ACLU nor the Adventists seem to have been aware of the other's efforts on behalf of Girouard.[36] M. L. Rice, President of the Atlantic Union Conference of the Seventh-day Adventists, the conference where Girouard lived, wrote to Girouard informing him that the General Conference had agreed to sponsor his case. It had retained David Coddaire to "prepare brief [sic] at once with full authorization to carry through. General Conference bearing expenses."[37] The very same day Forster wrote to Albert, informing him that the previous day the Supreme Court had decided *In re Summers*. In that light, "It is all the more urgent that the Girouard case be appealed." Roger Baldwin had insited that Albert "should have one of the ministers connected with your committee *personally* go over to see Girouard and discuss the matter with him. It is quite urgent that no papers be filed by Girouard's lawyer as they will probably bawl [sic] up the case." Albert was to "do everything you can to have our committee get the case for us. Please do not let any stone remain unturned."[38]

A few days later the General Conference informed Girouard that it was "planning to retain Mr. Coddaire as one of the attorneys in your case, and also associate with him a prominent attorney in Washington, D.C.," apparently a change from the original plans. The ACLU seems to have been unaware of these developments. Forster was eager for this case to go to the Supreme Court because "it is the best case around and has progressed the furthest." On 5 July 1945 Albert finally determined that Girouard's counsel intended to file a petition for certiorari to the Supreme Court. Asked whether they would welcome an *amicus curiae* brief from the ACLU, they agreed to think about it. Nothing had been done because Coddaire was in the hospital and his associate, William Fitzsimmons, would do nothing without his direction. The ACLU offered Coddaire and Fitzsimmons financial help and assistance on their brief. Alfred Albert wrote that, judging from their brief to the Court of Appeals, he was not confident that Coddaire and his associate could write an adequate brief to the Supreme Court, but he was sure the ACLU would be asked to help on the brief.[39]

As if the ACLU and the Seventh-day Adventists were two ships passing in the night, the latter asked Girouard to write a letter to Coddaire "asking him to arrange for the General Conference attorneys, Cummings & Stanley, to be associated in your naturalization appeal to the Supreme

Court." They even supplied the text of the letter Girouard was to send to Coddaire.[40] Later, apparently without any knowledge of the addition of the Cummings firm, Alfred Albert wrote to the ACLU that he had finally had a long talk with Coddaire, who was the dominant person in his firm. Coddaire absolutely refused any assistance from the ACLU, either in terms of assistance with his brief to the Supreme Court or the submission of an *amicus* brief. Albert said Coddaire refused to say why he adamantly refused ACLU help, but he surmised two things. First, his client had paid him $1,500 to argue the case and appeal it. (This is phrased as if Girouard had paid the fee, not the Seventh-day Adventist Church.) He probably thought that the appearance of anyone else on the briefs would compromise his position with his client. Secondly, he did not like the ACLU. "I have done all that I possibly can by way of talking to him and arguing with him, but to no avail. He has told me, however, that the petition for certiorari has been filed."[41]

If Coddaire said that, it was not true. What had been filed in the Supreme Court was a motion for an extension of time to file a petition for certiorari. The petition consisted of a brief summary of the issue in Girouard's case and its disposition by the District Court and the First Circuit Court of Appeals. It reminded the Supreme Court that it had been closely divided on the previous alien conscientious objector cases and that subsequently there had been some views different from the majority expressed in other cases, including the dissent in *Girouard* at the Court of Appeals level. The petition summarized the reasons that the question was ripe for reconsideration:

> Changes in judicial viewpoint, as well as current political and military developments and the history of non-combatants' participation in vital and dangerous functions of the military arm in the conflict just ended, make the question appropriate for reconsideration by this Court. The question is one which will undoubtedly recur, is obviously important, and should be now determined.

Girouard's counsel had requested an extension of time because his attorney had been in the hospital since the Court of Appeals decision, new counsel had been engaged, and counsel needed to do extensive research to write a petition for certiorari. The motion, signed by a lawyer in the firm of Cummings and Stanley, asked for two months' additional time after the normal deadline for submission of a petition. The Court granted the motion and extended the deadline for submitting a petition to 30 October 1945.[42]

It was mid-November before the ACLU knew or acknowledged that Homer Cummings had become Girouard's lead attorney. ACLU operatives found the news pleasing, especially since Cummings welcomed the ACLU's offer to write an *amicus* brief. That brief would be written by Julien Cornell, a New York attorney and counsel to the ACLU's committee on conscientious objectors. John W. Davis also had agreed to sign the brief. The Seventh-day Adventist Church financed the case. The General Conference Committee voted to pay Cummings and Stanley $3,000 for the preparation of the petition for certiorari and some other work and an additional $2,000 if the Supreme Court heard oral arguments in the case.[43]

Homer Cummings, a former Attorney General of the United States, brought a national reputation to Girouard's case. Born in Chicago in 1870, he was graduated from Yale in engineering and Yale Law School and spent much of the rest of his life in Connecticut, where he was active in politics. He served three terms as the mayor of Stamford. He chaired the national Democratic Party organization from 1914 to 1920. In 1932 he backed the candidacy of Franklin Delano Roosevelt for President. He served as Roosevelt's Attorney General from 1933 until 1939. When Roosevelt became disenchanted with the Supreme Court because it struck down so many of his New Deal programs, he tried to alter the nature of the Court through his "Court packing" plan. At FDR's request, Cummings drew up the Judicial Reorganization Act, which eventually went nowhere, but which elicited considerable criticism for Roosevelt. Cummings resigned as Attorney General in 1939. He continued to live in Washington, D.C., where he practiced law and dabbled in Connecticut politics until his death in 1956 at the age of 86. He was known as an aggressive litigator with a showy style in the courtroom.[44]

In beginning his petition for certiorari on behalf of James Louis Girouard, after a brief review of the facts of Girouard's application for citizenship and the history of the case, Cummings turned to the first of the two major points of his argument. The Court of Appeals had misapplied the decisions in *Schwimmer*, *Macintosh*, and *Bland* to Girouard. Those cases were decided about views that would have limited the war powers of Congress, whereas Girouard's views did no such thing. He and thousands of other Seventh-day Adventists were willing to serve in the military, thus affirming the war power of government. He did not seek to determine the conditions under which war should be fought and his support of the nation in time of war was absolute. His only request was to serve in the military as a noncombatant. Cummings then described each of the three cases to demonstrate how Girouard's case was different.

Schwimmer focused on a person who had objections to waging any war and who, the Court held, would impermissibly propagandize others to oppose war as well. Girouard and other Adventists did not fit that profile, so *Schwimmer* arguably did not properly serve as a precedent to deny Girouard his opportunity for citizenship, the Court of Appeals notwithstanding.

The subject of *Macintosh* wanted to make a judgment about the moral quality of a war before he would agree to participate in it. The applicant in *Bland* refused participation in all wars, but also wanted to modify the oath of allegiance before she would agree to swear to it. An examination of Girouard's application for citizenship showed no parallels with those cases. He was unequivocal in his recognition of the prerogative of the government to wage war in any and all circumstances the government found necessary and had no objection to the oath as written. Girouard requested only the right to serve in the military without taking up arms. Such an attitude did not diminish his patriotism and his willingness to give his life for his country. At that point Cummings included a long footnote describing the Seventh-day Adventist Church's attitude toward war and the role of the noncombatant in the waging of war. He pointed out that Adventists had served their country heroically even as noncombatants.[45] "Thus the cases relied on by the court below," Cummings concluded,

> offered no basis for denial of naturalization to petitioner [Girouard]. On the contrary, they indicated that a mere religious scruple against bearing arms standing alone is not to be regarded as presenting an insurmountable barrier. One who, subject to his religious inhibition against taking human life, recognizes the plenary authority of Congress under the war power and reserves no right to hinder or impair any exercise of that power but is ready to risk his life in the military forces and in other ways to uphold the hands of the authorities surely is not to be classed with those who would subvert the defense of the Government upon their own judgment that a war is morally unjustified. ... Here there is no question of petitioner's willingness to assume all the risks of a soldier in the contingency of war.[46]

In the second major point of his petition for certiorari, Cummings argued that the 1942 amendments to the Nationality Act of 1940 essentially rendered impotent holdings in *Schwimmer* and *Macintosh* that an applicant for citizenship must demonstrate the applicant's attachment to the principles of the Constitution by bearing arms in its defense. The dissenters in *Macintosh* argued that bearing arms is not necessary to demonstrate attachment to the principles of the Constitution. The 1942 legislation verified the dissenters' view, making it possible for noncombatant aliens to receive citizenship, indeed by expedited means, if they had served in the military. The laws did not apply to those who had not served in the military or refused to wear the uniform, and Girouard could not benefit directly from that legislation. Yet Congress had recognized that one could show attachment to the Constitution without taking up arms. "The important feature of the 1942 legislation," Cummings argued, "is that Congress, without abrogation or modification of the statutory requirements as to oath and attachment to the principles of the Constitution, has expressly recognized that such requirements may be fulfilled by an otherwise qualified alien applicant despite his religious conviction against bearing arms." In amending the Nationality Act, Congress had shown that this legislation and its predecessors, which had grounded the decisions in *Schwimmer* and *Macintosh*, "are not to be regarded as impliedly requiring as a condition of naturalization declaration by the applicant of willingness to bear arms."[47]

Cummings ended his petition by briefly pointing out that although *Schwimmer* and *Macintosh* were still the controlling cases, there had been considerable disagreement with them, in the dissents in the cases themselves, in scholarly commentary, and in lower court opinions such as *In re Kinloch*, *In re Losey*, and *In re Sawyer* and the dissent by Judge Woodbury in Girouard's own case. Many applications for naturalization by noncombatants were now awaiting a definitive decision from the Court about how the 1942 legislation by Congress might be understood and applied. For all these reasons, the Supreme Court should hear arguments and render a decision in this case.[48] Cummings filed the petition for certiorari on the deadline, 30 October 1945.[49]

Responding to the petition for certiorari, the government argued that the Court of Appeals was correct in its interpretation of *Schwimmer*, *Macintosh*, and *Bland*. It agreed that Girouard's case could be distinguished from the first two of those cases, but asserted that *Bland* was foursquare the same as *Girouard*. Both applicants objected to war because of religious belief; both were willing to defend the country if the country would conform to their religious scruples against bearing arms.

In the Nationality Act of 1940 Congress made several changes in the naturalization law, but did not change the oath of allegiance and did not specifically provide for admission to citizenship of noncitizens who were conscientious objectors. "This action on the part of Congress would seem to be a recognition and an acceptance of the majority opinions of this Court in the cases referred to."

In 1942 Congress amended the 1940 Act in order to grant expedited means for naturalization of aliens who had served in the American military, although they explicitly excluded aliens who had performed no military service. Girouard argued that this exclusion implied that conscientious objectors who did serve in the military were entitled to naturalization. Because the laws retained the language of the oath of allegiance, "they represent a congressional declaration that persons *willing* to perform noncombatant service in uniform may properly take the oath, despite religious scruples." The government argued that the statutes should be taken literally, rather than reading implications, as Girouard's petition did.[50]

Finally, the government acknowledged that some cases recently decided supported Girouard's argument, specifically *In re Kinloch* and *In re Sawyer*. But *In re Nielsen* supported the government's contention. Most important, the Court of Appeals in *Girouard* believed that the 1942 amendments granted the possibility of citizenship only to those conscientious objectors who had *actually* served in the military, not to those, like Girouard, who were *willing* to serve. "Since it is unlikely that Congress intended to make a fundamental change in the general requirements for citizenship without comment and by indirection, we do not think the 1942 amendments can be deemed to have limited the effect of the *Bland* decision."[51] In spite of the government's reply to Girouard's petition, the Supreme Court granted certiorari on 10 December 1945.[52]

Once the Supreme Court had agreed to hear the case, Cummings prepared a much more comprehensive argument to persuade the Justices to rule in favor of Girouard. He began by defining the question before the Court and, in the process, conceding some things at issue in the earlier cases, especially *Macintosh*. Cummings did not dispute "that naturalization is a privilege that may be granted or withheld at the sole discretion of the Congress." Girouard's counsel recognized "that Congress has power to fix such conditions as it may deem appropriate to the grant of the privilege, including exaction of a promise to bear arms" and "that Congress may, in its discretion, compel service in the army in time of war."

In Girouard's case, "The question presented is much narrower: Has the Congress by implication prescribed that as a condition to naturalization, the applicant shall expressly promise to bear arms?"[53] Girouard's answer to that question would, of course, be "No," and Cummings employed several arguments to make that point.

His first argument was most fundamental: the right to naturalization does not depend upon an expression of willingness to bear arms. When a person like Girouard is willing to accept the war powers of the government and the waging of specific wars authorized by Congress, to serve in the military in every way except the taking of human life and to take the oath to defend the Constitution and the laws of the land and "to bear true faith and allegiance to the same," his unwillingness to bear arms does not demonstrate that he is not attached to the principles of the Constitution. Such a person is not lacking in patriotism and love of country.[54]

Extending this theme, Cummings noted that the United States had historically and frequently recognized exclusively religious scruples against bearing arms and had exempted from military service those who held them. Also, oaths of office did not demand that one with religious objections against bearing arms should be barred from office. Dissenting in *Macintosh*, Chief Justice Hughes had shown that the oath for office holders was virtually identical to that required of applicants for citizenship. Persons with religious objections to fighting in war never were banned from public office by the oath. By extension, similarly situated applicants for citizenship should not be banned, either. Article 6, clause 3, of the Constitution prohibits a religious test for public office, reinforcing the point. Given the parallel between the oath of office and oath of naturalization, there should be no religious test for naturalization. Those holding religious objections to combatant service should not be denied citizenship.[55]

Americans, native and naturalized, may defend the Constitution and laws of the nation in a variety of ways; bearing arms is not the only way. American law has historically exempted conscientious objectors from military service. In a footnote Cummings cited all the conscientious objector colonial and state statutes, and in another all the appropriate state constitutions. He then detailed, in several pages, the federal selective service statutes that exempted conscientious objectors. If various state and federal statutes exempted conscientious objectors from military service, the governments must recognize that these persons could defend the Constitution and laws of the United States in ways other than military service.

Congress had recognized that exercise of its war powers must not infringe on constitutionally guaranteed individual liberties, such as free exercise of religion. When the question asked of Girouard, "If necessary, are you willing to take up arms in defense of this country?"

> is answered in the negative solely on religious grounds, and when it further appears that aside from actual combatant service involving the shedding of blood, the applicant is ready and willing to render full military service, then it seems clear that the negative answer cannot be made the basis for assertion that the applicant cannot in good faith take the oath.[56]

Cummings sounded another variation on this theme in arguing that the law requiring applicants for citizenship to be "attached to the principles of the Constitution" does not demand that applicants promise to bear arms. Certainly one of those "principles of the Constitution"—a rather loose, elastic phrase—is the right of religious freedom contained in the First Amendment.[57] Cummings pointed out that the Court had recently held that the liberties guaranteed by the First Amendment are preferred freedoms in the American system.[58] He also recognized that civil liberties could be restrained in times of national emergency. The balance between civil liberties and government's powers is delicate. Yet the government must always, in exercising its powers, be sensitive to the civil liberties of citizens.[59] Such general phrases as "the principles of the Constitution" should always be interpreted to accord with freedom of conscience. Illustrating this, Cummings again referred to laws that had historically exempted conscientious objectors from military service. In view of these statutes, "the omission of such an express requirement from the Nationality Act is highly significant," Cummings wrote. "It seems plain that the required showing that the applicant is 'attached to the principles of the United States,' was not intended by the Congress to include exaction of a promise to bear arms in derogation of the religious beliefs of the applicant."[60]

Next Cummings recapitulated his argument in his petition for certiorari about the effects of the 1942 amendments of the Nationality Act of 1940. He concluded his brief by repeating his opening argument from his petition for certiorari. The facts in *Schwimmer, Macintosh*, and *Bland* do not apply to the facts of *Girouard*. Now the government, in its memorandum opposing certiorari, had conceded that the first two of those cases could be distinguished from Girouard's. Cummings offered more detail than he had in his petition, especially about the differences between *Schwimmer* and *Girouard*, but the basic argument is the same.[61]

In contrast to its rather cursory reply to the petition for certiorari, the government answered Girouard's brief with a gigantic brief signed by Solicitor General J. Howard McGrath. It had four major points. First, Congress in the Nationality Act of 1940 had affirmed the earlier rule that willingness to bear arms was a prerequisite for becoming an American citizen. That understanding, of course, came from the Supreme Court's interpretation of the Nationality Act of 1906 in *Schwimmer, Macintosh*, and *Bland*. Those three cases were widely known to the general public and they were discussed in the popular press and in the commentaries of law journals. The government acknowledged that much of the commentary on the conclusions reached by the Supreme Court was negative. Given the widespread critique, Congress also surely knew the adverse responses to the opinions. Yet Congress did nothing to modify or overthrow the rule that bearing arms was a prerequisite to achieving citizenship, although it had opportunity to do that. For more than a decade, legislation before Congress—the Griffin Bill and its progeny—sought to grant citizenship to applicants who were conscientious objectors (see Chapter Six). Full hearings were held on two of the bills and speeches were made on the floor of Congress on behalf of those and other, similar, bills. The issue came before Congress virtually constantly from 1929 through 1940, yet none of the bills even made it out of committee. Congressional interest in changing the rule could not even muster a vote on any one of the bills. "We think it clear, therefore," Solicitor General McGrath concluded, "that Congress approved the rule laid down in the *Schwimmer, Macintosh* and *Bland* cases . . . through its failure to pass bills which would have permitted the naturalization of alien conscientious objectors."[62]

Against this background, the government's brief returned to the principal theme of its first point, that in the Nationality Act of 1940 Congress had reenacted the rule of naturalization articulated in *Schwimmer, Macintosh*, and *Bland*. In fact, the Act had given the oath of allegiance more status than it had before 1940. Although many features of the oath were in the Nationality Act of 1906, the exact language was administratively prescribed in the Naturalization Regulations of 1929, rule 8 (c). Yet the exact language of the oath was part of the statute in the Nationality Act of 1940. The language was the same as in the earlier oath.[63] By giving the language of the oath statutory authority, Congress adopted and reenacted the rule of the cases in question, namely that an alien must express willingness to bear arms in behalf of the country as a qualification as an applicant for citizenship.[64] In the government's reading, the legislative history of the Nationality Act of 1940 and congressional statements about it, in a context of controversial cases, would "certainly lend no support to the suggestion that Congress in 1940, at a time when our own national safety was recognized to be in danger, meant to leave the arms-bearing requirement open for future judicial considerations."[65] Those who drafted the bill, "who presumably were aware of the consistent refusal of Congress to pass bills which would have enacted the dissenting opinions in these cases, and who recommended legislative enactment of the former administrative oath," could not have "intended *sub silentio* to permit the then recognized content of the oath to remain open to change." The oath had rather acquired a formal dignity it did not previously possess. "We think it clear, therefore," government's lawyers concluded, "that whatever the original meaning of the oath, whatever the additional sanction it received through Congressional acquiescence, it stood on a new and independent legislative footing as a result of the enactment of the Nationality Act of 1940."[66]

In its second major point, the government's brief claimed that requiring an applicant for citizenship to be willing to bear arms was consistent with other parts of the naturalization law and did not contradict First Amendment freedoms. Naturalization is not a constitutional right, but dependent on congressional acts. The only constitutional command about naturalization is uniform law. If the rules of naturalization are uniform, the constitutional mandate has been satisfied. Congress makes the rules. In this case, the issue is not to determine what principles should be used to admit people to citizenship, but rather to determine what Congress has required.[67]

Next, Solicitor General McGrath denied that naturalization law requires that Girouard should be treated equally with native-born conscientious objectors. The law treats applicants for citizenship differently from citizens. Girouard "only wishes to be placed on a par with the natural born citizen and not come in on an unequal footing,"[68] but the Constitution and laws of the United States have never treated aliens and native-born citizens equally. For example, immigrants who suffer from mental illness or contagious diseases are excluded from admission, whereas obviously native-born persons with those problems are full citizens. Again, the United States does not deport native-born anarchists, felons, polygamists, prostitutes, paupers, or illiterates, but immigrants who

fall into any of those categories are not admitted or certainly not naturalized. Racial characteristics are also treated differently. Citizenship is
automatic for those born in America, regardless of their race, but immigration laws had created all sorts of quotas that implied exclusion, based on
race and nationality. Finally, according to the Constitution itself, even
after naturalization, a foreign-born person can never be President of the
United States and must wait after his naturalization seven years to be able
to be a representative and nine years to be a senator. Furthermore,
naturalized citizenship can be challenged in a court of law, as *Schneiderman* illustrates. None of these things are true of the native-born citizen.
"We have gone thus fully into these distinctions," the Department of
Justice concluded, "because we consider them essential to a clear
understanding of what is involved here—understanding that is befogged
by petitioner's insistence that he stand on a basis of equality with the
citizen." Girouard's argument "fails to distinguish what Congress has
demanded for citizenship from what Congress should demand."[69]

In the third part of its second major point, the government's brief
asserted that constitutionally guaranteed freedom of religion did not
include an exemption on religious grounds from military or combatant
service. Girouard's brief had argued throughout "that Congress lacks
constitutional power to exact full military service from individuals who
have religious scruples against bearing arms." The majority opinion in
Macintosh vigorously rejected any assertion of such a constitutional right,
based on religion or any other thing, to exemption from taking up arms in
defense of the country. The government's brief supplemented that
judgment by reviewing the history of the First Amendment. When James
Madison, on 8 June 1789, proposed the language that would later become
the Second Amendment, it contained the clause "but no person religiously
scrupulous shall be compelled to bear arms." The members of the first
Congress thoroughly debated the issue, and the clause was eventually
excised from the amendment and consequently does not appear in the
Constitution. The very point that the brief for Girouard seemed to rely on
so strongly was explicitly rejected by the authors of the Constitution.
Girouard's brief also seemed to hold that the rejected language should be
read into the First Amendment, so that religiously based objection to
participation in war is still a constitutionally guaranteed freedom. "What
petitioner is really saying, therefore, is that since the proposal was
advisedly rejected, we should read the First Amendment as though it had

been adopted. It would be difficult to imagine a more obvious *non sequitur*."[70]

Girouard's brief also had marshaled evidence that beginning with the Revolutionary War conscientious objectors had been exempted by statute from participation in war. According to the government, the evidence that Congress had made exemptions for conscientious objectors demonstrated that Congress could remove those exemptions. Likewise, Congress could decline to recognize religious scruples of applicants for naturalization. Indeed, since *Schwimmer* conscientious objectors had not been eligible for citizenship and, as the brief noted earlier, Congress had abundant opportunity to change that rule and had not done so.[71]

Homer Cummings, in his two previous briefs on behalf of Girouard, had argued that the 1942 amendments to the Nationality Act of 1940 had implicitly drawn noncombatants willing to serve in the military into their scope. That is, although the laws explicitly excluded people who had not served in the military, their language strongly suggested that Congress recognized that noncombatants who were willing to agree with the war powers of the government and to serve in the military should, by implication, receive the benefits of citizenship. The third major point of the government's brief explicitly rejected that contention; its argument was principally historical and linguistic.

The legislative history of the 1942 laws showed that Congress intended particularly to reward those noncitizens who had served in the American military during World War II and certain other previous wars. The reward set aside some of the requirements of the naturalization process to make the road to naturalization easier. Congress made it explicitly clear that the procedures applied only to those, including noncombatants, who had actually served. Those who had not served or had never worn the uniform were not covered by the law. That specification was not unique to the 1942 law. In 1926 Congress had passed a similar law to expedite naturalization for aliens who had served in the military in World War I. In that law, too, conscientious objectors were excluded from the expedited procedures. The United States had long recognized and rewarded the valiant military service some noncitizens gave to the country in some wars, but in every case the legislation excluded aliens who had not served in the military. To argue that the law included those willing to serve in the military in a noncombatant role, as Girouard's brief did, was hopefulness misplaced. Girouard's brief, relying on Judge Woodbury's dissent in the Court of Appeals, argued that the oath of allegiance could not mean one thing to an alien who served in the armed forces and another thing to one who had not given such service. The government's brief simply said the oath could and did mean different things to those two categories of people. As lower courts had held in *In re Kinloch* and *In re Sawyer*, "the noncombatant veteran is entitled to naturalization, the noncombatant nonveteran is not."[72]

In its fourth, and final, point, the government's brief claimed that the war experience of the nation since *Schwimmer*, *Macintosh*, and *Bland* were decided abundantly confirmed the rightness and wisdom of the judgments in these cases. The brief conceded what Girouard's brief had pointed out—at the time the cases were handed down there were not only strong dissents, but also unfavorable commentary in the press and professional journals. Yet those were times of peace. The Kellogg-Briand Peace Treaty had recently been approved. Pacifism was popular. In a sense, people had the luxury to be critical of the Court's ruling on alien conscientious objectors. Soon enough the world situation turned ugly. Evil, aggressive nations began to invade their neighbors and soon had designs on territory far away.[73] In December 1941 America was dragged into the conflagration. We and our allies won, but only because we were able to amass and use superior armed force. "The liberties which we in consequence can still enjoy, *and which petitioner can still enjoy*," the government asserted, "were preserved only through the exertion of millions of arms-bearing citizens, and through the costly sacrifice which over three hundred thousand Americans laid on the altar of freedom."[74]

Girouard was willing to do noncombatant service in the military. McGrath acknowledged the importance of noncombatants; certainly they had an important role to play in the effort of total war in which the United States was engaged. Yet noncombatants were only auxiliaries to those who fought the battles. It was not unreasonable for Congress to expect a "higher" level of service for those who wanted to become citizens of this great nation. "Those who seek the benefits of our citizenship may properly be called upon for willingness to meet its most arduous burdens."[75]

Moving toward a summary, and reflecting on "some fifteen years' hindsight," Solicitor General McGrath observed that "the requirements laid down by the decision of this Court" in *Schwimmer*, *Macintosh*, and *Bland* and "adopted" in congressional legislation "assume a prophetic wisdom that could not have been apparent to all in the peaceful years between the wars." Recent history had "amply justified" the government's position "that one who desires citizenship in a free republic must be prepared if need be to fight in defense of his country's freedom." Actual attacks from real enemies had made "the test of one's willingness to defend the Constitution against all enemies . . . more critical and more real." Now, the government concluded, "After the searing experiences of the past half-generation, there is certainly no occasion now to make available the priceless heritage of American citizenship to one who will not meet the price that Congress asks."[76]

In its *amicus curiae* brief on behalf of Girouard the ACLU bluntly asserted that *Schwimmer, Macintosh*, and *Bland* were wrongly decided and should not be followed as precedent in deciding *Girouard*. The ACLU justified that rather bold statement by positing the correctness of the dissents in those cases and by calling attention to what Congress had never done. Congress had never in any statute required an applicant for citizenship to bear arms, yet the Court had held that such a requirement existed. Not only had Congress not included the requirement in any law, but also an oath virtually identical was sworn by office holders, as Chief Justice Hughes had noted in his *Macintosh* dissent. No one had ever understood that oath to require the office holders to promise to take up arms.[77] The *amicus* brief now made the leap, without mentioning that most conscientious objection is religion-based or that Schwimmer's was not, to say that the Court, in its decisions in the three cases, had "imputed to Congress the intention to discriminate on a religious basis." Yet because Congress had never legislated a rule that prevented a conscientious objector from becoming a citizen, "it should be presumed that Congress did *not* intend to discriminate on religious grounds." At that point, the ACLU quoted Chief Justice Hughes's dissent in *Macintosh* that a statute "should be construed not in opposition to, but in accord with, the theory and practice of our government in relation to freedom of conscience."[78]

Since the dissents of Justice Holmes and Chief Justice Hughes were written, the ACLU observed, the mood of the Court toward civil liberties had changed so substantially that the philosophy of the dissents now prevailed. In that light, if the statutory interpretation recommended in the *amicus* brief were accepted, "the rule of the *Schwimmer, Macintosh* and *Bland* cases must now be overthrown."[79]

In its second point, the ACLU's brief argued that the 1942 amendment to the Nationality Act of 1940 did not intend to exclude conscientious objectors from naturalization. It applied to aliens who had served in the military during World War II and certain other wars. *In re Kinloch* showed that it applied to noncombatant veterans as well as to those who actually fought. "The amendment does not change the oath," the ACLU claimed, beginning an amazing verbal sleight of hand in favor of Girouard.

> It does not provide a special oath for conscientious objectors entitled to its benefits. They must take the same oath which this court declared Schwimmer, Macintosh and Bland could not take. Thus Congress has made it perfectly clear that the oath does not demand a willingness to bear arms. In granting privileges to conscientious objectors for attaining citizenship Congress clearly intended that the oath could be taken by them.
>
> Petitioner has not served in the armed forces and is not claiming the privileges of the amendment; he has fulfilled all the usual requirements for naturalization. But petitioner, or any other conscientious objector, can take the oath if, under the amendment, the oath can be taken by conscientious objectors who have served in the armed forces. For all conscientious objectors are alike in their ability to take the oath—they are all unwilling to make a promise to bear arms. And the words of the oath cannot mean one thing when applied to one person and another thing when applied to another person. The only possible interpretation which can be placed upon the 1942 amendment is that Congress did not intend to bar conscientious objectors from naturalization.[80]

The Supreme Court heard Girouard's case on 4 March 1946. Of the nine Justices who had heard *Macintosh* and *Bland* in 1931, only Justice Harlan Fiske Stone remained on the Court. In 1941 he had become Chief Justice. In a sense, with their briefs and oral arguments, lawyers for the government and for Girouard had a fresh audience. Homer Cummings's oral argument before the Court survives in manuscript,[81] but to have a manuscript is not necessarily to know what was said in Court. Justices often asked questions from the bench (as they do now), so it was entirely possible that counsel could be diverted from his or her planned argument and never get back to it. One can learn from a manuscript of an oral argument only what the lawyer intended to say to the Court. Not surprisingly, Cummings addressed most of the points that he or the ACLU had covered in their written briefs, but occasionally he made a new point, sometimes with a bit of jab at his opponent. "I pay tribute to the eloquent and, indeed, impassioned brief filed by the Government in this case—including its purple passages," Cummings declaimed, but he could not

> concede that the Schwimmer, Macintosh and Bland cases and their doctrines have been demonstrated by the recent World War to have

been as great a contributing cause to the final victory, as the devoted
services of the 12,000 or more Seventh Day Adventists who served as
non-combatants in the Military and Naval Forces of the United States.
Nor do I think that our country would have been stronger, if these
consecrated soldiers had not been available to us in our time of stress.

"Our country does not gain in strength or dignity," Cummings remarked,
"by shutting its doors to men like these."[82] Turning to the determining
precedents and supposed congressional affirmation of them, Cummings
noted that

my learned friend . . . seems to think that because Congress gave a
statutory basis to the oath of Allegiance in the Act of 1940 and did not
upset the Schwimmer, Macintosh, and Bland cases by direct and
specific legislation, these cases have somehow become sacrosanct and
that there is nothing this Court can do about it. They are embalmed
forever—a sort of Judicial Egyptian mummy, upon which no profane
hands may be laid.[83]

Remarkably, the Supreme Court of 1946 disinterred the precedents of
the preceding generation and laid its hands, profane or not, upon them. By
a vote of five to three—Justice Robert Jackson did not participate—a
Court still divided decided in favor of Girouard on 22 April 1946.

Justice William O. Douglas wrote for the majority. Justice Douglas
had been on the Court for seven years when he wrote *Girouard*. Born in
Minnesota in 1898, Douglas spent his childhood and youth in the state of
Washington. At age three he endured a nearly fatal encounter with polio.
For years he hiked in the woods to strengthen his weakened legs and, in
the process, developed a lifelong love for the wilderness and an interest in
the conservation of nature. His father, a Presbyterian minister, died when
William was six, so his childhood was burdened not only with the
aftermath of polio, but also by the deprivations of poverty. His strong
mother encouraged him to persevere and stimulated him intellectually; he
was graduated valedictorian of Yakima High School in 1916. In 1918
Douglas was rejected by the Navy because of color blindness, but his
patriotic persistence found a place in an Army training program before the
war ended. After working his way through Whitman College in Walla
Walla, Washington, Douglas was graduated Phi Beta Kappa in 1920. He
graduated second in his class from Columbia Law School in 1925. He
joined a Wall Street law firm and discovered he thoroughly disliked

corporate law. In 1927 he accepted a teaching position at Columbia Law School and the next year joined the faculty of Yale Law School, where he taught for five truly happy years.

Douglas had specialized in law school in the law of finance, corporate bankruptcy, reorganization, and receivership. In the aftermath of the crash of the stock market in 1929, the Securities and Exchange Commission was founded and Douglas was soon hired to its staff. He came to the notice of President Franklin Delano Roosevelt; he even frequented FDR's poker parties. In 1936 he was named a commissioner of the SEC and the next year he became its chairman. Roosevelt appointed him to the Supreme Court in 1939, where he began the longest term of any Justice in history, thirty-six years and seven months. He retired from the Court in 1975 and died in 1980. One side of his tombstone in Arlington National Cemetery reads, simply, "Private, United States Army."

Douglas was evolving, at the time he wrote *Girouard*, into a strong supporter of civil liberties. Later, along with Justice Hugo Black, particularly on the Warren Court (1953-1969), Douglas became an "absolutist" for the Bill of Rights, especially the First Amendment.[84] Toward the end of his career he wrote of "my conviction that the state existed for the individual, not the individual for the state—putting human rights first." Such rights "included the right to own property and enjoy it, as well as the right to stand for radical as well as rightist views and the right to become a vagabond." Government, for Douglas, "was an agency of people, a priesthood of a very special kind" requiring "a faithful commitment to law over and above all else." The governor's "task," Douglas thought, is "to tell the people what the national conscience—the Constitution— requires. The people can change it if they desire. But the main job of the Keepers of the Conscience is to make clear in a fearless way what the demands of civilization are."[85] Douglas's opinion in *Girouard* illustrates that he was well on his way to that consciousness.

After reciting the history and the facts of the case, Douglas noted that *Schwimmer*, *Macintosh*, and *Bland* had enshrined the rule that a noncitizen who refuses to take up arms in defense of the country will not be admitted to citizenship. "As an original proposition," Douglas responded, "we could not agree with that rule." Now the majority of the Court agreed more with the dissenting opinions of Justice Holmes in *Schwimmer* and Chief Justice Hughes in *Macintosh*. Douglas set about to demonstrate why this was so, drawing heavily from Cummings's brief for Girouard and the ACLU's *amicus* brief, although he tended to express his points more

eloquently than the briefs did. Observing that Congress had not promulgated the rule about bearing arms as a prerequisite to citizenship, Douglas
found many more ways to defend the nation than to bear arms. "Total war
in its modern form," he wrote, "dramatizes as never before the great
cooperative effort necessary for victory." There were "nuclear physicists
who developed the atomic bomb, the worker at his lathe, the seamen on
cargo vessels, construction battalions, nurses, engineers, litter bearers,
doctors, chaplains—these, too, made essential contributions. And many of
them made the supreme sacrifice." Douglas did not find "refusal to bear
arms" to be "necessarily a sign of disloyalty or a lack of attachment to our
institutions." Indeed, he argued, "Devotion to one's country can be as real
and as enduring among non-combatants as among combatants. One may
adhere to what he deems to be his obligation to God and yet assume all
military risks to secure victory."[86]

Applicants for citizenship who were conscientious objectors were
excluded from the oath of citizenship, while potential office holders with
the same beliefs could take the oath of office. Yet the oaths, Douglas
argued, are parallel. Girouard's religious scruples would not prevent him
from becoming a member of Congress; why should they prevent him from
being a citizen? The Constitution itself, in Article 6, forbids a religious
test for public office. "There is not the slightest suggestion," Douglas
wrote, rejecting the government's claims, "that Congress set a stricter
standard for aliens seeking admission to citizenship than it did for officials
who make and enforce the laws of the nation and administer its affairs."[87]

Congress had historically, in its various conscription laws, exempted
conscientious objectors from serving in the military. Congress had
therefore recognized that a noncombatant can still serve the country, that
even in time of war one can support and defend its institutions without
taking up weapons. By expediting naturalization for alien veterans, even
noncombatant veterans, in the 1942 amendments to the Nationality Act of
1940, Congress had taken note of the possibility of religiously based
pacifist service to the nation. In making this point, Douglas seems to refute
directly Justice Sutherland's famous dictum in *Macintosh* that the will of
the country and the will of God are the same. "The struggle for religious
liberty," Douglas wrote,

> has through the centuries been an effort to accommodate the demands
> of the State to the conscience of the individual. The victory for freedom
> of thought recorded in our Bill of Rights recognizes that in the domain

of conscience there is a moral power higher than the State. Throughout
the ages, men have suffered death rather than subordinate their
allegiance to God to the authority of the State.

"We conclude," Douglas declared, in the "punch line" of the decision,
"that the *Schwimmer, Macintosh* and *Bland* cases do not state the correct
rule of law."[88] Judicial precedent since 1929 was canceled. James Louis
Girouard's citizenship was restored.

But the opinion was not unanimous. Chief Justice Harlan Fiske Stone
dissented, joined by Justices Felix Frankfurter and Stanley Reed. (Justice
Robert H. Jackson did not participate. At the time *Girouard* was argued
and decided, Jackson had taken a leave from the Supreme Court to serve
as the lead United States prosecutor at the Nuremberg trials of Nazi war
criminals.[89]) Stone had been appointed to the Court by President Calvin
Coolidge in 1925. He was appointed Chief Justice, succeeding Charles
Evans Hughes, by President Franklin Roosevelt in 1941.[90]

After rehearsing the facts of the case, Stone recalled that he had
dissented in *Macintosh* and *Bland* for the very reasons that the Court now
reversed them in *Girouard*. Stone had, however, come to the conviction
that Congress had actually adopted the rule laid down in *Schwimmer*,
Macintosh, and *Bland*. "For that reason alone I think that the judgment [of
the Court of Appeals in *Girouard*] should be affirmed."[91]

Stone saw clear evidence that Congress had adopted the rule that
bearing arms was a prerequisite for naturalization. Almost immediately
after *Schwimmer* was handed down, Congressman Anthony Griffin had
introduced legislation to overturn that decision and make conscientious
objectors eligible for citizenship. Congress did not act on that bill, so
similar bills were introduced during succeeding sessions of Congress. Full
hearings were held on two versions of the Griffin bill. Yet none of the bills
ever got out of committee to face a vote in either the House or the Senate.
Congressional refusal to act on this legislation meant to Stone that
Congress had, in fact, approved the Court's holdings in the three cases
concerning naturalization of conscientious objectors. Any doubt about that
conclusion should have been allayed when, in 1940, Congress reenacted
unchanged the language of the oath of allegiance, which the Court had
earlier determined to require willingness to bear arms before conscientious
objectors could be naturalized. "By thus adopting and confirming this
Court's construction of what Congress had enacted in the Naturalization
Act of 1906," Stone wrote, "Congress gave that construction the same

legal significance as though it had written the very words into the Act of 1940."[92]

In reference to the 1942 amendments to the Nationality Act of 1940, Stone reviewed the arguments advanced by Cummings: Congress, by providing expedited citizenship for aliens—combatant and noncombatant—who had served in the military, showed that Congress, by implication at least, had made the oath of allegiance available to people like Girouard, those noncombatant aliens who were willing to serve in the military even though they had not. The oath could not mean different things to different groups of people. If Congress had truly wanted to exempt alien conscientious objectors such as Girouard from the rule of *Schwimmer, Macintosh*, and *Bland*, Stone responded, it certainly could have explicitly done so. It did not. For that reason, Cummings had to argue that his client came under the 1942 amendments by implication.

According to Stone, *In re Nielsen* showed that the same oath had to be taken by everyone, those who were conscientious objectors and those who were not. Although Congress had "recognized by indirection that those who had appeared in the role of conscientious objectors, might become citizens by taking the oath of allegiance and establishing their attachment to the principles of the Constitution," Stone wrote, such indirect recognition "does not show that Congress dispensed with the requirements of the oath as construed by this Court and plainly confirmed by Congress in the Nationality Act of 1940." He did not find in "the amendments and their legislative history" any "hint of any purpose of Congress to relax, a least for persons who had rendered no military service, the requirements of the oath of allegiance and proof of attachment to the Constitution as this Court had interpreted them and as the Nationality Act of 1940 plainly required them to be interpreted." Stone's conclusion was emphatic: "It is not the function of this Court to disregard the will of Congress in the exercise of its constitutional power."[93]

That Stone dissented in this case, joined by Frankfurter, appears exquisitely ironic. Stone was one of three persons appointed to a committee during World War I to examine the claims of conscientious objectors and determine whether or not they qualified (see Chapter One). Although the committee rejected the claims of many, Stone perceived that true conscientious objectors were people of principle and often exhibited an admirable mental toughness and courage. He also, as he pointed out in his dissent in *Girouard*, had joined the dissents in *Macintosh* and *Bland*.[94] In that role in *Macintosh* he endorsed many of the principles used by

Douglas to rule in favor of Girouard. Frankfurter, while a professor at Harvard Law School, was a national sponsor of the Griffin Bill Committee (his name appeared on its letterhead). During the time of discussion about language in the Griffin bill, Frankfurter wrote to Griffin to encourage him to change the language of his bill along the lines the ACLU had suggested. "I am, as you know," Frankfurter wrote in that letter, "in deep sympathy with the purpose behind your bill." Indeed, during the behind-the-scenes debate among the Supreme Court Justices about how to decide *Girouard*, Frankfurter wrote to Harold Burton that he, Frankfurter, thought that *Schwimmer* was wrongly decided.[95]

Why then did Stone and Frankfurter dissent in *Girouard*? The answer lies in the concluding sentence of Stone's dissent. Both men believed in "judicial restraint," that the Court should defer to the will of the elected legislative branch in disputed questions when the Court had reason to believe that the legislature's action could be as correct as any decision the Court might reach. If the legislature had the constitutional power to do what it did, the courts should not examine or second-guess the wisdom of the policy.[96] Both men, Frankfurter perhaps more than Stone, believed that the Court should usually yield to the judgment of the legislature when it legitimately—that is, within constitutional boundaries—exercised its power.[97] In *Girouard*, although both men had sympathy for conscientious objectors, Stone dissented and Frankfurter joined because they believed the record showed that Congress had essentially approved of the rule of *Schwimmer*, *Macintosh*, and *Bland*.[98] As Stone so carefully documented in his dissent, Congress had failed to act on the Griffin bill in its various versions for more than a decade and it had reenacted the traditional language of the oath in its 1940 legislation. That was enough to cause Stone and Frankfurter to disagree philosophically with the majority in *Girouard*, even though emotionally they would have liked to agree.[99]

Douglas answered the dissent in the majority opinion, saying that it is risky to conclude policy or law from the silence or inactivity of Congress. The history of the Nationality Act of 1940 "is at best equivocal." It did not obviously confirm the rule that bearing arms is a prerequisite for naturalization. It could as easily be interpreted as the intention on the part of Congress to leave the issue fluid as to have confirmed *Schwimmer*, *Macintosh*, and *Bland*. In 1942 Congress created expedited procedures for aliens who had served, even as noncombatants, in the military. "That was affirmative recognition," Douglas wrote, that one could be attached to the principles of our government and could support and defend it even though his religious convictions prevented him from bearing arms. And, as we have said, we cannot believe that the oath was designed to exact something more from one person than from another. Thus, the affirmative action taken by Congress in 1942 negatives any inference that otherwise might be drawn from its silence when it reenacted the oath in 1940.[100]

Stone himself unintentionally provoked an episode of high drama associated with the decision in *Girouard*, unrelated either to the issue or to the legal reasoning of the case. In the 1940s, when an opinion was announced, a Justice read his opinion aloud. Thus, Justice Douglas read the majority opinion of *Girouard* and Justice Stone read his dissent. In doing so, he spoke with less emphasis and in a lower tone of voice than was his custom. Alpheus Thomas Mason, Stone's biographer, suggests that Stone spoke with restraint because he dissented against a principle he had affirmed in *Macintosh* and *Bland*. Justice Hugo Black read some decisions, and then it was Stone's turn to read three decisions for which he had written the majority opinions. Silence filled the room. Justice Wiley Rutledge later said that when he looked at Stone, he was shuffling through his papers and mumbling something about staying or reconsidering the case. Then Justice Black banged the gavel and adjourned the Court until 2:30 P.M. (it was then 1:45). Stone was taken to a room behind the courtroom. A physician was summoned. His original diagnosis was indigestion. Stone's own physician was not so sure it was that simple, but allowed Stone to be taken home. At 6:45 P.M., without ever regaining consciousness, Stone died from a cerebral hemorrhage. The last coherent words Stone uttered represented "the polar star of the Supreme Court" so far as he was concerned. "It is not the function of this Court to disregard the will of Congress in the exercise of its constitutional power."[101]

F. D. Nichol, the editor of the Seventh-day Adventist *Review and Herald* magazine, and Emily Marx, the attorney who had taken Marie Averil Bland's case to the Supreme Court, wrote letters to Justice Douglas, thanking him for the reasoning and result in *Girouard*. Each expressed heartfelt gratitude for Douglas's opinion. In each case, Douglas wrote a perfunctory note of thanks at the bottom of the letter and returned it to the author.[102]

The *Girouard* case seems to have received much less media coverage than the frenzy after *Schwimmer* and *Macintosh/Bland*. Two local newspapers reported the story with primary emphasis on Girouard. They described the case, told of Justice Douglas's opinion and Justice Stone's dissent. Both mentioned that Girouard had been employed at the Adventist New England Sanitarium and Hospital.[103] Regional papers gave the story somewhat larger coverage, but still focused primarily on Girouard, his objections to taking human life based on his Adventist beliefs, and that his case was a reversal of earlier Court doctrine.[104] The ACLU issued a press release that summarized the case, quoted rather liberally from Douglas's majority opinion, mentioned Stone's dissent, and expressed considerable satisfaction with the result. ACLU attorneys saw noteworthy significance in Douglas's statement that the three previous cases no longer were the correct rule of law. Schwimmer was opposed to all war service, yet her case was now discredited, indicating that *Girouard* had significance far beyond the kind of conscientious objection Girouard himself proposed.[105] The *New York Times* ran two stories, one about the case itself and one about the death of Chief Justice Stone. The former was entirely descriptive, giving the background of the case and the essence of Douglas's majority opinion and of Stone's dissent. It did mention that the Immigration and Naturalization Service had held up the citizenship applications of about 150 conscientious objectors pending the decision in *Girouard*. Now these cases would be reviewed to see if they were covered by the Supreme Court's decision. The latter story told of Stone's becoming ill on the bench just after he had read his dissent in *Girouard*. It mentioned that Stone had prepared three majority opinions and two dissents for the day; a heavy schedule.[106] The *New York Herald Tribune* interviewed Rosika Schwimmer for her reaction. "'The only thing I am happy about is that I have lived to see this decision,' said Mrs. Schwimmer, who is sixty-nine and gravely ill. 'I always feared it would happen the day after I died. I only wish that Justice Holmes could have lived to see himself vindicated.'" This report never mentions Girouard's name, but relates that Schwimmer thought that she might now receive citizenship automatically. She had sent a telegram to Homer Cummings congratulating him on his victory, but she was fearful for the future of the world since atomic power had been discovered and unleashed.[107]

The *Washington Post* editorialized that *Girouard* was a correct decision. "It has taken the Court a long time to arrive at that conclusion, but we think that the present decision brings it into line with both the public conscience and the letter of the law." The *Post* pointed out that Girouard was willing to serve as a noncombatant in the military, as some 10,000 Adventists had done during World War II. "Surely that meets the requirement of supporting and defending the Constitution and what it stands for. . . . The Court has now at least done its duty in correcting its own mistake."[108]

A *Chicago Daily News* editorial took the other side, pointing out that Chief Justice Stone had been part of the committee evaluating conscientious objectors during World War I. "As an authority on the subject, his dissenting opinion deserves consideration." (The editorial did not mention that Stone had dissented in *Macintosh* and *Bland*.) The *Daily News* added that although the country had always been lenient to native-born conscientious objectors, it had barred applicants having religious objections to military service from citizenship. "This policy should be continued. . . . Conscientious objectors may be and often are good citizens. But the alien being naturalized, who must renounce a previous loyalty, should be held to a stern test of his sincerity." The *Cleveland Plain Dealer* disagreed with the Court, primarily on the grounds that it had invaded the prerogative of Congress. It strongly criticized "a Supreme Court which has too often of late been concerned with putting into congressional enactments words that Congress did not intend to be there."[109]

Radio commentators in 1946 reached millions with news and opinion almost immediately, a radical innovation since the decisions in *Schwimmer*, *Macintosh*, and *Bland* that had come to maturity in World War II. Robert Trout (1909-2000), one of the pioneers of broadcast journalism, offered a report within hours on the Columbia Broadcasting System, with perceptive analysis so moving that a friend of Rosika Schwimmer obtained a transcript and sent it to her.

> There was a dramatic moment in the great white, marble Supreme Court Building this afternoon when Harlan Fiske Stone, the Chief Justice of the United States, suddenly became ill. Two Associate Justices, Mr. Reed and Mr. Black, took him by the arms and assisted the seventy-three-year-old Chief Justice from the bench. His physician later issued a statement, saying it's nothing more serious than indigestion, but Chief Justice Stone must have complete rest at home for a few days.
>
> Before the Chief Justice became ill, there was a drama of another sort in the solemn, high-ceilinged room. The Court handed down a five to three decision, with the Chief Justice joining Justices Reed and Frankfurter, in disagreement of the majority opinion . . . an opinion read by Justice Douglas and finding that an alien does *not* have to promise to bear arms in order to become a citizen of the United States. The alien directly concerned in this case is James Louis Girard [*sic*], born in Canada, unwilling to bear arms, but perfectly willing to carry out

medical duties as a non-combatant. But James Girard is not the first to appeal—on this point—to the highest court in the land. Fifteen years ago there were other names linked in the news with this issue: Bland, MacIntosh [*sic*], Rosika Schwimmer. Fifteen years ago, the Supreme Court of the United States handed down its decision: the opposite of today's. Then the great Justice Oliver Wendell Holmes disagreed with the majority and, in disagreeing, wrote one of his famous "dissenting opinions." Today the majority quoted from Justice Holmes' famous dissent . . . quoted these words: "If there is any principle of the Constitution that more imperatively calls for attachment than any other, it is the principle of free thought. Not free thought for those who agree with us, but freedom for the thought that we hate. I think that we should adhere to the principle with regard to admission into, as well as to life within, this country."

So spoke Oliver Wendell Holmes fifteen years ago, "Justice Holmes dissenting." Today those words were read from the bench . . . now a part of the majority opinion, . . . famous words ringing out again, in changed circumstances, in the Supreme Court of the United States.[110]

In a commentary for the National Broadcasting Company, Walter W. Van Kirk found broad national and international significance in the case. "Religious circles throughout the country will rejoice in this action by the Supreme Court," Van Kirk declared.

Churchmen of all faiths will recall the statement once made by former Justice Oliver Wendell Holmes that the cherished principle of free thought should apply not only to "life within this country," but also to "admission into" it. The present is a time when the issue of man's fundamental freedoms is being discussed from one end of the earth to the other. During the San Francisco Conference, at which time the United Nations Charter was drafted, the American delegation pressed for the creation of a Commission on Human Rights. Such a Commission was established. It will hold its first meeting in New York City within the next few days. One can imagine the complications that would have arisen in the deliberations of this Commission as these deliberations bear upon the problem of religious freedom, had the Supreme Court rendered a different decision. In such an event the United States, as one of the most eloquent defenders of man's fundamental freedoms, would have been put in the position of denying in its own statutes the principles of religious liberty which it has espoused not only for itself but for the others nations of the world. This decision of the Supreme Court will be a boon to freedom the world over.[111]

The Christian Century, as was to be expected from its outrage after the earlier cases, expressed delight about *Girouard*. After a concise but accurate summary of the case and Douglas's decision, the *Century* called the case "a legal landmark," remarking that the decision was being hailed "in church circles and everywhere among men who are awake to the peril in which the individual conscience stands in a world of growing state totalitarianism." The *Century* was happy to join in that wide acclaim for the decision. Grant J. Verhulst in the Methodist *Christian Advocate* agreed. Now "the highest tribunal of the nation has reversed its previous position that subjected every citizen . . . to accept the voice of government as the voice of God," Verhulst wrote. "We can rejoice that the individual's right to exercise freedom of conscience has been re-established by law."[112]

Few other church periodicals appear to have reacted to *Girouard*. Even the Seventh-day Adventist Church was rather subdued in its expression of delight about the case. *Liberty* magazine, an Adventist publication emphasizing religious freedom, in one issue published the entire Supreme Court opinion of *Girouard* with an editorial sketching the facts of the case and publishing excerpts from other publications, secular and religious, that supported the decision. In another issue it disagreed with *The Christian Statesman*, the publication of the National Reform Association, which advocated that Christian moral principles should be made the law of the land through legislation or court opinion. The *Statesman* praised *Girouard* and saw it as an example of its own position, believing that in the case the Court had asserted the "supremacy of the moral laws of God in the political sphere." *Liberty* rejected that interpretation of *Girouard*, asserting that the state should never legislate religious law and impose it on citizens. *Liberty* firmly asserted that *Girouard* was not an example of such a process. "This decision recognizes two spheres—one in which the state has the perfect right to function, and one into which the state has no right to enter," *Liberty* declared. "The Supreme Court in the Girouard case struck a blow for religious liberty by denying the state a right to interfere in the purely religious relationship of a man with his God."[113]

The principal Adventist denominational magazine, *Review and Herald*, reviewed the facts of the case and expressed extreme satisfaction. "All Adventists naturally rejoice over the outcome of this case." The decision removed a stigma from Adventists. When they were barred from citizenship because of their traditional position on participating in combat, others had accused them of being disloyal and unwilling to do their part as American citizens. They no longer had to endure those charges. The article likened Girouard himself to biblical heroes of faith. "We read in the Scriptures of the boldness of men in standing for their beliefs when called in question by officers of civil governments," the *Review and Herald* reflected, "and we sometimes think that no such things occur now. But today, no less than then, God's people are called upon to make decisions that affect their personal welfare." While "Brother Girouard had lived in the United States for some time" and "there was a strong possibility that he would not even be called upon to bear arms, since he was not far from forty years of age," yet "rather than sacrifice a conviction, he was willing to sacrifice, if need be, whatever opportunities came with American citizenship." The article concluded with a reminder to Adventists about their traditional view of citizenship. Conscientious objection is not a license to avoid all civic duties. Adventist soldiers had objected to taking human life, but they did not use that belief to escape military duty altogether. Indeed "this fine decision places every Seventh-day Adventist under a new obligation carefully to observe the Master's command to 'render to Caesar the things that are Caesar's,'" the *Review and Herald* exhorted. "Good Christians are always good citizens. It is only when the demands of the state interfere with the rights of conscience that anyone must put obedience to God above every earthly duty."[114]

In reacting to *Girouard* some legal commentators wrote about conscientious objection and others wrote about the technical issue of whether the reenactment by Congress of a prior law incorporated the judicial interpretations of the earlier law. Predictably, more law journals commented on the latter—a critical concern of the dissent—than the former.

On conscientious objection itself, the *American Bar Association Journal* argued forcefully that it was not legitimate, taking that position not as much on legal grounds as on the character of objectors themselves. The *Journal* advanced some traditional arguments against naturalization for conscientious objectors. Exemption from military service for native-born citizens is not a right, but a concession of congressional grace. Applicants for citizenship should not be able to demand as a condition of their allegiance what citizens receive only as a grant. Persons who request citizenship in a country that endows citizens with political and religious freedoms should not receive it if they are not willing to fight for the freedoms they enjoy. Remarkably, the article contained slurs against the character of conscientious objectors. According to the *Journal*, those who

processed the applications for conscientious objector status during World
War II perceived

> that many who claimed the privileges of conscientious objectors were
> not in fact motivated by religious conviction but were dissembling for
> their own protection. There was something soft, effeminate, or furtive
> about many of them. They were frequently referred to by others as
> "yellow." Some were quite clearly the victims of a martyr complex.
> They posed and dramatized.

"The commendable principle of freedom of thought and religion should
not be so applied that it tends to pamper and pander to derelicts and
degenerates," the *Journal* concluded. "They should not be received into
citizenship upon exceptions which limit the *imperium* of government." In
light of the decision in *Girouard*, Congress should clearly declare itself
on this issue. Obviously the author believed that Congress should and
would reject *Girouard* and return to the *status quo ante* that excluded
conscientious objectors from citizenship.[115]

Not surprisingly, the article elicited considerable response. A
subsequent issue of the magazine presented a sample of many letters it
received. To its credit, the periodical published letters that criticized its
position as well as those that supported it. Julien Cornell, who had written
the ACLU's *amicus curiae* brief in support of Girouard, objected
strenuously to the article's characterization of conscientious objectors.[116]

Finally, the magazine solicited Earl G. Harrison, Dean of the
University of Pennsylvania Law School, to write an article taking the other
side of the issue. Harrison had been a Second Lieutenant in the infantry in
World War I and Commissioner of Immigration and Naturalization during
World War II. Harrison did not rise to the bait of the scurrilous language
used about conscientious objectors in the first article, but argued the legal
points, tracing the history of the issue. "*Nowhere* in the Congressional
requirements for naturalization was there to be found anything pertaining
to willingness to take up arms in defense of this country," Harrison wrote,
referring to the Supreme Court's action in *Schwimmer*. "*The Supreme
Court proceeded to write into the Congressional language just such a
requirement.*" *Macintosh* and *Bland* perpetuated that error. In *Girouard*,
the Court simply adopted the views expressed by Chief Justice Hughes in
Macintosh, which Harrison believed were exactly right. On the issue raised
by Chief Justice Stone's dissent in *Girouard*, that by not passing
legislation overturning *Schwimmer* and the rest, Congress had essentially

adopted their rule, Harrison simply declared that the silence of Congress cannot carry such weight. "My principal purpose here," he concluded, "has been to indicate that the excoriation of the majority opinion of the *Girouard* case in the earlier article was entirely unwarranted, and that a totally false impression of the whole 'issue' was given in that biased and one-sided exposition." Harrison found it "utterly and completely wrong to accuse the Supreme Court of judicial legislation in the *Girouard* case. All the Court did was to wipe out the judicial legislation of the *Schwimmer* case."[117]

Most law journal commentary that chose to take note of *Girouard* focused on the technical issue of Congress's reenactment of the language of the oath of allegiance from the Nationality Act of 1906 in the Nationality Act of 1940 and whether that included interpretation of the oath in *Schwimmer*, *Macintosh*, and *Bland*. It is not surprising that legal journals should concentrate on this conundrum, since it was the issue that divided the majority from the dissenters in *Girouard*. "I would paraphrase the argument about as follows," Harrison wrote:

> In 1929 and again in 1931 the Supreme Court read into the Naturalization Act a requirement that was not there. Since Congress subsequently re-enacted the same laws but without incorporating the requirement legislated by the Supreme Court, it must be presumed that Congress intended by its silence to have adopted it.[118]

Some law review articles only described the issue and did not agree with one side or the other.[119] Some authors argued that the majority opinion was right, that the action of Congress in the Nationality Act of 1940 did not carry forward the rule of the earlier naturalization cases and that the amendments to the Act in 1942 clearly did show that Congress intended to extend naturalization to noncombatants.[120] The majority of the authors who commented on the case disagreed with the decision in *Girouard* on the basis that Chief Justice Stone was correct in his dissent. The unwillingness of Congress to overturn the rule of *Schwimmer*, *Macintosh*, and *Bland* when it had abundant opportunity to do so for a decade showed that it agreed with the rule. For *Girouard* to overturn the rule and to declare the earlier cases no longer the rule of law was to usurp the role of Congress and engage in judicial legislation.[121]

The Christian Century, in its article praising the *Girouard* decision, raised a problem. It was not sure *Girouard* actually did apply to the conscientious objection of Professor Macintosh. The editor agreed with the Supreme Court that *Girouard* nullified *Schwimmer* and *Bland*, but he was not so sure about *Macintosh*. Macintosh was a selective conscientious objector; he wanted to make a judgment about the wars he would agree to fight in based on whether he found them to be just, on their moral quality. *The Christian Century* saw nothing in the language of *Girouard* that specifically applied to that situation.

> The right of individual conscience to pass on the judgment of Congress in voting a declaration of war seems untouched in the pronouncement written by Justice Douglas, and hence to remain in a sort of legal twilight zone.
>
> There is only one way, we believe, to get this issue completely cleared. That is for Dr. Macintosh to apply again for citizenship, making precisely the same reservation that he made fifteen years ago. We trust that he will do so without delay.[122]

We must now consider what indeed happened after *Girouard* restored "the correct rule of law" and *Schwimmer*, *Macintosh*, and *Bland* were declared to be good law no longer.

Notes

1. The form Girouard completed differed from earlier versions; the famous question was now number 26.

2. Transcript of Record, *Girouard v. United States*, 3-12.

3. The name on his birth certificate is Joseph Lewis Girouard. According to his granddaughter, Holly Medler Howes, Girouard's father was called Oliver in all the legal documents pertaining to this case, although he was named Joseph. Perhaps his name was Oliver Joseph. Girouard had a difficult relationship with his alcoholic father, and early in life apparently began calling himself James Louis. He also spelled his family name in two different ways, Girouard and Girard. On his naturalization application, question 3, he mentioned that he had used the other spelling. "I have used another name in this country than that given above. It was James Louis Girard. I used that name because members of family who preceded me to U.S. used short spelling of name." Two newspaper articles announcing his victory in the Supreme Court commented that he preferred the spelling "Girard" and had petitioned a court to change his name legally. His granddaughter is not sure whether that legal proceeding was ever final. In a brief autobiography, he called himself "Girard." Telephone conversation, Holly Howes with Ronald B. Flowers, 21 July 2001; copy of birth certificate, prepared in New Brunswick

Department of Health, 17 August 1939, provided by Holly Howes and Harvey Medler, grandchildren of Girouard, hereinafter indicated as "Family Archives"; Transcript of Record, 4; "Stoneham Man Wins Plea on Bearing Arms," *Boston Herald*, 23 April 1946; *Stoneham Independent*, 26 April 1946, 1; "*James Louis Girard*: A Brief Biography," no date, Family Archives.

4. Girouard, "*James Louis Girard*: A Brief Biography"; Personal Service Record of James Louis Girouard, New England Sanitarium and Hospital, Family Archives; Holly Howes interview with Ronald B. Flowers, November 23, 1992; Transcript of Record, 1-4.

5. King Whitney to Ronald B. Flowers, 3 July 1992. King Whitney's wife's mother was the sister of Mabel Girouard, wife of James Louis Girouard.

6. Transcript of Record, 1-7.

7. See generally Francis D. Nichol, *The Midnight Cry: A Defense of the Character and Conduct of William Miller and the Millerites, Who Mistakenly Believed That the Second Coming of Christ Would Take Place in the Year 1844* (Washington, D.C.: Review and Herald Publishing Association, 1944) and George R. Knight, *Millennial Fever and the End of the World: A Study of Millerite Adventism* (Boise, Id.: Pacific Press Publishing Association, 1993).

8. Francis McLellan Wilcox, *Seventh-day Adventists in Time of War* (Washington, D.C.: Review and Herald Publishing Association, 1936), 27-31, 37-39. Wilcox (45) summarized Jesus' commandment to give to Caesar and God what respectfully belongs to each. "The Christian has a dual duty—one toward God and another toward worldly powers. God's requirements never infringe on the legitimate claims of Caesar. Neither has Caesar the right to infringe on the demands of God. The two realms must ever be separate and distinct."

9. Wilcox, *Adventists in Time of War*, 23-24; Ronald Lawson, "Church and State at Home and Abroad: The Evolution of Seventh-day Adventist Relations with Governments," *Journal of the American Academy of Religion* 64 (Summer 1996): 284-85.

10. Lawson, "Church and State at Home and Abroad," 288-91.

11. Lawson, "Church and State at Home and Abroad," 291; "Noncombatancy," *Seventh-day Adventist Encyclopedia* (Washington, D.C.: Review and Herald Publishing Association, 1966), 871-72; see also Eric Syme, *A History of SDA Church-State Relations in the United States* (Mountain View, Calif.: Pacific Press Publishing Association, 1973), 69-78.

12. "In United States District Court, Sworn Statement of James Louis Girouard," Transcript of Record, 15-16. Many who knew him have said that Girouard was a quiet, soft-spoken man, perhaps accounting for the brevity of his remarks.

13. "Record of Selective Service Local Board No. 161, U. S. Department of Justice, Immigration and Naturalization Service," Transcript of Record, 16-17.

14. "Petition for Naturalization United States of America—Filed November 3, 1943," Transcript of Record, 7-11.

15. Edmund J. Brandon, United States Attorney, "Statement in Narrative Form of Petitioner's Testimony Before the Court, in Accordance with Rule 75(c)—Filed December 28, 1944," Transcript of Record, 13-15. This document was filed as part of the government's appeal to the First Circuit Court of Appeals (see Appendix V).

16. "In United States District Court, Order of Court—August 1, 1944," and "Notice of Exception and Order Thereon—Filed August 25, 1944," Transcript of Record, 11-13.

17. So I suppose, based on the text of this letter.

18. Forster to Freeman, 28 March 1945; Hays to Davis, 24 April 1945; Davis to Hays, 28 April 1945; "Issue of Citizenship for Alien Pacifist May Be Carried to Supreme Court," *ACLU Press Release*, 21 May 1945; Forster to Albert, 29 May 1945. ACLU Archives, vol. 2683.

19. Edmund J. Brandon, Unites States Attorney, "Notice of Appeal to Circuit Court of Appeals for First Circuit," Transcript of Record, 18-21.

20. Because no transcript of the District Court proceedings was made, Girouard's lawyers at that level are not mentioned in the Transcript of Record. Girouard's relative has this vague recollection: "As we remember the story, Jim was referred to a rather young lawyer from Haverhill, Massachusetts, who was a member of the state legislature. I believe the lawyer had done work for Luella's dad [Luella's mother was the sister of Girouard's wife] from time to time and it was he who recommended Jim go to this lawyer." King Whitney to Ronald B. Flowers, 24 June 1992. This reference does not name the lawyer, so I do not know if it were Coddaire or Fitzsimmons.

21. *United States v. Schwimmer* 279 U.S. 644 at 650 (1929).

22. *United States v. Macintosh* 283 U.S. 605 at 624 (1931); *United States v. Girouard* 149 F.2d 760 at 761-62 (1945).

23. *United States v. Girouard* 149 F.2d 760 at 763.

24. 54 *Statutes at Large* 887.

25. *United States v. Girouard* 149 F. 2d 760 at 763.

26. 54 *Statutes at Large* 1137.

27. 56 *Statutes at Large* 182.

28. *United States v. Girouard* 149 F.2d 760 at 763.

29. See 54 *Statutes at Large* 1137 at 1140-43, §§ 302-308.

30. *United States v. Girouard* 149 F. 2d 760 at 764-65.

31. *United States v. Girouard* 149 F. 2d 760 at 765.

32. *United States v. Girouard* 149 F. 2d 760 at 765.

33. *United States v. Girouard* 149 F. 2d 760 at 765-67.

34. At that point Judge Woodbury included a footnote citing several cases brought to the Supreme Court by Jehovah's Witnesses: *Cantwell v. Connecticut* 310 U.S. 296 (1940); *Jones v. Opelika* 316 U.S. 584 (1942); 319 U.S. 103 (1943); *Jamison v. Texas* 318 U.S. 413 (1943); *Murdock v. Pennsylvania* 319 U.S. 105 (1943); *Martin v. Struthers* 319 U.S. 141 (1943); *Taylor v. Mississippi* 319 U.S. 583 (1943); *West Virginia Board of Education v. Barnette* 319 U.S. 624 (1943);

Follett v. McCormick 321 U.S. 573 (1944).

35. *United States v. Girouard* 149 F.2d 760 at 767.

36. Albert to Forster, 2 June 1945, ACLU Archives, vol. 2683; Minutes of the 559th meeting of the General Conference Committee, 11 June 1945, Seventh-day Adventist Historical Society, hereafter cited as "SDA Archives." The resolution of the General Conference Committee noted that "one of our members, a Canadian, applied for and obtained naturalization as an American citizen, even though he went on record as unwilling to bear arms. However, the decision was later reversed. Appeal can now be made to the Supreme Court, if taken at once, but our brother is unable to finance the cost of such an appeal." The resolution authorized "the Religious Liberty Department to use the case of James Lewis [*sic*] Girouard, an employee of the New England Sanitarium and Hospital, as a test case before the United States Supreme Court, in an endeavor to obtain a modification of naturalization procedures which now bar from citizenship in the United States any one unwilling to bear arms in defense of the country, even though willing to serve in the military forces in a noncombatant capacity in time of war," and "to consult and employ lawyers to plead this case."

37. M. L. Rice to Girouard, 12 June 1945; SDA Archives.

38. Forster to Albert, 12 June 1945; ACLU Archives, vol. 2683.

39. Rice to Girouard, 20 June 1945; SDA Archives; Forster to Albert, 3 July 1945; Albert to Forster, 5 July 1945; Baldwin to Albert, 10 July 1945; Albert to Baldwin, 11 July 1945; ACLU Archives, vol. 2683.

40. Rice to Girouard, 27 July 1945, SDA Archives. Girouard was instructed to send this text:

"I have been told by the Rev. M. L. Rice, who is president of the Atlantic Union Conference of the Seventh-day Adventists, that the General Conference of Seventh-day Adventists has shown its interest in the appeal of my naturalization case by arranging for the General Conference attorneys, the firm of Cummings & Stanley, to appear in the case, and I am anxious that its desires for Cummings & Stanley to be co-counsel should be complied with.

"I am sure you will understand that since the General Conference advanced your fee, it seems only right that its wishes in this matter should be respected.

"Will you take whatever steps are necessary to establish the proper working arrangements between you and Cummings & Stanley?"

41. Albert to Forster, 17 August 1945; ACLU Archives, vol. 2683.

42. "Motion for Extension of Time Within Which to File Petition for Writ of Certiorari," date stamped 24 August 1945 by the office of the Clerk of the Supreme Court, Record Group 267, National Archives; Transcript of Record, *Girouard v. United States, Brief for Petitioner*, 1-2.

43. Forster to Harrop Freeman, 16 November 1945, "We may all consider it fortunate that the matter is now being handled by Homer Cummings of Washington, D.C."; Freeman to Forster, 22 November 1945, "Homer Cummings will be an excellent addition."; Arthur Garfield Hays to Homer Cummings, 11 December 1945, "We of course are very pleased to note that you have undertaken

to handle the citizenship case of James Louis Girouard, . . ."; Cummings to Hayes, 14 December 1945; Hays to Cummings, 11 January 1946; ACLU Archives, vol. 2683. Minutes of General Conference Committee, 27 November 1945, SDA Archives.

44. Michael E. Parrish, "Cummings, Homer Stillé," in *American National Biography*, John A. Garraty and March C. Carnes, eds. (New York: Oxford University Press, 1999) 5: 853-54. On Cummings's role in the "Court packing" plan, Justice William O. Douglas writes that it was essentially Cummings's idea. Cummings may have gotten the idea from a previous Attorney General, James C. McReynolds (who later served on the Supreme Court), but Douglas was not sure. Douglas was sure that Cummings was its principal advocate to the President. "None of us close to FDR was in on the idea of Court-packing. If the President had asked me for my advice, I would have told him I was opposed. *The Attorney General, Homer Cummings, sold the plan to him one night in a solo performance at the White House*." William O. Douglas, *Go East, Young Man, The Early Years: The Autobiography of William O. Douglas* (New York: Vintage Books, 1974), 318, 321. Emphasis added. Cummings's obituary agrees that he proposed the idea to Roosevelt. "Homer Cummings, Ex-U.S. Aide, Dies," *New York Times*, 11 September 1956, 35.

45. Transcript of Record, *Girouard v. United States, Petition for Writ of Certiorari*, 10 n2. Cummings summarized his point in a long footnote.

"The non-combatant is not a coward; he simply conscientiously objects to affirmative participation in the taking of human life; he dares, however, to assume any military risk necessary to save life.

"A Seventh Day Adventist non-combatant does not agitate against war. He recognizes that war is many times unavoidable in the preservation of the State. He does not arrogate to himself the prerogative of deciding whether the government is right or wrong in entering upon a war. He merely maintains an attitude and a conviction that war, whether right or wrong, whether justified or unjustified, whether of aggression or of defense, does not change his obligation of obedience to God."

46. *Petition for Writ of Certiorari*, 10, 11.

47. *Petition for Writ of Certiorari*, 12, 14-17.

48. *Petition for Writ of Certiorari*, 17-18.

49. Transcript of Record, *Girouard v. United States, Brief for Petitioner*, 2.

50. Transcript of Record, *Girouard v. United States, Memorandum for the United States*, 3-5. Emphasis added.

51. *Memorandum for the United States*, 5-6. This response by the government to Girouard's petition for certiorari was only six pages long. Whether its brevity means that government lawyers thought it inevitable that the Supreme Court would take the case, or whether they thought that Girouard's argument was without merit and the precedents of *Schwimmer*, *Macintosh*, and *Bland* were so strong that the Court would never take the case, is unclear.

52. 326 U.S. 714 (1945).

53. Transcript of Record, *Girouard v. United States, Brief for Petitioner*, 9.

54. *Brief for Petitioner*, 9-11.

55. *Brief for Petitioner*, 11-12. The constitutional provision for oaths of office and the prohibition of religious tests for office are juxtaposed; indeed, they are clauses of the same sentence. Article 6, clause 3, of the Constitution reads, "The Senators and Representatives before mentioned and the Members of the several State Legislatures, and all executive and judicial Officers, both of the United States and of the several States, shall be bound by Oath or Affirmation, to support this Constitution; but no religious test shall ever be required as a Qualification to any Office or public Trust under the United States." The oath of office read, "That I will support and defend the Constitution of the United States against all enemies, foreign and domestic; that I will bear true faith and allegiance to the same; that I take this obligation freely, without any mental reservation or purpose of evasion." See *Brief for Petitioner*, 11 n4.

56. *Brief for Petitioner*, 13-18.

57. "Congress shall make no law respecting an establishment of religion or prohibiting the free exercise thereof."

58. Cummings cited some of the recent Jehovah's Witness cases in which one Justice or another had referred to religious freedom as a "preferred freedom." *Schneider v. Irvington* 308 U.S. 147 at 161 (1939); *Cantwell v. Connecticut* 310 U.S. 296 (1940); *Prince v. Massachusetts* 321 U.S. 158 at 164 (1944).

59. At this point Cummings quoted a passage from a lower court pertaining to military service: "Congressional enactments having the purposes of raising or maintaining armed forces have high standing because of their importance. At the same time, they must not limit the constitutionally protected individual liberties of the citizen to any greater extent than is reasonably necessary and proper to accomplish the important allowable ends of preserving the life of the Government and the State and their orderly conduct." See *Dunne v. United States* 138 F.2d 137 at 141 (1943), cert. den. 320 U.S. 790 (1943).

60. *Brief for Petitioner*, 18-22.

61. *Brief for Petitioner*, 23-34.

62. Transcript of Record, *Girouard v. United States, Brief for the United States*, 15-23.

63. Homer Cummings's brief for Girouard mentioned this development, but only in a footnote. *Brief for Petitioner*, 9 n3.

64. To support the idea that Congress had in fact reenacted the language of the oath and the interpretation of the Supreme Court, the brief presciently quoted a passage from Chief Justice Harlan Fiske Stone: "The long time failure of Congress to alter the Act after it had been judicially construed, and the enactment by Congress of legislation which implicitly recognizes the judicial construction as effective, is persuasive of legislative recognition that the judicial construction is the correct one. This is the more so where, as here, the application of the statute . . . has brought forth sharply conflicting views on the Court and in Congress, and where after the matter has been fully brought to the attention of the public and the

Congress, the latter has not seen fit to change the statute." See *Apex Hosiery Co. v. Leader* 310 U.S. 469 at 488-89 (1940).

65. The government's brief attributed that suggestion to the dissent of Court of Appeals Judge Woodbury in *United States v. Girouard*. See *Brief for the United States*, 26-28. Ironically, Homer Cummings's *Brief for Petitioner* did not rely on Judge Woodbury's dissent at all, despite its strong support for Girouard's position.

66. *Brief for the United States*, 29-30, references omitted.

67. *Brief for the United States*, 30-33.

68. See *Brief for Petitioner*, 22-23 n10. This contention does not seem to have been a major part of Girouard's argument; the government brief exaggerates its importance.

69. *Brief for the United States*, 33-38.

70. *Brief for the United States*, 38-43.

71. *Brief for the United States*, 43-44.

72. *Brief for the United States*, 45-54.

73. McGrath described this rather lyrically, if one can be lyrical about oppression and destruction: "The forces of darkness, once loosed, swept relentlessly and remorselessly over Europe and Asia, crushing political freedom, crushing religious freedom, overwhelming with a destructive nihilism every human value and every aspect of human decency, until finally millions of human lives were ruthlessly extinguished in a series of scientific slaughter-houses by the side of which the most outrageous excesses of the Huns of Atilla and the Barbarian hosts of old pale by comparison into orderly decency." See *Brief for the United States*, 59-60.

74. *Brief for the United States*, 60; emphasis added.

75. *Brief for the United States*, 60-61.

76. *Brief for the United States*, 61.

77. Of course, Illinois had denied Clyde W. Summers the opportunity to practice law because he was a conscientious objector. According to the ACLU *amicus* brief, "The *Summers* case is an example of the disastrous effect on our civil liberties of following the *Schwimmer* and *Macintosh* cases." Transcript of Record, *Girouard v. United States, Brief of the American Civil Liberties Union, Amicus Curiae*, 9.

78. ACLU *Amicus* Brief, 8-9; emphasis in original.

79. ACLU *Amicus* Brief, , 9-10.

80. ACLU *Amicus* Brief, 10-11.

81. Such a manuscript is rare for this period in the Court's history, for it was not the custom in those days to transcribe oral arguments. Now, with electronic recording equipment, such transcripts are regularly made. I do not have a manuscript of the argument of Frederick Bernays Wiener, who argued *Girouard* for the government, or the manuscript of the argument of any other lawyer mentioned in this book. The Cummings manuscript exists because the Seventh-day Adventist Church apparently asked him for it. My copy is attached

to a form cover letter, 20 March 1946, to "Dear Brother," written by Heber H. Votaw, Secretary of the Religious Liberty Association, International Headquarters, an agency of the Seventh-day Adventist Church. The letter mentions that the General Conference had engaged Cummings to plead Girouard's case. "I thought you would be interested in what he had to say."

82. Homer Cummings's Oral Argument, *Girouard v. United States*, 5-6, SDA Archives.

83. Cummings's Oral Argument, 8.(For the complete text of Cummings's oral argument, see Appendix W.)

84. James C. Duram and Judith Johnson, "William O. Douglas," in *The Supreme Court Justices: Illustrated Biographies, 1789-1993*, Clare Cushman, ed. (Washington, D.C.: Congressional Quarterly, 1993), 391-95; *The Douglas Letters: Selections from the Private Papers of Justice William O. Douglas*, Melvin I. Urofsky, ed. (Bethesda, Md.: 1987), ix-xxii. See his two-volume autobiography, William O. Douglas, *Go East, Young Man, The Early Years: The Autobiography of William O. Douglas* (New York: Vintage Books, 1974) and *The Court Years, 1939-1975: The Autobiography of William O. Douglas* (New York: Vintage Books, 1980).

85. Douglas, *Go East, Young Man, The Early Years*, 308.

86. *Girouard v. United States* 328 U.S. 61 at 64 (1946). On the back of the draft of the opinion, Justice Harold Burton wrote to Douglas, "I agree. Congratulate you on its simplicity of statement." It was Burton who suggested to Douglas in this passage that he mention the people who made the atomic bomb. Papers of William O. Douglas, box 134, Library of Congress.

87. *Girouard v. United States* 328 U.S. 61 at 65-66.

88. *Girouard v. United States* 328 U.S. 61 at 68-69. On the back of the draft of the opinion, Justice Wiley Rutledge wrote to Douglas, underlining his statement, "I'm with you—and how!" Justice Frank Murphy wrote, "I agree." Papers of William O. Douglas, box 134, Library of Congress.

89. James M. Marsh, "Robert H. Jackson," in *The Supreme Court Justices: Illustrated Biographies, 1789-1993*, Clare Cushman, ed. (Washington, D.C.: Congressional Quarterly, 1993), 409.

90. Louis Lusky, "Harlan Fiske Stone," in *The Supreme Court Justices: Illustrated Biographies, 1789-1993*, Clare Cushman, ed. (Washington, D.C.: Congressional Quarterly, 1993), 361-65.

91. *Girouard v. United States* 328 U.S. 61 at 72-73.

92. *Girouard v. United States* 328 U.S. 61 at 72-76. Justice Felix Frankfurter joined in Stone's dissent, and suggested the passage directly quoted here. In the same letter, Frankfurter wrote to Stone, "I am happy about your opinion. Through the 1940 Act it is absolutely copper fastened." Frankfurter to Stone, 19 April 1946, papers of Harlan Fiske Stone, box 72, Library of Congress.

93. *Girouard v. United States* 328 U.S. 61 at 77-79.

94. Stone's biographer reports that he wrote a separate dissent, but, in the end, decided not to publish it, joining in Hughes's opinion instead. He perceived that Hughes wanted to "get his own way," so he withdrew his dissent. See Alpheus Thomas Mason, *Harlan Fiske Stone: Pillar of the Law* (New York: Viking Press, 1956), 317. That Stone wavered on this issue is supported in a letter that Rosika Schwimmer wrote in 1943, three years before *Girouard*, although it is based on hearsay information. "When citizenship was denied to me in 1929," Schwimmer wrote, "a New York lawyer friend of mine was told by a Columbia University professor that he had written Justice Stone, expressing his disappointment about his siding with the majority which denied citizenship to me. In response, Justice Stone wrote to his Columbia friend that he had been about to sign the minority opinion when he 'was requested to reread the story of R.S. I did so, and decided we'd better keep her out.' In the cases of Professor MacIntosh and the nurse, Miss Bland, which followed mine, Justice Stone sided with the liberal minority." See Schwimmer to Zechariah Chaffee, Jr., 9 February 1943; see also Walton Hamilton [Yale Law School] to Edith Wynner, 30 March 1946; Schwimmer-Lloyd collection, box G-24.

95. Frankfurter to Griffin, 22 January 1932, Schwimmer-Lloyd collection, Griffin bill files, box G-7; Frankfurter to Burton, 20 March 1946, papers of Harold Burton, box 153, Manuscript Division, Library of Congress. Stone had voted with the majority in *Schwimmer*, believing that Schwimmer's inclination to persuade others to pacifism was a sufficient reason to deny her citizenship. Indeed Stone suggested to Justice Pierce Butler some of the language he used in the majority opinion in making that point. He wanted to ground the opinion on her past and potential future actions and not just on her ideas, as Justice Holmes, in his dissent, suggested they were doing. In addition to Schwimmer's propagandizing, she based her pacifism on political principles. "As a Supreme Court Justice, he could do no more for Miss Schwimmer than he had for political recalcitrants as a member of the Board of Inquiry in 1918. A religious dissenter such as Professor Macintosh, on the other hand, could enlist his support." Mason, *Harlan Fiske Stone*, 519-23.

96. Urofsky, *Douglas Letters*, 74; Stanley C. Brubaker, "Judicial Self-Restraint," in *The Oxford Companion to the Supreme Court of the United States*, Kermit L. Hall, ed. (New York: Oxford University Press, 1992), 470-72.

97. Urofsky, *Douglas Letters*, 73-75; Peter Charles Hoffer, "Frankfurter, Felix" in *Oxford Companion to the Supreme Court*, 314-17; A. E. Kier Nash, "Stone, Harlan Fiske." in *Oxford Companion to the Supreme Court*, 838-40; Mason, *Harlan Fiske Stone*, 804-5.

98. Stone's biographer writes that Stone agonized over the conscientious objector cases, all the more so when the Court's finding in favor of Girouard brought the issue to a head for him. "I know from what he told me," Justice Douglas wrote of the effect of adjudicating these cases on Stone, "that it was for him a moving experience. Perhaps he learned from the quiet Quakers, or from those who are more impassioned, the full meaning of religious freedom. Perhaps he saw in the deep, burning eyes of some of the two thousand drafted men whom

he interviewed the message that there are some who will die rather than bear false witness to their religion." William O. Douglas, *An Almanac of Liberty* (New York: Doubleday, 1954), 352, quoted in Mason, *Harlan Fiske Stone*, 523.

99. "I would like to depart from the *Schwimmer* doctrine," Frankfurter wrote to Justice Burton, during deliberations on *Girouard*, "and therefore I am looking for arguments that entitle me to do so. But I cannot reject action of the Congress as clear as that expressed by what Congress has been asked to do and has impressively refused to do since 1929. Its intention is as clear to me as if it had used the words in the 1940 statute: 'By this Act we affirm the construction stated by the Supreme Court in the *Schwimmer*, *Macintosh* and *Bland* cases.'" Frankfurter to Burton, 20 March 1946; papers of Harold Burton, Manuscript Division, Library of Congress.

100. *Girouard v. United States* 328 U.S. 61 at 70. (The text of the Court's opinion is in Appendix X.)

101. *Girouard v. United States* 328 U.S. 61 at 79; Mason, *Harlan Fiske Stone*, 803-9. Justice Douglas (*The Court Years*, 224) later offered a somewhat more compressed memory of Stone's death: "Stone did not actually die on the bench, but he did have a fatal stroke in 1946 while I was reading *Girouard v. United States*, to which he had written a dissent. As I announced the decision I heard Stone mumbling, and when I finished I signaled to Black to do something, and we carried Stone off the bench and put him down on the couch in the Robing room. We then had a hurried Conference after we called the Capitol physician, and decided that since Stone was still alive, we should return and announce the remaining decisions; otherwise we might have had to put some cases down for rehearing."

102. Emily Marx wrote to Douglas, 26 April 1946, "Fifteen years is a long, long time to wait for judicial recognition of the merits of my brief in *U.S. v. Bland*; but your opinion is such a sound piece of work that it compensates (somewhat) for the long wait. I suppose I should add (deferentially, of course) that nothing less could be expected from one who has been exposed to the spirit and teachings of the Yale Law School." (Marx went to Yale, Douglas taught there.) Francis D. Nichol wrote to Douglas, 1 May 1946, "Please permit me to express my profound appreciation of the reasoning set forth in the decision you read on April 23, in the case of James Louis Girouard. You and those who joined with you in the decision have done a great service to the cause of religious liberty." Papers of William O. Douglas, Manuscript Division, Library of Congress.

103. "Supreme Court Rules on Case of Stoneham Man Favorably," *Stoneham Independent*, 26 April 1946, 1; "Stonehamite Wins Case In Supreme Court," *Stoneham Press*, 26 April 1946, 3. The latter article mentions that 25 employees of the Sanitarium, doctors and nurses, served in the Medical Corps during World War II and that one of those died of typhus while treating wounded soldiers in India.

104. "Stoneham Man Wins Plea on Bearing Arms," *Boston Herald*, 23 April 1946; "Do Not Have To Fight To Be Citizen," *Washington Post*, 23 April 1946.

105. "U.S. Supreme Court Holds Alien Pacifists Eligible for Citizenship," *American Civil Liberties Union Press Release*, Bulletin #1228, 29 April 1946; ACLU Archives, vol. 27!3.

106. Jay Walz, "New Citizen Freed of Oath to Fight," *New York Times*, 23 April 1946, 1; "Chief Justice Harlan Stone of Supreme Court Is Dead," *New York Times*, 23 April 1946, 1.

107. "Rosika Schwimmer, Pacifist, Expects U.S. Citizenship at Last," *New York Herald Tribune*, 27 April 1946; Schwimmer-Lloyd collection, box G-15. Schwimmer was not as hopeful about receiving citizenship as this story suggests (see Chapter Eight). The day after *Girouard* was handed down, Schwimmer did send a telegram to Homer Cummings thanking him for his victory: "With deep gratitude I congratulate you on your success in righting the great wrong done to American traditions of freedom of thought almost seventeen years ago by the Supreme Court decision in my citizenship case interpreting the oath of allegiance as requiring the bearing of arms. I am happy to have lived to see this reversal of the court's decision the effects of which will go far beyond the boundaries of the United States. You and your associates have revived my faith in the basic ideals and traditions of the United States to which I came self-exiled when my native land became a fascist country. . . . With best wishes for your continued success as a champion of human liberties." See Schwimmer to Cummings, 23 April 1946; Schwimmer-Lloyd collection, box G-18.

108. *Washington Post*, 23 April 1946, quoted in "Conscientious Objectors and Naturalization," *Liberty* 41 (Third Quarter 1946): 27; SDA Archives.

109. *Chicago Daily News*, 24 April 1946; "Can Allegiance Be Qualified?" *Cleveland Plain Dealer* 1 March 1947, reprinted in *American Bar Association Journal* 33 (April 1947): 325.

110. "Robert Trout with 'The News till Now,'" excerpt from script of 22 April 1946. Rosika Schwimmer filed this transcript with the notation, "Rec'd from Joe Wershba, May 4, 1946"; Schwimmer-Lloyd collection, box G-15.

111. Walter W. Van Kirk, "Religion in the News," 15/30 (Saturday, 27 April 1946), broadcast 6:45 to 7:00 p.m., National Broadcasting Company. A cover letter from Enid Jameson, secretary to Dr. Van Kirk, to Girouard, 22 May 1946, that said the transcript was being sent to Girouard because he might have some interest in it; SDA Archives.

112. "Dr. Macintosh—Apply Again!" *Christian Century* 63 (8 May 1946): 583-84; Grant J. Verhulst, "Freedom for Conscience," *Christian Advocate* 121 (16 May 1946): 611; see also "Conscientious Objectors and Naturalization," *Liberty* 41 (Fourth Quarter 1946): 27.

113. "Conscientious Objectors and Naturalization," *Liberty* 41 (Fourth Quarter 1946): 26-27; "A Misapplication of the Girouard Case," *Liberty* 41 (Fourth Quarter 1946): 33-34.

114. Heber H. Votaw, "Supreme Court Decides Noncombatant Adventists May Become Citizens," *Review and Herald* (16 May 1946): 7-8.

115. "American Citizenship: Can Applicants Qualify Their Allegiance?" *American Bar Association Journal* 33 (February 1947): 95-98.

116. "American Citizenship: Our Readers' Views of the Girouard Decision," *American Bar Association Journal* 33 (April 1947): 323-26.

117. Earl G. Harrison, "American Citizenship: 'Can Applicants Qualify Their Allegiance?'—A Reply," *American Bar Association Journal* 33 (June 1947): 540-43, emphasis in original.

118. Harrison, "American Citizenship: . . . —A Reply," 543.

119. "Statutes—Construction—Effect of Reenactment After Judicial Construction," *Minnesota Law Review* 31 (May 1947): 625-27. Joseph A. Bethel, ("Naturalization and Willingness to Take Up Arms," *Marquette Law Review* 30 [1946]: 130-37) does suggest that after *Girouard* no question about willingness to bear arms should appear in the application for naturalization.

120. "Constitutional Law—Naturalization: *Schwimmer* Case Overruled—Inapplicability of *Stare Decisis* When Prior Decision Incorrect," *New York University Law Quarterly Review* 21 (July 1946): 445-49; H. E. Kinney, "Naturalization—Willingness to Bear Arms Held Not to Be a Qualification for Citizenship," *Georgia Bar Journal* 9 (August 1946): 106-107; A. L. S., "Aliens—Constitutional Law—Naturalization—Promise to Bear Arms Not a Prerequisite to Naturalization," *George Washington Law Review* 14 (June 1946): 641-44.

121. George Brody, "Naturalization—Statutory Construction," *Michigan Law Review* 45 (1946): 227-30; "Statutory Construction: Change in Interpretation After Reenactment," *Indiana Law Review* 22 (1946): 94-97; "Statutes—Construction—Reenactment of Naturalization Oath as Evidence of Legislative Intent," *Columbia Law Review* 46 (September 1946): 886-87; Frank E. Horack, Jr., "Congressional Silence: A Tool of Judicial Supremacy," *Texas Law Review* 25 (June 1947): 247-61; William E. Aulgur, "Naturalization—Statutory Construction: *Girouard v. United States*," *Missouri Law Review* 11 (June 1946): 339-43; "Legislative Adoption of Prior Judicial Construction: The *Girouard* Case and the Reenactment Rule," *Harvard Law Review* 59 (1946): 1277-86. William O. Gilbreath ("Naturalization—Requirement of Willingness to Bear Arms," *Kentucky Law Journal* 35 [May 1947]: 334-380) offers a concise, clear summary of the issues—unlike most of these articles, which are virtually incomprehensible.

122. "Dr. Macintosh—Apply Again," *Christian Century*, 584.

Eight

Death and Legislation[1]

We might think that the *Girouard* decision should have profoundly influenced the lives of Rosika Schwimmer, Douglas Clyde Macintosh, and Marie Averil Bland. It did not. Even though *Girouard* declared that each of their cases was no longer good law, they did not benefit from the ruling.

Years before *Girouard* was decided, Schwimmer was urged to try again to gain citizenship. In 1939 Emily Marx, who had been Bland's lawyer, wrote to Schwimmer, offering to take her case before the Supreme Court. Marx supposed that the Court, "as presently constituted . . . would probably welcome the opportunity to admit you to citizenship." Schwimmer thanked Marx for the offer, but declined. She was weary and believed that others should take up the battle. "I am sorry I can't avail myself of your offer because I would not undergo the ordeal again," Schwimmer wrote. "When I was refused in 1927 I would not have applied if organizations and individuals interested in civil rights in the country had not urged me to make my case a test, which none of them expected to fail." Schwimmer had "done my share," and would let others "make now renewed attempts. I certainly do not want to push myself into citizenship."[2]

After *Girouard* nullified the decision that had denied her citizenship, the possibility of becoming a citizen became considerably more real to Schwimmer. Her correspondence hints that she had discussed the possibility with some people, but they had concluded that citizenship would not be forthcoming. In one letter Schwimmer lamented that her longtime friend and fellow pacifist Lola Maverick Lloyd, who died in 1944, "did not live to see this victory in a fight which she had been carrying on from the day when I was refused citizenship in 1929." Schwimmer had "thought this new decision will give me citizenship automatically, but lawyers who analyzed the situation said that I would have to go through the whole rigmarole again: asking for first papers, etc., etc." In another letter she wrote, "The reversal of the citizenship procedure here, of course, is a very great moral satisfaction. Unfortunately there is no practical benefit in it for me. . . . Of course, I don't want to go back to Hungary, but I would like to get out of the stateless status, which is a most agonizing condition." She thought with another friend about going yet again through the entire procedure of applying for citizenship and concluded that the process would take several years, "and I don't think I will live long enough to wait for that." Her current ailments—which were multiple, in addition to her thirty-year battle with diabetes—reinforced her fear.[3]

In late 1946 Schwimmer received a letter from a longtime friend, the women's suffrage leader Carrie Chapman Catt. Their relationship had been problematic since at least 1915, when Schwimmer was quite visibly involved in the Ford Peace Ship project. Some people had then accused Schwimmer of being a German sympathizer and she had become even more controversial. Catt had thought that negative accusations against Schwimmer would tarnish the suffrage movement if Catt or the movement were too closely identified with her. Catt withdrew from Schwimmer to avoid besmirching the suffrage movement any more than necessary. (It was controversial enough in its own right.) Although they continued to correspond, Catt's letters were usually characterized by a cold formality. After the Supreme Court denied Schwimmer citizenship, Catt did not join other feminists and pacifists in signing a statement in her support. When Schwimmer was given the unofficial World Peace Prize in 1937, Catt was only a reluctant supporter. Schwimmer was hurt and even embittered by Catt's attitude toward her, lukewarm at best.[4] But now, after *Girouard*, when they were both old and sickly, Catt wrote a long letter to Schwimmer. In Catt's mind, "the obstacle to your citizenship no longer exists." Schwimmer could "die if you wish as a woman without a country, but if that is not satisfactory you may have a country now by asking for it, and I think it may be written about you that you led the way." No woman before Schwimmer had been asked to bear arms, Catt thought, and none would again be asked. Their medicines were expensive, and Catt could imagine Schwimmer's reluctance to hire lawyers, "but I think I would like better than anything else to try to raise whatever it costs to give you citizenship in this country." For Schwimmer herself Catt now expressed warm, personal concern: "Dear Rosika, I hope you are not suffering too much, and that you find some joy in living." "I am very, very grateful for your effort to interest a woman lawyer to take up the problem of my citizenship," Schwimmer replied. "I have, unfortunately no money to pay for legal services. But if a lawyer friend of yours would undertake the work

I would be most grateful, indeed."[5] With Catt's encouragement, contrary to her earlier abject pessimism about the possibility of citizenship, Schwimmer now showed some interest in pursuing the project.

Soon Roger Baldwin of the ACLU wrote to Schwimmer that he had heard she was interested in pursuing citizenship and volunteered to provide her a lawyer, if she wished, at no cost to her. Schwimmer asked how Baldwin found out about her interest in the matter. She said she had expressed interest in a rather automatic process, since years ago a Federal Court of Appeals had unanimously ruled in favor of her citizenship and now the Supreme Court's decision had been nullified in *Girouard*. Several lawyers had told her that the automatic procedure was not possible. It would be necessary to reapply. "Since then, several people, amongst them . . . Mrs. Carrie Chapman Catt speak of spending all their energies to get citizenship for me. . . . Thank you for your offer to provide a lawyer without expenses to me, but, as I say, the matter at present is in Mrs. Catt's hand." Baldwin replied that he had heard of her interest from Judge Dorothy Kenyon, Mrs. Catt's lawyer. They had agreed that no court proceedings could be brought on Schwimmer's behalf at this late date, so many years after her case had been adjudicated. "The only possibility outside of beginning all over again is a special bill in Congress covering you, Professor Macintosh, and Miss Bland, . . . I will correspond with them and see whether they are willing to have that relief. If so, we will prepare a bill and get it introduced." In a later telephone conversation, Baldwin told Schwimmer that he had not received an answer from Miss Bland and that Professor Macintosh's wife explained that he had suffered a stroke and could not talk. They agreed to continue to try contact Bland. Since a bill in Congress would not require Macintosh to testify, his disability would not necessarily preclude an attempt to obtain citizenship for him. If Bland and/or Macintosh could not go forward, the bill would be prepared for Schwimmer alone.[6]

Schwimmer wrote to Catt, confidentially, that Baldwin tended to make things difficult. She had never had much confidence in him and never would have allowed the ACLU to carry forward her original case if they had not convinced her that her victory, which they absolutely expected, would be a contribution to American civil liberties. In a later letter to a different friend, Schwimmer commented that the ACLU had passed her case to a staff member, Miss Frances Levenson, given that Baldwin was out of town for an extended period. Miss Levenson was able and businesslike, much to Schwimmer's relief. Miss Levenson and Judge

Kenyon were going to draft the bill and then find a congressman to introduce it. Since Marie Averil Bland had died, it would apply to Macintosh and Schwimmer only. Carrie Chapman Catt had also died, on 9 March 1947, so Schwimmer hoped that Miss Levenson and Judge Kenyon could find a legislator close to Catt who would introduce the bill. "But whether such special legislators are available or others have to be found," Schwimmer wrote, "I suggest that in the introductory speech to the bill, they should refer to Mrs. Catt's desire to get citizenship for me and say that they introduce the bill to do justice to Professor Macintosh and me but also to honor Mrs. Catt, who did not live to see her wish materialize." The bill, she thought, should be enacted "in honor and memory of Mrs. Catt."[7]

It was not to be. Miss Levenson of the ACLU told Schwimmer that after considerable reflection "it would be inexpedient to have such a bill introduced at the present time." The problem "at the present time" was the pressure that had been brought to the Congress to pass the Dolliver bill.[8] The introduction of a bill on behalf of Macintosh and Schwimmer might increase support for that bill. In addition, Congress was never favorably disposed to pass private citizenship bills. Given the difficulties, Levenson wrote, "we are compelled to take the position that we can not sponsor the introduction of a private bill on your behalf at the present time."[9]

In July 1948 a group of women met at Seneca Falls, New York, to celebrate the centennial of the 1848 meeting that had launched the women's suffrage movement.[10] Schwimmer was too ill to go, but she sent a message urging continued activism for human rights and abolition of war. Her words reveal the enduring scar that denial of citizenship had left on her. "I myself acquired, in 1929," she wrote, "the dubious distinction of having been the first woman denied citizenship by a civilised nation, the United States of America, solely for having refused to promise to bear arms." She recalled ruefully that "the wits of the time" had sung, "I did not raise my grandmother to be a soldier." The decision had been reversed, but "the militarisation of women has not." Schwimmer saw, presciently, that "Women's rights, men's rights—human rights—all are threatened by the ever-present spectre of war so destructive now of human, material and moral values as to render victory indistinguishable from defeat." For advocates of human rights, the cause of peace should be equally compelling. "We who successfully freed one half the human race without violence must now undertake with equal devotion, perseverance and intelligence the supreme act of human statesmanship involved in the creation of institutions of government on a world scale."[11]

Probably because of her persistence in this cause, Schwimmer was nominated in 1948 for the Nobel Peace Prize by members of the parliaments of Great Britain, Sweden, France, Italy, and Hungary. Edith Wynner, Schwimmer's longtime friend, assistant, and protégée, in her capacity as vice-president of the World Movement for World Federal Government, issued a news release in June 1948 announcing that, in addition to the parliamentary nominators, many university presidents and professors of law and political science in those countries and in the United States had endorsed Schwimmer's candidacy for the prize. The Swedish, Swiss, and Hungarian sections of the Women's International League for Peace and Freedom also supported her. Schwimmer's considerable accomplishments made her, according to Wynner, an appropriate candidate for the peace prize. She urged supporters to write to the Nobel Committee in Oslo to promote Schwimmer's selection. Soon Wynner issued a similar, shorter appeal on the letterhead, "International Committee for the 1948 Nobel Peace Prize Candidacy of Rosika Schwimmer."[12]

The prize was to be announced in November. Rosika Schwimmer died 3 August 1948 of bronchial pneumonia,[13] having suffered for years from respiratory difficulties. (For a summary of her health problems toward the end of her life, see Appendix Z.) On 19 November, a *New York Times* headline announced, "No '48 Peace Prize; Suitable Person Lacking." The rules of the prize forbade "the prize to any but living persons."[14] Had death prevented her from receiving the prize she apparently coveted? No, it would have been awarded to Count Folke Bernadotte, a Swedish diplomat who had been appointed United Nations Mediator to Palestine on 21 May 1948. In June he had negotiated a cease-fire in the Israeli-Arab war, and had labored mightily for peaceful relations between the two sides. On 17 September, Bernadotte was assassinated in an ambush by "Jewish irregulars" and so could not receive the Nobel Peace Prize.[15] Schwimmer would not have received the prize if she had lived. After a life of disappointments, not the least of which was denial of American citizenship, death sheltered Rosika Schwimmer from still another great defeat.[16]

In the wake of *Girouard*, *The Christian Century* had begged Douglas Clyde Macintosh to reapply for citizenship. The *Century* and others hoped to see the wrong to him corrected. Yet the *Century* editors were not as sure as apparently even Justice William O. Douglas had been that *Girouard* actually made citizenship possible for Macintosh. It was not clear that the language of *Girouard* covered Macintosh's views on war. The *Century* found

> nothing in the actual text of the Girouard decision which deals with the vital issue raised by Dr. Macintosh. The right of individual conscience to pass on the judgment of Congress in voting a declaration of war seems untouched in the pronouncement written by Justice Douglas, and hence to remain in a sort of legal twilight zone.

It was imperative, then, that Macintosh reapply for citizenship. That was the only way for the issue to be clarified. "We trust that he will do so without delay."[17] But it was not to be.

On 3 May 1946 (*Girouard* had been handed down 22 April), Porter R. Chandler, a member of John W. Davis's law firm wrote to Macintosh, calling his attention to *Girouard* and indicating that the way seemed to be open for a reconsideration of his case and admission to citizenship, "if you still desire to obtain it." The firm had already asked one of its associates in Washington to inquire of the Clerk of the Supreme Court about procedure. They concluded that it would be impossible to request the Court to rehear the case after all these years. The associate also had inquired of the Immigration and Naturalization Commission, which had suggested that Macintosh would have to reapply for citizenship at the District Court level with the assumption that if everything else were acceptable, his religious objection to war would not be a barrier, since the Supreme Court had explicitly vacated his case. Davis's firm recommended that Macintosh should obtain counsel and file a new application at the U.S. District Court in New Haven, where he still lived.[18]

Another letter from Chandler, dated 9 May 1946 and addressed to Mrs. Macintosh, indicates that the Davis firm was aware that Professor Macintosh had retired, but had not known of his debilitating stroke. In light of his health problems, only he, of course, could decide to pursue naturalization. Mrs. Macintosh had asked in her reply to the first letter if there were any legal reason why a handicapped person could not seek naturalization. Chandler answered that the law would not make his physical condition an impediment if he were otherwise qualified. This appears to be the last correspondence between the Davis law firm and Mrs. Macintosh.[19]

Roger Baldwin of the ACLU wrote to Professor Macintosh on 22 January 1947 (the same day he had written to Schwimmer that he would be in touch with Macintosh and Bland), suggesting that a private bill should be introduced in Congress as an alternative to having Macintosh reapply and go through the entire naturalization process again. "Would you be willing to have your case so handled? Or have you taken other steps?" He wrote again on 30 January, this time to Mrs. Macintosh. She had replied to his earlier letter, telling him of her husband's precarious health. She apparently also said that at this late time in his life, Professor Macintosh still had great affection for Canada.[20] "I would hardly think it wise in view of his condition and his strong Canadian loyalties for him to apply again," Baldwin responded. "There ought to be an easy way to correct such an injustice in the light of the later wisdom of the court. But unhappily there is not." He wrote in pen at the bottom: "My warm regards to you both."[21] This appears to be the last correspondence from anyone about the possibility of American citizenship for Macintosh.

Professor Macintosh died 6 July 1948 at his home in New Haven. He was 71. An obituary described him as "one of the great empiricists of religion of the modern day," whose "reputation was world-wide." In considerable detail the article recounted books he had written, lectures he had given at great universities, and honorary degrees he had received, all to demonstrate his considerable reputation. Yet "Dr. Macintosh's reputation as a scholar . . . was over-shadowed, in the popular mind, by his unsuccessful two-year battle to gain American citizenship."[22] So it was that a man who accomplished so many things came to the end of his life unsuccessful in a cause of great import to him, because he held tenaciously to a principle based on his understanding of the will of God.

Death did not, however, bring an end to Dr. Macintosh's citizenship saga. In 1977 Paul Douglas Macintosh Keane enrolled in Yale Divinity School as a student. Mr. Keane's parents had been good friends with Professor Macintosh. Macintosh had been the sponsor of the youth group at the Baptist church in New Haven when Mr. Keane's parents were teenagers and had made enormous contributions to their lives. They named their son after Macintosh in gratitude for his ministry and friendship to them. Paul Keane had never met his namesake, but he knew much about him because of what his parents had told him. When he got to Yale, it dawned on him that a fitting memorial to Macintosh would be to gain citizenship for him posthumously. He discussed this with Roland Bainton, Titus Street Professor of Church History Emeritus, who had been a friend of Macintosh. A former student of Professor Bainton was John C. Danforth, at the time United States Senator from Missouri. Professor

Bainton approached Senator Danforth about the possibility of a bill in Congress to award Macintosh honorary citizenship posthumously. His letter to Danforth recalled the Supreme Court decision denying citizenship to Macintosh and that *Girouard* had declared the previous decision to be bad law. He also mentioned Macintosh would undoubtedly have pursued citizenship himself after *Girouard*, but was prevented by his frail health. "I trust the attempt will not lapse."[23]

On 24 March 1981, Senator Danforth introduced a resolution, S.J. Res. 55. After several "whereas" clauses that rehearsed Macintosh's military, professional, and legal history, it concluded: "*Resolved by the Senate and House of Representatives of the United States of America in Congress assembled*, That the president is authorized and directed to declare by proclamation that Douglas Clyde Macintosh is an honorary citizen of the United States." (For the text of the resolution, see Appendix AA.) The resolution was passed by the Senate. Senator Danforth wrote to Professor Bainton that he was pleased to be part of the effort to achieve honorary citizenship for Macintosh. The resolution would now go to the House Judiciary Committee. He hoped it would be enacted promptly.[24] It was not.

On 27 April 1981, Richard Fairbanks, the Assistant Secretary for Congressional Relations of the State Department, wrote to Peter Rodino, Chair of the House Judiciary Committee, about the Macintosh resolution. The United States, Fairbanks wrote, does not grant honorary citizenship. It had happened only once in U.S. history, when Winston Churchill, son of an American mother, was granted honorary citizenship in 1963 because of his extraordinary service to the world during World War II. More recently the State Department had opposed requests to grant citizenship to Alexander Solzhenitsyn and Christopher Columbus. The United States, Fairbanks asserted, regards honorary citizenship as the highest honor it can bestow and must bestow it sparingly. Only those who have made a contribution to world history and to the wellbeing of the United States should receive such an honor. The State Department had no doubt that Professor Macintosh was a man of exceptional intellect, high principle, and commitment to the welfare of the nation. Yet those things could be said of many, and the State Department opposed granting honorary citizenship in his case.

A member of the House Judiciary Committee, Lawrence J. DeNardis of Connecticut, responded to that opinion, saying that the effort to award posthumous citizenship to Macintosh was not to honor him so much as to correct a prior injustice, the Court's denial of his application for citizenship. After the Court's *Girouard* decision, Macintosh was physically unable to pursue his own citizenship, which he surely could have obtained had he been able. This resolution intended simply to redress that miscarriage and would not endanger the concept of high tribute in honorary citizenship that the State Department was so anxious to preserve. DeNardis encouraged the department to rethink and change its opposition to Macintosh. Senator Danforth also wrote to the State Department, repeating and endorsing the comments made by Representative DeNardis.

The State Department responded that it still did not favor posthumous honorary citizenship for Macintosh, but suggested another plan that it did support, posthumous naturalization. There was considerable precedent for that. Since the plan intended to rectify the Court's denial of citizenship,

> Special legislation to provide posthumous citizenship, rather than honorary citizenship, would specifically rectify that denial, thereby drawing particular attention to its reasons and more clearly accomplishing the purpose of the bill. At the same time, such legislation would avoid extending the status of honorary citizenship and preserve its symbolic nature as this country's ultimate official recognition of extraordinary contributions to the world.[25]

I have found no other correspondence or other indication that this initiative was ever considered again.

Information about Marie Averil Bland after *Girouard* is much less complete than that about Schwimmer or Macintosh. Indeed, it is virtually nonexistent. I do not know what happened to her after her case was adjudicated.[26] She disappeared, as if she had been swallowed by the earth. Her father's will, written in November 1936, does not mention her or even acknowledge her existence.[27] There is, however, some indirect evidence that she lived past 1931. Two documents in the Schwimmer-Lloyd collection at the New York Public Library, written in 1947, refer to Bland's death. One discussion of who might benefit from a bill brought before Congress to provide citizenship to those who had been denied by the Supreme Court simply says, "As Nurse Marie Bland died," without any time attribution. Another treatment of the same topic indicates that "Miss Bland died *a few years ago*."[28] New York City telephone books listed a Marie A. Bland until 1943. She is not listed in 1944 or thereafter.

That is not definitive evidence of when and where she died, but it does fit these two vague references.

James Louis Girouard became an American citizen in 1946, as the result of the Supreme Court's decision. He was extremely proud to be an American. Yet aside from the brief moment of fame afforded by publicity about the case, he lived the rest of his life as routinely as he had before the decision. He continued to work as an engineer at the New England Sanitarium and Hospital. He retired in 1964, completing forty years of service to that institution. He and Mabel Kierstead had married in 1923. For a while she worked as a practical nurse at the same hospital where Girouard worked, but was stricken with multiple sclerosis and afflicted with that disease for 35 of the 45 years of their marriage. During most of that time she was an invalid. Girouard uncomplainingly cared for her until she died in September 1968, when he was 66 years old. They had one child and three grandchildren. Twelve years later, when he was 78, Girouard married Helen Josephine McClintock. He was already blind from glaucoma, a condition he endured for the last ten years of his life. Helen died in 1999.

A quiet, unassuming, humble man, Girouard was a devoted Seventh-day Adventist and a deacon in his Stoneham, Massachusetts, church. He was a strong believer in the church's belief on noncombatancy. His son-in-law, Carroll Medler, had been in the Navy before he married Girouard's daughter, Louise. But Medler had worked in the engine room of his ship and Girouard considered that to be noncombatant duty.

Girouard died of cancer. He was hospitalized for a while in the hospital where he had worked for so long, but he did not want to prolong his life, so refused treatment. He died at home, by his request, on 12 June 1991, at the age of 89. His funeral, in the Stoneham Seventh-day Adventist Church, filled the sanctuary, standing room only, in recognition of the life of this quiet, pleasant, principled man. His granddaughter told me that his two victories in life were his court case and his great-granddaughter, Jamie, who was named after him.[29]

Justice Robert Jackson once wrote of an alien who was seeking admission to the United States as a man "who seems to have led a life of unrelieved insignificance."[30] James Louis Girouard seems to have led a life of unrelieved insignificance, except to his family and friends. Yet as a man of conviction, he found himself in the national spotlight in 1946, when his case reversed a long-standing judicial precedent and set the stage for changing part of the law of immigration in this country.

Actually, legislation about naturalization candidates and bearing arms was proposed before *Girouard* was decided on 22 April 1946. On 16 April, Representative James Dolliver of Iowa introduced H.R. 6147, which would require applicants for citizenship to express explicitly their willingness to bear arms in defense of the United States. Citizenship of any naturalized person who refused to bear arms would be revoked.[31] Edith Wynner, Rosika Schwimmer's longtime friend and assistant, said that the American Legion had encouraged Dolliver to file the bill; she thought it exceedingly strange that the bill had been introduced shortly before *Girouard* was decided. "I wonder how it was that the American Legion was tipped off that the Supreme Court decision was going against them in this case," she wrote in a letter to Girouard's attorney, Homer Cummings. "I am grateful for your efforts to restore the right to freedom of conscience to applicants for naturalization. April 22nd becomes one of the most important dates in American history. I hope the American Legion does not succeed in fouling it again."[32] Edward J. Shaughnessy, Special Assistant to the Commissioner of the U.S. Immigration and Naturalization Service, sounded a similar theme. In a speech to a group interested in immigration and naturalization issues, he called H.R. 6147 "interesting" and "debatable." He noted that the bill was sponsored by the American Legion and set forth a long-standing position of that organization, that applicants for naturalization should promise to bear arms. "It is most coincidental that a bill containing the 'bear arms' provision should be introduced in the Congress on April 16th, of this year, when considered with the opinion handed down by the Supreme Court on Monday of this week, April 22nd." He referred, of course to *Girouard v. United States*.[33]

Representative Dolliver introduced his bill twice in the next session of Congress, H.R. 1191, 21 January 1947, and H.R. 2286, 27 February 1947. Both bills were referred to the House Judiciary Committee, where they died.[34] This seems to have been the last bill introduced to prohibit the naturalization of conscientious objectors. That is not surprising, given the holding in *Girouard*.

The Internal Security Act of 1950 was, despite its title, principally concerned with immigration and naturalization. The bill linked immigration policy to national security. Immediately after World War II, Congress became obsessed with the possibility that Nazis and former Nazis would enter the United States. Proposed legislation sought to close the immigration quota for Germans in order to keep Nazis out. Some thought that was too severe, but favored strict screening of German immigrants to prevent Nazis from entering. In 1946 the House of Representatives passed such a bill, but the Senate rejected it. By 1949 the focus was on Communists more than Nazis. Senator Pat McCarran of Nevada introduced legislation that would exclude from the country any member of the Communist party or any of its subsidiaries. After the hearings the language of the bill was broadened to exclude Communists or those affiliated with any other totalitarian organization. At this time Congress initiated a process to study the entire corpus of immigration and nationalization laws with the view of writing a comprehensive bill to reform those laws. Many in Congress believed that the issue of internal security of the nation could not wait until that massive project was completed, so a separate bill was proposed with the characteristics just described. Provisions were added to the bill to exact penalties on Americans who engaged in subversive activities or collaborated with Communists, Fascists, or any other persons posing a threat to American security.

Finally, on 20 September 1950, the internal security bill was passed and sent to President Truman. On 22 September, he vetoed the bill. The President objected to the breadth of the immigration restrictions. He believed the bill excluded former subversives who had renounced their former ideology. "Instead of trying to encourage the free movement of people, subject only to the real requirements of national security, these provisions attempt to bar movement to anyone who is, or once was, associated with ideas we dislike, and in the process, they would succeed in barring many people whom it would be to our advantage to admit." On 23 September Congress overrode President Truman's veto and the Internal Security Act of 1950 became law.[35]

The Internal Security Act of 1950 broke new ground in its treatment of applicants for citizenship who were conscientious objectors. Although the law restricted immigrants perceived to be "dangerous to the national interest" (an argument once used about conscientious objectors who applied for naturalization), for the first time in American history Congress, after the *Girouard* decision, provided that conscientious objectors could be naturalized.

The Internal Security Act was a stopgap measure passed while Congress was preparing comprehensive legislation on immigration and naturalization. It grew out of a huge report on immigration and naturalization prepared by the Senate Judiciary Committee.[36] That report's section on the oath of allegiance briefly rehearsed the tradition of the expectation that an applicant for citizenship could not be naturalized if a conscientious objector. "However," the report added, "the decision in the recent Girouard case leaves no alternative but to redefine the intent of the Congress in this matter." Following that statement was a long review of the issues and conclusions in *Schwimmer*, *Macintosh*, *Bland*, and *Girouard*. Following that commentary were "conclusions and recommendations." Number seven in that list addressed the issue of the naturalization of conscientious objectors.

> The subcommittee has given careful and serious consideration to all of the arguments for and against requiring a petitioner for naturalization to promise to bear arms in defense of this country. The subcommittee realizes that religious freedom and freedom of conscience is [*sic*] basic in our political and social life. The subcommittee is not prepared to affirm that, in every case, an alien petitioner for naturalization who has conscientious and religious scruples against bearing arms, even in defense of his country, would not, in all other respects, make a good American citizen and contribute his full share to the American way of life.
>
> Nevertheless, the subcommittee recommends that the oath of allegiance be amended to require specifically that the alien shall promise to bear arms if defense of the United States shall so require, unless the alien is conscientiously opposed to participation in war in any form, by reason of his religious training and belief. In such cases, in lieu of a promise to bear arms, the alien shall take an oath to defend the United States in noncombatant service. When any alien shall assert his opposition to participation in war in any form because of his personal religious training and belief, his opposition and his religious training and belief shall be made to appear to the court by clear and convincing evidence.[37]

The actual law—based on a bill that came from the House, H.R. 9490, and another from the Senate, S. 4037[38]—was constructed by a conference committee from the two houses. The section of the final bill modifying the oath of naturalization to include conscientious objectors had been part of the Senate bill, as the language quoted from Senate Report 1515 suggests. It was not included in the original House bill.[39] A minority report appended to the Senate Report on S. 4037 suggested that changes in the naturalization oath pertaining to conscientious objectors and some other naturalization procedures be differentiated in a separate bill because these provisions might be overwhelmed by the anti-Communist features of the bill and not receive the attention they deserved.[40] That did not happen, and consequently the Internal Security Act of 1950 contained the first legislative language to implement *Girouard*, the first language ever to support an opportunity for alien conscientious objectors to become American citizens.[41]

The language of the part of the Act that pertains to the naturalization of conscientious objectors (see the full text in Appendix BB) presents two forms of the oath of naturalization. In the first form, the applicant swears that he or she will bear arms in defense of the country or that he or she will perform noncombatant duty *in* the military when required by law. The second form of the oath does not mention service in the military at all. Indeed, it is the traditional language of the oath that confronted Rosika Schwimmer, Douglas Clyde Macintosh, Marie Averil Bland, and James Louis Girouard. In their cases, because of the "bearing arms" question on the application questionnaire and the decisions of the Supreme Court for the first three, the process presumed that the oath demanded bearing arms in defense of the United States. Now, in the Internal Security Act, the same language had the opposite meaning. Because the first form of the oath presumed either combatant or noncombatant service in the military, the second form of the oath, the traditional language, now presumed the oath-taker would not serve in the military.[42] In order to be able to take that form of the oath that enabled one to avoid some form of military service, one's conscientious objection had to be based on "religious training or belief." This phrase was taken from the two selective service laws passed before the Internal Security Act of 1950.[43] A nonreligious, philosophical conscientious objector could not be naturalized under the Internal Security Act of 1950.

Simultaneously with the debate on the Internal Security Act, Congress conducted a thorough study of the immigration and naturalization laws. That report, published April 1950,[44] stimulated the language that appeared in the Internal Security Act, but the overhaul of the immigration and naturalization laws recommended in the report was far from complete. Subcommittees of the Committees on the Judiciary of both the House and Senate conducted joint hearings on. S. 716, introduced by Senator Pat McCarran, H.R. 2379, introduced by Representative Francis Walter, and H.R. 2816—a bill with much less emphasis on immigration quotas than the other two—introduced by Representative Emmanuel Celler.[45]

The subcommittees published a 727-page report of the hearings on the three proposed bills. Although the bills were huge, since each was to be a comprehensive immigration and naturalization law drawing much comment from expert witnesses, there is remarkably little reaction to the proposed section concerning naturalization of conscientious objectors. Indeed the language from opponents and proponents alike was not as emotional as it had been in the 1930s.

The Veterans of Foreign Wars of the United States opposed the bill, arguing not only that no person should be naturalized who objected to military service, but also that such persons should be deported.[46] The Disabled American Veterans joined in that view. Yet that group's opposition was not quite so absolute. It also recognized the effect of *Girouard*. It advocated that the new law should be consistent with that case, but not go any further. In stating that point, the representative who testified before Congress in these hearings was inconsistent with the resolution passed in 1950 by the DAV convention.[47] The American Legion representative touched the issue only lightly, noting that the section of the bills on the naturalization of conscientious objectors required that they swear to bear arms (completely ignoring the language immediately following that allowed such people to choose noncombatant service in the military or service of national importance under civilian control). The American Legion enthusiastically supported such language, saying that it had long been needed. The U.S. Justice Department stated that the Internal Security Act had enacted the possibility for conscientious objectors to be naturalized. The proposed bills eliminated the possibility and that was a good thing.[48]

Three persons from the National Council on Naturalization and Citizenship appeared at the hearings. Two of them addressed the issue of naturalization of conscientious objectors. They supported the language before Congress. They approved exemptions from military service based on religious training and belief. But the organization took issue with the proposed language of the oath, requiring, as it did, with the use of the word "and," that aliens swear to bear arms, do noncombatant service and work of national importance under civilian direction. It was impossible to do all three. Consequently, their testimony recommended that the word "and" be replaced with "or," so that the oath actually gave an alien applicant some choices as to what he or she might agree to do in service to the United States. Congress should either modify the language or simply retain the language of the International Security Act of 1950. A representative of several Jewish groups expressed the same view.[49] The ACLU also objected to the proposed language of the law and suggested retaining the language of the Internal Security Act. The ACLU representative emphatically supported the right of conscientious objectors to be naturalized. A Mennonite spokesman agreed with that argument, but the ACLU went further. It was not enough that the objection be based on "religious training and belief." Persons with humanitarian objections to war should be granted citizenship upon application, also.[50] The representative of Americans for Democratic Action pursued the last point vigorously. Naturalization should not be limited to those whose objections to war were religiously based, but should be extended to those who had philosophical or humanitarian objections as well. If it were just a matter of a person not wanting to fight, that person should not be awarded citizenship, but if one offered real, rational reasons for refusing to bear arms, he or she should be equally eligible for citizenship with persons who gave religiously based reasons.[51]

After the hearings were completed, the bills were modified and then reintroduced as S. 2055 and H.R. 5678. The House Report on the latter bill, referring to naturalization of conscientious objectors, acknowledged that *Girouard* had changed previous law. In light of that, the House declared,

> The bill is designed to place the naturalized citizen in the same position as the native-born citizen by requiring the naturalized citizen to promise to bear arms on behalf of the United States when required by law, or to perform noncombatant service in the Armed Forces of the United States when required by law, or to perform work of national importance under civilian direction when required by law.[52]

Since the debates, both public and in legal briefs, in the 1930s about the relation of candidates for citizenship to native-born citizens, the tone has changed. When *Schwimmer*, *Macintosh*, and *Bland* were being debated and briefed, opponents always argued that applicants for citizenship and native-born citizens were not the same, that the former had to meet a higher standard than the latter. Here the rationale for the proposed legislation is that they must be equally situated. This language also adds a third choice for the alien conscientious objector. In addition to bearing arms or serving as a noncombatant in the military, both of which were provided by the Internal Security Act of 1950, there is a possibility of work in service to the nation under civilian supervision, which was not part of the earlier Act.

These were truly choices because the different modes of service are separated by the word "or" rather than "and."[53] These points were confirmed in an exchange on the floor of the House of Representatives about the provision in the law for the naturalization of conscientious objectors. In that dialogue, the author of H.R. 5678, Representative Francis Walter, confirmed that an applicant for citizenship had three choices because the word "or" was used between the clauses setting forth the choices. These choices would make prospective citizens equal with the native-born in opportunities to avoid participating in war. Traditional pacifist groups such as Quakers and Mennonites were satisfied with the language of the bill.[54]

After congressional debate the Conference Committee with members from both the House and the Senate issued a final report on the law containing the final language of the bill. Both houses of Congress approved the bill and sent it to President Truman on 10 June 1952. The President vetoed the bill on 25 June, principally because he believed it retained a national origin quota system for the number of immigrants who could enter during any given year. He believed it was too restrictive. After a final, intense, debate, Congress overrode the veto and the Immigration and Naturalization Act, commonly known as the McCarran-Walter Act, became law on 27 June 1952.[55] The Act now clearly defined the process and requirements for naturalization of conscientious objectors.

Sec. 337. (a) A person who has petitioned for naturalization shall, in order to be and before being admitted to citizenship, take in open court an oath (1) to support the Constitution of the United States; (2) to renounce and abjure absolutely and entirely all allegiance and fidelity to any foreign prince, potentate, state, or sovereignty of whom or which the petitioner was before a subject or citizen; (3) to support and defend the Constitution and the laws of the United States against all enemies, foreign and domestic; (4) to bear true faith and allegiance to the same; and (5) (A) to bear arms on behalf of the United States when required by the law, or (B) to perform noncombatant service in the Armed Forces of the United States when required by the law, or (C) to perform work of national importance under civilian direction when required by the law. Any such person shall be required to take an oath containing the substance of clauses (1) through (5) of the preceding sentence, except that a person who shows by clear and convincing evidence to the satisfaction of the naturalization court that he is opposed to the bearing of arms in the Armed Forces of the United States by reason of religious training and belief shall be required to take an oath containing the substance of clauses (1) through (4) and clauses (5) (B) and (5) (C), and a person who shows by clear and convincing evidence to the satisfaction of the naturalization court that he is opposed to any type of service in the Armed Forces of the United States by reason of religious training and belief shall be required to take an oath containing the substance of clauses (1) through (4) and clause (5) (C). The term "religious training and belief" as used in this section shall mean an individual's belief in a relation to a Supreme Being involving duties superior to those arising from any human relation, but does not include essentially political, sociological, or philosophical views or a merely personal moral code.[56]

Although *Girouard* declared *Schwimmer* and *Macintosh* to be no longer good law, neither Rosika Schwimmer nor Douglas Clyde Macintosh would have been eligible for citizenship under this provision of the McCarran-Walter Act. Schwimmer would have been refused citizenship because the law specified that qualifying conscientious objection must be based on "religious training and belief" and not "political, sociological, or philosophical views or a merely personal moral code." As an atheist, Schwimmer was clearly a philosophical pacifist. Macintosh's conscientious objection was based on religious training and belief, but the law does not allow selective conscientious objection. When Professor Roland Bainton wrote to Senator John Danforth, asking his help in obtaining posthumous honorary citizenship for Macintosh, he said his primary interest was in vindicating the principle of selective conscientious objection. That did not happen. There is no language in the Naturalization Act that would allow one to make a decision about which wars in which to fight. One may not, as a prospective citizen, pick and choose the wars in which one will fight. Even after *Girouard* and the radical liberalization of the Naturalization Act and oath, Douglas Clyde Macintosh, with his particular religious objection to war, still could not have become an American citizen. Of the principals who were denied citizenship by decisions of the Supreme Court, only Marie Averil Bland would have benefitted from the modification of the law in the Internal Security Act of 1950 or the Immigration and Nationality Act of 1952.

The language of the statute has remained virtually intact since 1952. In its current form, the law reads:

Sec. 1448. Oath of renunciation and allegiance
(a) Public ceremony
A person who has applied for naturalization shall, in order to be and before being admitted to citizenship, take in a public ceremony before

the Attorney General or a court with jurisdiction under section 1421(b) of this title an oath (1) to support the Constitution of the United States; (2) to renounce and abjure absolutely and entirely all allegiance and fidelity to any foreign prince, potentate, state, or sovereignty of whom or which the applicant was before a subject or citizen; (3) to support and defend the Constitution and the laws of the United States against all enemies, foreign and domestic; (4) to bear true faith and allegiance to the same; and (5)(A) to bear arms on behalf of the United States when required by the law, or (B) to perform noncombatant service in the Armed Forces of the United States when required by the law, or (C) to perform work of national importance under civilian direction when required by the law. Any such person shall be required to take an oath containing the substance of clauses (1) to (5) of the preceding sentence, except that a person who shows by clear and convincing evidence to the satisfaction of the Attorney General that he is opposed to the bearing of arms in the Armed Forces of the United States by reason of religious training and belief shall be required to take an oath containing the substance of clauses (1) to (4) and clauses (5)(B) and (5)(C) of this subsection, and a person who shows by clear and convincing evidence to the satisfaction of the Attorney General that he is opposed to any type of service in the Armed Forces of the United States by reason of religious training and belief shall be required to take an oath containing the substance of said clauses (1) to (4) and clause (5)(C). The term "religious training and belief" as used in this section shall mean an individual's belief in a relation to a Supreme Being involving duties superior to those arising from any human relation, but does not include essentially political, sociological, or philosophical views or a merely personal moral code.[57]

Consequently, the language of the oath of naturalization itself now is:

I hereby declare, on oath, that I absolutely and entirely renounce and abjure all allegiance and fidelity to any foreign prince, potentate, state, or sovereignty, of whom or which I have heretofore been a subject or citizen; that I will support and defend the Constitution and laws of the United States of America against all enemies, foreign and domestic; that I will bear true faith and allegiance to the same: that I will bear arms on behalf of the United States when required by the law; that I will perform noncombatant service in the Armed Forces of the United States when required by the law; that I will perform work of national importance under civilian direction when required by the law; and that I take this obligation freely, without any mental reservation or purpose of evasion; so help me God.

The federal regulation that formulates this language of the oath also specifies that when an applicant for naturalization "is exempt from taking the oath . . . in its entirety, the inapplicable clauses shall be deleted and the oath shall be taken in such altered form."[58]

The language of the law requiring that objection to bearing arms must be based on religious training and belief was derived from the Selective Service Acts of 1940 and 1948. Those laws defined the phrase "religious training and belief" to mean "an individual's belief in a relation to a Supreme Being." That language is retained in the naturalization statute into the present, but the "Supreme Being" phrase was removed from the Selective Service law in 1967.[59] That change in the language emerged undoubtedly from the Supreme Court's interpretations of conscientious objector dimensions of the Selective Service laws during and after the Vietnam war. Those cases, *United States v. Seeger*[60] and *Welsh v. United States*[61] (see Chapter One) are pertinent here. They asked the Supreme Court to determine whether applicants for conscientious objector status in the draft could receive that status if their religious beliefs were unconventional, that is, if they did not believe in a personal "Supreme Being." The Court answered that they could be considered conscientious objectors. Congress had used "Supreme Being" rather than "God" in the statute to show that Congress did not have a narrow definition of religious training and belief in mind. To determine whether an unconventional believer's conscientious objection was based on religious training and belief, the Court formulated a test: "[D]oes the claimed belief occupy the same place in the life of the objector as an orthodox belief in God holds in the life of one clearly qualified for the exemption?"[62] I call this a "double sincerity test." The draft board compared the sincerity of belief of an unconventional believer against the sincerity of belief of a hypothetical (or real) person with a conventional belief in God who clearly qualified for conscientious objector status. If the quality of belief was comparable, the unconventional believer received the status. *Welsh* took this to the extreme of giving objector status to one who did not even know he was religious, but was religious under the expanded definition of *Seeger*.

Courts since the 1970s have used the *Seeger* and *Welsh* concept to interpret the "religious training and belief" language of the naturalization oath statute, allowing wide latitude in admission of applicants for citizenship who are conscientious objectors. Almost any sort of religious belief will meet the standard of religious training and belief. Indeed, the *Seeger* and *Welsh* formulations "have effectively eliminated the 'personal moral code' disqualifier in the statute, by restricting it to those situations in which it is the sole basis for the registrant's belief."[63] It is a development for which Rosika Schwimmer, Douglas Clyde Macintosh, and Marie Averil Bland struggled, but never lived to see.

Notes

1. With thanks to Richard Strauss (1864-1949), composer of *Death and Transfiguration*, (originally *Tod und Verklärung*), opus 24, 1889.

2. Marx to Schwimmer, 28 November 1939; Schwimmer to Marx, 10 January 1940; Schwimmer-Lloyd collection, box G-24.

3. Schwimmer to Margarete Schurgast, 4 August 1946; Schwimmer to Augusta Markowitz, 5 August 1946; Schwimmer to Judge Dorothy Kenyon, 4 August 1946; Schwimmer-Lloyd collection, box G-24.

4. Beth S. Wenger, "Radical Politics in a Reactionary Age: *The Unmaking of Rosika Schwimmer, 1914-1930*," *Journal of Women's History* 2 (Fall 1990): 80, 89-90.

5. Catt to Schwimmer, 15 October 1946; Schwimmer to Catt (1), 17 December 1946; Schwimmer to Catt (2), 17 December 1946; Schwimmer-Lloyd collection, box G-24. In a letter to Catt on 22 October 1946, Schwimmer discussed her citizenship dilemma in detail (see Appendix Y).

6. Baldwin to Schwimmer, 14 January 1947; Schwimmer to Baldwin, 16 January 1947; Baldwin to Schwimmer, 22 January 1947; Schwimmer's notes on a telephone conversation, Schwimmer and Baldwin, 11 February 1947; Schwimmer-Lloyd collection, box G-24.

7. Schwimmer to Catt, 11 February 1947; Schwimmer to Catt, 16 February 1947; Schwimmer to Alda Wilson, 24 March 1947; Schwimmer-Lloyd collection, box G-24. Jacqueline Van Voris, "Catt, Carrie Chapman" in *American National Biography*, John A. Garraty and Mark C. Carnes, eds. (New York: Oxford University Press, 1999) 4: 582-84.

8. That bill, H.R. 6147, strongly supported by the American Legion, had been introduced in Congress on 16 April 1946, six days before *Girouard* was handed down. It proposed to make the promise to bear arms mandatory for any applicant for citizenship and to cancel the citizenship of any person already naturalized who refused to bear arms. See Edith Wynner to Homer S. Cummings, 2 May 1946; Edward J. Shaughnessy, Special Assistant to the Commissioner, U.S. Immigration and Naturalization Service, a paper entitled "Nationality Legislation" read at the conference of the National Council on Naturalization and Citizenship, 26 April 1946; Schwimmer-Lloyd collection, box G-24.

9. Frances Levenson to Schwimmer, 5 May 1947; Schwimmer-Lloyd collection, box G-24.

10. S. C. Stanley, "Seneca Falls Woman's Rights Convention (July 198-20, 1848)," in *Dictionary of Christianity in America*, Daniel G. Reid, and others, eds. (Downers Grove, Ill.: InterVarsity Press, 1990), 1073.

11. Rosika Schwimmer, "We Must Not Fail in Our Pledge to End War," *Peace News for War-Resistance and World-Community* (23 July 1948); Schwimmer-Lloyd Collection, box G-24.

12. Edith Wynner, "Rosika Schwimmer," 737; Obituary, *Nation* 167 (14 August 1948): 171; Edith Wynner, Vice-President, World Movement for World Federal Government, "For Immediate Release," June 1948; Edith Wynner, Corresponding Secretary, International Committee for the 1948 Nobel Peace Prize Candidacy of Rosika Schwimmer," open letter, June 1948; Swarthmore Peace Collection.

13. On 9 August 1948 Franciska Schwimmer and Edith Wynner announced that

"With deep sorrow we inform you of the death of Rosika Schwimmer on August 3, 1948, in New York City, at the age of seventy.

"She had bequested her brain and body for the service of medical science and by her wish her remains were cremated without ceremony or memorial.

"Those of her friends who wish to honor her memory will help create a decent home for mankind within the framework of world federal government by giving moral and financial support to the world government organizations in their countries." Swarthmore Peace Collection.

14. "No '48 Peace Prize; Suitable Person Lacking," *New York Times*, 19 November 1948, 29.

15. "Bernadotte Is Slain in Jerusalem; Killers called 'Jewish Irregulars'; Security Council Will Act Today," *New York Times*, 18 September 1948, 1; Editorial, "Count Bernadotte; Responsibility for His Death to Be Shared by All," *New York Times*, 24 September 1948, 24.

16. In 1942 Schwimmer and Lola Maverick Lloyd gave their papers to the New York Public Library. Not until 1974 were the papers arranged, cataloged, and opened for research. They are a treasure trove of information about pacifism, the women's movement, efforts for women's suffrage, and a variety of other causes in which the two women were involved. From 16 May until 15 August 1979, the New York Public Library publicly displayed some materials from the collection. The exhibition, "Arms and the Woman: United States v. Rosika Schwimmer," marked the fiftieth anniversary of the United States Supreme Court decision that denied her citizenship. See Edith Wynner, "Schwimmer-Lloyd Papers Open for Research," *World Peace News* (February 1974): 6 and (March 1974): 4; Edith Wynner, Consultant, Schwimmer-Lloyd Collection of the New York Public Library, "Arms and the Woman: United States v. Rosika Schwimmer," *News Release* (May 1979)" 1-3; Schwimmer-Lloyd collection. As Beth Wenger ("Schwimmer, Rosika," in *Jewish Women in America: An Historical Encyclopedia*, Paula E. Hyman and Deborah Dash Moore, eds. [New York: Routledge, 1997]: 1222) has written, Schwimmer "emerged as one of the most powerful political players in the international feminist and pacifist movements, but

she also paid the price for living in an era of right-wing backlash, xenophobia, and anti-Semitism. Despite her many challenges and setbacks, Rosika Schwimmer never abandoned her unshakable devotion to achieving the goals of world peace and equality."

17. "Dr. Macintosh—Apply Again!" *Christian Century* 63 (8 May 1946): 583-84.

18. Porter R. Chandler to Macintosh, 3 May 1946; DCM Scrapbook. By this time the firm was known as Davis Polk Wardwell Sunderland & Kiendl.

19. Chandler to Mrs. Douglas C. Macintosh, 9 May 1946; DCM Scrapbook. Mrs. Macintosh usually noted on a letter the date she answered it. I find no such notation on the letter of 9 May.

20. "I was destined to be to the end 'a stranger within thy gates,'" Macintosh wrote in 1939. "I was to be *in* this American world, but not quite *of* it. But there is, perhaps, a bright side to the picture. I was to have two countries, the land of my birth and the land of my adoption. I can sing 'My country, 'tis of thee,' and mean part of it for Canada and part of it for the United States. These are my two countries, and I love them both." (Douglas Clyde Macintosh, *Social Religion* [New York: Charles Scribner's Sons, 1939], xi; emphasis in original.) Along the way Macintosh's affection for Canada began to intensify, so that by the time *Girouard* made citizenship possible, he was not interested. "Mr. Macintosh had stood for freedom of conscience no doubt since his boyhood," Mrs. Macintosh wrote to the Davis law firm, ". . . but with all he was a Canadian and a Britisher. . . . He was deeply disappointed with the Supreme Court decision, but in the depths there was profound compensation. The ancient loyalties could prevail." See William H. Harbaugh, *Lawyer's Lawyer: The Life of John W. Davis* (New York: Oxford University Press, 1973), 297-98.

21. Roger Baldwin to Macintosh, 22 January 1947; Baldwin to Mrs. Douglas C. Macintosh, 30 January 1947; DCM Scrapbook.

22. "Dr. Macintosh, Yale Theology Professor, Dies," *New York Herald Tribune*, 7 July 1948.

23. Telephone conversation, Ronald B. Flowers and Paul Douglas Macintosh Keane, 4 December 1999; Keane to Flowers, 6 December 1999; Bainton to Danforth, 19 February 1981; Roland Bainton papers, Yale Divinity School Library, manuscript group 75.

24. Danforth to Bainton, 27 March 1981; *Congressional Record: Daily Digest, Senate* 24 March 1981, D 300; Yale Divinity School Library, Bainton Papers, manuscript group 75.

25. Richard Fairbanks to Peter Rodino, 27 April 1981; Lawrence J. DeNardis to Fairbanks, 12 May 1981; Danforth to Fairbanks, 27 May 1981; Fairbanks to DeNardis, undated. All obtained from the United States Department of State under the Freedom of Information Act request # 9404254. Christopher R. Brewster, who was on Senator Danforth's staff at the time and drafted the language for S.J. Res. 55, confirms this story. According to Brewster, the House Judiciary Committee shared the State Department's misgivings about awarding citizenship through legislation, Representative DeNardis's letter notwithstanding. This may explain

why Peter Rodino, the chair of the Judiciary Committee, did not respond to the judgment of the State Department. Brewster recalls that no one opposed the bill on the basis that Macintosh had been a conscientious objector, or that he was in any way unworthy of citizenship. It was just the question of whether Congress should grant citizenship. The consensus was "No." Christopher R. Brewster to Ronald B. Flowers, 4 March 1994.

26. I have inquired of the archives of the General Synod of the Church of England, London; the Nursing Archives of the Mugar Memorial Library, Boston University; the Southwest Center for Nursing History, University of Texas at Austin; the Canadian Association for the History of Nursing; the Archives of the Episcopal Church; the Guild of Saint Barnabas for Nurses (Episcopal); the Royal College of Nursing, London; Grace Episcopal Church of New York; the Episcopal Peace Fellowship; the Swarthmore College Peace Collection; the United States Immigration and Naturalization Service, under the Freedom of Information Act; the Church of Jesus Christ of Latter-day Saints genealogical database; and two independent researchers. None of these, except the Swarthmore College Peace Collection, had even heard of Marie Averil Bland.

27. "Last Will and Testament of Edward Michael Bland," 6 November 1936, obtained through the Department of Public Records, London, England.

28. Schwimmer to Alda Wilson, 24 March 1947; Frieda Langer Lazarus to Senator Wayne Morse, 28 July 1947, emphasis added; Schwimmer-Lloyd collection, box G-24.

29. These paragraphs rely on telephone conversations with two friends of Girouard, David Stone and Robert Whitney, in 1990, and several phone conversations and personal visits with his two grandchildren, Holly Howes and Harvey Medler, 1990-2001.

30. Justice Robert H. Jackson, dissenting in *Shaughnessy v. Mezei* 345 U.S. 206 at 219. In this case the government opposed a man seeking entry to the United States, but would not reveal why, even in a court of law, pleading "national security." "This man, who seems to have led a life of unrelieved insignificance," Jackson wrote, "must have been astonished to find himself suddenly putting the Government of the United States in such fear that it was afraid to tell him why it was afraid of him."

31. "H.R. 6147. Mr. Dolliver: April 16, 1946 (Immigration and Naturalization)," *Digest of Public General Bills*, 79th Congress, 2d Session (Washington, D.C.: Library of Congress, 1946, #6), 86.

32. Wynner to Cummings, 2 May 1946; Schwimmer-Lloyd collection, box G-24.

33. Edward J. Shaughnessy, "Nationality Legislation," speech before the Annual Conference of the National Council on Naturalization and Citizenship, 16 April 1946; Schwimmer-Lloyd collection, box G-24. I have found no documentation that the American Legion supported this bill, however much members of the Legion may have sympathized with its denial of naturalization to conscientious objectors.

34. *Digest of Public General Bills*, 89th Congress, 1st Session (Washington, D.C.: Library of Congress, 1947, 4), 171, 218.

35. Robert A. Divine, *American Immigration Policy, 1924-1952* (New Haven: Yale University Press, 1957), 160-63. The law's citation is 64 *Statutes at Large* 987. Roscoe Baker, *The American Legion and American Foreign Policy* (New York: Bookman Associates, 1954), 103-104. The American Legion strongly supported the Internal Security Act and strenuously urged overturning Truman's veto.

36. "The Immigration and Naturalization Systems of the United States," *Report of the Committee on the Judiciary Pursuant to S. Res. 139: A Resolution to Make an Investigation of the Immigration System*, Senate Report 1515, 81st Congress, 2d Session, 20 April 1950, hereinafter referred to as "Senate Report 1515."

37. Senate Report 1515, 741-46.

38. *Digest of Public General Bills*, 81st Congress, 2d Session (Washington, D.C.: Library of Congress, 1951, 7), 46-47, 197.

39. "Internal Security Act of 1950," *Conference Report to Accompany H.R. 9490*, House of Representatives Report 3112, 81st Congress, 2d Session, 19 September 1950, 48, 52, 62.

40. "Protecting the Internal Security of the United States," *Report to Accompany S. 4037*, Senate Report 2369, Part 2, Minority Views, 81st Congress, 2d Session, 17 August 1950, 19.

41. 64 *Statutes at Large* 987; Divine, *American Immigration Policy*, 162-63.

42. "Internal Security Act of 1950," (*Conference Report to Accompany H.R. 9490*, House of Representatives Report 3112, 81st Congress, 2d Session, 19 September 1950, 62) explicitly spells out this conclusion. "Section 29 of the conference substitute amends section 335 of the Nationality Act of 1940 to provide that there shall be included in the oath required for naturalization a provision that the petitioner will bear arms on behalf of the United States or perform noncombatant service when required by law. However, if the petitioner satisfies the naturalization court that he is opposed to bearing arms or to performing noncombatant service by reason of religious training or belief, he may take an oath which does not include a promise to bear arms or to perform noncombatant service."

43. Selective Service Act of 1940: "Nothing contained in this Act shall be construed to require any person to be subject to combatant training and service in the land or naval forces of the United States who, by reason of religious training and belief, is conscientiously opposed to participation in war in any form" (54 *Statutes at Large* 885 at 889 § 5[g]).

Selective Service Act of 1948: "Nothing contained in this title shall be construed to require any person to be subject to combatant training and service in the armed forces of the United States who, by reason of religious training and belief, is conscientiously opposed to participating in war in any form. Religious training and belief in this connection means an individual's belief in a relation to a Supreme Being involving duties superior to those arising from any human relation, but does not include essentially political, sociological, or philosophical views or a merely personal moral code" (62 *Statutes at Large* 604 at 612-613 § 6[j]). The explanation of "religious training and belief" in the 1948 law quotes verbatim a phrase from Chief Justice Charles Evans Hughes's dissent in *United States v. Macintosh* 283 U.S. 605 at 633-34.

44. Senate Report 1515.

45. "Revision of Immigration, Naturalization, and Nationality Laws," *Joint Hearings Before the Subcommittees of the Committees on the Judiciary, Congress of the United States on S. 716, H.R. 2397, and H.R. 2816*, 82nd Congress, 1st Session, 6-21 March and 9 April 1951. Hereinafter cited as *Joint Hearings*.

46. Statement of Omar B. Ketchum, Legislative Director of the Veterans of Foreign Wars of the United States, *Joint Hearings*, 9-10.

47. Statement of Charles E. Foster, Assistant Legislative Director of the Disabled American Veterans. The DAV resolution read:

"Whereas the Supreme Court of the United States held on April 22, 1946, that it is not a prerequisite of citizenship that an alien applicant be willing to bear arms in the defence of this country; and

"Whereas the Disabled American Veterans is concerned about the future welfare and security of this Nation: Now, therefore, be it

"*Resolved*, That the Disabled American Veterans, assembled in its twenty-ninth national convention in San Francisco, Calif., August 13-19, 1950, urge the Congress to enact legislation making it mandatory for any alien seeking citizenship in the United States to affirmatively state under oath that he will support and defend the Constitution of the United States, and, if necessary, bear arms to protect the liberty and freedom which this country has enjoyed for more than 150 years" (*Joint Hearings*, 13-14, 15).

48. Statement of A. Luke Crispe, Chairman of the National Americanism Commission of the American Legion, *Joint Hearings*, 27; Statement by Peyton Ford, Deputy Attorney General, *Joint Hearings*, 720.

49. Statement of Mrs. Ruth Z. Murphy, Member of the Legislative Committee of the National Council on Naturalization and Citizenship, *Joint Hearings*, 84-85; Statement of Henry F. Butler, Washington, D.C., Appearing as a Member of the Legislative Committee of the National Council on Naturalization and Citizenship, *Joint Hearings*, 98-100, 110-11; Statement of Simon H. Rifkind on Behalf of the Synagogue Council of America, the American Jewish Committee, the American Jewish Congress, the Anti-Defamation League of B'nai B'rith, the Jewish Labor Committee, the Jewish War Veterans of the United States, and 27 Local Community Councils, Comprising the National Community Relations Advisory Council, the Hebrew Immigrant Aid Society (HIAS), and United Service for New Americans (USNA), *Joint Hearings*, 594.

50. Statement of Edward J. Ennis, on Behalf of the American Civil Liberties Union, *Joint Hearings*, 147-48; Statement of J. Harold Sherk, Executive Secretary of the Peace Section, Mennonite Central Committee, Akron, Pa., *Joint Hearings*, 760-61.

51. Statement of Stanley H. Lowell, Appearing on Behalf of Americans for Democratic Action, Washington, D.C., *Joint Hearings*, 438-40, 450.

52. "Revising the Laws Relating to Immigration, Naturalization, and Nationality," *Report to Accompany H.R. 5678*, House of Representatives Report 1365, 82d Congress, 2d Session, 14 February 1952, 82; for a short history of the legislation see 27-28.

53. These comparisons can be seen in House Report 1365, 286-87, where the proposed law and the existing law are printed in parallel columns.

54. "Revision of Laws Relating to Immigration, Naturalization, and Nationality," *Congressional Record—House*, 25 April 1952, 4422-23.

55. "Immigration and Nationality Act," *Conference Report to Accompany H.R. 5678*, House of Representatives Report 2096, 9 June 1952; Divine, *American Immigration Policy*, 183-86; 66 *Statutes at Large* 163 (1952).

56. 66 *Statutes at Large* 258, § 337(a).

57. 8 U.S.C § 1448(a).

58. 8 *Code of Federal Regulations* § 337.1 (a)(b), 1 January 2001 edition.

59. "Nothing contained in this title shall be construed to require any person to be subject to combatant training and service in the armed forces of the United States who, by reason of religious training and belief, is conscientiously opposed to war in any form. As used in this subsection, the term 'religious training and belief' does not include essentially political, sociological or philosophical views, or a merely personal moral code" (81 *Statutes at Large* 100 at 104 § [7]).

60. 380 U.S. 163 (1965).

61. 398 U.S. 333 (1970).

62. *United States v. Seeger* 380 U.S. 163 at 184. At 178 the Court expressed the test "in these words: A sincere and meaningful belief which occupies in the life of its possessor a place parallel to that filled by the God of those admittedly qualifying for the exemption comes within the statutory definition."

63. "Aliens and Citizens," 3C *American Jurisprudence 2d*, (Saint Paul, Minn.: West Group, 1962-), § 2854, 288-89; "Naturalization," 2A *Immigration Law Service: The Immigration and Naturalization Process* (Deerfield, Ill.: Clark, Boardman, Callaghan, rev. 1996) § 30:89, 75-76. For a full treatment of the "Oath of Renunciation and Allegiance," which contains the issue of conscientious objection, see 3C *American Jurisprudence 2d*, §§ 2850-61, 285-91 and 2A *Immigration Law Service*, "Oath of Renunciation and Allegiance," §§ 30:84-30:93, 71-77.

Epilogue

Learning the Lessons
of Life, Peace, and Justice

Coming to the end of this study, we should ask what it all means; what is its significance? These are stories about people of conviction who are significant for the history of pacifism, immigration and naturalization, jurisprudence, and even women's history and American religious history. In addition to their human interest and their contributions to various historical records, these stories may offer other values.

Recently Jeffrey M. Anderson[1] has distinguished between two views of religion in the tension between religion and civic duty, a subject of many of the Supreme Court's church-state cases. One view is that religion imposes on a believer an obligation to behave in a moral and ethical way. The believer derives a moral imperative from his or her religious faith. Religious behavior is a duty to serve God. The other understanding perceives religion as merely a choice one makes between a number of "lifestyle options." One chooses religious behavior as casually as one chooses paper or plastic at the supermarket, or one chooses a particular flavor of ice cream from among thirty-one. Far from being a duty, religious identity is merely a personal choice. According to Anderson, the *Macintosh* and *Bland* cases show that the Court's decisions have frequently understood religion as a personal choice. The Court denied Macintosh and Bland citizenship in part because the Justices could not distinguish the basis for their conscientious objection from that of Rosika Schwimmer. The *Macintosh* and *Bland* opinions recognized that their conscientious objections to war were based on religion, whereas Schwimmer's was not. Yet the Court concluded that their scruples were merely a matter of choice, a lifestyle decision indistinguishable from Schwimmer's, rather than a duty imposed by religious commitment and identity. Although Macintosh and Bland argued that their objections to war were based squarely on their Christian religious faith, the Court held that *Schwimmer* controlled their cases, implying that all ideological objections to war were merely personal preference. Only the dissents by Chief Justice Charles Evans Hughes recognized the depth of faith in religious objectors. Only he comprehended that religious duty, an obedience to God that would allow them to do no other, was the ground of Macintosh's and Bland's conscientious objection.[2]

Anderson argues that although *Girouard* overturned *Schwimmer*, *Macintosh*, and *Bland*, it did not assert an understanding of religion as duty over against the Court's view of religious behavior as casual personal choice. *Girouard* effectively lumped the three cases together. In overruling them, Justice William O. Douglas did not distinguish between *Schwimmer*, in which the objection to war was based on personal philosophy, and *Macintosh* and *Bland*, in which the objections were based on religious duty. Justice Douglas quoted Justice Holmes's dissent in *Schwimmer* and Chief Justice Hughes's dissent in *Macintosh*, yet Holmes had said that Schwimmer should not have been denied citizenship because she held unpopular views; free thought is a precious American liberty. Free thought implies personal choice more than response to a commitment to religious duty, in Anderson's view. In his conclusion, Holmes equated the conscientious objection of the atheist Schwimmer with that of the obviously religious Quakers, implicitly equating religious expression with atheist expression. "Douglas's *equal* importation of Hughes and Holmes in the *Girouard* opinion reveals an inclination to treat religious convictions as if they were ordinary political opinions," Anderson writes. On the one hand, "*Girouard* signals a profound disagreement with the reasoning of the earlier Courts." On the other, Douglas's "*equal* reliance upon the Holmes dissent in *Schwimmer*, which ignored the religion question, and the Hughes dissent in *Macintosh*, which confronted it forcefully, renders it difficult to ascribe to the *Girouard* Court any coherent understanding of religious conviction."[3]

Anderson overstates his case somewhat. Justice Douglas did not invoke Holmes and Hughes equally in his *Girouard* decision. Although he did rely on Justice Holmes, he relied on Chief Justice Hughes more. Douglas did, however, cite a famous passage from Holmes's *Schwimmer* dissent.

> [I]f there is any principle of the Constitution that more imperatively calls for attachment than any other it is the principle of free thought—not free thought for those who agree with us but freedom for thought that we

hate. I think that we should adhere to that principle with regard to admission into, as well as to life within this country.[4]

Anderson argues that Douglas's invocation of that passage and free-thought language generally suggests a free-choice concept of religious behavior rather than a grasp of religious duty. That interpretation is not inevitable. One could easily argue that free thought is simply (not that it is trivial) the political context in which one can respond to religious duty. It does not have to imply mere personal choice. Douglas indirectly made that point in the language directly following his quotation of Holmes. "The struggle for religious liberty," he wrote,

> has through the centuries been an effort to accommodate the demands of the State to the conscience of the individual. *The victory for freedom of thought recorded in our Bill of Rights recognizes that in the domain of conscience there is a moral power higher than the State.* Throughout the ages, men have suffered death rather than subordinate their allegiance to God to the authority of the State. Freedom of religion guaranteed by the First Amendment is the product of that struggle. As we recently stated in *United States v. Ballard*, "Freedom of thought, which includes freedom of religious belief, is basic in a society of free men."[5]

Borrowing some language from Hughes's dissent, Douglas speaks of duty, even citing martyrdom, and yet connects it to the concept of freedom of thought, thereby suggesting that Anderson has too easily equated freedom of thought with mere personal choice.

Of course, the "punch line" in *Girouard* is, "We conclude that the *Schwimmer, Macintosh* and *Bland* cases do not state the correct rule of law."[6] Because "the *Girouard* decision explicitly overruled *Schwimmer* as well as *Macintosh* and *Bland*, despite the fact that everyone agreed that Schwimmer's objection to military service was not religiously grounded at all," Anderson concludes that "Douglas relied upon a notion of 'freedom of thought' that included religious belief but did not distinguish religious convictions from other kinds of beliefs."[7] That the three cases are mentioned together in denunciation suggests to Anderson that Douglas did not have a clear sense of conscientious objection as the result of religious duty. Again, I am not sure that is an inevitable conclusion. Just prior to the "punch line," Douglas had written, "The test oath is abhorrent to our tradition. Over the years, Congress has meticulously respected that tradition and even in time of war has sought to accommodate the military requirements to the religious scruples of the individual." Therefore the Court could "not believe that Congress intended to reverse that policy when it came to draft the naturalization oath. Such an abrupt and radical departure from our traditions should not be implied. Cogent evidence would be necessary to convince us that Congress took that course."[8] Douglas wrote these sentences in the same paragraph with the religious-duty language I have previously quoted. Indeed, Douglas referred in this passage to Congress's attempt to accommodate persons' religious principles. Douglas saw a connection between government's recognition of religious duty and the rejection of test oaths in the nation's laws. The statement that *Schwimmer, Macintosh,* and *Bland* were no longer good law follows hard on that paragraph. One can argue that it illustrates abhorrence of test oaths as easily as one can argue that rejection of those three cases illustrates that Douglas was ambiguous in his understanding of the role of religion in naturalization cases involving conscientious objectors.

Having argued that Anderson overstated his case, I must acknowledge that his argument is reasonable and plausible. There is no doubt that in more recent church-state decisions, the Supreme Court has succumbed to a reductionism that conflates religious freedom with freedom of speech. Anderson succinctly describes the process. "The Court denies that there is anything different about religion," making "a conviction concerning the character of God and God's laws . . . substantially equivalent to an opinion about a political leader or the tax code." Such an equivalence effectively reduces freedom of religion to freedom of expression, denying "any of the special status suggested by its particular mention in the text of the First Amendment."[9]

In a case in which the Court did commingle religious freedom and free speech, the Court majority accepted "the proposition that because religious worship uses speech, it is protected by the Free Speech Clause of the First Amendment." The Court found such speech not only "protected," but also that "religious worship *qua* speech is not different from any other variety of protected speech as a matter of constitutional principle." In a vehement dissent, Justice Byron White affirmed " that this proposition is plainly wrong. Were it right, the Religion Clauses would be emptied of any independent meaning in circumstances in which religious practice took the form of speech."[10] In spite of this warning from one of the more "conservative" Justices of the recent Court, protesting the kind of reductionism Anderson describes, the Court has entered this forbidden territory.[11]

Although I am not as convinced as Anderson that *Girouard* is ambiguous on the question of religious duty, it may be that the cases described in this book, with the exception of Chief Justice Hughes's dissent in *Macintosh*, are precursors of the more recent Court's unwillingness to consider seriously that "free exercise of religion" received special mention in the Constitution.

I am writing this Epilogue in May 2002, eight months after devastating terrorist attacks on the United States. Even prior to those tragic events, Americans were debating immigration and the role of immigrants. That debate is nothing new. Native-born Americans (themselves children of previous generations of immigrants) have always been uneasy about how many and what kinds of immigrants should be allowed to enter the United States. Often have children of immigrants attempted to keep out other immigrants of particular national origins, such as Chinese. In time of war immigrants from the "enemy" country living in America have been harassed, if not physically harmed, as happened to persons with German names or appearance during World War I. "What goes around, comes around." As the result of the attack by Middle Eastern, Muslim terrorists on 11 September 2001, there is an attitude of hostility in the land toward persons who are "Arab-looking," who have "Arab names,"or who are Muslim. Many Americans are trying to learn more about the Middle East and Islam in order to make America a more hospitable place for immigrants from that part of the world. But others study these subjects so that they might understand better the threat these people pose to the freedoms and customs of America and Americans.[12] Terrorist attacks in 2001 have exacerbated the broader debate about immigration as did military attacks in 1941.[13]

Opposition to immigration in the past has often been based on thinly veiled (or overt) racism. It still is. Political maven and sometime presidential candidate Pat Buchanan has argued that traditional American values are being eroded by militant liberalism, enemies of religion, and those who have a "one world" view of global politics and a "multicultural" image of American society. In his recent book, *The Death of the West: How Mass Immigration, Depopulation and a Dying Faith Are Killing Our Culture and Country*, Buchanan claims that immigration into Western Europe and America by non-Westerners (read: non-Caucasians) portends the death of Western society.[14] Buchanan and his allies perpetuate the kind of racial attitudes that prevailed in the 1924 legislation that brought open immigration into America to an end and set rigid quotas based, in large part, on race. With small exceptions, only Northern Europeans were welcome. The events of 11 September 2001 have revived that debate.

This book can propose no answer to the large and complicated issue of immigration. It opens a window on a relatively small and obscure issue in American naturalization policy. Yet this book does say at least one thing about immigration. The Internal Security Act of 1950 and the Immigration and Nationality Act of 1952 (the McCarran-Walter Act) were restrictive and racist. Although they focused on excluding Communists and other subversives, they were still racist (particularly the 1952 legislation), so much so that President Truman vetoed them on that ground, among others. In spite of this regression, and influenced by the Supreme Court's *Girouard* decision, Congress enacted for the first time a process whereby conscientious objectors could be naturalized. Even in the midst of restrictionist and racist attitudes, Congress treated candidates for naturalization more humanely, at least on the issue of conscientious objection to war, than it had ever been willing to do before. I do not know the answers to the questions of immigration, or what they should be. But perhaps, in 2002 and beyond, the United States will choose to act on the questions of immigration and naturalization with humanity and compassion, granting dignity and hope to the "alien." The stories told in this book show there is some precedent for that.

I now call four witnesses—two of them committed adherents, two of them not—to the role of the historic "peace churches" in the formation of the national mind and spirit.

> The Quaker pacifist, even when he is humble enough not to claim that he presents a viable position for the state *now*, has the right to recognize that he, also, is a contributor. By his extreme position he is helping the state to avoid settling back into a mood in which war and the preparation for war are taken for granted. He is the gadfly of his civilization, somewhat as Socrates was the gadfly of the Athenian civilization. It is right that some, without being censorious of others, and being genuinely loving, should, in the course of their present lives, provide a modicum of the pattern "which nations are to expect and travel towards." The position of the conscientious objector is morally justified if he makes peace more likely, not today, but in the long run.[15]

We who allow ourselves to become engaged in war need this testimony of the absolutist against us, lest we accept the warfare of the world to be normative, lest we become callous to the horror of war, and lest we forget the ambiguity of our own actions and motives and the risk we run of achieving no permanent good from this momentary anarchy in which we are involved.[16]

The responsibility of carrying the torch of moral idealism is a responsibility greater than the responsibility of bearing arms, which millions are induced to do when bands begin to play and the drums begin to beat.[17]

Numbering less than half a million adherents, the historic peace churches have kept before the other 240 million of us the vision of a world without war. . . . It has been the not-always-adequately-appreciated gift of the peace churches to keep before us this vision that might lead us beyond the self-defeating toils of enmity to a better way.[18]

I was not a pacifist when I began this study, nor have I become one. More precisely, I am a pacifist in my gut, but not in my head. My emotions tell me that humankind would be much better off if all people were pacifists. Yet my mind tells me that, on this side of paradise, sinful human nature being what it is, not everyone will commit to peace. Wars will be fought—we may hope that they will be fought according to "just war" criteria[19]—and nations will hasten to prepare for war. Yet I strongly believe, with the statements I have quoted, that the ideal of life without war must, always, be lifted up before all, in word and flesh. Dorothy Day, founder of the Catholic Worker movement and an absolute pacifist during World War II, has taught us that pacifism is not the choice between good and evil, but between good and better.[20] We may counter that pacifism is a thoroughly "idealistic" concept. It is, but a world without idealism is an impoverished world. Peace churches and individual conscientious objectors such as Rosika Schwimmer, Douglas Clyde Macintosh, Marie Averil Bland, and James Louis Girouard help us to "keep our eyes on the prize." Their struggle is more than mere lip service to an "ideal." They believed that the "ideal" is real and attainable. I have told their stories here, not only to rescue them from obscurity, but also to learn what I can about the sanctity of human life, the futility of war, and the pursuit of justice. These lessons I commend to every reader.

Notes

1. Jeffrey M. Anderson, "Conscience in the Court, 1931-1946: Religion as Duty and Choice" *Journal of Supreme Court History* 26 no. 1 (2001): 25-52. Anderson's article won the 2000 Hughes-Gossett Student Essay Prize of the Supreme Court Historical Society; see *Journal of Supreme Court History* 26 no. 1 (2001): 95 and "Celebration of Twenty-sixth Annual Meeting,"*Supreme Court Historical Society Quarterly* 22 no. 2 (2001): 6.

2. Anderson, "Conscience in the Court," 29-42.

3. Anderson, "Conscience in the Court," 41-42; emphasis added.

4. *Girouard v. United States* 328 U.S. 61 at 68, quoting *United States v. Schwimmer* 279 U.S. 644 at 654-55.

5. 328 U.S. 61 at 68-69, citations omitted; emphasis added.

6. 328 U.S. 61 at 69.

7. Anderson, "Conscience in the Court," 41.

8. 328 U.S. 61 at 69.

9. Anderson, "Conscience in the Court," 42.

10. *Widmar v. Vincent* 454 U.S. 263 at 284 (1981).

11. See *Widmar v. Vincent* 454 U.S. 263 (1981); *Lamb's Chapel v. Center Moriches Union Free School District* 508 U.S. 384 (1993); *Rosenberger v. Rector and Visitors of the University of Virginia* 515 U.S. 819 (1995); *Good News Club v. Milford Central School* 533 U.S. 98 (2001).

12. See Richard D. Lamm, "Terrorism and Immigration: We Need a Border," *Vital Speeches of the Day* 68 (1 March 2002) : 298-300.

13. For a comprehensive view of post-September 11 immigration policy and problems, see Tamar Jacoby, "Too Many Immigrants?" *Commentary* 113 (April 2002): 33-44.

14. Patrick J. Buchanan, *The Death of the West: How Mass Immigration, Depopulation and a Dying Faith Are Killing Our Culture and Country* (New York: Saint Martin's Press, 2002); for a favorable review see Dwight D. Murphy, "Book Review" *St. Croix Review* 35 (April 2002): 59-62; for an unfavorable review see Philip A. Klinkner "The Base Camp of Christendom," *Nation* 274 (11 March 2002): 25-27, 29.

15. D. Elton Trueblood, *The People Called Quakers* (New York: Harper and Row, 1966), 206.

16. Reinhold Niebuhr, *Christianity and Power Politics* (New York: Charles Scribner's Sons, 1940), 31.

17. Statement of Joseph B. Matthews, Secretary of the Fellowship of Reconciliation, *Hearings Before the Committee on Immigration and Naturalization, House of Representatives, on H. R. 3574*, 8-9 May 1930, 82-83.

18. Dean M. Kelley, "Introduction," in *The Politics of Conscience: The Historic Peace Churches and America at War, 1917-1955*, Albert N. Keim and Grand M. Stoltzfus, eds. (Scottsdale, Pa.: Herald Press, 1988), 10.

19. See the sermon of Christopher Bryan, "'Father, Forgive . . .'" *Sewanee Theological Review* 45 no. 1 (Christmas 2001): 3-8.

20. Sandra Yocum Mize, "'We Are Still Pacifists'; Dorothy Day's Pacifism During World War II," *Records of the American Catholic Historical Society of Philadelphia* 108 (Spring-Summer 1997): 6.

Appendix A

Woman's Peace Party
Preamble and Platform

WE, WOMEN OF THE UNITED STATES, assembled in behalf of World Peace, grateful for the security of our own country, but sorrowing for the misery of all involved in the present struggle among warring nations, do hereby band ourselves together to demand that war be abolished.

Equally with men pacifists, we understand that planned-for, legalized, wholesale, human slaughter is today the sum of all villainies.

As women, we feel a peculiar moral passion of revolt against both the cruelty and the waste of war.

As women, we are especially the custodian of the life of the ages. We will not longer consent to its reckless destruction.

As women, we are particularly charged with the future of childhood and with the care of the helpless and the unfortunate. We will not longer endure without protest that added burden of maimed and invalid men and poverty-stricken widows and orphans which war places upon us.

As women, we have builded by the patient drudgery of the past the basic foundation of the home and of peaceful industry. We will not longer endure without a protest that must be heard and heeded by men, that hoary evil which in an hour destroys the social structure that centuries of toil have reared.

As women, we are called upon to start each generation onward toward a better humanity. We will not longer tolerate without determined opposition that denial of the sovereignty of reason and justice by which war and all that makes for war today render impotent the idealism of the race.

Therefore, as human beings and the mother half of humanity, we demand that our right to be consulted in the settlement of questions concerning not alone the life of individuals but of nations be recognized and respected.

We demand that women be given a share in deciding between war and peace in all the courts of high debate within the home, the school, the church, the industrial order, and the state.

So protesting, and so demanding, we hereby form ourselves into a national organization to be called the Woman's Peace Party.

We hereby adopt the following as our platform of principles, some of the items of which have been accepted by a majority vote, and more of which have been the unanimous choice of those attending the conference that initiated the formation of this organization. We have sunk all differences of opinion on minor matters and given freedom of expression to a wide divergence of opinion in the details of our platform and in our statement of explanation and information, in a common desire to make our woman's protest against war and all that makes for war, vocal, commanding and effective. We welcome to our membership all who are in substantial sympathy with that fundamental purpose of our organization, whether or not they can accept in full our detailed statement of principles.

Platform

THE PURPOSE of this Organization is to enlist all American women in arousing the nations to respect the sacredness of human life and to abolish war. The following is adopted as our platform:

1. The immediate calling of a convention of neutral nations in the interest of early peace.

2. Limitation of armaments and the nationalization of their manufacture.

3. Organized opposition to militarism in our own country.

4. Education of youth in the ideals of peace.

5. Democratic control of foreign policies.

6. The further humanizing of governments by the extension of the franchise to women.

7. "Concert of Nations" to supersede "Balance of Power."

8. Action toward the gradual organization of the world to substitute Law for War.

9. The substitution of an international police for rival armies and navies.

10. Removal of the economic causes of war.

11. The appointment by our Government of a commission of men and women, with an adequate appropriation, to promote international peace.

Woman's Peace Party, *Preamble and Platform, Adopted at Washington, January 10, 1915*, quoted in Marie Louise Degen, *The History of the Woman's Peace Party* (Baltimore: John's Hopkins Press, 1939; New York: Garland Publishing, 1972), 40-42.

Appendix B

Kellogg-Briand Peace Treaty

Also known as: Kellogg-Briand Pact, Pact of Paris
Date of signature: August 27, 1928
Place of signature: Paris
Signatory states: Germany, United States, Belgium, French Republic, Great Britain, Ireland and the British Dominions, India, Italy, Japan, Poland, Czechoslovakia
Accessions: Afghanistan, Abyssinia, Albania, Austria, Bulgaria, Chile, China, Costa Rica, Cuba, Denmark, Free City of Danzig, Dominican Republic, Egypt, Estonia, Finland, Greece, Guatemala, Haiti, Honduras, Hungary, Iceland, Latvia, Liberia, Lithuania, Luxembourg, Mexico, the Netherlands, Nicaragua, Norway, Panama, Paraguay, Peru, Persia, Portugal, Roumania, Kingdom of the Serbs, Croats and Slovenes, Siam, Spain, Sweden, Switzerland, Turkey, Soviet Union, Venezuela

[The signatories],
deeply sensible of their solemn duty to promote the welfare of mankind;

Persuaded that the time has come when a frank renunciation of war as an instrument of national policy should be made to the end that the peaceful and friendly relations now existing between their peoples may be perpetuated;

Convinced that all changes in their relations with one another should be sought only by pacific means and be the result of a peaceful and orderly process, and that any signatory Power which shall hereafter seek to promote its national interests by resort to war should be denied the benefits furnished by this Treaty;

Hopeful that, encouraged by their example, all the other nations of the world will join in this humane endeavour and by adhering to the present Treaty as soon as it comes into force bring their peoples within the scope of its beneficient provisions, thus uniting the civilized nations of the world in a common renunciation of war as an instrument of their national policy;

Have decided to conclude a Treaty and . . . have agreed upon the following articles:

Article I

The High Contracting Parties solemnly declare in the names of their respective peoples that they condemn recourse to war for the solution of international controversies, and renounce it as an instrument of national policy in their relations with one another.

Article II

The High Contracting Parties agree that the settlement or solution of all disputes or conflicts of whatever nature or of whatever origin they may be, which may arise among them, shall never be sought except by pacific means.

Article III

The present Treaty shall be ratified by the High Contracting Parties named in the Preamble in accordance with their respective constitutional requirements, and shall take effect as between them as soon as all their several instruments of ratification shall have been deposited at Washington.

This Treaty shall, when it has come into effect as prescribed in the preceding paragraph, remain open as long as may be necessary for adherence by all the other Powers of the world. Every instrument evidencing the adherence of a Power shall be deposited at Washington and the Treaty shall immediately upon such deposit become effective as between the Power thus adhering and the other Powers parties hereto.

It shall be the duty of the Government of the United States to furnish each Government named in the Preamble and every Government subsequently adhering to this Treaty with a certified copy of the Treaty and of every instrument of ratification or adherence. It shall also be the duty of the Government of the United States telegraphically to notify such Governments immediately upon the deposit with it of each instrument of ratification or adherence.

In faith whereof the respective Plenipotentiaries have signed this Treaty in the French and English languages both texts having equal force, and hereunto affix their seals.

World Encyclopedia of Peace, Linus Pauling and others, eds. (Oxford: Pergamon Press, 1986) 3: 45-46.

Appendix C

Rosika Schwimmer,
*An Adventure in Citizenship**

1 The United States had a perfect right to deny citizenship to me; but they owe me a Ph.D. That was my first thought when I recovered from the stunning blow of the United States Supreme Court decision.

Over a long period the Chicago District Director of Naturalization requested written statements as to my beliefs and opinions on a variety of questions. They seemed a bit far-fetched for a decision in citizenship, rather like theses for Ph.D. dissertations. More amused than angered I answered the absurd questions. I do not refer to those on official forms every applicant is obliged to answer.

As a prospective loyal citizen I conscientiously filled out the printed questionnaire. I did not mind revealing to the authorities whether I had come to this country as a stowaway, a deserting seaman or as a passenger. Nor was I reluctant to tell that I was not "a believer in the practice of polygamy." I could assure the authorities "I had never been arrested," nor "been an inmate of an insane asylum." Never having "been charged with a violation of the prohibition law" I was ready "to abjure all allegiance and fidelity to Hungary," and declared myself willing to take the oath of allegiance which demanded: "that I will support and defend the Constitution and Laws of the United States of America against all enemies, foreign and domestic, and that I will bear true faith and allegiance to the same."

There were two questions I did not answer. I thought they were addressed to men. Number 22 asked: "If necessary, are you willing to take up arms in defense of this country?" Number 23 inquired: "Did **2** you file a questionnaire with a draft board during the war? If so, answer the following: Date filled in. Address at that time . . . . . Address of draft board . . . . . Board Division No. . . . . . Your order No. . . . . . Your serial No. . . . . . Class in which you were placed . . . . . Division . . . . . Date of classification . . . . . Did you claim exemption because you were an alien? For any other reason? Why? . . . . ."

My petition was duly sent to Washington and I looked forward to citizenship in the country I had chosen when the country of my birth and ancestors became intolerable to me.

Instead of an invitation to become a citizen the questionnaire came back with the stern demand to answer question number 22.

This demand marked a new epoch in the naturalization principles of the U.S.A., and my negative answer to it was destined to have far-reaching consequences.

The legal side of the question has been discussed by lawyers, in law faculties of colleges and universities all over the country. The press searchlight was fully turned on it. Yet little is known of the play behind the scenes and the forces turning the trend of American naturalization traditions.

A process of world importance because it puts the finishing seal on the world's militarization, League of Nations, Kellogg Peace Pacts, notwithstanding.

The final decision, closing the legal battle around my negative answer to question No. 22, clearly exposed to what extent the militarist spirit superseded the traditional anti-militarist attitude of America. Prussia may well be proud. If imitation is the best form of flattery, the U.S.A. paid Prussia the supreme compliment of surpassing it in the militarization of its own people, beyond the wildest dreams the wildest Prussian general may have indulged in.

3 Now that the door has been slammed in the face of applicants for naturalization who come to this country for other than commercial reasons, it is of interest to scrutinize the forces responsible for the exclusion of a type that used to be desirable citizenship timber. By now there are enough of us to form a *salon des refusés*.

Not the least defect of the Gerard list of America's rulers is the absence of men and women who rule the country's militarist policies. I came across many of them in the course of my naturalization proceedings. All of them worked in frenzied patriotism to keep closed the door at which I had in the innocence of my fifty years politely knocked for entrance.

To present them in the order of their appearance, I must introduce first the Amazons of the New World, the Ladies Auxiliary of the American Legion.

In May 1924 a patriotic bird whispered the frightful news into their shocked ears that I had applied in November 1921 for first papers and was entitled to apply for citizenship in August 1926. The gallant ladies immediately passed a resolution of protest against my naturalization. From the metropolis of the Ku Klux Klan, Indianapolis. They sent the resolution to the Secretary of Labor and to all those who were to be warned of the danger. *Two and a quarter years before I was entitled to apply for citizenship.*

In the last analysis these valiant ladies can claim full credit for having saved the U.S.A. from destruction by my admission to citizenship. A heroic deed worthy to go down in history along with the saving of the Capitol by the patriotic Roman geese.

Next in the line of defense and importance Mr. Schlotfeldt. In appearance as in name typically German. Of the *gutmütig* and *gemüttlich* type. Always pleasant and friendly when I had to call on him.

4 During my Chicago residence I got repeated invitations for lecture tours in Europe but could not accept them as I had no passport to travel. Living in Vienna as a political refugee from Hungary I had an emergency passport from the Austrian government. On this I came to America with a special permit of the United States' State department. The emergency passport having expired I was anxious to get some American paper permitting me to travel.

Consulting the District Director of Naturalization he seemed sincerely anxious to be helpful. The only suggestion, however, for a short-cut to American citizenship was his advice to marry an American, which would have enabled me to apply after one year. Having had more than my share in melodramatic situations—which I loathe—I did not feel like adding a marriage *de convenance.*

Finally Mr. Schlotfeldt rendered a tangible service to hasten my citizenship. *He suggested* my filing the "Preliminary form of petition for naturalization" *more than a year before I was formally entitled to it.* This could and would not have led to my citizenship before the legally necessary 5 years residence. But it would have made it possible for him to call me for examination the day I fulfilled the time requirement. There was a constant list of ten thousand applicants waiting for final examination, and kept waiting one year or more for lack of personnel to take care of them. Purgatory extended.

I gratefully handed my preliminary petition on December 26, 1924, and Mr. Schlotfeldt filed it ahead of time. He knew clearly who I was. We had long political conversations on world affairs. He knew of my uncompromising pacifism which had made me a political refugee from Hungary. Yet he favored my petition as a humanitarian *would* in circumstances as wretched as mine. He seemed to have a good sense of humor and repeatedly congratulated me on being able to laugh where **5** "even men would easily cry."

I was certainly unprepared for Mr. Schlotfeldt's metamorphosis, evident when the questionnaire came back from Washington with the fateful Question 22 to be filled out. He had learned I was persona non grata with the patriotic organizations. Outwardly the same kindly old man. Still trying to help me into citizenship, but on a different basis.

When I unscrewed my pen to answer Number 22, he urged me not to be rash. First he tried to persuade me to an affirmative answer, in other words to lie myself into citizenship; then to take the questionnaire home and "think it over."

When I [undecipherable] an immediate negative answer, he solemnly declared I had signed away my American citizenship. He lectured me on the patriotic duty of bearing arms and we discussed endlessly. Mr. Schlotfeldt's last advice was to withdraw my petition. "You have not the ghost of a chance," he said prophetically, "why expose yourself to a denial of citizenship?"

Having, as I now know, obsolete ideas about Americanism, I insisted on going through the whole process of examination, unable to believe the U.S.A. would be the first civilized country to compel women to take up arms.

On the 22nd of September, 1926—in favored position as to time, created by Mr. Schlotfeldt's early filing of my petition—I appeared for examination.

Mr. Schlotfeldt was extremely polite also to my two sponsors and my lawyer. He personally dusted the chairs for us, a symbolic action for the dust to be thrown in our eyes. With all outward politeness he tried to confuse my witnesses with methods usually applied by bullying lawyers in cross-examination.

6 He urged once more my withdrawal of the petition. Then decreed he could not advise my admission to citizenship because of the contradiction between my willingness to take the oath of allegiance, and refusal to bear arms in defense of the country. "If the oath to defend the Constitution and the Laws implied defense by arms, it would be unnecessary to ask separately whether applicants are willing to take up arms" was my last verbal retort. Though for years Mr. Schlotfeldt had not considered me inadmissible, he now faithfully obeyed the militarist opposition to my citizenship.

The final decision was in the hands of the Federal Judge before whom I was to appear after the legally prescribed interval of ninety days. Mr. Schlotfeldt requested me to make a written statement as to my interpretation of the oath of allegiance. The whole question came down to the interpretation of the word defend. To Mr. Schlotfeldt and later to 7 out of 13 federal judges who passed in three courts on my case the word absolutely implied the use of weapons to kill.

"The lawyer defends his client by arguing, not by shooting. It would be denying the force of spiritual influences, of mental energies, if we defined the word 'defense' solely as a physical act." This was the gist of the first of my labours on which I base my claim for a Ph.D.

Instead of ninety days nearly a year elapsed before I was admitted for final hearing and then only on utmost pressure by the two lawyers representing me. I had meantime moved to New York and was kept busy answering Mr. Schlotfeldt's conundrums.

His inquiry of December 17th, 1926 is a specimen that would adorn Mr. Mencken's column of Americana:

"Dear Madam: I find that it will be impossible to hear your petition for citizenship until sometime in January, and therefore ask that you furnish me with a statement as to your so-called pacifist theory or 7 inability to defend the country as per our conversation last September. If you have any lectures you have delivered on this subject, I should be glad to have a copy; also a copy of any lectures or paper you may have prepared on the question of the organization of national governments as distinguished from world governments, if any. A copy of anything you may have which discloses your present beliefs on the organization of the Government or conduct of the Government will be appreciated.

Yours very truly,
(signed) Fred J. Schlotfeldt,
District Director."

I have never written speeches nor made notes for them, so I had to write another essay for the naturalization authorities. The gist of it was: "The trend of governmental evolution is best demonstrated in the organization of the United States of America. In the evolution from the jungle to civilized human cooperation the founders of the United States of America have demonstrated the greatest genius in statecraft. I believe that national governments will continue on individual basis, as the States have, that form the North American Union. I believe the national governments will increasingly organize for peaceful cooperation, as the States have developed into a Union of 48 States. I believe that future generations will arrive at something like the United States of the World. Such an organization, to my mind, will permit every State to develop on its national lines, keep its own language and individual type of culture. Within all this variety, however, I believe the elements of common interest to all mankind will be ultimately organized so that all human differences can be solved without resort to war. The forty-eight States of the North American Union prove that this can be done."

Knowing that "no more is demanded of an alien who becomes a citizen than from a natural born citizen" I finished declaring: "If however, it is a fact that the Government of the United States can compel its women citizens to take up arms in defense of the country—something that no other civilized government has ever attempted—I would not be **8** able to comply with this requirement of American citizenship. In this case I would recognize the right of the Government to deal with me as it is dealing with its male citizens who for conscientious reasons refuse to take up arms."

Mr. Schlotfeldt had hardly read this "piece" of mine when he favored me with a new inquiry.

"Dear Madam: 1. Since my previous communication my attention has been called to a communication of yours to Col. L.A. Stone under date of September 19, 1925 in which you say: 'I am an uncompromising pacifist for whom even Jane Addams is not even enough of a pacifist. I am an absolute atheist. I have no sense of nationalism, only a cosmic consciousness of belonging to the human family.' Does this correctly state your principles or do you desire to add thereto. You will understand my motive in writing you at this time is that we may have a correct statement of your views."

This introduces another important *persona dramatis* and also discloses militarist activities of which people are unaware in peace time. Chicago boasts of a Military Intelligence Association organized and led by Lieutenant Colonel Lee Alexander Stone. In private life a physician, he used his ample spare time to place spies at danger points and to warn his people of the espied perils. The gem of my vast collection of slanders and libels, printed and written about my dangerous person is Mr. Ralph Duncan's spy report to Colonel Stone. This spy report was used to frighten timid women's clubs from engaging me as a speaker. It frightened them successfully. Engagements were withheld or canceled and Mr. Feakins's agency threatened with a boycott of his entire speakers list if I was kept on it. The leader of the Illinois Federation of Women's Clubs gave away the show. In her patriotic rage she sent a copy of Colonel Stone's Duncan-report to harassed Mr. Feakins. This enabled me at last to trace the source of much trouble.

In a personal interview Colonel Stone declared himself convinced he and his military *confrères* had done me a terrible injustice and volunteered to do everything in his power to mend the wrong. I have the Colonel's handwritten statement of many pages refuting his accusations. **9** I was to use it any way I pleased. He promised to broadcast it over the radio. On my request he brought a full fledged Military Commission of four to question me in my own home. He arranged for my addressing a luncheon meeting of his cherished Military Intelligence Association. Colonel Stone and the other three men were to do everything to amend the wrong caused by their over zealous patriotism. And they were all "so pleased you are to become one of us" they assured me when my application for citizenship was mentioned.

After Mr. Schlotfeldt's decision to disapprove of my citizenship Colonel Stone stormed: "We military men don't want women to fight, we want them to uphold us when we are fighting. I will go up personally to Schlotfeldt and tell him so." At the same time however he advised me to withdraw my negative answer to question 22. "Why not say yes? What do you care as long as you get citizenship?" The same remarkable irreverence for truthfulness as the Naturalization Director's. These patriots will knock the hat off your head if you do not salute the flag, but the advice to lie yourself into citizenship does not conflict with their patriotism.

And now a passage lifted out of a three page private letter thrown as another stumbling block in my path to citizenship. On my telegraphed question to Colonel Stone how Mr. Schlotfeldt got hold of the letter he telegraphed he had shown it to him in an effort to help me. He advised again to change my negative answer.

In the opus answering Mr. Schlotfeldt's latest inquiry I did not confine myself to his question. Not being an exhibitionist I wanted the naturalization authorities to know the reason for those obnoxious revelations about myself. In consequence of Colonel Stone's helpful services my atheism and "cosmic consciousness of belonging to the human family" were discussed in the examination before Federal Judge Carpenter, in the Government's argument against my admission before the Supreme

Court of the United States, and played an important role in the **10** appellate decision of Prof. Macintosh and Nurse Bland's citizenship. It figures in all the briefs about these cases and is spread all over the legal literature dealing with them.

Generous and chivalrous Colonel Stone sent the same private letter to his pal Fred R. Marvin to help the defense in my libel suit against the superpatriot.

The remarkable thing about the next act in the naturalization drama, Federal Judge Carpenter, is that he refused to consider my atheism as detrimental to my citizenship aspirations. Previous to my examination he had exhibited an entirely unjudicial temper about my case and the questions he asked during examination were branded as conundrums by the three federal judges who reversed his decision.

Would I shoot, he asked, if I were a nurse and saw an enemy creep into the tent, trying to shoot the officer I was nursing. I would not, though I was supposed to have a pistol in my nursing hands. But I would try to hit the pistol out of the enemy's hand, or to throw myself in front of my patient to save him. This was not to the point. The question was shooting. Suppose I was ten feet away and could not protect my patient in the suggested way and someone handed me a pistol, would I shoot? It was a sad moment for a Chicago judge to face someone so depraved as I proved by my negative answer. "No gun, no citizenship" said a sarcastic newspaper. That Judge Carpenter referred to the U.S.A. as "this Great United Corporation," called its native citizens "Stockholders" and aspirants for citizenship "partners or stockholders" seems in the light of Mr. Gerard's theory the correct terminology.

But though sorely disappointed by the refusal and in a most perplexing situation as "a woman without a country" I would not have moved a finger to push myself into "partnership in this Great United Corporation." There is such a thing as to be too proud to fight and also to be too disgusted.

11 Mr. Harold Fields, Director of the League for American Citizenship, Roger Baldwin and his Civil Liberties Union, and other anxious to uphold traditional American ideals urged me to appeal. They insisted the denial on the ground of my refusal to bear arms was unconstitutional. An appeal against the decision would be a civic service.

The interlude between Judge Carpenter's denial and the filing of my appeal was filled with Mr. Schlotfeldt's playful attempt to outwit my lawyers. By not all too legal technical steps he nearly succeeded in preventing the appeal. Then Judges Anderson, Alschuler and Balsess decried: "A petitioner's rights are not to be determined by putting conundrums to her" and ordered my admission. This decision deserves special place in the history of recent naturalization proceedings. Its liberalism is clear cut. Devastating to the alleged liberalism of the three New York appellate judges who granted citizenship to Professor Macintosh and Miss Bland emphatically distinguishing between God-fearing applicants and atheists.

Mr. Schlotfeldt, requested to set a date for my taking the oath of allegiance, informed us the Secretary of Labor had submitted the case to the Attorney General for advice, whether the Government could appeal to the Supreme Court against my admission.

The greatest legal authorities considered that step impossible, yet Mr. Sargent did advise appeal. Solicitor General W. D. Mitchell wrote and signed the Government's petition for a Writ of [undecipherable] 12 my case. A really noble deed.

In due time the Supreme Court decided to hear the case, and gave the great legal authorities another chance for a wrong guess.

There was again a little interlude for Mr. Schlotfeldt to try a stunt. In a national conference of the District Directors of Naturalization he urged them to include the famous question No. 22 in the questionnaire. After the war the majority of districts had discarded it with other questions not compulsory according to Congressional requirement. Mr. Schlotfeldt's attempt failed.

Instead of Mr. Mitchell, who meantime had become Attorney General, his successor, Solicitor General Wheat argued the case before the Supreme Court.

The sole issue was the interpretation of the word "defense" in the oath of allegiance. Yet Mr. Wheat argued with great emotional heat about the hazard of the U.S.A. would be taking by admitting a woman of my "intellectual accomplishments." He literally declared my refusal to bear arms would not matter if I were "a plain, ordinary housewife," but was menace to this country because of the influence I could exert as a writer and lecturer.

My attorney, Mrs. Olive H. Rabe of Chicago, stressed in her strictly legal argument the point that the Naturalization authorities "wish to deny citizenship to a woman because she refuses to do what the laws of the country do not permit her to do."

The great legal authorities did not miss this last chance to make a mistake in their prognosis of the decision.

The majority opinion was written by Justice Butler, former law partner of Attorney General Mitchell. The six judges included Chief Justice Taft, who once organized a League to Enforce **13** Peace, and Justice Stone in whom my liberal friends had unbounded confidence.

A New York university professor wrote to one of the majority justices, a former colleague of his: "I missed your signature on the minority opinion." He had been on the verge to sign it, but reread my record and considered it "safer to keep her out." The battle was over. The militarists had won, in midst of the general admonition to take the Kellogg Peace Pact seriously.

How the matter looks to the world cannot be better illustrated than by a letter Professor Einstein wrote to a mutual European friend who had mentioned the case to him:

"I consider the stand taken by Madam Schwimmer highly valuable" wrote Einstein "and she certainly deserves the support of all humanitarians.

"Governments are the representatives of people still devoted to the outworn traditions of military duties. The world's sorely needed pacification cannot be achieved without the struggle of the most intelligent against the authorities which depend on forces that have to be defeated. Those who are convinced of this necessity are therefore in duty bound to stand by their convictions publicly and shoulder the burden of the conflict with authority. A result can only be achieved if many people sufficiently influential show the moral courage to take this stand.

"Such an attitude is revolutionary. But no unendurable bondage of the individual has ever been broken except by rebellion. Here too this road is unavoidable. All credit is due Madam Schwimmer for having recognized this and for having acted courageously in accordance with this understanding."

14 Reviewing the strange parade it is gratifying to note that the military interpretation of the oath of allegiance was received with universal consternation by the people of the press. Justice Holmes's classic minority opinion was generally hailed as the real expression of true Americanism. After the Supreme Court's decision a great number of applicants had to be refused under growing uneasiness of the public. A turn might be just around the corner.   July 30, 1930

*Bold numbers indicate pagination in original typescript.

Appendix D

Rosika Schwimmer's Naturalization Hearing*

In the District Court of the United States for the Northern District of Illinois Eastern Division

In Re. Petition of Rosika Schwimmer for Naturalization

Proceedings had and evidence taken in the above entitled cause before the Honorable George A. Carpenter, one of the judges of said court, Thursday, October 13, 1927, at the hour of 10 o'clock A.M.

Mr. A. Jordan,
appeared for the Government:
Mr. William B. Gemmill and
Mrs. Olive H. Rabe,
appeared for the petitioner.

———

MR. JORDAN: Mr. Schlotfeldt is out of town and asked me to handle this for him.

THE COURT: Is this matter on argument or—

MR. JORDAN: There has been no preliminary hearing, your Honor. Direct testimony should be taken. There has been no preliminary hearing at all.

THE COURT: You mean in your office?

MR. JORDAN: In our office. The Court is to hear the entire case.

THE COURT: Go ahead. Let the applicant and the witnesses be sworn.

ROSIKA SCHWIMMER, the petitioner herein, called as a witness in her own behalf, having been first duly sworn, was examined by Mr. Jordan, and testified as follows:

Q. What is your full name, please?

A. Rosika Schwimmer.

Q. You were born in Hungary?

A. Hungary, Budapest.

Q. For how long have you been living continuously in the U.S. now?

A. Since August, 1921.

Q. You had been in the United States prior to that, hadn't you?

A. I have been here three times.

Q. Is it your intention to remain in the United States permanently?

A. It is.

Q. Is there anything in our form of government that you are not in sympathy with?

A. Nothing.

Q. You have read the oath of allegiance?

A. I did.

Q. Are you able to take that oath without any reservation?

A. I am.

2 Q. I would like for you to inform the Court that this is the information sheet you filled out in connection with your application for citizenship (handing document to the witness).

A. Yes.

Q. And in answer to question 22, "If necessary, are you willing to take to arms in defense of this country?" You have answered, "I would not take up arms personally."

A. Yes.

Q. And that is correct, is it?

A. Yes.

Q. Now, on January 11, 1927, Mr. Schlotfeldt wrote you a letter, didn't he?

A. Yes.

Q. About some statement you had made to Colonel Stone?

A. Well, it wasn't a statement. It was part of a letter. It wasn't a statement at all.

Q. And in that you also reiterated to Mr. Schlotfeldt to this effect: "I am an uncompromising pacifist for whom even Jane Addams is not enough of a pacifist. I am an absolute atheist. I have no sense of nationalism."

A. Yes.

Q. Is that correct?

A. Yes, that is correct.

THE COURT: What do you mean by "no sense of nationalism?"

A. I mean that if I had a sense of nationalism I could not want to leave the Hungarian nationality into which I was born.

Q. This has nothing to with war. I am asking you what you mean when you say you have no sense of nationalism, because nationalism is a very comprehensive term and includes more than war.

A. I didn't speak now of war. Perhaps I didn't express myself well enough, your Honor. I say I meant when I said this, if I had a feeling of nationalism, then being born a Hungarian, I would have such a feeling of Hungarian nationality that I would not want to leave that nationality, whatever the things are that are displeasing me.

Q. In other words, if something came up between Hungary and the United States, your sympathies would still be with Hungary?

A. No, to the contrary they would not be. I said I have no sense of nationality that would bind me to Hungary.

Q. Of course, I do not believe the time is ever coming when this country, this Government, is going to send its women to fight. We have not as yet a regiment of Amazons.

A. I hope you don't have.

Q. But we may have to send them as nurses to look after our fighters. We may have to send them in the various religious organizations, like the Y.M.C.A. or the Knights of Columbus, to give succor and aid to our fighters. Now, are you willing to be sent on missions of that sort by this Government to look after the boys that are fighting for this country?

A. I am willing to do everything that an American citizen has to do, except fighting.

3 Q. Well, our women do not fight. We do not expect you to shoulder a musket.

A. Oh, I am willing to obey every law that the American Government compels citizens to do.

Q. Are you willing to do anything that an American woman is called upon to do? I mean an American citizen, a woman of this country.

A. Yes, I am, because I have not found that anything was asked that was against—I mean it is only the fighting question. That is, if American women would be compelled to do that, I would not do that.

Q. You say you are an uncompromising pacifist?

A. Yes.

Q. How far does that go? Does it refer only to yourself?

A. Yes.

Q. That you are not going to use your fists on somebody?

A. Yes.

Q. Or that you disapprove of the Government fighting?

A. It means that I disapprove of the Government asking me to fight.

Q. You mean fight personally?

A. Yes, physically.

Q. Carrying a gun?

A. Yes.

Q. Is that as far as it goes?

A. That is as far as it goes.

Q. Or is it more deep seated?

A. No.

Q. Really, of course, none of us wants war—

A. Yes.

Q. But there are a great many of us when war comes and our country is in danger who get our backs to the wall—

A. Yes.

Q. And we fight until there is nothing but the wall left.

A. Yes.

Q. Now are you willing to do that?

A. I am afraid, your Honor, I did not catch the point of the question. I am awfully sorry.

Q. I don't mean to bear arms for the country.

A. Yes

Q. The time will never come, I venture to say, when the women of the United States will have to bear arms.

A. Well, I am not willing to bear arms. In every other single way, civic way, I am ready to follow the law and do everything that the law compels American citizens to do. I am willing to do that. That is why I say I can take the oath of allegiance because as far as I, with the able help of my lawyers, could find out there is nothing that I could be compelled to do that I could not do.

Q. Your lawyer can't search into your heart any more than I can. You are the only one that can answer these questions.

A. I am opening my heart very frankly because there is nothing to hide. As I said when the question came up, if it is a question of fighting, as much as I desire American citizenship I would not seek the citizenship.

4 Q. Now, is it a question of fighting personally?

A. Yes.

Q. You yourself?

A. Myself.

Q. You do not care how many other women fight?

A. I don't care because I consider it a question of conscience. If there are women fighters, it is their business.

Q. Do you expect to spread this propaganda throughout this country with other women?

A. Which propaganda may I ask?

Q. That you are an uncompromising pacifist and will not fight.

A. Oh, of course, I am always ready to tell that to anyone who wants to hear it.

Q. What is your occupation, Madame?

A. I am a writer and lecturer.

Q. And in your writings and in your lectures you take up this question of war and pacifism?

A. If I am asked for that, I do.

Q. You know we have a great deal to give—at least we think so—

A. I think so, too.

Q. —when we confer citizenship upon people of other countries.

A. I think so, too.

Q. And we expect when we do that that they come in on an equal footing, and out of regard to the other stockholders in this Great United corporation we have to see to it that any partners or stockholders coming in are willing to do what those who are already here are willing to do. Now, it seems that your general views—

Now, I am not at all against people writing. There are a great many American citizens who are now decrying the possibility of the occurrence of war. They are against it. We have a great many pacifists in this country, but when the time comes, and they are called out for the country, they forget all their views, all of the things they have been talking about, and start in on the defense of the home.

Now, you can't come in half way. You must come in the whole distance, because there you are and under that flag is our country, and you can't get under that flag unless you promise to do every single thing that the citizens of this country not only have permission to do, but are willing to do.

A. Well, I can only repeat what I said: that I am willing to everything that, to my knowledge to this day, American women are asked to do.

THE COURT: Well, can we ask anything more than that?

MR. JORDAN: I would just like, your Honor, to bring out a few things in Madame Schwimmer's letter to Mr. Schlotfeldt, and also excerpts from one of her radio speeches.

In the letter here, "My answer to question 22 in my petition for final examination demonstrated that I am an uncompromising pacifist." A little further down: "Highly as I prize the privilege of American citizenship, I could not compromise my way into it by giving an untrue answer to question 22, though for all practical purposes I might have done so."

Then there are a few little excerpts here from the radio talks I would like the Court to hear: "I cannot see that a woman's refusal to take up arms is a contradiction to the oath of allegiance, promising to support and defend the Constitution and laws of the United States of America. I have for the fulfillment of this duty other ways and means in mind."

5 MRS. RABE: Would you mind reading the rest of that statement right there?

MR. JORDAN: That finishes that paragraph, I believe.

MRS. RABE: Oh, does it? I thought she spoke about having written in favor of our Constitution.

THE COURT: Let me ask you this one question:—

A. Yes, sir.

Q. If you were called to the service, and the kind of work that women usually can perform better than the men can—say as a nurse or as some one to give cheer to the soldiers—and you were at some place in a war, which I hope never will come, and you saw someone coming in the headquarters or the barracks, wherever it was, with a pistol in his hand to shoot the back of an officer of our country, and you had a pistol handy by, would you kill him?

A. No, I would not.

THE COURT: The application is denied.

MR. GEMMILL: Just a moment, your Honor. We would like to perfect our record. We expect to go up on this case, your Honor.

MRS. RABE: And I would like the witnesses to be heard.

MR. GEMMILL: I think, unless we may have a stipulation here that all the qualifications of the applicant are granted, with the exception of question 22—

THE COURT: Otherwise, except on this one point, I think the Government will admit that the applicant is entirely qualified.

MR. GEMMILL: As to the residence and good moral character—

MR. JORDAN: There is no question about those things. The only things are the three points she made; that she is an uncompromising pacifist, and the question of being an atheist—

THE COURT: That I may not agree with you on, because we have some of our own people—

MR. JORDAN: That is true enough, but we have decisions here from the Supreme Court on that.

THE COURT: I don't care for that.

MR. JORDAN: Then the question where she says she is an unqualified atheist—whether that would have a bearing on her oath of allegiance.

THE COURT: I think under the Constitution that religious liberty is guaranteed.

MR. JORDAN: Yes, Sir.

THE COURT: And therefore the contrary is.

MR. JORDAN: Then there would be no question on that. The other thing would be with reference to that question 22.

THE COURT: Yes.

MR. JORDAN: Whether or not she is a conscientious objector.

THE COURT: Exactly.

MR. GEMMILL: I would like to ask Mrs. Schwimmer one question.

Q. What do you mean, Mrs. Schwimmer, when you say you can take the oath and you are willing to support and defend the Constitution and the Laws of the United States.

A. I mean the things that I have practically already done; that I was in many meetings in which it was said that it would be far better to have a Soviet regime—"that is a far better kind of regime"—and myself having lived under Soviet regime in Hungary, I could get up and tell the people—as I have practically 6 done—"Don't think you change to something better." To this day there is no better form of government than that of the United States, which is by the people, for the people, as the great saying is, and that Sovietism is nothing but tyranny under another name,—old fashioned tyranny under a new name; and I wrote these things, and I said these things, and I can prove it by writings which I can get from Hungary; so that is what I meant; that there are other means to defend the Constitution and the institutions of this country.

Q. Is it your belief, Mrs. Schwimmer, your own personal belief, that you would not take the life of any one?

A. Yes.

Q. Of any animal?

A. Animals, no. I have no objections against taking the life of animals. I personally wouldn't shoot, but I have no objections against that; but I would not shoot. Even if a pistol was pointed to me, I would not shoot.

Q. Is that what you had in mind when you answered the Court's last question—

A. Yes.

Q. —relative to the shooting of the officer?

A. Yes, of course, I couldn't.

THE COURT: What do you mean by that?

MR. GEMMILL: I mean to say, your Honor, I am trying to explain her answer. It wasn't cold blooded murder of the United States officer that Mrs. Schwimmer had in mind. It was her feeling against the killing of any one.

THE WITNESS: Yes.

THE COURT: I raised a question that might arise in any war, and asked her what she would do if in order to save the life of an officer of this country, whether it was a general officer or the lowest man in the ranks, and she had the opportunity to kill the enemy before he killed our soldier would she do it, and she said "No."

THE WITNESS: Yes.

MR. GEMMILL: May I ask one or two more questions?

THE COURT: Yes.

MR. GEMMILL: Under that same case, Mrs. Schwimmer, would you have given the officer any warning, if it was possible?

A. Certainly.

Q. So that he could defend himself?

A. Certainly.

THE COURT: That is, you would have given him—

A. I would try to hit the pistol out of the man's hand who tries to shoot. That is what I would try to do.

Q. Let me ask you this: Would you have thrown yourself on the assailant?

A. Yes, I might do that.

Q. And run the risk of being shot yourself?

A. Yes, I might do that. Yes.

MR. JORDAN: You say you might do that?

A. Well, I speak of a possibility. I can't say I would do that. We speak of hypothetical things. I can't say I "will" do that, because there is no occasion for it.

7 THE COURT: One never can tell until the occasion arises what will be done.

THE WITNESS: If it would happen this moment I would do it.

THE COURT: But my first question referred not to your trying to stop the man from reaching the American soldier.

THE WITNESS: I understand.

THE COURT: —because he may have been ten feet off—

THE WITNESS: I understand.

THE COURT: —and the American soldier would have been killed before you could have reached his assailant.

THE WITNESS: Yes.

THE COURT: I am asking if you had the weapon, if it were handy by—

THE WITNESS: Yes.

THE COURT: —would you have killed the assailant—

THE WITNESS: No.

THE COURT: —before he reached the American soldier?

THE WITNESS: No.

THE COURT: Then I am of the same opinion.

MR. GEMMILL: Supposing that pistol had been pointed at you and you had a pistol?

A. I would not defend myself. I mean I wouldn't take a pistol to defend myself even if you handed it to me; under no circumstances.

THE COURT: That question is not involved at all. This is a very close question, gentlemen, and I am really refusing this because the Government, I think, has no appeal, but it is an attitude,—the attitude of the applicant—that I think is not common with the women of this country.

Is there anything more, gentlemen?

MR. GEMMILL: I just want to be a little careful about this record.

THE COURT: Suppose it is written up and then we will reduce it to an agreed statement of facts?

MR. GEMMILL: That is satisfactory.

MR. JORDAN: Do you care, your Honor, to take the statements of the witnesses so that they will not be required further?

THE COURT: Oh, yes. Let both witnesses step forward, please. Have you examined them before?

MR. JORDAN: Only one of them: Frances Bird, I believe.

FRANCES BIRD called as a witness, having been first duly sworn, was examined by Mr. Jordan, and testified as follows:

Q. You were born in this country?

A. Yes, sir.

Q. How long have you known Madame Schwimmer?

A. I have known her since the latter part of August or early September, 1921.

Q. And you can vouch for her character?

A. Yes.

8 Q. And do you believe that she would make a good citizen?

A. An excellent citizen.

Q. There is nothing in what she has said and done that would lead you to say otherwise?

A. No.

FLORENCE HOLBROOK called as a witness, having been first duly sworn, was examined by Mr. Jordan, and testified as follows:

Q. Where were you born?

A. Illinois.

Q. You are single?

A. Yes.

Q. How long have you known Madame Schwimmer?

A. Since 1914 on occasions, and continuously since August, 1921.

Q. That is, since she came back here to live in 1921?

A. Yes.

Q. And you have seen her frequently, have you?

A. Yes.

Q. What do you say about her qualifications for citizenship?

A. I think she would make a first-class citizen.

THE COURT: Both of the witnesses believe that the applicant is a thoroughly good woman.

MRS. BIRD: Yes.

MISS HOLBROOK: Yes, I do.

THE COURT: That is all. That is what we want to know.

MR. JORDAN: The witnesses may be excused then.

MR. GEMMILL: I suppose in this kind of a case a motion for a new trial first should be made.

THE COURT: No, I think not.

MR. GEMMILL: Motion in arrest, or pray an appeal then.

THE COURT: Let us delay the final order until you get your agreed statement of facts. You confer with the Department, because it sounds absurd to the Court that you suggest a motion in arrest of judgment.

MR. GEMMILL: I understand that an appeal lies as in all other cases, and I thought I had better make my motions regardless.

THE COURT: We will give you everything because I want this question reviewed.

MR. GEMMILL: Yes, your Honor.

THE COURT: But it is amusing to have you refer to some good old common law phrases which never had anything to do with naturalization petitions.

MR. GEMMILL: That is quite true. I realize though that there is only one way of appeal and that is to make your motions first. If we will get an agreed statement of facts and bring them to your Honor for his approval, then we will pray our appeal.

THE COURT: Exactly, and put in your prayer and make all the orders you can think of that will protect the applicant here on the appeal on the seventh floor.

MR. JORDAN: May we have a date or shall we come in on motion?

THE COURT: Come in on motion when it is ready.

9 You understand, Madame, that while the Court may have said some things that shock, perhaps, your views of nationalism, we are here to administer the law as we see it. We have taken an oath for that purpose and we try to live up to it. There is nothing personal about it all.

MADAME SCHWIMMER: I realize that, your Honor.

MR. GEMMILL: Just one more remark, if the Court please. Mrs. Rabe, who is counsel for Mrs. Schwimmer, has prepared a very fine brief, in my opinion. I want your Honor at some time or other before the final order is entered to either hear her on that or look at that brief, if you will. I realize it is a matter of discretion and opinion. However, there are certain authorities—

THE COURT: I will be very glad to see it. It is a matter of education for me.

*Bold numbers designate original pagination of the typescript.

Appendix E

Statement of Rosika Schwimmer in "Agreed Statement of Facts"*

10 On the 22nd of September, 1926, I appeared before District Director of Naturalization for Chicago, Mr. Fred I. Schlotfeldt, with my two sponsors, Miss Florence Holbrook, principal of the Philip Wendell Junior High School and Miss Frances Bird. I was also accompanied by my friend Mrs. Olive H. Rabe, attorney at law at Chicago.

Mr. Schlotfeldt found a contradiction in my answer to two **11** questions of the Preliminary Form for Petition for Naturalization. I had answered question No. 22 in the negative. As I was unable to see a connection between the two questions, while Mr. Schlotfeldt considered them organically connected, he requested me to make a written statement as to my interpretation of the oath of allegiance (question No. 20).

Complying with Mr. Schlotfeldt's request, I am hereby submitting my interpretation of the oath of allegiance to be presented to the Federal Judge before whom I am going to appear for final examination.

I declare that I have wholeheartedly and without any reservation answered "Yes" to question No. 20, which reads:

"Have you read the following oath of allegiance? 'I hereby declare, on oath, that I absolutely and entirely renounce and abjure all allegiance and fidelity to any foreign prince, potentate, state or sovereignty, and particularly to the Kingdom of Hungary of whom I have theretofore been a subject; that I will support and defend the Constitution and laws of the United States of America against all enemies, foreign and domestic; and that I will bear true faith and allegiance to the same.' Are you willing to take this oath in becoming a citizen?"

I could and can say "Yes" because I do not want to remain a subject of Hungary and because choosing an adoptive country I found the Constitution and the institutions of the United States of America nearest to my ideals of a democratic republic governed by the people for the people on the basis of independence and tolerance.

I have no prospect to share the material benefits America offers its citizens. My desire to become an American citizen is based on ideal considerations. Like so many foreign born men and women through America's history I have chosen to apply for American citizenship because the United States of America seemed to me a haven of refuge from a country where social prejudices and feudal institutions have grown intolerable to self-respecting men and women. I am therefore whole-heartedly prepared to "bear true faith and allegiance." And just as unreservedly am I ready "to support and defend the Constitution and the laws against all enemies foreign and domestic."

This is the point where Mr. Schlotfeldt considered me inconsistent, because I gave a negative answer to question No. **12** 22, which reads: "If necessary, are you willing to take up arms in defense of this country?"

First I had not answered this question at all because I thought it applied only to men, like question No. 23 about draft-board, service in the war, etc. As Mr. Schlotfeldt, however, explained that women too have to answer question No. 22, I wrote: "I would not take up arms personally."

I cannot see that a woman's refusal to take up arms is a contradiction to the oath of allegiance. Promising to support and defend the Constitution and the laws of the United States of America I have—for the fulfillment of this duty—other ways and means in mind.

I am keenly interested in every aspect of civic life. I read papers, magazines of every shade of opinion, attend lectures and meetings dealing with civic problems. As I know a number of languages I occasionally glance through Hungarian, French, German, Dutch, Scandinavian, and Italian publications. I can imagine finding in meetings and publications attacks against the American form of government and praise of undemocratic forms, in which I do not believe.

According to my conception of "support and defense" I would in such cases consider it my duty to uphold most emphatically the American constitution [sic] and the American form of government in which I believe, and to oppose such forms of government which are not based on Democracy and Self-government. Both my theoretical convictions and my practical experiences qualify me to take this stand. I have lived under feudal, under Soviet, and under White Terror regimes in the country of my birth. I found all three systems intolerable.

No argument whatsoever has ever been able to sway me from my deep-rooted opposition to any undemocratic form of government, like the dictatorship of the proletariate, or dictatorship of Fascism, or the rule of White Terror, or Military dictatorship. All my past work proves that I have always served democratic ideals and fought—though not with arms—against undemocratic institutions.

It would be denying the force of spiritual influences, of mental energies, if we defined the word "defense" solely as a physical act.

My "support of the Constitution and the laws of the United States of America" I could and would prove in participating in civic activities which are in accord with the laws of the country.

13 I defended and upheld American institutions long before I even dreamed of applying for American citizenship. When during the war-years America was maligned and misrepresented as selfish scheming, etc., in the opposite belligerent and in the neutral countries, I made it my particular task to lecture and write in those countries about America's idealism and democracy. So much so, that malicious sources spread the rumour I was paid by America for that service. A great number of lectures all over Hungary, a few in Austria, Switzerland, the Netherlands, and in the Scandinavian countries, many articles in the leading daily papers of these countries gave me an opportunity to uphold American ideals and institutions.

During my four months as minister from Hungary to Switzerland at the end of the war—the only time in my life that I accepted an office—I worked for the preparation of a constitution modelled [*sic*] after the American and the Swiss constitutions. I hoped Hungary would become a Democracy like the United States of America and Switzerland. The representatives of the American Government in Berne at the time, Mrs. Vira B. Whitehouse (Mrs. Norman R. de W.), her successor, Mr. Hugh Smith, the Military attaché, Colonel Godson, and others who co-operated with me during this time in Hungarian matters can testify to that. Also to the fact that I was vehemently opposed to Bolshevism, as a terroristic and undemocratic rule.

More recently I had an opportunity to "Defend" America in the sense in which I consider the word defense. During an international pacifist congress of women in 1924 in Washington, D.C., the question of Pan-Europe was discussed. I see in Pan-Europe the only real danger and possibility of a successful attack against the United States of America. I explained my stand against the Pan-European idea on this ground. And since the Pan-European movement, led by Count Coudenhouve-Kalergi started—curiously enough said to be financed by shortsighted Americans—I take every chance to oppose it with the explanation that it is the way to a world fight against the United States.

If, however, it is a fact that the Government of the United States can compel its women citizens to take up arms in the defense of the country—something that no other civilized government has ever attempted, I would not be able to comply with this requirement of American citizenship. In this case I would recognize the right of the government to deal **14** with me as it is dealing with its male citizens who for conscientious reasons refuse to take up arms.

My application expresses my hope to share the privileges but also the duties and obligations of American citizenship.

Transcript of Record, *Court of Appeals for the Seventh Circuit, Schwimmer v. United States*, 10

*Bold numbers indicate the original page numbers in the Transcript of Record.

Appendix F

Rosika Schwimmer
*What Price American Citizenship?**

/1/ The puzzle "Is she, or is she not an American citizen?" has become one of the minor parlor games since contradicting rumors, correct and incorrect reports about my citizenship have bobbed up in the press. I am not so conceited to believe that the tremendous American and international interest in my citizenship is due to my person. I feel sure it is due to the importance of the underlying principle.

Though Naturalization Director Schlotfeldt had predicted it to me I was stunned when Federal Judge Carpenter on October 13, 1927 denied my petition on ground of my intransigent pacifism. Keenly as I desired American citizenship I was ready to acquiesce in the decision, because I felt too proud to fight myself into the citizenship of a country that did not want me.

But individuals and organizations, like the leaders of the League for American Citizenship and the American Civil Liberties Union and prominent Quakers urged me to appeal against the verdict as a test whether compulsory bearing arms can be made a condition for a woman's citizenship. When the Court of Appeals on June 29, 1928, reversed the verdict practically the whole American press hailed my admittance as a gesture of true Americanism. Only two organs differed from the general opinion. The Chicago Tribune and the late President Harding's paper the "Marion Star."

On the 22nd of September my attorney, Mrs. Olive H. Rabe, Chicago informed me that the Government has appealed against the ruling which granted me citizenship.

I have renounced Hungarian citizenship, because my native country returned to feudalism, semi-dictatorship and Monarchism, after having been under the Karolyi regime a democratic republic. I disliked this reactionary condition much as the Bolshevik dictatorship which had followed the Karyoli regime. I chose the U.S.A. as adoptive country [*sic*] because it is a democracy, a republic and in its peaceful co-operative union of 48 states to my mind the most magnificent example of statecraft existing. That this country should deny me citizenship because of my pacifist principles is utterly bewildering. The Kellogg treaties have just heralded to the world that /2/ the U.S.A. believes in the supreme pacifist principle of solving international differences by reasoning instead of fighting. Even if I should never be accepted into American citizenship I feel in spirit distinctly American. I consider it an American duty to stand the ordeal of further legal proceedings which might make it appear as if I wished to push myself into a family that does not want me. I am facing this unfavorable appearance because the essential issue is not whether the outcome will fulfill my heart's desire to become an American citizen, but whether the U.S.A. are pioneering in the demanding that women bear arms.

The date 23 September 1928 is written in Schwimmer's hand at the top of the page. Schwimmer-Lloyd collection, box G-5.
*Bold numbers represent original pagination of typescript.

Appendix G

United States v. Schwimmer*

279 U.S. 644

CERTIORARI TO THE CIRCUIT COURT OF APPEALS FOR THE SEVENTH CIRCUIT

No. 484. Argued April 12, 1929—Decided May 27, 1929.

646 *Mr. Alfred A. Wheat*, with whom *Attorney General Mitchell*, *Assistant Attorney General Luhring*, and *Mr. Harry S. Ridgely* were on the brief, for the United States.

Mrs. Olive H. Rabe for respondent.

MR. JUSTICE BUTLER delivered the opinion of the Court.

Respondent filed a petition for naturalization in the District Court for the Northern District of Illinois. The court found her unable, without mental reservation, to take the prescribed oath of allegiance, and not attached to the principles of the Constitution of the United States, and not well disposed to the good order and happiness of the same; and it denied her application. The Circuit Court of Appeals reversed the decree, and directed the District Court to grant respondent's petition. 27 F. (2d) 742.

The Naturalization Act of June 29, 1906, requires:

"He (the applicant for naturalization) shall, before he is admitted to citizenship, declare on oath in open court . . . that he will support and defend the Constitution and laws of the United States against all enemies, foreign and domestic, and bear true faith and allegiance to the same." U.S.C. Tit. 8, § 381.

"It shall be made to appear to the satisfaction of the court . . . that during that time (at least five years preceding the application) he has behaved as a man of good moral character, attached to the principles of the Constitution of the United States, and well disposed to the good order and happiness of the same. . . ." § 382.

Respondent was born in Hungary in 1877 and is a citizen of the country. She came to the United States in August, 1921, to visit and lecture, has resided in Illinois since the latter part of that month, declared her intention to become a citizen the following November, and filed petition for naturalization in September, 1926. On a preliminary form, she stated that she understood the prin647ciples of and fully believed in our form of government, and that she had read, and in becoming a citizen was willing to take, the oath of allegiance. Question 22 was this: "If necessary, are you willing to take up arms in defense of this country?" She answered: "I would not take up arms personally."

She testified that she did not want to remain subject to Hungary, found the United States nearest her ideals of a democratic republic, and that she could whole-heartedly take the oath of allegiance. She said: "I cannot see that a woman's refusal to take up arms is a contradiction to the oath of allegiance." For the fulfillment of the duty to support and defend the Constitution and laws, she had in mind other ways and means. She referred to her interest in civic life, to her wide reading and attendance at lectures and meetings, mentioned her knowledge of foreign languages, and that she occasionally glanced through Hungarian, French, German, Dutch, Scandinavian, and Italian publications, and said that she could imagine finding in meetings and publications attacks on the American form of government, and she would conceive it her duty to uphold it against such attacks. She expressed steadfast opposition to any undemocratic form of government, like proletariat, fascist, white terror, or military dictatorships. "All my past work proves that I have always served democratic ideals and fought—though not with arms—against undemocratic institutions." She stated that before coming to this country she had defended American ideals, and had defended America in 1924 during an international pacifist congress in Washington.

She also testified: "If . . . the United States can compel its women citizens to take up arms in the defense of the country—something that no other civilized government has ever attempted—I would not be able to comply with this requirement of American citizenship. In this **648** case I would recognize the right of the government to deal with me as it is dealing with its male citizens who for conscientious reasons refuse to take up arms."

The district director of naturalization by letter called her attention to a statement made by her in private correspondence: "I am an uncompromising pacifist. . . . I have no sense of nationalism, only a cosmic consciousness of belonging to the human family." She answered that the statement in her petition demonstrated that she was an uncompromising pacifist. "Highly as I prize the privilege of American citizenship, I could not compromise my way into it by giving an untrue answer to question 22, though for all practical purposes I might have done so, as even men of my age—I was 49 years old last September—are not called to take up arms. . . . That 'I have no nationalistic feeling' is evident from the fact that I wish to give up the nationality of my birth and to adopt a country which is based on principles and institutions more in harmony with my ideals. My 'cosmic consciousness of belonging to the human family' is shared by all those who believe that all human beings are the children of God."

And at the hearing she reiterated her ability and willingness to take the oath of allegiance without reservation and added: "I am willing to do everything that an American citizen has to do except fighting. If American women would be compelled to do that, I would not do that. I am an uncompromising pacifist. . . . I do not care how many other women fight, because I consider it a question of conscience. I am not willing to bear arms. In every other single way I am ready to follow the law and do everything that the law compels American citizens to do. That is why I can take the oath of allegiance, because, as far as I can find out there is nothing that I could be compelled to do that I cannot do. . . . With reference to spreading propaganda among the women throughout 649 the country about my being an uncompromising pacifist and not willing to fight, I am always ready to tell any one who wants to hear it that I am an uncompromising pacifist and will not fight. In my writings and in my lectures I take up the question of war and pacifism, if I am asked for that."

Except for eligibility to the Presidency, naturalized citizens stand on the same footing as do native-born citizens. All alike owe allegiance to the government, and the government owes to them the duty of protection. These are reciprocal obligations, and each is a consideration for the other. *Luria v. United States*, 231 U.S. 9, 22. But aliens can acquire such equality only by naturalization according to the uniform rules prescribed by the Congress. They have no natural right to become citizens, but only that which is by statute conferred upon them. Because of the great value of the privileges conferred by naturalization, the statutes prescribing qualifications and governing procedure for admission are to be construed with definite purpose to favor and support the government. And, in order to safeguard against admission of those who are unworthy, or who for any reason fail to measure up to required standards, the law puts the burden upon every applicant to show by satisfactory evidence that he has the specified qualifications. *Tutun v. United States*, 270 U.S. 568, 578. And see *United States v. Ginsberg*, 243 U.S. 472, 475.

Every alien claiming citizenship is given the right to submit his petition and evidence in support of it. And, if the requisite facts are established, he is entitled as of right to admission. On applications for naturalization, the court's function is "to receive testimony, to compare it with the law, and to judge on both law and fact." *Spratt v. Spratt*, 4 Pet. 393, 408. We quite recently declared that: "Citizenship is a high privilege, and when doubts exist concerning a grant of it, generally at least, **650** they should be resolved in favor of the United States and against the claimant." *United States v. Manzi*, 276 U.S. 463, 467. And when, upon a fair consideration of the evidence adduced upon an application for citizenship, doubt remains in the mind of the court as to any essential matter of fact, the United States is entitled to the benefit of such doubt and the application should be denied.

That it is the duty of citizens by force of arms to defend our government against all enemies whenever necessity arises is a fundamental principle of the Constitution.

The common defense was one of the purposes for which the people ordained and established the Constitution. It empowers Congress to provide for such defense, to declare war, to raise and support armies, to maintain a navy, to make rules for the government and regulation of the land and naval forces, to provide for organizing, arming, and disciplining the militia, and for calling it forth to execute the laws of the Union, suppress insurrections and repel invasions; it makes the President commander in chief of the army and navy and of the militia of the several states when called into the service of the United States; it declares that, a well-regulated militia being necessary to the security of a free state, the right of the people to keep and bear arms shall not be infringed. We need not refer to the numerous statutes that contemplate defense of the United States, its Constitution and laws, by armed citizens. This Court, in the *Selective Draft Law Cases*, 245 U.S. 366, speaking through Chief Justice White, said (p. 378) that "the very conception of a just government and its duty to the citizen includes the reciprocal obligation of the citizen to render military service in case of need. . . ."

Whatever tends to lessen the willingness of citizens to discharge their duty to bear arms in the country's defense detracts from the strength and safety of the Government. **651** And their opinions and beliefs as well as their behavior indicating a disposition to hinder in the performance of that duty are subjects of inquiry under the statutory provisions governing naturalization and are of vital importance, for if all or a large number of citizens oppose such defense the "good order and happiness" of the United States cannot long endure. And it is evident that the views of applicants for naturalization in respect of such matters may not be disregarded. The influence of conscientious objectors against the use of military force in defense of the principles of our government is apt to be more detrimental than their mere refusal to bear arms. The fact that, by reason of sex, age or other cause, they may be unfit to serve does not lessen their purpose or power to influence others. It is clear from her own statements that the declared opinions of respondent as to armed defense by citizens against enemies of the country were directly pertinent to the investigation of her application.

The record shows that respondent strongly desires to become a citizen. She is a linguist, lecturer, and writer; she is well educated and accustomed to discuss governments and civic affairs. Her testimony should be considered having regard to her interest and disclosed ability correctly to express herself. Her claim at the hearing that she possessed the required qualifications and was willing to take the oath was much impaired by other parts of her testimony. Taken as a whole, it shows that her objection to military service rests on reasons other than mere inability because of her sex and age personally to bear arms. Her expressed willingness to be treated as the Government dealt with conscientious objectors who refused to take up arms in the recent war indicates that she deemed herself to belong to that class. The fact that she is an uncompromising pacifist, with no sense of nation**652**alism, but only a cosmic sense of belonging to the human family, justifies belief that she may be opposed to the use of military force as contemplated by our Constitution and laws. And her testimony clearly suggests that she is disposed to exert her power to influence others to such opposition.

A pacifist, in the general sense of the word, is one who seeks to maintain peace and to abolish war. Such purposes are in harmony with the Constitution and policy of our Government. But the word is also used and understood to mean one who refuses or is unwilling for any purpose to bear arms because of conscientious considerations and who is disposed to encourage others in such refusal. And one who is without any sense of nationalism is not well bound or held by the ties of affection to any nation or government. Such persons are liable to be incapable of the attachment for and devotion to the principles of our Constitution that are required of aliens seeking naturalization.

It is shown by official records and everywhere well known that during the recent war there were found among those who described themselves as pacifists and conscientious objectors many citizens—though happily a minute part of all—who were unwilling to bear arms in that crisis and who refused to obey the laws of the United States and the lawful commands of its officers and encouraged such disobedience in others. Local boards found it necessary to issue a great number of noncombatant certificates, and several thousand who were called to camp made claim because of conscience for exemption from any form of military service. Several hundred were convicted and sentenced to imprisonment for offenses involving disobedience, desertion, propaganda and sedition. It is obvious that the acts of such offenders evidence a want of that attachment to the principles of the Constitution of which **653** the applicant is required to give affirmative evidence by the Naturalization Act.

The language used by respondent to describe her attitude in respect of the principles of the Constitution was vague and ambiguous; the burden was upon her to show what she meant and that her pacifism and lack of nationalistic sense did not oppose the principle that it is a duty of citizenship by force of arms when necessary to defend the country against all enemies, and that her opinions and beliefs would not prevent or impair the true faith and allegiance required by the act. She failed to do so. The District Court was bound by the law to deny her application.

The decree of the Circuit Court of Appeals is reversed. The decree of the District Court is affirmed.

MR. JUSTICE HOLMES, dissenting.

The applicant seems to be a woman of superior character and intelligence, obviously more than ordinarily desirable as a citizen of the United States. It is agreed that she is qualified for citizenship except so far as the views set forth in a statement of facts "may show that the applicant is not attached to the principles of the Constitution of the United States and well disposed to the good order and happiness of the same, and except in so far as the same may show that she cannot take the oath of allegiance without a mental reservation." The views referred to are an extreme opinion in favor of pacifism and a statement that she would not bear arms to defend the Constitution. So far as the adequacy of her oath is concerned I hardly can see how that is affected by the statement, inasmuch as she is a woman over fifty years of age, and would not be allowed to bear arms if she wanted **654** to. And as to the opinion, the whole examination of the applicant shows that she holds none of the now-dreaded creeds but thoroughly believes in organized government and prefers that of the United States to any other in the world. Surely it cannot show lack of attachment to the principles of the Constitution that she thinks that it can be improved. I suppose that most intelligent people think that it might be. Her particular improvement looking to the abolition of war seems to me not materially different in its bearing on this case from a wish to establish cabinet government as in England, or a single house, or one term of seven years for the President. To touch a more burning question, only a judge mad with partisanship would exclude because the applicant thought that the Eighteenth Amendment should be repealed.

Of course the fear is that if a war came the applicant would exert activities such as were dealt with in *Schenck v. United States*, 249 U.S. 47. But that seems to me unfounded. Her position and motives are wholly different from those of Schenck. She is an optimist and states in strong and, I do not doubt, sincere words her belief that war will disappear and that the impending destiny of mankind is to unite in peaceful leagues. I do not share that optimism nor do I think that a philosophic view of the world would regard war as absurd. But most people who have known it regard it with horror, as a last resort, and even if not yet ready for cosmopolitan efforts, would welcome any practicable combinations that would increase the power on the side of peace. The notion that the applicant's optimistic anticipations would make her a worse citizen is sufficiently answered by her examination which seems to me a better argument for her admission than any that I can offer. Some of her answers might excite popular prejudice, but if there is any principle of the Constitution that more imperatively calls for attachment than any other it is the principle of free **655** thought—not free thought for those who agree with us but freedom for the thought that we hate. I think that we should adhere to that principle with regard to admission into, as well as to life within this country. And recurring to the opinion that bars this applicant's way, I would suggest that the Quakers have done their share to make the country what it is, that many citizens agree with the applicant's belief and that I had not supposed hitherto that we regretted our inability to expel them because they believed more than some of us do in the teachings of the Sermon on the Mount.

MR. JUSTICE BRANDEIS concurs in this opinion.

MR. JUSTICE SANFORD, dissenting.

I agree, in substance, with the views expressed by the Circuit Court of Appeals, and think its decree should be affirmed.

*Bold numbers represent original pagination of typescript.

Appendix H

Rosika Schwimmer's Reaction to Denial of Citizenship

New York American, 31 May 1929 (excerpt from longer article)

"Pacifist Not Bitter; Fate Puzzles Her"

CAN'T UNDERSTAND

"Mine is a queer sensation, a feeling I can hardly describe. I had come to believe myself an American citizen. Now it is hard to believe that if I look into the street and see it dirty I may not say to myself: 'Well, I will see the commissioner about it.' No, I must say: 'Madame, it is none of your business. You are an alien; at best a guest.'

"And it is hard to think that because I, a woman of fifty-two, do not want to fight, this great country of ideals should refuse me citizenship.

"As a child in Hungary I read avidly of Washington and Lincoln and Benjamin Franklin. Franklin was my favorite. I never tired of reading about him.

"I used to thrill at the thought of a young, vigorous, forward-looking country, where the ideals of liberty and freedom were exalted. It appealed to me tremendously. When I left Hungary, I considered carefully where I should go. I have no strong nationalistic feelings, but I endeavored, to use an Old-World saying to 'choose my parents wisely.' I chose the United States."

"AL CAPONE ALL RIGHT"

"But I have fought all my life for peace, for an end of war. I am opposed to killing. Al Capone is all right; he is ready to shoot. But I am dangerous."

Mme. Schwimmer's situation is an anomalous one. She last entered the country in 1921 legally, and, under the law which makes her residence legal after five years, she is not endangered with deportation. In fact, she

398

is expatriated from Hungary, and there would be no place in the world to which she might be deported, although that question never has been raised. She said:

"When I returned to the United States in 1921 I was amazed at the horrible stories being spread about me. I was called a Red and a Communist and many lectures cancelled because a military intelligence association in Chicago accused me privately of circulating Communistic propaganda.

.   .   .   .

DENIES COWARDICE

"Many people have erroneous ideas about pacifists. They believe a pacifist shrinks from physical violence because of cowardice. It is not so. I don't believe in suffering injustice, physical or mental. I'm a fighter. I am a pacifist, but not passively so.

"What I have been saying is what Nicholas Murray Butler is saying, what the Kellogg Treaty says, what everybody says. Yet I am dangerous because I say it."

Appendix I

The Naturalization Act of 1906

The Naturalization Act of 1906, operative at the time of Macintosh's application, reads in pertinent part:

"Sec. 4: That an alien may be admitted to become a citizen of the United States in the following manner and not otherwise:

. . . .

"Third. He shall, before he is admitted to citizenship, declare on oath in open court that he will support the Constitution of the United States, and that he absolutely and entirely renounces and abjures all allegiance and fidelity to any foreign prince, potentate, state, or sovereignty, and particularly by name to the prince, potentate, state, or sovereignty of which he was before a citizen or a subject; that he will support and defend the Constitution and laws of the United States against all enemies, foreign and domestic, and bear true faith and allegiance to the same.

"Fourth. It shall be made to appear to the satisfaction of the court admitting any alien to citizenship that immediately preceding the date of his application he has resided continuously within the United States five years at least, and within the State or Territory where such court is at the time held one year at least, and that during that time he has behaved as a man [*sic*] of good moral character, attached to the principles of the Constitution of the United States and well disposed to the good order of the same."

34 Stat. 596, c. 3592; 8 U.S.C. §§ 372, 381, 382

Appendix J

Macintosh's Description of His Objection to War

SUPPLEMENTARY STATEMENT FOR THE INFORMATION OF THE JUDGE OF THE UNITED STATES DISTRICT COURT AT NEW HAVEN, JUNE 24, 1929.

I am not a pacifist—at least in the extreme sense in which that word is now commonly used. I am not certain that under no possible circumstances would I support a defensive war. At the same time I am very strongly of the opinion that no events are likely to occur within my lifetime such as would justify a declaration of war on the part of the United States of America. Moreover I am in agreement with what seems to be the best judgment of well-informed persons that any major war in the future would be so absolutely disastrous to the human race that it is scarcely possible to exaggerate the importance of our doing everything that can reasonably be done now to secure the future peace of the world. To this end it has seemed to me that full freedom to oppose unjustified war is of the first importance.

In accordance with this view I am taking the liberty of stating explicitly a reservation without which I cannot truthfully give an affirmative answer to Question 22 in the Preliminary Form for Petition for Naturalization ("If necessary, are you willing to take up arms in defense of this country?"), and a similar reservation which I could not but have in mind in taking the oath of allegiance to the United States of America in the form in which it occurs in Question 20 of the same document. These are the reservations:

1. I claim the right, conscientiously and in the light of the relevant facts (which ought to be truthfully and adequately made known by the government), to decide for myself whether or not the taking up of arms in defense of my country is "necessary" for the true well-being of the nation

and of the world.

2. If the promise to "support and defend the Constitution and laws of the United States of America against all enemies, foreign and domestic," has reference, among other things, to the use or to a support and defense of the use of military force in acts of war, I am not willing to take the oath of allegiance in this form, except with the distinct understanding that I shall be under obligation to take or to support and defend such military action only if I can at the time honestly believe it to be in the best interests of my country and of humanity in general.

I am willing, however, to pledge full loyalty, as I understand loyalty, to my country. By this I mean that I recognize the duty of placing the true well-being of my country above all private and selfish interests, and that I would strive to act in accordance with this ideal. But I do not recognize any duty to place the outward prosperity or military success of my country above the true well-being of humanity; and because it must always remain somewhat uncertain, before the event, just what action any government will take with regard to peace and war, I have to say that I am not willing to declare beforehand that I will do what I should very probably be unable to do conscientiously at the time.

If then I am permitted to become a citizen of the United States of America at this time, it will be with the distinct understanding that taking the oath of allegiance does not necessarily imply any contract either to use military force or to support and defend the use of military force at the dictation of the government of the day. And I should want it to be understood that if and when I take the oath of allegiance to the United States on any future occasion (as in applying for a passport, for example), it may be and is very likely to be with this same reservation.

I recognize not only the duty of loyal citizenship but that this loyalty involves due regard for the Constitution and laws of the country. Not selfish pleasure or mere individual preference, but only the furthering of the true well-being of humanity, could justify the citizen in acting in opposition to the Constitution and laws of his country. I am not asking recognition of any right of the citizen to refuse obedience to the Constitution and laws of his country if and when his motives are of an individualistic and selfish nature; I am only asking to be allowed to refuse such obedience if and when, after fair consideration of the available facts in the case, I honestly believe such refusal to be in the best interests of humanity.

from Douglas Clyde Macintosh Scrapbook

Appendix K

United States v. Macintosh*

283 U.S. 605

Certiorari to the Circuit Court of Appeals for the Second Circuit

No. 504. Argued April 27, 1931—Decided May 25, 1931.

607 *Solicitor General Thacher*, with whom *Assistant Attorney General Dodds* and *Messers. Whitney North Seymour* and *Harry S. Ridgley* were on the brief, for the United States.

610 *Mr. John W. Davis*, with whom *Messers. Charles E. Clark, Allen Wardwell*, and *W. Charles Poletti* were on the brief, for respondent.

613 Mr. Justice SUTHERLAND delivered the opinion of the Court.

The respondent was born in the Dominion of Canada. He came to the United States in 1916, and in 1925 declared his intention to become a citizen. His petition for naturalization was presented to the federal District Court for Connecticut, and that court, after hearing and consideration, denied the application upon the ground that, since petitioner would not promise in advance to bear arms in defense of the United States unless he believed the war to be morally justified, he was not attached to the principles of the Constitution. The Circuit Court of Appeals reversed the decree and directed the District Court to admit respondent to citizenship. 42 F.(2d) 845.

The Naturalization Act, § 4, c. 3592, 34 Stat. 596 (U.S C. Title 8, § 372 *et seq.*), provides that an alien may be admitted to citizenship in the manner therein provided and not otherwise. By section 3 of the same act, jurisdiction to naturalize aliens is conferred upon the District Courts of the

United States and other enumerated courts of record. U.S.C., Title 8, § 357. The applicant is required to make **614** and file a preliminary declaration in writing setting forth, among other things, his intention to become a citizen of the United States and to renounce all allegiance to any foreign prince, etc. Section 4 of the act (U.S.C., Title 8, §§ 381, 382 provides:

"Third. He shall, before he is admitted to citizenship, declare on oath in open court that he will support the Constitution of the United States, and that he absolutely and entirely renounces and abjures all allegiance and fidelity to any foreign prince, potentate, state, or sovereignty, and particularly by name to the prince, potentate, state or sovereignty of which he was before a citizen or subject; that he will support and defend the Constitution and laws of the United States against all enemies, foreign and domestic, and bear true faith and allegiance to the same.

"Fourth. It shall be made to appear to the satisfaction of the court admitting any alien to citizenship that immediately preceding the date of his application he has resided continuously within the United States, five years at least, and within the State or Territory where such court is at the time held one year at least, and that during that time he has behaved as a man of good moral character, attached to the principles of the Constitution of the United States, and well disposed to the good order and happiness of the same. In addition to the oath of the applicant, the testimony of at least two witnesses, citizens of the United States, as to the facts of residence, moral character, and attachment to the principles of the Constitution shall be required, . . ."

Section 9 of the act, 34 Stat. 599 (U.S.C., Title 8, § 398), requires that every final hearing upon a petition for naturalization shall be had in open court; that every final order upon the petition shall be under the hand of the court; and that "upon such final hearing of such petition the applicant and witnesses shall be examined under **615** oath before the court and in the presence of the court." By § 11, 34 Stat. 599 (U.S.C., Title 8, § 399), it is provided that the United States shall have the right to appear in the proceeding for the purpose of cross-examining the petitioner and witnesses produced in support of the petition "concerning any matter touching or in any way affecting his right to admission to citizenship, and shall have the right to call witnesses, produce evidence, and be heard in opposition to the granting of any petition in naturalization proceedings."

By the petition for naturalization, a case is presented for the exercise of the judicial power under the Constitution, to which the United States is a proper, and always a possible, adverse party. *Tutun v. United States*, 270 U.S. 568, 576-77.

Naturalization is a privilege, to be given, qualified, or withheld as Congress may determine, and which the alien may claim as of right only upon compliance with the terms which Congress imposes. That Congress regarded the admission to citizenship as a serious matter is apparent from the conditions and precautions with which it carefully surrounded the subject. Thus, among other provisions, it is required that the applicant not only shall reside continuously within the United States for a period of at least five years immediately preceding his application, but shall make a preliminary declaration of his intention to become a citizen at least two years prior to his admission. He must produce the testimony of witnesses as to the facts of residence, moral character, and attachment to the principles of the Constitution, and in open court take an oath renouncing his former allegiance and pleading future allegiance to the United States. At the final hearing in open court, he and his witnesses must be examined under oath, and the government may appear for the purpose of cross-examining in respect of "any matter touching or in any way affecting his right to **616** admission," introduce countervailing evidence, and be heard in opposition.

In specifically requiring that the court shall be satisfied that the applicant, during his residence in the United States, has behaved as a man of good moral character, attached to the principles of the Constitution of the United States, etc., it is obvious that Congress regarded the fact of good character and the *fact* of attachment to the principles of the Constitution as matters of the first importance. The applicant's behavior is significant to the extent that it tends to establish or negative these facts.

But proof of good behavior does not close the inquiry. Why does the statute require examination of the applicant and witnesses in open court and under oath, and for what purpose is the government authorized to cross-examine concerning any matter *touching* or in any way *affecting* the right of naturalization? Clearly, it would seem, in order that the court and the government, whose power and duty in that respect these provisions take for granted, may discover whether the applicant is fitted for citizenship;—and to that end, by actual inquiry, ascertain, among other things, whether he has intelligence and good character; whether his oath to support and defend the Constitution and laws of the United States, and to bear true faith and allegiance to the same, will be taken without mental reservation or purpose inconsistent therewith; whether his views are compatible with the obligations and duties of American citizenship; whether he will upon his own part observe the laws of the land; whether he is willing to support the government in time of war, as well as in time of peace, and to assist in the defense of the country, not to the extent or in the manner that he may choose, but to such extent and in such manner as he lawfully may be required to do. These, at least, are matters which are of the essence of the statutory requirements, and in respect of which the mind and conscience of the applicant **617** may be probed by pertinent inquiries, as fully as the court, in the exercise of a sound discretion, may conclude is necessary.

The settled practice of the courts having jurisdiction in naturalization proceedings has, from the beginning, been in accordance with this view. *In re Bodek*, 63 Fed. 813; *In re Meakins*, 164 Fed. 334; *In re Madurri*, 176 Fed. 465, 466; *In re Ross*, 188 Fed. 685; *United States v. Bressi*, 208 Fed. 369, 372; *Schurmann v. United States*, 264 Fed. 917, 920; *In re Sigelman*, 268 Fed. 217. And it finds support in the decisions of this Court. As early as 1830, in *Spratt v. Spratt*, 4 Pet. 393, 407, Chief Justice Marshall, speaking for the Court, said:

"The various acts upon the subject submit the decision on the right of aliens to admission as citizens to courts of record. They are to receive testimony, to compare it with the law, and to judge on both law and fact." *United States v. Schwimmer*, 279 U.S. 644, 649.

With the foregoing statutory provisions and the scope of the powers and duties of the courts of first instance in respect thereof in mind, we come to a consideration of the case now before us. The applicant had complied with all the formal requirements of the law, and his personal character and conduct were shown to be good in all respects. His right to naturalization turns altogether upon the effect to be given to certain answers and qualifying statements made in response to interrogatories propounded to him.

Upon the preliminary form for petition for naturalization, the following questions, among others, appear: "20. Have you read the following oath of allegiance? (which is then quoted). Are you willing to take this oath in becoming a citizen?" "22. If necessary, are you willing to take up arms in defense of this country?" In response to the question designated 20, he answered "Yes." In response to the question designated 22, he answered, "Yes; but I should want to be free to judge of the neces**618**sity." By a written memorandum subsequently filed, he amplified these answers as follows:

"20 and 22. I am willing to do what I judge to be in the best interests of my country, but only in so far as I can believe that this is not going to be against the best interests of humanity in the long run. I do not undertake to support 'my country, right or wrong' in any dispute which may arise, and I am not willing to promise beforehand, and without knowing the cause for which my country may go to war, either that I will or that I will not 'take up arms in defense of this country,' however 'necessary' the war may seem to be to the Government of the day.

"It is only in a sense consistent with these statements that I am willing to promise to 'support and defend' the Government of the United States 'against all enemies, foreign and domestic.' But, just because I am not certain that the language of questions 20 and 22 will bear the construction I should have to put upon it in order to be able to answer them in the affirmative, I have to say that I do not know that I can say 'Yes' in answer to these two questions."

Upon the hearing before the District Court on the petition, he explained his position more in detail. He said that he was not a pacifist; that, if allowed to interpret the oath for himself, he would interpret it as not inconsistent with his position and would take it. He then proceeded to say that he would answer question 22 in the affirmative only on the understanding that he would have to believe that the war was morally justified before he would take up arms in it or give it his moral support. He was ready to give to the United States all the allegiance he ever had given or ever could give to any country, but he could not put allegiance to the government of any country before allegiance to the will of God. He did not anticipate engaging in any propaganda against the prosecution of a war which the **619** government had already declared and which it considered to be justified; but he preferred not to make any absolute promise at the time of the hearing, because of his ignorance of all the circumstances which might affect his judgment with reference to such a war. He did not question that the government under certain conditions could regulate and restrain the conduct of the individual citizen, even to the extent of imprisonment. He recognized the principle of the submission of the individual citizen to the opinion of the majority in a democratic country; but he did not believe in having his own moral problems solved for him by the majority. The position thus taken was the only one he could take consistently with his moral principles and with what he understood to be the moral principles of Christianity. He recognized, in short, the right of the government to restrain the freedom of the individual for the good of the social whole; but was convinced, on the other hand, that the individual citizen should have the right respectfully to withhold from the government military services (involving, as they probably would, the taking of human life), when his best moral judgment would compel him to do so. He was willing to support his country, even to the extent of bearing arms, if asked to do so by the government, in any war which he could regard as morally justified.

There is more to the same effect, but the foregoing is sufficient to make plain his position.

These statements of the applicant fairly disclose that he is unwilling to take the oath of allegiance, except with these important qualifications: That he will do what he judges to be in the best interests of the country only in so far as he believes it will not be against the best interests of humanity in the long run; that he will not assist in the defense of the country by force of arms or give any war his moral support unless he believes it to be morally justified, however necessary the war might **620** seem to the government of the day; that he will hold himself free to judge of the morality and necessity of the war, and, while he does not anticipate engaging in propaganda against the prosecution of a war declared and considered justified by the government, he prefers to make no promise even as to that; and that he is convinced that the individual citizen should have the right to withhold his military services when his best moral judgment impels him to do so.

Thus stated, the case is ruled in principle by *United States v. Schwimmer, supra.* In that case the applicant, a woman, testified that she would not take up arms in defense of the country. She was willing to be treated on the basis of a conscientious objector who refused to take up arms in the recent war, and seemed to regard herself as belonging in that class. She was an uncompromising pacifist, with no sense of nationalism, and only a cosmic sense of belonging to the human family. Her objection to military service, we concluded, rested upon reasons other than her inability to bear arms because of sex or age; and we held that her application for naturalization should be denied upon the ground, primarily, that she failed to sustain the burden of showing that she did not oppose the principle making it a duty of citizens, by force of arms when necessary, to defend their country against its enemies. At page 650 we said:

"That it is the duty of citizens by force of arms to defend our government against all enemies whenever necessity arises is a fundamental principle of the Constitution.

"The common defense was one of the purposes for which the people ordained and established the Constitution. . . . We need not refer to the numerous statutes that contemplate defense of the United States, its Constitution and laws, by armed citizens. This Court, in the *Selective Draft Law Cases*, 245 U.S. 366, speaking through Chief Justice White, said (p. 378) that 'the very concep**621**tion of a just government and its duty to the citizen includes the reciprocal obligation of the citizen to render military service in case of need. . . .'

"Whatever tends to lessen the willingness of citizens to discharge their duty to bear arms in the country's defense detracts from the strength and safety of the government. And their opinions and beliefs as well as their behavior indicating a disposition to hinder in the performance of that duty are subjects of inquiry under the statutory provisions governing naturalization and are of vital importance, for if all or a large number of citizens oppose such defense the 'good order and happiness' of the United States cannot long endure. And it is evident that the views of applicants for naturalization in respect of such matters may not be disregarded. The influence of conscientious objectors against the use of military force in defense of the principles of our government is apt to be more detrimental than their mere refusal to bear arms. The fact that, by reason of sex, age or other cause, they may be unfit to serve does not lessen their purpose or power to influence others. It is clear from her own statements that the declared opinions of respondent as to armed defense by citizens against enemies of the country were directly pertinent to the investigation of her application."

And see *In re Roeper* 274 Fed. 490; *Clarke's Case*, 301 Pa. 321, 152 Atl. 92.

There are few finer or more exalted sentiments than that which finds expression in opposition to war. Peace is a sweet and holy thing, and war is a hateful and an abominable thing, to be avoided by any sacrifice or concession that a free people can make. But thus far mankind has been unable to devise any method of indefinitely prolonging the one or of entirely abolishing the other; and, unfortunately, there is nothing which seems to afford **622** positive ground for thinking that the near future will witness the beginning of the reign of perpetual peace for which good men and women everywhere never cease to pray. The Constitution, therefore, wisely contemplating the ever-present possibility of war, declares that one of its purposes is to "provide for the common defense." In express terms Congress is empowered "to declare war," which necessarily connotes the plenary power to wage war with all the force necessary to make it effective; and "to raise . . . armies," which necessarily connotes the like power to say who shall serve in them and in what way.

From its very nature, the war power, when necessity calls for its exercise, tolerates no qualifications or limitations, unless found in the Constitution or in applicable principles of international law. In the words of John Quincy Adams,—"This power is tremendous; it is strictly constitutional; but it breaks down every barrier so anxiously erected for the protection of liberty, property and of life." To the end that war may not result in defeat, freedom of speech may, by act of Congress, be curtailed or denied so that the morale of the people and the spirit of the army may not be broken by seditious utterances; freedom of the press curtailed to preserve our military plans and movements from the knowledge of the enemy; deserters and spies put to death without indictment or trial by jury; ships and supplies requisitioned; property of alien enemies, theretofore under the protection of the Constitution, seized without process and converted to the public use without compensation and without due process of law in the ordinary sense of that term; prices of food and other necessities of life fixed or regulated; railways taken over and operated by the government; and other drastic powers, wholly inadmissible in time of peace, exercised to meet the emergencies of war.

623 These are but illustrations of the breadth of the power; and it necessarily results from their consideration that whether any citizen shall be exempt from serving in the armed forces of the nation in time of war is dependent upon the will of Congress and not upon the scruples of the individual, except as Congress provides. That body, thus far, has seen fit, by express enactment, to relieve from the obligation of armed service those persons who belong to the class known as conscientious objectors; and this policy is of such long standing that it is thought by some to be beyond the possibility of alteration. Indeed, it seems to be assumed in this case that the privilege is one that Congress itself is powerless to take away. Thus it is said in the carefully prepared brief of respondent:

"To demand from an alien who desires to be naturalized an unqualified promise to bear arms in every war that may be declared, despite the fact that he may have conscientious religious scruples against doing so in some hypothetical future war, would mean that such an alien would come into our citizenry on an unequal footing with the native born, and that he would be forced, as the price of citizenship, to forego a privilege enjoyed by others. That is the manifest result of the fixed principle of our

Constitution, zealously guarded by our laws, that a citizen cannot be forced and need not bear arms in a war if he has conscientious religious scruples against doing so."

This, if it means what it seems to say, is an astonishing statement. Of course, there is no such principle of the Constitution, fixed or otherwise. The conscientious objector is relieved from the obligation to bear arms in obedience to no constitutional provision, express or implied; but because, and only because, it has accorded with the policy of Congress thus to relieve him. The **624** alien, when he becomes a naturalized citizen, acquires, with one exception, every right possessed under the Constitution by those citizens who are native-born (*Luria v. United States*, 231 U.S. 9, 22); but he acquires no more. The privilege of the native-born conscientious objector to avoid bearing arms comes, not from the Constitution, but from the acts of Congress. That body may grant or withhold the exemption as in its wisdom it sees fit; and, if it be withheld, the native-born conscientious objector cannot successfully assert the privilege. No other conclusion is compatible with the well-nigh limitless extent of the war powers as above illustrated, which include, by necessary implication, the power, in the last extremity, to compel the armed service of any citizen in the land, without regard to his objections or his views in respect of the justice or morality of the particular war or of war in general. In *Jacobson v. Massachusetts*, 197 U.S. 11, 29, this Court, speaking of the liberties guaranteed to the individual by the Fourteenth Amendment, said:

". . . and yet he may be compelled, by force if need be, against his will and without regard to his personal wishes or his pecuniary interests, or even his religious or political convictions, to take his place in the ranks of the army of his country, and risk the chance of being shot down in its defense."

The applicant for naturalization here is unwilling to become a citizen with this understanding. He is unwilling to leave the question of his future military service to the wisdom of Congress, where it belongs, and where every native-born or admitted citizen is obliged to leave it. In effect, he offers to take the oath of allegiance only with the qualification that the question whether the war is necessary or morally justified must, so far as his support is concerned, be conclusively determined by reference to his opinion.

625 When he speaks of putting his allegiance to the will of God above his allegiance to the government, it is evident, in the light of his entire statement, that he means to make his own interpretation of the will of God the decisive test which shall conclude the government and stay its hand. We are a Christian people (*Holy Trinity Church v. United States*, 143 U.S. 457, 470-71), according to one another the equal right of religious freedom, and acknowledging with reverence the duty of obedience to the will of God. But, also, we are a nation with the duty to survive; a nation whose Constitution contemplates war as well as peace; whose government must go forward upon the assumption, and safely can proceed upon no other, that unqualified allegiance to the nation and submission and obedience to the laws of the land, as well those made for war as those made for peace, are not inconsistent with the will of God.

The applicant here rejects that view. He is unwilling to rely, as every native-born citizen is obliged to do, upon the probable continuance by Congress of the long-established and approved practice of exempting the honest conscientious objector, while at the same time asserting his willingness to conform to whatever the future law constitutionally shall require of him; but discloses a present and fixed purpose to refuse to give his moral or armed support to any future war in which the country may be actually engaged, if, in his opinion, the war is not morally justified, the opinion of the Nation as expressed by Congress to the contrary notwithstanding.

If the attitude of this claimant, as shown by his statements and the inferences properly to be deduced from them, be held immaterial to the question of his fitness for admission to citizenship, where shall the line be drawn? Upon what ground of distinction may we hereafter reject another applicant who shall express his willingness to re626spect any particular principle of the Constitution or obey any future statute only upon the condition that he shall entertain the opinion that it is morally justified? The applicant's attitude, in effect, is a refusal to take the oath of allegiance except in an altered form. The qualifications upon which he insists, it is true, are made by parol and not by way of written amendment to the oath; but the substance is the same.

It is not within the province of the courts to make bargains with those who seek naturalization. They must accept the grant and take the oath in accordance with the terms fixed by the law, or forego the privilege of citizenship. There is no middle choice. If one qualification of the oath be allowed, the door is opened for others, with utter confusion as the probable final result. As this Court said in *United States v. Manzi*, 276 U.S. 463, 467:

"Citizenship is a high privilege, and when doubts exist concerning a grant of it, generally at least, they should be resolved in favor of the United States and against the claimant."

The Naturalization Act is to be construed "with definite purpose to favor and support the government," and the United States is entitled to the benefit of any doubt which remains in the mind of the court as to any essential matter of fact. The burden was upon the applicant to show that his views were not opposed to "the principle that it is a duty of citizenship by force of arms when necessary to defend the country against all enemies, and that (his) opinions and beliefs would not prevent or impair the true faith and allegiance required by the act." *United States v. Schwimmer*, *supra*, 279 U.S. 649, 650 , 653. We are of opinion that he did not meet this requirement. The examiner and the court of first instance who heard and weighed the evidence and saw the applicant and witnesses so concluded. That conclusion, if we were in **627** doubt, would not be rejected except for good and persuasive reasons, which we are unable to find.

The decree of the Court of Appeals is reversed and that of the District Court is affirmed.

MR. CHIEF JUSTICE HUGHES, dissenting.

I am unable to agree with the judgment in this case. It is important to note the precise question to be determined. It is solely one of law, as there is no controversy as to the facts. The question is not whether naturalization is a privilege to be granted or withheld. That it is such a privilege is undisputed. Nor, whether the Congress has the power to fix the conditions upon which the privilege is granted. That power is assumed. Nor, whether the Congress may in its discretion compel service in the army in time of war or punish the refusal to serve. That power is not here in dispute. Nor is the question one of the authority of Congress to exact a promise to bear arms as a condition of its grant of naturalization. That authority, for the present purpose, may also be assumed.

The question before the Court is the narrower one whether the Congress has exacted such a promise. That the Congress has not made such an express requirement is apparent. The question is whether that exaction is to be implied from certain general words which do not, as it seems to me, either literally or historically, demand the implication. I think that the requirement should not be implied, because such a construction is directly opposed to the spirit of our institutions and to the historic practice of the Congress. It must be conceded that departmental zeal may not be permitted to outrun the authority conferred by statute. If such a promise is to be demanded, contrary to principles which have been respected as fundamental, the Congress should exact it in unequivocal **628** terms, and we should not, by judicial decision, attempt to perform what, as I see it, is a legislative function.

In examining the requirements for naturalization, we find that the Congress has expressly laid down certain rules which concern the opinions and conduct of the applicant. Thus it is provided that no person shall be naturalized "who disbelieves in or who is opposed to organized government, or who is a member of or affiliated with any organization entertaining and teaching such disbelief in or opposition to organized government, or who advocates or teaches the duty, necessity, or propriety of the unlawful assaulting or killing of any officer or officers, either of specific individuals or of officers generally, of the Government of the United States, or of any other organized government, because of his or their official character, or who is a polygamist." Act of June 29, 1906, c. 3592, § 7; 34 Stat. 596, 598; U.S.C., Tit. 8, § 364. The respondent, Douglas Clyde Macintosh, entertained none of these disqualifying opinions and had none of the associations or relations disapproved. Among the specific requirements as to beliefs, we find none to the effect that one shall not be naturalized if by reason of his religious convictions he is opposed to war or is unwilling to promise to bear arms. In view of the questions which have repeatedly been brought to the attention of the Congress in relation to such beliefs, and having regard to the action of the Congress when its decision was of immediate importance in the raising of armies, the omission of such an express requirement from the naturalization statute is highly significant.

Putting aside these specific requirements as fully satisfied, we come to the general conditions imposed by the statute. We find one as to good behavior during the specified period of residence preceding application. No applicant could appear to be more exemplary than Macintosh. A Canadian by birth, he first came to the United **629** States as a graduate student at the University of Chicago, and in 1907 he was ordained as a Baptist minister. In 1909 he began to teach in Yale University and is now a member of the faculty of the Divinity School, Chaplain of the Yale Graduate School, and Dwight Professor of Theology. After the outbreak of the Great War, he voluntarily sought appointment as a chaplain with the Canadian Army and as such saw service at the front. Returning to this country, he made public addresses in 1917 in support of the Allies. In 1918, he went again to France, where he had charge of an American Y.M.C.A. hut at the front until the armistice, when he resumed his duties at Yale University. It seems to me that the applicant has shown himself in his behavior and character to be highly desirable as a citizen, and, if such a man is to be excluded from naturalization, I think the disqualification should be found in unambiguous terms and not in an implication which shuts him out and gives admission to a host far less worthy.

The principal ground for exclusion appears to relate to the terms of the oath which the applicant must take. It should be observed that the respondent was willing to take the oath, and he so stated in his petition. But, in response to further inquiries, he explained that he was not willing "to promise beforehand" to take up arms, "without knowing the cause for which my country may go to war," and that "he would have to believe that the war was morally justified." He declared that "his first allegiance was to the will of God"; that he was ready to give to the United States "all the allegiance he ever had given or ever could give to any country, but that he could not put allegiance to the government of any country before allegiance to the will of God." The question then is whether the terms of the oath are to be taken as necessarily implying an assurance of willingness to bear arms, so that one whose conscientious convictions or belief of su630preme allegiance to the will of God will not permit him to make such an absolute promise cannot take the oath and hence is disqualified for admission to citizenship.

The statutory provision as to the oath which is said to require this promise is this: "that he will support and defend the Constitution and laws of the United States against all enemies, foreign and domestic, and bear true faith and allegiance to the same." Act of June 29, 1906, c. 3592 , § 4, 34 Stat. 596, 598; U.S.C. Tit. 8, § 381. That these general words have not been regarded as implying a promise to bear arms notwithstanding religious or conscientious scruples, or as requiring one to promise to put allegiance to temporal power above what is sincerely believed to be one's duty of obedience to God, is apparent, I think, from a consideration of their history. This oath does not stand alone. It is the same oath in substance that is required by act of Congress of Civil officers generally (except the President, whose oath is prescribed by the Constitution). The Congress, in prescribing such an oath for civil officers, acts under Article

VI, section 3, of the Constitution, which provides: "The Senators and Representatives before mentioned, and the Members of the several State Legislatures, and all executive and judicial Officers, both of the United States and of the several States, shall be bound by Oath or Affirmation, to support this Constitution; but no religious Test shall ever be required as a Qualification to any Office or public Trust under the United States." The general oath of office, in the form which has been prescribed by the Congress for over sixty years, contains the provision "that I will support and defend the Constitution of the United States against all enemies, foreign and domestic; that I will bear true faith and allegiance to the same; that I take this obligation freely, without any mental reservation or purpose of evasion." Rev. St. § 1757 (U.S.C., Tit. 5, § 16). It goes without **631** saying that it was not the intention of the Congress in framing the oath to impose any religious test. When we consider the history of the struggle for religious liberty, the large number of citizens of our country from the very beginning who have been unwilling to sacrifice their religious convictions, and, in particular, those who have been conscientiously opposed to war and who would not yield what they sincerely believed to be their allegiance to the will of God, I find it impossible to conclude that such persons are to be deemed disqualified for public office in this country because of the requirement of the oath which must be taken before they enter upon their duties. The terms of the promise "to support and defend the Constitution of the United States against all enemies, foreign and domestic," are not, I think, to be read as demanding any such result. There are other and most important methods of defense, even in time of war, apart from the personal bearing of arms. We have but to consider the defense given to our country in the late war, both in industry and in the field, by workers of all sorts, by engineers, nurses, doctors and chaplains, to realize that there is opportunity even at such a time for essential service in the activities of defense which do not require the overriding of such religious scruples. I think that the requirement of the oath of office should be read in the light of our regard from the beginning for freedom of conscience. While it has always been recognized that the supreme power of government may be exerted and disobedience to its commands may be punished, we know that with many of our worthy citizens it would be a most heart-searching question if they were asked whether they would promise to obey a law believed to be in conflict with religious duty. Many of their most honored exemplars in the past have been willing to suffer imprisonment or even death rather than to make such a promise. And we also know, in particular, that a promise to engage **632** in war by bearing arms, or thus to engage in a war believed to be unjust, would be contrary to the tenets of religious groups among citizens who are of patriotic purpose and exemplary conduct. To conclude that the general oath of office is to be interpreted as disregarding the religious scruples of these citizens and as disqualifying them for office because they could not take the oath with such an interpretation would, I believe, be generally regarded as contrary not only to the specific intent of the Congress but as repugnant to the fundamental principle of representative government.

But the naturalization oath is in substantially the same terms as the oath of office to which I have referred. I find no ground for saying that these words are to be interpreted differently in the two cases. On the contrary, when the Congress reproduced the historic words of the oath of office in the naturalization oath, I should suppose that, according to familiar rules of interpretation, they should be deemed to carry the same significance.

The question of the proper interpretation of the oath is, as I have said, distinct from that of legislative policy in exacting military service. The latter is not dependent upon the former. But the long-established practice of excusing from military service those whose religious convictions oppose it confirms the view that the Congress in the terms of the oath did not intend to require a promise to give such service. The policy of granting exemptions in such cases has been followed from colonial times and is abundantly shown by the provisions of colonial and state statutes, of state Constitutions, and of acts of Congress. See citations in the opinion of the Circuit Court of Appeals in the present case. 42 F.(2d) 845, 847, 848. The first Constitution of New York, adopted in 1777, in providing for the state militia, while strongly emphasizing the duty of defense, added: "That all such of the inhabitants of this State (being of the people called Quakers) **633** as, from scruples of conscience, may be averse to the bearing of arms, be therefrom excused by the legislature; and to pay to the State such sums of money, in lieu of their personal service, as the same may, in the judgment of the legislature, be worth." Art. XL. A large number of similar provisions are found in other states. The importance of giving immunity to those having conscientious scruples against bearing arms has been emphasized in debates in Congress repeatedly from the very beginning of our government, and religious scruples have been recognized in draft acts. Annals of Congress (Gales), 1st Congress, vol. I, pp. 434, 436, 729, 731; vol. II, pp. 1818-1827; Acts of February 24, 1864, 13 Stat. 6, 9; January

21, 1903, 32 Stat. 775; June 3, 1916, 39 Stat. 166, 197; May 18, 1917, 40 Stat. 76, 78. I agree with the statement in the opinion of the Circuit Court of Appeals in the present case that: "This federal legislation is indicative of the actual operation of the principles of the Constitution, that a person with conscientious or religious scruples need not bear arms, although, as a member of society, he may be obliged to render services of a noncombatant nature."

Much has been said of the paramount duty to the state, a duty to be recognized, it is urged, even though it conflicts with convictions of duty to God. Undoubtedly that duty to the state exists within the domain of power, for government may enforce obedience to laws regardless of scruples. When one's belief collides with the power of the state, the latter is supreme within its sphere and submission or punishment follows. But, in the forum of conscience, duty to a moral power higher than the state has always been maintained. The reservation of that supreme obligation, as a matter of principle, would unquestionably be made by many of our conscientious and law-abiding citizens. The essence of religion is belief in a relation to God involving duties superior to those 634 arising from any human relation. As was stated by Mr. Justice Field, in *Davis v. Beason*, 133 U.S. 333, 342: "The term 'religion' has reference to one's views of his relations to his Creator, and to the obligations they impose of reverence for his being and character, and of obedience to his will." One cannot speak of religious liberty, with proper appreciation of its essential and historic significance, without assuming the existence of a belief in supreme allegiance to the will of God. Professor Macintosh, when pressed by the inquiries put to him, stated what is axiomatic in religious doctrine. And, putting aside dogmas with their particular conceptions of deity, freedom of conscience itself implies respect for an innate conviction of paramount duty. The battle for religious liberty has been fought and won with respect to religious beliefs and practices, which are not in conflict with good order, upon the very ground of the supremacy of conscience within its proper field. What that field is, under our system of government, presents in part a question of constitutional law, and also, in part, one of legislative policy in avoiding unnecessary clashes with the dictates of conscience. There is abundant room for enforcing the requisite authority of law as it is enacted and requires obedience, and for maintaining the conception of the supremacy of law as essential to orderly government, without demanding that either citizens or applicants for citizenship shall assume by oath an obligation to regard allegiance to God as subordinate to allegiance to civil power. The attempt to exact such a promise, and thus to bind one's conscience by the taking of oaths or the submission to tests, has been the cause of many deplorable conflicts. The Congress has sought to avoid such conflicts in this country by respecting our happy tradition. In no sphere of legislation has the intention to prevent such clashes been more conspicuous than in relation to the bearing of arms. It would require strong evidence **635** that the Congress intended a reversal of its policy in prescribing the general terms of the naturalization oath. I find no such evidence.

Nor is there ground, in my opinion, for the exclusion of Professor Macintosh because his conscientious scruples have particular reference to wars believed to be unjust. There is nothing new in such an attitude. Among the most eminent statesmen here and abroad have been those who condemned the action of their country in entering into wars they thought to be unjustified. Agreements for the renunciation of war presuppose a preponderant public sentiment against wars of aggression. If, while recognizing the power of Congress, the mere holding of religious or conscientious scruples against all wars should not disqualify a citizen from holding office in this country, or an applicant otherwise qualified from being admitted to citizenship, there would seem to be no reason why a reservation of religious or conscientious objection to participation in wars believed to be unjust should constitute such a disqualification.

Apart from the terms of the oath, it is said that the respondent has failed to meet the requirement of "attachment to the principles of the Constitution." Here, again, is a general phrase which should be construed, not in opposition to, but in accord with, the theory and practice of our government in relation to freedom of conscience. What I have said as to the provisions of the oath I think applies equally to this phase of the case.

The judgment in *United States v. Schwimmer*, 279 U.S. 644, stands upon the special facts of that case, but I do not regard it as requiring a reversal of the judgment here. I think that the judgment below should be affirmed.

Mr. Justice HOLMES, Mr. Justice BRANDEIS, and Mr. Justice STONE concur in this opinion.

*Bold numbers represent original pagination in *United States Reports*.

Appendix L

Statement of the Texas Baptist Convention

The Baptist General Convention of Texas, representing more than 500,000 white Baptists, takes notice of the fact that since our last annual session the Supreme Court of the United States, by a decision of five against four, declared Douglas Clyde Macintosh, a Baptist minister and professor in the divinity school of Yale University, ineligible for citizenship for the sole reason that he could not promise in advance to bear arms in any war in which the United States may be engaged "unless he believed the war to be morally justified."

We declare first of all our profound respect for this highest court of our great country. We also call attention to the fact that in the past our Baptist people have been loyal supporters of the laws of our land; that in times of war they have been among the first volunteers to serve in its defense and honor, and that they will without doubt be equally patriotic in the future.

But since we believe that the decision referred to above violates the principles of freedom of conscience, and since Baptists have always held and do now hold that the conscience must be free, and that no earthly authority of king, government or church can be acknowledged as paramount over that which a Christian yields his Lord, and since we agree with the four judges of the minority in their statement, written by Chief Justice Hughes, in which they contend that "in the forum of conscience duty to a moral power higher than the state has always been maintained," and that "the reservation of that supreme obligation, as a matter of principle, would unquestionably be made by many of our conscientious and law-abiding citizens":

Be it resolved:

1. That we place on record our most solemn protest against the conscience-oppressing interpretation of the Constitution involved in this decision;

2. That we repudiate the pagan doctrine of the supremacy of the state over the Christian conscience therein asserted;

3. That we re-assert the ancient Baptist principle that Christ is Lord in every sphere of life, and that there must be liberty of conscience in determining what obedience to him involves;

4. That we insist that when we must choose between the authority of men, even men administering human government, and the authority of Christ, we are bound to say, "We must obey God rather than man;"

5. That we pledge ourselves to work for the reversal of this decision with its unchristian implications, or in case we fail in this effort, to seek an amendment to the Constitution of the United States which will make citizenship harmonize with Christian principles;

6. That we express to Prof. Macintosh and others in like position our sincere sympathy, and the hope that our country will soon admit to the full rights of citizenship all, who like them have no disqualification except that they will not violate the integrity of conscience and disobey that they believe to be the will of God.

from the Douglas Clyde Macintosh Scrapbook

Declaration of an American Citizen

Whereas, the Supreme Court of the United States has refused citizenship to Professor Douglas Clyde Macintosh on the ground that he was unwilling to promise to subject his conscience to an act of Congress in the event of a war which he believed to be unjust and contrary to the will of God; and

Whereas, the ground upon which the Court's decision rested was the alleged fact that every native-born citizen of the United States has impliedly made the identical promise which Mr. Macintosh refused to make, and that to admit Mr. Macintosh with such a reservation of conscience would give him a privileged status as a citizen in comparison with the status of native-born citizens; and

Whereas, the Supreme Court's decision, together with the argument on which it rests, affects not only an applicant for naturalization but every native-born citizen, whether he be willing or unwilling to bear arms in event of war, and lends itself to a justification of any form of tyranny over the free conscience of American citizens; and

Whereas, the Supreme Court, referring to Professor Macintosh, says:

"When he speaks of putting his allegiance to the will of God above his allegiance to the government, it is evident . . . that he means to make his own interpretation of the will of God the decisive test. . . . We are a Christian people. . . . But we are also a nation with the duty to survive, . . . a nation whose government must go forward upon the assumption . . . that unqualified allegiance to the nation and submission and obedience to the laws of the land, as well those made for war as those made for peace, are not inconsistent with the will of God"; and

Whereas, it is a fundamental principle of democracy that conscience shall not be sacrificed to the state, but that the state accepts the responsibility of so fashioning its policies that it will enlist the support of the free consciences of its citizens; and

Whereas, no principle contributes so much to the moral dignity and to the purifying and stabilizing of democracy as the guarantee of a free conscience to all its citizens and an unhindered right to worship and serve God according to the dictates of a free conscience; and

Whereas, in his dissenting opinion in this same case Chief Justice Charles Evans Hughes, with the concurrence of Justices Brandeis, Holmes and Stone, denied that the Constitution and the oath of allegiance can rightly be made to bear the interpretation advanced by the majority of the Court, and affirmed the contrary view as follows:

"In the forum of conscience, duty to a moral power higher than the state has always been maintained. The reservation of that supreme obligation, as a matter of principle would unquestionably be made by many of our conscientious and law abiding citizens. The essence of religion is belief in a relation to God involving duties superior to those arising from any human relation. . . . One cannot speak of religious liberty, with proper appreciation of its essential and historic significance, without assuming the existence of a belief in supreme allegiance to the will of God"; and

Whereas, in so far as citizens assent to the doctrine advanced by the Court's decision they consent to the nullification of the most basic principle of ethical religion, and surrender their own and the church's freedom to preach and practice that truth which is the vital breath of any spiritual faith, namely, that God alone is Lord of the conscience, and that we must obey God rather then men; and

Whereas, if native-born American citizens allow the imputation of such an obligation to pass without protest, they thereby acquiesce in a ruling which is not only, in the language of Chief Justice Hughes, "repugnant to the fundamental principle of representative government," but which radically modifies the spirit of our democracy and smothers spiritual religion by setting up the state as the supreme object of devotion beyond which religion dare not go; and

Whereas, it is required of citizens when entering upon public office, whether federal or state, and when applying for passports, and on many other occasions, to take the oath of allegiance which, under this decision, now implies the giving of an absolute pledge to hold their personal consciences in subservience to the will of Congress as the final interpretation of the will of God; now

Therefore, I, a native-born citizen of the United States, solemnly refuse to acknowledge the obligation which the supreme court [*sic*] declares to be binding upon native-born citizens. I have not promised, expressly or tacitly, to accept an act of Congress as the final interpretation of the will of God, and I will not do so. In my allegiance to my country I withhold nothing, not even my life. But I cannot give my conscience. That belongs to God. I repudiate the obligation which the Supreme Court's decision would impose upon me, and declare that the imposition of such an obligation is the essence of tyranny. I refuse to be bound by it.

I further solemnly declare that until this intolerable restriction upon conscience and religion has been removed, I will not take the oath of allegiance upon any occasion without adding thereto a reservation of the right of conscience and of my supreme allegiance to the will of God.

And I further solemnly declare that I will use whatever influence is within my power, in my personal relations or in public address, to inform others and to awaken them to the peril in which this decision involves their traditional and most fundamental liberty, and I will do all that lies within my power to secure a reversal of this decision by the court itself or its correction through adequate legislation by Congress.

The Christian Century 49 (20 January 1932): 75
Copyright 1932 Christian Century Foundation. Reprinted by permission from the January 20, 1932, issue of *The Christian Century*.

Appendix N

Petition of Religious Leaders

The recent decision of the Supreme Court, which denies the right of citizenship to persons who refuse to abdicate their conscience on the question of participation in armed conflict, forces us, the undersigned citizens, to notify the constituted authorities of our nation that we share the convictions of those who have been denied citizenship.

Some of the undersigned find it impossible, because of religious and moral scruples, to render any kind of combatant service in time of war. Others share the conviction of one of the persons denied citizenship in the recent Supreme Court decision and cannot promise support to the government until we have had the opportunity of weighing the moral issues involved in an international struggle.

We concur in the minority opinion of the Supreme Court that in the forum of conscience, duty to a moral power higher than the state has always been maintained. The reservation of that supreme obligation, as a matter of principle, would undoubtedly be made by many of our conscientious citizens. The essence of religion is belief in a relation to God involving duties superior to those arising from any human relation.

The statement was signed by the following: Abernethy, W. S., minister, Calvary Baptist Church, Washington; Ainslie, Peter, minister, Christian Temple, Baltimore; Anderson, William F., Bishop, Methodist Episcopal Church, Boston; Ashworth, Robert A., editor, *The Baptist*, Chicago; Boddy, William H., minister, First Presbyterian Church, Chicago; Bowie, W. Russell, rector, Christ Church, New York City; Brewster, Benjamin, Bishop of Maine, Protestant Episcopal Church; Brummitt, Dan B., editor, *Northwestern Christian Advocate*, Chicago; Burleson, Hugh L., Bishop of South Dakota, Protestant Episcopal Church; Cadman, S. Parkes, radio minister, Federal Council of Churches of Christ; Cavert, Samuel McCrea, general secretary, Federal Council of Churches of Christ; Coffin, Henry Sloane, president Union Theological Seminary; Cronbach, Abraham, professor Hebrew Union College, Cincinnati;

Dieffenbach, A. C., editor, *The Christian Register*, Boston; Eddy, Sherwood, New York City; Fisher, Fred B., minister Methodist Episcopal Church, Ann Arbor, Mich; Fitch, Albert Parker, minister Park Avenue Presbyterian Church, New York City; Fosdick, Harry Emerson, minister Riverside Church, New York City; Gilkey, Charles W., dean of the chapel, University of Chicago; Gilroy, William E., editor, *The Congregationalist*, Boston; Hartman, L. O., editor, *Zion's Herald*, Boston; Herring, Hubert C., Committee on Cultural Relations with Latin America; Holmes, John Haynes, minister Community Church, New York City; Huston, S. Arthur, Bishop, Protestant Episcopal Church, Seattle; Hutchinson, Paul, managing editor, *The Christian Century*, Chicago; Israel, Edward L., chairman Central Conference of American Rabbis, Baltimore; Jenkins, Burris, minister Linwood Boulevard Christian Church, Kansas City; Lathrop, John Howland, minister Church of the Savior, Brooklyn; Leinbach, Paul S., editor, *The Reformed Church Messenger*, Philadelphia; Luccock, Halford E., professor Yale University Divinity School, New Haven; Mann, Louis L., rabbi Sinai Temple, Chicago; McConnell, Francis J., president Federal Council of Churches of Christ; Marshall, Harold, manager, *The Christian Leader*, Boston; Morrison, C. C., editor, *The Christian Century*, Chicago; Nicholson, Mrs. Thomas, president Woman's Foreign Missionary Society of Methodist Episcopal Church, Detroit; Niebuhr, Reinhold, professor, Union Theological Seminary; Page, Kirby, editor, *The World Tomorrow*; Palmer, Albert W., president, Chicago Theological Seminary, Chicago; Parsons, Edward L., Bishop, Protestant Episcopal Church, San Francisco; Patton, Carl S., moderator, Congregational General Council, Los Angeles; Scarlett, William, Bishop Coadjutor, Protestant Episcopal Church, St. Louis; Shipler, Guy Emery, editor, *The Churchman*; Sockman, Ralph W., minister Madison Avenue Methodist Episcopal Church, New York City; Stearly, Wilson R., Bishop of Newark, Protestant Episcopal Church; Tittle, Ernest Fremont, minister First Methodist Episcopal Church, Evanston, Ill; Weigle, Luther A., dean Yale University Divinity School, New Haven; Wise, Stephen S., rabbi Free Synagogue, New York City; Woolley, Mary E., president Mount Holyoke College, South Hadley, Mass.

"Churchmen Ask Action to Annul Macintosh Bar,"
New York Times, 24 September 1931.

Appendix O

Hearing Before the Naturalization Examiner

United States District Court,
Southern District of New York

In the Matter of
The Petition of MARIE AVERIL BLAND to be admitted to become a
citizen of the United States of America

Preliminary hearing before J. A. G. Stitzer, Designated Examiner, in
the office of the District Director of Naturalization, 132 Nassau Street,
New York City, on April 24, 1930.

Present:
J. A. G. STITZER, Designated Examiner.
CHARLES P. MULLER, Assistant District Director of Naturalization.
LOUIS WEINBERGER, Assistant Chief Examiner.
EMILY MARX, Attorney for the Petitioner.
MARIE AVERIL BLAND, Petitioner.
SARAH PESSIN, Stenographer.

By Mr. Muller: Miss Marx, your client, Miss Bland, has been
requested to call at this office today for a further preliminary hearing
before the Designated Examiner in order that there may be no question as
to the facts in her case, so that the issues may be clarified and so that they
may be presented to the Court without any resulting ambiguity. I take it
you have no objection to proceeding with the hearing?

By Miss Marx: But I understand that this examination is merely going
to be used as a basis for the recommendation of the Examiner?

By Mr. Muller: That is correct.

By Miss Marx: And is not to be final at all on the petitioner as far as
the court proceedings are concerned. In other words, if the Court should

determine, if you should recommend, that the petition be dismissed, she will have another opportunity to be examined before the Court?

By Mr. Muller: Precisely so; the statute provides for that. This is a preliminary hearing, and on the evidence adduced and on all other evidence in the case the Designated Examiner will make a finding and recommendation to the Court, and it is for the Court to decide whether or not the petition is to be granted.

(Petitioner sworn by Mr. Stitzer.)

By Mr. Muller:

Q. What is your full name?

A. Marie Averil Bland.

Q. And you reside at 1000 Park Avenue, New York City?

A. Yes.

Q. You filed your petition for citizenship, No. 156508, in the United States District Court, New York City, on May 21, 1929, is that correct?

A. Yes.

Q. I show you an affidavit which purports to have been verified by you on April 22, 1930, before John F. Kelley, Notary Public, and ask you whether the signature appearing thereon is your signature?

A. Yes, that is my signature.

Q. And this affidavit was verified by you on the date stated therein?

A. Yes.

Q. Did you read this affidavit before you verified it?

A. I did.

Q. Carefully?

A. Carefully.

Q. You recall at this time all the statements contained in the affidavit?

A. Yes.

Q. Are all those statements true?

A. Yes.

Q. I will offer this in evidence if there is no objection.

By Miss Marx: There is no objection. (Affidavit marked "Exhibit I.")

By Mr. Muller:

Q. Miss Bland, you were born in Canada, is that correct?

A. Yes.

Q. And you have lived all your life in Canada and the United States?

A. And a great deal in England.

Q. And English is your native tongue?

A. Yes.

Q. What education have you had?

A. Private school education.

Q. Would you say that you have the equivalent of a high school education?

A. Yes, decidedly.

Q. At least that?

A. At least.

Q. I show you a blank original petition for citizenship and call your attention to the oath of allegiance on the reverse thereof which you will be required to take in the event you are admitted to citizenship. Will you please read that oath carefully.

A. (Reads the oath.)

Q. If there is no objection, Miss Marx, I will offer the text of the oath of allegiance in evidence so that it may be of record.

(Text of oath of allegiance marked "Exhibit II.")

Q. As I understand it from your affidavit of April 22, 1930, you took the position that you could not take this oath in its entirety without modification or mental reservation. Am I correct in that assumption?

A. You are.

Q. Will you please indicate specifically which part or parts of the oath you feel you could not take freely.

A. From "I will support and defend the Constitution and laws of the United States of America against all enemies foreign and domestic; that I will bear true faith and allegiance to the same; and that I take this obligation freely, without any mental reservation or purpose of evasion."

Q. Am I to understand that you cannot unqualifiedly subscribe and swear to the parts of the oath which you have just read?

A. Yes.

Q. What do you find objectionable in the parts of the oath which you have just read?

A. I understand that when you swear to defend the country that it means to carry arms and I would refuse to carry arms.

Q. Am I to understand that if admitted to become a citizen of the United States you would refuse to carry arms in defense of the country without regard to circumstances, without regard to whether or not you felt the cause in which the United States was engaged to be just, without regard to whether a war of aggression was waged against this country, and without regard as to whether the life of the country depended upon your bearing arms?

A. Yes.

Q. In other words, regardless of circumstances or conditions, and even though it were in your own hands by bearing arms to save the existence of this country, you would decline to do so?

A. I could not do it.

Q. And you would not do it?

A. No.

Q. Would you describe yourself as a person who refuses to or is unwilling for any purpose to bear arms because of conscientious considerations?

A. Yes. According to the ethics of Christ, I would not conscientiously bear arms.

Q. And does your belief in that respect go so far, in your estimation, as to justify you in the event of a war in which this country were to become embroiled for you to encourage others to believe as you do?

A. If I were asked personally what my views are I would say, "Personally, I would not bear arms."

Q. But what I am trying to find out is whether your views on that subject are so deep-seated that in the event of a war you would proselyte or endeavor to sway others to accept your views and beliefs?

A. No, except so far as my own personal character might influence others.

Q. Are you a member of or affiliated with any religious organization which includes in its creed or tenets of faith such views on war as you have heretofore expressed in your affidavit and at this hearing?

A. I belong to Grace Episcopal Church, New York City, and my personal interpretation of the gospel preached in that church is opposition to war.

Q. I have never heard that the Episcopal Church advocates or teaches the views on personally engaging in a war in defense of one's country which you have enunciated here.

A. I don't stand or hold any brief for the Episcopal Church. I am expressing my own views and interpretation of my faith.

Q. Then, as I understand it, your views are not based upon the tenets of the church with which you are affiliated, but are solely and entirely your own personal views.

A. I think that is rather a difficult question to answer because I believe ethically the church is against war, but I have no authority; I am not representing the Episcopal Church, I represent one individual in that church and that's my feeling. I think there are many in the church who would support my views.

Q. This antipathy which you would have and this avowed refusal which you would make to bearing arms in defense of the United States if admitted to citizenship, is your personal interpretation of the tenets of your church and not the church's interpretation.

A. Insofar as I can state, yes.

Q. The United States Supreme Court has enunciated the principle that it is the duty of citizens by force of arms to defend our government against all enemies whenever necessity arises and that that is a fundamental principle of the Constitution. Do I understand you to say that it is your belief, view, and opinion that if you were admitted to citizenship you could not and would not subscribe to that fundamental principle of the Constitution as enunciated by the Supreme Court?

A. I could not personally subscribe to it, yes.

Q. And in so far as that principle of the Constitution is concerned, do I understand that you are not attached to that principle?

A. I am not.

Q. The Supreme Court of the United States has also said in an opinion rendered by that Court that "The very conception of a just government and its duty to the citizens includes the reciprocal obligation of the citizens to render military service in case of need." Am I correct in concluding that you disagree with that conception, and that you disapprove of that reciprocal obligation?

A. I feel that my duty to my God is higher than my duty to any man-made laws in regard to carrying arms.

Q. And if admitted to citizenship of the United States you would decline to render the reciprocal obligation to render military service in case of need?

A. Yes, I would have to. I would render service to the Government in anything but a combatant capacity, and would be willing to help nurse the wounded anywhere in time of war.

Q. But you would decline and refuse to render military service by force of arms even in case of need?

A. Yes.

Q. Would you describe yourself as a conscientious objector against the use of military force in defense of the principles of our government?

A. If conscientious objector is used in the strict sense of the word, conscientiously I could not, and I say yes to that statement.

Q. If admitted to citizenship would you consider yourself to be bound or held by ties of affection to this country?

A. I certainly would.

Q. Any more than to any other country?

A. I can't say that; I have too great a world feeling; and I have always been a loyal Canadian, but my loyalty to this country would be just as great as my loyalty to my own country was.

Q. If admitted to citizenship would your loyalty be any greater to the United States than it would be or has been to Canada?

A. Yes, it would be, because it would be a matter of duty if not of inclination. I don't take the laws of citizenship lightly.

Q. How do you feel that there would be any opportunity for you to show any greater loyalty to the United States than to Canada or any other country for that matter, if, as you say, you couldn't even take up arms to defend the United States in case of an aggression?

A. My idea of loyalty does not take that form; I think you can be loyal in ideals and ethics and you can work for the real spiritual welfare of a country even though you don't defend it by force of arms.

Q. You have stated in effect that if the United States were to become engaged in a war you would not proselyte or attempt to cause others generally to refuse to take up arms?

A. I have said so, yes.

Q. Let me ask you this. Under such circumstances, if someone were to approach you and ask for advice as to whether that person should or should not take up arms in defense of this country, what would you say then?

A. I would tell them their own conscience would have to decide that.

Q. If you were admitted to citizenship, would you demand, as a condition precedent to the taking of the oath of allegiance which you have read in the course of this hearing, that such oath be modified?

A. Yes. I would like to have inserted that I would according to my conscience as a Christian would allow to defend.

Q. So, then, you would not even take the oath of allegiance with a mental reservation; you would require it to be modified as to its language and text to accord with your views, is that correct?

A. My understanding is that you are supposed to have no mental reservations, the oath itself says so, therefore I could not subscribe to it because I have very strong mental reservations on the subject of bearing arms.

Q. I show you the text of the oath of allegiance again and ask you to say just what modification of the oath you would demand before you took the oath if admitted to citizenship? Read the whole oath and substitute, deleting in your reading from it the parts which you would require to be deleted and add to it the parts which you would require to be added.

A. I would require the oath to be amended to read as follows: "I hereby declare, on oath, that I absolutely and entirely renounce and abjure all allegiance and fidelity to any foreign prince, potentate, state, or sovereignty, and particularly to * * * of whom I have heretofore been subject or citizen, that I do solemnly affirm I will support the Constitution of the United States and will as far as my conscience as a Christian will allow defend it against all enemies foreign and domestic; that I will bear true faith and allegiance to the same and that I take this obligation freely, without any mental reservation or purposes of evasion, so help me God."

Q. So that, unless the oath of allegiance were modified in the respects in which you have modified it, you would not accept the gift of American citizenship?

A. I am afraid I would have to refuse regretfully.

Q. In the event that you should be admitted to citizenship and the United States became embroiled in a war, and if in the course of such war you were drafted to serve in a combatant capacity in the military or naval forces of the United States, what would your attitude be?

A. Does this suppose that I have been admitted on the regular oath or on my own oath?

Q. On any oath?

A. Well, I suppose I would go to prison.

Q. You would unqualifiedly refuse to serve?

A. Certainly.

Q. For how long a period have you entertained the views with reference to serving in war and defending the country of your allegiance as enunciated in your testimony here today?

A. It has been a growing conviction since the last war. It has been a very gradual change in my attitude.

Q. And since when would you say those views became firmly fixed in the definite form in which you have expressed them today?

A. That's very difficult to answer. I can't definitely state it; I should say at least two to three years.

By Miss Marx:

Q. On April 22, when you appeared before an examiner of this office, you stated that Dr. Bowie, the minister of the Grace Episcopal Church at Broadway and Tenth Street, had been preaching to his congregation that war was wrongful from an ethical and religious point of view and that the duty of the members of his congregation toward their Maker was to refrain from bearing arms, is that correct?

A. That is.

Q. Have your views on the question of bearing arms been influenced by those preachings of Dr. Bowie?

A. Undoubtedly so, and also from a great many other sources.

By Mr. Muller:

Q. The preachings of Dr. Bowie along the lines which you have just indicated, however, are not within the tenets and the creed of the Episcopal Church, are they?

A. No.

Q. They are his personal views?

A. Yes.

Q. Do I understand that Dr. Bowie has advocated in his preachings that persons who are citizens shall refuse to bear arms when called to do so, or that it would be proper for them to so refuse?

A. Yes, I think you can. He feels that in times of peace and since the great war that the conscience of the people should be aroused to the evil, terrible devastation that war produces.

Q. Of course, I think we are all agreed in times of peace we should do everything possible to avert wars, but has he preached that in time of war it would be proper for persons who owe allegiance to the United States to decline and refuse to take up arms in defense of the country?

A. That would be my understanding of what he has said, although he has never said it in so many words.

Q. Is that your understanding?

A. He didn't use that specific phrase, "refuse to bear arms," but he feels that the people should stand against war even in the event of war; I mean that their true spirit of Christ, the manifestation of their belief in the ethics of Christ, should be expressed in time of war in that manner.

By Miss Marx:

Q. Have you personally discussed this matter with Dr. Bowie?

A. No, I have not.

By Mr. Muller:

Q. Is it a fact then that your ideas of the teachings and beliefs of Dr. Bowie are based solely on the interpretation which you yourself placed upon his public addresses?

A. Yes.

Q. And that in those public addresses he never said unqualifiedly in your hearing that it would be proper or that he advocated that citizens of this country should decline to perform combatant military service if called upon to do so?

A. Not specifically; by inference, rather than specifically.

By Mr. Weinberger:

Q. Miss Bland, if you were admitted to citizenship, would you be prepared to give up, foreswear, every bit of allegiance you have heretofore owed to any other country, or sovereignty or state without any qualifications whatsoever?

A. Why, certainly.

Q. What is your individual conception if admitted to citizenship, of the duties, obligations, responsibilities you would owe to the United States Government?

A. To obey the laws, even the Prohibition Law, and to do your utmost to improve conditions, industrially and socially and morally, to take an interest in civic affairs and to put the whole weight of your ideals into making the country even better than it is.

Q. Would you exclude any of the present recognized duties or obligations or responsibilities that go hand in hand with citizenship?

A. I would exclude the obligation to bear arms.

Q. Do I rightly assume then that that is the only duty or recognized obligation that you would exclude?

A. Yes, unless there be some obligation of which I have no knowledge.

Q. Do you intend to make the United States your permanent home?

A. So far as I know, yes.

Q. Have you any present thought of taking up residence in any country other than the United States?

A. No, never.

I hereby certify that I have carefully read the foregoing transcript of testimony of the hearing accorded me in the office of the District Director of Naturalization on April 24, 1930, in connection with my pending petition for citizenship, and that the said transcript is true and correct in all respects.

Dated, April 25, 1930.

(Signed) MARIE AVERIL BLAND

Appendix P

Affidavit of Petitioner

(Exhibit I of Examination before Examiner)

State of New York
County of New York

Marie Averil Bland, residing at No. 1000 Park Avenue, New York City, being duly sworn, deposes and says:

I filed a petition for naturalization No. 156508 in the United States District Court, New York, N.Y., on May 21, 1929 and my petition came on before the Court for final hearing on April 14, 1930. On this date I appeared in Court and together with many others I was asked to raise my right hand in order that the Oath of Allegiance might be administered to me.

As instructed by the Clerk of Court, I raised my right hand and swore that I renounce all allegiance to any foreign power of which I had been a citizen or subject. At this point, or as soon as the Clerk began to say "that I will support and defend the Constitution and Laws of the United States of America against all enemies," I dropped my hand to indicate that I did not approve of that portion of the oath and that I held a mental reservation against personally bearing arms. When the Clerk of the Court had concluded administering the Oath of Allegiance, I stepped forward and asked to see the Judge. The Clerk asked me why and I stated to him that I refused to take the oath because I had mental reservations regarding personally bearing arms. I asked that the oath administered to Quakers by the passport bureau be administered to me instead of the one administered to the group in Court. This oath substituted for "I will support and defend the Constitution of the United States" the words, "I will support the Constitution of the United States and will, as far as my conscience as a Christian will allow, defend it against all enemies." I was not granted an interview by the Judge.

I arrived in the United States from England on February 10th, 1914. I was born in Ingersoll, Province of Ontario, Canada. During the European war I never gave much thought to the question of my possible obligation to personally bear arms in defense of the country. The day the Armistice was signed I went to France as a member of the reconstruction unit of the United States Government and performed the duties of a nurse in the psychiatric department at Brest, France. For nine months I nursed shell shocked soldiers. Since my return from France, I have been giving more and more thought to the horrors of war and to the necessity of working toward the ultimate abolition of war as a means of settling international disputes. Being a nurse by profession and neither a lecturer nor a propagandist, I merely kept my personal views to myself and have at no time discussed this with anyone except perhaps with some of my personal friends. Since the date of my return from France, I have come to realize that the abolition of war is in accord with the teachings of Jesus Christ and that He would have condemned fighting and bearing arms. I am a member of Grace Episcopal Church of New York City. My father is a minister of the Church of England and is at present in charge of a church in Lincolnshire, England. I believe that it is my duty as a Christian to refuse to bear arms or kill my fellow men, even in the event of a war. However, I am perfectly aware of the fact that the abolition of war can only be brought about by a gradual change of public opinion. I have never delivered a lecture in my life and have no present intention of doing so.

I have been informed that the word "defend" in the Oath of Allegiance as administered by this Court, has been construed by the United States Supreme Court to include an obligation to bear arms personally. I therefore deem it incumbent upon me to draw the attention of the judge who administered the Oath of Allegiance to the fact that my religious convictions would prevent my taking the usual oath to "defend" the Constitution, without a mental reservation. Since I believe that my obligations to my Maker impose upon me a duty to refrain from personally bearing arms, I cannot take the Oath of Allegiance without a mental reservation that as to me, personally, the word "defend" does not mean personally bearing arms. In the event of a war, I would willingly contribute my knowledge, experience and services as a nurse to the care of the wounded, wherever my services would be needed. But I would not personally take a gun in my hand and shoot any of my fellow men.

MARIE AVERIL BLAND

Appendix Q

Testimony in District Court

United States District Court,
Southern District of New York

Before Hon. William Bondy, J.

In the Matter
of
The Petition of MARIE AVERIL
BLAND to be admitted to become a citizen of the United States of
America

New York, April 28, 1930
11:10 A.M.

APPEARANCES:

For the Petitioner: EMILY MARX.

For the United States Department of Labor: J. A.
G. STITZER, Designated Examiner.

MARIE AVERIL BLAND, the above named petitioner, having been first
duly sworn, was examined and testified as follows:

Direct Examination by Mr. Stitzer:
  Q. What is your name?
  A. Marie Averil Bland.
  Q. Where do you reside?
  A. 1000 Park Avenue.
  Q. How long have you been in the United States?

A. Since 1914, in February.

Q. Have you been in court for final hearing prior to this date?

A. Yes.

Q. When?

A. On the 14th, I think, of February; two weeks ago—I mean, of April.

Q. Why were you not admitted to citizenship?

A. Because I refused to take an oath of allegiance swearing to bear arms.

Q. Why did you refuse to take the oath of allegiance?

A. Because I could not conscientiously bear arms for the United States or any other country.

The Court: Can you not conceive of any circumstances under which you would?

The Witness: No, I could not.

The Court: If you actually believed that the security of the homes of Americans was threatened, would you take up arms?

The Witness: No, I could not—not even then.

The Court: Are you a married woman?

The Witness: No.

Miss Marx: What is your reason for not wanting to take up arms?

The Witness: My reason is that I could not, according to my conscience as a Christian, bear arms. It is against my ethics—the ethics of Christ.

The Court: To bear arms?

The Witness: Yes.

The Court: If a person threatened you with violence, what would you do? Let him exercise violence?

The Witness: They would have to.

The Court: If a person threatened to kill you, with a gun in his hand, would you let him kill you?

The Witness: Certainly.

Miss Marx: You said that your religion forbids you bearing arms?

The Witness: Yes.

Miss Marx: For the purposes of the record, will you explain what you mean by your religion?

The Witness: Well, my religion, as far as I can explain it, is living according to the ethics of Christ, and what Christ taught—my interpretation of the Gospel.

The Court: Your interpretations are different from those of the majority of people, are they not?

The Witness: They may be. I could not say.

The Court : Is there any further examination or cross-examination?

Mr. Stitzer: I want to offer the objections. This is a report of the proceedings held before me on the 24th of April, 1930. I offer that in evidence, and also an affidavit that the petitioner filed, and I think there is the formal form of oath, as an exhibit, with my final recommendation that the petition be denied, on the ground that the petitioner is not entitled to citizenship in the United States.

The Court: Why does not the Schwimmer case apply?

Miss Marx: It does not, because the Schwimmer case—in that case you will find that Mrs. Schwimmer stated that she had no national feeling; that she not only did not want to bear arms herself, but she was in the business of lecturing and propagandering [sic], and she was going around and telling everybody not to bear arms. You will find by the testimony here that this petitioner is entirely different from Mrs. Schwimmer. First of all, she is a nurse by profession; she is not a lecturer. Secondly, these ideas are only her own, and she intends to keep them to herself, and just govern her own conduct by them, and she has no intention of telling anybody else about them. Mr. Stitzer asked her specifically what she would do in the event of war, if someone would come to her and ask her, "Shall I bear arms?" and she said she would answer and tell that person that his own conscience would have to govern his own actions. In addition, this petitioner specifically shows that she is imbued with a national feeling to become a citizen of the United States, and to work for our ideals and our country; whereas, Mrs. Schwimmer specifically stated that she had a cosmic conscience and no national feeling whatever. As a matter of fact, the government attorney in the Schwimmer case pointed out that that was not a case of religious conviction at all. I have given you a memorandum. Now, assuming that the Supreme Court is correct, though I do not agree with that decision—

The Court (Interposing): You disagree with the Supreme Court?

Miss Marx: I do not admit that the Constitution requires the bearing of arms. They say in this opinion that one of the principles of the Constitution is to bear arms in defense of the country, but I do not think that is so. That was not a decision of the Supreme Court, but merely dictum. But assuming that it is a principle of the Constitution to bear arms, there is another principle involved here, and that is religious freedom, which was not involved in the Schwimmer case; and, you will find that this conflict has come up many times before, in the Revolutionary War, and the Civil War, and every single time they have allowed these so-called conscientious objectors on religious grounds to get out of the draft and out of military service. My contention is that this principle of religious freedom is much more important than any principle of bearing arms, and that, so far as our country is concerned, we have always insisted that if a person had religious opinions which they honestly believed, and those opinions did not conflict with our public policy, they were entitled to them.

The Court: There is a great difference whether one is a citizen and has conscientious scruples about bearing arms and the conditions upon which a person, an alien, is to be admitted to citizenship.

Miss Marx: I do not think there is.

The Court: Oh, yes. The conditions under which a person may become a citizen and the rights of people who are citizens are somewhat different.

Miss Marx: The objection on the part of the Government is that for three years before this petition was filed the petitioner was not attached to the principles of the Constitution. They admit that she is well qualified in every other way.

The Court: I understand that. The only difficulty is that she does not want to subscribe to the oath that she would bear arms in defense of the United States, and she says she would not do so under any circumstances.

Miss Marx: That is right.

The Court: Then, that is the only issue. The only issue before the Court is whether the United States will admit to citizenship a person who says that because of conscientious or religious scruples they will not bear arms in defense of the United States—and this woman says she would not bear arms even in self-defense. That is true, is it not?

The Witness: Yes, sir.

Miss Marx: But the Government says that this refusal to bear arms shows that she is not attached to the principles of the Constitution. Now, I say that whether she is a citizen or an alien the principle does not change.

The Court: That is true.

Miss. Marx: And I think that this principle of religious freedom is more important than the principle of bearing arms.

The Court: I understand the issue, and I will see what the law is and follow that.

Mr. Stitzer: We raised a question as to the competency of the witnesses—in view of the fact that she is not attached to the principles of the Constitution, that her witnesses are not competent to testify. They are here?

Miss Marx: Only one. The other is ill.

The Court: Why are the witnesses not competent?

Mr. Stitzer: They have said that they are attached to the Constitution—

The Court (Interposing): They are competent, but you do not think their testimony is sufficient evidence of the fact?

Mr. Stitzer: That is it.

The Court: It is conceded that the witness would give her opinion that she is qualified.

Mr. Stitzer: Yes.

Miss Marx: It is conceded that she is otherwise qualified.

Mr. Stitzer: Yes, counsel for the petitioner would like to have a copy of the proceedings held before me?

Miss Marx: No, I have that.

Mr. Stitzer: Then, she can have a copy of these proceedings.

Miss Marx: Yes. I would also like a copy of the recommendations of the Examiner.

The Court: Give her a copy of all the proceedings.

Mr. Stitzer: Yes.

Appendix R

United States v. Bland*

283 U.S. 636

CERTIORARI TO THE CIRCUIT COURT OF APPEALS FOR THE SECOND CIRCUIT

No. 505. Argued April 27, 1931—Decided May 25, 1931.

Solicitor General Thacher, with whom *Assistant Attorney General Dodds* and *Messers. Whitney North Seymour* and *Harry S. Ridgely* were on the brief, for the United States.

Miss Emily Marx for respondent.

MR. JUSTICE SUTHERLAND delivered the opinion of the Court.

This case is ruled by the decision just announced in *United States v. Macintosh*, 283 U.S. 605.

The respondent, an applicant for citizenship, was a native of Canada and came to the United States in 1914. She had duly declared her intention to become a citizen. She refused to take the oath of allegiance prescribed by the statute to defend the Constitution and laws of the United States against all enemies, etc., except with the written interpolation of the words, "as far as my conscience as a Christian will allow." It is unnecessary to review her testimony. The only difference between the position she took, and that taken by the respondent in the *Macintosh* case, is that, in addition to refusing positively to bear arms in defense of the United States under any **637** circumstances, she required an actual amendment of the oath as already stated, instead of reserving the point by parol. As we said in the *Macintosh* case, this is a circumstance which has no distinguishing

443

effect. The substance of the oath has been definitely prescribed by Congress. The words of the statute do not admit of the qualification upon which the applicant insists. For the court to allow it to be made is to amend the act and thereby usurp the power of legislation vested in another department of the government.

The examiner reported against the applicant, and the court of first instance, after a full hearing, denied the application. We think its decree was right.

The decree of the Court of Appeals is reversed and that of the District Court is affirmed.

MR. CHIEF JUSTICE HUGHES, dissenting.

What I have said in the case of *United States v. Macintosh*, with respect to the interpretation of the provisions of the Naturalization Act and of the prescribed oath, I think applies also to this case. The petitioner is a nurse who spent nine months in the service of our government in France, nursing United States soldiers and aiding in psychiatric work. She has religious scruples against bearing arms. I think that it sufficiently appears that her unwillingness to take the oath was merely because of the interpretation that had been placed upon it as amounting to a promise that she would bear arms despite her religious convictions. It was the opinion of the Circuit Court of Appeals that the appellant may properly take the oath according to its true significance and should be permitted to take it. 42 F.(2d) 842, 844, 845. I think that the judgment below should be affirmed.

MR. JUSTICE HOLMES, MR. JUSTICE BRANDEIS, and MR. JUSTICE STONE concur in this opinion.

*Bold numbers represent original pagination in *United States Reports*.

Appendix S

Resolution of the Chamber of Commerce of New York

At the regular monthly meeting of the Chamber of Commerce of the State of New York, held March 6, 1930, the following preamble and resolutions were unanimously adopted:

Liberalizing Our Naturalization Laws as Proposed in H. R. 3547 Is Opposed

To the Chamber of Commerce:

Whereas a bill, H. R. 3547, has been introduced by Representative Griffin to amend our naturalization laws by adding the following new sentence:

"Except that no person mentally, morally, and otherwise qualified shall be debarred from citizenship by reason of his or her religious views or philosophical opinions with respect to the lawfulness of war as a means of settling international disputes"; and

Whereas the allegiance of a citizen to a State to which he belongs means nothing if he is unwilling for philosophical reasons both to defend its honor as well as protect its territory from military invasion, should the need arise; and

Whereas philosophical reasoning can well be the theoretical ideal for settling international disputes and controlling violence, the fact remains, however, that violence in our present world civilization can not thus be controlled; and that without the existence of a physical power to resist violence exerted against us we would sooner or later cease to be a free and independent Nation; and

Whereas citizenship is not a right to be claimed or demanded of us by an alien but is a favor granted or withheld according to any conditions a nation may wish to impose; and

Whereas it is most repugnant to the Constitution and our form of government that aliens seeking the advantages of United States citizenship should be accorded exemptions, benefits, or privileges of any kind not also possessed by our native-born or descendants of early settlers, who have for generations been devoted to our Nation's progress and the defense of its sovereignty in peace and war; and

Whereas those sincere, conscientious objectors who were bona fide members of recognized religious sects during the World War were recognized in our conscription laws, and were exempt from combatant service, have been found to be exceedingly small in number, approximately 4,000; and

Whereas it seems absurd now to open the floodgates for conscientious objectors of all varieties and thereby make possible by statutory enactment two classes of citizens—one class who can sit idly by, exempt from hazardous service in times of great national danger, and the other class compelled to risk their lives for the protection of our country and homes from possible invasion:

Therefore be it

Resolved, That the Chamber of Commerce of the State of New York is opposed to H. R. 3547 or any similar measure to amend the naturalization laws so as to grant citizenship to aliens possessing political views repugnant to our form of government or to extend to aliens exemptions, privileges, or benefits other than those enjoyed by the great body of our citizenry; and be it further

Resolved, That copies of this preamble and resolution be sent to the President of the United States and the Members of Congress, and that the president of the chamber be authorized to appoint representatives to appear at hearings and otherwise oppose legislation of this character.

LEONOR F. LOREE. *President.*
CHARLES T. GWYNNE,
Executive Vice President.

JERE D. TAMBLYN. *Secretary.*

Hearings Before the Committee on Immigration and Naturalization, House of Representatives, Seventy-first Congress, second session, on H.R. 3547, 8-9 May 1930, 60-61.

Appendix T

Women's Patriotic Conference on National Defense

Whereas it is fundamental that all citizens owe an alike allegiance to the Government of the United States, and the Government likewise owes its citizens protection; and

Whereas it is the duty of citizens by force of arms if necessary to uphold the Constitution of the United States; and

Whereas organized groups of propagandists have undertaken a campaign to nullify this solemn obligation resting upon our citizens; and

Whereas to remove the obligation of national defense as required in the oath of allegiance from aliens seeking American citizenship, notwithstanding the fact that native Americans loyally adhere to this obligation; and

Whereas a nation can not tolerate individual rebellion to that fundamental principle embodied in the Constitution of the United States as expressed in the oath of allegiance administered to aliens seeking citizenship; therefore be it

Resolved, That the Women's Patriotic Conference on National Defense does hereby indorse as a fundamental obligation of citizenship the oath of allegiance now required to be taken by aliens seeking naturalization; and be it further

Resolved, That this conference go on record as opposed to any attempt to weaken or nullify the oath of allegiance required from aliens before admission to citizenship; and be it further

Resolved, That this conference commend the courage and patriotism of the Naturalization Bureau of the Department of Labor in defending and upholding this American principle against the attack of those who are now attempting to nullify the oath of allegiance now required by the naturalization laws of our country.

January, 1932

Presented by Mrs. William S. Walker of the Daughters of the American Revolution, *Hearings Before the Committee on Immigration and Naturalization, House of Representatives*, Seventy-first Congress, second session, on H.R. 3547, 8-9 May 1930, 185.

Appendix U

Representative Resolutions Against the Griffin Bill

Resolved, That the advisory board of the American Coalition of Patriotic Societies [representing 75 patriotic societies] is emphatically opposed to any modification of our laws, or Constitution, whereby an alien may secure citizenship with any qualification as to his loyalty and duty to serve in the armed forces of the United States in time of war; and be it further

Resolved, That the advisory board of the American Coalition of Patriotic Societies urge upon Congress the enactment of positive legislation that will make the granting of citizenship to any alien seeking naturalization, with any reservation whatsoever as to his or her obligation to serve in or with the armed forces of the United States in time of war, absolutely impossible.

Washington, D.C., October 1931
Hearings on H. R. 297, 87

Resolved, That we believe American citizenship is a privilege to be conferred only upon those who wholly accept the responsibility involved, and not upon those who demand or propose special terms; and consequently we believe that no person should be admitted to citizenship in our United States who is unwilling to take an unqualified oath of allegiance to our Government

American Legion, Boston, Massachusetts convention, 1930
Hearings on H. R. 297, 99

Be it resolved by the American Legion in thirteenth national convention assembled, That we memorialize the United States Congress to amend the naturalization laws to specifically require that all applicants for citizenship be required to promise under oath that "they will bear arms in defense of this country" as a condition of the grant of naturalization; and be it further

Resolved, That the national legislative committee make this a major objective in its legislative program.

Detroit, Michigan, September 1931
Hearings on H. R. 297, 99

This is to certify that the following is an extract from Resolution No. 7, adopted by the national convention of the Military Order of the World War, on October 9, 1931, under the title of "Americanism."

Be it further resolved, That the Military Order of the World War, in convention assembled, October, 1931, lend our full and undivided efforts toward "American and Americans" in all of its phases. To this end we urge—

1. Early naturalization of those who intend to make the United States their domicile for any appreciable length of time, and that those applying for naturalization be required to subscribe to the customary oath of allegiance and service to this country now in use and without reservation, verbal or mental.

2. The reservation of all aliens.

3. Deportation of all aliens, illegally in this country, and those who have been found guilty of seditious propaganda, or otherwise undesirable activities.

Edwin S. Bettelheim, Jr.,
Adjutant General
Hearings on H. R. 297, 110

Resolved, by the thirty-second National Encampment, Veterans of Foreign Wars of the United States, That this organization does hereby condemn most bitterly the attitude of any and all organizations, religious or otherwise, throughout the United States in their advocacy of abolishing the pledge requiring naturalized citizens to bear arms in defense of our country.

Kansas City, September 1931
Hearings on H. R. 297, 125

Hearings Before the Committee on Immigration and Naturalization, House of Representatives, Seventy-second Congress, first session, on H.R. 297 and H.R. 298, January 1932, 26-27.

Appendix V

James Girouard's Testimony Before the District Court

In United States District Court

Statement in Narrative Form of
Petitioner's Testimony Before the Court,
in Accordance with Rule 75(c)
—Filed December 28, 1944

In accordance with Rule 75(c) of the Federal Rules of Procedure, Edmund J. Brandon, United States Attorney for the District of Massachusetts, for and on behalf of the United States of America now comes and makes this condensed statement of petitioner's testimony before the Court.

Statement

The appellee, James Louis Girouard, a native and former resident of Canada, entered the United States in 1923, and has since resided in this country. In 1940 he filed a declaration of intention to become a citizen of the United States, and in 1943 a petition for naturalization.

In answer to the question, on the preliminary form of application, as to whether be was willing to take up arms in defense of this country, the said appellee answered: "No, (Seventh Day Adventist, non-combatant)."

On preliminary examination the appellee, then the petitioner, stated to the Examiner that this answer was based on purely religious grounds. In his Selective Service questionnaire he had claimed exemption from both combatant and non-combatant military service as a conscientious objector. On March 9, 1943, he made a sworn statement before George F. Sears, Immigrant Inspector, which is included in the Designation of Contents of Record, and marked "4." This also was presented to the Judge at the hearing. At the time of the hearing before the Court the Naturalization Examiner recommended that the petition of said appellee, James Louis Girouard, be denied.

This hearing was held before the Court on August 1, 1944, at which time the District Court Judge interrogated the appellee, James Louis Girouard. No transcript of this examination was made, but it appears that the appellee testified that he was a member of the Seventh Day Adventist sect, of whom he said there were apparently 10,000 serving in the armed forces of the United States as non-combatants, especially in the Medical Corps, and that he was willing to serve in the army as such non-combatant, but would not bear arms. The Court ordered him admitted to citizenship.

To this ruling a Notice of Exception was immediately filed with the Court by a representative of the United States Immigration and Naturalization Service, which the Judge ordered noted and instructed that same be filed. The ruling reads as follows:

"That since the Selective Service and Training Act permits, as a matter of right, an applicant for the draft to express a willingness to serve in the armed forces of the United States, but as a non-combatant, then this petitioner by exercising that right is still a person who can take an unqualified oath of allegiance to the United States, and is therefore eligible to citizenship."

Edmund J. Brandon, United States Attorney;
Arthur J. B. Cartier, Assistant United States Attorney.

Transcript of Record
James Louis Girouard v. United States, 13-15

Appendix W

Oral Argument of Homer Cummings

If the Court Please:

This case is here on a writ of Certiorari to the Circuit Court of Appeals for the First Circuit, granted December 10, 1945. The jurisdiction of this Court is invoked under Section 240 (a) of the Judicial Code as amended by the Act of February 13, 1925. It has to do with the proposed Naturalization of the petitioner, a native of Canada and a British citizen, who, at the age of 21, entered this country in 1923 and has resided here ever since. He is an engineer and has a family consisting of a wife and daughter.

The question involved is whether the religious scruples of the petitioner against taking human life and, therefore, against bearing arms, debar him from taking the prescribed oath of allegiance or indicate such a lack of attachment to the principles of the Constitution that he cannot be admitted as a citizen, despite his willingness to serve in the Military Forces in any capacity save as an actual combatant. In all other respects he is fully qualified and would make an exemplary, useful and law-abiding citizen.

The District Court of Massachusetts, over the objection of the Naturalization Examiner, entered an order directing that the petitioner be admitted to citizenship.

The Circuit Court (Judge Woodbury dissenting) reversed the decision of the District Court.

The facts are relatively simple. The petitioner is a Seventh Day Adventist. He stated, in his petition for Naturalization, filed January 26, 1943, that he understood the principles of the Government of the United States, believed in its form of Government and was willing to take the prescribed oath of allegiance.

This oath of allegiance, it will be recalled, contains the following words, *viz.*:

"I will support and defend the Constitution and laws of the United States of America against all enemies, foreign and domestic; that I will bear true faith and allegiance to the same; and that I take this obligation freely without any mental reservations or purpose of evasion."

It further appears that in answer to Question 26 in the Preliminary Form, namely, "If necessary, are you willing to take up arms in defense of the country?" the petitioner answered, "No (Non-combatant) Seventh Day Adventist."

Later, in his sworn testimony before the acting Naturalization Examiner, March 9, 1943, he further explained his answer to Question 26 by saying, "It is purely a religious matter with me. I have no political or personal reasons other than that."

At a hearing before the District Judge on August 1, 1944, he testified that he was a member of the Seventh Day Adventist Denomination, of whom several thousand were then serving in the Armed Forces of the United States as non-combatants, especially in the Medical Corps; and that he was willing to serve in the Army but would not bear arms. The District Court ruled, "that since the Selective Service and Training Act permits, as a matter of right, an applicant for the draft to express a willingness to serve in the Armed Forces of the United States, but as a non-combatant, then this petitioner by exercising that right is still a person who can take an unqualified oath of allegiance to the United States and is therefore eligible to citizenship." Evidently the District Judge felt that there was not much logic or common sense in denying citizenship to an applicant, merely because he made the same statement he could lawfully make if admitted as a citizen.

The majority opinion of the Circuit Court held that the case fell under the doctrines of the Schwimmer, Macintosh and Bland cases, although conceding that the amendment to the Naturalization laws enacted March 27, 1942, required the conclusion that conscientious objectors who are veterans may take the oath despite their religious scruples against bearing arms.

Judge Woodbury, in his dissent, pointed out that Congress could not be deemed to have intended to have the same words of the same oath mean one thing to a conscientious objector who had served as non-combatant in the military forces and something else to one who is equally willing to serve, but who has had no opportunity to do so.

Moreover, he took the view that the Congressional enactments of 1942 show that the Schwimmer, Macintosh and Bland cases do not presently reflect the intent of Congress, no longer express the law, and would not be followed by this Court today.

That the petitioner is earnestly "attached to the principles of the Constitution of the United States" is, I think, not in serious dispute. So far as necessary this aspect of the matter has been dealt with in our brief, and we have particularly stressed the principles set forth in Schneiderman v. U.S. 320 U.S. 118, 137, 138, 139.

We are thus confronted with but one narrow issue, namely: Does the prescribed oath of allegiance imply that every petitioner shall expressly and unqualifiedly promise in advance to bear arms in defense of the country?

That there is no such express requirement in the oath of allegiance is undisputed. If there be such a requirement it must be read into the form of oath and made a necessary corollary of the words, "Support and defend the Constitution and Laws of the United States of America against all enemies, foreign and domestic."

It should be noted that at no time in our entire history has Congress ever made any specific requirement that the oath of allegiance should include a promise to bear arms. Such a requirement was originally the brain-child of the Immigration and Naturalization Service, and secured its present alleged status by virtue of the decisions in the Schwimmer, Macintosh and Bland cases.

The oath of allegiance, in substantially its present form, has been prescribed since the adoption of the Constitution. This oath does not stand alone. It is the same oath, in substance, that is required by Act of Congress of Civil Officers generally, and has been so required for seventy-five years. This Civil Oath has been taken freely by innumerable lawyers, civil service employees and public officials who entertained religious scruples against bearing arms. Never has it been interpreted or understood to include a promise to bear arms.

Nor do I think that it could be so interpreted in view of Article VI, clause 3 of the Constitution, prohibiting religious tests "as a qualification for any office or public trust under the United States." It is impossible, by any process of logic, to give differing interpretations to these two parallel, statutory oaths. Moreover, under the Civil Service Rules this Civil oath has been interpreted by the Commission as not excluding conscientious objectors from Civil Service.

In addition to this, the Armed Forces have permitted a similar oath of Allegiance to be taken by persons unwilling to bear arms and it has been taken by literally thousands of conscientious objectors serving as non-combatants under the Selective Training and Service Act of 1940. This oath contains these words:

> "I will bear true faith and Allegiance to the United States of America. I will serve them honestly and faithfully against all their enemies whomsoever."

From the very beginning down to date our Government has exhibited special solicitude for those who, because of religious scruples, are unwilling to bear arms as combatants, but who are willing to serve as non-combatants. Nowhere has the reason for not insisting upon the promise to bear arms been more effectively stated than by Mr. Chief Justice Hughes in his dissenting opinion in the Macintosh case. I have never been able to find any adequate answer to that powerful dissent.

Of course, I pay tribute to the eloquent and, indeed, impassioned brief filed by the Government in this case—including its purple passages. But I cannot concede that the Schwimmer, Macintosh and Bland cases and their doctrines have been demonstrated by the recent World War to have been as great a contributing cause to the final victory, as the devoted services of the 12,000 or more Seventh Day Adventists who served as non-combatants in the Military and Naval Forces of the United States. Nor do I think that our country would have been stronger, if these consecrated soldiers had not been available to us in our time of stress.

Man for man they are precisely like the petitioner, save that they were privileged to serve in the war, and most of them undoubtedly are citizens. How many of them are aliens, like the petitioner, will probably never be known. Our country does not gain in strength or dignity by shutting its doors to men like these.

The theory expounded in the Government's brief would require the exclusion from citizenship of every one of these patriotic citizens had they been seeking Naturalization, prior to the World War.

Their record in the recent World War is a source of pride to all patriotic citizens. Of these men who served, 45 received the Bronze Star Medal, 6 received Oak Leaf Clusters, 12 received the Silver Star Medal, one received the Gold Star Medal, 6 received special Commendations, one received the Air Medal, 16 received Presidential Citations, and others

received Meritorious Service Placques, Legion of Merit Awards, Certificates of Merit, the Croix de Guerre, and the Congressional Medal of
Honor. Many of them gave their lives: According to our latest information
there were more than one hundred awards—a remarkable showing for such
a relatively small number.

The Seventh Day Adventists are amongst our finest citizens. Their
position is not anti-militarism, it is not pacifism. Indeed, they are not
conscientious objectors at all, in any proper sense or as the term is
ordinarily understood. They do not condemn those who take part in War,
nor do they criticize the Government for waging it. They willingly wear the
uniform. They subject themselves to military jurisdiction. As members of
the Medical Corps they have, in large numbers, assumed all the risks of
front line combat. Indeed, it may well be that the moral courage with which
they have assumed these risks, though totally unarmed, is attributable to
the same religious faith which the Government now urges as a reason for
excluding the petitioner from Citizenship. They do not hold their own
judgment as superior to that of their Government. They accept the
decisions of the Congress in matters relating to War as binding upon them
and upon all other citizens. They realize that War may be necessary. They
do not agitate against War.

But they also believe in the teachings of Jesus Christ and the
scriptural admonition, "Thou shalt not kill"; and they will not personally
take human life. This is part of their deep religious faith and their measure
of their duty to God.

Only the extreme compulsion of an unequivocal and specific
Congressional enactment should lead us to deny citizenship to such
persons, when thousands far less worthy are freely admitted. Much less
should such a conclusion be reached by surmise, conjecture or implication.

As we have sought to point out in our Brief, and as the Government
admits, the Schwimmer and Macintosh cases are, on the facts, easily
distinguishable from the present case. Indeed, I am not convinced that the
Bland case is not also distinguishable. In any event, the present case
presents a much more sharply defined issue of religious liberty.

I note that my learned friend leans heavily upon the doctrine of
Congressional affirmation by acquiescence. He seems to think that because
Congress gave a statutory basis to the oath of Allegiance in the Act of
1940 and did not upset the Schwimmer, Macintosh and Bland cases by
direct and specific legislation, these cases have somehow become
sacrosanct and that there is nothing this Court can do about it. They are

embalmed forever—a sort of Judicial Egyptian mummy, upon which no profane hands may be laid.

I think this is carrying a salutary rule much too far. Because Congress did not affirmatively reverse this Court by changing the form of oath affords but slight evidence that it approved of what this Court had done.

Common sense and common knowledge indicate that the issue which divided this Court also divided the people generally and the Congress also. It became what might be described as a political "hot potato"; so Congress dropped it. This is a familiar technique and should not be taken too seriously. Congress took no affirmative action either way. If the split decisions of this Court in the three famous cases had been the other way, there is no reason in the world to assume that Congress would have done anything whatever about that either.

What the Congress did was to preserve the oath as it had been in existence, in substantially the same form, since the earliest days of our Government. To change it, in the manner the Government's Brief suggests, would be to throw it out of harmony with the form of oath required by Civil Officers.

It would be dangerous indeed to assume that the oath of Allegiance was intended by Congress to be at odds with and different in content, form, and meaning from the oath required by Article VI, clause 3 of our Constitution. Nor can it be assumed that Congress desired to approve by inaction an interpretation running counter to our fundamental political concepts. Moreover, to draw a line between complete conscientious objectors who will not perform any military duty whatever and will not wear the uniform, as against those who are unwilling to bear arms because of deep religious scruples, but who are prepared to enter the army as non-combatants and wear the uniform and obey military authority, would be a task of considerable delicacy. All these things were left where they were before—within the province and jurisdiction of the Courts.

The rule upon which the Government relies is, at best, as this Court has said, "but one of many aids" to statutory construction.

And again, it will be noted that the present case is clearly distinguishable from both the Schwimmer and the Macintosh cases.

We have only the Bland case to consider. And, as this Court has said, "one decision (only) construing an Act does not approach the dignity of a well-settled interpretation." We find support for this proposition in U.S. vs. Raynor, 302 U.S. 540, 522, and in White vs. Winchester Club, 315 U.S. 32, 40.

In U.S. vs. Missouri Pacific Railroad Company, 278 U.S. 269, 280 it is said that:

> "the rule that the re-enactment of a statute after it has been construed by officers charged with its enforcement impliedly adopts that construction, applies only when the construction is not plainly erroneous and only to cases presenting the same precise conditions of the cases passed on prior to the re-enactment."

and in: F.C.C. vs. Columbia Broadcasting System, 311 U.S. 132, 137 this Court said:

> "We are not, however, willing to rest decision on any doctrine concerning the implied enactment of a judicial construction upon re-enactment of a statute. The persuasion that lies behind that doctrine is merely one factor in the total effort to give fair meaning to language."

But whatever may be said of these three famous cases, the issue is resolved for us here by the Amendatory Legislation of 1942. We contend that this legislation shows that Congress did not mean to require upon the part of applicants for Naturalization a collateral promise to bear arms. The provisions of the two amendments of 1942 facilitate the naturalization of aliens who have served in the armed forces. Those provisions, in substance, apply to any such alien, regardless of age, and waive declaration of intention, period of residence, venue, command of the English language, handwritten signature, and fees. Clearly those enactments apply to conscientious objectors who have served as non-combatants as well as those who have served in combatant capacities. To this effect, see in Re: Kinlock 53 Fed. Supp. 521. That they apply to such conscientious objectors is demonstrated by the fact that they do not apply "to any conscientious objector who performed no military duty whatever or refused to wear the uniform."

It will be noted that this legislation does not change the form of the oath of allegiance. It does not provide a special oath for conscientious objectors entitled to its benefits.

On the contrary, each of the two amending statutes exacts "compliance with all the requirements of the naturalization laws," except for the specified dispensations. Such compliance involves the taking of the same oath, in the same language as proscribed by the same statutory provision that is here involved. Thus it is clear that the oath does not demand, by implication or otherwise, a promise to bear arms.

True, the petitioner cannot take advantage of these 1942 amendments for he has not actually seen service in the armed forces.

The important, the outstanding fact of the 1942 legislation is that Congress, without modifying the requirements as to the oath, has expressly recognized that such oath may properly be taken by an otherwise qualified alien applicant despite his religious conviction against bearing arms. There is no occasion to give this legislation a strained or narrow meaning. The attempt to interpret this legislation as altering the oath as to those who served, but not as to those who have not served, will not endure analysis.

Manifestly all conscientious objectors and persons with religious scruples are alike in their ability or inability to take the oath—they are all unwilling to make a collateral promise to bear arms. The words of the same oath cannot possibly mean one thing when applied to one person and another thing when applied to another person. If Congress had intended, or deemed it necessary, in the 1942 amendments, to relax the requirements of the oath of allegiance as to the specified veterans, as the Government suggests would have been essential, it certainly would have done so by words as unequivocal as those employed in relaxing the other requirements.

The Government seeks to break the compelling force of these arguments based upon the 1942 amendments by suggesting that they are not new, but stem from the Act of 1926, which antedates the three famous decisions. From this is drawn the conclusion that the Act of 1926 was known to this Court at the time the decisions were rendered and was, therefore, taken into account. It will be noted, however, that nowhere, either in the majority or minority opinions, is it referred to; and a careful examination of the voluminous briefs filed in these cases discloses that it was not brought to the attention of this Court by counsel on either side. This circumstance is an added reason for a re-survey of all three cases, particularly the Bland case.

It is highly desirable that we get back upon the firm ground of consistent interpretation, in harmony with the settled principles of our Government. General phrases (and that is what we are dealing with), as Mr. Chief Justice Hughes so well observed,

> "should be construed not in opposition to, but in accord with, the theory and practice of our Government in relation to Freedom of conscience."

We therefore respectfully submit that the Schwimmer, Macintosh and Bland cases be distinguished or over-ruled and that the petitioner be admitted to citizenship.

Appendix X

Girouard v. United States*

328 U.S. 61

CERTIORARI TO THE CIRCUIT COURT OF APPEALS FOR THE FIRST CIRCUIT

No. 572. Argued March 4, 1946—Decided April 22, 1946

Homer Cummings and *William D. Donnelly* argued the case for the petitioner. With them on the brief was *David J. Coddaire.*

Frederick Bernays Wiener argued the case for the United States. With him on the brief were *Solicitor General McGrath, Robert S. Erdahl* and *Leon Ulman.*

MR. JUSTICE DOUGLAS delivered the opinion of the Court.

In 1943 petitioner, a native of Canada, filed his petition for naturalization in the District Court of Massachusetts. He stated in his application that he understood the prin62ciples of the government of the United States, believed in its form of government, and was willing to take the oath of allegiance (54 Stat. 1157, 8 U.S.C. 735(b), 8 U.S.C.A. 735(b), which reads as follows:

> "I hereby declare, on oath, that I absolutely and entirely renounce and abjure all allegiance and fidelity to any foreign prince, potentate, state, or sovereignty of whom or which I have heretofore been a subject or citizen; that I will support and defend the Constitution and laws of the United States of America against all enemies, foreign and domestic; that I will bear true faith and allegiance to the same; and that I take this obligation freely without any mental reservation or purpose of evasion: So help me God."

To the question in the application "If necessary, are you willing to take up arms in defense of this country?" he replied, "No (Non-combatant) Seventh Day Adventist." He explained that answer before the examiner by saying "it is a purely religious matter with me, I have no political or personal reasons other than that." He did not claim before his Selective Service board exemption from all military service, but only from combatant military duty. At the hearing in the District Court petitioner testified that he was a member of the Seventh Day Adventist denomination, of whom approximately 10,000 were then serving in the armed forces of the United States as non-combatants, especially in the medical corps; and that he was willing to serve in the army but would not bear arms. The District Court admitted him to citizenship. The Circuit Court of Appeals reversed, one judge dissenting. 149 F.2d 760. It took that action on the authority of *United States v. Schwimmer*, 279 U.S. 644; *United States v. Macintosh*, 283 U.S. 605, and *United States v. Bland*, 283 U.S. 636, saying that the facts of the present case brought it squarely within the principles of those cases. The case is here on **63** a petition for a writ of certiorari which we granted so that those authorities might be re-examined.

The *Schwimmer*, *Macintosh* and *Bland* cases involved, as does the present one, a question of statutory construction. At the time of those cases, Congress required an alien, before admission to citizenship, to declare on oath in open court that "he will support and defend the Constitution and laws of the United States against all enemies, foreign and domestic, and bear true faith and allegiance to the same."[1] It also required the court to be satisfied that the alien had during the five year period immediately proceeding the date of his application "behaved as a man of good moral character, attached to the principles of the Constitution of the United States, and well disposed to the good order and happiness of the same."[2] Those provisions were reenacted into the present law in substantially the same form.[3]

While there are some factual distinctions between this case and the *Schwimmer* and *Macintosh* cases, the *Bland* case on its facts is indistinguishable. But the principle emerging from the three cases obliterates any factual distinction among them. As we recognized in *In re Summers*, 325 U.S. 561, 572, 577 they stand for the same general rule—that an alien who refuses to bear arms will not be admitted to citizenship. As an original proposition, we could not agree with that rule. The fallacies underlying **64** it were, we think, demonstrated in the dissents of Mr. Justice Holmes in the *Schwimmer* case and of Mr. Chief Justice Hughes in the *Macintosh* case.

The oath required of aliens does not in terms require that they promise to bear arms. Nor has Congress expressly made any such finding a prerequisite to citizenship. To hold that it is required is to read it into the Act by implication. But we could not assume that Congress intended to make such an abrupt and radical departure from our traditions unless it spoke in unequivocal terms.

The bearing of arms, important as it is, is not the only way in which our institutions may be supported and defended, even in times of great peril. Total war in its modern form dramatizes as never before the great cooperative effort necessary for victory. The nuclear physicists who developed the atomic bomb, the worker at his lathe, the seaman on cargo vessels, construction battalions, nurses, engineers, litter bearers, doctors, chaplains—these, too, made essential contributions. And many of them made the supreme sacrifice. Mr. Justice Holmes stated in the *Schwimmer* case (279 U.S. p. 655) that "the Quakers have done their share to make the country what it is." And the annals of the recent war show that many whose religious scruples prevented them from bearing arms, nevertheless were unselfish participants in the war effort. Refusal to bear arms is not necessarily a sign of disloyalty or a lack of attachment to our institutions. One may serve his country faithfully and devotedly, though his religious scruples make it impossible for him to shoulder a rifle. Devotion to one's country can be as real and as enduring among non-combatants as among combatants. One may adhere to what he deems to be his obligation to God and yet assume all military risks to secure victory. The effort of war is indivisible; and those whose religious scruples prevent them from killing are no less patriots than those whose special traits or handicaps result in their **65** assignment to duties far behind the fighting front. Each is making the utmost contribution according to his capacity. The fact that his role may be limited by religious convictions rather than by physical characteristics has no necessary bearing on his attachment to his country or on his willingness to support and defend it to his utmost.

Petitioner's religious scruples would not disqualify him from becoming a member of Congress or holding other public offices. While Article VI, Clause 3 of the Constitution provides that such officials, both of the United States and the several States, "shall be bound by Oath or Affirmation, to support this Constitution," it significantly adds that "no religious Test shall ever be required as a Qualification to any Office or public Trust under the

United States." The oath required is in no material respect different from that prescribed for aliens under the Naturalization Act. It has long contained the provision "that I will support and defend the Constitution of the United States against all enemies, foreign and domestic; that I will bear true faith and allegiance to the same; that I take this obligation freely, without any mental reservation or purpose of evasion." As Mr. Chief Justice Hughes stated in his dissent in the *Macintosh* case (283 U.S. p. 631) "the history of the struggle for religious liberty, the large number of citizens of our country from the very beginning who have been unwilling to sacrifice their religious convictions, and, in particular, those who have been conscientiously opposed to war and who would not yield what they sincerely believed to be their allegiance to the will of God"—these considerations make it impossible to conclude "that such persons are to be deemed disqualified for public office in this country because of the requirement of the oath which must be taken before they enter upon their duties."

There is not the slightest suggestion that Congress set a stricter standard for aliens seeking admission to citizen66ship than it did for officials who make and enforce the laws of the nation and administer its affairs. It is hard to believe that one need forsake his religious scruples to become a citizen but not to sit in the high councils of state.

As Mr. Chief Justice Hughes pointed out (*United States v. Macintosh*, 283 U.S., p. 633), religious scruples against bearing arms have been recognized by Congress in the various draft laws. This is true of the selective Training and Service Act of 1940 (54 Stat. 889, 50 U.S.C. App. § 305(g)[4] as it was of earlier acts. He who is inducted into the armed services takes an oath which includes the provision "that I will bear true faith and allegiance to the United States of America; that I will serve them honestly and faithfully against all their enemies whomsoever ... "[5] 41 Stat. 809, 10 U.S.C. § 1581. Congress has thus recognized that one may adequately discharge his obligations as a citizen by rendering non-combatant as well as combatant services. This respect by Congress over the years for the conscience of those having **67** religious scruples against bearing arms is cogent evidence of the meaning of the oath. It is recognition by Congress that even in time of war one may truly support and defend our institutions though he stops short of using weapons of war.

That construction of the naturalization oath received new support in 1942. In the Second War Powers Act, 56 Stat. 176, 182, 8 U.S.C. Supp. IV, § 1001, Congress relaxed certain of the requirements for aliens who served honorably in the armed forces of the United States during World War II and provided machinery to expedite their naturalization.[6] Residence requirements were relaxed, educational tests were eliminated, and no fees were required. But no change in the oath was made; nor was any change made in the requirement that the alien be attached to the principles of the Constitution. Yet it is clear that these new provisions cover non-combatants as well as combatants.[7] If petitioner had served as a non-**68**combatant (as he was willing to do), he could have been admitted to citizenship by taking the identical oath which he is willing to take. Can it be that the oath means one thing to one who has served to the extent permitted by his religious scruples and another thing to one equally willing to serve but who has not had the opportunity? It is not enough to say that petitioner is not entitled to the benefits of the new Act since he did not serve in the armed forces. He is not seeking the benefits of the expedited procedure and the relaxed requirements. The oath which he must take is identical with the oath which both non-combatants and combatants must take. It would, indeed, be a strange construction to say that "support and defend the Constitution and laws of the United States of America against all enemies, foreign and domestic" demands something more from some than it does from others. That oath can hardly be adequate for one who is unwilling to bear arms because of religious scruples and yet exact from another a promise to bear arms despite religious scruples.

Mr. Justice Holmes stated in the *Schwimmer* case (279 U.S. pp. 654-55): "if there is any principle of the Constitution that more imperatively calls for attachment than any other it is the principle of free thought—not free thought for those who agree with us but freedom for the thought that we hate. I think that we should adhere to that principle with regard to admission into, as well as to life within this country." The struggle for religious liberty has through the centuries been an effort to accommodate the demands of the State to the conscience of the individual. The victory for freedom of thought recorded in our Bill of Rights recognizes that in the domain of conscience there is a moral power higher than the State. Throughout the ages men have suffered death rather than subordinate their allegiance to God to the authority of the State. Freedom of religion guaranteed by the First Amendment is the product of that struggle. As we **69** recently stated in *United States v. Ballard*, 322 U.S. 78, 86, "Freedom of thought, which includes freedom of religious belief, is basic in a society of free men. *West Virginia State Board of Education v. Barnette*, 319 U.S. 624." The test oath is abhorrent to our tradition. Over the years Congress has meticulously respected that tradition and even in time of war has sought to accommodate the military requirements to the religious scruples of the individual. We do not believe that Congress intended to reverse that policy when it came to draft the naturalization oath. Such an abrupt and radical departure from our traditions should not be implied. See *Schneiderman v. United States*, 320 U.S. 118, 132. Cogent evidence would be necessary to convince us that Congress took that course.

We conclude that the *Schwimmer*, *Macintosh* and *Bland* cases do not state the correct rule of law.

We are met, however, with the argument that even though those cases were wrongly decided, Congress has adopted the rule which they announced. The argument runs as follows: Many efforts were made to amend the law so as to change the rule announced by those cases; but in every instance the bill died in committee. Moreover, in 1940 when the new Naturalization Act was passed, Congress reenacted the oath in its pre-existing form, though at the same time it made extensive changes in the requirements and procedure for naturalization. From this it is argued that Congress adopted and reenacted the rule of the *Schwimmer*, *Macintosh*, and *Bland* cases. Cf. *Apex Hosiery Co. v. Leader*, 310 U.S. 469, 488-89.

We stated in *Helvering v. Hallock*, 309 U.S. 106, 119, that "It would require very persuasive circumstances enveloping Congressional silence to debar this Court from reexamining its own doctrines." It is at best treacherous to find in Congressional silence alone the adoption of a controlling rule of law. We do not think under the circumstances of this legislative history that we can properly **70** place on the shoulders of Congress the burden of the Court's own error. The history of the 1940 Act is at most equivocal. It contains no affirmative recognition of the rule of the *Schwimmer*, *Macintosh* and *Bland* cases. The silence of Congress and its inaction are as consistent with a desire to leave the problem fluid as they are with an adoption by silence of the rule of those cases. But for us, it is enough to say that since the date of those cases Congress never acted affirmatively on this question but once and that was in 1942. At that time, as we have noted, Congress specifically granted naturalization privileges to non-combatants who like petitioner were prevented from bearing arms by their religious scruples. That was affirmative recognition that one could be attached to the principles of our government and could support and defend it even though his religious convictions prevented him from bearing arms. And, as we have said, we cannot believe that the oath was designed to exact something more from one person than from another. Thus the affirmative action taken by Congress in 1942 negatives any inference that otherwise might be drawn from its silence when it reenacted the oath in 1940.

Reversed.

MR. JUSTICE JACKSON took no part in the consideration or decision of this case.

MR. CHIEF JUSTICE STONE dissenting.

I think the judgment should be affirmed, for the reason that the court below, in applying the controlling provisions of the naturalization statutes, correctly applied them as earlier construed by this Court, whose construction Congress has adopted and confirmed.

In three cases decided more than fifteen years ago, this Court denied citizenship to applicants for naturalization who had announced that they proposed to take the pre71scribed oath of allegiance with the reservation or qualification that they would not, as naturalized citizens, assist in the defense of this country by force of arms or give their moral support to the government in any war which they did not believe to be morally justified or in the best interests of the country. See *United States v. Schwimmer*, 279 U.S. 644 , *United States v. Macintosh*, 283 U.S. 605, *United States v. Bland*, 283 U.S. 636.

In each of these cases this Court held that the applicant had failed to meet the conditions which Congress had made prerequisite to naturalization by § 4 of the Naturalization Act of June 29, 1906, c. 3592, 34 Stat. 596, the provisions of which, here relevant, were enacted in the Nationality Act of October 14, 1940. See c. 876, 54 Stat. 1137, as amended by the Act of March 27, 1942, c. 199, 56 Stat. 176, 182-183, and by the Act of December 7, 1942, c. 690, 56 Stat. 1041, 8 U.S.C.A. §§ 707, 735. Section 4 of the Naturalization Act of 1906, paragraph "Third," provided that before the admission to citizenship the applicant should declare on oath in open court that "he will support and defend the Constitution and laws of the United States against all enemies, foreign and domestic, and bear true faith and allegiance to the same." And paragraph "Fourth" required that before admission it be made to appear "to the satisfaction of the court admitting any alien to citizenship" that at least for a period of five years immediately preceding his application the applicant "has behaved as a man of good moral character, attached to the principles of the Constitution of the United

States, and well disposed to the good order and happiness of the same." In applying these provisions in the cases mentioned, this Court held only that an applicant who is unable to take the oath of allegiance without the reservations or qualifications insisted upon by the applicants in those cases manifests his want of attachment to the principles of the Constitution and his unwillingness to meet 72 the requirements of the oath, that he will support and defend the Constitution of the United States and bear true faith and allegiance to the same, and so does not comply with the statutory conditions of his naturalization. No question of the constitutional power of Congress to withhold citizenship on these grounds was involved. That power was not doubted. See *Selective Draft Law Cases*, 245 U.S. 366, *Hamilton v. Regents*, 293 U.S. 245. The only question was of construction of the statute which Congress at all times has been free to amend if dissatisfied with the construction adopted by the Court.

With three other Justices of the Court I dissented in the *Macintosh* and *Bland* cases, for reasons which the Court now adopts as ground for overruling them.[1] Since this Court in three considered earlier opinions has rejected the construction of the statute for which the dissenting Justices contended, the question, which for me is decisive of the present case, is whether Congress has likewise rejected that construction by its subsequent legislative action, and has adopted and confirmed the Court's earlier construction of the statutes in question. A study of Congressional action taken with respect to proposals for amendment of the naturalization laws since the decision in the *Schwimmer* case, leads me to conclude that Congress has adopted and confirmed this Court's earlier con73struction of the naturalization laws. For that reason alone I think that the judgment should be affirmed.

The construction of the naturalization statutes, adopted by this Court in the three cases mentioned, immediately became the target of an active, publicized legislative attack in Congress which persisted for a period of eleven years, until the adoption of the Nationality Act in 1940. Two days after the *Schwimmer* case was decided, a bill was introduced in the House, H.R. 3547, 71st Cong., 1st Sess., to give the Naturalization Act a construction contrary to that which had been given to it by this Court and which, if adopted, would have made the applicants rejected by this Court in the *Schwimmer*, *Macintosh* and *Bland* cases eligible for citizenship. This effort to establish by Congressional action that the construction which this Court had placed on the Naturalization Act was not one which Congress had adopted or intended, was renewed without success after the decision in the

Macintosh and Bland cases, and was continued for a period of about ten years.[2] All of these measures were of substantially the same pattern as H.R. 297, 72d Cong., 1st Sess., introduced December 8, 1931, at the first session of Congress, after the decision in the *Macintosh* case. It provided that no person otherwise qualified "shall be debarred from citizenship by reason of his or her religious views or philosophical opinions with respect to the lawfulness of war as a means of settling international disputes, but every alien admitted to citizenship shall be subject to the same obligation as the native-born citizen." H.R. 3547, 71st Cong., 1st Sess., **74** introduced immediately after the decision in the *Schwimmer* case, had contained a like provision, but with the omission of the last clause beginning "but every alien." Hearings were had before the House Committee on Immigration and Naturalization on both bills at which their proponents had stated clearly their purpose to set aside the interpretation placed on the oath of allegiance by the *Schwimmer* and *Macintosh* cases.[3] There was opposition on each occasion.[4] Bills identical with H.R. 297 were introduced in three later Congresses.[5] None of these bills were reported out of Committee. The other proposals, all of which failed of passage (see footnote 2, *ante*), had the same purpose and differed only in phraseology.

Thus, for six successive Congresses, over a period of more than a decade, there were continuously pending before Congress in one form or another proposals to overturn the rulings in the three Supreme Court decisions in question. Congress declined to adopt these proposals after full hearings and after speeches on the floor advocating the change. 72 Cong. Rec. 6966-7; 75 Cong. Rec. 15354-7. In the meantime the decisions of this Court had been followed in *Clarke's Case*, 301 Pa. 321, 152 A. 92; *Beale v. United States*, 71 F.2d 737; *In re Warkentin*, 93 F.2d 42. In *Beale v. United States*, the court pointed out that the proposed amendments affecting the provisions of the statutes relating to admission to citizenship had failed saying: "We must conclude, therefore, that these statutory requirements as construed ***75** by the Supreme Court have Congressional sanction and approval."

Any doubts that such were the purpose and will of Congress would seem to have been dissipated by the reenactment by Congress in 1940 of Paragraphs "Third" and "Fourth" of § 4 of the Naturalization Act of 1906, and by the incorporation in the Act of 1940 of the very form of oath which had been administratively prescribed for the applicants in the *Schwimmer*, *Macintosh* and *Bland* cases. See Rule 8(c), Naturalization Regulations of July 1, 1929.[6]

The Nationality Act of 1940 was a comprehensive, slowly matured and carefully considered revision of the naturalization laws. The preparation of this measure was not only delegated to a Congressional Committee, but was considered by a committee of Cabinet members, one of whom was the Attorney General. Both were aware of our decisions in the *Schwimmer* and related cases and that no other question pertinent to the naturalization laws had been as persistently and continuously before Congress in the ten years following the decision in the *Schwimmer* case. The modifications in the provisions of Paragraphs "Third" and "Fourth" of § 4 of the 1906 Act show conclusively the careful attention which was given to them.

76 In the face of this legislative history the "failure of Congress to alter the Act after it had been judicially construed, and the enactment by Congress of legislation which implicitly recognizes the judicial construction as effective, is persuasive of legislative recognition that the judicial construction is the correct one. This is the more so where, as here, the application of the statute . . . has brought forth sharply conflicting views both on the Court and in Congress, and where after the matter has been fully brought to the attention of the public and the Congress, the latter has not seen fit to change the statute." *Apex Hosiery Co. v. Leader*, 310 U.S. 469, 488-89. And see to like effect *United States v. Ryan*, 284 U.S. 167-175; *United States v. Elgin, J. & E.R. Co.*, 298 U.S. 492, 500; *Missouri v. Ross*, 299 U.S. 72, 75; cf. *Helvering v. Winmill*, 305 U.S. 79, 82, 83. It is the responsibility of Congress, in reenacting a statute, to make known its purpose in a controversial matter of interpretation of its former language, at least when the matter has, for over a decade, been persistently brought to its attention. In the light of this legislative history, it is abundantly clear that Congress has performed that duty. In any case it is not lightly to be implied that Congress has failed to perform it and has delegated to this Court the responsibility of giving new content to language deliberately readopted after this Court has construed it. For us to make such an assumption is to discourage, if not to deny, legislative responsibility. By thus adopting and confirming this Court's construction of what Congress had enacted in the Naturalization Act of 1906 Congress gave that construction the same legal significance as though it had written the very words into the Act of 1940.

The only remaining question is whether Congress repealed this construction by enactment of the 1942 amend**77**ments of the Nationality Act. That Act extended special privileges to applicants for naturalization who were aliens and who have served in the armed forces of the United

States in time of war, by dispensing with or modifying existing requirements, relating to declarations of intention, period of residence, education, and fees. It left unchanged the requirements that the applicant's behavior show his attachment to the principles of the Constitution and that he take the oath of allegiance. In adopting the 1942 amendments Congress did not have before it any question of the oath of allegiance with which it had been concerned when it adopted the 1940 Act. In 1942 it was concerned with the grant of special favors to those seeking naturalization who had worn the uniform and rendered military service in time of war and who could satisfy such naturalization requirements as had not been dispensed with by the amendments. In the case of those entitled to avail themselves of these privileges, Congress left it to the naturalization authorities, as in other cases, to determine whether, by their applications and their conduct in the military service they satisfy the requirements for naturalization which had not been waived.

It is pointed out that one of the 1942 amendments, 8 U.S.C. Supp. IV, § 1004, provided that the provisions of the amendment should not apply to "any conscientious objector who performed no military duty whatever or refused to wear the uniform." It is said that the implication of this provision is that conscientious objectors who rendered noncombatant service and wore the uniform were, under the 1942 amendments, to be admitted to citizenship. From this it is argued that since the 1942 amendments apply to those who have been in noncombatant, as well as combatant, military service, the amendment must be taken to include some who have rendered **78** noncombatant service who are also conscientious objectors and who would be admitted to citizenship under the 1942 amendments, even though they made the same reservations as to the oath of allegiance as did the applicants in the *Schwimmer*, *Macintosh* and *Bland* cases. And it is said that although the 1942 amendments are not applicable to petitioner, who has not been in military service, the oath cannot mean one thing as to him and another as to those who have been in the noncombatant service.

To these suggestions there are two answers. One is that if the 1942 amendment be construed as including noncombatants who are also conscientious objectors, who are unwilling to take the oath without the reservations made by the applicants in the *Schwimmer*, *Macintosh* and *Bland* cases, the only effect would be to exempt noncombatant conscientious objectors from the requirements of the oath, which had clearly been made applicable to all objectors, including petitioner, by the Nationality Act of 1940, and from which petitioner was not exempted by the 1942 amendments. If such is the construction of the 1942 Act, there is no constitutional or statutory obstacle to Congress' taking such action. Congress if it saw fit could have admitted to citizenship those who had rendered noncombatant service, with a modified oath or without any oath at all. Petitioner has not been so exempted.

Since petitioner was never in the military or naval forces of the United States, we need not decide whether the 1942 amendments authorized any different oath for those who had been in noncombatant service than for others. The amendments have been construed as requiring the same oath, without reservations, from conscientious objectors, as from others. *In re Nielsen*, 60 F.Supp. 240. Not all of those who rendered noncombatant service were conscientious objectors. Few were. There were others in the noncombatant service who had announced their con79scientious objections to combat service, who may have waived or abandoned their objections. Such was the experience in the First World War. See "Statement Concerning the Treatment of Conscientious Objectors in the Army," prepared and published by direction of the Secretary of War, June 18, 1919. All such could have taken the oath without the reservations made by the applicants in the *Schwimmer*, *Macintosh* and *Bland* cases and would have been entitled to the benefits of the 1942 amendments provided they had performed military duty and had not refused to wear the uniform. The fact that Congress recognized by indirection, in 8 U.S.C. Supp. IV, § 1004, that those who had appeared in the role of conscientious objectors, might become citizens by taking the oath of allegiance and establishing their attachment to the principles of the Constitution, does not show that Congress dispensed with the requirements of the oath as construed by this Court and plainly confirmed by Congress in the Nationality Act of 1940. There is no necessary inconsistency in this respect between the 1940 Act and the 1942 amendments. Without it repeal by implication is not favored. *United States v. Borden Co.*, 308 U.S. 188, 198-99, 203-6; *Georgia v. Pennsylvania R. Co.*, 324 U.S. 439, 457; *United States Alkali Ass'n v. United States*, 325 U.S. 196, 209. The amendments and their legislative history give no hint of any purpose of Congress to relax, at least for persons who had rendered no military service, the requirements of the oath of allegiance and proof of attachment to the Constitution as this Court had interpreted them and as the Nationality Act of 1940 plainly required them to be interpreted. It is not the function of this Court to disregard the will of Congress in the exercise of its constitutional power.

MR. JUSTICE REED and MR. JUSTICE FRANKFURTER join in this opinion.

Notes (for the Majority Opinion)

1. Naturalization Act of 1906, § 4, 34 Stat. 596.

2. *Id.*

3. We have already set forth in the opinion the present form of the oath which is required. It is to be found in the Nationality Act of 1940, 54 Stat. 1137, 1157, 8 U.S.C. § 735(b). Sec. 307(a) of that Act, 8 U.S.C. § 707(a), provides that no person shall be naturalized unless he has been for stated periods and still is "a person of good moral character, attached to the principles of the Constitution of the United States, and well disposed to the good order and happiness of the United States."

4. Sec. 305(g) provides in part:

"Nothing contained in this Act shall be construed to require any person to be subject to combatant training and service in the land or naval forces of the United States who, by reason of religious training and belief, is conscientiously opposed to participation in war in any form. Any such person claiming such exemption from combatant training and service because of such conscientious objections whose claim is sustained by the local board shall, if he is inducted into the land or naval forces under this Act, be assigned to noncombatant service as defined by the President, or shall, if he is found to be conscientiously opposed to participation in such noncombatant service, in lieu of such induction, be assigned to work of national importance under civilian direction."

For earlier Acts see Act of February 21, 1864, 13 Stat. 6, 9; Act of January 21, 1903, 32 Stat. 775; Act of June 3, 1916, 39 Stat. 166, 197; Act of May 18, 1917, 40 Stat. 76, 78.

5. And see *Billings v. Truesdell*, 321 U.S. 542, 549-50; Army Regulations No. 615-500, August 10, 1944, § II, 15(f) (2).

6. Comparable provision was made in the Act of December 7, 1942, 56 Stat. 1041, 8 U.S.C. Supp. IV, § 723a, for those who served honorably in World War I, in the Spanish American War, or on the Mexican Border.

7. *In re Kinloch*, 53 F.Supp. 521, involved naturalization proceedings of aliens, one of whom, like petitioner in the present case, was a Seventh Day Adventist. He had been inducted into the army as a non-combatant. His naturalization was opposed by the Immigration Service on the ground that he could not promise to bear arms. The court overruled the objection, stating, page 523:

"If conscientious objectors, who are aliens, performing military duty, and wearing the uniform, are not granted the privileges of citizenship under this act, then the act would be meaningless. It would be so made if an applicant, being a conscientious objector, who has attained the status of a soldier, performs military duty, and honorably wears the uniform (as is admitted in the instant cases), is denied citizenship. If the oath of allegiance is to be construed as requiring such applicant to agree, without mental reservation, to bear arms, then the result would be a denial of citizenship, even though Congress has conferred such privilege upon him."

And see *In re Sawyer*, 59 F.Supp. 428.

Notes (for the Dissent)

1. In the opinion of the writer there was evidence in *United States v. Schwimmer*, 279 U.S. 644, from which the district court could and presumably did infer that applicant's behavior evidenced a disposition, present and future, actively to resist all laws of the United States and lawful commands of its officers for the furthering of any military enterprise of the United States, and actively to aid and encourage such resistance in others, and this the district court presumably concluded evidenced a want of attachment of the applicant to the principles of the Constitution which the naturalization law requires to be exhibited by the behavior of the applicant, preceding the application for citizenship.

2. H.R. 3547, 71st Cong., 1st Sess., 71 Cong. Rec. 2184; H.R. 297, 72d Cong., 1st Sess., 75 Cong. Rec. 95; H.R. 298, 72d Cong., 1st Sess., 75 Cong. Rec. 95; S. 3275, 72d Cong., 1st Sess., 75 Cong. Rec. 2600; H.R. 1528, 73d Cong., 1st Sess., 77 Cong. Rec. 90; H.R. 5170, 74th Cong., 1st Sess., 79 Cong. Rec. 1356; H.R. 8259, 75th Cong., 1st Sess., 81 Cong. Rec. 9193; S.165, 76th Cong., 1st Sess., 84 Cong. Rec. 67.

3. Hearings on H.R. 3547, pp. 12, 22, 29-57, 73-109, 169, 180; Hearings on H.R. 297, pp. 4-7, 10, 12, 15-19, 41-48, 53-56, 66-81, 147, 148.

4. Hearings on H.R. 3547, pp. 57-65, 73, 146-169, 181-212; Hearings on H.R. 297, pp. 85-140.

5. H.R. 1528, 73d Cong., 1st Sess.; H.R. 5170, 74th Cong., 1st Sess.; H. R. 8259, 75th Cong., 1st Sess.

6. Section 307(a) of the Nationality Act, 8 U.S.C. § 707(a), provides that no person shall be naturalized unless for a period of five years preceding the filing of his petition for naturalization he "has been and still is a person . . . attached to the principles of the Constitution of the United States, and well disposed to the good order and happiness of the United States." Section 335(a) of the Nationality Act, 8 U.S.C. § 735(a), provides that before an applicant for naturalization shall be admitted to citizenship, he shall take an oath in open court that inter alia he will "support and defend the Constitution and laws of the United States against all enemies, foreign and domestic, . . . and . . . bear true faith and allegiance to the same."

*Bold numbers represent original pagination in *United States Reports*.

Appendix Y

Rosika Schwimmer to Carrie Chapman Catt

October 22, 1946

Dear Mrs. Catt:

. . . .

I appreciate very much your offer to help me to get American citizenship. Yes, I would like to get it because statelessness is a very agonizing condition.

When I was refused citizenship by the Supreme Court it was done because the Auxiliary of the American Legion had, two years before I could apply for second papers, passed a resolution and sent it to the Labor Department demanding that I be refused citizenship when I applied for it. I learned about this from a Wisconsin newspaper clipping but all the people to whom I showed it pooh poohed it and declared such a refusal will never occur. You will find the details of this story in Edith Wynner's as yet unpublished manuscripts which I enclose and beg you to return when you are finished with it.

When this un-American decision was reversed recently in the Girouard Case I thought I might now get citizenship right away on the following ground:

The Federal Court of Appeals in Chicago granted me citizenship by unanimous decision which contained the much-quoted comment: "A petitioner's rights are not to be determined by putting conundrums to her." This Court ordered citizenship papers to be issued to me.

The American Legion was mad and put pressure on the Department of Labor to appeal against the decision. The Labor Department was reluctant and tc ok quite a long time before it yielded to the pressure. Then everyone said the Supreme Court will refuse to hear the appeal. Many famous professors of law of most important universities told me and wrote me that the appeal is absurd and the Supreme Court won't deal with it.

But the American Legion was and has been ever since more powerful than people seem to realize and got its way.

My lawyer's brief probed and the conclusion of her argument was that I was asked to do something that the laws forbade me to do since all the laws referring to military service spoke of "able-bodied men." But logic and the law had no place in the proceedings and America's traditional naturalization laws were changed to the amazement of the whole world which knew of no other country that compelled women to bear arms.

Since the Supreme Court has now reversed itself, I thought having passed all the examinations and even having been granted citizenship by the Federal Court of Appeals that now citizenship papers should automatically be granted to me without my having to go through the tiresome formalities involved if I had to apply again for first papers, then wait two years, then go through all the examinations and hearings again.

I have no lawyer because the woman lawyer who did the much-admired groundwork in my case has moved years ago for reasons of health to Colorado and the New York lawyer who was at my disposal without charging me is now in the Navy's Japanese service. He had gone through the diplomatic school way back and Japanese was his hobby. He was of a wealthy family and could travel. When the war with Japan started he entered the naval service and as I haven't heard from him for quite a while I think he must be over in Japan.

Since I cannot afford to pay a lawyer I cannot consult one to attend to getting me citizenship on the ground that I had passed all the formalities and was granted citizenship prior to the Supreme Court decision reversing it. And also having lived here as a "tolerated alien" I have led a most strictly correct life obeying all rules and orders which had become particularly aggravating after Hungary became involved in war with the United States. At that time I was considered a Hungarian and all the restrictions were put on me that applied to enemy aliens although I was no longer a Hungarian having renounced Hungarian citizenship when I applied for my first papers.

But everything is made so hard for people who are strictly honest and do their utmost to live decently. I am no longer an enemy alien but I am stateless.

So if you could help me through your lawyer to analyze the situation and find out whether I could claim citizenship papers on the grounds I described I would be very happy. In that case, I would of course furnish all the pertinent documents.

Another step had been suggested. Way back when Einstein was harassed by the Woman Patriots who strangely enough got the support of the German Consulate here in Berlin [*sic*] trying to have the State Department refuse Einstein a visa to the United States, someone suggested the introduction of a special bill to give him American citizenship.

Now, since this recent reversal, someone suggested finding a Senator and Congressman who would introduce a joint resolution in my interest. I suggested that such a bill should include Professor Macintosh, Nurse Marie Bland and all others who since the decision in my case have been refused citizenship for refusal to promise to bear arms.

The lady who suggested such a step for me, however, didn't know anyone in Congress whom she could ask to introduce the resolution either for me alone, or, as I suggested, for all those who have been wronged by the 1929 decision.

So there would be a second way in which you might be helpful if I could not get it on the first-mentioned ground. Of course, Congress will reassemble on in January but if legislators could be found willing to introduce such a bill the publicity about the intended step could help to rouse public opinion to favor such a bill.

Your very kind offer to help me achieve American citizenship reminds me of an incident at the organizing meeting of the Women's Peace Party in January 1915 in Washington. At one of the gala meetings, different leaders presided over the addresses of different speakers. You presided when I spoke and introduced me by saying: "And I hope she will become an American citizen and be one of us."

I answered that I do not intend to change formally my nationality because I feel at home wherever I am in the world but I am so much in love with the United States that I think I will put up a pied à terre here and spend a part of every year in this country. So to say commuting between the United States and Europe.

Editing the report of the meeting, they left out your remark and my answer which I often regretted.

It would be an act of poetic justice if you managed to help make me an American citizen. Looking forward to hearing what you decide to do, as always,

Affectionately,

Rosika
Schwimmer-Lloyd collection, box G-24.

Appendix Z

Rosika Schwimmer's
Health in March 1947

March 8, 1947

My dear Mrs. Catt:

Your letter of February 11, caught me at the door when I was rushing to the railroad station. I was off for a few days' conference on world government in Asheville, North Carolina and read your letter on the train. I would have loved to dash off an answer but I am a bad traveler and cannot write while riding in train, bus or airplane.

After the very strenuous conference and an absence of nearly a week, I returned with serious obligations to attend to a few exceedingly urgent matters. It is only today that I am free to answer your confidential inquiry about Mme. Schwimmer's health and needs.

There is, alas, nothing good I can tell you about her physical condition. Her thirty-one year old diabetes has reached the stage where even 160 daily units of insulin cannot control it.

That mysterious sleeping sickness which for a few years she could control through benzedrine for a few hours every day is also resisting this drug and every other means her physician has tried. This means that there is every day less and less time when she is able to work.

But I who have worked with her for twelve years can say that even in the short periods of working ability which she now has, her creative thinking is as clear and sharp as it ever was. I am sure she could serve the world even in her deplorable physical condition better than any of those active today with full-time use of all their faculties.

Amongst ailments in addition to her diabetes and sleeping sickness there are a few that should be attended to even if we must let her carry out her decision "to let go" and not to seek further medical attempts to ameliorate her condition or at least to half further deterioration. The two things she must have are new dental palates and a dermatologist's continued burning off of skin cancer spots.

As you know, my dear Mrs. Catt, Mme. Schwimmer used to go for annual hospitalization to the Chicago Presbyterian Hospital where she was under the care of the greatest specialists during all these decades. Most of them gave their services free or at greatly reduced rate. The dermatologist, Dr. Mitchell, whose wife remembered Mme. Schwimmer's work for peace and woman suffrage in 1914/15, started the skin cancer treatment and urged her very emphatically to continue it in New York. She has not done so because she doesn't want to spend any more of the little money at her and her sister's disposal on herself.

But Miss Franciska and I are greatly worried that we cannot break her resistance at least about new dental plates and a dermatologist's attention.

Shall I tell you about all her other troubles? It would really need a medical encyclopedia. She has chronic bronchitis for which she would need vacations among pine trees. She has a chronic diverticulitis over the whole bowel system against which nothing can be done except observation of diet restrictions and constant use of an expensive medicine. Her arthritis has grown quite bad. Her inflamed joints are very painful and she would need a series of sulphur baths. The cataract on her eyes has grown to a stage where she has in general great difficulty in reading and writing and sometimes days go by when her vision is too blurred to read at all.

Since contact with Europe has opened, she has directed Miss Schwimmer's and my work for giving and securing help to surviving leaders and co-workers of the causes to which she had devoted her life. You kindly responded to her first appeal for the Hungarian feminists for whom you had done so much since you helped them to get organized in 1904.

Former suffragists and pacifists in many countries are provided with at least minimum help through Mme. Schwimmer's efforts. A considerable part of the legacy Mrs. Lola Maverick Lloyd left her was spent on the action to secure help for them. Today Mme. Schwimmer has only money enough left to carry her and her sister for about three-fourths or one year longer. And then—

May I tell you in deepest confidence that I am exerting myself to the utmost to earn money enough to take over Mme. and Miss Schwimmer as "my dependents." But so far I haven't moved an inch towards achieving that. The situation of those who work for a cause, in my case peace through world government, is that there is plenty of work but never adequate pay for it, often not even covering expenses.

For instance, after delivering eighty lectures in five weeks in 1944, I earned lots of money for the American Friends Service Committee, the sponsoring organization, but hardly covered expenses for myself.

In addition to all this, Miss Franciska's health is also far from satisfactory but she does not submit herself to medical examination and works more than six persons should. Because of the high cost of household help we haven't had an hour's help in the last three years and from scrubbing bathroom and kitchen floors to diet cooking we have to do everything ourselves. The same holds for clerical help and this holds up attending to the tremendous international mail which is coming in. And so on and so on.

This is a frightful indictment of our so-called civilization that women who have spent their lives in service to mankind should be hampered in securing their minimum needs by lack of money.

In summarizing the situation I must say that Mme. Schwimmer's condition is much worse than she permitted you to know and which on your request I describe to you very sketchily with a desperate feeling that even a few thousand dollars are not available for her most urgent needs.

You asked me a confidential question. May I beg you not to let Mme. Schwimmer know about this correspondence.

Hoping you may have some advice as to what could be done for her, possibly undertaking steps to secure the Nobel peace Prize or something similar which would make it possible to prolong her life. I would appreciate your permission to visit you to discuss this problem with you in the near future.

Respectfully yours,

Edith Wynner

Mrs. Carrie Chapman Catt
120 Paine Avenue
New Rochelle, New York

Schwimmer-Lloyd collection, box G-24.
[Note: Carrie Chapman Catt died 9 March 1947, the day after this letter was written.]

Appendix AA

Senate Joint Resolution 55

Whereas Douglas Clyde Macintosh, a native of Canada and a Baptist minister, distinguished himself as an outstanding theologian and respected teacher in more than thirty years of service on the faculty of the Yale Divinity School, and as a visiting lecturer in philosophy and religion at the Universities of California, Chicago, Calcutta, and Harvard;

Whereas in World War I Douglas Clyde Macintosh voluntarily saw service as a chaplain with the Canadian Army at Vimy Ridge and in the Battle of the Somme, lectured on behalf of the Allies in the United States, and operated an American Y.M.C.A. outpost at the front until the Armistice in 1918;

Whereas in 1931 the Supreme Court of the United States, in the case of United States v. Macintosh, 283 U.S. 605 (1931), affirmed the decision of the Federal District Court of Connecticut denying Douglas Clyde Macintosh's petition for naturalization as a citizen of the United States because he would not promise to bear arms in defense of the United States unless he believed the war to be morally justified;

Whereas in proceedings before the District Court Douglas Clyde Macintosh stated that he was ready to give to the United States all the allegiance he had ever given or ever could give any country, but could not put allegiance to the government of any country before allegiance to the will of God;

Whereas in 1946, in the case of Girouard v. United States, 328 U.S. 61 (1946), the Supreme Court of the United States overruled the decision of United States v. Macintosh;

Whereas Douglas Clyde Macintosh suffered an incapacitating stroke in 1942 making him unable to renew his petition for naturalization;

Whereas one of the cardinal principles upon which this Nation was founded is the unalienable right to the free exercise of religion, according to the dictates of conscience; and

Whereas Douglas Clyde Macintosh died in 1948 without receiving vindication for his personal sufferings on behalf of that principle: Now, therefore, be it

Resolved by the Senate and House of Representatives of the United States of America in Congress assembled, That the President is authorized and directed to declare by proclamation that Douglas Clyde Macintosh is an honorary citizen of the United States.

Congressional Record—Senate, March 24, 1981, D 300.

Appendix BB

Internal Security Act of 1950

64 *Statutes at Large* 987 (September 23, 1950)

Amending Section 335 of Nationality Act of 1940

Sec. 29. Section 335 of the Nationality Act of 1940, as amended, is amended to read:

"Sec. 335. (a) A person who has petitioned for naturalization shall, before being admitted to citizenship, take in open court one of the oaths set forth in subsection (b) of this section (1) to support the Constitution of the United States; (2) to renounce and abjure absolutely and entirely all allegiance and fidelity to any foreign prince, potentate, state, or sovereignty of whom or which the petitioner was before a subject or citizen; (3) to support and defend the Constitution and the laws of the United States against all enemies, foreign and domestic; (4) to bear true faith and allegiance to the same; and (5) to bear arms on behalf of the United States when required by law, or to perform noncombatant service in the Armed Forces of the United States when required by law: *Provided,* That any such person shall be required to take the oath prescribed in subsection (b) (1) of this section unless by clear and convincing evidence he can show to the satisfaction of the naturalization court that he is opposed to the bearing of arms or the performance of noncombatant service in the Armed Forces of the United States by reason of religious training and belief: *Provided further,* That in the case of the naturalization of a child under the provisions of section 315 or 316 of this Act the naturalization court may waive the taking of either of such oaths if in the opinion of the court the child is unable to understand their meaning.

"(b) As provided in subsection (a) of this section, the petitioner for naturalization shall take one of the following oaths:

"(1) I hereby declare, on oath, that I absolutely and entirely renounce and abjure all allegiance and fidelity to any foreign prince, potentate, state, or sovereignty of whom or which I have heretofore been a subject or citizen; that I will support and defend the Constitution and laws of the United States of America against all enemies, foreign and domestic; that I will bear true faith and allegiance to the same; that I will bear arms on behalf of the United States or perform noncombatant service in the Armed Forces of the United States when required by law; and that I take this obligation freely without any mental reservation or purpose of evasion: So help me God. In acknowledgment whereof I have hereunto affixed my signature; or

"(2) I hereby declare, on oath, that I absolutely and entirely renounce and abjure all allegiance and fidelity to any foreign prince, potentate, state, or sovereignty of whom or which I have heretofore been a subject or citizen; that I will support and defend the Constitution and laws of the United States of America against all enemies, foreign and domestic; that I will bear true faith and allegiance to the same; and that I take this obligation freely and without any mental reservation or purpose of evasion: So help me God. In acknowledgment whereof I have hereunto affixed my signature."

64 *Statutes at Large* 1017-18

Bibliography

Primary Sources: Books

Bowie, Walter Russell. *Learning to Live.* Nashville, Tenn.: Abingdon Press, 1969.

Darrow, Clarence *The War.* New York: The National Security League, 1917.

Fox, George. *The Journal,* ed. Nigel Smith. London: Penguin Books, 1998.

Griffin, Anthony J. *The War and Its Aftermath: Speeches of Hon. Anthony J. Griffin of New York in the House of Representatives During the 65th, 66th, and 67th Congresses.* Washington, D.C.: n.p., 1922.

Hearings Before the Committee on Immigration and Naturalization, House of Representatives, Seventy-First Congress, Second Session, on H.R. 3547. 8-9 May 1930.

Hearings Before the Committee on Immigration and Naturalization, House of Representatives, Seventy-Second Congress, First Session, on H.R. 297, H. R. 298. 26 January 1931.

"Immigration and Nationality Act." *Conference Report to Accompany H.R. 5678,* House of Representatives Report 2096. 9 June 1952.

"Internal Security Act of 1950." *Conference Report to Accompany H.R. 9490,* House of Representatives Report 3112, 81st Congress, 2d Session. 19 September 1950.

Macintosh, Douglas Clyde. *God in a World at War.* London: George Allen & Unwin, 1918.

———. *Social Religion.* New York: Charles Scribner's Sons, 1939.

"Protecting the Internal Security of the United States." *Report to Accompany S. 4037.* Senate Report 2369, Part 2, Minority Views, 81st Congress, 2d Session. 17 August 1950.

"Revising the Laws Relating to Immigration, Naturalization, and Nationality." *Report to Accompany H.R. 5678.* House of Representatives Report 1365, 82nd Congress, 2d Session. 14 February 1952.

"Revision of Immigration, Naturalization, and Nationality Laws." *Joint Hearings Before the Subcommittees of the Committees on the Judiciary, Congress of the United States on S. 716, H.R. 2397, and H.R. 2816.* 82nd Congress, 1st Session. 6-21 March and 9 April 1951.

"Revision of Laws Relating to Immigration, Naturalization, and Nationality." 4422-23 in *Congressional Record—House*, 25 April 1952.

Rosika Schwimmer, World Patriot: A Biographical Sketch. Odhams Press, London: International Committee for World Peace Prize Award to Rosika Schwimmer, 1937; rev. and enl. ed., 1947.

Schwimmer, Rosika. *Union Now for Peace or War?: The Danger of the Plan of Clarence Streit.* New York: Author, 1939.

——— and Edith Wynner. *Memorandum on Immediate Action for World Government.* New York, n.p., 1945.

The Case of Rosika Schwimmer: Alien Pacifists Not Wanted! New York: American Civil Liberties Union, 1929.

The Complete Writings of Menno Simons, c. 1496-1561, trans., Leonard Verduin, ed. J. C. Wenger. Scottdale, Pa.: Herald Press, 1984.

"The Immigration and Naturalization Systems of the United States." *Report of the Committee on the Judiciary Pursuant to S. Res. 139: A Resolution to Make an Investigation of the Immigration System.* Senate Report 1515, 81st Congress, 2d Session. 20 April 1950.

The Journal of George Fox, ed. John H. Nickalls. Cambridge, England: Cambridge University Press, 1952.

Wynner, Edith, and Georgia Lloyd, *Searchlight on Peace Plans: Choose Your Road to World Government.* New York: E. P. Dutton, 1949.

———. *World Federal Government, Why?, What?, How?* Afton, N.Y.: Fedonot Press, 1954.

Primary Sources: Articles

Griffin, Anthony J. "A Dialogue Between a Citizen and a Soldier on H.R. 3547." *Congressional Record—House*, 72 (11 April 1930): 6966-67.

Griffin, Anthony J. "H.R. 297—An Appeal for Religious Liberty and Freedom of Thought." *Congressional Record—House* 75 (14 July 1932): 15354-57.

Lloyd, Lola Maverick. *The Griffin Bill.* New York: Griffin Bill Committee, n.d., 1-8.

Macintosh, Douglas Clyde. "God and History." 22-32 in *Religion and the War: By Members of the Faculty of the School of Religion, Yale University*, ed. E. Hershey Sneath. New Haven, Conn.: Yale University Press, 1918.

————. "Toward a New Untraditional Orthodoxy." 277-319 in *Contemporary American Theology: Theological Autobiographies*, Vol. I, ed. Vergilius Ferm. New York: Round Table Press, 1932.

Schwimmer, Rosika. "The Nobel Peace Prize," *World Tomorrow* 15 (January 1932): 20-22.

"Trial and Martyrdom of Michael Sattler." 136-44 in *Spiritual and Anabaptist Writers*, vol 25 of *The Library of Christian Classics*, ed. George H. Williams. Philadelphia: Westminster Press, 1957.

"Women and War." *Outlook* 109 (24 March 1915): 676-77.

Secondary Sources: Books

Abrams, Ray H. *Preachers Present Arms*. New York: Round Table Press, 1933, Scottdale, Pa.: Herald Press, 1969.

Allen, Joseph L. *War: A Primer for Christians*. Nashville, Tenn.: Abingdon Press, 1991.

Alonso, Harriet Hyman. *Peace as a Women's Issue: A History of the U.S. Movement for World Peace and Women's Rights*. Syracuse, N.Y.: Syracuse University Press, 1993.

Bainton, Roland H. *Christian Attitudes Toward War and Peace: A Historical Survey and Critical Re-evaluation*. Nashville, Tenn.: Abingdon Press, 1960.

Baker, Liva. *The Justice from Beacon Hill: The Life and Times of Oliver Wendell Holmes*. New York: HarperCollins, 1991.

Baker, Roscoe. *The American Legion and American Foreign Policy*. New York: Bookman Associates, 1954.

Barash, David P. *Introduction to Peace Studies*. Belmont, Calif.: Wadsworth Publishing, 1991.

Bennett, Marion T. *American Immigration Policies: A History*. Washington, D.C.: Public Affairs Press, 1963.

Billington, Ray Allen. *The Protestant Crusade, 1800-1860: A Study of the Origins of American Nativism*. Chicago: Quadrangle Books, 1938, 1952, 1964.

Blumhofer, Edith L. *Aimee Semple McPherson: Everybody's Sister.* Grand Rapids, Mich.: William B. Eerdmans, 1993.

Brock, Peter. *The Quaker Peace Testimony, 1660 to 1914.* York, England: Sessions Book Trust, 1990.

————.*Twentieth-Century Pacifism.* New York: Van Nostrand Reinhold, 1970.

————. *Varieties of Pacifism: A Survey from Antiquity to the Outset of the Twentieth Century.* Syracuse, N.Y.: Syracuse University Press, 1998.

Buchanan, Patrick J. *The Death of the West: How Mass Immigration, Depopulation and a Dying Faith Are Killing Our Culture and Country.* New York: Saint Martin's Press, 2002.

Byler, Dennis. *Making War and Making Peace.* Scottdale, Pa.: Herald Press, 1989.

Cady, Duane L. *From Warism to Pacifism: A Moral Continuum.* Philadelphia: Temple University Press, 1989.

Chatfield, Charles. *For Peace and Justice: Pacifism in America, 1914-1941.* Knoxville: University of Tennessee Press, 1971.

————, ed. *Peace Movements in America.* New York: Schocken Books, 1973.

————. *The American Peace Movement: Ideals and Activism.* New York: Twayne Publishers, 1992.

Cushman, Clare, ed. *The Supreme Court Justices: Illustrated Biographies, 1789-1993.* Washington, D.C.: Congressional Quarterly, 1993.

Danelski, David J., and Joseph S. Tulchin, eds. *The Autobiographical Notes of Charles Evans Hughes.* Cambridge, Mass.: Harvard University Press, 1973.

Degen, Marie Louise. *The History of the Woman's Peace Party.* Baltimore, Md.: Johns Hopkins Press, 1939; New York: Garland Press, 1972.

Divine, Robert A. *American Immigration Policy, 1924-1952.* New Haven, Conn.: Yale University Press, 1957.

Douglas, William O. *Go East, Young Man, the Early Years: The Autobiography of William O. Douglas.* New York: Vintage Books, 1974.

————. *The Court Years, 1939-1975: The Autobiography of William O. Douglas.* New York: Vintage Books, 1980.

Franklin, Frank George. *The Legislative History of Naturalization in the United States*. Chicago: University of Chicago Press, 1906; repr., New York: Arno Press, 1969.

Gaustad, Edwin Scott. *A Religious History of America*. Rev. ed., New York: Harper and Row, 1990.

———— and Philip Barlow. *New Historical Atlas of Religion in America*. New York: Oxford University Press, 2001.

Gavan, Lettie. *American Women in World War I: They Also Served*. Niwot: University Press of Colorado, 1997.

Gettys, Luella. *The Law of Citizenship in the United States*. Chicago: University of Chicago Press, 1934.

Handlin, Oscar. *The Uprooted: The Epic Story of the Great Migrations That Made the American People*. New York: Grosset and Dunlap, 1951.

Hansen, Marcus Lee. *The Immigrant in American History*. Cambridge, Mass.: Harvard University Press, 1940; New York: Harper and Row, Harper Torchbooks, 1964.

Harbaugh, William H. *Lawyer's Lawyer: The Life of John W. Davis*. New York: Oxford University Press, 1973; University Press of Virginia, 1990.

Hawkley, Louise, and James C. Juhnke, eds. *Nonviolent America: History Through the Eyes of Peace*. North Newton, Kans.: Bethel College, 1993.

Hershberger, Guy Franklin. *War, Peace, and Nonresistance*. Scottdale, Pa.: Herald Press, 1981.

Hershey, Burnet. *The Odyssey of Henry Ford and the Great Peace Ship*. New York: Taplinger Publishing, 1967.

Hill, Frank Ernest. *The American Legion Auxiliary: A History: 1924-1934*. Indianapolis: American Legion Auxiliary, 1935.

Horsch, John. *The Principle of Nonresistance as Held by the Mennonite Church*. Scottdale, Pa.: Mennonite Publishing House, 1951.

Hutchinson, Edward P. *Legislative History of American Immigration Policy, 1798-1965*. Philadelphia: University of Pennsylvania Press, 1981.

Irons, Peter. *The Courage of Their Convictions: Sixteen Americans Who Fought Their Way to the Supreme Court*. New York: Penguin Books, 1988, 1990.

Jones, Maldwyn Allen. *American Immigration*. Chicago: University of Chicago Press, 1960, 2d ed., 1992.

Jones, Richard Seelye. *A History of the American Legion*. Indianapolis, Ind.: Bobbs-Merrill, 1946.

Josephson, Harold, Sandi E. Cooper, Solomon Wank, and Lawrence S. Wittner, eds. *Biographical Dictionary of Modern Peace Leaders*. Westport, Conn.: Greenwood Press, 1985.

Keim, Albert N., and Grant M. Stoltzfus. *The Politics of Conscience: The Historic Peace Churches and America at War, 1917-1955*. Scottdale, Pa.: Herald Press, 1988.

Kettner, James H. *The Development of American Citizenship, 1608-1870*. Chapel Hill: University of North Carolina Press, 1978.

Kraft, Barbara S. *The Peace Ship: Henry Ford's Pacifist Adventure in the First World War*. New York: Macmillan, 1978.

Kraut, Alan M. *The Huddled Masses: The Immigrant in American Society, 1880-1921*. Arlington Heights, Ill.: Harlan Davidson, 1982.

Lavery, Emmet. *The Magnificent Yankee: A Play in Three Acts*. New York: Samuel French, 1945, 1946.

Lieberman, Mark. *The Pacifists: Soldiers Without Guns*. New York: Praeger Publishers, 1972.

Littell, Franklin H. *The Origins of Sectarian Protestantism: A Study of the Anabaptist View of the Church*. New York: Macmillan, 1964.

Long, Edward LeRoy, Jr. *War and Conscience in America*. Philadelphia: Westminster Press, 1968.

Manual for Noncommissioned Officers and Privates of Cavalry of the Army of the United States. Washington, D.C.: Government Printing Office, 1917.

Mason, Alpheus Thomas. *Harlan Fiske Stone: Pillar of the Law*. New York: Viking Press, 1956.

Miller, Robert Moats. *American Protestantism and Social Issues: 1919-1939*. Chapel Hill: University of North Carolina Press, 1958.

————. *Harry Emerson Fosdick: Preacher, Pastor, Prophet*. New York: Oxford University Press, 1985.

Moley, Raymond, Jr. *The American Legion Story*. New York: Duell, Sloan, and Pearce, 1966.

Moorehead, Caroline. *Troublesome People: The Warriors of Pacifism*. Bethesda, Md.: Adler and Adler, 1987.

Niebuhr, Reinhold. *Christianity and Power Politics*. New York: Charles Scribner's Sons, 1940.

Noll, Mark A. *A History of Christianity in the United States and Canada*. Grand Rapids, Mich.: William B. Eerdmans, 1992.

Novick, Sheldon M. *Honorable Justice: The Life of Oliver Wendell Holmes*. New York: Dell Laurel, 1989.

Pauling, Linus, Ervin Laszlo, and John Youl Yoo, eds. *World Encyclopedia of Peace*. Oxford, England: Pergamon Press, 4 vols., 1986.

Peters, Shawn Francis. *Judging Jehovah's Witnesses: Religious Persecution and the Dawn of the Rights Revolution*. Lawrence: University of Kansas Press, 2000.

Pierce, Nathaniel W., and Paul L. Ward. *The Voice of Conscience: A Loud and Unusual Noise?: The Episcopal Peace Fellowship 1939-1989*. Charlestown, Mass.: Episcopal Peace Fellowship, 1989.

Roche, John P. *The Early Development of United States Citizenship*. Ithaca, N.Y.: Cornell University Press, 1949.

Rumer, Thomas A. *The American Legion: An Official History, 1919-1989*. New York: M. Evans, 1990.

Steinson, Barbara J. *American Women's Activism in World War I*. New York: Garland, 1982.

Strayer, Martha. *The D.A.R.: An Informal History*. Westport, Conn.: Greenwood Press, 1958, 1973.

Syme, Eric. *A History of SDA Church-State Relations in the United States*. Mountain View, Calif.: Pacific Press, 1973.

Trueblood, D. Elton. *The People Called Quakers*. New York: Harper and Row, 1966.

Urofsky, Melvin I. ed., *The Douglas Letters: Selections from the Private Papers of Justice William O. Douglas*. Bethesda, Md.: Adler and Adler, 1987.

Walker, Samuel. *In Defense of American Liberties: A History of the ACLU*. New York: Oxford University Press, 1990.

Wells, Ronald A., ed. *The Wars of America: Christian Views*. Macon, Ga.: Mercer University Press, 1991.

White, G. Edward. *Justice Oliver Wendell Holmes: Law and the Inner Self*. New York: Oxford University Press, 1993.

Wilcox, Francis McLellan. *Seventh-Day Adventists in Time of War*. Washington, D.C.: Review and Herald Publishing Association, 1936.

Wiltsher, Anne. *Most Dangerous Women: Feminist Peace Campaigners of the Great War*. London: Pandora Press, 1983.

Secondary Sources: Articles

"Aliens and Citizens," in 3C *American Jurisprudence 2d*. Saint Paul, Minn.: West Group, 1962- , § 2854, 288-89.

"American Citizenship: Can Applicants Qualify Their Allegiance?" *American Bar Association Journal* 33 (February 1947): 95-98.

"American Citizenship: Our Readers' Views of the Girouard Decision." *American Bar Association Journal* 33 (April 1947): 323-26.

Anderson, Jeffrey M. "Conscience in the Court, 1931-1946: Religion as Duty and Choice." *Journal of Supreme Court History* 26 no. 1 (2001): 25-52.

Aulgur, William E. "Naturalization—Statutory Construction: *Girouard v. United States*." *Missouri Law Review* 11 (June 1946): 339-43.

Bernard, William S. "A History of U.S. Immigration Policy." 75-105 in *Immigration: Dimensions of Ethnicity*, edited by Stephan Thernstrom. Cambridge, Mass.: Belknap Press of Harvard University Press, 1982.

Bethel, Joseph A. "Naturalization and Willingness to Take Up Arms." *Marquette Law Review* 30 (1946): 130-37.

Boyer, Richard O. "The Gentleman in the Pulpit." *New Yorker* 14 (22 October 1938): 27-33.

Brody, George. "Naturalization—Statutory Construction." *Michigan Law Review* 45 (1946): 227-30.

Brown, Elmer "Aliens—Right of Naturalization—Unwillingness to Bear Arms." *Boston University Law Review* 9 (November 1929): 263-65.

Bryan, Christopher. "'Father Forgive . . .'" *Sewanee Theological Review* 45 (Christmas 2001): 3-8.

Brubaker, Stanley C. "Judicial Self-Restraint." 470-72 in *The Oxford Companion to the Supreme Court of the United States*, edited by Kermit L. Hall. New York: Oxford University Press, 1992.

Burner, David. "Pierce Butler." 1081-90 in *The Justices of the United States Supreme Court: Their Lives and Major Opinions*, edited by Leon Friedman and Fred L. Israel. New York: Chelsea House, 1997.

Chambers, John Whiteclay II. "Conscientious Objectors and the American State from Colonial Times to the Present." 23-46 in *The New Conscientious Objection: From Sacred to Secular Resistance*, edited by Charles C. Moskos and John Whiteclay Chambers II. New York: Oxford University Press, 1993.

Chatfield, Charles. "Pacifists and Their Publics: The Politics of a Peace Movement." *Midwest Journal of Political Science* 13 (May 1969): 298-312.

———. "Thinking About Peace in History." 36-51 in *The Pacifist Impulse in Historical Perspective*, edited by Harvey L. Dyck. Toronto: University of Toronto Press, 1996.

Childress, James F. "Conscientious Objection." 118-20 in *The Westminster Dictionary of Christian Ethics*, edited by James F. Childress and John Macquarrie. Philadelphia: Westminster Press, 1986.

———. "Pacifism." 446-48 in *The Westminster Dictionary of Christian Ethics*, edited by James F. Childress and John Macquarrie. Philadelphia: Westminster Press, 1986.

"Constitutional Law—Naturalization: *Schwimmer* Case Overruled—Inapplicability of *Stare Decisis* When Prior Decision Incorrect." *New York University Law Quarterly Review* 21 (July 1946): 445-49.

Cook, Blanche Wiesen. "Democracy in Wartime, Antimilitarism in England and the United States, 1914-1918." 39-56 in *Peace Movements in America,* edited by Charles Chatfield. New York: Schocken Books, 1973.

"Cutting, Bronson Murray." *The National Cyclopædia of American Biography*. New York: James T. White, 1937, 26: 443.

Daniels, Roger. "What Is an American? Ethnicity, Race, the Constitution and the Immigrant in Early American History." 29-47 in *The Immigration Reader: America in a Multidisciplinary Perspective*, edited by David Jacobson. Malden, Mass.: Blackwell Publishers, 1998.

Duram, James C., and Judith Johnson, "William O. Douglas." 391-95 in *The Supreme Court Justices: Illustrated Biographies, 1789-1993*, edited by Clare Cushman. Washington, D.C.: Congressional Quarterly, 1993.

Easterlin, Richard A. "Economic and Social Characteristics of the Immigrants." 1-34 in *Immigration: Dimensions of Ethnicity*, edited by Stephan Thernstrom. Cambridge, Mass.: Belknap Press of Harvard University Press, 1982.

"Emily Marx," *Who's Who of American Women*. Chicago: Marquis—Who's Who: 3d edition, 1964-65, 655.

Endy, Melvin B., Jr. "War and Peace." 1409-28 in *Encyclopedia of the American Religious Experience: Studies of Traditions and Move-

ments, edited by Charles H. Lippy and Peter W. Williams. New York: Charles Scribner's Sons, 1988, Vol. III.

Flowers, Ronald B. "In Praise of Conscience: Marie Averil Bland." *Anglican and Episcopal History* 62 (March 1993): 37-57.

————. "Government Accommodation of Religious Based Conscientious Objection," *Seton Hall Law Review* 24 no. 2 (1993): 695-735.

———— and Nadia M. Lahutsky. "The Naturalization of Rosika Schwimmer." *Journal of Church and State* 32 (Spring 1990): 343-66.

Fuchs, Lawrence H. "Immigration Policy." 1093-1101 in *The Encyclopedia of the United States Congress*, edited by Donald C. Bacon, Roger H. Davidson, and Morton Keller. New York: Simon and Schuster, 1995, Vol. II.

Garver, Newton. "Pacifism." 925-27 in *Encyclopedia of Ethics*, edited by Lawrence C. and Charlotte B. Becker. New York: Garland Publishing, 1992, Vol. II.

Gilbreath, William O. "Naturalization—Requirement of Willingness to Bear Arms." *Kentucky Law Journal* 35 (May 1947): 334-38.

Gray, Herman A. "Willingness to Bear Arms as a Prerequisite to Naturalization," *New York University Law Quarterly Review* 7 (March 1930): 723-27.

Harrison, Earl G. "American Citizenship: 'Can Applicants Qualify Their Allegiance?'—A Reply." *American Bar Association Journal* 33 (June 1947): 540-43.

Hazard, Henry B. "'Attachment to the Principles of the Constitution' as Judicially Construed in Certain Naturalization Cases in the United States." *American Journal of International Law* 23 (October 1929): 783-808.

————. "Supreme Court Holds Madam Schwimmer, Pacifist, Ineligible to Naturalization." *American Journal of International Law* 23 (July 1929): 626-32.

Hazenhyer, Ida May. "A History of the American Physiotherapy Association." *The Physiotherapy Review* 26 (January-February 1946): 3-5, reprinted in *The Beginnings: Physical Therapy and the APTA*. Alexandria, Va.: American Physical Therapy Association, 1979, 60-62.

Hoffer, Peter Charles. "Frankfurter, Felix." 314-17 in *The Oxford Companion to the Supreme Court of the United States*, edited by Kermit L. Hall. New York: Oxford University Press, 1992.

Holloway, Vernon H. "A Review of American Pacifism." *Religion in Life* 19 (Summer 1950): 367-79.

Horack, Frank E., Jr. "Congressional Silence: A Tool of Judicial Supremacy." *Texas Law Review* 25 (June 1947): 247-61.

Everett E. Gendler. "War and the Jewish Tradition." 78-102 in *A Conflict of Loyalties: The Case for Selective Conscientious Objection*, edited by James Finn. New York: Pegasus, 1968.

Jacobson, David. "Introduction: An American Journey." 1-16 in *The Immigration Reader: America in a Multidisciplinary Perspective*, edited by David Jacobson. Malden, Mass.: Blackwell Publishers, 1998.

Jacoby, Tamar. "Too Many Immigrants?" *Commentary* 113 (April 2002): 37-44.

Josephson, Harold. "The Search for Lasting Peace: Internationalism and American Foreign Policy, 1920-1950." 204-21 in *Peace Movements and Political Cultures*, edited by Charles Chatfield and Peter van den Dungen. Knoxville: University of Tennessee Press, 1988.

Kinney, H. E. "Naturalization—Willingness to Bear Arms Held Not to be a Qualification for Citizenship." *Georgia Bar Journal* 9 (August 1946): 106-07.

Klinkner, Philip A. "The Base Camp of Christendom." *Nation* 274 (11 March 2002): 25-27, 29.

Kraft, Barbara S. "Peacemaking in the Progressive Era: A Prestigious and Proper Calling." *Maryland Historian* 1 (Fall 1970): 121-44.

Lamm, Richard D. "Terrorism and Immigration: We Need a Border." *Vital Speeches of the Day* 68 (1 March 2002): 298-300.

Lawson, Ronald. "Church and State at Home and Abroad: The Evolution of Seventh-day Adventist Relations with Governments." *Journal of the American Academy of Religion* 64 (Summer 1996): 279-311.

"Legislative Adoption of Prior Judicial Construction: The *Girouard* Case and the Reenactment Rule," *Harvard Law Review* 59 (1946): 1277-86.

Leisy, Elva Krehbiel. "Women and Peace." 302-15 in *War—Peace—Amity*, edited by Henry P. Krehbiel. Newton, Kans.: Author, 1937.

Lief, Alfred. "Pacifist Citizens Wanted." *Arbitrator: A Monthly Digest of News of Social Significance* 13 (February 1931): 1-2.

Lusky, Louis. "Harlan Fiske Stone." 361-65 in *The Supreme Court Justices: Illustrated Biographies, 1789-1993*, edited by Clare Cushman. Washington, D.C.: Congressional Quarterly, 1993.

Lutzker, Michael A. "Themes and Contradictions in the American Peace Movement, 1895-1917." 320-40 in *The Pacifist Impulse in Historical Perspective*, edited by Harvey L. Dyck. Toronto: University of Toronto Press, 1996.

M., W. E. ""Naturalization—Effect of Woman Applicant's Expression of Unwillingness to Personally Bear Arms." *Virginia Law Review* 16 (December 1929): 169-74.

McClymer, John F. "Schwimmer, Rosika." 272-3 in *European Immigrant Women in the United States: A Biographical Dictionary*, edited by Judy Barrett Litoff and Judith McDonnell. New York: Garland Publishing, 1994.

Marsh, James M. "Robert H. Jackson." 406-10 in *The Supreme Court Justices: Illustrated Biographies, 1789-1993*, edited by Clare Cushman. Washington, D.C.: Congressional Quarterly, 1993.

Messinger, I. Scott. "Legitimating Liberalism: The New Deal Image-makers and Oliver Wendell Holmes, Jr." *Journal of Supreme Court History* (1995): 57-72.

Millard, Ruth. "Will Women Bear Arms in Next War?" *New York World*, Women's Section, 4 May 1930.

Mize, Sandra Yocum. ""We Are Still Pacifists': Dorothy Day's Pacifism During World War II." *Records of the American Catholic Historical Society of Philadelphia* 108 (Spring-Summer 1987): 1-12.

Murphey, Dwight D. "Book Review." *St. Croix Review* 35 (April 2002): 59-62.

Nash, A. E. Kier. "Stone, Harlan Fiske." 838-40 in *The Oxford Companion to the Supreme Court of the United States*, edited by Kermit L. Hall. New York: Oxford University Press, 1992.

"Naturalization." § 30:89 75-76 in 2A *Immigration Law Service: The Immigration and Naturalization Process*. Deerfield, Ill.: Clark, Boardman, Callaghan, revised 1996.

"Noncombatancy." *Seventh-Day Adventist Encyclopedia*. Washington, D.C.: Review and Herald Publishing Association, 1966, 871-72.

Noonan, John T., Jr. "The Catholic Justices of the United States Supreme Court." *Catholic Historical Review* 67 (July 1981): 369-85.

"Oath of Renunciation and Allegiance." §§ 2850-61, 285-91 in 3C *American Jurisprudence 2d*. Saint Paul, Minn.: West Group, 1962-.

"Oath of Renunciation and Allegiance." §§ 30:84-93, 71-77 in 2A *Immigration Law Service*, Deerfield, Ill.: Clark, Boardman, Callaghan, rev. 1996.

"O'Day, Caroline Love Goodwin." *The National Cyclopædia of American Biography.* New York: James T. White, 1942, current volume F, 1939-42, 281.

Parrish, Michael E. "Cummings, Homer Stillé." 853-54 in *American National Biography*, edited by John A. Garraty and March C. Carnes. Vol. 5. New York: Oxford University Press, 1999.

Patterson, David. "Citizen Peace Initiatives and American Political Culture, 1865-1920." 187-203 in *Peace Movements and Political Cultures*, edited by Charles Chatfield and Peter van den Dungen. Knoxville: University of Tennessee Press, 1988.

Pride, David T. "James C. McReynolds." 326-30 in *The Supreme Court Justices: Illustrated Biographies, 1789-1993*, edited by Clare Cushman. Washington, D.C.: Congressional Quarterly, 1993.

Pugh, Robert C. "Pacifism and Citizenship—The Case of Rosika Schwimmer." *University of Cincinnati Law Review* 3 (November 1929): 462-71.

Purcell, Richard J. "Mr. Justice Pierce Butler." *Catholic Educational Review* 42 (April 1944): 193-215.

"Recollections and Reminiscences from Former Reconstruction Aides." 10-28 in *The Beginnings: Physical Therapy and the APTA*. Alexandria, Va.: American Physical Therapy Association, 1979.

Reilly, William. "Pierce Butler." 351-55 in *The Supreme Court Justices: Illustrated Biographies, 1789-1993*, edited by Clare Cushman. Washington, D.C.: Congressional Quarterly, 1993.

Ruyter, Knut Willem. "Pacifism and Military Service in the Early Church." *Cross Currents* 32 (Spring 1982): 54-70.

S., A. L. "Aliens—Constitutional Law—Naturalization—Promise to Bear Arms Not a Prerequisite to Naturalization." *George Washington Law Review* 14 (June 1946): 641-44.

Schaeffer, Amy. "Meet Miss Marx!" *Barnard College Alumni Monthly* (30 January 1941): 12-13.

Stanley, S. C. "Seneca Falls Woman's Rights Convention (July 198-20, 1848)." 1073 in *Dictionary of Christianity in America*, edited by Daniel G. Reid, and others. Downers Grove, Ill.: InterVarsity Press, 1990.

"Statutes—Construction—Effect of Reenactment after Judicial Construction." *Minnesota Law Review* 31 (May 1947): 625-27.

"Statutes—Construction—Reenactment of Naturalization Oath as Evidence of Legislative Intent." *Columbia Law Review* 46 (September 1946): 886-87.

"Statutory Construction: Change in Interpretation After Reenactment." *Indiana Law Review* 22 (1946): 94-97.

Stevenson, Janet. "Lola Maverick Lloyd: 'I Must Do Something for Peace!'" *Chicago History* 9 (Spring 1980): 47-57.

Stockwell, Rebecca S. "Bertha von Suttner and Rosika Schwimmer: Pacifists from the Dual Monarchy." 141-56 in *Seven Studies in Medieval English History and Other Historical Essays*, edited by Richard H. Bowers. Jackson: University of Mississippi Press, 1983.

Ueda, Reed. "Naturalization and Citizenship." 106-54 in *Immigration: Dimensions of Ethnicity*, edited by Stephan Thernstrom. Cambridge, Mass.: Belknap Press of Harvard University Press, 1982.

Urofsky, Melvin I. "Justice Louis Brandeis." 9-34 in *The Jewish Justices of the Supreme Court Revisited: Brandeis to Fortas*, edited by Jennifer M. Low. Washington, D.C.: Supreme Court Historical Society, 1994.

Van Voris, Jacqueline. "Catt, Carrie Chapman." 582-84 in *American National Biography*, edited by John A. Garraty and Mark C. Carnes. New York: Oxford University Press, 1999, vol. 4.

Vellacott, Jo. "Women, Peace and Internationalism, 1914-1920: 'Finding New Words and Creating New Methods.'" 106-24 in *Peace Movements and Political Cultures*, edited by Charles Chatfield and Peter van den Dungen. Knoxville: University of Tennessee Press, 1988.

Wenger, Beth. "Radical Politics in a Reactionary Age: The Unmaking of Rosika Schwimmer, 1914-1930." *Journal of Women's History* 2 (Fall 1990): 66-99.

———. "Rosika Schwimmer (1877-1948)." 1220-22 in *Jewish Women in America: An Historical Encyclopedia*, edited by Paula E. Hyman and Deborah Dash Moore. New York: Routledge, 1997, vol. 2.

Williams, William H. A. "Immigration as a Pattern in American Culture." 19-28 in *The Immigration Reader: America in a Multidisciplinary Perspective*, edited by David Jacobson. Malden, Mass.: Blackwell Publishers, 1998.

Personal correspondence, papers, and documents in library and archival collections.

American Civil Liberties Union Archives
Seeley G. Mudd Manuscript Library
Princeton University
Princeton, New Jersey

Citizenship and Conscience Papers
Swarthmore College Peace Collection
Swarthmore, Pennsylvania

Douglas Clyde Macintosh Papers, Manuscript Group Number 50
John C. Danforth File in the Roland Bainton Papers, Manuscript Group
Number 75
Special Collections
Yale Divinity School Library
New Haven, Connecticut

Information on Federal Bureau of Investigation's Investigation on the
Immigration Status of Rosika Schwimmer and Her Activities in America
Freedom of Information Act Request Number 302395
Federal Bureau of Investigation
Washington, D.C.

Information on State Department Involvement Pertaining to the Posthumous
Granting of U.S. Citizenship to Douglas Clyde Macintosh S.J. Res. 55
(1981)
Freedom of Information Act Request Number 9404254
United States Department of State
Washington, D.C.

Schwimmer-Lloyd Collection
Rare Books and Manuscripts Division
New York Public Library
Astor, Lenox, and Tilden Foundations
New York City, New York

United States v. Schwimmer 279 U.S. 644 (1929)
United States v. Macintosh 283 U.S. 605 (1931)
United States v. Bland 283 U.S. 636 (1931)
Girouard v. United States 328 U.S. 61 (1946)
Appellate Case File, Records of the Supreme Court of the United States
Record Group 267
National Archives
Washington, D.C.

CASE INDEX

NAME INDEX

Addams, Jane, 57-58, 63, 89, 91, 108-9, 123, 368, 374
Albert, Alfred, 272, 276-78
Alexander II, Czar, 10
Ambrose, Bishop of Milan, 42
Anderson, Jeffrey M., 347-50
Augustine, Bishop of Hippo, 42, 44
Auman, Rev. Lester Ward, 177

Bailey, Forrest, 95, 109-11, 120, 154, 206-7
Bailie, Helen Tufts, 237
Bainton, Roland, 325-26, 336
Baldwin, Roger, 72, 95, 110-11, 120, 154, 156, 176, 199, 208-9, 216, 218, 235-39, 245, 277, 321, 324-25, 370
Barnes, Harry Elmer, 237
Bernadotte, Count Folke, 323
Black, Justice Hugo L., 75, 254-55, 293, 298, 300
Bland, Augusta, 196
Bland, Edward Michael, 196, 327
Bland, Marie Averil, xi, 123, 173-76, 181, 197-227, 230, 235, 237-38, 248, 253, 255, 274, 291-92, 299, 301, 319, 321-22, 325, 327, 332, 336, 339, 347-48, 353, 370-71, 427-28, 435-36, 438, 443, 454-58, 460-61, 470, 478; brief to District Court, 202-4, brief to Supreme Court, 210-212; death, 327-28, government brief to Supreme Court, 212-14, hearing before District Court, 204-5, 438-42, petition for rehearing, 216-18; question 22, 218-19
Boe, Mary, 234

Bondy, Judge William, 204-5, 438
Borchard, Edwin, 238
Bowie, Dr. Walter Russell, 123, 198, 214, 425, 434-35
Brandeis, Justice Louis D., 118-19, 128, 172-73, 215, 250, 397, 420, 423, 444
Briand, Aristide, 65
Broun, Heywood, 153, 174
Brown, Elmer, 125
Buchanan, Pat, 351
Burrows, Judge Warren B., 150, 152-54, 156, 178
Burton, Justice Harold, 297
Butler, Justice Pierce, 115-17, 157, 175, 215, 372, 390

Calvert, Bruce T., 159
Carnegie, Andrew, 55, 59
Carpenter, Judge George A., 96-99, 110, 369-70, 373, 388
Catt, Carrie Chapman, 57, 129, 320-22, 476, 480-81
Celler, Rep. Emmanuel, 332; H.R. 2816, 332
Chandler, Porter R., 324
Charles I, 3, 48
Charles II, 3
Churchill, Winston, 326
Clark, Charles E., 154, 173, 403
Clark, Justice Tom, 74
Cleveland, President Grover, 16
Coddaire, David J., 272, 277-78, 462
Coffin, Dr. Henry Sloane, 122, 425
Columbus, Christopher, 326
Constantine, Emperor, 42, 46
Coolidge, President Calvin, 155, 170, 295

SUBJECT INDEX

ABOUT THE AUTHOR

Ronald B. Flowers is John F. Weatherly Professor of Religion at Texas Christian University, where he has taught in the Religion Department since 1966. He was educated at Texas Christian University (B.A. 1957), Vanderbilt University Divinity School (B.D. 1960; S.T.M. 1961), and the School of Religion of the University of Iowa (Ph.D. 1967). During his service at TCU he won several teaching awards. Of those he is most proud are the Honors Program Faculty Recognition Award (1976) and the Chancellor's Award for Distinguished Teaching (1998). Ordained in the Christian Church (Disciples of Christ), Dr. Flowers served several student churches and as the minister of the Crofton (Kentucky) Christian Church (1961-63). While in graduate school, studying religion in a state university, he developed an interest in church-state relations, which has been a career-long specialty. He has published numerous articles and two other books on church-state matters, particularly the church-state cases of the United States Supreme Court. He is a member of the American Academy of Religion and the Supreme Court Historical Society. He and Leah Elizabeth Flowers have been married forty-three years and have three grown children, Jennifer, Philip, and Paul, and two grandchildren, Jessica and Jodi.